The Law and Regulation of Internationa

The Law and Regulation of International Finance

Professor Ravi C Tennekoon
Law School, Kings College, London

Formerly, Partner, Herbert Smith,
London; Executive Director,
Legal Directorate, ABN AMRO Bank,
London; and Lecturer and Tutor
in Laws, Trinity College, Oxford.

Tottel publishing

Tottel Publishing Ltd
Maxwelton House
41-43 Boltro Road
Haywards Heath
West Sussex
RH16 1BJ

© Tottel Publishing Ltd 1991

Reprinted 2006, 2008 (Twice), 2009

All rights reserved. No part of this publication may be reproduced in any material form (including photocopying or storing it in any medium by electronic means and whether or not transiently or incidentally to some other use of this publication) without the written permission of the copyright owner except in accordance with the provisions of the Copyright, Designs and Patents Act 1988 or under the terms of a licence issued by the Copyright Licensing Agency Ltd., Saffron House, Kirby Street, London, England EC1N 8TS. Applications for the copyright owner's written permission to reproduce any part of this publication should be addressed to the publisher.

Warning: The doing of unauthorised act in relation to a copyright work may result in both a civil claim for damages and criminal prosecution.

Crown copyright material is reproduced with the permission of the Controller of HMSO and the Queen's Printer for Scotland. Parliamentary copyright material is reproduced with the permission of the Controller of Her Majesty's Stationery Office on behalf of Parliament. Any European material in this work which has been reproduced from EUR-lex, the official European Communities legislation website, is European Communities copyright.

British Library Cataloguing-in-Publication Data.
A catalogue record for this book is available from the British Library.

ISBN: 978-1-84592-392-1

Printed and bound in Great Britain by
CPI Antony Rowe, Chippenham and Eastbourne

*This book is dedicated to my mother, and to my father,
Roland Tennekoon, whose courtroom advocacy inspired me
and many others*

Preface

This book is an examination of the legal issues which arose in the context of the explosive growth of the new international financial markets that developed in London in the 1960s and 1970s.

Much has happened since the book was first conceived. The Financial Services Act 1986 created the first comprehensive, and more importantly, institutionalised regime of regulation for the financial markets of the United Kingdom, including, of course, the international financial markets to which London is at present the 'host' city. Furthermore, in 1990 the United States Securities and Exchange Commission promulgated Regulation S, which provides a framework for international securities issues acceptable to the Commission and in accordance with the policy underlying US securities regulation.

London has become host city to the world's international markets notwithstanding the fact that New York and Tokyo are the financial capitals of the world's two largest economies. Consequently, in the absence of an international code or regime of international law, English lawyers and English law have been prominent in shaping the legal framework and structures governing international financing transactions.

For the purposes of the discussion in the book the pattern that I have adopted is first, to describe the financial nature and structure of a transaction and the procedures used in the markets to set up the transaction; second, to examine the legal framework which has been used to give legal effect to the transaction and the issues arising in this context; third, to consider the regulatory aspects of the financing transaction, which are, of course, extremely important in practice. Relevant aspects of international taxation are not covered, since taxation is a subject in itself.

Readers should not expect to find within this book precedents for, say, a bond issue or loan agreement. It will be seen that in relation to the legal documents effecting such financing transactions the emphasis lies upon analysis and discussion of existing legal structures and clauses commonly used.

My approach to the subject of international finance mirrors that of major City firms that seek to ensure the validity and effectiveness of the international financial transaction and to minimise the likelihood of such a transaction devolving into a mass of worldwide litigation. Consequently, the book is based on what may be termed a 'structuralist' or 'constructive' approach, rather than a 'breakdown' or 'litigation' approach to international financing transactions. This is perhaps also justified by the near absence of litigation in the context of the international financial markets.

The book is focused on the law and regulation affecting the two financing transactions which are the standard bearers of the modern international financial markets based in London: the international or 'Euro' bond issue and the international syndicated loan. A section is also devoted to the law and regulation of the Euro Commercial Paper market, and its progenitors, the Revolving Underwriting Facility and the Note Issuance Facility.

Constraints of time and space mean that I have not attempted to deal with currency and interest swaps, although it is a subject closely allied to those dealt with in this book, nor have I dealt with the subjects of project finance, aircraft and ship finance nor indeed with Sovereign debt and debt restructuring (which is a subject in itself).

My thanks are due to a number of practitioners and academics with whom I have discussed on various occasions the law relating to many of the areas covered in this book though not necessarily its contents: Richard Youard, Martin Read, Rupert Beaumont, David Frank, Colin Hall, The Hon Nigel Boardman, Richard Slater, Chris Fitzgerald, Tim Freshwater, Robert Welsford, Ruth Fox, Jonathan Haw, Chris Smith, Chris Saunders, Andrew Balfour, John Macaskill, James Cripps, Simon Robinson, William Underhill, James Featherby, John Crosthwaite, Andrew Hougie, all of Slaughter and May; Philip Wood, Tony Humphrey, Tony Herbert, of Allen & Overy; Hugh Piggott, Keith Clark, Michael Bray, Tim Herrington, of Clifford Chance; Richard Morrissey of Sullivan and Cromwell; Tom Cashel formerly of Simpson Thatcher and Bartlett; Derek Davies of St Catherine's College, Oxford; Professor A G Guest, CBE, QC, Professor Francis Jacobs QC, Advocate-General of the European Court, Richard Plender QC, Professor David Hayton, Professor Jill Martin, Robin Morse, all of King's College, University of London; Professor Trevor Hartley of the London School of Economics; Professor Roy Goode, QC, Professor Ross Cranston, of Queen Mary and Westfield College, University of London; Jane Welch, Andrew Whittaker, of the Securities and Investments Board.

I owe a debt of gratitude to Beatrice without whose help and encouragement this book would not have been possible. My thanks also to Helen Griffiths who assisted in many ways and to my secretary who was patient with my endless amendments.

The opinions and statements concerning the law expressed in this book do not necessarily represent those of Herbert Smith or of any individual partner of Herbert Smith or of any other firm of lawyers or partner in any similar firm, and should not be relied on as such.

For all errors, omissions and shortcomings, the writer alone is responsible. The law is stated as of 1 August 1991.

Ravi C Tennekoon
August 1991
[Preface as amended for 1994 reprint]

Contents

Preface vii
Table of statutes xix
Table of statutory instruments, rules and regulations xxiii
Table of US statutes, rules and regulations xxvii
Table of European and foreign enactments xxxi
Table of cases xxxiii

Chapter 1 The international financial markets: introduction 1

I   A description of the international financial market 1
II   The development of the international financial market in London 5
     1 Development of the Eurocurrency markets 5
     2 The growth of the international or Eurobond market 8
     3 The centre of the international financial market 10

PART I GOVERNING LAW IN INTERNATIONAL FINANCE 13

Chapter 2 The nature and scope of a governing law 15

I   The necessity for a governing law 15
II   Choice of law: the legal and commercial factors 16
     1 Freedom of choice under the prospective proper law 17
     2 Certainty and result predictability under legal documents 20
     3 Conceptual sophistication of the system 23
     4 Language 23
     5 The forum of potential litigation 23
     6 Familiarity 24
III   Aspects of a transaction controlled by the proper law 25
IV   Limits to the control of a transaction by the proper law 27
     1 Corporate capacity 27
     2 Illegality subsequent to contract 30

V   The proper law and the effect of Exchange Control Regulations: art VIII(2)(b) of the IMF Agreement   34
VI   The proper law, exchange control laws and the 'Act of State' doctrine   38
VII Other possible limitations on the doctrine of the proper law   40
     1   Negotiability of bond instruments   40
     2   Creation of security interests   41
     3   Mergers and acquisitions   41

PART II   INTERNATIONAL SYNDICATED LOANS   43

Chapter 3   The lead manager and the syndications process   45

I   The background   45
II   The role of the lead manager in the syndications process   46
III   Liability of the lead manager   48
      1   The information memorandum   48
      2   Loan documentation   55

Chapter 4   The lead manager as agent bank   58

I   Certification of compliance with conditions precedent by the borrower   58
II   Duties as paying agent   59
III   'Monitoring' loan covenants   61
IV   Duty to act on the occurrence of default   61
V   The agent bank as a fiduciary   64

Chapter 5   Structure and contents of a syndicated loan agreement   68

I   Conditions precedent   68
II   Representations and warranties   71
III   Financial arrangements   73
      1   Currency of the loan and currency of repayment   73
      2   Statement of purpose and use of proceeds of loan   74
      3   Prepayment   75
      4   Funding mechanisms in the international market: need for special clauses   77
      5   Interest payments and withholding tax   79
      6   Funding and increased costs   81
IV   Covenants   82
      1   Financial covenants   84
      2   The financial information covenant   86
      3   Asset disposal covenant   86
      4   Merger control covenants   86
      5   The pari passu covenant   89
      6   Negative pledge   89
      7   Default and cross default   98
      8   Sharing clauses and relationship between syndicate banks inter se   100

Chapter 6 Sales of loan assets and securitisation: legal structures and mechanisms 103

I   Purposes of loan 'sales' 103
II   Types of asset sales 104
      1   Loan 'sales' 104
      2   'Sales' of a loan facility 104
      3   'Risk participations' 105
III   Techniques of 'selling' bank assets 105
IV   The traditional methods 106
      1   Assignment 106
      2   Novation 107
      3   Sub-participation 108
      4   Comparison of assignment and sub-participation methods 109
V   Supervisory treatment 115
VI   New methods of transfer: TLCs and TLIs 116
      1   The TLC 116
      2   Issue and transfer mechanics 117
      3   The TLI 119
      4   Issue and transfer mechanics 120
      5   The nature of a TLI 122
VII   TPCs 123

Chapter 7 The impact of UK and US regulation on syndicated loans and loan sales 124

I   Syndicated loans and the UK Financial Services Act 1986 124
      1   Is a syndicated loan a para 2 or para 3 'investment'? 124
      2   Do activities associated with a syndicated loan constitute 'investment business' under Part II of FSA Sch 1? 127
      3   Do the prohibitions on unsolicited calls (s 56) and investment advertisements (s 57) apply in respect of syndicated loans? 129
      4   Syndicated loans as collective investment schemes 130
II   Sale of loan assets and the FSA 134
      1   Novation and assignment 134
      2   Sub-participations 137
      3   Conclusions on loan sales by traditional methods 138
      4   The FSA and the use of TLCs, TLIs and TPCs 138
III   US securities regulation 139
      1   The Glass-Steagall Act 141

PART III INTERNATIONAL OR 'EURO' BONDS 143

Chapter 8 Background and issue procedures 145

I   Background 145
      1   The issuer's perspective 145
      2   The investor's perspective 146
      3   The investment bank's perspective 146

xii *Contents*

    4   The international or 'Euro' bond issue, the 'foreign' bond issue and the 'domestic' bond issue   147
II Issue procedures in the international bond markets   149
    1   Mandate   152
    2   Launch   152
    3   Stabilisation   155
    4   Signing   156
    5   Allotment   157
    6   The closing   158
    7   The 'lock-up' period   159

Chapter 9   Negotiability and governing law   161

I   Negotiability of the Eurobond   162
    1   Doors to negotiability   163
II   Conflicts of laws and Eurobonds   165
III Negotiability and the Euroclear/Cedel clearance system   169
    1   Mechanics of transfer in the international clearance systems   169
    2   Legal issues   171
IV The temporary global bond   174

Chapter 10   Legal framework of marketing and distribution   177

I   The documents   177
    1   The subscription agreement   178
    2   The agreement between managers and the underwriting agreement   184
    3   The selling group agreement   189

Chapter 11   The bond instrument: the legal relationship between issuer and Eurobond holder   193

I   Rights and obligations arising on the bond instrument   193
    1   Payment of interest and principal   193
    2   Repayment of principal and early redemption provisions   195
    3   Taxation and payments of interest and principal   198
    4   Covenants in the bond instrument   198
    5   Events of default   202
    6   Limitation period   203
II Default, acceleration and enforcement   204
    1   Enforceability of trust deed provisions restricting individual bondholder rights   205
    2   Bondholder control of trustee powers   207
    3   Efficacy of the 'no action' clause   210
    4   Rationale for trustee control over acceleration and enforcement   212

III Types of bonds 213
    1 Interest rate 213
    2 Maturity and redemption 215
    3 Bonds linked to equity and other assets 217

Chapter 12 The role of fiscal agents in a Eurobond issue 218

I General 218
II The role of the fiscal agent 218
    1 Delivery of bonds 219
    2 Principal paying agent 219
    3 Redemption of bonds 220
    4 Replacement of bonds 220
    5 The position of bondholders 221
    6 Bondholder meetings 222

Chapter 13 Trustees under Eurobond trust deeds 224

I Preliminary 224
II Nature of the trust 225
III Functions and powers of the Eurobond trustee 228
IV Eurobond trustee's immunities, duties and liabilities 236
    1 Duty to act with due skill and diligence 237
    2 Duty of trustee not to allow his duty as trustee to conflict with his own interests 243
    3 Duty of trustees to provide information about matters affecting the trust 245
    4 Duty not to delegate the trustee's duties or powers 245
    5 Rationale for trustee in a Eurobond issue 246
    6 Regulation of the contents of trust deeds 248

Chapter 14 Convertible Eurobonds and bonds with warrants 251

I Introduction 251
II Equity convertibles 253
    1 Financial features of equity convertibles 253
    2 Attractions of convertibles 254
    3 The conversion privilege 256
    4 Protecting the conversion privilege 262
    5 Conditions precedent to conversion and conversion procedure 272
    6 Right to interest and dividends on conversion 273
III Bonds with equity warrants 274
    1 The equity warrant 274
    2 The subscription right 275
    3 The deed poll 276
    4 Conditions precedent to and procedure for exercise of the subscription right 277
    5 Issue of shares 277

PART IV REGULATION OF THE INTERNATIONAL CAPITAL MARKETS: (A) REGULATION OF INTERNATIONAL BOND ISSUES UNDER UNITED KINGDOM LAWS 279

Introduction 281

Chapter 15 The requirement of 'authorisation' under the Financial Services Act 1986 283

I   Authorisation to carry on investment business in the UK   283
   1   'Investment business'   284
   2   Investment business carried on in the UK   289
II   Offshore entities: the 'overseas person'   290
   1   Exception for transactions 'with or through' certain persons   291
   2   Paragraph 27, Schedule 1 exception   293

Chapter 16 The regulation in the UK of advertising and marketing of Eurobond issues 297

I   Regulation of advertisements   297
   1   The prohibition in FSA s 57   298
   2   FSA s 160 prohibition on advertisements   305
   3   Provisions in the Companies Act 1985 Part III (to be repealed)   308
II   Regulation of cold calling   310
III   Misleading statements   314

Chapter 17 The listing of Eurobonds 317

I   Why are Eurobonds listed?   317
II   Regulatory background to a London listing   318
   1   Provisions of FSA 1986   319
III   Listing rules: the legal basis   320
IV   The requirements for listing   321
   1   Basic requirements   321
   2   Preconditions to a listing application   321
   3   Requirements as to time and documents   322
   4   Registration and publication of listing particulars   322
   5   Determining the contents of listing particulars   323
   6   FSA section 146   324
   7   Section 7 of the Yellow Book   324
   8   Requirements of disclosure: contents of listing particulars   325
   9   Other requirements of listing   327
V   Supplementary listing particulars: FSA s 147   328
VI   Liability for false or misleading listing particulars and supplementary listing particulars   329
   1   Criminal liability   329
   2   Civil liability   329
VII   Advertisements in connection with listing particulars   331

VIII Listing under the 'mutual recognition' provisions of the Admissions Directive 333
    1 Special provisions applicable to a London listing of convertibles or equity warrants 335
IX Continuing obligations 336

Chapter 18 Regulation of stabilisation 340

I An introduction to stabilisation 340
II The statutory provisions of FSA 1986 s 47(2) 341
III Stabilisation and insider dealing legislation 343
IV The SIB's stabilisation rules 347
    1 Securities which may be stabilised 348
    2 The stabilising manager 350
    3 The stabilising period 350
    4 Pre-conditions to lawful stabilisation: legends and warnings 351
    5 Pre-stabilisation ramping 352
    6 Permitted stabilising transactions 353
    7 Price limits applicable to stabilisation 355
    8 The stabilisation register 356
    9 SFA Rules on stabilisation 356
    10 The extraterritorial impact of s 47(2) and international stabilisation 357

PART V REGULATION OF THE INTERNATIONAL CAPITAL MARKETS: (B) IMPACT OF US SECURITIES LAWS ON INTERNATIONAL BOND ISSUES 359

Introduction 361

Chapter 19 The legislative framework of US securities laws 363

I Securities Act 1933 ('SA 1933') 363
    1 Section 5 363
    2 Consequences of breach 365
    3 'Anti-fraud' provisions 367
II The Securities Exchange Act 1934 ('SEA 1934') 369
    1 Section 15: broker dealer registration 369
    2 Other provisions of SEA 1934 370
    3 Anti-fraud provision of SEA 1934: r 10 (b)-5 371
III Regulation of stabilisation during an issue or distribution of securities: r 10(b)-6 and r 10(b)-7 372
    1 Remedies and enforcement 376
IV The Trust Indenture Act 1939 ('TIA 1939') 378

xvi *Contents*

Chapter 20 Extraterritoriality of US securities laws 380

I Introduction 380
II The 'effects' doctrine 382
III 'Conduct' based jurisdiction 384
IV The SEC and extraterritoriality 387
V SEC Release 4708 of July 1964 388

Chapter 21 Regulation S r 15(a)-6 and other provisions 393

I Regulations S 393
   1 The prohibition on 'directed selling efforts' 395
   2 Requirement of 'off-shore transaction' 397
   3 Issuer conditions 399
   4 Foreign issuers with no substantial US market interest (category(a)) 400
   5 Reporting issuers and issuers of debt securities (category (b)) 403
   6 All other issuers (category (c)) 406
II The interaction of Regulation S and US tax laws 409
   1 TEFRA D Regulations 409
   2 Impact of TEFRA D on Regulation S 413
   3 TEFRA C Regulations 415
III SEA 1934 r 15(a)-6 416
   1 Unsolicited transactions 417
   2 Furnishing of research reports 417
   3 Inducing or attempting to induce transactions with major US institutional investors or US institutional investors including banks, savings and loan associations and insurance companies 419
   4 Effecting transactions in securities with certain other specified persons 419
   5 Interaction of r 15(a)-6 with Regulation S 420
   6 Exemptions for 'comparably regulated' foreign broker dealers 420
IV Summary: US securities laws and TEFRA 420
V Rule 144A, PORTAL and private placements 422
   1 Interaction of Regulation S, TEFRA D and r 144A 425
   2 The PORTAL system and r 144A 425

Chapter 22 Participation by US commercial banks in the international capital markets: the Glass-Steagall Act 427

I The Glass-Steagall Act 427
II The rationale for the Glass-Steagall provisions 429
III Applicability of Glass-Steagall to Eurobonds and Euro Commercial Paper 430

Contents xvii

PART VI EURO COMMERCIAL PAPER AND EURO NOTES 435

Chapter 23 Definitions and structure 437

I What are Euro Commercial Paper and Euro Notes? 437
II The market for Euro Commercial Paper and Euro Notes 440
III Structure and procedure in respect of a Euro Commercial Paper Programme 441
IV Legal documents 442
   1 The Programme Agreement 442
   2 The Issuing and Paying Agency Agreement ('IPA') 445
   3 The global note and deed poll 446

Chapter 24 The regulation of Euro Commercial Paper and Euro Note issues 449

I UK securities regulation 449
   1 Banking Act 1987 449
   2 Companies Act 1985 457
   3 Financial Services Act 1986 ('FSA') 459
   4 Control of Borrowing Order (COBO) 461
   5 The information memorandum and liability for misstatements 461
II US securities regulation and banking legislation 465
   1 US Securities Act 1933 and the Securities Exchange Act 1934 465
   2 The Glass-Steagall Act 469

Chapter 25 Note issuance facilities (NIFs) and revolving underwriting facilities (RUFs) 471

I Note issuance facilities (NIFs) 471
   1 The manager and tender panel members 475
   2 The tender agent and the facility agreement 475
II Revolving underwriting facilities (RUFs) 477

Index 481

Table of statutes

References in this Table to *Statutes* are to Halsbury's Statutes of England (Fourth Edition) showing the volume and page at which the annotated text of the Act may be found. Page references printed in **bold** type indicate where the section of the Act is set out in part or in full.

	PAGE
Banking Act 1979	452
s 1(5)(a)	451
Banking Act 1987 (4 *Statutes* 527)	
	128, 453, 472, 473
s 1(1)	450
(5)(a)	451
3	**449**, 451, 452, 454, 455
(1)	450, 455
(2), (3)	450
4	454
(4)	453
5	**450**
(1), (2)	454
(3)	451
6	**451**
(1) (a), (b)	452
(2) (a), (b)	452
32 (1)	455
(3)	457
(5), (6)	**455**
(7)	**456**
34(1), (3), (4)	457
35	**462**, 463
Bills of Exchange Act 1882 (5 *Statutes* 334)	122, 163, 167, 175, 439
s 3	164
(1)	164
9(1)(a)–(c)	164
59(2)	198
72	166
83	**164**, 438
Bills of Sale Act 1878 (5 *Statutes* 394)	91
Bills of Sale Act (1878) Amendment Act 1882 (5 *Statutes* 409)	91, 127
s 17	125, 126

	PAGE
Borrowing (Control and Guarantees) Act 1946 (30 *statutes* 65)	
s 1	449
3(4)	449
Bretton Woods Agreement Act 1945:	28
Civil Jurisdiction and Judgments Act 1982 (22 *Statutes* 344)	
Sch 1 Convention on Jurisdiction and the Enforcement of Judgements in Civil and Commercial Matters	24, 25
Companies Act 1862	
s 20	299
Companies Act 1948	
s 88	237
Companies Act 1985 (8 *Statutes* 104):	125, 198, 440, 449
s 1	459
35, 35A	**28**, 29
35B	**29**
(Pt II ss 43–55)	459
s 43–48	459
(Pt III ss 56–79)	182, 308, 310, 319, 322, 439, 473, 474
s 56(1), (2)	309
58	309, 457
(1)	**308**, 309, **457**, 458
59, 60	459
(Pt III, Ch 11 ss 72–79)	309
s 72	309, 457
75, 77	309
79(1)	458
(2)	309, 310, 458, 459, 474
81	439, 459
89–91	258, 264
92	258, 264, 272

Table of statutes

	PAGE
Companies Act 1985—contd.	
s 93	258, 264
94	258, 264, 272
(3)	272
100	272
(2)	270
101	271
117(1)	270
118	271
(1)	270
121	28
191	248
192	234, 237, 238, 239, 240, 242
(1)	**237**
193	**215**
194	198
263	266
(1)	259
264	259, 266, 314
395, 396	97
(Pt XIII ss 425–430)	87
s 425–427	87
427A	**87**
428	261, 264
(1)	87
735	28
736, 736A	261
744	237, 248, 439
Companies Act 1989 (8 *Statutes* 819)	
s 93, 105	97
144(1)	261
193	313
194	63
198(1)	308, 319
(4)	308
202	309, 458
207	448
Company Securities (Insider Dealing) Act 1985 (8 *Statutes* 749):	264
s 1	245, 345, 347, 348
(2)	**344**, 345
(7)	344
3(2)	**345**
4	345, 346, 347, 348
(1)	**346**
5	347
6	347, 348
9	344
10	343, 344
12(a), (b)	345, 346
(c)	346
13(3)	347
14	**87**, 261
16	345, 346
(1)	344
(3)	346
Contracts (Applicable Law) Act 1990	
(11 *Statutes* 237)	17, 278
s 2(2)	18, 26, 31, 291
3(3)	166
(a)	18

	PAGE
Contracts (Applicable law) Act 1990—contd.	
Sch 1 (Rome Convention on the law applicable to obligations 1980)	34, 226
art 1	19, 40
(1)	**18**
(2)	168
(c)	**18**, 19
(e), (f)	27
3	26, 31, 42
(1)	**18**, 26, 291
(3)	18
4	31
(2) (c)	40
5, 6	31
7(1)	18, 291
(2)	**18**, 35, 37, 291
8	26
9(2)	26
10	26, 41
(1)(b)	31
(d)	31, 42
(e)	31
12	31
16	31, 35
31	18
Exchange Control Act 1947	35
Financial Services Act 1986 (8 *Statutes* 805, 19 *Statutes* 179, 30 *Statutes* 162)	64, 177, 182, 191, 449, 473
s 1	64, 124
(1)	284
(2)	127, 284
(3)	287, **289**, 290
(b)	290
3	183, 283, 287, 289, 291, 303, 459, 460
4	283
(2)	283
5	283
(1)	**283**
(7)	283
7	284
31	**295**
32	295
36	287, 302, 304, 346
(1)	287
37	288, 302
(1)	306
38	304
39	288
40	346, 453
(2)(a),(c)	288
42	304
43	304, 460
44	304
(9)	129, 138, 283, **299**, 300, 329
45	304
46	304
(1)	459, 463

Table of statutes xxi

Financial Services Act 1986—contd.
s 47 . . . . 316, 329
   (1) 192, **314**, 315, 316, 329, 463
   (2) 187, 197, **341**, 342, 343, 348,
                350, 352, 353, 356, 357, 363
   (3) 329, 341
   (4) 315
      (b), (c) 316
   (5) 357
48 304
   (2)(e) 304
   (7) 156, 197, 343, 347, 348, 349,
                            351, 357
56 . . . . 129, 130, 139, 183, 293, 294, 295,
                     311, 457, 459, 461
   (1)(a)(b) **310**, 311
   (2), (4) 311
   (8) **310**
57 . . . . .129, 130, 139, 293, 294, 295,
          297, 300, 301, 303, 306, 319,
          320, 459, 460, 461, 474
   (1) **298**
   (2) **298**, 299, 455
   (3), (5) 298
58 (1) **303**, 305
      (a)–(c) 304
      (d) (ii) **301**, 302, 304, 319
   (2) 305
   (3) 301, 302
61 322
   (1) 298
      (a),(i) 357
   (3) **298**, 332, 357
   (4) **298**
62 332
   (2) 307, 357
62A 307, 313, 357
63A 63, 64, 294, 311, 356
75 . . . . 130, 132, 134
   (1) 130, 131
   (2) 130, 133
   (3) 130, 133
      (a) 132
   (6) 132, 133
      (b) **133**
76 133
   (3) 133
77 133
(Pt IV ss 142–157) 183, 301, 302, 305,
                  306, 308, 309, 315,
                  320, 322, 439, 457
s 142 302
   (1), (2) 305
   (3) 321
      (c) 305
   (6) 320
143(1) 320
144(2), (3) 321
145(2) 321
146 . . . . 154, 180, **324**, 328, 329, 330
147 . . . . .180, 328, 329, 330

Financial Services Act 1986—contd.
s 147(1) 328
   (b) 328
   (2) 324, 328
   (3) 328
148 . . . . 324, 328, 330
   (1) 328
   (b) 324
   (2) 324, 328
149(1) 322
   (3) 323
150 . . . . 315, 329, 330
151 . . . . 329, 330
   (1) 330
152 . . . . 315, 324, **330**
   (1) 331
   (d) 331
   (3) (5) 331
   (16) 148, 149, 331
153 . . . . 315, 321
154 . . . . 332, 333
   (1) **331**
   (b) 332
   (2) 331
   (4) 332
(Pt V ss 158–171) 183, 304, 305, 306,
                308, 315, 319, 439, 457,
                          459, 474
s 158(1) 305
   (b) 306
   (4) **306**
   (6) 306
159 . . . . 305, 306
   (1) 306, 307
160 . . . . 297, 305, 307, 308, 319
   (1) 306, **319**
   (2),(3) **306**
   (4) **307**
   (6)–(9) 308
160A **308**
   (1)(c) 319
   (2) 319
161(1), (2) 305
166, 168 315
171 307
   (1), (3), (6) 307
172(1) 87, 261
(Pt VII ss 173–178) 343
174(4)(b) 347
175 347
192 320
195 . . . . 309, 458
207(2) **297**
   (3) 300, **301**, 456
212(3) 309, 439
Sch 1 64
(Pt I paras 1–11) . 124, 127, 135, 284, 439
   para 1 . . . . . . 305, 306, 341, 348, 355
      2 . . .124, 125, 126, 128, 132, 133,
           135, 136, 138, 284, 305, 306,
           348, 355, 439, 440, 459

	PAGE		PAGE
Financial Services Act 1986—contd.		Foreign Judgments (Reciprocal	
Sch 1—contd.		Enforcement) Act, 1933 (22	
Pt I—contd.		Statutes 283)	24
para 1 note (a)	440	Insolvency Act 1986 (4 Statutes 71)	
3 . . .122, 124, 128, **284**, 305, 348,		s 175	199
349, 355, 440		221(5)	199
note 1	303, 314	386	199
4 . . . 252, 284, 305, 306, 348, 355		Sch 6	199
5	305, 306, 348, 355	International Organisations Act 1968	
(b)	284, 348	(10 Statutes 595)	28
(c)	252, **348**, 349	Law of Property Act 1925 (37	
7	252, 349	Statutes 72)	
9	289	s 56	276
11	135	(1)	276
12	138, 285	136(1)	**106**, 107, 135
notes 1,2	138	Misrepresentation Act 1967 (29	
13	285	Statutes 724)	
note 4	138	s 2	50
15	128, **285**, 460	(1)	29, **30**, 48, 49, 463, 464
(Pt III paras 17–25) . . . 283, 284, 289, 299,		3	52, 192
300, 303		Recognition of Trusts Act 1987 (48	
para 17	138, **285**, 286	Statutes 361)	
(1)	**137**	Schedule Convention on the Law	
(2)	137	applicable to Trusts and on	
(e)	288	their Recognition	226
23	303	Ch II	
24	128	art 6, 8	207, 225
25A	162	Ch III	
25B	287	art 11	207
(2)	**288**	Sale of Goods Act 1979 (39 Statutes	
(3)(4)	288	106)	
(Pt IV paras 26–27) . . . 283, 284, 289, 290,		s 16	173
291, 299, 300		39	90
para 26	290, **291**, **292**, 311	61	105
27	291, 293, 294, 295	Trustee Act 1925 (48 Statutes 221)	
(1) (a)	294	s 23	245, 246
(Pt V paras 28–35)		(1)	246
para 28	136, 138, 460	(2)	245, 246
(1)	136	36	235
(c)	285, 292	(1)	235
(d)	286	(2)	236
(2)(b)	286	41	235
(c)	136	(1)	236
(3)	128, 138, 286, 287	46, 58	236
(7)(c)	290	61	242
35	**132**	69(2)	231
Sch 5	460	Unfair Contract Terms 1977 (11	
para 1	460	Statutes 220)	
2(2)(b)	460	s 1(1)	243
Sch 11		2	52, 53, 55, 57
para 20, 22B	311	(2)	52, 243
Sch 12	261	3	55
Sch 17		27(1)	55, 57
Pt I	439	Variation of Trusts 1958 (48 Statutes	
		323)	231
		Weights and Measures Act 1963	
		s 24(2)	299

Table of statutory instruments, rules and regulations

References in the right-hand column are to division and paragraph numbers. Paragraph references printed in **bold** type indicate where the statutory instrument, etc is set out in part or in full.

	PAGE
Statutory instruments	
Banking Act 1987 (Advertisements) Regulations 1988, SI 1988/645 .	455
reg 2 (1)–(5)	456
Banking Act 1987 (Exempt Transactions) Regulations 1988, SI 1988/646	455
art 8, 9	454
13(a) (b)	453
(d)	454
Sch 2	453
Sch 3	454
Banking Act 1987 (Exempt Transactions) (Amendments) Regulations 1990, SI 1990/20	455
Bretton Woods Agreement Order 1946 SR&O 1946/36	35
Companies Act 1989 (Commencement No 6 and Transitional and Saving Provision) Order 1990, SI 1990/1392	
art 4	448
Contracts (Applicable Law) Act 1990 (Commencement No 1) Order 1991, SI 1991/907	18
Control of Borrowing Order 1958, SI 1958/1208	449, 461
art 8A(1), (2)	461
Exchange Control (General Exemption) Order 1979, SI 1979/660 .	34
Financial Services Act 1986 (Commencement No 3) Order 1986, SI 1986/2246	
art 5	309
Sch 4	309
Financial Services Act 1986 (Commencement No 8) Order 1988:	281

	PAGE
Financial Services Act 1986 (Investment Advertisements) (Exemptions) Order 1988, SI 1988/316	
art 9 .... 294, 302, 303, 460	
(3) . . .129, 130, **302**, 303, 304, 461, 474	
Financial Services Act 1986 (Restriction of Right of Action) Regulations 1991, SI 1991/489	
reg 2 .... 307, 313, 357	
(1)	313
Financial Services Act 1986 (Restriction of Scope of Act) Order 1988, SI 1988/318	127, 287
Financial Services Act 1986 (Restriction of Scope of Act and Meaning of Collective Investment Scheme) Order 1988, SI 1988/803	127
Financial Services Act 1986 (Restriction of Scope of Act and Meaning of Collective Investment Scheme) Order 1990, SI 1990/349	
art 7	132
Insider Dealing (Recognised Stock Exchange) Order 1989, SI 1989/2165	345
Insider Dealing (Recognised Stock Exchange) (No 2) Order 1990, SI 1990/47	346
Reciprocal Enforcement of Foreign Judgments (Australian Capital Territory) Order 1955, SI 1955/559	24
Reciprocal Enforcement of Foreign Judgments (Austria) Order 1962, SI 1962/1339	24

xxiii

xxiv Table of statutory instruments etc

	PAGE
Reciprocal Enforcement of Foreign Judgments (Guernsey) Order 1973, SI 1973/610	24
Reciprocal Enforcement of Foreign Judgments (India) Order 1958, SI 1958/425	24
Reciprocal Enforcement of Foreign Judgments (Isle of Man) Order 1973, SI 1973/611	24
Reciprocal Enforcement of Foreign Judgments (Israel) Order 1971, SI 1971/1039	24
Reciprocal Enforcement of Foreign Judgments (Jersey) Order 1973, SI 1973/612	24
Reciprocal Enforcement of Foreign Judgments (Norway) Order 1962, SI 1962/636	24
Reciprocal Enforcement of Foreign Judgments (Pakistan) Order 1958, SI 1958/141	24
Reciprocal Enforcement of Foreign Judgments (Suriname) Order 1981, SI 1981/735	24
Reciprocal Enforcement of Foreign Judgments (Tonga) Order 1980, SI 1980/1523	24
Reciprocal Enforcement of Judgments (Administration of Justice Act 1920. Pt II) (Amendment) Order 1985, SI 1985/1994	24
Rules and regulations	
Bank of England's Notice to Institutions authorised under the Banking Act 1987, BSD 1988/3	104
Bank of England's Notice to Institutions authorised under the Banking Act 1987, BSD 1989/1:	104, **115**
Common Unsolicited Calls Regulations 1991	130, 294, 295, 310
reg 1	311
4(1)(e)	313
14	311, 313
Conflict of Laws Rules (Dicey and Morris)	
r 3	79
115	246
146, 148	25
150, 151	25, 41, 93
152	26
174	**27**
180	**16**
184	25
195	163, 167
196	167
210	74
212	35
(1)	**234**
(2)	**235**
Financial Services (Client's Money) Regulations 1987	288

	PAGE
Financial Services (Financial Records) Rules 1987	288
Financial Services (Financial Resources) Rules 1987	288
Financial Services (Glossary and Interpretation) Rules and Regulations 1991	134
Financial Services (Interim) (Service Companies) Rules and Regulations 1988	288
Financial Services (Miscellaneous Amendments) (No 17) Rules and Regulations 1991	
r 3.11	352, 354
Financial Services (Promotion of Unregulated Collective Investment Schemes) Regulations 1991	133
London International Stock Exchange	
London International Stock Exchange Rules	
r 300	344, 345
326	352
(1)	347
535	352, 453
Blue Book (*Eurocurrency Debt Securities, Guide to listing*)	317, 325
para 5.2	323
6	323
Sch 1	325, 331
Sch 2	326
Sch 5	
para 2, 3	337
Sch 6	324
Listing Rules of the London International Stock Exchange (*Admission of Securities to Listing*) Yellow Book	302, 320
s 1	
Ch 1	
para 1.4	322
Ch 2	321
para 20	335, 336
s 2	
Ch 1	
para 2.1	322
4	322
5	322
5.8	322
9	322, 333
10	197
Ch 3	
para 3.8	332
3.11	332
s 3	
Ch 2	
Pt 1	325
para 1.7, 1.8	330
Pt 2	325
Pts 4, 5	326

Table of statutory instruments etc xxv

	PAGE
Listing Rules of the London International Stock Exchange—*contd.*	
s 3—*contd.*	
Ch 2—*contd.*	
Pt 8	325
Ch 3	
Pt 3	
para 3.16	326
s 5	197
Ch 1	336
Ch 2	337
para 4(b)	337
17	197
Ch 3	337
para 1	336
2–9	337
11–15	338
Ch 4	
para 1,2	339
3(a)	339
4–7, 11	339
s 7	332
Ch 1	
para 1	324, 325
2	321
4.3	322
5	323
5.4	303, 305, 320
6.3	330, 331
(d)	326
6.4	336
6.4 (iii)	327
7	336
Ch 2	195
Ch 3	
para 3	349
s 8	
Ch 2	
para 2	334
3(d)	**334**
(e)	334
4	335
s 9	
Ch 2	224
para 3.2	223
3.3	222
3.4	223
3.5	223
Ch 4	162, 327
para 2	197

	PAGE
The Securities Association (TSA) Rules 1987/The Securities and Futures Authority (SFA) Rules	
Ch III Financial Regulations	
r 10.01	150, **151**
The Securities and Investments Board: Financial Services (Conduct of Business Rules 1987	
r 1.05	
Practice Note	314
The Securities and Investments Board: Financial Services (Conduct of Business) Rules 1990	314
r 10.01(2)	348
(a), (b)	349
(3)	352, 354
10.02	350, 351, 353, 354, 355, 356
(1)	353
(2)(b)	352
(3)	356
10.03	353, 354, 355, 356
(2)(a)(i)(ii)	355
(b)	355
(3)	356
10.04	351, 352, 356, 357
(2)(b)	352
(c)	**353**
Table S1	351
note 5	352
10.05	355
Table S 2	355, 356
note 4	348
(3)	349
10.07	**348**, 350, 351
Pt 16	
r 16.18	**356**
Core Conduct of Business Rules 1991	
Core rule 5	304
6	294, 304
29	347, 356
36	64
(2)	64
Ch IV	
Pt XV	
r 1220.01	63
1110	356
Unsolicited Calls Regulations 1987	294, 295, 313
see also Common Unsolicited Calls Regulations 1991 *supra*	

Table of US statutes, rules and regulations

Page references in this Table printed in **bold** type indicate where the material is set out in part or in full.

	PAGE
Statutes	
Bank Holding Company Act 1956	142, 430
s 4	428
(c)(18)	428
Banking Act 1933	362, 429, 430
s 2	465
(10), (11)	468
3(a)(3)	**465**, 466, 467, 468, 469
(10)	469
4(2)	467
5	469
12(1)	469
(2)	468
16	141, 427, 428, 431, 432, 469
20	141, 427, 469
21	141, 428, 431, 432, 469
32	141, 428, 469
Depository Institution Deregulation and Monetary Control Act 1980	
s 326(a)	7
Federal Reserve Act 1916	432
para 20	427
25, 25A	432
Foreign Assets Control Law 1917	7
Glass Steagall Act see Banking Act 1933	
Internal Revenue Code	
s 150.4(a)(b)	411
163(f)	409
(2)(B)	409, 410
(13)	411
871	411
(a), (h)	410
895	412
4701	409
7701	411
(a)(30)	411
International Banking Act 1978	6

	PAGE
Investment Advisors Act 1940	361, 423
s 203	418
206	378
Investment Company Act 1940	361, 362, 423, 467
Model Business Corporation Act	
s 2, 40	259
Public Law 97–320	
s 326(a)	7
Public Utility Holding Company 1935	361, 369
Restatement on Foreign Relations Law (2d)	
s 17	382
18	382, 383
Restatement on Torts (2d)	
para 26	226
Restatement on Trusts (2d)	30
Securities Act 1933	139, 183, 371, 427
s 2	141, **361**, 393
(1)	**139**, 140, 141
(3)	**364**
(7)	**362**, 381
(12)	364, 408
(13)	423
3(a)(2)	
(5)(A)	424
4	393
(2)	141, 422, 423
(3)	364, 365
(a)	425
5	364, 365, 366, 378, 381, 388, 389, 390, 393, 394, 404, 408, 409, 415, 420, 422, 423, 424, 425, 426
(a)	**363**
(c)	**363**, 364
10, 11	367
12	366, 367

xxvii

xxviii Table of US statutes, etc

	PAGE
Securities Act 1933—contd.	
s 12(1)	365, 366, 367
(2)	367, 368, 421
14, 15	366
17	**368**, 372
(a)(1)	371, 377
(2)	372, 377
(3)	371, 377
(b)	369
19	393
20	365, 387
(a)(b)	369
24	365, 369, 387
Sch A	364
Sch B	364
Securities Exchange Act 1934	139, 361, 363, 366, 394, 418, 427
s 3	141
(a)(4),(5)	369
(a)(10)	139, 361, 374, 465
(a)(12)(A)	374
(a)(12)	381
(17)	362
9	371, 372
10(b)	371, 372, 374, 377, 381, 385
12	364, 371
(a)	370
(b)	403
(g)	403
(1)	370
(3)	370
(5)	400, 402
13	371, 423, 424
14(e)	378
15	369, 370, 381, 388, 393, 416, 420, 421
(a)	388, 389
(c) 1, 2, 3	381
(d)	403, 423, 424
21	387
(a)	370, 376
29	370
30	370, 380
(b)	380
32	370, 387
(a)	376
Tax Equity and Fiscal Responsibility Act 1982	409
Tax Reform Act 1984	409
Trust Indenture Act 1939	212, 248, 361, 409
preamble	**249**
s 77 bbb	**249**
77 ddd(a)	211
77 eee	249
77 fff	**249**
77 ppp(b)	211
78 jj	249
302	378
306	378, 408, 409

	PAGE
Uniform Commercial Code	
s 1–105	20
(1)	**19**
8–320	171
New York	
General Obligations Law title 14	
5–1401	**20**
Business Corporations Law	
s 622	258
Virginia	
Corporations Law 1956	
s 43	259
Rules and Regulations	
Regulations of the Board of the Federal Reserve Bank	
Regulation D	81
s 204(1)(c)(5)	8, 82
2 204(2)(e)(i)	8
Regulation K	142, 432, 470
s 211.3(b)	433
211.5(d)	433
(4),(13)	432
Regulation Q	
s 217	7
Securities and Exchange Commission (SEC) Rules	
r 10(b)–5	264, 371, 372, 373, 378, 381, 382, 386, 387, 421, 469
(b)	372
(5)	**373**
10(b)-6	371, 372, 373, 421
(b)	373
(6)(a)(b)	373
10(b)–7	371, 372, 373, **374**; 421
(B)	375
(C)	376
(E)	374
(G)	375
(J)	376
(K)	374
(L)	375
12(g)3–2	370, 371
3–2(b)	403, 424, 425
5–1	400, 402
–1(a)(5)	402
15(a)(vi)	397
15a–6	388, 393, 396, 416, 417, 420, 421
15a–6(a)(1)	417, 418
(a)(2)	418
(a)(3)	419
15a–6(b)(7)(4)	419
15c–1(6)(8)	372, 375
15(c)(2)–11	423
17(a)–2	372
144	422, 423
(c)(1)(2)	423
(d)(e)	423
144A	364, 393, 422, 423, 424, 425, 426
(a)(1)–(4)	424
(d)(3)(i)	424
(d)(4)(i)	425

Table of US statutes etc

	PAGE
Regulation D	
s 501(a)	467
502(a)	468
506	**467**
Regulation S	141, 159, 183, 388, 390, 393, 394, 409, 411, 414, 416, 421, 425, 465, 468
s 901	394
902(a)(1)	363, 399
(b)	395
(1)	395
(2), (3)	396
(4)	397
(6)	396
(c)	403
(e)	394
(f)	400
(g)	400, 402
(i)	397, 398
(2)	406
(3)	398
(l)	404
(m)	403, **405**
(n)	400
(1)	401, 402
(2)	400
(o)	397, 401, 405
(1)(v)(viii)	406
(2)	397, 398, 406
(6)	405
(7)	397, 398, 406
Regulation S—contd.	
s 903	394, 395, 409, 422
(a), (b)	406
(c)(1)(i)	399, 400
(1)(i)(D)(c)	401
(ii)(iii)	399
(2)	183, 191, 390, 397, 399, 403
(3)	184, 391, 397, 399, 404, 406, 407
(4)	400, 401
(ii)	**401**
904	394, 395, 409
Regulation S–K	364, 371
s 502(d)	374
Regulation S–X	364
Regulation Y	428
US Codes	
12 USC s 461(6)	8
26 USC s 4911–3	9
US Treasury Regulations TEFRA c	
s 1.163.5(c)(2)(c)	415
US Treasury Regulations TEFRA d	184, 219, 390, 409, 410, 411, 413, 414, 416, 421, 422, 425, 426
s 1.163(2)(i)(D)(1)–(3)	412
1.163(2)(i)(D)(4)	411
1.163(2)(i)(D)(5)	412
1.163–5	413
165–12c(1)(v)	**412**
US Treasury Regulations TEFRA a and b	410

Table of European and foreign enactments

Page references in this Table printed in **bold** type indicate where the material is set out in part or in full

	PAGE
Basle Convergence Agreement December 1987	103, 104, 115
Belgian Royal Decree No 62, 10 November 1967	172, 173
Brussels Convention on Jurisdiction and the Enforcement of Judgments in Civil and Commercial Matters 1968 Cmnd 7395 see Civil Jurisdiction and Judgments Act 1982, Sch 1	
EC Council Directive (Admissions Directive) 79/279 OJ L66, 16.3.79, p 21	318, 320, 333, 334
EC Council Directive 89/646 (Second Banking Coordination) Directive OJ L 386 30.12.89,	295
EC Council Directive (First Company Law Directive 68/151, OJ L65, 14.3.68, p 8 (5 Edn 1968 (1) p 41)	
art 9	29
EC Council Directive (Second Company Law Directive) 77/91 OJ L26, 31.1.77, p 1	270, 272
EC Council Directive (Interim Reports Directive) 82/121 OJ 48 20.2.82, p 26	318, 320
EC Council Directive (Listing Particulars Directive) 80/390 OJ L100, 17.4.80, p 1	318, 320
art 4(1)	324
24	333, 334
EC Council Directive (Prospectus Directive) 89/298 OJ L124 5.5.89 p 8	**148**
Euroclear System-Operating Procedures November 1990	
s 1	159
2	169
3	170
5	159, 196
9	196

	PAGE
s 10	169
Euroclear System – Terms and Conditions Governing Use December 1982	172
art 4	170, **173**
French Civil Code	21, 23
art 1184	22
part 3	22
1156	22
1689	105
2312	20
Hague Convention on the Law applicable to Trusts and their Recognition Cmnd 9494 see Recognition of Trusts Act 1987, Schedule	
International Monetary Fund Agreement	
art VIII (2)(a)	37
(b)	31, 33, 34, **35**, 36, 37, 38, 71
XXX(d)	37
International Primary Markets Association Recommendations:	153, 181, 187
s 1	148
1.1	**153**
1.2	157, 158, 341, 347
1.3	158, 347, 351
1.7	187, 347
1.8(3)	188
App A, App c	154
Italian Civil Code	
art 25	20
1455	22
Rivista di Diritto Internazionale Privato e Processuale 1977, 1981	36
Rome Convention on the law applicable to contractual obligations 80/934: Misc 5(1982) Cmnd 8489: OJ L266, 9.10.80 pl see Contracts (Applicable Law) Act 1990	

xxxi

Table of cases

PAGE

A

Aaron v SEC 446 US 680 (1980) 376
Aas v Benham [1891] 2 Ch 244, 65 LT 25, CA 244
Aberfoyle Plantations Ltd v Cheng [1960] AC 115, [1959] 3 All ER 910, [1959] 3 WLR 1011, 103 Sol Jo 1045, PC 70
Adams v National Bank of Greece SA [1960] 1 QB 64, [1959] 2 All ER 362, [1959] 2 WLR 800, 103 Sol Jo 431, CA; revsd [1961] AC 255, [1960] 2 All ER 421, [1960] 3 WLR 8, 104 Sol Jo 489, HL 41, 258, 260, 277
Adelaide Electric Supply Co Ltd v Prudential Assurance Co Ltd [1934] AC 122, [1933] All ER Rep 82, 103 LJ Ch 85, 150 LT 281, 50 TLR 147, 77 Sol Jo 913, 39 Com Cas 119, HL 73
Affiliated Ute Citizens of Utah v United States 406 US 128 (1972) . . 377
Affréteurs Réunis SA v Leopold Walford (London) Ltd [1919] AC 801, 88 LJKB 861, 121 LT 393, 35 TLR 542, 14 Asp MLC 451, 24 Com Cas 268, HL . . 226
Agra and Masterman's Bank, Re, ex p Waring (1866) 36 LJ Ch 151 . . . 61
Aid Auto Stores Inc v Cannon 525 2d 468 (2nd Circ, 1975) . . . 366
Alcock v Smith [1892] 1 Ch 238, 61 LJ Ch 161, 66 LT 126, 8 TLR 222, 36 Sol Jo 199, CA 166, 168
Alexander v Rayson [1936] 1 KB 169, [1935] All ER Rep 185, 105 LJKB 148, 154 LT 205, 52 TLR 131, 80 Sol Jo 15, CA 75
Allied Bank International v Banco Credito Agricola de Cartago 23 ILM 742 (1984) . 39
Allied Bank International v Banco Credito Agricola de Cartago 566 F Supp 1440 (SDNY, 1983); affd 733 F 2d 23 (2nd Circ, 1984) . . . 38
Alton Box Board Co v Goldman Sachs & Co 560 F 2d 916 (8th Circ, 1977) . . 368
Aluminium Industrie Vaassen BV v Romalpa Aluminium Ltd [1976] 2 All ER 552, [1976] 1 WLR 676, 119 Sol Jo 318; affd [1976] 2 All ER 552, [1976] 1 WLR 676, 120 Sol Jo 95, [1976] 1 Lloyd's Rep 443, CA 72
Amfac Manufacturing Corpn v Arizona Malle of Temple 583 F 2d 426 (9th Circ, 1978) 140
Anctil v Manufacturers Life Insurance Co [1899] AC 604, [1895-9] All ER Rep 1238, 68 LJCP 123, 81 LT 279, PC 235
Andrabell Ltd (in liquidation), Re, Airborne Accessories Ltd v Goodman [1984] 3 All ER 407, [1984] BCLC 522 72
Anemone, The. See Clipper Maritime Ltd v Shirlstar Container Transport Ltd, The Anemone
Anns v Merton London Borough Council [1978] AC 728, [1977] 2 All ER 492, [1977] 2 WLR 1024, 141 JP 526, 121 Sol Jo 377, 75 LGR 555, 5 BLR 1, 243 Estates Gazette 523, 591, [1977] JPL 514, HL 57
Arab Monetary Fund v Hashim (No 3) [1991] 2 AC 114, [1991] 1 All ER 871, [1991] 2 WLR 729, HL 28

xxxiv *Table of cases*

	PAGE
Archbolds (Freightage) Ltd v S Spanglett Ltd (Randall, Third Party) [1961] 1 QB 374, [1961] 1 All ER 417, [1961] 2 WLR 170, 105 Sol Jo 149, CA	75
Armar Shipping Co Ltd v Caisse Algérienne d'Assurance et de Réassurance, The Armar [1981] 1 All ER 498, [1981] 1 WLR 207, 125 Sol Jo 79, [1980] 2 Lloyd's Rep 450, CA	233
Ashby v Blackwell and Million Bank Co (1765) Amb 503, 2 Eden 299	241
Attenborough v Mackenzie (1856) 25 LJ Ex 244	198

B

BSF Co v Philadelphia National Bank 42 Del Ch 106, 204 A 2d 746 (Sup Ct, 1964)	267
Badische Co Ltd, Re [1921] 2 Ch 331, 91 LJ Ch 133, 126 LT 466	78
Banco de Bilbao v Sancho [1938] 2 KB 176, [1938] 2 All ER 253, 107 LJKB 681, 159 LT 369, 54 TLR 603, 82 Sol Jo 254, CA	27
Banco Nacional de Cuba v Sabbatino 376 US 398 (1964)	38
Bank of England v Vagliano Bros [1891] AC 107, [1891-4] All ER Rep 93, 60 LJQB 145, 64 LT 353, 55 JP 676, 39 WR 657, 7 TLR 333, HL	164
Banque Keyser Ullmann SA v Skandia (UK) Insurance Co Ltd [1990] 1 QB 665, [1989] 3 WLR 25, 133 Sol Jo 817, [1988] NLJR 287, [1989] 26 LS Gaz R 33, sub nom Banque Financière de la Cité SA v Westgate Insurance Co Ltd [1989] 2 All ER 952, [1988] 2 Lloyd's Rep 513, CA; affd sub nom Banque Financière de la Cité SA (formerly Banque Keyser Ullman SA) v Westgate Insurance Co Ltd (formerly Hodge General and Mercantile Co Ltd) [1990] 2 All ER 947, [1990] 3 WLR 364, 134 Sol Jo 1265, [1990] 2 Lloyd's Rep 377, [1990] NLJR 1074, HL	50
Baraka v Bancomer SA 762 F 2d 222 (1985)	39
Barclays Bank International Ltd v Levin Bros (Bradford) Ltd [1977] QB 270, [1976] 3 All ER 900, [1976] 3 WLR 852, 120 Sol Jo 801, [1977] 1 Lloyd's Rep 51	73, 74
Barclays Bank Ltd v Quistclose Investments Ltd [1970] AC 567, [1968] 3 All ER 651, [1968] 3 WLR 1097, 112 Sol Jo 903, HL	60
Bartlett v Barclays Bank Trust Co Ltd [1980] Ch 515, [1980] 1 All ER 139, [1980] 2 WLR 430, 124 Sol Jo 85	237
Bartlett v Barclays Bank Trust Co Ltd (No 2) [1980] Ch 515, [1980] 2 All ER 92, [1980] 2 WLR 430, 124 Sol Jo 221	234
Bechuanaland Exploration Co v London Trading Bank Ltd [1898] 2 QB 658, 67 LJQB 986, 79 LT 270, 14 TLR 587, 3 Com Cas 285	163, 165, 175
Becker (A G) Inc v Board of Governors of Federal Reserve System 224 US App DC 21, 693 F 2d 136 (1982)	431
Becker (A G) Inc v Board of Governors of the Federal Reserve System 519 F Supp 602 (1981)	431
Bence v Shearman [1898] 2 Ch 582, 67 LJ Ch 513, 78 LT 804, 47 WR 350, CA	163
Bersch v Drexel Firestone Inc 519 F 2d 974 (2nd Circ); cert den 423 US 1017 (1975)	383, 384
Beswick v Beswick [1968] AC 58, [1967] 2 All ER 1197, [1967] 3 WLR 932, 111 Sol Jo 540, HL	276
Bigos v Bousted [1951] 1 All ER 92	75
Birtchnell v Equity Trustee Executors and Agency Co Ltd (1929) 42 CLR 384	65
Blackwell v Benstein 203 F 2d 690 (5th Circ, 1953)	368
Blue Chip Stamps v Manor Drugstores 421 US 723 (1975)	377
Boardman v Phipps. See Phipps v Boardman	
Boissevain v Weil [1949] 1 KB 482, [1949] 1 All ER 416, 65 TLR 197, 93 Sol Jo 133, CA; affd [1950] AC 327, [1950] 1 All ER 728, 66 (pt 1) TLR 771, 94 Sol Jo 319, HL	17
Bond Worth Ltd, Re [1980] Ch 228, [1979] 3 All ER 919, [1979] 3 WLR 629, 123 Sol Jo 216	72
Bonython v Commonwealth of Australia [1951] AC 201, 66 (pt 2) TLR 969, 94 Sol Jo 821, PC	55
Borden (UK) Ltd v Scottish Timber Products Ltd (1978) 122 Sol Jo 825, [1979] 2 Lloyd's Rep 168; revsd [1981] Ch 25, [1979] 3 All ER 961, [1979] 3 WLR 672, 123 Sol Jo 688, [1980] 1 Lloyd's Rep 160, CA	72
Boulting v Association of Cinematograph, Television and Allied Technicians [1963] 2 QB 606, [1963] 1 All ER 716, [1963] 2 WLR 529, 107 Sol Jo 133, CA	67

Table of cases xxxv

PAGE

Boulton v Jones (1857) 2 H & N 564, 27 LJ Ex 117, sub nom Bolton v Jones 30 LTOS 188, 3 Jur NS 1156, 6 WR 107 119
Branca v Cobarro [1947] KB 854, [1947] 2 All ER 101, [1948] LJR 43, 177 LT 332, 63 TLR 408, CA 46
Brandts (William) Sons & Co v Dunlop Rubber Co Ltd [1905] AC 454, [1904-7] All ER Rep 345, 74 LJKB 898, 93 LT 495, 21 TLR 710, 11 Com Cas 1, HL . 109, 227
Bray v Ford [1896] AC 44, [1895-9] All ER Rep 1000, 65 LJQB 213, 73 LT 609, 12 TLR 119, HL 65
Brice v Bannister (1878) 3 QBD 569, 47 LJQB 722, 38 LT 739, 26 WR 670, CA . 111, 114
British India Steam Navigation Co v IRC (1881) 7 QBD 165, 50 LJQB 517, 44 LT 378, 29 WR 610 . . . . 440, 459
British Vacuum Cleaner Co Ltd v New Vacuum Cleaner Co Ltd [1907] 2 Ch 312, 76 LJ Ch 511, 97 LT 201, 23 TLR 587, 51 Sol Jo 553, 14 Mans 231, 24 RPC 641 . 299
Broad v Rockwell International Corpn 454 US 965, 642 F 2d 929 (1981) . . 262
Brogden, Re, Billing v Brogden (1888) 38 Ch D 546, [1886-90] All ER Rep 927, 59 LT 650, 37 WR 84, 4 TLR 521, CA 240
Brunswick (Duke) v King of Hanover (1844) 6 Beav 1, 6 State Tr NS 33, 13 LJ Ch 107, 2 LTOS 306, 8 Jur 253; affd (1848) 2 HL Cas 1 . . . . 38, 40
Bunge Corpn v Tradax SA [1981] 2 All ER 513, [1981] 1 WLR 711, 125 Sol Jo 373, [1981] 2 Lloyd's Rep 1, HL 21
Burbridge v Manners (1812) 3 Camp 193 198
Business Computers Ltd v Anglo-African Leasing Ltd [1977] 2 All ER 741, [1977] 1 WLR 578, 120 Sol Jo 201 163
Buttes Gas and Oil Co v Hammer (No 3) [1982] AC 888, [1981] 3 All ER 616, [1981] 3 WLR 787, 125 Sol Jo 776, HL 40

C

CNS Enterprises Inc v G & G Enterprises Inc 508 F 2d 1354 (7th Circ); cert denied 423 US 825 (1975) 139
Cable (Lord), Re, Garratt v Waters [1976] 3 All ER 417, [1977] 1 WLR 7, 120 Sol Jo 317 81
Cady v Murphy 113 2d 988 (1st Circ, 1940) 366
Callejo v Bancomer SA 764 F 2d 1101 (5th Circ, 1985) 37, 39
Campbell v Walker (1800) 5 Ves 678, 5 RR 135 243
Campbell Discount Co Ltd v Bridge [1961] 1 QB 445, [1961] 2 All ER 97, [1961] 2 WLR 596, 105 Sol Jo 232, CA; revsd sub nom Bridge v Campbell Discount Co Ltd [1962] AC 600, [1962] 1 All ER 385, [1962] 2 WLR 439, 106 Sol Jo 94, HL . 76
Caparo Industries plc v Dickman [1990] 2 AC 605, [1990] 1 All ER 568, [1990] 2 WLR 358, 134 Sol Jo 494, [1990] BCLC 273, [1990] BCC 164, [1990] NLJR 248, [1990] 12 LS Gaz R 42, HL 30, 49, 50, 57, 191, 464
Carl Zeiss Stiftung v Rayner and Keeler Ltd (No 2) [1967] 1 AC 853, [1966] 2 All ER 536, [1966] 3 WLR 125, 110 Sol Jo 425, [1967] RPC 497, HL 27
Carlill v Carbolic Smoke Ball Co [1892] 2 QB 484, 61 LJQB 696, 56 JP 665, 8 TLR 680, 36 Sol Jo 628; affd [1893] 1 QB 256, [1891-4] All ER Rep 127, 62 LJQB 257, 67 LT 837, 57 JP 325, 41 WR 210, 9 TLR 124, 4 R 176, CA . . . 117
Case (JI) Co v Borak 377 US 426 (1964) 378
Charge Card Services Ltd, Re [1987] Ch 150, [1986] 3 All ER 289, [1986] 3 WLR 697, 130 Sol Jo 801, [1987] BCLC 17, [1986] BTLC 195, 2 BCC 99, 373; on appeal [1989] Ch 497, [1988] 3 All ER 702, [1988] 3 WLR 764, 132 Sol Jo 1458, [1988] BCLC 711n, 4 BCC 524, [1988] NLJR 201, CA 94
Chaudhry v Prabhakar [1988] 3 All ER 718, [1989] 1 WLR 29, 133 Sol Jo 82, [1988] NLJR 172, [1989] 6 LS Gaz R 44, CA 62
Citibank v Wells Fargo Asia Ltd 110 S Ct 2034 (1990) 39
City of London Brewery Co v IRC [1899] 1 QB 121, 68 LJQB 62, 78 LT 39, 648, 47 WR 216, 15 TLR 49, 43 Sol Jo 61, CA 125
Clark v Balm, Hill & Co [1908] 1 KB 667, 77 LJKB 369, 15 Mans 42 . . 125, 126
Clipper Maritime Ltd v Shirlstar Container Transport Ltd, The Anemone [1987] 1 Lloyd's Rep 546 46

xxxvi *Table of cases*

PAGE

Clough Mill Ltd v Martin [1984] 1 All ER 721, [1984] 1 WLR 1067, 128 Sol Jo 564, [1984] BCLC 97, [1984] LS Gaz R 2375; revsd [1984] 3 All ER 982, [1985] 1 WLR 111, 128 Sol Jo 850, [1985] BCLC 64, [1985] LS Gaz R 116, CA . . 72
Collett v Co-operative Wholesale Society Ltd [1970] 1 All ER 274, [1970] 1 WLR 250, 134 JP 227, 114 Sol Jo 9, 68 LGR 158 299
Collins v Signetics 605 F 2d 110 (3rd Circ, 1979) 367
Commercial Discount Corpn v Lincoln Trust Commercial Corpn 445 F Supp 1263 (SDNY, 1978) 140
Constantine (Joseph) SS Line Ltd v Imperial Smelting Corpn Ltd, The Kingswood [1942] AC 154, [1941] 2 All ER 165, 110 LJKB 433, 165 LT 27, 57 TLR 485, 46 Com Cas 258, HL 271
Continental Grain Australia Pty Ltd v Pacific Oilseeds Inc 592 F 2d 409 (8th Circ, 1979) 386
Coomber, Re, Coomber v Coomber [1911] 1 Ch 723, 80 LJ Ch 399, 104 LT 517, CA 64
Cowan v Scargill [1985] Ch 270, [1984] 2 All ER 750, [1984] 3 WLR 501, [1984] ICR 646, 128 Sol Jo 550 237
Coxen, Re, McCallum v Coxen [1948] Ch 747, [1948] 2 All ER 492, [1948] LJR 1590, 92 Sol Jo 442 . . . . 235, 241
Crédit Français International SA v Sociedad Financiera de Comerco SA 490 NYS 2d 670 (1985) 20, 101
Cremdean Properties Ltd v Nash (1977) 244 Estates Gazette 547, CA . . . 192
Cundy v Lindsay (1878) 3 App Cas 459, [1874-80] All ER Rep 1149, 38 LT 573, 42 JP 483, 26 WR 406, 14 Cox CC 93, sub nom Lindsay & Co v Cundy 47 LJQB 481, HL 119
Cunningham v Pressed Steel Car Co 238 App Div 624, 265 NY Supp 256 (1933) . 205
Curtis v Chemical Cleaning and Dyeing Co Ltd [1951] 1 KB 805, [1951] 1 All ER 631, [1951] 1 TLR 452, 95 Sol Jo 253, CA 50

D

Dave v Rosenfeld 229 F 2d 855 (2nd Circ, 1956) 367
Davison v Donaldson (1882) 9 QBD 623, 47 LT 564, 31 WR 277, 4 Asp MLC 601, CA 60
Dearle v Hall (1823-28) 3 Russ 1, [1824-34] All ER Rep 28 . . . 107, 110, 163
De Mattos v Gibson (1859) 4 De G & J 276, 28 LJ Ch 498, 33 LTOS 193, 5 Jur NS 555, 7 WR 514 96
Denmark Productions Ltd v Boscobel Productions Ltd [1969] 1 QB 699, [1968] 3 All ER 513, [1968] 3 WLR 841, 112 Sol Jo 761, CA 227
Derry v Peek (1889) 14 App Cas 337, [1886-90] All ER Rep 1, 58 LJ Ch 864, 61 LT 265, 54 JP 148, 38 WR 33, 5 TLR 625, 1 Meg 292, HL 49
Des Brisay v Goldfield Corpn 549 F 2d 133 (9th Circ, 1977) . . . 382, 383
Drexel Burnham Lambert Group Inc v Galadari 610 F Supp 114, 777 F 2d 877 . 39
Dundee General Hospitals Board of Management v Walker [1952] 1 All ER 896, sub nom Dundee General Hospitals v Bell's Trustees 1952 SLT 270, 1952 SC (HL) 78 . . . . 210, 232, 241
Dunlop Pneumatic Tyre Co Ltd v New Garage and Motor Co Ltd [1915] AC 79, [1914-15] All ER Rep 739, 83 LJKB 1574, 111 LT 862, 30 TLR 625, HL . . 75
Durham Bros v Robertson [1898] 1 QB 765, [1895-9] All ER Rep 1683, 67 LJQB 484, 78 LT 438, CA 110, 114

E

Edelstein v Schuler & Co [1902] 2 KB 144, [1900-3] All ER Rep 884, 71 LJKB 572, 87 LT 204, 50 WR 493, 18 TLR 597, 46 Sol Jo 500, 7 Com Cas 172 . 163, 164
Edgington v Fitzmaurice (1885) 29 Ch D 459, [1881-5] All ER Rep 59, 55 LJ Ch 650, 53 LT 369, 50 JP 52, 33 WR 911, 1 TLR 326, CA 50
Edmonds v Blaina Furnaces Co (1887) 36 Ch D 215, [1886-90] All ER Rep 581, 56 LJ Ch 815, 57 LT 139, 35 WR 798 125
Ehrlich-Boher & Co v University of Houston 49 NY 2d 574, 427 NYS 2d 817 (1980) 19
Elafi, The. See Karlshamns Oljefabriker v Eastport Navigation Corpn, The Elafi

Table of cases xxxvii

	PAGE
Ellis v Carter 291 F 2d 870 (9th Circ, 1961)	362
Embiricos v Anglo-Austrian Bank [1905] 1 KB 677, 74 LJKB 326, 92 LT 305, 53 WR 306, 21 TLR 268, 49 Sol Jo 281, 10 Com Cas 99, CA	166, 168
Emerald Construction Co v Lowthian [1966] 1 All ER 1013, [1966] 1 WLR 691, 110 Sol Jo 226, CA	97
Emery's Investments' Trusts, Re, Emery v Emery [1959] Ch 410, [1959] 1 All ER 577, [1959] 2 WLR 461, 103 Sol Jo 257	79
English and Scottish Mercantile Investment Co Ltd v Brunton [1892] 2 QB 1; affd [1892] 2 QB 700, 62 LJQB 136, 67 LT 406, 41 WR 133, 8 TLR 772, 4 R 58, CA	125
Ernst & Ernst v Hochfelder 425 US 185 (1976)	377
Eugenia, The. See Ocean Tramp Tankers Corpn v V/O Sovfracht, The Eugenia	
Euro-Diam Ltd v Bathurst [1990] 1 QB 1, [1987] 2 All ER 113, [1987] 2 WLR 1368, 131 Sol Jo 775, [1987] 1 Lloyd's Rep 178, 1987 FLR 247, [1987] LS Gaz R 1732; affd [1990] 1 QB 1, [1988] 2 All ER 23, [1988] 2 WLR 517, 132 Sol Jo 372, [1988] 1 Lloyd's Rep 228, [1988] 9 LS Gaz R 45, CA	32
European Assurance Society, Re, Miller's Case (1876) 3 Ch D 391, CA	234
Exchange National Bank v Touche Ross & Co 544 F 2d 1126 (2d Circ, 1976)	140, 141

F

FOF Proprietary Funds Ltd v Arthur Young & Co 400 F Supp 1219 (SDNY, 1975)	385
First Russian Insurance Co v London and Lancashire Insurance Co [1928] Ch 922, 97 LJ Ch 445, 140 LT 337, 44 TLR 583, 31 Ll L Rep 151	27
Fletcher v Fletcher (1844) 4 Hare 67, 14 LJ Ch 66, 8 Jur 1040, 67 RR 6	226
Forrer v Nash (1865) 35 Beav 167, 6 New Rep 361, 11 Jur NS 789, 14 WR 8	96
Forster v Baker [1910] 2 KB 636, 79 LJKB 664, 102 LT 29, 26 TLR 243; on appeal [1910] 2 KB 636, [1908-10] All ER Rep 554, 79 LJKB 664, 102 LT 522, 26 TLR 421, CA	107
Franklin Savings Bank of New York v Levy 551 F 2d 521 (2nd Circ, 1977)	367, 469
Friedman v Airlift International Inc 355 NYS 2d 613 (1974)	211, 212
Fuller v Krogh 15 Wis 2d 412 (1962)	258

G

Gardner and Florence Call Cowles Fund v Empire Inc 589 F Supp 669 (1984)	260, 262
Gisborne v Gisborne (1877) 2 App Cas 300, [1874-80] All ER Rep Ext 1698, 46 LJ Ch 556, 36 LT 564, 25 WR 516, HL	209
Glegg v Bromley [1912] 3 KB 474, [1911-13] All ER Rep 1138, 81 LJKB 1081, 106 LT 825, CA	110
Goldsmith v Rodger [1962] 2 Lloyd's Rep 249, CA	50
Goodwin v Robarts (1875) LR 10 Exch 337, 44 LJ Ex 157, 33 LT 272, 23 WR 915, Ex Ch; affd (1876) 1 App Cas 476, [1874-80] All ER Rep 628, 45 LJQB 748, 35 LT 179, 24 WR 987, HL	163, 165
Gorringe v Irwell India Rubber and Gutta Percha Works (1886) 34 Ch D 128, [1886-90] All ER Rep Ext 1643, 56 LJ Ch 85, 55 LT 572, 35 WR 86, CA	107
Gould v Tricon Inc 272 F Supp 385 (SDNY, 1967)	368
Gray v Portland Bank 3 Mass 364 (1807)	258
Guaranty Trust Co of New York v Hannay & Co [1918] 2 KB 623, [1918-19] All ER Rep 151, 87 LJKB 1223, 119 LT 321, 34 TLR 427, CA	90
Guardian Depositors Corpn v David Stott Flour Mills Inc 291 Mich 180 (1939)	205
Gurney v Behrend (1854) 3 E & B 622, [1843-60] All ER Rep 520, 23 LJQB 265, 23 LTOS 89, 18 Jur 856, 2 WR 425	163

H

Haag v Barnes 9 NY 2d 554, 216 NYS 2d 65 (1961)	19
Halle v Van Sweringen Corpn 37 Del 491	211
Hallett's Estate, Re, Knatchbull v Hallett (1880) 13 Ch D 696, [1874-80] All ER Rep 793, 49 LJ Ch 415, 42 LT 421, 28 WR 732, CA	220
Harff v Kerkorian 324 A 2d 215 (Del Ch, 1974); revsd 347 A 2d 133 (Del, 1975)	262, 267

	PAGE
Harmer v Armstrong [1934] Ch 65, [1933] All ER Rep 778, 103 LJ Ch 1, 149 LT 579, CA	276
Harris v Wyre Forest District Council [1988] QB 835, [1988] 1 All ER 691, [1988] 2 WLR 1173, 132 Sol Jo 91, 87 LGR 19, 20 HLR 278, [1988] 1 EGLR 132, [1988] 05 EG 57, [1988] NLJR 15, [1988] 7 LS Gaz R 40, CA; revsd [1990] 1 AC 831, [1989] 2 All ER 514, [1989] 2 WLR 790, 133 Sol Jo 597, 87 LGR 685, 21 HLR 424, 17 Con LR 1, [1989] 1 EGLR 169, [1989] 17 EG 68, 18 EG 99, [1989] NLJR 576, HL	243
Hawkesley v May [1956] 1 QB 304, [1955] 3 All ER 353, [1955] 3 WLR 569, 99 Sol Jo 781	208
Hedley Byrne & Co Ltd v Heller & Partners Ltd [1964] AC 465, [1963] 2 All ER 575, [1963] 3 WLR 101, 107 Sol Jo 454, [1963] 1 Lloyd's Rep 485, HL	30, 49, 50, 52, 444, 464
Helby v Matthews [1895] AC 471, [1895-9] All ER Rep 821, 64 LJQB 465, 72 LT 841, 60 JP 20, 43 WR 561, 11 TLR 446, 11 R 232, HL	91
Hendy Lennox (Industrial Engines) Ltd v Grahame Puttick Ltd [1984] 2 All ER 152, [1984] 1 WLR 485, 128 Sol Jo 220, [1984] 2 Lloyd's Rep 422, [1984] BCLC 285, [1984] LS Gaz R 585	72
Henry v Hammond [1913] 2 KB 515, [1911-13] All ER Rep Ext 1478, 82 LJKB 575, 108 LT 729, 29 TLR 340, 57 Sol Jo 358, 12 Asp MLC 332	61
Hill York Corpn v American International Franchises Inc 448 F 2d 680 (5th Circ, 1971)	368
Holder v Holder [1968] Ch 353, [1968] 1 All ER 665, [1968] 2 WLR 237, 112 Sol Jo 17, 205 Estates Gazette 211, CA	243
Hollandia, The [1983] 1 AC 565, [1982] 3 All ER 1141, [1982] 3 WLR 1111, 126 Sol Jo 819, [1983] 1 Lloyd's Rep 1, [1983] Com LR 44, HL	291
Hong Kong Fir Shipping Co Ltd v Kawasaki Kisen Kaisha Ltd [1962] 2 QB 26, [1962] 1 All ER 474, [1962] 2 WLR 474, 106 Sol Jo 35, [1961] 2 Lloyd's Rep 478, CA	21, 73
Hopkins (John) University v Hutton 422 F 2d 1124 (4th Circ, 1970)	367
Howard Marine and Dredging Co Ltd v A Ogden & Sons (Excavations) Ltd [1978] QB 574, [1978] 2 All ER 1134, [1978] 2 WLR 515, 122 Sol Jo 48, 9 BLR 34, [1978] 1 Lloyd's Rep 334, CA	49
Hughes v Pump House Hotel Co [1902] 2 KB 190, [1900-3] All ER Rep 480, 71 LJKB 630, 86 LT 794, 50 WR 660, 18 TLR 654, CA	110

I

IIT v Cornfeld 619 F 2d 909 (2nd Circ, 1980)	385
ITT v Vencap 519 F 2d 1001 (2nd Circ, 1975)	384
Independent Automatic Sales Ltd v Knowles and Foster [1962] 3 All ER 27, [1962] 1 WLR 974, 106 Sol Jo 720	97
Indian and General Investment Trust Ltd v Borax Consolidated Ltd [1920] 1 KB 539, [1918-19] All ER Rep 346, 89 LJKB 252, 122 LT 547, 36 TLR 125, 64 Sol Jo 225	79
Interfoto Picture Library Ltd v Stiletto Visual Programmes Ltd [1989] QB 433, [1988] 1 All ER 348, [1988] 2 WLR 615, 132 Sol Jo 460, [1988] BTLC 39, [1987] NLJ Rep 1159, [1988] 9 LS Gaz R 45, CA	76

J

Jackson v Oppenheim 533 F 2d 826 (2nd Circ, 1976)	368
Jackson and Bassford Ltd, Re [1906] 2 Ch 467, 75 LJ Ch 697, 95 LT 292, 22 TLR 708, 13 Mans 306	97
Janred Properties Ltd v Ente Nazionale Italiano per il Turismo [1989] 2 All ER 444, CA	27, 30, 72
Japha v Delaware Valley Utilities Co 15 Atlantic Reporter 2d 432	211
Johnson v Agnew [1980] AC 367, [1979] 1 All ER 883, [1979] 2 WLR 487, 123 Sol Jo 217, 39 P & CR 424, 251 Estates Gazette 1167, HL	119
Johnson v Kearley [1908] 2 KB 514, 77 LJKB 904, 99 LT 506, 24 TLR 729, CA	61
Jones v Lock (1865) 1 Ch App 25, 35 LJ Ch 117, 13 LT 514, 11 Jur NS 913, 14 WR 149	227

K

Kahler v Midland Bank Ltd [1950] AC 24, [1949] 2 All ER 621, [1949] LJR 1687, 65 TLR 663, HL 16, 25, 31, 32, 35
Karlshamns Oljefabriker v Eastport Navigation Corpn, The Elafi [1982] 1 All ER 208, [1981] 2 Lloyd's Rep 679, [1981] Com LR 149 173
Kessler v General Cable Corpn 155 Cal Rptr 94 . . . . . 261, 262
Kingsley v Sterling Industrial Securities Ltd [1967] 2 QB 747, [1966] 2 All ER 414, [1966] 2 WLR 1265, 110 Sol Jo 267, CA 91
Kleinwort Sons & Co v Ungarische Baumwolle Industrie Akt [1939] 2 KB 678, [1939] 3 All ER 38, 108 LJKB 861, 160 LT 615, 55 TLR 814, 83 Sol Jo 437, 44 Com Cas 324, CA 30, 42, 278
Klug v Klug [1918] 2 Ch 67, 87 LJ Ch 569, 118 LT 696, 62 Sol Jo 471 . . . 208
Knight v Knight (1840) 3 Beav 148, 9 LJ Ch 354, 4 Jur 839, 52 RR 74; affd sub nom Knight v Boughton (1844) 11 Cl & Fin 513, 8 Jur 923, HL . . . 225
Kremezi v Ridgway [1949] 1 All ER 662, 93 Sol Jo 287 233

L

Leasco Data Processing Equipment Corpn v Maxwell 468 F 2d 1326 (2nd Circ, 1972) 381, 383
Lee v Showmen's Guild of Great Britain [1952] 2 QB 329, [1952] 1 All ER 1175, [1952] 1 TLR 1115, 96 Sol Jo 296, CA 235
Lehigh Valley Trust Co v Central National Bank of Jacksonville 409 F 2d (5th Circ, 1969) 141
Lemon v Austin Friars Investment Trust Ltd [1926] Ch 1, [1925] All ER Rep 255, 95 LJ Ch 97, 133 LT 790, 41 TLR 629, 69 Sol Jo 762, CA . . 125, 440, 459
Levy v Abercorris Slate and Slab Co (1887) 37 Ch D 260, [1886-90] All ER Rep 509, 57 LJ Ch 202, 58 LT 218, 36 WR 411, 4 TLR 34 . . . 122, 125, 439, 459
Libra Bank Ltd v Banco Nacional de Costa Rica 570 F Supp 870 (SDNY, 1983) . 36, 38
Libyan Arab Foreign Bank v Bankers Trust Co [1989] QB 728, [1989] 3 All ER 252, [1989] 3 WLR 314, 133 Sol Jo 568, [1988] 1 Lloyd's Rep 259 . 6, 7, 32, 81, 278, 452
Libyan Arab Foreign Bank v Manufacturers Hanover Trust Co (No 2) [1989] 1 Lloyd's Rep 608 . . . . 8, 34, 81, 246
Lines Bros Ltd, Re [1983] Ch 1, [1982] 2 All ER 183, [1982] 2 WLR 1010, 126 Sol Jo 205, CA 74
Lipton Ltd v Ford [1917] 2 KB 647, 86 LJKB 1241, 116 LT 632, 33 TLR 459, 15 LGR 699 78
Lissberger, Re 71 NYS 2d 585 (1947); affd 78 NYS 2d 199 (1948) . . . 258
Liverpool City Council v Irwin [1977] AC 239, [1976] 2 All ER 39, [1976] 2 WLR 562, 120 Sol Jo 267, 13 HLR 38, 74 LGR 392, 32 P & CR 43, 238 Estates Gazette 879, 963, HL 22, 23
Lloyd's v Harper (1880) 16 Ch D 290, 50 LJ Ch 140, 43 LT 481, 29 WR 452, CA . 226
Locabail International Finance Ltd v Agroexport, The Sea Hawk [1986] 1 All ER 901, [1986] 1 WLR 657, 130 Sol Jo 245, [1986] 1 Lloyd's Rep 317, CA . . 96
Londonderry's Settlement, Re, Peat v Walsh [1965] Ch 918, [1964] 3 All ER 855, [1965] 2 WLR 229, 108 Sol Jo 896, CA 208, 240
Love (Gregory) & Co, Re, Francis v Gregory Love & Co [1916] 1 Ch 203, [1914-15] All ER Rep Ext 1215, 85 LJ Ch 281, 114 LT 395, 32 TLR 210, 60 Sol Jo 221, [1916] HBR 42 97
Loveridge v Dreagoux 678 F 2d 870 (10th Circ, 1982) 362
Lucking's Will Trusts, Re, Renwick v Lucking [1967] 3 All ER 726, [1968] 1 WLR 866, 112 Sol Jo 444 . . . . 237, 246
Lumley v Wagner (1852) 1 De GM & G 604, [1843-60] All ER Rep 368, 21 LJ Ch 898, 19 LTOS 264, 16 Jur 871 97
Luxor (Eastbourne) Ltd v Cooper [1941] AC 108, [1941] 1 All ER 33, 110 LJKB 131, 164 LT 313, 57 TLR 213, 85 Sol Jo 105, 46 Com Cas 120, HL . . . 23

M

	PAGE
Macdonald v Law Union Insurance Co (1874) LR 9 QB 328, 43 LJQB 131, 30 LT 545, 38 JP 485, 22 WR 530	276
McEntire v Crossley Bros Ltd [1895] AC 457, [1895-9] All ER Rep 829, 64 LJPC 129, 72 LT 731, 2 Mans 334, 11 R 207, [1895] 1 IR 308, HL	91
McKenty v Van Horenback (1911) 21 Man R 360	172
McPhail v Doulton [1971] AC 424, [1970] 2 All ER 228, [1970] 2 WLR 1110, 114 Sol Jo 375, HL	227
Mangles v Dixon (1852) 3 HL Cas 702, [1843-60] All ER Rep 770, 19 LTOS 260, 88 RR 296	163
Manisty's Settlement, Re, Manisty v Manisty [1974] Ch 17, [1973] 2 All ER 1203, [1973] 3 WLR 341, 117 Sol Jo 665	209
Maritime National Fish Ltd v Ocean Trawlers Ltd [1935] AC 524, [1935] All ER Rep 86, 104 LJPC 88, 153 LT 425, 79 Sol Jo 320, 18 Asp MLC 551, PC	271
Martin-Baker Aircraft Co Ltd v Canadian Flight Equipment Ltd [1955] 2 QB 556, [1955] 2 All ER 722, [1955] 3 WLR 212, 99 Sol Jo 472, 72 RPC 236	227
Mathew v Brise (1845) 15 LJ Ch 39, 7 LTOS 1, 10 Jur 105, 63 RR 69	246
Merkur Island Shipping Corpn v Laughton [1983] 2 AC 570, [1983] 1 All ER 334, [1983] 2 WLR 45, [1983] ICR 178, 126 Sol Jo 745, [1983] IRLR 26, [1983] 1 Lloyd's Rep 154, CA; affd [1983] 2 AC 570, [1983] 2 All ER 189, [1983] 2 WLR 778, [1983] ICR 490, 127 Sol Jo 306, [1983] IRLR 218, [1983] 2 Lloyd's Rep 1, HL	97
Merrill Lynch Pierce Fenner & Smith Inc v Curran 102 S Ct 1825 (1982)	378
Middleton v Pollock, ex p Elliott (1876) 2 Ch D 104, 45 LJ Ch 293	227
Miliangos v George Frank (Textiles) Ltd [1976] AC 443, [1975] 3 All ER 801, [1975] 3 WLR 758, 119 Sol Jo 774, [1975] 2 CMLR 585, [1976] 1 Lloyd's Rep 201, HL	74
Miller (James) & Partners Ltd v Whitworth Street Estates (Manchester) Ltd [1970] AC 583, [1970] 1 All ER 796, [1970] 2 WLR 728, 114 Sol Jo 225, [1970] 1 Lloyd's Rep 269, 214 Estates Gazette 111, HL	17, 169, 233
Miller's Case. See European Assurance Society, Re, Miller's Case	
Milroy v Lord (1862) 4 De GF & J 264, [1861-73] All ER Rep 783, 31 LJ Ch 798, 7 LT 178, 8 Jur NS 806, 135 RR 135	225
Monterosso Shipping Co Ltd v International Transport Workers' Federation, The Rosso [1982] 3 All ER 841, [1982] ICR 675, [1982] IRLR 468, 126 Sol Jo 591, [1982] 2 Lloyd's Rep 120, [1982] Com LR 152, CA	53
Moorcock, The (1889) 14 PD 64, [1886-90] All ER Rep 530, 58 LJP 73, 60 LT 654, 37 WR 439, 5 TLR 316, 6 Asp MLC 373, CA	22
Morgan Crucible Co plc v Hill Samuel & Co Ltd [1991] Ch 295, [1991] 2 WLR 655, [1990] NLJR 1605, sub nom Morgan Crucible Co plc v Hill Samuel Bank Ltd [1991] 1 All ER 148, [1991] BCLC 178, CA	49, 51, 57, 191
Morley v Morley (1858) 25 Beav 253, 6 WR 360	121
Murphy v Brentwood District Council [1991] 1 AC 398, [1990] 2 All ER 908, [1990] 3 WLR 414, 134 Sol Jo 1076, 22 HLR 502, 50 BLR 1, 21 Con LR 1, [1990] NLJR 1111, HL	57, 191
Myzel v Fields 386 F 2d 718 (8th Circ, 1967)	362

N

National Bank of Commerce v All American Assurance Co 583 F 2d 1295 (5th Circ, 1978)	139
National Bank of Greece and Athens SA v Metliss [1958] AC 509, [1957] 3 All ER 608, [1957] 3 WLR 1056, 101 Sol Jo 972, HL	41, 87, 258, 259, 260
National Courier Association v Board of Governors of the Federal Reserve System 516 F 2d 1229 (DC Circ, 1975)	428
New York Life Insurance Co v Public Trustee [1924] 2 Ch 101, 93 LJ Ch 449, 131 LT 438, 40 TLR 430, 68 Sol Jo 477, CA	246
New Zealand and Australian Land Co v Watson (1881) 7 QBD 374, 50 LJQB 433, 44 LT 675, 29 WR 694, CA	61
New Zealand Netherlands Society Oranje Inc v Kuys [1973] 2 All ER 1222, [1973] 1 WLR 1126, 117 Sol Jo 565, [1974] RPC 272, [1973] 2 NZLR 163, PC	65, 66

	PAGE
Newfoundland Government v Newfoundland Rly Co (1888) 13 App Cas 199, 57 LJPC 35, sub nom A-G for Newfoundland v Newfoundland Rly Co 58 LT 285, 4 TLR 292, PC	163
Noble v European Mortgage Investment Co 19 Del Ch 216 (1933)	205, 211
North and South Trust Co v Berkeley [1971] 1 All ER 980, [1971] 1 WLR 470, 115 Sol Jo 244, [1970] 2 Lloyd's Rep 467	67

O

Oatway, Re, Hertslet v Oatway [1903] 2 Ch 356, 72 LJ Ch 575, 88 LT 622	220
Ocean Tramp Tankers Corpn v V/O Sovfracht, The Eugenia [1964] 2 QB 226, [1964] 1 All ER 161, [1964] 2 WLR 114, 107 Sol Jo 931, [1963] 2 Lloyd's Rep 381, CA	271
Okura & Co Ltd v Navara Shipping Corpn SA [1982] 2 Lloyd's Rep 537, CA	46
Ooregum Gold Mining Co of India v Roper [1892] AC 125, 61 LJ Ch 337, 66 LT 427, 41 WR 90, 8 TLR 436, 36 Sol Jo 344, HL	272
Osofsky v Zipf 645 F 2d 107 (2nd Circ, 1981)	377
Overbrooke Estates Ltd v Glencombe Properties Ltd [1974] 3 All ER 511, [1974] 1 WLR 1335, 118 Sol Jo 775	192
Owen (Edward) Engineering Ltd v Barclays Bank International Ltd [1978] QB 159, [1978] 1 All ER 976, [1977] 3 WLR 764, 121 Sol Jo 617, [1978] 1 Lloyd's Rep 166, 6 BLR 1, CA	105
Ozalid Group (Export) Ltd v African Continental Bank Ltd [1979] 2 Lloyd's Rep 231	74

P

Pacific Colcotronis, The. See UBAF Ltd v European American Banking Corpn, The Pacific Colcotronis	
Page One Records Ltd v Britton (trading as The Troggs) [1967] 3 All ER 822, [1968] 1 WLR 157, 111 Sol Jo 944	95
Pagnan SpA v Feed Products Ltd [1987] 2 Lloyd's Rep 601, CA	46
Pauling's Settlemeht Trusts (No 2), Re, Younghusband v Coutts & Co [1963] Ch 576, [1963] 1 All ER 857, [1963] 2 WLR 838, 107 Sol Jo 395, [1963] TR 157, 42 ATC 97	236
Peachdart Ltd, Re [1984] Ch 131, [1983] 3 All ER 204, [1983] 3 WLR 878, 127 Sol Jo 839, [1983] BCLC 225, [1984] LS Gaz R 204	72
Perry v Suffields Ltd [1916] 2 Ch 187, 85 LJ Ch 460, 115 LT 4, 60 Sol Jo 494, CA	46
Pethybridge v Unibifocal Co Ltd [1918] WN 278	210
Pharo v Smith 621 F 2d 656 (5th Circ, 1980)	367
Phillips v Eyre (1870) LR 6 QB 1, 10 B & S 1004, 40 LJQB 28, 22 LT 869, Ex Ch	30
Phillips Products Ltd v Hyland [1987] 2 All ER 620, [1987] 1 WLR 659n, 129 Sol Jo 47, Tr L 98, [1985] LS Gaz R 681, CA	243
Phipps v Boardman [1965] Ch 992, [1965] 1 All ER 849, [1965] 2 WLR 839, 109 Sol Jo 197, CA; affd sub nom Boardman v Phipps [1967] 2 AC 46, [1966] 3 All ER 721, [1966] 3 WLR 1009, 110 Sol Jo 853, HL	65, 243, 244, 446
Photo Production Ltd v Securicor Transport Ltd [1980] AC 827, [1980] 1 All ER 556, [1980] 2 WLR 283, 124 Sol Jo 147, [1980] 1 Lloyd's Rep 545, 130 NLJ 188, HL	21
Picker v London and County Banking Co (1887) 18 QBD 515, 56 LJQB 299, 35 WR 469, 3 TLR 444, CA	163, 165
Piper v Chris-Craft Industries 430 US 1 (1977)	378
Port Line Ltd v Ben Line Steamers Ltd [1958] 2 QB 146, [1958] 1 All ER 787, [1958] 2 WLR 551, 102 Sol Jo 232, [1958] 1 Lloyd's Rep 290	96
Proudfoot v Montefiore (1867) LR 2 QB 511, 8 B & S 510, 36 LJQB 225, 16 LT 585, 15 WR 920, 2 Mar LC 512	61

R

R v Caldwell (1980) 71 Cr App Rep 237, CA; affd sub nom Metropolitan Police Comr v Caldwell [1982] AC 341, [1981] 2 WLR 509, sub nom R v Caldwell [1981] 1 All ER 961, 145 JP 211, 125 Sol Jo 239, 73 Cr App Rep 13, HL	315
R v Cunningham [1957] 2 QB 396, [1957] 2 All ER 412, [1957] 3 WLR 76, 121 JP 451, 101 Sol Jo 503, 41 Cr App Rep 155, CCA	315

xlii Table of cases

PAGE

R v International Trustee for Protection of Bondholders AG [1937] AC 500, [1937] 2 All ER 164, 106 LJKB 236, 156 LT 352, 53 TLR 507, 81 Sol Jo 316, 42 Com Cas 246, HL 16
R v Lawrence [1982] AC 510, [1981] 1 All ER 974, [1981] 2 WLR 524, 145 JP 227, 125 Sol Jo 241, [1981] RTR 217, 73 Cr App Rep 1, [1981] Crim LR 409, HL . 315
Rae (Inspector of Taxes) v Lazard Investment Co Ltd [1963] 1 WLR 555, 107 Sol Jo 474, 41 TC 1, [1963] TR 149, 42 ATC 84, HL 27
Ralli Bros v Cia Naviera Sota y Aznar [1920] 2 KB 287, [1920] All ER Rep 427, 89 LJKB 999, 123 LT 375, 36 TLR 456, 64 Sol Jo 462, 2 Ll L Rep 550, 15 Asp MLC 33, 25 Com Cas 227, CA 34
Rampell (A S) Inc v Hyster Co 3 NY 2d 369, 165 NYS 2d 475 (1957) . . . 19
Read v Joannon (1890) 25 QBD 300, 59 LJQB 544, 63 LT 387, 38 WR 734, 6 TLR 407, 2 Meg 275, DC 126
Redgrave v Hurd (1881) 20 Ch D 1, [1881-5] All ER Rep 77, 57 LJ Ch 113, 45 LT 185, 30 WR 251, CA 463
Regal (Hastings) Ltd v Gulliver (1942) [1967] 2 AC 134n, [1942] 1 All ER 378, HL . 65
Regazzoni v K C Sethia (1944) Ltd [1958] AC 301, [1957] 3 All ER 286, [1957] 3 WLR 752, 101 Sol Jo 848, [1957] 2 Lloyd's Rep 289, HL . . . 31, 75
Richards v Delbridge (1874) LR 18 Eq 11, 43 LJ Ch 459, 22 WR 584 . . 227
Risdon Iron and Locomotive Works v Furness [1906] 1 KB 49, 75 LJKB 83, 93 LT 687, 54 WR 324, 22 TLR 45, 50 Sol Jo 42, 11 Com Cas 35, CA . . . 277
Rogers & Co v British and Colonial Colliery Supply Association (1898) 68 LJQB 14, 6 Mans 305, sub nom Stewart, Rogers & Co v British and Colonial Colliery Supply Association 79 LT 494 . . . . 205, 210
Rosso, The. See Monterosso Shipping Co Ltd v International Transport Workers' Federation, The Rosso
Rumasa SA v Multinvest (UK) Ltd [1986] AC 368, [1985] 2 All ER 208, [1985] 3 WLR 501, 129 Sol Jo 573; affd [1986] AC 368, [1985] 2 All ER 619, [1985] 3 WLR 501, 129 Sol Jo 573, CA; on appeal [1986] AC 368, [1986] 1 All ER 129, [1986] 2 WLR 24, 130 Sol Jo 37, HL 40

S

SCF Finance Co Ltd v Masri (No 2) [1987] QB 1002, [1987] 1 All ER 175, [1987] 2 WLR 58, 131 Sol Jo 74, [1986] 2 Lloyd's Rep 366, [1987] LS Gaz R 492, CA . 452
SEC v Gulf Intercontinental Finance Corpn 223 F Supp 987 (SD Fla 1963) . . 384
SEC v Kasser 548 F 2d 109 (3d Circ, 1977) 384, 386
SEC v Texas Gulf Sulphur Co 258 F Supp 262 (1966); revsd 401 F 2d 833 (1968) . 372
SEC v United Financial Group Inc 474 F 2d 354 (9th Circ, 1973) . . . 381
SEC v United Financial Group Inc 474 F 2d 591 (3rd Circ, 1976) . . . 384
SEC v W J Howey Co 328 US 293 (1946) 140
SIAT di dal Ferro v Tradax Overseas SA [1980] 1 Lloyd's Rep 53, CA . . . 206
Sanders v John Nuveen & Co 463 F 2d 1075 (7th Circ); cert denied 409 US 1009 (1972) 469
Sanders v John Nuveen & Co Inc 619 F 2d 1222 (7th Circ, 1980) 367
Saunders v Vautier (1841) Cr & Ph 240, [1835-42] All ER Rep 58, 4 Beav 115, 10 LJ Ch 354, 54 RR 286 231
Schoenbaum v Firstbrook 405 F 2d 200 (1986) 0000
Sea Hawk, The. See Locabail International Finance Ltd v Agroexport, The Sea Hawk
Securities Industry Association v Board of Governors of the Federal Reserve System 468 US 137, 104 S Ct 2979 (1989) 429, 430
Security Industry Association v Board of Governors 627 F Supp 695 (1986) . . 431
Security Industry Association v Board of Governors of the Federal Reserve System (Bankers Trust II) 807 F 2d 1052 (DC Circ, 1986) cert denied 483 US 1005, 107 S Ct 3228 (1987) 431
Services Europe Atlantique Sud (SEAS) v Stockholms Rederiaktiebolag SVEA, The Folias [1979] AC 685, [1979] 1 All ER 421, [1978] 3 WLR 804, 122 Sol Jo 758, [1979] 1 Lloyd's Rep 1, HL 74
Sharif v Azad [1967] 1 QB 605, [1966] 3 All ER 785, [1966] 3 WLR 1285, 110 Sol Jo 791, CA 36

Table of cases xliii

PAGE

Shell UK Ltd v Lostock Garage Ltd [1977] 1 All ER 481, [1976] 1 WLR 1187, 120
Sol Jo 523, CA 23
Shoenbaum v Firstbrook 405 F 2d 200 (2nd Circ, 1968) 380, 382
Simons v Cogan 542 A 2d 785 (Del Ch, 1987) 262
Sinclair's Life Policy, Re [1938] Ch 799, [1938] 3 All ER 124, 107 LJ Ch 405, 159 LT
189, 54 TLR 918, 82 Sol Jo 545 276
Slavenburg's Bank NV v Intercontinental Natural Resources Ltd [1980] 1 All ER 955,
[1980] 1 WLR 1076, 124 Sol Jo 374 . . . . 125, 126
Smart's Goods, Re [1902] P 238, 71 LJP 123, 87 LT 142, 18 TLR 663, 46 Sol Jo 587 . 205
Smith v Eric S Bush [1988] QB 743, [1987] 3 All ER 179, [1987] 3 WLR 889, 131 Sol
Jo 1423, 19 HLR 287, [1987] BTLC 242, [1987] 1 EGLR 157, 282 Estates
Gazette 326, [1987] NLJ Rep 362, [1987] LS Gaz R 3260, CA; affd [1990] 1 AC
831, [1989] 2 All ER 514, [1989] 2 WLR 790, 133 Sol Jo 597, 87 LGR 685, 21
HLR 424, 17 Con LR 1, [1989] 1 EGLR 169, [1989] 17 EG 68, 18 EG 99, [1989]
NLJR 576, HL 52
Smith v Manausa 385 F Supp 443; affd 535 F 2d 353 (6th Circ, 1976) . . . 366
Smith v South Wales Switchgear Ltd [1978] 1 All ER 18, [1978] 1 WLR 165, 8 BLR
1, 122 Sol Jo 61, HL 205
Snook v London and West Riding Investments Ltd [1967] 2 QB 786, [1967] 1 All ER
518, [1967] 2 WLR 1020, 111 Sol Jo 71, CA 91
Sophie, The (1842) 1 Wm Rob 368, 1 Notes of Cases 393, 3 LT 153, 6 Jur 351, 166
ER 610 90
Speed v Transamerican Corpn 235 F 2d 369 (3rd Circ, 1956) 262
Speight v Gaunt 9 App Cas 1, 53 LJ Ch 419, 50 LT 330, 48 JP 84, 32 WR 435, HL . 246
Spellman v Spellman [1961] 2 All ER 498, [1961] 1 WLR 921, 105 Sol Jo 405, CA . 112
Standard Manufacturing Co, Re [1891] 1 Ch 627, [1891-4] All ER Rep 1242, 60 LJ
Ch 292, 64 LT 487, 39 WR 369, 7 TLR 282, 2 Meg 418, CA 126
Steel Wing Co Ltd, Re [1921] 1 Ch 349, [1920] All ER Rep 292, 90 LJ Ch 116, 124
LT 664, 65 Sol Jo 240, [1920] B & CR 160 107
Stocks v Dobson (1853) 4 De GM & G 11, 22 LJ Ch 884, 21 LTOS 189, 17 Jur 539 . 111,
114
Stoneleigh Finance Ltd v Phillips [1965] 2 QB 537, [1965] 1 All ER 513, [1965] 2
WLR 508, 109 Sol Jo 68, CA 91
Straub v Vaisman and Co Inc 540 F 2d 591 (3rd Circ, 1976) 384
Superintendent of Insurance v Bankers Life and Casualty Co 404 US 6 (1971) . . 377
Swiss Bank Corpn v Lloyds Bank Ltd [1979] Ch 548, [1979] 2 All ER 853, [1979] 3
WLR 201, 123 Sol Jo 536; revsd [1982] AC 584, [1980] 2 All ER 419, [1980] 3
WLR 457, 124 Sol Jo 741, CA; affd [1982] AC 584, [1981] 2 All ER 449, [1981] 2
WLR 893, 125 Sol Jo 495, HL 97
Sydney Municipal Council v Bull [1909] 1 KB 7, [1908-10] All ER Rep 616, 78 LJKB
45, 99 LT 805, 25 TLR 6 79
Szalatnay-Stacho v Fink [1947] KB 1, [1946] 2 All ER 231, 115 LJKB 455, 175 LT
336, 62 TLR 573, 90 Sol Jo 442, CA 30

T

Tailby v Official Receiver (1888) 13 App Cas 523, [1886-90] All ER Rep 486, 58
LJQB 75, 60 LT 162, 37 WR 513, 4 TLR 726, HL 110
Tate v Williamson (1866) 2 Ch App 55, LR 1 Eq 528, 15 LT 549, 15 WR 321; on
appeal 2 Ch App 55, CA 54
Tempest v Lord Camoys (1882) 21 Ch D 571, 51 LJ Ch 785, 48 LT 13, 31 WR 326,
CA 209
Tesco Supermarkets Ltd v Nattrass [1972] AC 153, [1971] 2 All ER 127, [1971] 2
WLR 1166, 135 JP 289, 115 Sol Jo 285, 69 LGR 403, HL 62
Tilley's Will Trusts, Re, Burgin v Croad [1967] Ch 1179, [1967] 2 All ER 303, [1967] 2
WLR 1533, 111 Sol Jo 237 220
Tolhurst v Associated Portland Cement Manufacturers (1900) Ltd [1902] 2 KB 660,
71 LJKB 949, 87 LT 465, 51 WR 81, 18 TLR 827, CA; affd [1903] AC 414,
[1900-3] All ER Rep 386, 72 LJKB 834, 89 LT 196, 52 WR 143, 19 TLR 677,
HL 109
Tomlinson v Gill (1756) Amb 330 226

	PAGE
Topham v Greenside Glazed Fire-Brick Co (1887) 37 Ch D 281, 57 LJ Ch 583, 58 LT 274, 36 WR 464	125
Toprak Mahsulleri Ofisi v Finagrain Cie Commerciale Agricole et Financière SA [1979] 2 Lloyd's Rep 98, CA	31
Torkington v Magee [1902] 2 KB 427, [1900-3] All ER Rep 991, 71 LJKB 712, 87 LT 304, 18 TLR 703; revsd [1903] 1 KB 644, 72 LJKB 336, 88 LT 443, 19 TLR 331, CA	105, 109
Torni, The [1932] P 27, 48 TLR 195; affd [1932] P 78, [1932] All ER Rep 384, 101 LJP 44, 147 LT 208, 48 TLR 471, 43 Lloyd LR 78, 18 Asp MLC 315, CA	26
Tournier v National Provincial and Union Bank of England [1924] 1 KB 461, [1923] All ER Rep 550, 93 LJKB 449, 130 LT 682, 40 TLR 214, 68 Sol Jo 441, 29 Com Cas 129, CA	111
Trans Trust SPRL v Danubian Trading Co Ltd [1952] 2 QB 297, [1952] 1 All ER 970, [1952] 1 TLR 1066, 96 Sol Jo 312, [1952] 1 Lloyd's Rep 348, CA	69
Transamerica Mortgage Advisors v Lewis 447 US 11 (1979)	378
Trollope and Colls Ltd v North West Metropolitan Regional Hospital Board [1973] 2 All ER 260, [1973] 1 WLR 601, 117 Sol Jo 355, 9 BLR 60, HL	23
Tsakiroglou & Co Ltd v Noblee Thorl GmbH [1962] AC 93, [1961] 2 All ER 179, [1961] 2 WLR 633, 105 Sol Jo 346, [1961] 1 Lloyd's Rep 329, HL	78
Tuck's Settlement Trusts, Re, Public Trustee v Tuck [1976] Ch 99, [1976] 1 All ER 545, [1976] 2 WLR 345, 119 Sol Jo 868; affd [1978] Ch 49, [1978] 1 All ER 1047, [1978] 2 WLR 411, 121 Sol Jo 796, CA	209, 232, 235, 241
Tulk v Moxhay (1848) 1 H & Tw 105, [1843-60] All ER Rep 9, 2 Ph 774, 18 LJ Ch 83, 13 LTOS 21, 13 Jur 89	96
Turner v Shearer [1973] 1 All ER 397, [1972] 1 WLR 1387, 137 JP 191, 116 Sol Jo 800, DC	299

U

UBAF Ltd v European American Banking Corpn, The Pacific Colcotronis [1984] QB 713, [1984] 2 All ER 226, [1984] 2 WLR 508, 128 Sol Jo 243, [1984] BCLC 112, [1984] 1 Lloyd's Rep 258, [1984] LS Gaz R 429, CA	49, 53, 56, 475
US v Aluminium Co of America 148 F 2d 416 (2nd Circ, 1945)	381
US v Cook 573 F 2d 281 (5th Circ); cert denied 439 US 836 (1978)	384
Underhill v Hernandez 168 US 250 (1897)	38
Union Planters National Bank of Memphis v Commercial Credit Business Loans Inc 651 F 2d 1174 (6th Circ); cert denied 454 US 1124 (1981)	140
United American Bank v Gunter 620 F 2d 1108 (5th Circ, 1980)	139, 140
United California Bank v THC Financial Corpn 557 F 2d 1351 (9th Circ, 1977)	140
United City Merchants (Investments) Ltd and Glass Fibres and Equipments Ltd v Royal Bank of Canada, Vitrorefuerzos SA and Banco Continental SA (incorporated in Canada) [1983] 1 AC 168, [1982] 2 All ER 720, [1982] 2 WLR 1039, 126 Sol Jo 379, [1982] 2 Lloyd's Rep 1, [1982] Com LR 142, HL	36, 90
United Dominions Trust (Commercial) Ltd v Eagle Aircraft Services Ltd [1968] 1 All ER 104, [1968] 1 WLR 74, 111 Sol Jo 849, CA	70
United Dominions Trust (Commercial) Ltd v Parkway Motors Ltd [1955] 2 All ER 557, [1955] 1 WLR 719, 99 Sol Jo 436	112

V

Vandepitte v Preferred Accident Insurance Corpn of New York [1933] AC 70, [1932] All ER Rep 527, 102 LJPC 21, 148 LT 169, 49 TLR 90, 76 Sol Jo 798, PC	226
Van Genert v Boeing Co 520 F 2d 1373 (2nd Circ, 1975)	262
Van Lynn Developments Ltd v Pelias Construction Co Ltd (formerly Jason Construction Co Ltd) [1969] 1 QB 607, [1968] 3 All ER 824, [1968] 3 WLR 1141, 112 Sol Jo 819, CA	107
Vickery, Re, Vickery v Stephens [1931] 1 Ch 572, [1931] All ER Rep 562, 100 LJ Ch 138, 144 LT 562, 47 TLR 242	245
Visser, Re, Queen of Holland v Drukker [1928] Ch 877, [1928] All ER Rep 305, 97 LJ Ch 488, 139 LT 658, 44 TLR 692, 72 Sol Jo 518	81

Vita Food Products Inc v Unus Shipping Co Ltd [1939] AC 277, [1939] 1 All ER 513, 108 LJPC 40, 160 LT 579, 55 TLR 402, 83 Sol Jo 295, 44 Com Cas 123, 19 Asp MLC 257, PC 17, 169

W

Wagg (Helbert) & Co Ltd's Claim, Re [1956] Ch 323, [1956] 1 All ER 129, [1956] 2 WLR 183, 100 Sol Jo 53 . . . . 16, 17, 35
Wait and James v Midland Bank (1926) 31 Com Cas 172 173
Wale v IRC (1879) 4 Ex D 270, 48 LJQB 574, 41 LT 165, 27 WR 916 . . . 136
Walker v Bradford Old Bank Ltd (1884) 12 QBD 511, 53 LJQB 280, 32 WR 644 . 110
Warner Bros Pictures Inc v Nelson [1937] 1 KB 209, [1936] 3 All ER 160, 106 LJKB 97, 155 LT 538, 53 TLR 14, 80 Sol Jo 855 95
Waterman's Will Trusts, Re, Lloyds Bank Ltd v Sutton [1952] 2 All ER 1054, [1952] 2 TLR 877, 96 Sol Jo 850 237
Watts v Missouri-Kansas-Texas Railroad Co 383 F 2d 571 (5th Circ, 1967) . 204, 205, 211, 212
Westerton, Re, Public Trustee v Gray [1919] 2 Ch 104, 88 LJ Ch 392, 122 LT 264, 63 Sol Jo 410 107
Weston Banking v Turkaye Garanti Bankasi 446 NE 2d 1195 (NY, 1982) . . 37
White v Bijou Mansions Ltd [1938] Ch 351, [1938] 1 All ER 546, 107 LJ Ch 212, 158 LT 338, 54 TLR 458, 82 Sol Jo 135, CA 276
Wilkes' (Beloved) Charity, Re (1851) 3 Mac & G 440, 20 LJ Ch 588, 17 LTOS 101 . 208
Williams v Evans (1866) LR 1 QB 352, 35 LJQB 111, 13 LT 753, 30 JP 692, 14 WR 330 60
Williams & Humbert Ltd v W & H Trade Marks (Jersey) Ltd [1986] AC 368, [1985] 2 All ER 208, [1985] 3 WLR 501, 129 Sol Jo 573; affd [1986] AC 368, [1985] 2 All ER 619, [1985] 3 WLR 501, 129 Sol Jo 573, CA; on appeal [1986] AC 368, [1986] 1 All ER 129, [1986] 2 WLR 24, 130 Sol Jo 37, [1986] NLJ Rep 15, [1986] LS Gaz R 37, HL 40
Williamson v Tucker 645 F 2d 404 (5th Circ); cert denied 454 US 897 (1981) . . 139
Wilson Smithett and Cope Ltd v Terruzzi [1976] QB 683, [1976] 1 All ER 817, [1976] 2 WLR 418, 120 Sol Jo 116, [1976] 1 Lloyd's Rep 509, CA . . . 36
Winn v Bull (1877) 7 Ch D 29, 47 LJ Ch 139, 42 JP 230, 26 WR 230 . . . 46
Wonneman v Stratford Securities Co CCH Fed Sec L Rep 91 (SDNY, 1961) . . 366
Wrightson, Re, Wrightson v Cooke [1908] 1 Ch 789, [1908-10] All ER Rep Ext 1399, 77 LJ Ch 422, 98 LT 799 236

Z

Zahn v Transamerica Corpn 162 F 2d 36 (3rd Circ, 1947) 262
Zeevi (J) & Sons Ltd v Grindlays Bank (Uganda) Ltd 37 NY 2d 2220, 333 NE 2d 168 (1975) 37
Zeller v Bogue Electric Manufacturing Corpn 476 F 2d 795 (2nd Circ); cert denied 414 US 908 (1973) 469
Zivnostenska Banka National Corpn v Frankman [1950] AC 57, [1949] 2 All ER 671, HL 32

CHAPTER 1
The international financial markets: introduction

I A DESCRIPTION OF THE INTERNATIONAL FINANCIAL MARKET

This book seeks to examine the law and regulation affecting the raising of finance in the international financial markets. It does not deal with all forms of international financial transactions, but is focused on the primary markets for international syndicated loans and international issues of debt securities. This chapter considers what are the international financial markets and how they developed.

US economists Dufey and Giddy in *The International Money Market*[1] (hereafter *Dufey and Giddy*) have distinguished transactions in the domestic financial markets from those in the international financial markets. They state:

> 'Only one type of transaction can occur in a domestic financial market: a domestic lender provides funds (via domestic financial intermediaries or directly through organised regulated securities markets) to domestic borrowers. In an international financial market however three additional types of transactions may occur: (1) between foreign lenders and domestic borrowers (2) between domestic lenders and foreign borrowers and (3) between foreign lenders and foreign borrowers.'

International finance in the traditional sense as understood in the nineteenth century encompassed the first two types of transactions, but not the third. In the traditional sense international finance was confined to financial centres in the mature western economies which had a surplus of domestic capital which could be continuously supplied to foreign borrowers. Dufey and Giddy have pointed out that 'London was clearly the leader in this traditional international market, its leadership only occasionally challenged by Paris during the nineteenth century'.[2]

The traditional forms of 'international' finance would typically involve

---

1 Prentice Hall, Foundations of Finance Series, 1978, ch 2, app 2.
2 See *Dufey and Giddy* p 36.

2   *The international financial markets: introduction*

British or other European banks lending funds to foreign borrowers either in London, Paris or Berlin, or through overseas colonial banks to borrowers overseas. Capital was also raised through traditional 'international' bond issues where foreign borrowers raised capital in the British capital markets in sterling or in the French capital markets in French francs. As Fisher in his work on *International Bonds* (hereafter *Fisher*)[3] has pointed out, 'almost all bond issues in the nineteenth century were linked to national capital markets, and thus by definition foreign bonds', and 'the main international bond centres were principally located in countries which enjoyed a surplus in their balance of payments'. Fisher[4] has also pointed out that:

> '[the] chief capitals of the international bond markets in the nineteenth century were London, Paris, Berlin and later New York. The capital exported from these European centres through bond issues was used to finance railroad and industrial expansion in the US and the railways of Russia, South America and China.'

However, after the weakening of the British economy after the First World War, New York surpassed London as the net exporter of capital to foreign borrowers. New York became the leading international financial centre in the traditional sense where foreign borrowers obtained financing by way of international bank loans or the issue of dollar denominated bonds.[5]

International finance in its modern sense (Dufey and Giddy's third form) concerns the provision of finance at a financial centre by foreign lenders to foreign borrowers largely in a currency which is not the currency of the financial centre.[6]

It is in this modern sense that the term 'international finance' is used in this work. Dufey and Giddy[7] have pointed out that 'international finance' in this sense has two distinct and independent markets.

The first is the 'Eurocurrency' or international banking market and the second is the international or 'Euro' bond market. These markets have also been termed 'the first bona fide supranational market' by Professor Samuel Hayes of the Harvard Business School and Philip Hubbard in their work, *Investment Banking: A Tale of Three Cities*.[8]

The Eurocurrency or international banking market is a market where finance is raised in various currencies by transnational corporations, sovereign states and other entities through multinational syndicates of banks which obtain the funds for such loans from a vast pool of currencies lying on deposit *outside the home state of those currencies* (*ie outside the state in which the currency is legal tender*).[9] The source of funds for the syndicate banks is a pool of currencies lying 'off-shore' from their state of issue. This

---

3   Euromoney Publications 1981.
4   See *Fisher* ch 1.
5   See *Dufey and Giddy* p 36; *Fisher* p 15.
6   See *Dufey and Giddy* p 36.
7   At p 36.
8   See Hayes and Hubbard *Investment Banking, A Tale of Three Cities* (Harvard Business School, 1990) ch 14, p 339.
9   See as to what constitutes legal tender Dr F A Mann *The Legal Aspects of Money* ch 1.

'off-shore' feature makes this type of financing unique and different from the traditional provision of finance by syndicates of foreign and local banks, which lend domestic currency to foreign borrowers (for instance, a US dollar loan in New York to a Mexican borrower).[10]

American economists, like Dr Marcia Stigum in her major work *The Money Market*[11] and Dufey and Giddy in their book on the *International Money Markets*,[12] recognise that London has established itself as the major centre for the Eurocurrency and international banking markets which developed in the 1960s and 1970s. In the 'Eurocurrency' or international banking markets, Japanese, American, German, Canadian, Swiss, English and French banks as well as banks from other countries form lending syndicates in London to lend US dollars, German deutschmarks, Swiss francs, French francs, Japanese yen or pounds sterling, and other currencies, in 'international syndicated loans' to borrowers from across the world. The total volume of such loans increased from US $4.7bn in value in 1970 to US $459bn in value in 1988.[13]

As far as the international or 'Euro' bond markets are concerned, London has emerged as the pre-eminent centre for this market too.[14] The total volume of Eurobonds traded at year end 1990 was US $6.2 *trillion* in value,[15] of which 60% was traded in the UK by AIBD member firms.[16] Bond issues in US dollars, Japanese yen, Swiss francs, Australian dollars, Canadian dollars, French francs and ECUs are effected in London and bonds are sold to institutional, corporate and individual investors worldwide (except the US: see p 159–160 and Part V) by underwriting syndicates of investment banks from Japan, the US, the UK, Germany, France, Canada and other countries. The total volume of international bonds issued in 1988 reached US $175.8bn in value.[17]

The key features of the 'international' bond issue are that (a) the currency of the bond is not that of the place of issue; (b) the bonds are not sold in the capital markets of one country, but are distributed worldwide; (c) the issue of the bonds is underwritten by a syndicate of investment banks drawn from different countries; and (d) the issuers of bonds are foreign to the place of issue.

Dufey and Giddy[18] would add to this list the fact that bonds are 'placed' rather than formally issued and that the bonds are not subject to withholding tax.

The features of the international or Euro issue which distinguish such an issue from the 'foreign' issue are (a) and (b) above. Thus issues of US

---

10 See the discussion by Dr Marcia Stigum in ch 6 *The Money Market* (revised edn, Dow Jones Irwin, New York, 1983).
11 Revised edn, 1983, p 139.
12 At pp 40–45.
13 See the Euromoney 20th Anniversary Supplement (June 1989) *The Euromarket in Figures* p 163. The figure includes Euronote facilities.
14 See *Fisher* ch 1.
15 See article by John Langton, chief executive of the Association of International Bond Dealers writing in the *Sunday Observer* of 14 July 1991 in an article entitled '$6 trillion market with a crucial capital role'.
16 According to Langton, above, British firms accounted only for 24% of this.
17 See the Euromoney 20th Anniversary Supplement (June 1989) *The Euromarket in Figures*, p 163.
18 At pp 19–20.

dollar bonds by non-US entities in New York would not be regarded as an international issue in the modern sense, but rather a 'foreign issue' in the domestic capital markets in the US. So too an issue in Tokyo of yen bonds by a non-Japanese issuer would not constitute an issue in the international markets but rather a foreign issue in the domestic capital markets of Japan. In both cases the currency of the issue is the domestic currency of the place of issue and the bonds are sold only to investors in the capital markets of the place of issue. Such foreign issues in the domestic capital markets have rather colourful names such as: Yankee Issues for US dollar issues in New York; Samurai Issues for Japanese yen issues in Japan; Bulldog Issues for sterling issues in London; Matador Issues for peseta issues in Madrid. Sterling bond issues in London aimed at investors overseas, rather than at the UK domestic capital markets, are however regarded as international or Euro sterling issues. Such issues accounted for US $23.8bn in value in 1988 in a year when total Eurobond new issue volume was US $175.6bn in value.[19]

The international or Eurobond market for new issues in London is by no means a 'British' market. According to Euromoney,[20] in the two years 1988 and 1989, there were only two British merchant banks in the top twenty banks in the Euromoney tables for lead managers of Eurobond issues ('book runners'). In 1988 five of the top ten investment banks which acted as lead manager were Japanese while in 1989 there were four Japanese houses in the top ten. Nomura Securities had been the lead manager in the largest number of issues in volume terms and in terms of the number of issues in both years. The American investment banks included elite names such as Goldman Sachs, Salomon Brothers, J P Morgan Securities and Morgan Stanley; while the European banks whose names appear in the tables were Deutsche Bank (German), Banque Paribas (French), Union Bank of Switzerland (Swiss), Commerz Bank (German), and Dresdner Bank (German); the English merchant banks whose names appeared in this table were the elite S G Warburg, Baring Bros and Hambros Bank; while the investment bank which led the consolidated tables for 1980–88 was the Swiss-American bank, Credit Suisse First Boston.[1] As regards international syndicated loans, the Euromoney tables for 1980–88[2] evidence a predominance of US banks and the tables are dominated by Citcorp, Chase Investment Bank, J P Morgan Bank of America, Manufacturers Hanover and Chemical Bank.

It will be seen from the above that while the centre of the international financial market, properly so called, is in London, the market is dominated by foreign investment and commercial banks and the currencies used are predominantly foreign.

It is apparent from the above that the epithets 'Euromarket', 'Eurobond' and 'Eurocurrency' are completely misleading. Neither the borrowers nor the lenders, nor even the currencies in these markets, are wholly or substan-

---

19 See Euromoney 20th Anniversary Supplement (June 1989).
20 20th Anniversary Supplement.
 1 See Euromoney 20th Anniversary Supplement. The truly international nature of the people who shaped and developed this international market can be gathered from Kerr *A History of the Eurobond Market* (Euromoney, 1984).
 2 Euromoney 20th Anniversary Supplement.

tially European. Commentators have repeatedly pointed out that the so-called 'Euro' markets are the only true international markets.[3]

II THE DEVELOPMENT OF THE INTERNATIONAL FINANCIAL MARKET IN LONDON[4]

How London became the centre of both the Eurocurrency and the Eurobond markets and thus of the international financial markets, rather than New York or Tokyo, is a question which has intrigued many economists and bankers alike.

London's position is curious since the traditional assumption of economics is that an international financial centre is located in a country which is a net exporter of capital, and whose economy is sufficiently large to support all the financing demands of foreign borrowers who come to that centre. The United Kingdom is not such an economy[5] in relation to the funds raised in the London international markets. However it has been convincingly demonstrated by Dufey and Giddy[6] that with the advent of internationalisation of capital and financial markets and the free movement of capital across national boundaries, this traditional assumption is no longer correct. An international financial centre need not be located in or supported by an economy which exports the capital required by borrowers. The existence of a pool of currency deposits outside their home states and the ability of capital to move freely across national boundaries has enabled London to re-emerge as the centre of the modern international financial markets in the 1970s even though it is located in a country which is a medium-sized economy by global standards.[7]

1 Development of the Eurocurrency markets

In the view of most writers on the subject the growth of the international financial markets occurred in the 1960s and was fuelled by events in the 1950s.[8] However, Einzig[9] has suggested that there is evidence of 'Euro market' type activity even in the 1920s and 1930s.[10]

The development of the Eurocurrency markets is generally said to have

---

3 See the views of Dr Stigum in *The Money Market* ch 6 and *Dufey & Giddy* ch 1.
4 The literature is extensive on this subject. The writer has drawn on the works listed in the bibliography at the end of the chapter.
5 The Gross National Product of the United Kingdom in 1990 was just over US $1,000 billion, roughly the same as that of Italy and France; by comparison the United States had a GNP of US $5,390 billion and Japan of US $2,940 billion. See the *Economist* of 17–23 August 1991, p 91, citing the OECD.
6 See chs I, and VI.
7 See *Dufey and Giddy* p 41.
8 See Stigum *The Money Market* ch 6; *Dufey and Giddy* ch 1; *Fisher* ch 1; McDonald *International Syndicated Loans* (Euromoney Publications 1982) chs 2 and 3 (hereafter *McDonald*). McDonald has included at pp 26–27 an extremely useful table of events which operated as catalysts for the growth of the international markets.
9 *The Eurodollar System* (St Martin's Press, New York, 5th edn, 1970).
10 See for some early assessments of the international markets, Klopstock 'The International Money Market: Structure, Scope and Instruments' Jo of Finance, May 1965, pp 183–205; Johnson *Eurodollars in the New International Money Market* (First National City Bank, New York, 1964); Einzig *The Eurodollar System*, (St Martin's Press, New York, 1964).

6 *The international financial markets: introduction*

its roots in the growth of the pool of 'Eurodollars' in Europe after the Second World War.

'Eurodollars' are US dollars lying on deposit with banks outside the US including foreign branches of US banks.[11] Staughton J in *Libyan Arab Foreign Bank v Bankers Trust Co*[12] gave judicial recognition in English law to this concept of Eurodollars. Dr Marcia Stigum in the *Money Market*[13] states: 'Eurodollars are simply dollars held on deposit in a bank or branch located outside the United States ...' but further includes within the definition US dollars held on deposit with an international banking facility ('IBF') set up under the International Banking Act 1978 of the US.[14]

Karlik[15] has pointed out that, from an economist's viewpoint, 'Eurodollar deposits ... are not money in a strictly defined sense; they are time rather than demand deposits and cannot be drawn upon to make payments.'[16]

The growth of the pool of Eurodollar deposits in Europe is attributed by economists[17] to a number of factors:

(i) A large amount of dollars was poured into Europe after the Second World War to reconstruct Europe. As far back as 1953 there was a dollar pool of around US $13,000m on deposit in Europe. Parallel to this, by that date private investment had been made in Europe from US sources amounting to some US $8,000m.[18]

(ii) The US ran a balance of payments deficit during the 1950s and much of the 1960s which resulted in US dollars flooding into Europe. According to McDonald,[19] the deficits averaged US $1.4bn from 1952 to 1956 and US $3bn between 1958 and 1963. Dr Stigum[20] and Karlik[21] have, however, pointed out that while this phenomenon may partially explain the growth of the dollar pool, other factors had a greater impact and that dollars held by European corporations and other entities could equally well have been placed on deposit in New York rather than in London.

(iii) The USSR and other countries in the Eastern bloc moved their dollar holdings from New York to London[22] due to the intensification of the Cold War and a fear that the US might 'freeze' their assets in

---

11 See also *McDonald* ch 2, p 20.
12 [1988] 1 Lloyd's Rep 259 at 263.
13 Ch 6.
14 Dr Stigum has pointed out (at p 188) that by 1 December 1981 New York and eleven, other states had passed enabling legislation permitting domestic US banks and foreign bank branches to open IBFs. US dollar deposits held in IBFs are not subject to reserve requirements and the IBF need not pay insurance premiums to the federal deposit insurance scheme, the FDIC. IBFs create in her words (at p 188) 'a species of free trade zone for international money – primarily Eurodollars'.
15 Senior Economist, Joint Economic Committee of the US Congress.
16 See some 'Questions and Brief Answers about the Eurodollar Market', Papers of the Joint Economic Committee of the US Congress (1977).
17 See the articles and works cited below at p 11.
18 See *McDonald* at p 18 citing 'Survey of Current Business: International Investment Position of the United States', May 1954, and statistics from the US Department of Commerce Office of Business Economics, 1954.
19 Fn 18 above, at p 19.
20 *The Money Market* pp 138–139.
21 Fn 16 above.
22 See Stigum, fn 20 above, at p 136 and Karlik, fn 16 above.

New York. The action of the US Treasury in 1948 when it blocked the transfer of gold valued at US $20m belonging to the Government of Czechoslovakia operated as a catalyst for Eastern bloc countries to move dollar deposits from New York to London and other European cities.[1]

(iv) Dollars held by Middle Eastern countries in New York were also moved in substantial amounts to London due to the fear of assets being frozen after the US Treasury froze the assets of the Egyptian Government in 1956.[2] The assets totalled US $62m.[3]

This practice of keeping dollar deposits in London was graphically illustrated in the *Libyan Arab Foreign Bank* case[4] where it appeared that on a daily basis the Libyan Arab Foreign Bank moved all US dollar balances above US $500,000 lying to their account with Bankers Trust in New York to Bankers Trust in London, where the dollars were eventually held on deposit.

The practice of Middle Eastern and Arab states referred to above assumed major significance in 1974 when the Organisation of Petroleum Exporting Countries ('OPEC') virtually quadrupled the price of oil, and oil-producing states in the Middle East began to hold billions of dollars in oil revenues. These dollars were largely deposited in London.[5]

According to Dr Stigum,[6] the accumulated dollar pool was first put to use for international trade financing after 1957 by British bankers. This was due to the fact that the Bank of England in 1957 restricted the use of sterling for financing international trade between countries outside the 'non-sterling area'.

Certain US regulations also provided a stimulus to the growth of the international market in Eurocurrencies:

(i) One such regulation which induced even US corporate entities to place dollars on deposit in London according to both Stigum[7] and Karlik[8] was the US Federal Reserve Bank's Regulation Q[9] introduced in the year 1968.[10] Regulation Q imposed a ceiling on the interest payable by US banks to depositors of US dollars within the US. The consequence was that US banks began taking their US dollar deposits in London. Interest rate controls under Regulation Q were subsequently phased out under the Depository Institution Deregulation and Monetary Control Act 1980.[11]

(ii) Financing in Eurodollars in London also proved to be cheaper than financing in New York due to the impact of Regulation D of the US

---

1 See *McDonald* p 19.
2 Under the Foreign Assets Control Law of 1917.
3 *McDonald* p 19 citing the New York Times of 1 August 1956.
4 [1988] 1 Lloyd's Rep 259.
5 See *Fisher* p 17; and Karlik, fn 16 above, item 5 where he points out that the Eurocurrency markets grew by one third that year.
6 See *The Money Market* pp 136–137.
7 Fn 8 above at p 138.
8 Fn 16 above, item 5.
9 12 CFR 217.
10 *McDonald* at p 24 points out that the first syndicated loans in the Eurocurrency markets were effected in the year 1968.
11 Public Law 97–320 s 326(a), enacted by Congress. See also the Report of the Senate Committee no 96–368 which discusses the 'Phaseout of Regulation Q'.

8 *The international financial markets: introduction*

Federal Reserve.[12] Regulation D imposed a reserve which stood at 3% of the amount of net transaction accounts from $0–$40.5m and 12% of the amount of net transaction accounts of over $40.5m. This meant that, for net US dollar amounts held by US banks on time deposit and 'demand deposit' accounts (deposits payable within seven days),[13] US banks were compelled to keep 3% or 12% of net deposits with the Federal Reserve in the form of non-interest bearing deposits (or in the form of vault cash). This percentage amount was not available for lending. This had two consequences. First, depositors would be paid less than they would otherwise get in respect of a deposit, in order to enable the bank to maintain such non-interest bearing deposits with the Federal Reserve. Second, when the remaining amounts of net deposits were lent to borrowers, the interest rate payable by such a borrower could be higher than otherwise such as to enable the bank to make up the loss of interest caused by Regulation D. The US Congress has exempted from such reserve requirements 'deposits payable only outside the States of the United States and the District of Columbia...'[14] Regulation D[15] itself states that 'a deposit that is payable only at an office located outside the United States' is not subject to reserve requirements.

The result was that in the 'Eurodollar' markets, US banks could pay competitive rates to depositors and consequently, provide dollar financing to borrowers at cheaper rates than in the US domestic markets.

The growth of the Eurodollar pool and the uses to which such dollars were put by London bankers saw a parallel development in European currencies which had been made convertible after 1958.[16] A pool of European currencies developed in London and were put to the same uses as the Eurodollar pool, namely the provision of finance, initially for trade, but subsequently for syndicate bank loans. Subsequently, these developments were mirrored in respect of Japanese yen, as well as Australian, Canadian and New Zealand dollars. It is nevertheless the case that the Eurodollar remained the major source of finance, accounting for over 80% of deposits in London's Eurocurrency markets[17] up to 1970, although that figure had fallen to 73% by 1980.[18] The Eurodollar still remains the principal currency on deposit in the international markets.

In 1981 the gross size of the total Eurocurrency market had grown to US $1930 *billion* in value though the figure net of inter-bank transactions was US $540 *billion* in value.

2 The growth of the international or Eurobond market

As observed above the pool of 'Eurodollars' and 'Eurocurrencies' placed on deposit in such vast amounts gave rise to the international syndicated

---

12   12 CFR Part 204; the impact of Regulation D was discussed in detail in *Libyan Arab Foreign Bank v Manufacturers Hanover Trust Co* (No 2) [1989] 1 Lloyd's Rep 608 especially at pp 623–624.
13   See definitions 12 CFR s 204.2(e)(1).
14   12 USC section 461(b)(6).
15   12 CFR s 204.1(c)(5).
16   See *McDonald* p 20.
17   See *Fisher* Exhibit 1.1 at p 17.
18   See *Fisher*, fn 3, p 2 above.

loans market in London. A parallel but distinct segment of the international financial market is the international (or 'Euro') bond market. As Fisher has pointed out,[19] the pool of Eurodollars outside the US made the issue of the first Eurobonds possible. However, as Dufey and Giddy[20] have pointed out, Eurodollar or Eurocurrency deposits cannot be used by banks to effect a bond issue in the same way that banks used Eurodollar deposits to effect international syndicated loans. The growth of the international bond markets is thus a linked but distinct development from the growth of the Eurocurrency and syndicated loans market.

The first Eurobond issue is now generally agreed to be that for the Italian Autostrada company made on 1 July 1963, guaranteed by Institute per la Ricostruzione Industriale (IRI) and lead managed by S G Warburg and Co.[1]

The catalyst for the modern international bond market was the imposition in the US of Interest Equalisation Tax ('IET') in 1964[2]. This tax sought to discourage foreign issuers of bonds from raising long-term capital in the US domestic capital markets. It imposed a tax on any US investor who purchased a foreign bond which ranged from 2.75% to 15% depending on the 'life' of the bond. This was a strong disincentive to the issue of dollar denominated bonds in New York and compelled prospective issuers to look for an alternative to US domestic capital markets. The alternative was London's fledgling international markets. IET was in fact abolished in 1972 but this made no difference to the explosive growth of the international bond market in London from a mere US $5.2bn in value in 1972 to US $175.8bn in 1988.[3]

Dr Stigum has pointed out that the programme of restraints on capital outflows introduced by the US administration resulted in the explosive growth of the entire international financial markets in London and not simply the Eurobond market. The programme included not only IET but also the Foreign Credit Restraint Programme in 1965 which limited the amount of credit which US banks could extend to foreign borrowers; this was followed in 1968 by the Foreign Investment Programme which restricted the amount of funds which domestic US corporations could raise in the US for purposes of investment.

There is another factor which is regarded as having assisted the growth of the international bond markets in London and their continued presence in London rather than New York even after abolition of IET in 1972. This factor is the comparative burden of securities regulation in the two centres as perceived by investment bankers and international issuers of bonds. New York has always been perceived as a heavily regulated securities market[4] with a vast and complex network of securities laws. An issue of securities in the US domestic capital markets was perceived by foreign issuers as cumbersome, time-consuming and expensive, whereas until 1988 London did not have a formalised system of regulation of securities. Equally, with regard

---

19 See *Fisher* ch 1.
20 *Dufey and Giddy* p 19.
1   See *Fisher* p 19; Bowe *Eurobonds* (Dow Jones Irwin, Illinois, 1988) p 14; Hayes and Hubbard *Investment Banking: A Tale of Three Cities* (Harvard Business School, 1990); and Kerr *History of the Eurobond Market* (Euromoney, 1984).
2   26 USC section 4911-31; see *Fisher* p 19; *McDonald* p 23; Kerr *History of the Eurobond Market* p 17.
3   See Euromoney 20th Anniversary Supplement (June 1989) *The Euromarket in Figures*.
4   See on US securities regulation, Part V.

10 *The international financial markets: introduction*

to the 'Eurocurrency' or international banking markets, Dr Stigum has said:[5] 'Some of the many factors that contributed to London's development as an international financial centre were the freedom and flexibility with which financial institutions were permitted to operate there.'

Curiously, the absence of a detailed and all-embracing system of securities regulation in the international markets has not led to substantial defaults. According to Euromoney statistics there were nearly 11,000 Eurobond issues over the 25 years from 1963–1988[6] while Kerr writing in 1984 stated that there were 36 defaults up to that date.[7]

3 The centre of the international financial market

The American economists Dufey and Giddy[8] were able to declare in 1978 that 'London is clearly the dominant international banking centre in the world'[9] while another leading American economist, Dr Marcia Stigum, after a survey of the international markets concludes, 'In truth, that square mile of London known as the City of London or more often as just *the City* is and has been since the nineteenth century the financial capital of the world'. Professor Hayes of the Harvard Business School and Hubbard writing in 1990 in their work on investment banking[10] conclude that neither New York nor Tokyo, although homes to the largest domestic capital markets, match the City of London as an international financial centre and are unlikely to do so in the near future.[11]

---

5 *The Money Market* p 139.
6 See Euromoney 20th Anniversary Supplement (June 1989) *The Euromarket in Figures*. The total has been arrived at by adding up the figures published by Euromoney.
7 See Kerr *History of the Eurobond Market*.
8 *Dufey and Giddy* p 40.
9 *The Financial Times* on 7 February 1991 reported that there were 478 foreign banks in London compared with 277 in Paris and 247 in Frankfurt while the Bank of England has stated in the Bank of England Quarterly Bulletin, November 1989 ('London as an International Financial Centre' at 517) that the number of foreign banks in London rose from around 330 in 1975 to 521 in February 1989 although this figure includes representative offices; in January 1991 the number of foreign banks was 541 of which EC countries accounted for 162, North America 76 and Japan 57: see the Bank of England Banking Act Report for 1990/1991.
10 '*Investment Banking: A Tale of Three Cities*' (Harvard Business School, 1990) ch 14.
11 The Bank of England in its *Quarterly Bulletin* for November 1989 in an article entitled 'London as an International Financial Centre' provided the following data which is interesting in this context.

Three quarters of all trades in dollar denominated international bonds (amounting to US $358bn in the first quarter of 1989) occurs in London; 80 of the 114 dealers reporting prices to the Association of International Bond Dealers were located in London. While London's Stock Exchange is the fourth largest in the world by market capitalisation its turnover in *foreign* equities totalling US $71bn in value was nearly one and a half times that of New York and ten times that of Tokyo, and measured half of global foreign equity turnover. In comparison, domestic equity turnover was a mere 5% of global turnover representing the relatively small size of the UK domestic economy.

In foreign exchange, London's net daily turnover in April 1989 was US $187bn compared with US $129bn in New York and US $115bn in Tokyo.

In the area of fund management the journal *The Banker* (March 1991), provided the following statistics with regard to equities under management in 1990 (the figures were also quoted in the *Financial Times* of 16 May 1991): Tokyo was the largest centre and accounted for US $2,192.3bn; New York, the second largest centre, accounted for US $406.6bn; London occupied third place with US $365.3bn; Geneva and Zurich accounted for US $283.4bn and 257.1bn respectively; Paris occupied 11th position with total equities under management of US $81.3bn.

The law and regulations governing the raising of long-term finance in the international financial markets of London is the scope of the following chapters. No attempt is made to consider the legal aspects of foreign transactions in the domestic capital and financial markets of New York and Japan, despite their importance, nor in the (relatively) small domestic markets of Great Britain.

BIBLIOGRAPHY

Bell *The Euro-dollar Market and the International Financial System* (Halsted Press, 1974).
Bloch 'Eurodollars: An Emerging International Money Market' Bulletin no 39, Institute of Finance, NYU (April 1966).
Carli et al, 'Eurodollars: A Paper Pyramid' (1971) Banca Nazionale de Lavoro, Quarterly Review 95–109.
Chalmers *Readings in the Eurodollar* (Griffith and Sons, London 1969).
Clendenning *Eurodollar Market* (Oxford, 1970).
Dach 'Legal Nature of the Euro-Dollar System' (1964) Am Jo of Comp Law 13.
de Grauwe 'The Development of the Eurocurrency Market' Finance and Development vol 12, no 3 (September 1975) 14–16.
Einzig 'Dollar Deposits in London' (1960) The Banker 110.
Einzig and Quinn *Roll-Over Credits – The System of Adaptable Interest Rates* (St Martin's Press, New York 1973).
   'Statistics and Dynamics of the Eurodollar Market' (1961) Economic Journal 71.
   'Some Recent Changes in the Euro-dollar System' Jo of Finance 19 (1964) 443–449. 'The Euro-Currency Business of Banks in London' Bank of England, Quarterly Bulletin, March 1970, June 1971, March 1972.
   'Euro-Dollars: A Changing Market' Federal Reserve Bulletin, October 1969.
Hugon 'Why the Eurodollar?' (1978) 222 Bankers Magazine.
   'Past and Future of the Euro-Money Market' FAJ 27, September/October 1971, 21–24.
Johnson *Euro-dollars in the New International Money Market* (First National City Bank, New York 1964).
Klopstock 'The International Money Market: Structure, Scope and Instruments' Jo of Finance 20 (1965).
   'Outlook for the Euromarket: 1' International Currency Review, March/April 1973.
   'The Use of Eurodollars by US Banks' in Herbert Prochnow (ed) *The Eurodollar* (Rand McNally, New York 1970).
   'The Wiring of the Eurodollar Market' Euromoney, August 1970.
Lee 'The Eurodollar Market Revisited' The Bankers Magazine, Autumn 1973.
Little 'The Eurodollar Market: Its Nature and Impact' Federal Reserve Bank of Boston, New England Economic Review, May/June 1960.
   Eurodollars: The Money Market Gypsies (1975).
Lutz, 'The Eurocurrency System' Banca Nazionale de Lavoro Quarterly Review vol 27, no 110 (September 1974) 183–200.

Machlup 'Five Errors about Eurodollars' Euromoney, July 1972.
Madden and Nadler *The International Money Markets* (Greenwood, 1968).
Martenson *The Eurodollar Market* (Bankers Publishing Company, Boston, 1964).
Mayer 'The BIS Concept of the Eurocurrency Market' Euromoney, May 1976, 60–66.
Mikesell 'The Eurodollar Market and the Foreign Demand for Liquid Dollar Assets' Jo of Money, Credit and Banking, August 1972.
Quinn *The New Euromarkets* (1975).
Sakaibara 'The Eurocurrency Market in Perspective' Finance and Development vol 12, no 3 (September 1975) 11–13, 41.
Shaw *The London Money Market* (2nd edn, 1978).
Woodworth 'Understanding the Eurodollar Market' The Bankers Magazine, August 1971.

Part I
Governing law in international finance

CHAPTER 2
The nature and scope of a governing law

I THE NECESSITY FOR A GOVERNING LAW

International finance in all its forms necessarily involves the potential applicability of many systems of law.

Thus in a syndicated loan the transnational banks active in this market, although based in London, are drawn from a range of countries including the United States, Japan, Germany, France, Great Britain, and Switzerland amongst others;[1] the borrowers may be corporations, banks and state corporations from a large number of nations; sovereign states themselves are frequent borrowers in the international markets; the currencies in which the lending is effected may be in US dollars, German deutschmarks, Swiss francs, Japanese yen or some other major currency.[2]

Similarly, in an international (or 'Euro') bond issue[3] the issuers of bonds as well as the investment banks who place or sell the international bonds on behalf of an issuer are drawn from a similar range of countries.[4] There are other characteristics of a Eurobond issue which make such an issue more international in character than an international syndicated loan. Thus the bonds are sold to investors resident in a range of countries; they will be traded in the international markets[5] by persons and entities resident in different countries; and payment of interest and principal in respect of the bonds will occur wherever the offices of paying agents[6] are located.

Given the above context there is the possibility that rules and regulations of different systems of law may apply to an international financial transaction. The potential applicability of a number of different legal systems introduces a significant element of uncertainty, first as to the intrinsic validity, enforceability and interpretation of the legal documents which constitute or give effect to an international transaction, and secondly, as to the rights and liabilities of parties to such a transaction. In order to reduce such uncer-

---

1 See Part II on syndicated loans and Euromoney 20th Anniversary Supplement *The Euromarket in Figures* p 163.
2 See Euromoney Supplement, fn 1 above, at p 163.
3 See ch 8 on Eurobonds.
4 See Euromoney Supplement, fn 1 above, at p 163.
5 Under the rules of the Association of International Bond Dealers.
6 These are banks specially appointed for the purposes of transfer of funds.

tainty to a minimum, an attempt is made in practice to apply one system of law to the transaction and to exclude as far as possible the applicability of other systems of law with which the transaction may have some connection. This is generally sought to be achieved in practice by a 'choice of law' clause which subjects to one governing system of law – 'the proper law' – the validity, enforceability and interpretation of the contractual and other legal documents which constitute the transaction.

In the English conflict of laws according to Dicey and Morris in *The Conflict of Laws*,[7] 'the term "proper law of the contract" means a system of law by which the parties intended the contract to be governed, or, where their intention is neither expressed nor to be inferred from the circumstances, the system of law with which the transaction has its closest and most real connection'. It is also fundamental to recognise that once a contractual proper law has been chosen by the parties 'this law and, exceptions apart, this law alone, can affect the contractual obligation and thus, for example, modify, discharge or annul a debt based upon the contract'.[8]

From a practical point of view the purpose of a choice of law clause is to seek to control the following:

(a) the validity, enforceability and interpretation of all legal documents evidencing and constituting the transaction, eg in a syndicated loan, the syndicated loan agreement; in a bond issue the subscription agreement, the trust deed, the agreement between managers, the selling group agreement and the bond instruments themselves;
(b) the legal rights and obligations of the various parties to an international financing transaction;
(c) the extent to which other systems of law will affect the transaction.

The end purpose is to achieve certainty and result predictability in respect of the above three factors by cocooning the transaction in the chosen system of law.

In the absence of such a clause the international financing transaction may be subject to and be affected by a number of legal systems, including in particular the law of the place where the legal documents are formally signed, the law of the place where a borrower (in the case of a syndicated loan) or an issuer (in the case of an international bond issue) is incorporated or is deemed to be resident, or even the law of the country in which any dispute is subsequently litigated.

II CHOICE OF LAW: THE LEGAL AND COMMERCIAL FACTORS

In determining which law should be chosen as the controlling or governing law of an international financial transaction, a number of factors need to be considered:

---

7 11th edn, 1989, see r 180.
8 See *Dicey and Morris* r 180 at p 1163; see also *R v International Trustee For Protection of Bondholders AG* [1937] AC 500 HL; *Kahler v Midland Bank Ltd* [1950] AC 24 HL; *Re Helbert Wagg & Co Ltd's Claim* [1956] Ch 323.

1 Freedom of choice under the prospective proper law

A fundamental question which needs to be considered is the extent to which a particular legal system will permit parties to a transaction to choose that system of law to govern the validity and enforceability of an agreement as well as the rights and liabilities of parties to that agreement: the question of 'party autonomy'. In particular, it is necessary to determine whether a particular legal system will permit that system of law to be chosen to govern a transaction with which it has little or no connection. A legal system may require that it may not be chosen to govern a transaction unless, for instance, the transaction was entered into within the territory in which that system of law operates; or that the currency of the transaction is the legal tender of the territory in which that system of law operates; or that one of the parties was a national or resident of the country of that legal system.

It is not proposed to consider party autonomy by reference to every system of law, but to consider the question by reference to the two major systems of law which govern international financial transactions in practice: English law and, to a lesser extent, New York law.

i The position under English law

The position under the English common law before the Contracts (Applicable Law) Act 1990 was reasonably clear. English law would give effect to an express choice of law clause which seeks to subject the legal aspects and incidents of an agreement to English law, even if the transaction to which the agreement related had little or no connection with England: *Vita Food Products Inc v Unus Shipping Co Ltd*.[9] Lord Wright in that case clearly stated that there is no necessity to establish any connection between the contractual transaction and English law, before English courts would recognise a choice of law expressly made by the parties.[10] This ruling is also supported by the decision of the House of Lords in *Miller & Partners Ltd v Whitworth Street Estates (Manchester) Ltd*[11] even though there are some notable dicta in other cases to the contrary.[12]

The position under the English common law as to party autonomy was, however, not entirely without qualification. Lord Wright himself in the *Vita Food Products* case stated that the choice of law must be 'bona fide and legal' and, further, that there should be 'no reason for avoiding the choice on the ground of public policy'.[13] This qualification is, however, of doubtful value. Dicey and Morris take the view[14] that the expression 'legal' in the formula used by Lord Wright was probably redundant. They have also pointed out that the apparent limitation has never been applied by an English court, in the fifty years since the *Vita Food Products* case, to strike down a choice of law clause whether English or foreign; and that therefore it can only mean that the choice of law must not be 'capricious' or 'a mere pretence'.

---

9   [1939] AC 277, PC.
10 See [1939] AC 277 at 290.
11 [1970] AC 583, HL, especially per Lord Reid at 603.
12 See *Re Helbert Wagg & Co Ltd's Claim* [1956] Ch 323 and *Boissevain v Weil* [1949] 1 KB 482, CA.
13 See [1939] AC 277 at 290.
14 See *Dicey and Morris* p 1172 and an article by Dr F A Mann (1953) ICLQ 60.

The position under the common law has generally speaking been retained by the Contracts (Applicable Law) Act 1990 which gives effect to the EEC Convention on the Law Applicable to Contractual Obligations (The Rome Convention), and the relevant provisions of which came into effect on 1 April 1991.[15]

Article 3 of the Rome Convention[16] preserves the freedom of parties to a contract to select a system of law to control the validity and enforceability of a transaction and the rights and obligations of parties thereunder. Article 3 of the Rome Convention provides that:

> '(i) A contract shall be governed by the law chosen by the parties. The choice must be expressed or demonstrated with reasonable certainty by the terms of the contract or the circumstances of the case. By their choice the parties can select the law applicable to the whole or a part only of the contract.'

Article 3(3), however, provides that the fact that the parties to a contract have chosen a foreign law does not prevent application of mandatory rules of a country with which 'all the other elements relevant to the situation at the time of the choice are connected'. Under art 7(1) 'effect may be given to the mandatory rules of the law of another country' with which the situation has a close connection in precedence over the chosen law, 'if and in so far as, under the law of the latter country, those rules must be applied whatever the law applicable to the contract'. Article 7(1) does not, however, have the force of law in the UK due to s 2(2) of the Contracts (Applicable Law) Act 1990 under which the UK excluded the applicability of art 7(1).

Consequently, the only mandatory rules which the English courts would be required to apply would be those applicable under the conflicts rules of the English common law where English law is the law of the forum. This is the effect of art 7(2) read with art 3 of the Rome Convention read with s 2(2) of the Contracts (Applicable Law) Act 1990.

There is, however, an important exception to the applicability of the Rome Convention which is relevant to international bonds. Article 1 of the Rome Convention provides that 'The rules of this convention shall apply to contractual obligations in any situation involving a choice between the laws of different countries' but shall not apply to 'obligations arising under bills of exchange, cheques and promissory notes and other negotiable instruments to the extent that the obligations under such other negotiable instruments arise out of their negotiable character': art 1(2)(c). Two points need to be noted with regard to this provision. First, it is only those obligations which arise 'out of the negotiable character' of negotiable instruments, which fall outside the rules of the Convention. The Giuliano and Lagarde Report[17]

---

15 By the Contracts (Applicable Law) Act 1990 (Commencement no 1) Order 1991, SI 1991/707 (c 16). The Act itself was enacted on 26 July 1990. The Rome Convention was opened for signature on 19 June 1980 and signed by the UK on 7 December 1981. See, on the Rome Convention, C G J Morse 'The EEC Convention on the Law Applicable to Contractual Obligations' in *The Yearbook of European Law* vol 2 (1982) p 107.
16 Sch 1 of the Contracts (Applicable Law) Act 1990.
17 OJ 1980 No C282/1. The Report may be relied on by an English court for the purposes of interpreting the convention under s 3(3)(a) of the Contracts (Applicable Law) Act 1990.

which accompanies the Rome Convention states that art 1(2)(c) does not include the contracts pursuant to which such instruments are issued and contracts for the sale and purchase of such instruments.[18] Thus, for instance, the subscription agreement in an international bond issue will not be within art 1(2)(c). Secondly, whether a document is to be characterised as a negotiable instrument for the purposes of art 1(2)(c) is to be determined by the law of the forum: the Giuliano and Lagarde Report provides that 'whether a document is characterised as a negotiable instrument is not governed by this convention and is a matter for the law of the forum (including its rules of private international law)'.

The exclusion in art 1 of the Rome Convention means that at least with regard to obligations under negotiable instruments which 'arise out of their negotiable character' an English court would apply common law rules. The negotiability of Eurobonds[19] or Eurocommercial paper[20] and the obligations arising under the bond instrument would consequently not be subject to the rules in the Rome Convention.[21]

ii   *The position under New York law*

Section 1-105(1) of the US Uniform Commercial Code states that:

'Except as provided hereafter in this section, when a transaction bears a reasonable relation to this state and also to another state or nation the parties may agree that the law either of this state or of such other state or nation shall govern their rights and duties. Failing such agreement this Act applies to transactions bearing an appropriate relation to this state.'

The provisions of the Code, however, apply only to transactions governed by the Code and many financial agreements, including loan agreements, fall outside the Code. Nevertheless, a test similar to that in s 1-105 of the Code is applied by the New York courts, even when parties have expressly chosen a system of law to govern a transaction. The court in *A S Rampell Inc v Hyster Co*[1] gave effect to a governing law clause in a distribution agreement on the basis that it had 'a reasonable relation' to the state (Oregon) chosen by the clause. It appears that where New York law is chosen as the governing law, New York courts interpret the requirement of 'reasonable relation' liberally because of 'New York's recognised interest in maintaining and fostering its undisputed status as the prominent commercial financial centre of the Nation and the world': *Ehrlich-Boher & Co v University of Houston*.[2] Nevertheless, the New York courts in *Haag v Barnes* in 1961[3] applied the test of which jurisdiction had 'the most signifi-

---

18   Giuliano and Lagarde, Report para 4, (1980) OJ C282., 31.10.80.
19   See ch 9.
20   See ch 23.
21   See p 18, above.
1   3 NY 2d 369, 165 NYS 2d 475 (1957).
2   49 NY 2d 574, 427 NYS 2d 817 (1980).
3   9 NY 2d 554, 216 NYS 2d 65 (1961).

cant contacts with the matter in dispute' even though the parties had expressly chosen a law to govern the agreement.[4]

If the rule requiring a 'reasonable relation' to New York were applied to transactions in international finance it would restrict the choice of New York law as the proper law.

Consequently, a specific rule applies to commercial transactions which have a value of $250,000 or more, entered into after 19 July 1984. It is contained in s 5-1401 of the General Obligations Law of New York.[5] This provides that

> 'The parties to any contract, agreement or undertaking contingent or otherwise, in consideration of, or relating to any obligation arising out of a transaction covering in the aggregate not less than $250,000, including a transaction otherwise covered by subsection 1 of section 1-105 of the Uniform Commercial Code may agree that the law of this state shall govern their rights and duties in whole or in part, whether or not such contract, agreement or undertaking bears a reasonable relation to this state.'

While there are a number of exceptions to this rule, they do not prevent its applicability to contractual agreements in respect of international financing transactions. Consequently, both a syndicated loan agreement and the agreements which provide for the marketing and distribution of international bonds can be subject to the laws of New York provided the transaction value is $250,000 or more.

iii The position in civil law systems

It appears that under art 2312 of the French Civil Code a freedom of choice ('autonomie de la volonté') similar to that found in English and New York law is applicable in international contracts. In Italy, art 25 of the 1942 Civil Code seems to contain a similar freedom.

Apart from the fundamental consideration discussed above as to the freedom of choice permitted by a system of law, there are a number of other quasi-legal and practical factors which influence the choice of law in international finance, and these are considered below.

2 Certainty and result predictability under legal documents

In practice this is perhaps the most important consideration from the point of view of the parties to the transaction. It is of great value if the legal

---

4   This case was concerned with a child support agreement rather than a commercial agreement and relied on the ruling in *Auten v Auten* 308 NY 155 (1954), another case concerned with an agreement in the context of family relationships. In *A S Rampell & Co v Hyster Co* (above) the court ignored the ruling in *Auten v Auten*. See Gruson 'Governing law clauses in commercial agreements – New York's approach' 18 Columbia Jo of Transnational Law 323 (1979); and also *Crédit Français International SA v Sociedad Financiera de Comerco SA* 490 NYS 2D 670 (1985); Uniform Commercial Code s 1-105; the American ReStatement s 187(2)(a); see also, Gruson 'Controlling Choice of Law' in *Sovereign Lending: Managing Legal Risk* (Euromoney Publications 1984) ch 5.
5   Title 14: Enforceability of clauses respecting choice of law and choice of forum in certain transactions.

consequences of particular clauses used in a contractual document are capable of certain or near certain prediction under a given legal system. The parties to a transaction become capable of dealing with virtually every foreseeable eventuality or occurrence by express clauses at the time of contracting. To the extent that parties to a transaction do not have this capability at the time of contracting, the legal consequences of any subsequent occurrence or eventuality will be unpredictable and will depend on litigation and, in the final analysis, on a court's conception of reasonableness, fairness or policy.

A good example of the need for certainty and predictability is to be found in the context of a syndicated loan. It is of great practical value to be able to specify with certainty in a syndicated loan agreement the circumstances which confer an immediate and unqualified right to the syndicate of banks to terminate the loan agreement and demand repayment of all outstanding debt prior to maturity ('acceleration').[6] Could such a right be specified in a syndicated loan agreement in a manner which would not be capable of interference and qualification by a court? Under English law at least, it is possible to state that a particular term of a contract, for example the obligation to pay interest on a particular date, is an essential 'condition'[7] of the contract, a breach of which would confer on the banks a right to terminate the loan agreement and to demand repayment of all loan outstandings prior to their scheduled maturity. An English court will be bound to give effect to this provision regardless of considerations such as materiality, fairness, or whether the syndicate has suffered any loss in consequence of the breach. The English courts have committed themselves to this position in no uncertain terms in the House of Lords ruling in *Bunge Corpn v Tradax SA*.[8]

Another important example of a 'condition' is the right provided for in a subscription agreement in a bond issue[9] which gives the managing underwriters the power to terminate an issue on the occurrence of certain specified events. Once again it is imperative that this right conferred on the managing underwriters is not capable of being diluted because the applicable law requires materiality or evidence of loss before the right can be exercised.

Under many systems of law based on the French Civil Code, courts do have a power to interfere with such a contractual right on the basis that

---

6 On default and acceleration see ch 5, p 98, below.
7 For the confusion caused in the minds of continental lawyers by the use of this expression, see Zweigert and Kötz: *Introduction to Comparative Law* vol II (Clarendon Press, Oxford, 1987, 2nd edn) ch 13, p 195. Translated from the German text by Tony Weir.
8 [1981] 1 WLR 711, HL, especially at 724 per Lord Roskill; and in *Photo Production Ltd v Securicor Transport Ltd* [1980] AC 827, HL, especially Lord Diplock at 849; in *Bunge Corpn v Tradax SA*, the House of Lords clarified much of the dicta in *Hong Kong Fir Shipping Co v Kawasaki Kisen Kaisha Ltd* [1962] 2 QB 26 where the Court of Appeal seems to have said that it was not every breach which would give rise to a right to terminate a contract. The House of Lords in *Bunge* unequivocally stated that a test of materiality or the seriousness of the consequences of breach would not be applied to a term of the contract which had been expressly classified by the parties to the contract as being a 'condition' and/or for a breach of which the parties had expressly conferred a right to terminate the contract. The test of the seriousness of the consequences of the breach expounded in the *Hong Kong Fir* case was to be applied only to 'innominate' terms of a contract which the parties had not expressly classified or in respect of which the parties had not specified the remedy for breach.
9 See ch 10 below.

the breach was not serious or because of the absence of proven loss or on grounds of reasonableness or fairness, or a combination of these factors.[10] Indeed under French law there is a formal requirement in art 1184 of the French Civil Code that, in the event of breach, a contract can only be set aside by court judgment, and under art 1184 para 3 a judge has a power to confer a period of grace on the party in breach; however, the rules have been whittled down by the rulings of the Cour de Cassation.[11]

The need for certainty and result predictability is also important in another context. It is important that the circumstances in which a court will imply clauses additional to those which the parties have expressly included in a contract are extremely limited. If a legal system permits a wide freedom to its judges to imply terms into written contracts, and perhaps even rewrite the contract for the parties according to the judge's perception of the intention of parties, certainty and result predictability cannot be achieved at the time of contracting by the parties to a commercial transaction. Zweigert and Kötz[12] have pointed out that the extent of this freedom depends on the approach of legal systems to the construction of contracts.

There are two conflicting approaches to the construction of contracts. The first is the 'expressionist' approach, which emphasises that a contract must be interpreted strictly and literally, in accordance with the external expressions of the parties; the judge is concerned primarily with the objective meaning of words used in a contract, and the intention of the parties is relevant only in so far as it is reflected in the objective meaning of the words used. This is the approach of the English common law and systems based on it such as New York, Canadian and Australian law. The second approach is to regard the purpose of construction as a search for the subjective intention of the parties, so that a court may disregard the actual written words of a contract to give effect to the perceived intention of the parties. This approach is exemplified by codes based on the French Civil Code. Art 1156 of the French Civil Code thus gives primacy to 'la commune intention des parties contractantes' over the written word.

Under English law, where the parties to a commercial transaction have expressed their rights and obligations by the use of clearly drafted clauses, effect will be given to the plain and ordinary meaning of the words used, and English courts cannot read into a commercial or contractual agreement additional clauses which would make the agreement 'fair' or 'reasonable'. The House of Lords in *Liverpool City Council v Irwin*[13] held that an English court would not imply a term into the contract unless it appeared that the contract or transaction would lack business efficacy without the implication of such a term. In effect, the House of Lords reaffirmed the approach of the Court of Appeal in *The Moorcock*.[14] An English court will rarely imply a term 'where the parties have entered into a carefully drafted written contract

---

10   See, for instance, art 1455 of the Italian Civil Code. See also art 1184 of the French Civil Code; see also Zweigert and Kötz *Introduction to Comparative Law* vol II, (Clarendon Press, Oxford, 2nd edn 1987) ch 13.
11   See Zweigert and Kötz, above, at pp 188–189.
12   *Introduction to Comparative Law* vol II, ch 7.
13   [1977] AC 239.
14   (1889) 14 PD 64.

containing detailed terms agreed between them'.[15] The basic rule therefore is that unless the implication of the term is both obvious and necessary to give the transaction such business efficacy as is absolutely necessary,[16] the courts will not imply a term merely because it would be 'reasonable' to do so,[17] nor will the courts 'improve the contract which the parties have made for themselves, however desirable the improvement might be'.[18]

The problem with the approach in systems based on the French Civil Code is that it deprives a carefully drafted and detailed contractual agreement of its commercial integrity and exposes it to judicial interference on the basis of a judge's perception of the intention of the parties. One of the consequences of this is that the international financial community has preferred to use a system such as English law based on the more pragmatic and commercial expressionist approach.[19]

3 Conceptual sophistication of the system

It is also important that any system of law chosen to govern the international financing transaction must be such as to be capable of accommodating sophisticated and complex concepts, transactions, and structures within the framework of its legal terminology and legal rules.

4 Language

A factor which also influences the choice of law decision is the language in which the international financial market operates and the language in which financing techniques are developed. English is in practice the language of the international financial markets at present and, consequently, there is a preference for English law or New York law on this basis.

5 The forum of potential litigation

It is extremely convenient if the courts which are likely to be chosen by the parties to decide any disputes arising from the international financial transaction are also the courts of the country of the chosen system of law. For instance, it will be less desirable to choose English law as the chosen system of law, if the parties desire that the courts of Japan or Poland should be conferred jurisdiction to decide any dispute arising from the transaction. Consequently, factors affecting the choice of the courts (or choice of the forum) which will have jurisdiction to decide disputes arising in relation to the transaction also influence the question of choice of law.

---

15 *Shell UK Ltd v Lostock Garages Ltd* [1976] 1 WLR 1187 at 1200.
16 *Luxor (Eastbourne) Ltd v Cooper* [1941] AC 108 at 137, HL.
17 *Liverpool City Council v Irwin* [1977] AC 239.
18 *Trollope & Colls Ltd v North West Metropolitan Regional Hospital Board* [1973] 1 WLR 601, HL. For the different approaches to construction of contracts in Germanic and civilian jurisdictions, see Zweigert and Kötz *Introduction to Comparative Law* vol II ch 7. See generally, *Chitty on Contracts* (26th edn, 1989) vol 1, ch 13 on the approach of English law to the implication of terms into a contract.
19 See also the comments of Zweigert and Kötz, above, at p 88, ad fin in ch 7.

The choice of forum or choice of jurisdiction depends very much on the perception in the international financial markets as to the sophistication and impartiality of the courts of a given country. The selection of the court which would have primary jurisdiction over any disputes is also influenced by the following:

(a) the existence of speedy and effective judicial remedies in the event of a breach of the agreement relating to the international financial transaction;
(b) whether or not there is a special court which is staffed by judges who are experienced in deciding and who regularly decide not merely ordinary commercial disputes, but financial and business disputes with an international dimension. The Commercial Court of the High Court of England and the Courts of the Southern District of New York are generally regarded as having such a status;
(c) the extent to which the judgments of that court will be recognised and enforced by the courts of other countries.[20]

In practice the consideration of these criteria has led to a choice of the High Court of England (which comprises within it the English Commercial Court) as a favoured forum for the purposes of conferring jurisdiction in international financial transactions. The only other competing forum has generally been the Southern District Court of New York, especially the Second Circuit.

6 Familiarity

Transnational banks, investment banks, securities dealers, borrowers of funds and issuers of securities also prefer to choose a system of law which has traditionally been used to govern such transactions. Equally, there is a preference, when choosing the court which is to have jurisdiction over the dispute, to select court with which such entities are familiar.

On the basis of the above considerations, the law usually chosen in practice to govern transactions in the international financial markets (properly so called)[1] in a large majority of cases is English law.

---

20 Recognition of judgments of the High Court is based on reciprocal recognition treaties based on the Foreign Judgments (Reciprocal Enforcement) Acts of 1920 and of 1933. The countries to which the 1920 Act applies are to be found in SI 1985/1994 and such countries would in turn recognise and enforce judgments of the UK; the 1933 Act provides for recognition and enforcement of judgments of 'recognised courts' of a country which has been designated by statutory instrument. The provisions of the 1933 Act have been extended to India (SI 1958/425), Pakistan (SI 1958/141), the Australian Capital Territory (SI 1955/559), Guernsey, Isle of Man and Jersey (SIs 1973/610, 611 and 612), Austria (SI 1962/1339), Israel (SI 1971/1039), Norway (SI 1962/636), Suriname (SI 1981/735) and Tonga (SI 1980/1523); the 1933 Act also covered Belgium, the Federal Republic of Germany, France, Italy and the Netherlands but the applicability of the 1933 Act to these countries has been superseded by the Civil Jurisdiction and Judgments Act 1982 which gives effect to the Brussels Convention on Jurisdiction and Enforcement of Judgments in Civil and Commercial Matters of 1968. See also *Awards in the Commonwealth*, (Butterworths, London, 1984); Platto (ed) *Enforcement of Foreign Judgments Worldwide* (1989); Patchett *Recognition of Commercial Judgments and Awards in the Commonwealth* (Butterworths, London, 1984).
1 See the discussion in ch 1, above.

In the context of this market practice, the remainder of this section is consequently devoted to considering what matters are controlled by the proper law and what matters are governed by other systems of law, under conflicts rules of English law. This section will not consider the related question as to the circumstances in which a court would assert jurisdiction in respect of a dispute arising from or connected with an international financial transaction. The latter is essentially a question to be determined by the conflict of laws of the particular jurisdiction in question whether it is England, the United States, Japan, Germany or France.[2]

III ASPECTS OF A TRANSACTION CONTROLLED BY THE PROPER LAW

Under English common law the following matters are regarded as being governed by the proper law of the contract.[3]

(a) The question whether a contract has been formed, including whether requirements such as offer and acceptance, consideration and reality of consent are satisfied, is governed by the proper law of the contract.[4]

(b) The interpretation of a contract and the effect of a contract (ie the rights and obligations of the parties to the contract), are both to be determined in accordance with the proper law of the contract.[5]

(c) The question whether a contract is formally valid, in the sense that it has complied with all necessary formalities, is governed by the law of the country where the contract is made (*lex loci contractus*) or by the proper law of the contract. This means that if the contract is formally valid under one system or the other the contract is regarded as being formally valid.[6]

(d) The material or essential validity of a contract is governed by the proper law of the contract.[7] Essentially this means that if a contract is unlawful by the law which the parties have chosen to apply to it then it will be illegal and void.[8] There was some authority for the

---

2 With regard to the jurisdictional rules applicable in England and Continental Europe see the Brussels Convention on Jurisdiction and the Enforcement of Judgments in Civil and Commercial Matters of 1968. The 1968 Convention as amended by the Accession Convention of 1978 is given effect to in the Civil Jurisdiction and Judgments Act of 1982 as far as the UK is concerned. See also *Dicey and Morris* vol 1, Part 3: Jurisdiction and Foreign Judgments.
3 See *Dicey and Morris* ch 28.
4 See *Dicey and Morris* r 146.
5 See *Dicey and Morris* rr 150 and 151 and the cases cited under those rules.
6 See *Dicey and Morris* r 148.
7 See *Dicey and Morris* r 184 at p 1213 and the cases cited under that rule.
8 *Kahler v Midland Bank Ltd* [1950] AC 24 at 27, HL, where the court said 'the courts of this country will not compel the performance of a contract if by its proper law performance is illegal'.

proposition that a contract which is valid under its proper law will nevertheless be void under English law if it was illegal at the time it was entered into under the *lex loci contractus*: *The Torni*.[9] However, in view of the ruling of the Privy Council in *Vita Food Products Inc v Unus Shipping Co Ltd*, it seems that even where an agreement is unlawful by the law of the place where the agreement was entered into or by the law of the place of incorporation of a transacting party[10] the contract would be valid if it is valid by the proper law of the contract.

Nevertheless, it must be remembered that in the *Vita Food Products* case, Lord Wright said that the choice of law must be bona fide and legal and not contrary to English public policy. In practice, therefore, if the entry into the agreement by the issuer of bonds or the borrower in a syndicated loan is unlawful by the law of the place of incorporation of the issuer or of the borrower, the agreement may run the risk of being struck down as not being 'bona fide and legal'. This is particularly so if the choice of law is perceived by a court as an attempt to evade the consequences of illegality at the time of contracting[11] under the law of the place of incorporation of the issuer or of the borrower.[12]

(e) The question whether a contract has properly been performed or whether it has been discharged or terminated by frustration is also determined in accordance with the proper law of the contract.[13]

The Rome Convention which supersedes the English common law rules[14] provides in art 8 that 'the existence and validity of a contract or of any term of a contract shall be determined by the law which would govern it under this Convention if the contract or term were valid'. Consequently where there is an express choice of law this would be given effect to under art 3(1), and consequently, the law chosen by the parties in accordance with the Convention would govern existence and validity of the contract as well as its individual terms. Under art 9(2) a contract concluded between persons who are in different countries is formally valid if it satisfies the formal requirements of the law which the parties have chosen under the Convention or of the law of one of the countries in which the parties are resident. Under art 10(e), the law chosen by the parties under art 3 will govern the following: the interpretation of the contract, all questions as to performance of the contract, the consequences of breach including the assessment of damages and the methods of discharge of contract including prescription and limitation. Under art 10(e), the Rome Convention also attributes the consequences of nullity of the contract to the proper law but this provision is not applicable in the UK due to the reservation made by s 2(2) of the Contracts (Applicable Law) Act 1990.[15]

---

9 [1932] P27; affd [1932] P78, CA.
10 Such as an issuer of bonds or a borrower of funds.
11 Cf the position with regard to supervening illegality.
12 See the discussion in *Dicey and Morris* at p 1216.
13 See *Dicey and Morris* r 152 and the cases cited under that rule.
14 See p 18 above.
15 See also p 18 above.

IV LIMITS TO THE CONTROL OF A TRANSACTION BY THE PROPER LAW

There are a number of important matters which are not subject under English conflicts rules to the control of the proper law of an agreement, including a proper law expressly chosen by the parties. Those which are important in practice in the context of international financial transactions are as follows.

1 Corporate capacity

The Rome Convention does not govern questions which relate to corporate capacity and presumably whether or not proper internal procedures and authorisation have been followed and obtained by a corporate entity.[16] Consequently, even after the Rome Convention became operative as law in the UK, the question of corporate capacity will be governed by the conflicts rules of the English common law.

In *Janred Properties Ltd v ENIT*[17] the Court of Appeal affirmed r 139 in *Dicey and Morris*[18] which states that the capacity of a corporation to enter into any legal transaction is governed both by the constitution of the corporation and by the law of the country which governs the transaction in question; and that all matters concerning the constitution of a corporation are governed by the law of the place of incorporation.

Consequently, where English law governs an agreement or document concerning an international loan or bond issue, the question whether a borrower or an issuer is properly constituted and possesses the corporate power to enter into the transaction in question, is determined by the rules of legal system to which the corporate entity owes its legal existence.[19] Similarly, all matters relating to questions, such as, which officials of a corporation are authorised to act on its behalf, are also governed by the legal system to which the corporate entity owes its legal existence.[20]

If a corporate entity had no capacity under that law to enter into a contractual agreement, the contractual agreement becomes unenforceable under English law (as the proper law) against that party and is probably void. It seems that while the question whether a corporate entity has capacity is decided by reference to the legal system to which the corporate entity owes its legal existence, nevertheless, the *effect* of the absence of corporate capacity to enter into a transaction is probably decided by reference to the proper law of the contract under English conflict of laws rules. There

---

16 See art 1(2)(e) and (f).
17 [1989] 2 All ER 444.
18 10th edn, 1980 now r 174 of *Dicey & Morris* (11th edn, 1987).
19 See *First Russian Insurance v London and Lancashire Insurance Co* [1928] Ch 922 at 935; *Rae (Inspector of Taxes) v Lazard Investment Co Ltd* [1963] 1 WLR 555 at 573, HL; *Dicey and Morris* r 139.
20 See *Banco de Bilbao v Sancho* [1938] 2 KB 176, CA; *Carl Zeiss Stiftung v Rayner and Keeler Ltd* (no 2) [1967] 1 AC 853, HL.

does not seem to be a case directly in point but it would seem to follow from the general policy underlying the concept of the proper law.

As far as supra-national international organisations are concerned, their capacity and status will be governed by treaty provisions. However, unless such provisions are recognised as a matter of domestic English law the entity has no legal status under English law. As Lord Templeman in *Arab Monetary Fund v Hashim*[1] pointed out 'the courts of the United Kingdom cannot enforce treaty rights but they can recognise legal entities created by the laws of one or more sovereign states. A treaty cannot create a corporation but a sovereign state which is a party to a treaty can ...'. Lord Templeman, delivering the judgment of the House of Lords in *Arab Monetary Fund v Hashim*, stated that there were three gateways through which English law could recognise the legal capacity of an international corporate entity set up by treaty. Firstly on the basis of an Order in Council issued under the International Organisations Act 1968 or its predecessors. Secondly, where Parliament has declared that the provisions of an international treaty are to have the force of law in the UK. This was done with the International Monetary Fund by the Bretton Woods Agreement Act 1945. Thirdly, where the UK is not party to the treaty establishing the international entity, the courts may recognise the entity on the basis that it is created and exists as a domestic corporate entity in a foreign country.

Many systems of law do, however, provide that companies may not plead absence of corporate capacity as against third parties who enter into transactions with a company. Thus s 35 of the UK Companies Act 1985[2] states that: 'The validity of an act done by a company shall not be called into question on the ground of lack of capacity by reason of anything in the company's memorandum'. This provision, however, applies only with regard to companies formed and registered under the UK Companies Acts.[3]

Sections 35A and 35B of the Companies Act 1985 further state as follows:

'**35A. Power of directors to bind the company**
(1) In favour of a person dealing with a company in good faith, the power of the board of directors to bind the company, or authorise others to do so, shall be deemed to be free of any limitation under the company's constitution.
(2) For this purpose—
    (a) a person "deals with" a company if he is a party to any transaction or other act to which the company is a party;
    (b) a person shall not be regarded as acting in bad faith by reason only of his knowing that an act is beyond the powers of the directors under the company's constitution; and
    (c) a person shall be presumed to have acted in good faith unless the contrary is proved.
(3) The references above to limitations on the directors' powers under the company's constitution include limitations deriving—
    (a) from a resolution of the company in general meeting or a meeting of any class of shareholders; or

---

1 (no 3) [1991] 1 All ER 871 at 878, HL.
2 Inserted by s 108 of the Companies Act 1989.
3 See s 735 of the Companies Act 1985.

(b) from any agreement between the members of the company or of any class of shareholders.'

35B. No duty to enquire as to capacity of company or authority of directors
A party to a transaction with a company is not bound to enquire as to whether it is permitted by the company's memorandum or as to any limitation on the powers of the board of directors to bind the company or authorise others to do so.'[4]

Generally, and in particular where provisions similar to ss 35, 35A and 35B of the Companies Act 1985 are not available, the following techniques are adopted to minimise the risk of unenforceability due to lack of corporate capacity or authority.

First, the borrower or the issuer, as the case may be (and guarantor, if any) will be required to submit all constitutional documents as well as all internal authorisations necessary under the law of the place of incorporation as a condition precedent to the obligations of the banks in a syndicate loan or bond issue or other transaction.

Secondly, the borrower or the issuer, as the case may be (and the guarantor, if any) are required as a condition precedent to obtain legal opinions from lawyers in the state of incorporation of the borrower or issuer[5] as to whether it is a duly incorporated and duly organised entity which is lawfully in existence.

Thirdly, it is also invariably a condition precedent to require legal opinions from lawyers of the country of incorporation of the borrower or the issuer (and guarantor, if any) stating that the entry into and the execution of the agreement, and in the case of an issue of debt securities, the issue, execution and delivery of the bonds or other debt securities, has been duly authorised by all necessary corporate action and that all necessary corporate authorisations have been given to such action.

Fourthly, the borrower or issuer (and the guarantor, if any) are required to give a representation and warranty that the entity is duly incorporated, duly organised and is lawfully in existence and that all necessary internal authorisations and corporate resolutions have been taken and passed in order to give effect to the entry, execution and due performance of all contractual agreements and to the execution, issue and delivery of all debt instruments.

The practice of requiring a representation (as well as a contractual warranty) is based on the premise that in the event that the contract or security instrument becomes unenforceable or void, because the corporate entity had no capacity, the representation may give rise to an action for damages. Such actions may be brought in English law under s 2(1) of the Misrepresen-

---

4 See also the Prentice Report *Reform of the Ultra Vires Rule, a Consultative Document*, July 1986. Provisions similar to these may be expected to exist in member states of the European Community seeking to give effect to art 9 of the First Company Directive of the Council of European Economic Community no 68/151 dated 9 March 1968.
5 See on the use of foreign legal opinions Gruson and Kutschera *Legal Opinions and International Transactions*, (Graham and Trotman Ltd and the International Bar Association, 1987).

tation Act 1967[6] or under English tort rules relating to negligent misrepresentation laid down by the House of Lords in *Hedley Byrne and Co Ltd v Heller & Partners Ltd*[7] as explained by the House of Lords in *Caparo Industries v Dickman Ltd*.[8]

The action for misrepresentation will lie if the misrepresentation is committed in England. Where the agreement containing the misrepresentation is entered into in England, it seems that the misrepresentation would be made in England and therefore the tort of misrepresentation would also be committed in England. In such circumstances even if all the parties to the transaction are foreign, liability will be determined by reference to English rules on torts: *Szalatnay-Stacho v Fink*.[9]

There is another reason for a representation as to due incorporation to be included. In *Janred Properties v ENIT*[10] it was held that conduct and representations with regard to corporate capacity, may give rise under English law to an estoppel. Such an estoppel may prevent the company from relying on absence of capacity under the law of the place of incorporation. *Janred Properties* was concerned with a case where the absence of capacity rendered the contract voidable under Italian law (nullita relativa) rather than wholly void abinitio. As to whether such an estoppel could be pleaded in a case where the contract was wholly void is an open question. Nourse LJ obiter thought that no estoppel would lie where the entity against whom the estoppel is pleaded is a statutory body and the absence of capacity renders the contract void.[11]

2 Illegality subsequent to contract

Since the decision of the Court of Appeal in *Kleinwort Sons & Co v Ungarische Baumwolle Industrie Akt*,[12] it was clear under English common law that even if the performance of a contract governed by English law would result in the violation of the law of a country in which a party to a contract

---

6 This provision reads:

> 'where a person has entered into a contract after a misrepresentation has been made to him by another party thereto and as a result thereof he has suffered loss then if the person making the misrepresentation would be liable to damages in respect thereof had the misrepresentation been made fraudulently, that person shall be so liable notwithstanding that the misrepresentation was not made fraudulently, unless he proves that he had reasonable ground to believe and did believe up to the time the contract was made that the facts represented were true.'

This is essentially an action for loss resulting from a negligent misrepresentation.

7 See [1964] AC 465.
8 [1990] 2 AC 605.
9 [1947] KB 1, CA; see also for the leading case which applies *lex loci delicti*: *Phillips v Eyre* (1870) LR 6 QB 1, Exch. Nevertheless there are fine questions as to which is the *locus delicti* in a case where a representation which is false is made in England but the resulting damage occurs elsewhere. It appears that there are no decided English cases on this point. In the US the Second Restatement requires an enquiry into the system of law with which the tort is most closely connected in preference to the *lex loci delicti*. In effect this means the US courts would, generally speaking, consider both the place where the conduct occurred and the place where the effect of such conduct was felt.
10 [1989] 2 All ER 444.
11 See [1987] 2 FTLR 179 at 185.
12 [1939] 2 KB 678.

was incorporated (or resident) because of a change in that law after the contract was entered into, the contract must be performed according to its terms; the subsequent illegality is irrelevant unless the latter system of law was also the proper law of the contract.[13] This rule had two related exceptions which are discussed below. The ruling in the *Ungarische Baumwolle* case (above) is of fundamental practical importance in the context of international financial transactions. The rule prevents the obligation of the borrower of funds or the issuer of bonds to pay interest and principal under agreements and instruments governed by an English proper law from being nullified or modified partially or wholly by the law of the place of incorporation or residence of the borrower or the issuer. If such laws are given effect to in precedence over the chosen proper law, it would expose rights of the lending banks under syndicated loan agreements and bond holders in bond issues to the unpredictable changes in the law of the debtor's country of incorporation or residence. This exposure carries even greater risks where the borrower or issuer is a state corporation or other entity which has special protection in the state of incorporation. The English law rule stated above therefore provides an important protection to lenders and investors where the proper law of the agreements or the bond instruments is English law.

It is submitted that this rule has survived the incorporation of the Rome Convention into UK law by the Contracts (Applicable Law) Act 1990. Article 10 of the Convention[14] provides that the law applicable to a contract under arts 3 to 6 and 12 of the Convention, governs both 'performance'[15] and 'the various ways of extinguishing obligations'.[16] Consequently, it would seem that unless performance becomes illegal under the proper law, extinguishing the obligation under the contract, illegality by reference to other systems is irrelevant under English conflicts rules (subject to what is said below).

As an exception to the above rule, there were two cases under the conflicts rules of the English common law where an English court applying an English proper law would give effect to illegality under a foreign law. These cases were embodied in two distinct but parallel rules of the English conflict of laws: the rule in *Regazzoni v K C Sethia (1944) Ltd*[17] and the rule in *Kahler v Midland Bank Ltd*.[18]

It is submitted that these rules may be given effect to by an English court, under art 16 of the Rome Convention as the public policy of the forum.[19] It is submitted that both rules were part of English public policy, and should now be applied under art 16.

The rule in *Regazzoni v K C Sethia (1944) Ltd*[20] was explained by Gough LJ in *Toprak Mahsulleri Ofisi v Finagrain Commerciale Agricole et Financière SA*:

---

13 See also, however, the discussion below with regard to the extent to which art VIII(2)(b) of the International Monetary Fund Agreement affects this rule.
14 See Sch 1 of the Contracts (Applicable Law) Act 1990.
15 Art 10(1)(b).
16 Art 10(1)(d). Both art 10(1)(b) and art 10(1)(d) are operative in the UK unlike art 10(1)(e). See s 2(2) of the Contracts (Applicable Law) Act 1990.
17 [1958] AC 301, HL.
18 [1950] AC 24, HL.
19 Art 16 dealing with public policy, and art 7(2) dealing with mandatory law are part of UK law unlike art 7(1) of the Convention: see s 2(2) of the Contracts (Applicable Law) Act 1990.
20 [1958] AC 301, HL.

'An English contract should and will be held invalid on account of illegality if the real object and intention of the parties necessitates them joining in an endeavour to join in a foreign and friendly country some act which is illegal by the law of such country notwithstanding that there may be in a certain event alternative modes or places of performing which permit the contract to be performed legally.'[1]

In *Regazzoni's* case the plaintiff had agreed to buy 500,000 jute bags from the defendants c.i.f. Genoa. Although the defendants could have shipped such cargo from any port in the world, both parties knew that the jute would be obtained from India and intended to re-export the jute to South Africa. Both parties were also aware that it was illegal under Indian law to export goods from India destined to South Africa, directly or indirectly. The court held that despite the fact that the c.i.f. contract was governed by English law, the violation of Indian law rendered the contract unlawful under the conflicts rules of English law.

Secondly, it also seems to be clear that regardless of the proper law, 'the law of England will not require an act to be done in performance of an English contract if such act would be unlawful by the law of the country in which the act has to be done': Lord Reid in *Kahler v Midland Bank Ltd*.[2] In *Zivnostenska Banka National Corpn v Frankman*[3] the court went on to say that English law would not require a party to do an act in performance of a contract which would be an offence under the law of the place where that act had to be done, whatever the proper law, whether English or otherwise. In *Libyan Arab Foreign Bank v Bankers Trust Co*[4] Staughton J elaborated on this rule by stating that it applies not only where the actual act of performance becomes illegal by the law of the place of performance, but also where performance 'necessarily involves' doing an act which is unlawful by the law of the place where the act has to be done.[5] The domain of control of the proper law does not therefore extend to subsequent illegality under the law of the place of performance.

The ramifications of the second rule were explored in some detail in the context of the international markets in *Libyan Arab Foreign Bank v Bankers Trust Co* (above):

(i) Staughton J held that either the act of performance itself or some act which necessarily involves performance of the contractual obligation must be unlawful by the law of the place of performance; it is not sufficient that activity which is *merely incidental* to performance is rendered unlawful by the law of the place of performance. 'It is immaterial whether one party has to equip himself for performance by an illegal act in another country.'[6] It is of course not easy to draw a line as between equipping for performances on the one side and performance or acts necessarily involving performance on the other.

(ii) The place of performance in respect of the obligation to pay interest or principal in a particular currency need not necessarily be the country

---

1 [1979] 2 Lloyd's Rep 98, CA; followed by Staughton J in the *Libyan Arab Foreign Bank v Bankers Trust Co* [1988] 1 Lloyd's Rep 259 at 270.
2 [1950] AC 24 at 48, HL.
3 [1950] AC 57 at 78, HL.
4 [1988] 1 Lloyd's Rep 259.
5 See at 268 citing *Euro-Diam Ltd v Bathhurst* [1987] 1 Lloyd's Rep 178.
6 See the *Libyan Arab Foreign Bank* case at 269 per Staughton J.

which is the home state of that currency. The place of performance of a debt obligation is the place where the creditor has a right to demand repayment of a debt. Such location is expressly specified in most international loan agreements and in international bond instruments. Usually this would be the place where the borrower or the issuer (as the case may be) is required to pay interest and principal. Consequently, the place of performance would be such location(s) rather than the home state of the currency of the loan or bond. As a result, where English law is the proper law of a contract or debt security, only illegality by the law of such location(s) is capable of having an effect on a debtor's obligation to pay: *Kahler v Midland Bank* (p 31 above).

This ruling of Staughton J is of some significance. It has the effect that (subject to what is said below about art VIII (2)(b) of the International Monetary Fund Agreement) the regulations of the central bank or monetary authority of the home state of a particular currency cannot, as a matter of English law, interfere with a debtor's obligation to make payment of interest or principal in that currency unless parties have expressly chosen the home state as the *only* place of repayment. In arriving at this conclusion the court rejected an argument advanced on the basis of the views of the distinguished economist, Dr Marcia Stigum, to the effect that a debt denominated in a currency can only be repaid in the home state of that currency; that, for instance, in the case of dollars the place of payment of a US dollar denominated obligation could only be the US.[7] The Court held that whatever the position as a matter of economics, the position as a matter of English law was that the place of performance of a debt obligation in whatever currency was the place where the creditor had a right to demand repayment. Thus in that case the right to demand repayment of a dollar deposit placed with Bankers Trust (in London) was England.

(iii) The Court also rejected an argument that repayment of a debt denominated in a particular currency *necessarily* involves the use of the clearing and settlement mechanisms provided by the central bank (or other monetary authority) of the home state of that currency. Thus the repayment of a dollar denominated debt did not necessarily involve the clearing and settlement system of the US Federal Reserve Bank. The Court arrived at this conclusion by holding that under English law it was always open to a creditor to demand repayment of a debt denominated in a Eurocurrency by tender of sterling where repayment in the currency of the debt was not practicable.[8]

The result of this conclusion is also that the regulations of a central bank or monetary authority of the home state of a currency will have no effect on the obligations of a debtor under English conflicts rules to repay interest and principal – even though its clearance and settle-

---

[7] She was quoted as saying that 'dollars deposited and dollars lent in wholesale Eurodollar transactions never leave the United States'. See the *Libyan Arab Foreign Bank* case at p 272.

[8] Staughton J accepted, however, that the general rule was that a debtor may only be required to pay in the currency of the debt and indeed cannot tender repayment of a debt in another currency.

ment systems would usually be used to make repayment of principal or payment of interest in that currency.

In the *Libyan Arab Foreign Bank* case the facts were that the Libyan Arab Bank kept Eurodollar time deposits in London with a branch of Bankers Trust Co which was an entity incorporated in the US but with a branch in London. On 8 January 1986 the deposits totalled some $131.5m. On that day President Reagan issued an executive order with immediate effect which had the force of law blocking 'all property and interests in property of the government of Libya, its agencies, instrumentalities and controlled entities and the Central Bank of Libya that are in the United States ... or come within the possession or control of US persons *including overseas branches of US persons*' (emphasis added). On the basis of this decree Bankers Trust refused to repay the deposit[9] to the Libyans. The Court concluded that the account in London was subject to English law and, consequently, considered whether US law was the law of the place of performance. Bankers Trust could have refused to repay the principal amount due on the deposit if this was the case. Applying the above principles the court concluded that the US was not the place of performance in respect of the Eurodollar deposit nor did performance necessarily involve any act in the US. It was consequently held that the Reagan decree had no effect on the obligations of Bankers Trust to repay the deposits placed with them in London.[10]

V THE PROPER LAW AND THE EFFECT OF EXCHANGE CONTROL REGULATIONS: ART VIII(2)(b) OF THE IMF AGREEMENT

A distinction needs to be drawn between exchange control legislation which exists at the time parties enter into a transaction, and such legislation which is enacted subsequent to parties entering into a transaction. An example of the former would be a law which prevents an entity from borrowing foreign currency; an example of the latter would be a law which prohibited a borrower from repaying principal on a foreign currency loan lawfully entered into.

The basic rule with regard to the latter under English conflicts rules formulated by *Dicey and Morris* prior to the enactment of the Rome Convention as part of English law, was as follows:

'(i) a contractual obligation may be invalidated or discharged by exchange control legislation if—
   (a) such legislation is part of the proper law of the contract; or
   (b) it is part of the law of the place of performance; or
   (c) it is part of English law and the relevant statute or statutory instrument is applicable to the contract.'[11]

---

9 The 'deposit' could, of course, equally be regarded as a loan made by the Libyans to Bankers Trust.
10 The case was cited and followed on the applicability of English law as the proper law in *Libyan Arab Foreign Bank v Manufacturers Hanover Trust Co (No 2)* [1989] 1 Lloyd's Rep 608 by Hirst J.
11 See r 212(1) and *Ralli Bros v Cia Naviera Sota y Aznar* [1922] 2 KB 287, CA.

It is submitted that, in the light of the discussion above, subject to art VIII (2)(b) of the IMF agreement, the position is the same even after the enactment of the Rome Convention as part of English law. As regards (c) above, while the Exchange Control Act 1947 remains in force, all exchange controls were abolished in the UK in 1979 by statutory instrument.[12]

The principles applicable under English conflicts rules are therefore much the same as those discussed above with regard to subsequent illegality.

In addition, even if exchange control laws are to be given effect as part of the law of the place of performance, nevertheless 'if it is used not with the object of protecting the economy of the foreign state but as an instrument of oppression or discrimination' the English courts would not recognise such exchange control legislation.[13] This rule, it is submitted, is still applicable as part of English public policy under art 16 of the Rome Convention.

As regards exchange control legislation which subsists at the time at which parties enter into a transaction if a loan agreement or the agreements in respect of a bond issue are governed by English law the exchange control legislation of the country of incorporation of the borrower or of the issuer of bonds will have no impact on the validity and enforceability of the contractual agreements or the bonds. Where the legislation exists at the time the agreements are entered into and the legislation affects the capacity of the borrower or issuer to enter into the transaction, it must follow that the English proper law would give effect to the legislation on the basis of the rules discussed above.[14] It is, however, difficult to draw the line between those exchange control laws which affect corporate capacity and those which do not. In practice, therefore, the obtaining of necessary exchange control permissions and consents is a condition precedent to the obligations of banks to lend in a syndicated loan agreement, or the obligation to underwrite funds in an international bond issue.

Article VIII(2)(b) of the International Monetary Fund Agreement[15] is of paramount significance of the effect of exchange control legislation in international transactions. It provides as follows:

> 'Exchange contracts which involve the currency of any member and which are contrary to the exchange control regulations of any member maintained or imposed consistently with this agreement shall be unenforceable in the territories of any member.'[16]

This agreement is part of English law by virtue of art 3 of the Bretton Woods Agreement Order in Council 1946,[17] made under the Bretton Woods Agreement Act 1945.

As far as an English Court is concerned, if English law is the proper law of a contract or agreement, art VIII(2)(b) will be given effect to as part of the English proper law in accordance with art 3 of the Rome Convention. Further, even if English law is not the proper law, an English court

---

12 SI 1979/1660; see generally, Parker *Exchange Control*, (Jordans, 3rd edn, 1978) as to the position prior to abolition.
13 *Dicey and Morris* r 212 at p 1466; *Re Helbert Wagg & Co Ltd's Claim* [1956] Ch 323; *Kahler v Midland Bank Ltd* [1950] AC 24, HL.
14 See pp 27–30.
15 Referred to as the Bretton Woods Agreement.
16 See for an 'in depth' analysis Dr F A Mann *Legal Aspects of Money* (4th edn 1982, ch XIV); see also Goode *Payment Obligations in Commercial and Financial Transactions* (Sweet and Maxwell, 1983) pp 43–44.
17 SR & O 1946/36.

may give effect to art VIII 2(b) as mandatory law of the forum under Art 7(2) of the Rome Convention.

The key question, however, is the extent to which art VIII(2)(b) affects the rights and obligations of parties to agreements in international loans and bond issues.

There are a number of requirements which must be satisfied before art VIII(2)(b) can be relied on to render an agreement unenforceable.

First, it is only an *'exchange contract'* which may be rendered unenforceable by that article on the basis that it is contrary to the exchange control regulations of any member state. The question therefore arises as to the meaning of the phrase 'exchange contract'. There are two views as to the meaning of this phrase. The first view is that laid down by the English Court of Appeal in *Wilson Smithett and Cope Ltd v Terruzzi*,[18] where the Court of Appeal held that[19] an exchange contract is a contract to exchange the currency of one country for the currency of another country. This view has now been affirmed by the House of Lords in *United City Merchants (Investments) Ltd v Royal Bank of Canada*.[20] The New York courts in *Libra Bank Ltd v Banco Nacional de Costa Rica*[1] also came to the same conclusion. The reasoning in *Terruzzi* and the *Royal Bank of Canada* cases leaves no room for doubt that as far as the English courts are concerned, a loan agreement or the agreements giving effect to an international bond issue and the bond instruments themselves are not 'exchange contracts' for the purposes of art VIII(2)(b). This analysis would render art VIII(2)(b) irrelevant to international syndicated loan agreements and to issues of international debt securities.

The second approach is that an exchange contract is 'any contract which in any way affects the country's exchange resources'.[2] This view is strongly supported by Dr F A Mann[3] and by Sir Joseph Gold.[4] It also had the support of Lord Denning in *Sharif v Azad*[5] although his Lordship subsequently took the opposite view in *Terruzzi*.

It is submitted that the approach taken by the English courts in the *Royal Bank of Canada* case and the New York courts in the *Libra Bank* case represents the better view. On the one hand it is hard to disagree with Gold that such an interpretation would erode the objective of art VIII(2)(b), namely, the protection of scarce foreign exchange resources of poorer debtor nations from the claims of foreign banks and creditors. On the other hand, it would nevertheless seem that the arteries of the international financial markets would become clogged if art VIII(2)(b) is given the wider interpretation favoured by writers such as Gold and Mann. Debtor nations could modify or even nullify obligations under international loan agreements by appropriate legislation. It appears that the courts on the Continent of Europe, including France, Germany and Italy, take the wider view of the phrase

---

18 [1976] QB 683 at 703.
19 The ruling of the Court of Appeal was refused recognition in Italy by the Court of Appeal in Milan and the Corte di Cassazione. See Rivista di Diritto Internazionale Privato e Processuale 1977 and 1981.
20 [1983] 1 AC 168 per Lord Diplock.
1 570 F Supp 870 (SDNY, 1983).
2 See ibid at 613–614.
3 In his major work *Legal Aspects of Money* (4th edn ch XIV, pp 387–391) and in two articles: (1949) 26 BYIL 259 and (1982) 98 LQR 526.
4 Formerly General Counsel to the IMF, in (1984) 33 ICLQ 777.
5 [1967] 1 QB 605. CA.

'exchange contract'.[6] The views of the continental European courts were rejected by the Court of Appeal in *Terruzzi* as being contrary to 'ordinary intelligence' and dismissed as constituting 'not interpretation but mutilation'.[7]

Secondly, before art VIII(2)(b) applies another key point is that the exchange control regulations must '*involve the currency of that member state*'. Sir Joseph Gold[8] has argued that a currency of a member state is involved if that member's balance of payments would in any way be affected by the payment or transfer required under the exchange contract as widely defined by him. A narrow view of the phrase 'involve the currency of that member state' is that it is only where payment or transfer is required in the currency of the member state imposing the exchange control regulations by the 'exchange contract' that art VIII(2)(b) is triggered. Thus, for instance, where a Turkish corporation borrows Euro Swiss francs from a syndicate bank, and subsequently repayments of principal are prohibited by Turkish exchange control regulations[9] art VIII(2)(b) should have no application because the contract does not involve the currency of Turkey. On the basis of the narrow view, repayment would involve the currency of Turkey only where the repayment is to be made in Turkish currency.

Thirdly, the question arises whether art VIII(2)(b) applies in respect of exchange control regulations adopted after the making of 'the exchange contract'. In the *Libra Bank* case the District Court of the Southern District of New York, rejecting the view of Gold to the contrary,[10] held that if a loan agreement was valid and enforceable when made, it could not be rendered unenforceable by an intervening exchange control regulation by reference to art VIII(2)(b).[11]

Fourthly, before art VIII(2)(b) applies it must be shown that the exchange controls in question are 'maintained or imposed consistently with' the IMF Agreement. While there does not seem to be any English authority on the point, the US courts[12] have insisted that there must be proof that the exchange control regulation is indeed consistent with the fund agreement. This may mean that it may be necessary to show that the fund's approval had been obtained under art VIII(2)(a) which requires IMF approval for any legislation which imposes 'restrictions on the making of payments and transfers for current international transactions'. This includes the payment of interests on loans[13] and repayments of loans. The US courts in *Callejo v Bancomer SA*[14] regarded such approval or advice from the fund to be a necessary precondition to the activation of art VIII(2)(b).[15] There is, however, an exception to the requirement of fund approval contained in art VIII(2)(a) where there is a scarcity of a member's currency.

It is interesting to speculate how a French or German court would apply art VIII(2)(b) after the enactment of the Rome Convention, in respect of

---

6 See Dr F A Mann *Legal Aspects of Money* ch 15.
7 See per Shaw LJ [1976] QB 683 at 719 ff.
8 *The Fund Agreement in the Courts* (1986) vol 3.
9 See the facts of *Weston Banking v Turkaye Garanti Bankasi* 446 NE 2D 1195 (NY 1982).
10 See Gold *The Fund Agreement in the Courts*.
11 This view was also acted on in *J Zeevi & Sons Ltd v Grindlays Bank (Uganda) Ltd* 37 NY 2d 2220, 333 NE 2d 168 (1975).
12 See *Libra Bank Ltd v Banco Nacional de Costa Rica* above.
13 See art XXX(d).
14 764 F 2d 1101 (5th Circ 1985).
15 The comments in the *Callejo* case were, however, by way of dicta.

a contract where the proper law is English. Dr F A Mann has argued that art VIII(2)(b) is part of the substantive rules of English law rather than a conflicts rule.[16] The practical consequence of this is that a French or German court determining a dispute in respect of a contract governed by English law should apply art VIII(2)(b) in the sense in which it is understood in English law. The German courts, however, treat art VIII(2)(b) as a procedural rule.[17] On the other hand a continental European court applying the Rome Convention could apply art VIII(2)(b) of the IMF Agreement as part of the mandatory law of the forum (that is the German or French interpretation) under art 7(2) of the Rome Convention.

VI THE PROPER LAW, EXCHANGE CONTROL LAWS AND THE 'ACT OF STATE' DOCTRINE[18]

In *Allied Bank International v Banco Credito Agricola de Cartago*,[19] an attempt was made to give effect to exchange control laws which modify or nullify the repayment obligations of the borrower in an international syndicated loan, on the basis of the Act of State doctrine recognised by the US courts. In that case a syndicate of banks brought an action in the New York courts to recover loans made on the basis of a series of promissory notes evidencing a syndicated loan made to three Costa Rican banks. Payments were to be made in New York City. After the loan agreement was entered into, the Costa Rican government imposed exchange controls in response to an economic crisis, under which the approval of the Central Bank was required for any foreign exchange transaction on the part of the banks. Such permission was refused in respect of payments to the syndicate. At first instance,[20] Griesa J in the US District Court for the Southern District of New York held that the defence of 'Act of State' succeeded in that case because payment was prevented due to directives of the Costa Rican Central Bank, its President and the Ministry of Finance which were public in character and which were 'undertaken in response to a serious national economic crisis and were of the type which some governments undertake to assist in such a crisis, ie, restrictions upon foreign currency transactions'. The court did not refer to art VIII(2)(b) of the International Fund Agreement. The court of first instance, in arriving at its conclusion, relied on the doctrine laid down by the US Supreme Court in *Banco Nacional de Cuba v Sabbatino*.[1] The court relied on the early ruling of Fuller CJ in the US Supreme Court in *Underhill v Fernandez*[2] where the court said that the US judiciary would not 'examine the validity of a taking of property within its own territory by a foreign sovereign government extant and recognised by this country

---

16 See *Legal Aspects of Money* (4th edn) p 374.
17 See case cited by Dr Mann, above, at p 375.
18 See also Noyes Leech, 'International Banking: Effects of Nationalisations and Exchange Controls' (1986) 8 Journal of Comparative Business and Capital Market Law 123–147 (Elsevir Science Publishers BV (North Holland)); Joseph Gold, 'Exchange Control: Act of State, Public Policy, the IMF's Articles of Agreement, and other Complications' in the Houston Journal of International Law, vol 7, August 1984.
19 566 F Supp 1440 (SDNY, 1983) affd, 733 F 2d 23 (2b Circ 1984).
20 Reported in 566 F Supp 144a (SDNY, 1983).
1 376 US 398 (1964).
2 168 US 250 (1897), which relies on the old English case of *Duke of Brunswick v King of Hanover* (1844) 6 Beav 1; affd (1848) 2 HL Cas 1.

at the time of suit ... even if the complaint alleges that the taking violates customary international law'.[3]

If the ruling in the *Allied Bank* case represented the common law, it would mean that exchange controls of a borrower's home state would be given effect to, at least by the US courts in New York, on the basis that exchange controls represented an 'Act of State'.[4] However, in *Libra Bank Ltd v Banco Nacional de Costa Rica*[5] the US District Court for the Southern District of New York on virtually the same facts involving the exchange control regulations of Costa Rica came to a different conclusion. In that case Libra Bank was the agent bank in a syndicated loan of $40m to a Costa Rican bank which was wholly owned by the government of Costa Rica; Libra Bank sued to enforce payment of interest and principal in respect of that loan. Banco de Costa Rica claimed that it had been denied permission to make payments in foreign currency under the exchange control law of Costa Rica; and that therefore it was entitled not to make any payments and, secondly, that the US courts were barred from enforcing payment due to the Act of State doctrine recognised as being applicable in the *Allied Bank* case. The court in the *Libra Bank* case held that although the right of the syndicate banks to payment and interest was a contractual right which is property for the purposes of the Act of State doctrine, nevertheless the doctrine applied only where such property was located within the jurisdiction of the state whose legislation or decrees were pleaded as an Act of State. In this case, since payment of interest and principal was to be made at the offices of Libra Bank in New York it was held that the property in question (consisting of the contractual right to payment of principal and interest) was located within the US and not within the jurisdiction of Costa Rica. Consequently, it was held that the Act of State doctrine did not apply.[6]

The *Libra Bank* ruling may be regarded as representing New York law since the US Court of Appeals for the Second Circuit in *Allied Bank International v Banco Credito Agricola de Cartago*[7] held that where the situs of the debt repayment of obligation was outside the jurisdiction of the state whose laws seek to nullify that obligation or 'expropriate' the creditors' assets, a US court will not apply the Act of State doctrine.[8] The Court of Appeal consequently reversed the decision of Griesa J in the US District Court for the Southern District of New York, referred to above.

It seems therefore that so long as the place of payment of interest and principal in an international syndicated loan is in London or New York or some other money centre, it is unlikely that an exchange control regulation

---

3 At p 428.
4 The President of the Federal Reserve Bank of New York was apparently quoted in the *Wall Street Journal* of 4 May 1984 to the effect that 'the ruling effectively allows troubled, debtor countries to unilaterally stop paying their debts, leaving lending banks without legal recourse'.
5 570 F Supp 870 (SDNY, 1983).
6 See for a critique of the *Libra Bank* decision Sir Joseph Gold: 'Exchange Control: Act of State Public Policy, the IMF's Articles of Agreement, and Other Complications' in the Houston Jo of International Law vol 7, Autumn 1984.
7 757 F 2d 516 (2nd Circ, 1985), 77 ALR Fed 281.
8 See also *Citibank v Wells Fargo Asia Ltd* 110 US S Ct 2034 (1990); *Baraka v Bancomer* 762 F 2d 222 (1985); *Drexel Burnham Lambert Group Inc v Galadari* 610 F Supp 114 777 F 2d 877; *Callejo v Bancomer SA* 764 F 2d 1101 (5th Circ, 1985).

enacted by governments with serious financial problems would be given effect to in the US courts on the basis of the Act of State doctrine.

As far as English law is concerned, the concept of 'Act of State' has been used in two senses. As Lord Wilberforce explained in *Buttes Oil and Gas Co v Hammer (No 3)*,[9] the first 'concerns action by an officer of the Crown taken outside this country against foreigners otherwise than under the colour of legal right'. In this more traditional sense the doctrine has little application to foreign exchange control laws. However, Lord Wilberforce clearly recognised a second version of the 'Act of State' doctrine 'which is concerned with the applicability of foreign municipal legislation *within its own territory* and with the examinability of such legislation – often but not invariably arising in cases of confiscation of property' and concluded that an act of state doctrine, similar to that applied by the US courts, existed in English law. He was prepared to characterise the doctrine as a general principle 'that the courts will not adjudicate upon the transactions of foreign sovereign states' and said that it was a principle 'for judicial restraint or abstention' in examining the validity of foreign sovereign legislation.

It is submitted that if the doctrine of Act of State as developed by the American courts on the basis of early English precedents such as *Duke of Brunswick v King of Hanover*[10] is to be adopted by the English courts in the context of international finance, it must be applied with the restriction recognised by the New York courts, namely, that it applies only where the debt obligation which is modified or negated is located within the territory of the country enacting the exchange control legislation. Consequently, it would be applicable only where the place of payment of an international debt obligation is solely within the jurisdiction of the state whose exchange control laws modify or nullify the debt obligation.[11]

VII OTHER POSSIBLE LIMITATIONS ON THE DOCTRINE OF THE PROPER LAW

1 Negotiability of bond instruments

The question whether instruments traded in the international capital markets (such as Eurobonds and Euro commercial paper) qualify as negotiable instruments may not necessarily be determined by the law expressly chosen by the parties involved in the issue of such instruments. Article 1 of the Rome Convention does not apply to 'obligations arising under... negotiable instruments to the extent that the obligations under such other negotiable instruments arise out of their negotiable character.'[12] The Giuliano and Lagarde Report accepts that whether a document is characterised as a negotiable instrument is not governed by the Rome Convention and is a matter for the law of the forum. In practice an express clause is included in such instruments which seeks to subject the instrument to English (or other governing) law. The question is discussed in detail below.[13]

---

9 [1982] AC 888, HL.
10 (1848) 2 HL Cas 1.
11 See also dicta of Nourse J in *Williams & Humbert Ltd v W & H Trade Marks (Jersey) Ltd*; and *Rumasa SA v Multinvest (UK) Ltd* [1986] AC 368.
12 See art 1(2)(c).
13 See ch 9.

2 Creation of security interests

For the purpose of determining whether a borrower in a syndicated loan or issuer of bond instruments has complied with his obligations under a negative pledge clause,[14] it is necessary to decide whether the borrower or issuer has created a 'security interest' or 'a charge, pledge, mortgage, hypothecation or lien'. The question whether a security interest etc has been created is probably not determined by the proper law of a loan agreement or bond instrument. This is discussed below.[15]

3 Mergers and acquisitions

Clauses in syndicated loan agreements and bond instruments usually prohibit the merger of the corporate borrower or the corporate issuer of bonds with another legal entity without the prior consent of the syndicate banks or of the trustee in a bond issue, as the case may be.[16]

In such an event the question arises which law determines whether such a prohibited transaction has occurred. It is submitted that there are in fact two questions in this type of case. First, there is the question of interpretation of the word 'merger' in a contract governed by English law. This is a matter for the proper law under art 10 of the Rome Convention.[17] The second question concerns the legal nature and effect of the transaction between the borrower or issuer and another corporate entity which is alleged to affect the legal status of the borrower or issuer. It is submitted that this question is generally a matter for the law of the place of incorporation of the borrower or issuer because of the rulings of the House of Lords in *National Bank of Greece and Athens SA v Metliss*[18] and *Adams v National Bank of Greece SA*.[19] The Rome Convention does not control the law applicable to this issue. In *Metliss*, the question was whether English law would recognise the merger of two banks incorporated in Greece by a decree of the Government of Greece. The Greek decree provided for the merger and also for universal succession to the rights and liabilities of those two banks in a newly created bank, the National Bank of Greece and Athens SA. The House of Lords held that the creation and legal existence of the National Bank of Greece and Athens SA was a matter for Greek law, since that Bank owed its very existence to Greek law. The House of Lords held that the National Bank was liable on a guarantee governed by English law issued by one of the banks to which the National Bank was a successor under Greek law[20].

The control of the law of the place of the incorporation over the legal consequences of merger (as distinct from the nature of the transaction alleged to constitute a merger) must, however, not be over-emphasised. After the ruling in the *Metliss* case the Greek Government purported to issue a further

---

14 Discussed in detail at pp 25–27 above.
15 See pp 92–94.
16 See ch 5 below in respect of syndicated loans and ch 13 below in respect of bonds.
17 See also r 150 and r 151 and the cases cited in the notes to those rules in ch 28 of *Dicey and Morris*.
18 [1958] AC 509.
19 [1961] AC 255.
20 The guarantee had been given in respect of sterling bonds issued by another Greek bank.

decree which declared that the National Bank did not assume any liabilities of the banks to which it succeeded. This decree was to have retroactive effect so that it was operative as from the moment when the National Bank came into existence. The House of Lords held in *Adams v National Bank of Greece SA* (above) that the Greek decree was inoperative to affect the rights and obligations under a guarantee governed by English law under the principles laid down in *Kleinwort Sons & Co v Ungarische Baumwolle Industrie Akt*.[1] Greek law could control the status and capacity of an entity or whether an entity had succeeded to another entity, but it could not extinguish the rights and obligations under an English contract. It must be noted that the Greek Government had first provided for universal succession in the decree creating the National Bank of Greece and later by a subsequent decree purported to declare with retroactive effect that the National Bank had not succeeded to the liabilities of the two banks to whose assets it succeeded. The House of Lords ruling emphasised this point in coming to its conclusion. It is not clear how the House of Lords would have decided the case if the first Greek decree creating the National Bank of Greece did not provide for universal succession, but merely for a succession to the assets of the two banks and further terminated the legal existence of the two banks to which the National Bank of Greece succeeded. If an English bond-holder sued the National Bank of Greece on the guarantee of the 'dead' bank, it is submitted that the action would have failed since the status and capacity of the National Bank would have been determined by the Greek decree creating it. Nevertheless, the English bond-holder could have sued the 'dead' bank in an English court and obtained execution against any asset which belonged to it. The reason is that the Greek decree could not extinguish the rights and obligations under an English contract.

It is submitted that under the Rome Convention the result would be the same due to art 3 and art 10(1)(d) of that Convention which refers to the chosen proper law the question whether a contractual obligation is extinguished.

---

1 [1939] 2 KB 678, CA.

Part II

International syndicated loans

CHAPTER 3
The lead manager and the syndications process

I THE BACKGROUND

The term 'syndicated loan' describes a structure whereby a large number of banks lend funds for a long period of time to a single borrower. According to McDonald[1] this type of lending vehicle evolved in the domestic capital markets in the US in the 1950s. The evolution of syndicated loans in the international capital markets of London occurred very much later in the 1960s.[2] By 1972 it appears that syndicated loan volume in the international markets in London had reached $11.4bn, while 1973 saw the first syndicated loan for over $1bn;[3] by 1981 the volume of international syndicated loans had reached $178bn and by 1989 the London international markets saw a volume of over US $459bn.[4] The international nature of the syndications market in London was underpinned by the fact that lending was effected in all major convertible currencies unlike in the US domestic markets in Wall Street[5] where loans were being made only in US dollars albeit to foreign borrowers. The dollar was nevertheless the pre-eminent vehicle of lending in the international markets. In many such loans – referred to as 'multi-currency' loans – the funds are made available not simply in one currency but in several currencies at the option of the borrower.

As a matter of legal structure the international syndicated loan appears to be a number of separate loans made by individual banks to the same borrower, which are subject to the same terms and conditions. Each lender is obliged to lend funds to the borrower and each lender possesses individual rights to interest and principal from the borrower. The borrower's obligation to repay is owed to each of the syndicate banks in specified amounts and is not owed to any one bank under the conventional structure of a syndicated loan. Despite this apparent simplicity the syndicated loan raises legal issues which are more complex than those which would arise where a number of separate and individual loans are conveniently embodied in the same

---

1 See McDonald *International Syndicated Loans* (Euromoney Publications, 1982) p 24 (hereafter *McDonald*).
2 *McDonald* suggests that the first 'Eurocurrency' syndicated loans were made in 1968.
3 See the table at p 27 in *McDonald*.
4 See the Euromoney 20th Anniversary Supplement *Euromarket in Figures* p 163.
5 See *McDonald* ch 4.

45

legal document subject to identical terms and conditions. The procedures used to syndicate a loan, the sources of funding the terms relating to syndicate democracy and the pro rata sharing clause result in a structure more complex than a collection of individual loans to a single borrower.[5A]

II THE ROLE OF THE LEAD MANAGER IN THE SYNDICATIONS PROCESS

At the centre of the syndications process is a major international bank which will act as the lead bank or 'lead manager'. It will usually obtain a mandate from a borrower to organise a syndicate of banks to provide the finance required by the borrower.[6]

The lead manager initiates the syndications process by approaching potential borrowers, which may range from multinational corporations to sovereign states with a proposal for the provision of finance. A firm proposal of finance is usually contained in a 'term sheet' or 'offer document' on the basis of which the prospective borrower will grant 'a mandate' to the bank to organise a group of banks which will form the lending syndicate to the borrower. The term sheet or offer document will generally speaking specify the amount of the loan, the interest rate, the duration, currency and other terms and conditions on which the lead manager will organise a syndicate of banks to lend funds to the borrower.[7]

Both these documents are capable of giving rise to contractual liability under English law, unless appropriate clauses are inserted. The formula 'subject to contract' is generally used for this purpose. This formula is traditionally used in agreements for the sale of land under English law in order to prevent the creation of legal obligations. Such a clause should generally be sufficient to prevent legal obligations from arising until a formal contract, namely the syndicated loan agreement, has been signed by the parties.[8] In the absence of such a formula the question whether a legally binding contract could arise as a matter of law depends on the intention of the parties and the surrounding circumstances. Indeed, it has been held that a document containing terms and conditions but which is to be embodied in a formal written document may nevertheless constitute a complete and binding agreement.[9]

A 'term sheet' or 'offer document' could therefore result in binding legal obligations if care is not taken to exclude an intention to be legally bound.[10]

5A See the following discussion.
6 The syndications process described in 1982 by *McDonald* Section 2 and Section 3 and by Slater in 'Syndicated Bank Loans', (1982) Jo Business Law 173, largely reflects current market practice in respect of conventional syndicated loans.
7 See *McDonald* (p 78) for an example of an offer and document and (p 98) for an example of a telex containing the grant of a mandate.
8 In the case of sales of land this rule dates back to the ruling of the Court of Appeal in *Winn v Bull* (1877) 7 Ch D 29.
9 See *Branca v Cobarro* [1947] KB 854; *Clipper Maritime Ltd v Shirlstar Container Transport Ltd, The Anemone* [1987] 1 Lloyd's Rep 546.
10 On the other hand, it has also been held that where the agreement is incomplete there is no legal liability on the part of either party: *Perry v Suffields Ltd* [1916] 2 Ch 187 and *Pagnan SpA v Feed Products Ltd* [1987] 2 Lloyd's Rep 601. In both cases it was held that there was a complete contract even though a number of commercially important points had not been settled in the preliminary agreement. See also *Okura & Co Ltd v Navara Shipping Corpn SA* [1982] 2 Lloyd's Rep 537.

If intention to create legal relations is effectively excluded by appropriate clauses, there is no legal commitment on the part of the lead manager to provide the finance required by the borrower even after the mandate is given. However, regardless of the legal position, once a mandate is granted, a lead manager would usually consider itself obliged as a matter of good market practice to organise a syndicate and obtain the finance for the borrower.

After obtaining a mandate the lead manager would usually form a small group of banks, called the managing group, who will agree in principle to lend most or sometimes all of the funds required by the borrower. Where the managing group does not propose to provide all the finance required by the borrower such amounts of finance as may be necessary will be provided by a second group of banks invited by the managing group to join the syndicate. Neither the lead manager nor the banks in the managing group generally give any 'underwriting commitment' to provide the funds required by the borrower. This contrasts with the position of the managing underwriters in an international bond issue[11] who, in the subscription agreement, warrant that they will procure purchasers for the issuers' bonds and, failing which, will purchase the bonds themselves.

The lead manager is also responsible at this stage for the preparation of two sets of documents. First, there are the legal documents which will embody the final agreement as between the syndicate and the borrower and as between syndicate banks inter se. These would generally be prepared by external lawyers of the lead manager rather than 'in house' counsel. The lead manager together with the prospective borrower will in some cases also prepare an information memorandum containing details about the loan and, more importantly, information about the financial condition and business profile of the borrower. This document is prepared, generally speaking, only in the case of borrowers who are new to the international syndicated loans market or who do not come to the market frequently. Both these documents will be distributed in draft form to those banks which have indicated a clear interest to join in the syndication. It has been observed[12] that the information memorandum though prepared with reasonable care is not accompanied by the rather more thorough and strict procedures adopted in respect of prospectuses and offering circulars used to market international bonds.

The lead manager's role in the preparation of the legal documents and the information memorandum may expose the lead manager to legal obligations which are discussed in some detail below.[13]

Once the borrower and the syndicate banks have agreed on the form of the syndicated loan agreement the document will be formally signed by all parties. The disbursement of funds under the syndicated loan agreement, however, will not occur, even after the signing of the agreement, until the satisfaction of a number of conditions precedent which are common in such agreements. Most of these relate to the delivery of the borrowers' constitutional documents, as well as documents relating to internal corporate auth-

---

11 See ch 11 below.
12 By Richard Slater writing in 1982 in his article on syndicated loans in (1982) Jo of Business Law p 173 at 176.
13 See ch 4.

orisations, as well as external authorisations such as exchange control permission for the borrower to borrow. The conditions precedent also include the delivery of legal opinions from lawyers in the borrower's country certifying that the borrower is properly incorporated and has the status and capacity to enter into the syndicated loan agreement. The reason for such conditions precedent were explained in the previous section.[14]

Once conditions precedent have been satisfied by the borrower the bank designated as the 'agent bank', which is usually, although not necessarily, the lead manager, will certify to the syndicate that conditions precedent have been satisfied. Thereafter, disbursement of funds will occur through a process whereby the syndicate banks transfer such amounts as they have agreed to lend to an account held with the agent bank. The agent bank then transfers to the borrower the aggregate amount of funds required to be disbursed to the borrower under the syndicated loan agreement. The lead manager's role as the agent bank does not, however, cease at this point and continues during the 'life' of the loan until final maturity. The role of the agent bank requires the bank in question to carry out a number of administrative duties and generally 'monitor' the loan in a broad sense on behalf of the syndicate. The role of the agent bank is discussed later.[15]

III LIABILITY OF THE LEAD MANAGER[16]

1 The information memorandum

The information memorandum:

(a) contains information concerning the financial and business position of the borrower;
(b) is circulated by the lead manager to prospective participants in the syndicate;
(c) syndicate participants may rely at least partially on the information provided in deciding to participate in the syndication.

Consequently, it is a potential source of liability for the lead manager if the information memorandum contains inaccuracies or misleading information.

Under English law the liability of the lead manager to other members of the syndicate may be based on the provisions of the Misrepresentation Act 1967 or under the common law of tort.

First, s 2(1) of the Misrepresentation Act 1967 provides that:

'Where a person has entered into a contract after a misrepresentation has been

---

14 See ch 4 (a) below.
15 See ch 4 below.
16 See on this subject Clarke and Farrar 'Defining Rights and Duties of Managing and Agent Banks to Co Lenders' in *Sovereign Lending: Managing Legal Risk* (Gruson edn, Euromoney Publications); Lehane 'Role of Managing and Agent Banks: Duties, Liabilities, Disclaimer Clauses' in *Current Issues of International and Financial Law* p 230; and Cates 'The Role of Managers and Agents in Syndicated Loans' in International Financial Law Review, June 1982, p 21.

made to him by another party thereto and as a result thereof he has suffered loss, then, if the person making the misrepresentation would be liable to damages in respect thereof had the misrepresentation been made fraudulently, that person shall be so liable notwithstanding that the misrepresentation was not made fraudulently, unless he proves that he had reasonable grounds to believe and did believe up to the time the contract was made that the facts represented were true.'[17]

It has been said that liability under s 2(1) is not one based in negligence and that the Act imposed an absolute obligation not to make inaccurate representations. However, a representor can escape liability if he can prove that he had reasonable grounds for believing the representation at the time the representation was made.[18] It seems clear therefore that liability under s 2(1) is also based in negligence. Consequently, if the information memorandum contains inaccuracies which could have been avoided by the use of reasonable care there is potential liability to other members of the syndicate.

Secondly, liability for such inaccuracies in the information memorandum could also be based in the common law of negligence on the principles laid down in *Hedley Byrne & Co Ltd v Heller & Partners Ltd*[19] and restated by the House of Lords in *Caparo Industries plc v Dickman*.[20]

Thirdly, liability may also be based on the common law of tort relating to fraudulent misrepresentation laid down in *Derry v Peek*.[1]

A borrower who provides the information contained in the memorandum is, of course, also potentially liable under these heads. In practice, the primary remedy against the borrower for any inaccuracies in the information memorandum will be contained in the syndicated loan agreement itself. An express clause will provide that any inaccurate or misleading information in the information memorandum will constitute an 'event of default' on the part of the borrower which will give rise to an immediate right in the syndicate to call default and demand repayment of all outstanding amounts ('accelerate' the loan prior to maturity). This right against a borrower may in many cases be of little value, since misinformation may come to light only when the borrower gets into financial difficulties. In such an event the syndicate banks may not have any practical likelihood of obtaining repayment from the borrower by calling default. Syndicate banks may then look to the lead manager as the only realistic source from which to recover the loans which they have not been able to recover from the borrower. This exposure is more than a theoretical possibility in the light of *Colcotronis Tanker Security-litigation*.[2]

While it is not the purpose of a work of this nature to provide an explana-

---

17 See on this *Chitty on Contracts* (26th edn 1989) vol I, s 437 ff.
18 See *Howard Marine and Dredging Co Ltd v A Ogden & Sons (Excavations) Ltd* [1978] QB 574.
19 [1964] AC 465.
20 [1990] 2 AC 605; see also the ruling of the Court of Appeal in *Morgan Crucible Co plc v Hill Samuel Bank Ltd* [1991] 1 All ER 148, CA.
1 (1889) 14 App Cas 337. A representation is fraudulent if it is false, and the person making it either knows it to be false or has no honest belief in its truth or makes it 'recklessly careless whether it may be true or false'. See *Derry v Peek* (1889) 14 App Cas 377.
2 See *Re Colcotronis Tanker Security-litigation* 420 F Supp 998 (SDN 1976) and *UBAF v European American Banking Corpn* [1984] QB 713, CA.

tion of the basic principles applicable in the English law of negligent misrepresentation[3] certain points need emphasis.

First, for the purposes of the principle in *Hedley Byrne v Heller*[4] and *Caparo Industries plc v Dickman*[5] and s 2 of the Misrepresentation Act 1967, there must be a statement which is inaccurate or a failure to state a material fact which renders a statement in the information memorandum misleading before liability can ensue;[6] a complete failure to disclose a material fact in the information memorandum would not by itself seem to give rise to liability under those cases or the Misrepresentation Act 1967.[7] In practice, however, a court could easily construe a failure to disclose material facts as a material misrepresentation on the basis that such an omission renders the statements or information contained in the information memorandum misleading.[8] The result is that in practice a very high standard of disclosure of material facts is required in respect of an information memorandum in a syndicated loan agreement. Consequently, an information memorandum is dispensed with in practice whenever possible as a practical means of avoiding liability.

Secondly, it is a requirement of both an action for negligent misrepresentation under the principle in *Hedley Byrne v Heller & Partners*[9] (above) and under the Misrepresentation Act 1967, that there must be reliance by the syndicate banks on the material misstatement. As a matter of market practice it has been observed by McDonald that 'Perhaps up to 75% of the information memoranda sent upon request are ignored by the recipient.'[10] On the other hand, he remarks that most bankers in the international markets would wish to see an information memorandum before joining a syndicate of lending banks. As a matter of law, it seems that even if partial reliance is placed on the statements or information in the memorandum such reliance would be sufficient for the purposes of liability on the part of the lead manager either under the Misrepresentation Act 1967 or in the common law of tort.[11]

Thirdly, for the purposes of maintaining an action under the principles laid down in *Hedley Byrne* it is now clear that it is not sufficient merely to establish that the defendant could reasonably foresee that the plaintiff would suffer loss if the information was inaccurate; there must be a further element of 'proximity' between the plaintiff and the defendant: *Caparo Industries plc v Dickman*[12] (above). This latter concept is also to be found in the judgments in *Hedley Byrne* where the House of Lords said that there must be 'a special relationship' between plaintiff and defendant. This require-

---

3 See on the Misrepresentation Act 1967 the section in *Chitty on Contracts* cited above, and as regards negligent misrepresentation in tort *Clerk and Lindsell on Tort* (Sweet and Maxwell, 1989, 16th edn).
4 [1964] AC 465, p 49 above.
5 [1990] AC 605, p 49 above.
6 *Goldsmith v Roger* [1962] 2 Lloyd's Rep 249, CA.
7 See *Banque Financière de la Cité SA v Westgate Insurance Co Ltd* [1988] 2 Lloyd's Rep 513 at 555, CA.
8 See, for an example of such construction, the facts and decision in *Goldsmith v Roger* [1962] 2 Lloyd's Rep 249, CA; and the facts of *Curtis v Chemical Cleaning and Dyeing Co Ltd* [1951] KB 805, CA.
9 [1964] AC 465, p 49 above.
10 See *McDonald* p 206.
11 See *Edgington v Fitzmaurice* (1885) 29 Ch D 459, CA; *Chitty on Contracts* s 426.
12 [1990] AC 605, p 49 above.

ment perhaps means that it is not sufficient that the plaintiff belongs to an unidentified class of persons whom the defendant may reasonably foresee as being recipients of the memorandum; the plaintiff should be an identified person whom the defendant has in direct contemplation: *Morgan Crucible Co plc v Hill Samuel Bank Ltd.*[13] Even if the test in *Hedley Byrne* as explained in *Caparo Industries plc v Dickman* by the House of Lords is construed in this narrow sense, it is submitted that the lead manager is potentially liable. The information memorandum is distributed to identified and named banks in the markets who are prospective participants and, consequently, it is submitted that the requirement of 'proximity' would in most cases be satisfied.

i *Disclaimers and Contractual Clauses*

In order to reduce the potential liability of the lead manager under these heads, market practice has adopted two techniques. First, there are disclaimer notices in the information memorandum, and secondly, there are contractual clauses in the loan agreement aimed at dealing with the problem.

It is market practice to include a prominent disclaimer at the beginning of the information memorandum for the benefit of the lead manager. An example is provided by McDonald.[14]

> 'The managers listed on the cover of this information memorandum (the 'Memorandum') have been authorised by (the 'Borrower') to arrange a credit facility (the 'Credit Facility') described in this Memorandum and to distribute this Memorandum to potential lenders in the credit facility.
>
> All information set forth herein relating to the Borrower has been supplied by the Borrower and the contents have not been independently verified by the Managers, nor have they verified that all information material to an evaluation of the Credit Facility has been included. No representation or warranty, express or implied, is made by the managers with respect to the completeness or accuracy of this Memorandum or as to any other matter mentioned in the statements herein concerning the borrower.
>
> The managers do not undertake to review the financial condition or affairs of the Borrower nor to advise any lender in the Credit Facility of any information coming to its attention.
>
> The Memorandum is not intended by the Managers to provide the sole basis of any credit or other evaluation, and should not be considered as a recommendation by the Managers that any recipient of this Memorandum participate in the Credit Facility. In determining whether to participate in the Credit Facility, each potential lender is urged to make its own assessment of the relevance and adequacy of the information contained in this Memorandum and to make such independent investigation as it deems necessary for the purposes of such determination.
>
> This Memorandum is submitted to selected banks specifically in reference to the Credit Facility and may not be reproduced or used, in whole or in part, for any purpose, nor furnished to any person other than those to whom copies have been sent by the Managers.'

---

13 [1991] 1 All ER 148, CA.
14 See *McDonald* ch 10, p 205; see also the example given by Lehane at p 234 in *Current Issues in International and Financial Law* (1985).

52 The lead manager and the syndications process

How effective are such disclaimers under English law?

First, it seems that if the misrepresentation is fraudulent the court is unlikely to give any effect to such an exemption clause.

Secondly, in the case of negligent misrepresentation the effect of such clauses would necessarily depend on the precise words and content of the disclaimer. The objective of such clauses is to eliminate any reliance being placed on the lead manager by syndicate banks for the accuracy of the contents of the memorandum.

The clause from McDonald seeks:

(a) to deny any authorship on the part of the lead manager for the contents or statements in the information memorandum; it seeks to make the lead manager a 'postman' or 'conduit pipe' transmitting the information contained in the memorandum;
(b) to state that the lead manager has not verified any of the statements in the information memorandum; in other words, it seeks to shift the burden of verification of information onto each syndicate participant;
(c) to require that any recipient should verify all facts and statements himself; in other words, it seeks to negate any reliance by a syndicate participant on the information contained in the memorandum;
(d) to prevent responsibility for any further dissemination of the information memorandum and thus any liability to a secondary recipient who may rely on it for other purposes.[15]

Clauses of this type may be sufficient as a matter of common law to exempt the lead manager from liability.[16] It is necessary to consider, however, the provisions of the Unfair Contract Terms Act 1977 ('UCTA') under English law. If such clauses are subject to UCTA they may be struck down as void by an English court unless they satisfy a test of reasonableness.

It has been stated[17] that these clauses in the information memorandum would be caught by s 3 of the Misrepresentation Act 1967[18] under English law and would therefore need to satisfy a test of reasonableness. It is difficult to understand how s 3 of the Misrepresentation Act 1967[19] can have any application to such a notice contained in the information memorandum. The reason is that s 3 applies only to *a term in a contract* which seeks to exclude or restrict liability from misrepresentations and the information memorandum is not a contractual document.

Section 2 of UCTA, however, applies not only to contractual terms but also to notices which may not have any contractual force.[20] Section 2(2) of UCTA provides that a person cannot by reference to any contract term

---

15 In the light of the ruling in *Caparo Industries plc v Dickman*, it is unlikely that the lead manager will be liable to an unidentified secondary recipient of the information memorandum who uses the information memorandum for some purpose other than becoming a member of the syndicate.
16 See *Hedley Byrne & Co Ltd v Heller & Partners Ltd* [1964] AC 465 at 492, HL per Lord Reid and at 504 per Lord Morris. See also Dillon LJ in *Smith v Eric Bush* [1987] 3 All ER 179 at p 183, CA.
17 See Penn, Shea and Arora *Law and Practice of International Banking* (Sweet and Maxwell, 1987) p 124 and Lehane, fn 10 above, at p 234.
18 As amended by s 8 of UCTA.
19 As amended by s 8 of UCTA.
20 See *Chitty on Contracts* (26th edn 1989) ch 14, s 6 at p 602.

or *to a notice* given to persons generally or to particular persons exclude or restrict liability for negligence except in so far as the notice satisfies a requirement as to reasonableness.

The question whether UCTA applies in the first place to such a notice contained in the information memorandum will depend on conflicts rules of English law. If the action is based in tort, the law applicable under English conflicts rules may be the law of the place where the tort was committed (*lex loci delicti*) or the proper law of the tort as the case may be.[1] The validity of the disclaimer should logically be referred to this system of law and this law may not be English law. On this basis UCTA would have no application to the validity of the disclaimer.

It may, however, be the case that an English court would apply s 2 of UCTA regardless of the proper law or the *lex loci delicti* on the basis that it represents the public policy or 'mandatory' laws of the forum.[2]

Even if it is assumed that English law will determine the validity of the disclaimer it is submitted that such a clause would seem to be reasonable in all the circumstances. The following factors would be relevant to the question of reasonableness as between the lead manager and other banks in the syndicate: the sophistication of the recipients of the information memorandum; their access to legal and financial resources; the ability of such syndicate banks to make an independent evaluation of the borrower and of the information memorandum with the aid of such resources; the general practice that information memoranda are not relied on by syndicate banks to a great degree.[3] One factor which operates to the contrary is that in practice there may be little time for the prospective participant in the syndicate to make an independent evaluation of the borrower or of the information memorandum.

While it may be possible to exclude liability in negligence or negligent misrepresentation by a reasonable and appropriately drafted clause as discussed above, there is another potential basis of liability. The Court of Appeal in *UBAF Ltd v European American Banking Corpn*[4] obiter said that a lead manager also owes fiduciary duties to other members of the syndicate in respect of the contents of the information memorandum. It may not be possible to eliminate completely such a fiduciary duty which may be imposed by a court on a lead manager.

The weight of academic writing, however, seems to be against the imposition of such duties.[5] It is submitted that it would be wholly inappropriate to impose fiduciary duties on a lead manager in the context of an international syndicated loan for the benefit of other major international banks in the market place. While it is difficult to state precisely the circumstances in which an English court will impose fiduciary duties, outside certain estab-

---

1 See Dicey and Morris *Conflict of Laws* (11th edn) ch 35; and Cheshire and North *Private International Law* (11th edn) ch 20.
2 See *Monterosso Shipping Co Ltd v International Transport Workers' Federation, The Rosso* [1982] 2 Lloyd's Rep 120, CA.
3 See *McDonald* p 206.
4 [1984] QB 713.
5 See Gabriel *Legal Aspects of Syndicated Loans*, (Butterworths, 1986) p 147; Clarke and Farrar 'Defining Rights and Duties of Managing Agent Banks to Co-lenders' in *Sovereign Lending: Managing Legal Risk*. See also Penn, Shea and Arora in *Law and Practice of International Banking*, p 129, who concede that fiduciary duties may be imposed on a lead manager in respect of the negotiation of loan documentation.

lished categories such as solicitor and client, it is likely that such duties would be imposed 'wherever two persons stand in such a relation that while it continues, confidence is necessarily reposed by one, and the influence which naturally grows out of that confidence is possessed by the other ...'.[6] The extensive literature on fiduciary relationships[7] seems to conclude that there must necessarily be some element of superior skill, knowledge or bargaining power as between two parties or a 'reposing of confidence' which gives rise to elements of influence by one party on another before an English court will impose fiduciary duties outside the traditional categories of fiduciaries. In the context of the international syndicated loans market it is difficult to disagree with Clarke and Farrar[8] that the relationship between a lead manager and the syndicate banks 'is not fundamentally different from the relationship between IBM and the purchaser of a large computer system', because 'the members of a syndicate are buying a product developed, marketed, and serviced by the lead manager'. The question whether a lead manager owes fiduciary duties to the other members of a syndicate also arises in the context of the negotiation of loan documentation and in the context of the role of the lead manager as the agent bank once a syndication has been set up.[9]

ii *Contractual Provisions*

In addition to these disclaimer notices in the information memorandum, the lead manager's position with regard to the discharge of his duties to the other banks in the syndication is also strengthened by a number of warranties given by the borrower in the loan documents which are negotiated by the lead manager. The borrower would usually warrant that all statements constituting factual statements contained in the information memorandum do not contain any untrue statements of material fact and that they do not omit to state any material fact necessary to make the statements therein not misleading. Secondly, the borrower is also required to warrant that he is not aware of any other material facts or circumstances which have not been disclosed to the banks. Thirdly, with regard to all estimates, forecasts and opinions the borrower is required to warrant that they are made in good faith on the basis of available information at the time of the estimate forecast or opinion.

In the final analysis, however, there seems to be no clear substitute for the exercise of due care and diligence by the lead manager to ensure that in practice all statements in the information memorandum are accurate and that no material omissions have been made.

The lead manager's liability to the syndicate banks with regard to the contents of the information memorandum can and should also be dealt with by express clauses in the syndicated loan agreement drafted in language similar to that in a notice usually contained in the information memorandum. These clauses should require each syndicate bank to warrant that it takes

---

6 See *Tate v Williamson* (1866) 2 Ch App 55.
7 See Finn *Fiduciary Obligations* (1977); Meagher Gummow and Lehane *Equity, Doctrines and Remedies* (2nd edn, 1984) ch 5; Sealy 'Fiduciary Relationships' (1962) CLJ 69.
8 See fn 5 above.
9 See ch 4 below.

sole responsibility to verify the accuracy and adequacy of all information contained in the information memorandum; that each bank does not expect the lead manager to verify any of the information or statements in the information memorandum; and that each bank does not rely on the lead manager to provide it with information for purposes of entering into the loan agreement.

Such clauses may be liable to a test of 'reasonableness' under ss 2 or 3 of UCTA.

Provisions of UCTA will not, however, apply to a contractual clause of this type simply because English law has been expressly chosen as the proper law of the contract by the parties. Before UCTA provisions can apply, s 27(1) of UCTA requires that English law must be the proper law of the contract independently of the express choice of English law clause.[10] Whether English law would be regarded as the proper law of a contract independently of an express choice of law will depend on a number of factors.[11] 'The court is required in such cases to consider the system of law by reference to which the contract was made or that with which the transaction has the closest and most real connection': *Bonython v Commonwealth of Australia*.[12] It may be the case that the proper law of many international loan agreements is English law only because of the customary express choice of English law clause. If this express choice is disregarded the relevant factual and legal connections with England would probably be that: the loan agreement was drafted by reference to English law and signed in London; the loan itself was syndicated in London's international markets; many of the syndicate banks would have offices in London. These connections may not always be sufficient to establish English law as the proper law independently of the choice of law clause. Consequently, it may be the case that UCTA has no application at all to such syndicated loan agreements. Even if it does apply, it is submitted that such clauses should be considered reasonable on the basis of the arguments advanced previously in respect of the validity of disclaimer notices.[13]

2 Loan documentation

The question here is whether the lead manager may become liable to syndicate participants for any defect in the validity or enforceability of the loan agreement or the sufficiency of protection afforded to lenders in the syndicated loan agreement. The type of problem which may arise and give rise to difficulty ranges from the complete nullity of the syndicated loan agreement to the insufficiency of financial controls imposed on a borrower for the purpose of ensuring that the borrower will be able to meet his obligations to pay interest and principal. In practice the lead manager usually negotiates the content and form of the syndicated loan agreement with the borrower and through their respective legal counsel. Nevertheless, it seems clear that at least in the later stages of negotiating the contents of the syndicated

---

10 See Mann (1977) 26 ICLQ 903; (1978) ICLQ 661.
11 See on these factors: *Dicey and Morris* p 1190. Now see art 4 of the Rome Convention.
12 [1951] AC 201 at 219, PC. See also the discussion in Cheshire and North *Private International Law* (11th edn) pp 461–466.
13 See p 53 above.

loan agreement, the lead manager is not acting simply on his own behalf but is also acting on behalf of the prospective members of the syndicate of banks which will lend funds to the borrower upon signing of the loan agreement. Under ordinary principles of agency even if the lead manager did not have authority at the time to act for the prospective banks who eventually form the syndicate he may be liable to such banks as an agent when his acts are subsequently ratified.[14] It therefore seems that a duty of due care, skill, and diligence is owed on the basis of agency to the banks who will eventually form the syndicate.[15]

It may also be the case that a court adopting the approach in *UBAF v European American Banking Corpn*[16] may impose fiduciary duties on the lead manager not only with regard to the preparation and dissemination of the information memorandum but also with regard to the negotiation of the contents of the syndicated loan agreement for the benefit of the banks who eventually become members of the syndicate.

Some writers[17] have taken the view that fiduciary duties or agency duties will not be imposed on a lead manager for the benefit of co-lenders in a syndicate in respect of the negotiation of loan documentation. It is submitted that the risk that a court will impose fiduciary or agency duties on a lead manager cannot altogether be ruled out. However, the content of such agency or fiduciary duty may consist only of an obligation to select experienced and skilled lawyers to draft the syndicated loan agreement. Suppose, however, that the financial controls and other covenants imposed on a borrower are overly lax when compared to the norms and practices in the international markets with regard to a similar borrower for a similar transaction. Could it be argued that there is a breach of the lead manager's duties of skill and diligence? It is submitted that this argument cannot be sustained. First, the syndicate participants are principal parties to the loan agreement; it is not an agreement entered into by the lead manager acting as agent for syndicate participants. Secondly, even if there is some room to argue the agency point, it would be difficult to show a breach of duty if there is a tightly drafted cross default clause which gives the syndicate the ability to call default when other lenders can.[18]

The second basis on which a lead manager may be exposed to the risk of an action by co-lenders in a syndicate is in the tort of negligence. This will be on the basis that the lead manager owed a duty of reasonable care to prospective co-lenders when negotiating the syndicated loan agreement so as to ensure that it is valid and effective in law and that it contains terms and conditions which are sufficient in the context of market conditions to protect the position of the syndicate banks. In essence this would be a claim in pure financial loss sustained in consequence of the negligence of the lead manager. As such, the question whether an action will lie should be determined by reference to the new approach to such actions laid down

---

14 See *Bowstead on Agency* (15th edn) ch 2, p 29 and art 16–18.
15 See generally, *Bowstead on Agency* (15th edn 1985), and *Chitty on Contracts* (26th edn) vol II, s 1 as to circumstances in which an agency can arise by implication.
16 [1984] QB 713.
17 Gabriel *Legal Aspects of Syndicated Loans* (Butterworths, 1986) and Clarke and Farrar 'Defining Rights and Duties of Managing and Agent Banks to Co-lenders' in *Sovereign Lending: Managing Legal Risk* (Gruson edn, Euromoney Publications).
18 See ch 5, p 98 below.

by the House of Lords in two cases – *Caparo Industries plc v Dickman*[19] and *Murphy v Brentwood District Council*.[20] Both cases emphasise that the mere foreseeability of financial loss being inflicted on a defendant is by itself insufficient to create liability; there must be 'proximity' between the plaintiff and defendant. It is submitted, however, that both criteria are satisfied and that a duty is owed by the lead manager to the prospective members of the syndicate.[21] In practice the lead manager controls both the appointment of lawyers who draft the loan agreement, and to a large extent the contents of the loan agreement. Given that level of control it seems that it is reasonably foreseeable that if due care is not exercised prospective members of the syndicate may suffer loss if the loan becomes irrecoverable either wholly or partially due to the invalidity or inefficacy of the loan documentation. The degree of proximity required by the decisions in the above cases seems to exist because the identity of the prospective participants is known to the lead manager during the time that the loan documents are negotiated in final form.[1] It seems clear after the ruling of the House of Lords in *Murphy v Brentwood District Council*[2] that the circumstances in which English law will impose liability for pure economic loss (ie where there is no physical injury to person or property) is not to be determined on the basis of reasonable foresight and any restrictive policy criteria applicable to the range of actionable damage as laid down in the two-tier test of Lord Wilberforce in *Anns v Merton London Borough Council*.[3] It seems that each case would have to be judged on its own merits before a court would be prepared to hold that liability would be imposed.

Liability of the lead manager for the validity, adequacy and sufficiency of the legal documents is in practice usually the subject of express clauses. These clauses would generally seek to negate any reliance by the syndicate bank on the lead manager to ensure the validity, adequacy and sufficiency of the loan agreement and its contents. The adequacy of these clauses would once again be subject to the test of reasonableness under s 2 of the Unfair Contract Terms Act 1977, if English law is the proper law of the syndicated loan agreement disregarding, for the purpose of determining the proper law, any express choice of law clause.[4] Here again, in the context of the relative sophistication of the parties and their access to legal and financial resources, it is submitted that a court should not find it difficult to conclude that any express exclusion of liability on the part of the lead manager was reasonable.

---

19 [1990] 2 AC 605.
20 [1990] 2 All ER 908.
21 See also the ruling in *Morgan Crucible Co plc v Hill Samuel Bank Ltd* [1991] 1 All ER 148, CA.
1 See also the ruling in *Morgan Crucible Co plc v Hill Samuel Bank Ltd* [1991] 1 All ER 148, CA.
2 [1990] 2 All ER 908.
3 [1978] AC 728, HL.
4 Unfair Contract terms Act 1977 s 27(1). See also the discussion above at p 55.

CHAPTER 4
The lead manager as agent bank[1]

In practice a lead manager would also assume the role of the agent bank in the syndicated loan after the signing of the formal legal documents. The agent bank's role is to act as the agent for the syndicate. Express clauses in the loan agreement usually make it clear that the agent bank does not act on behalf of the borrower and as such does not owe any duties as agent to the borrower. The contractual duties of an agent bank in practice are broadly as follows:

(a) certification that the borrower has complied with conditions precedent;
(b) acting as a paying bank in respect of transfers of funds between the borrower and the syndicate;
(c) 'monitoring' the covenants of the loan agreement;
(d) taking appropriate action in the case of default by the borrower.

In addition to these the agent bank performs other minor ancillary duties such as receiving formal notices and financial information from the borrower including the borrower's annual report and accounts (in the case of a company).

I CERTIFICATION OF COMPLIANCE WITH CONDITIONS PRECEDENT BY THE BORROWER

The certification of compliance with conditions precedent requires a lead manager to examine a number of documents relating to the status and capacity of the borrower and to internal and external authorisations which are necessary to empower the borrower to enter into the loan transaction. The agent bank in practice is not able to form a view as to the sufficiency of

---

1 See on this subject Clarke and Farrar 'Defining Rights and Duties of Managing and Agent Banks to Co-lenders' in *Sovereign Lending: Managing Legal Risk* (Gruson edn, Euromoney Publications); Lehane 'Role of Managing and Agent Banks : Duties, Liabilities, Disclaimer Clauses' in *Current Issues of International and Financial Law* p 230; and Cates 'The Role of Managers and Agents in Syndicated Loans' IFLR, June 1982, p 21.

these documents since they would involve matters of foreign law. Consequently, the agent bank is empowered to take action on the basis of legal opinions in relation to the status and capacity of the borrower and internal and external authorisation for the borrowing. A borrower is required to deliver such legal opinions as a condition precedent to drawdown of funds. Given the fact that disbursement of funds will usually be made immediately upon the certification by the agent bank of the satisfaction of conditions precedent, the agent bank is exposed to actions in negligence in the performance on such certification. Consequently, clauses are generally included exempting the agent bank from liability for any action taken or not taken on the basis of such legal opinions and advice.[2]

II DUTIES AS PAYING AGENT

All funds which are to be disbursed by the syndicate banks to the borrower will in practice be transmitted by each syndicate bank into an account held by the agent bank and then transferred by the agent to an account designated by the borrower. Equally, all payments of interest and principal made by the borrower to the syndicate will be effected through a single payment by the borrower to the agent bank who will immediately transfer such payments to the members of the syndicate in accordance with their respective entitlements.

A number of practical problems can arise in this context. The first problem arises due to the times at which transfers of funds are effected. The transfers from the syndicate banks to the agent bank of loan funds and the transfer by the agent bank of such funds to the borrower are effected on the same day. The funds transfer by the agent bank is made in circumstances where the agent bank may not know for certain whether it has received the loan funds due from the syndicate banks. The agent bank is therefore exposed to the danger that while it may instruct the transfer of the full loan amount to the borrower it may not receive into its own accounts all funds due from one or more of the participant banks. This problem is overcome by a 'clawback' clause which enables the agent bank to demand repayment from the borrower of any funds which the agent bank itself has not received from any member or members of the syndicate. This mechanism is a logical corollary of the legal structure of a syndicated loan as an aggregation of several and separate loans effected by each syndicate bank to the borrower. The liability to lend is that of each bank; it is neither a joint liability of the syndicate banks nor is it the liability of the agent bank.

Secondly, there is also a theoretical exposure of the borrower to the insolvency of the agent bank which has received loan funds from the syndicate banks. The exposure of the borrower to the insolvency of the agent bank is not of commercial significance in practice due to the financial stature of agent banks active in the international syndicated loans market. However,

---

2 See, for example, the draft clauses in Cresswell, Blair, Hill and Wood *Encyclopaedia of Banking Law* paras K2126 and 2127.

if it were to occur, the transfer of funds by a principal to his agent for purposes of payment to a third party does not by itself absolve the principal from any obligation to make payments to the third party, if the agent fails to pay. The syndicate remains liable to lend to the borrower.[3] It may of course be the case that the borrower may be regarded as having elected to look to the agent bank *alone* for the payment of funds in which case the rule seems different[4] but this is unlikely to be the case in practice.

Thirdly, where the borrower makes payment of interest or principal to the agent bank the latter may fail to transfer such funds to members of the syndicate due to the insolvency or default of the agent. Here the question is whether the syndicate banks may sue the borrower for interest and/or principal. In this situation at least the borrower may not have any exposure under English law to the syndicate banks. It seems clear that where a creditor has required a debtor to make payment to his agent, and the debtor pays the agent the debtor has no further liability to the principal creditor.[5] The borrower therefore is not placed in double jeopardy due to the default or insolvency of the agent bank. On the other hand, the position of the syndicate banks in this situation is far from clear. Could they recover the funds paid by the borrower from the agent bank's receiver or liquidator in an insolvency? Much depends on the law governing the insolvency. However, if English law were to be applied, one analysis is that since the funds were transferred by the borrower to the agent bank for a particular purpose such funds would be impressed with a resulting or constructive trust for the benefit of the members of the syndicate on the basis of the ruling in *Barclays Bank Ltd v Quistclose Investments Ltd.*[6] Before a court applies the analysis in that case to funds held by an agent bank, such funds would need to have been kept in a separate account and not co-mingled with the funds of the agent bank. Reynolds[7] has suggested a more functional approach to the problem and suggests that we ask whether funds were required to be held separately by the agent; whether funds were received as part of a general account or in respect of a given transaction; whether it was contemplated that the funds could be used by the agent as part of his normal cash flow. It is submitted that on this approach the answer must be that syndicate banks would have proprietary rather than contractual remedies in the event of an insolvency governed by English law.

The second analysis is that the relationship between the agent bank and the members of a syndicate in respect of funds received from the borrower is that of debtor and creditor, in which case the syndicate banks' remedies would lie only in contract.

The practical answer may be that if the syndicate members wish to be protected against the insolvency of the agent bank after receipt of funds from the borrower the agent bank must be declared a trustee under English law in respect of such funds. In the absence of such a clause there is generally

---

3 See *Davison v Donaldson* (1882) 9 QBD 623, CA; see also *Bowstead on Agency* (15th edn, 1985) art 84 and Comments.
4 See Bowstead, above, art 84.
5 See *Williams v Evans* (1866) LR 1 QB 352. See also art 85 of *Bowstead on Agency* (15th edn).
6 [1970] AC 567, HL.
7 In *Bowstead on Agency* (15th edn) p 162.

a judicial reluctance to impose a trust in the context of ordinary commercial relationships.[8]

III 'MONITORING' LOAN COVENANTS

It is usual in practice for an agent bank in a syndicated loan to be dispensed from actively monitoring compliance by the borrower of all covenants in the syndicated loan agreement. Such a clause would usually be in the following form:

> 'The agent shall not be required to ascertain or enquire as to the performance or observance by the borrower of the terms of this agreement or any other document in connection herewith.'[9]

Express clauses would usually also remove the duty of the agent bank to keep the syndicate banks informed of all matters affecting the position of the borrower.

In the absence of such clauses the common law would impose on the agent bank a duty of due diligence to monitor the covenants in a loan agreement for the benefit of the other members of the syndicate as its principals and to keep them properly informed.[10]

IV DUTY TO ACT ON THE OCCURRENCE OF DEFAULT

In practice an agent bank is required under many syndicated loan agreements to call default and demand repayment of all outstanding interest and principal from the borrower only when required to do so by a majority of the syndicate banks.

Some syndicated loan agreements, however, confer upon the agent bank a power to call default on the occurrence of an 'event of default'[11] without waiting for a decision by a majority of banks to call a default. This format would provide that the agent bank may call a default of his own motion if he becomes aware of the occurrence of an event of default but *must* do so if so required by a majority of banks. The problem with conferring such discretion on an agent bank is that the agent bank becomes exposed to

---

8 See *New Zealand and Australian Land Co v Watson* (1881) 7 QBD 374, CA; *Henry v Hammond* [1913] 2 KB 515; *Re Agra and Mastermans Bank, ex p Waring* (1866) 36 LJ Ch 151.
9 See Cresswell, Blair, Hill and Wood, *Encyclopaedia of Banking Law* para K2125; see also para K2129 for an example of a clause which excludes the obligation of an agent to provide information to the members of the syndicate.
10 See *Bowstead on Agency* (5th edn) p 147; *Proudfoot v Montefiore* (1867) LR 2 QB 511; *Johnson v Kearley* [1908] 2 KB 514, CA; Clarke and Farrar 'Defining Rights and Duties of Managing and Agent Banks to Co-lenders' in *Sovereign Lending: Managing Legal Risk* (Gruson and Reisner edn) p 126.
11 As to events of default, see p 98 below.

actions by the syndicate banks on the basis of a breach of an agent's duties of due care, skill and diligence;[12] equally it is exposed to actions in negligence by the borrower, on the ground that the discretion has been unreasonably or negligently exercised. On the other hand the absence of such a discretion means that the agent bank cannot act swiftly on the occurrence of an event of default to crystallise the right of the syndicate to demand repayment of outstanding principal, but must wait until the syndicate members have been canvassed to determine whether a majority are in favour of calling default.

Where the agent bank is conferred a discretion to call default of its own motion, a further question arises under English law as to when the agent may be regarded as being 'aware' of the occurrence of an event of default. Is the agent obliged to call default only if it actually becomes aware of an occurrence of a default; or is it under a duty to be vigilant and use reasonable care in discovering whether an event of default has occurred? This question could arise because an agent under ordinary principles of the English law of agency would owe such a duty of reasonable care.[13] Such questions could also arise where the agent bank is not conferred an express power or discretion to call default of its own motion but there is no prohibition on the agent bank so acting. In such a case the agent may have an implied power to call default of his own motion.[14]

The problem is dealt with in practice by an express clause which provides that the agent bank does not have any duties to monitor compliance by the borrower of the covenants in the loan agreement. The agent is required to call default if it has actual knowledge of the occurrence of an event of default, or, if the agent bank is given express notice by a member of the syndicate or by the borrower of the occurrence of an event of default. This means that at least as a matter of contract law the agent bank need not assume the role of a 'watchdog' nor be vigilant as to the occurrence of default nor be required to take decisions in respect of complex technical questions as to whether or not a loan covenant has been breached.

What constitutes 'actual knowledge' for these purposes is itself a difficult question. Suppose that a department or division within the agent bank, eg the foreign exchange division or currency swap division, becomes aware that the borrower has defaulted on a large foreign exchange transaction or a large currency swap; suppose that this occurrence is a breach of the syndicated loan agreement. Could the agent bank be regarded as having actual knowledge of the occurrence of an event of default under the syndicated loan agreement?

If the foreign exchange or swap division, as the case may be, is part of the same legal entity as the agent bank, it seems clear from the ruling in *Tesco Supermarkets Ltd v Nattrass*[15] that the knowledge of directors or central management is attributed by English law to the corporate entity.[16] Consequently, the agent bank would be under a duty to take action by virtue of the clauses in the syndicated loan agreement where its directors or senior management become aware that the borrower has defaulted. It

---

12 See art 42 of *Bowstead on Agency* (15th edn) p 144.
13 See art 42 of *Bowstead on Agency* and *Chaudhry v Prabhakar* [1988] 3 All ER 718, CA.
14 See pp 64–66 as to when a court will imply a power.
15 [1972] AC 153, HL.
16 *Quaere*: would the *Nattrass* ruling apply equally to a foreign corporate entity? Probably yes, since the syndicated loan and hence the agent's liability is governed by English law.

would need to consider calling default if it had such power, and it would clearly need to notify other syndicate members of the occurrence of the default. Such a duty would be extremely onerous in practice due to the fact that it is likely that the division responsible for the syndicated loan would be separated by a Chinese Wall[17] from the swaps or foreign exchange or other division, so that officers in the syndicated loans division would be prevented by internal bank procedures from receiving or having access to such information.

The problem is one which can arise in practice in respect of the borrower's obligations other than the payment of interest and principal. It is sometimes sought to deal with the difficulty by including a clause in the syndicated loan agreement to the effect that the agent bank shall not be deemed to have knowledge of the occurrence of the event of a default (other than a failure to make a payment of interest or principal) unless the department of the agent bank having specific responsibility for the syndicated loan agreement has received written notice from a party to the agreement stating that an event of default has occurred and describing such an event of default.[18] A clause of this nature would further provide that when such a notice of default has been received by the agent bank from a member of the syndicate or from the borrower the agent bank should notify all other members of the syndicate and request directions as to whether or not the borrower should be put in default and whether all amounts outstanding under the loan agreement should be accelerated.

It is submitted that such a clause should be given effect to by a court so as to prevent the agent bank from coming under a duty to act on the occurrence of an event of default of which any senior manager in a division of the agent bank has actual knowledge. While the agent bank may owe fiduciary duties (qua agent) to other members of the syndicate, there seems to be no reason why this fiduciary duty should not be restricted in the manner set out in such a clause. Such an analysis has greater force where transmission of the information to the division responsible for the syndicated loan is inhibited by the practice of Chinese Wall procedures and arrangements under the regulatory system introduced by the UK Financial Services Act 1986[19] since members of the syndicate would be aware in practice of the existence of such Chinese Wall procedures within the agent bank.

If it were the case that the clause is ineffective and the agent bank is treated as an indivisible legal entity for purposes of determining actual know-

---

17 See rule 1220 of *Conduct of Business Rules of The Securities and Futures Authority* (SFA Rule Book July 1987, 3rd edn 1988) which describes a Chinese Wall as a system of written procedures and arrangements which inhibits the flow of confidential information from one group of employees of a member firm engaged in one type of activity, eg corporate finance, to another group of employees, for example, those engaged in syndicated loans. These rules are to be replaced with similar rules pursuant to the promulgation of the Securities and Investments Board's Core Rules under s 63A of the Finance Services Act 1986 (which was inserted by s 194 of the Companies Act 1989).
18 See *Encyclopaedia of Banking Law* at para K2125 for an example of such a clause.
19 See explanation of Chinese Walls in note 17 above.

ledge, there is a further difficulty, if the agent bank is required to act on the basis of such knowledge.

The agent bank may have come into possession of such information in a confidential capacity, eg it may have been obtained by the bank's advisory or trust department from the borrower. In such a situation the agent bank is in an intractable position since it involves a conflict of duties: it owes a duty of confidentiality to the borrower not to disclose such information to the syndicate banks or anyone else and not to use the information for a purpose other than that in respect of which that information was received. It may not, for instance, use the information to call a default. On the other hand, the agent bank owes a duty to the other members of the syndicate to inform them of the occurrence of an event of default of which it has actual knowledge. The practical answer to this dilemma is a clause such as that suggested by Lehane[20] which provides that the agent bank is not obliged to disclose information to the syndicate or to make use of such information relating to the borrower, if such disclosure or use would or might *in the opinion of* the agent bank constitute a breach of any law or duty of secrecy or of confidence.

In this context, the existence of a Chinese Wall between the division responsible for the syndicated loan and other divisions within the agent bank may also be of legal significance. Where information constituting a default is received by a division of the agent bank which is lawfully carrying on 'investment business'[1] and this information is not transmitted to the division responsible for the syndicate in consequence of a Chinese Wall, it is possible that Rule 36 of the Securities and Investment Board's *Core Conduct of Business Rules*[2] enables the agent bank not to transmit or use such information for the purposes of its duties qua agent bank. However, Core Rule 36 does not seem to provide the agent bank with the ability to overcome the difficulty created by conflicting fiduciary duties where the information is not received in the course of carrying on 'investment business' as defined in the Financial Services Act 1986.[3]

V THE AGENT BANK AS A FIDUCIARY

It seems clear from the above that due to the structure of international syndicated loan agreements, the agent bank is indeed a true agent as that term is understood in English law. It has been pointed out by Meagher, Gummow and Lehane[4] that all agents who act on behalf of another party owe fiduciary obligations.[5] There is no reason to doubt this view, and

---

20 'Role of Managing and Agent Banks: Duties, Liabilities, Disclaimer Clauses', in *Current Issues in International Financial Law* (1985).
1 As defined in s 1 of the Financial Services Act 1986 read with Sch 1 to the Act.
2 See Release 94 of the Securities and Investment Board dated 30 January 1991, framed under s 63A of the Financial Services Act 1986.
3 See Core r 36(2).
4 *Equity, Doctrines and Remedies* (2nd edn, 1984) p 538.
5 See also *Re Coomber, Coomber v Coomber* [1911] 1 Ch 723, CA.

The agent bank as a fiduciary 65

it is necessary to consider the exact scope and ambit of the fiduciary obligations of the agent bank.

It seems clear that the scope and content of fiduciary obligations arising out of any particular relationship depends on the nature of the activities and functions undertaken by the fiduciary.[6]

The core of the fiduciary duty, however, is to be found in the obligations imposed by English law:

(a) a fiduciary must at all times act in the best interests of the person to whom a fiduciary duty is owed and, in particular, must not allow his own interest to conflict with his fiduciary duty and, in particular, he must not make a secret profit.[7] It also seems clear that the rule against making a profit out of a fiduciary position operates with equal force regardless of the absence of fraud or *mala fides*;[8]

(b) a fiduciary must show the same level of skill, care and diligence as he would in respect of his own affairs.

There are additional fiduciary duties imposed on an agent such as the duty to keep his principal fully and completely informed.

The duty not to allow his interest to conflict with his duty (including for this purpose the duty not to make a secret profit), causes difficulties in the practicalities of international business. Consequently specific and detailed attention must be given to this duty.

In the context of a syndicated loan the agent bank may be in a position where there is conflict of interest and duty:

(a) where the agent bank becomes a lender in another context to the borrower or;

(b) where in consequence of acting as agent the agent bank subsequently develops a role as the financial adviser to the borrower or;

(c) where the agent bank is an entity within a financial conglomerate and the agent bank or other subsidiaries of the conglomerate (eg those engaged in securities trading, investment management or corporate finance) have been able to obtain business with the borrower due to the contract which the agent bank has with the borrower.

In this type of situation the agent bank is open to the allegation that it made profits by virtue of its position as agent bank in the syndicated loan by dealing with the borrower outside the framework of the syndicated loan; it may also be open to the allegation that it did not exercise its discretion

---

6 See *Re Coomber* (above); *New Zealand Netherlands Society Oranje Inc v Kuys* [1973] 2 All ER 1222, PC; *Birtchnell v Equity Trustee Executors and Agency Co Ltd* (1929) 42 CLR 384.

7 It is a fundamental principle with regard to every fiduciary that he ought not to allow interest to conflict with his duties as a fiduciary or to make a profit from his office. Lord Herschel in *Bray v Ford* [1986] AC 44 at 51–52, HL said: 'It is an inflexible rule of a court of equity that a person in a fiduciary position ... is not, unless otherwise expressly provided, entitled to make a profit; he is not allowed to put himself in a position where his interest and duty conflict.' See also the statements of the House of Lords to the same effect in *Boardman v Phipps* [1967] 2 AC 46, and the statement of Lord Denning MR in the Court of Appeal in *Phipps v Boardman* [1965] Ch 992, CA and Lord Russell of Killowen in *Regal (Hastings) Ltd v Gulliver* [1942] 1 All ER 378 at 386.

8 See *Regal (Hastings) Limited v Gulliver* [1942] 1 All ER 378.

to call default in a balanced and unbiased fashion, ie in the best interests of the syndicate due to the business interest which it has with the borrower.

It seems clear from the ruling in the *New Zealand Netherlands Society Oranje Inc v Kuys*[9] that the disclosure by a fiduciary agent of material facts relating to those interests which may conflict with his duties satisfies the requirements of equity with regard to the fiduciary agent's duties. Consequently if full disclosure is made of all material facts as to the agent bank's interests which may conflict with his duties to the syndicate and the consent of the syndicate banks is obtained in respect of all such activities the demands of equity would be satisfied. For these purposes would a clause in the syndicated loan agreement such as that given in Cresswell, Blair, Hill and Wood[10] suffice? The clause provides:

> 'The agent and each manager may accept deposits from, lend money to and generally engage in any kind of banking, trust, advisory or other business whatsoever with the borrower and its related entities and accept and retain any fees by the borrower or any of its related entities for its own account in connection herewith without liability to account therefore to any bank or other manager.'

There are two difficulties with regard to such clauses. First, Lehane[11] has argued that since such clauses are more in the form of a notice rather than a detailed and complete disclosure of the facts and circumstances constituting the material interest, such clauses may not be sufficient to enable the agent bank to discharge its duties to the syndicate banks. Secondly, an agent who is empowered to act without having regard to the best interests of his principal is a contradiction in terms.

It is submitted, however, that such clauses should be held by a modern court of equity as being sufficient to discharge the fiduciary's obligation of disclosure. It seems clear that the obligations owed by fiduciary agents can vary depending on the framework of the relationship between the parties. Consequently, given the bargaining power, skill, sophistication and resources of the banks active in the syndicated loans market the level of disclosure achieved in the clause above should suffice to discharge the agent bank's fiduciary duties; detailed factual disclosure of each transaction giving rise to a conflict should not be regarded by a court as being necessary.

An allied problem which arises with regard to the role of the agent bank is the case where his duty to one syndicate conflicts with his duties to another syndicate of which it is also the agent bank. This is a case of conflict of duties and must be distinguished from a case of the conflict of the agent bank's own interests with its duties owed to the banks in the syndicate.[12] It is clear, however, that the mere fact that an agent bank of a syndicate subsequently takes on the duties of agent bank for another syndicate by itself does not constitute such a conflict. There must be a real conflict on

---

9 [1973] 1 WLR 1126, PC.
10 *Encyclopaedia of Banking Law* para K2130.
11 'Role of Managing and Agent Bank: Duties, Liabilities, Disclaimer Clauses' in *Current Issues of International and Financial Law* (1985) at pp 24–25.
12 See also the discussion of this problem in the context of the knowledge of the agent bank at p 64 above.

The agent bank as a fiduciary 67

the facts rather than a potentiality of conflict.[13] Once again informed consent on the part of the principal can obviate the difficulty.[14]

Could this type of conflict of duty with duty be eliminated by a clause common in practice which empowers the agent to act as if the agent bank were not an agent? Lehane[15] has, as observed earlier, cast doubt on the ability of a fiduciary agent to cast aside his role as fiduciary. It is submitted, however, that such an ability is necessary in the context of the practicalities of international finance except where *mala fides* or gross incompetence is involved.

Another context in which a conflict of duty may arise is in the context of the transfer of information obtained from the borrower to the syndicate banks and was discussed previously.[16]

In the final analysis, it is submitted that the efficacy of clauses in syndicated loan agreements which seek to negative the existence of fiduciary duties must be determined in the commercial context of major international financial transactions. The parties are sophisticated and major transnational financial institutions with adequate legal and other resources to deal with each other on an arm's length basis. Case law and broad judicial formulations determining the nature and extent of fiduciary obligations in the context of family trusts or ordinary commercial transactions must therefore be viewed with some caution and not applied uncritically in the arena of international finance. Except where an agent bank wishes to shield itself from conduct which is not bona fide or which manifests gross negligence, such clauses should be given effect by an English court.

---

13 See *Boulting v ACTAT* [1963] 2 QB 606, CA.
14 See *North and South Trust Co v Berkeley* [1971] 1 WLR 470.
15 Fn 11 above.
16 See p 64.

CHAPTER 5
Structure and contents of a syndicated loan agreement

An international syndicated loan agreement would generally speaking consist of a large number of provisions which can be grouped under the following headings:

(a) conditions precedent;
(b) representations and warranties;
(c) financial arrangements;
(d) covenants;
(e) default;
(f) choice of law and jurisdiction.

The first four items (a), (b), (c) and (d) will be dealt with in this chapter while (e) is dealt with in the next chapter.[1] Choice of laws was considered in Chapter 2.

I CONDITIONS PRECEDENT

These are conditions which must be satisfied by the borrower before the obligation of the lending banks to disburse funds is triggered. The borrower would usually be required to provide various documents relating to its constitution, its powers, its status and capacity, internal authorisations and exchange control permissions (where necessary) as well as legal opinions from specified lawyers with regard to these and other matters. These conditions precedent seek to ensure that the loan agreement is a valid and enforceable legal agreement and that the borrower has the power and all necessary authorisations to enter into the agreement. As explained previously,[2] these are also necessitated by the fact that such matters as status and capacity of the borrower cannot be determined solely by reference to the chosen proper law and need to be verified by reference to the law of the place of incorporation of the borrowing entity.[3]

A further condition precedent is that no events of default have

---
1 See p 103.
2 See ch 2.
3 See ch 2, p 27, above. The reader is referred to these sections on conditions precedent.

occurred[4] during the period between the signing of the loan agreement and the making of the first disbursement of funds.

While it seems clear that the syndicate banks are under no obligation to disburse funds until satisfaction of the conditions precedent there are a number of questions which need to be considered as to the effect of these conditions precedent. First, may the borrower decide to refrain from making best efforts in satisfying the conditions precedent after the loan agreement is signed, or 'walk away' from (ie renounce) the agreement without incurring any legal liability? Secondly, prior to the satisfaction of the conditions precedent by the borrower may the syndicate banks withdraw from their commitment to lend? The answers to these questions depend on the construction of the clauses in each particular syndicated loan agreement.

As a matter of construction it will be necessary to determine first whether the 'conditions precedent' in an international syndicated loan agreement are true conditions precedent as understood in the common law. They may be 'promissory conditions' and not true conditions precedent in the sense of 'contingent conditions'.[5] If on a proper construction the 'conditions precedent' found in international syndicated loan agreements are promissory conditions, there is in fact a valid and binding agreement from the moment of signing. Neither the syndicate nor the borrower has a right to withdraw without incurring liability for breach of contract.

Many commentators on the conditions precedent in a syndicated loan agreement have proceeded on the basis that the usual clause containing the conditions precedent in fact constitutes a contingent condition.[6] This is by no means a necessary conclusion. It may be that, unless carefully drafted, conditions precedent may in effect amount to promissory conditions on the part of a borrower. Consequently, failure by the borrower to satisfy such conditions precedent may in fact expose the borrower to an action in damages for breach of contract; equally, the syndicate banks may not legally be able to 'walk away' from the syndicated loan agreement until the time specified

---

4 On events of default see p 98 below.
5 See on the distinction *Chitty on Contracts* (16th edn) para 795 at p 505. The distinction was summarised by Denning LJ in an oft quoted passage in *Trans Trust SPRL v Danubian Trading Co Ltd* [1952] 2 QB 297, at 304, CA:

'What is the legal position of such a stipulation? Sometimes it is a condition precedent to the formation of a contract, that is, it is a condition which must be fulfilled before any contract is concluded at all. In those cases the stipulation "subject to the opening of a credit" is rather like a stipulation "subject to contract". If no credit is provided there is no contract between the parties. In other cases, a contract is concluded and the stipulation for a credit is a condition which is an essential term of the contract. In those cases the provision of the credit is a condition precedent not to the formation of the contract, but to the obligation of the seller to deliver the goods. If the buyer fails to provide the credit, the seller can treat himself as discharged from any further performance of the contract and can sue the buyer for damages for not providing the credit.'

This case involved a c.i.f. contract whereby the buyer was required to provide a letter of credit and the seller's obligations to ship the cargo and perform his other obligations under the c.i.f. contract were made 'subject to the opening of a credit'. In that case Denning LJ thought that the stipulation 'subject to the opening of a credit' was not a contingent condition (ie a true condition precedent) but a promissory condition, failure to perform which gave rise to an action for damages for breach of the c.i.f. contract.
6 See Gabriel *Legal Aspects of Syndicated Loans* p 44; Penn Shea and Arora *The Law and Practice of International Banking* pp 101–102.

(if any) for the satisfaction of conditions precedent has lapsed, or until the borrower has had a reasonable time to satisfy such conditions precedent. Both parties are therefore bound by an existing contractual obligation to lend and to borrow from the moment of the signing of the loan agreement.

If the clause providing for the conditions precedent is drafted so as not to constitute a promissory condition, the question whether the borrower or lenders may 'walk away' prior to the time permitted to satisfy the conditions precedent is again a matter of construction of the legal nature of the 'condition precedent'.

The legal nature of a condition precedent may vary in English law and the position is succinctly summarised by the editors of *Chitty on Contracts*:[7]

'The failure of a condition precedent may have one of a number of effects. It may in the first place, suspend the rights and obligations of both parties, as, for instance, where the parties enter into an agreement on the express understanding that it is not to become binding on either of them unless the condition is fulfilled.

Secondly, one party may assume an immediate unilateral binding obligation, subject to a condition. From this he cannot withdraw; but no bilateral contract binding on both parties comes into existence until the condition is fulfilled.

Thirdly, the parties may enter into an immediate binding contract, but subject to a condition, which suspends all or some of the obligations of one or both parties pending fulfilment of the condition. These conditions precedent are, however, contingent and not promissory, and neither party will be liable to the other if the condition is not fulfilled.'

In deciding into which of the above categories the conditions precedent of any particular syndicated loan agreement fall, it is necessary to draw a distinction between cases where a condition precedent is at least partially outside the control of either party to the contract (eg exchange control permission being conferred by the central bank of the borrower's home state) and cases where the condition precedent is within the control of one of the parties (eg delivering a document which is lawfully in the possession of a party to the agreement). In a syndicated loan agreement the satisfaction of conditions precedent are generally within the control of the borrower. Consequently, it is submitted that in most syndicated loan agreements the conditions precedent are likely to fall into either the second or the third of the categories described in *Chitty*. Generally speaking, this is because the format of the conditions precedent clause in international syndicated loan agreements is couched in the form of language which suspends only the obligations of the syndicate banks until conditions precedent are satisfied by the borrower.[8] Therefore the borrower or lenders should not be able to 'walk away' before the condition is satisfied. It may also be the case that the borrower should make 'best efforts' to satisfy the conditions precedent which are within his power to satisfy. 'Best efforts' may of course be made an obligation of the borrower by virtue of an appropriate clause.

The conditions precedent are also in practice made applicable in respect of each 'drawdown' of funds where the syndicated loan provides for disburse-

---

7 See 16th edn para 796 at pp 506–507.
8 See for an example of this type of condition precedent *United Dominions Trust (Commercial) Ltd v Eagle Aircraft Services Ltd* [1968] 1 WLR 74, CA and compare with *Aberfoyle Plantations Ltd v Cheng* [1960] AC 115, PC.

ment of funds in respect of the loan to be made in a series of tranches rather than in one lump sum disbursement. The banks' obligations to lend in such circumstances is therefore subject to proper satisfaction of conditions precedent prior to each drawdown rather than to the first of the series of drawdowns.

In certain types of syndicated loan agreements, referred to as 'revolving' facilities, the borrower has a right during the period of the loan not only to borrow funds, but also to repay such funds and re-borrow up to an aggregate amount specified in the loan agreement. In such loans the conditions precedent are also made applicable to each such re-borrowing.

II REPRESENTATIONS AND WARRANTIES

The section entitled 'Representations and Warranties' in a syndicated loan agreement constitutes the substratum of facts on the basis of which the syndicate makes the loan facility available to the borrower. These must be distinguished from the covenants of the loan agreement which constitute the requirements which the borrower must comply with in the future during the subsistence of the loan agreement until final maturity of the loan.

In practice representations and warranties fall into a number of groups. The first group includes a number of representations and warranties which are virtually identical with the conditions precedent. They require that the borrower represents and warrants that it has the legal status and capacity to enter into the loan agreement and that all internal and external authorisations including exchange control permission have been obtained so as to enable the borrower to enter into a loan agreement which is legally valid and binding. These representations and warranties are interlinked with others which require the borrower to represent and warrant that all obligations of the borrower contained in the loan agreement are legal, valid and binding commitments. Equally the borrower is required to represent and warrant that the performance of the obligations under the syndicated loan agreement will not violate any provisions in its constitutional documents or any laws in the home state of the borrower or any exchange control law[9] or any contract to which the borrower is a party.

The purpose of having this group of representations and warranties is that if they are untrue or inaccurate, the syndicate has either:

(a) a right to terminate the agreement and demand immediate repayment of all outstanding funds (ie 'accelerate' the loan prior to maturity – this right is contained in the loan agreement itself); or

(b) if the result of the inaccuracy is such that the entire agreement is null and void (for instance, where the borrower has no legal capacity to borrow), the representations may provide grounds for an action in

---

9 On the effect of the violation of an exchange control law by a borrower when entering into a loan agreement, see p 34 below. Generally speaking the violation of an exchange control law, other than one which is part of the proper law of the agreement, would not affect the validity of the agreement under English conflicts rules. See, however, the discussion of art VIII(2)(b) of the International Monetary Fund Agreement on pp 34–40 above.

damages under English common law rules for fraudulent or negligent misrepresentation as the case might be.[10]

The borrower may also be estopped from pleading absence of capacity or absence of authorisation: *Janred Properties Ltd v ENIT*.[11]

The second group of representations and warranties relates to the financial and business position of the borrowing entity. The syndicate would normally have obtained all necessary financial reports and accounts from the borrower, as necessary, prior to the entry into the loan agreement. The borrower is therefore required to represent and warrant the accuracy of all financial statements and information submitted by the borrower to the syndicate banks. In addition, the borrower will be required to represent and warrant that litigation or similar proceedings are not pending against it which would have a material adverse effect on its financial or business condition. The borrower is also required to represent and warrant that it is not in default of any other loan agreement or other financing agreement to which it is a party. This would include the borrower's obligations under bond issues, project financings, leasing agreements and similar agreements. Finally, the borrower is required to represent and warrant that it has title to the assets appearing on its balance sheet. The latter is somewhat difficult to police in the case of most borrowers who are major multinational corporations, since their assets are situated in different countries and difficult questions of law may arise with regard to title to assets in such countries. Thus, for instance, under title retention clauses common in international sale contracts, particularly where continental European sellers are involved, difficult questions have arisen as to title to goods as between buyer and seller.[12]

Where the syndicated loan takes the form of a 'revolving'[13] credit facility these representations and warranties are required to be repeated by the borrower prior to each new drawdown in the same way that conditions precedent are made applicable prior to each drawdown in such a facility. Similarly, the borrower may be required to repeat the representations and warranties prior to each drawdown in a syndicated loan where the funds are to be disbursed in a series of tranches.

In circumstances where the syndicated loan agreement is valid and legally enforceable the consequence of a breach of one of the 'representations and warranties' is that the syndicate banks are given a right to terminate the loan agreement with immediate effect and to demand repayment of all outstanding borrowings if any. This is achieved by making a breach of a representation or warranty an 'event of default'.[14] The use of the word 'warranty' is therefore somewhat misleading since that term is generally

---

10 See p 27 above for a discussion of this aspect.
11 [1989] 2 All ER 444, CA and p 27 above.
12 See the difficulty which arose in respect of determining title in *Aluminium Industrie Vaassen BV v Romalpa Aluminium Ltd* [1976] 2 All ER 552; *Borden (UK) Ltd v Scottish Timber Products Ltd* [1979] 2 Lloyd's Rep 168; revsd [1979] 3 All ER 961, CA; *Re Bond Worth Ltd* [1979] 3 All ER 919; *Re Peachdart Ltd* [1983] 3 All ER 204; *Clough Mill Ltd v Martin* [1984] 1 All ER 721; *Hendy Lennox (Industrial Engines) Ltd v Grahame Puttick Ltd* [1984] 1 WLR 485; Re *Andrabell Ltd (in liquidation) Airborne Accessories Ltd v Goodman* [1984] 3 All ER 407.
13 See p 79 below.
14 See p 98 below on events of default.

used to refer to a term of a contract the breach of which may give rise to a claim for damages but not to a right to treat the contract as repudiated,[15] though this makes little difference in practice.

III FINANCIAL ARRANGEMENTS

This section of the syndicated loan agreement deals with the mechanics and procedures for the transfer of funds, the payment of interest and other administrative aspects. It also deals with certain fundamental aspects of the loan including:

(a) the currency of the loan;
(b) the period of the loan;
(c) the amount of the loan;
(d) arrangements with regard to disbursement of funds by the syndicate, ie, 'drawdown' of funds, including whether drawdown is to be in one tranche or a number of tranches;
(e) repayment of the loan;
(f) prepayment of the loan.

Some of these aspects require detailed discussion while others are self-explanatory.

1 Currency of the loan and currency of repayment

Availability of funds may be specified to be in one currency or a number of currencies.

Where the funds are to be made available in more than one currency these currencies need to be specified with accuracy. The maximum amount available to the borrower is, however, usually stipulated in US dollars.

Such loans are referred to as 'multi-currency' loans. In such loans additional provision is usually made to deal with a case where the funds borrowed subsequently exceed the stipulated US dollar maximum due to currency fluctuations. The syndicate is usually conferred a right to require repayment of the excess. Sometimes this right is subject to an exempt level of currency fluctuation.

Express provision needs to be made to ensure that the currency of repayment is the same as the currency of borrowing. This is particularly true in the case of multi-currency facilities. The reason for this is that where a debtor owes a debt expressed in a foreign currency, the general rule under English law is that the debtor may choose whether to pay in the foreign currency in question or in sterling.[16] It has been argued that this rule had

---

15 See *Hong Kong Fir Shipping Co Ltd v Kawasaki Kisen Kaisha Ltd* [1962] 2 QB 26 at 70, CA.
16 See *Chitty on Contracts* (16th edn) vol 1, para 2194 and *Adelaide Electric Supply Co Ltd v Prudential Assurance Co Ltd* [1934] AC 122, HL; *Barclays Bank International Ltd v Levin Bros (Bradford) Ltd* [1977] QB 270 at 277.

been swept away by the ruling of the Court of Appeal in *Miliangos v George Frank (Textiles) Ltd*[17] but this was rejected by Oliver LJ in *Re Lines Bros Ltd*.[18] Dicey and Morris state, however, that this rule is confined to cases where payment must be made in England.[19] If this is accurate the position seems to be that unless payment of interest and principal is required to be made by the borrower at an account of the agent bank[20] in England the rule will not apply. Nevertheless, given the uncertainty of the rule, it is essential that the currency of repayment be specified to accord with the currency of the loan.

There is no difficulty in enforcing payment in foreign currency after the ruling of the House of Lords in *Miliangos v George Frank (Textiles) Ltd*.[1] The House of Lords held that an English court would have jurisdiction to give judgment expressed in a foreign currency where the payment of the debt is due in that currency. However, some doubts still remained as to whether *Miliangos* would be applied (a) where the law applicable to a foreign money obligation was not the law of the place in which the currency was legal tender, and (b) where the claim was not for a foreign money debt. It now seems that English courts will give judgments in foreign currency in respect of claims other than in debt (for instance, in breach of contract: *The Folias*)[2] and in respect of claims under contracts governed by English law where the currency of payment was a foreign currency: *Barclays Bank International Ltd v Levin Bros (Bradford) Ltd*.[3]

It was held by Staughton J in the *Libyan Arab Bank* case[4] that if payment by the borrower becomes impossible in the currency of the debt, the debtor had an obligation to make payment in sterling if a demand was made by the creditor for payment in sterling.[5] Consequently, the purpose of the repayment clause must be such as to compel the borrower to make repayment in the currency of the loan agreement except where the syndicate banks require repayment in sterling or other substitute currency due to the fact that in the view of the banks payment in the currency of the loan has become impossible.

2 Statement of purpose and use of proceeds of loan

It is usual to include a specific clause stating the purpose for which the loan is made and the use to which proceeds of the loan are to be utilised.

In a syndicated loan agreement subject to English law, this statement is not strictly necessary as a matter of law. Nevertheless, it is extremely useful for purposes of avoiding the risk of illegality (*ab initio*) of the loan transaction under its English proper law. Under English law contracts may

---

17 [1976] AC 443.
18 [1983] Ch 1.
19 *Conflict of Laws* (11th edn) r 210.
20 On functions of the agent bank see ch 4 above.
1 [1976] AC 443.
2 [1979] AC 685.
3 [1977] QB 270.
4 See pp 32–34 above.
5 See also to the same effect Donaldson J in *Ozalid Group (Export) Ltd v African Continental Bank Ltd* [1979] 2 Lloyd's Rep 231. However, Professor Goode, in *Payment Obligations in Commercial and Financial Transactions* (Sweet & Maxwell, London, 1983) p 140, has argued that the contrary ought to be the rule.

be unlawful as formed (and thus void *ab initio*) or they may be unlawful as performed.[6] Where the purpose of a contract is to further an objective which is unlawful under English law, and that purpose is shared by both parties, the contract is unlawful as formed and neither party may enforce it or derive rights under it.[7] It is equally clear that where the syndicated loan agreement is itself not unlawful as formed, but the borrower intended to use the loan for an unlawful purpose, the syndicate banks will be able to enforce the loan agreement against the borrower if the banks were unaware of the unlawful purpose of the loan contract.[8]

The statement as to the purpose of the loan and the use of loan funds therefore has a dual objective. First, it ensures that the contract is not illegal as formed. Secondly, even if the borrower uses the loan proceeds for an unlawful purpose it enables the syndicate to assert that they were unaware of the illegal purpose for which the borrower used and intended to use the proceeds. It is also the practice to include a further statement to the effect that neither the agent bank nor the other members of the syndicate shall be bound to enquire as to the use of the proceeds of the loan and that they shall not be responsible for the application of the proceeds of the loan. It is submitted, however, that while this clause eliminates the need for enquiry as to the use of proceeds, if the syndicate were in fact aware that the loan proceeds were to be used for some unlawful purpose, for example arms shipments to a country which is at war with Britain, the syndicate banks will not be able to rely on this clause to enforce the loan agreement.[9]

3 Prepayment

It is usual in practice to provide for a 'premium' or a 'penalty' to be paid by the borrower to the syndicate banks in the event of prepayment of the loan prior to stated maturity. In so far as such 'premiums' or 'penalties' simply cover the costs and losses incurred by the bank as a result of the prepayment, there is no objection under English law. But if the sum payable is grossly disproportionate to the actual loss suffered or costs incurred by the banks the clause runs the risk of being struck down as a 'penalty' clause: *Dunlop Pneumatic Tyre Co Ltd v New Garage and Motor Co Ltd*.[10] The locus classicus on this subject was formulated in that case by Lord Dunedin[11] with the following propositions of law:

> '(1) Though the parties to a contract who use the words "penalty" or "liquidated damages" may prima facie be supposed to mean what they say, yet the expression used is not conclusive. The court must find out whether the payment stipulated is in truth a penalty or liquidated damages.
> (2) The essence of a penalty is a payment of money stipulated as in terrorem of the offending party; the essence of liquidated damages is a genuine pre-estimate of damage.

---

6 See *Chitty on Contracts* (16th edn) ch 16, para 1135.
7 *Alexander v Rayson* [1936] 1 KB 169, CA; *Bigos v Bousted* [1951] 1 All ER 92.
8 See *Archibolds (Freightage) Ltd v S Spanglett Ltd* [1961] 1 QB 374, CA.
9 See also the related issues discussed at pp 30–34 below in the context of *Regazzoni v K C Sethia (1944) Ltd* [1958] AC 301, HL.
10 [1915] AC 79, HL.
11 At 86–88.

(3) The question whether a sum stipulated is a penalty or liquidated damages is a question of construction to be decided upon the terms and inherent circumstances of each particular contract, judged of at the time of the making of the contract, not as at the time of the breach.

(4) To assist this task of construction various tests have been suggested which, if applicable to the case under consideration, may prove helpful or even conclusive. Such are:

(a) It will be held to be a penalty if the sum stipulated for is extravagant and unconscionable in amount in comparison with the greatest loss which could conceivably be proved to have followed from the breach.

(b) It will be held to be a penalty if the breach consists only in not paying a sum of money and the sum stipulated is a sum greater than the sum which ought to have been paid.

(c) There is a presumption (but no more) that it is a penalty when a single lump sum is made payable by way of compensation, on the occurrence of one or more or all of several events, some of which may occasion serious and others but trifling damage.

On the other hand:

(d) It is no obstacle to the sum stipulated being a genuine pre-estimate of damage that the consequences of the breach are such as to make precise pre-estimation almost an impossibility. On the contrary, that is just a situation when it is probable that pre-estimated damage was the true bargain between the parties.'

It has, however, been held in hire purchase cases that the law on penalties is not applicable when the sum is payable on the occurrence of an event other than a breach of contract: *Campbell Discount Co Ltd v Bridge*.[12] The ruling of the Court of Appeal in *Campbell Discount* on this point was not dissented from in the House of Lords where the decision was based on different grounds.[13] It seems, therefore, that the requirement that the borrower should pay a premium or penalty over and above the costs incurred or losses suffered by the syndicate banks on a prepayment is a legally enforceable provision, provided that the prepayment does not constitute a breach of contract by the borrower. Syndicated loan agreements therefore usually give the borrower a power to prepay without breaching the obligations of the loan agreement subject to the payment of the premium, and this should be sufficient to take such clauses outside the ambit of the penalty doctrine laid down in the *Dunlop Pneumatic Tyre Co* case.[14] Some doubt about the efficacy of such clauses emerges from certain dicta expressed recently by Bingham LJ in *Interfoto Picture Library Ltd v Stiletto Visual Programmes Ltd*.[15] It is submitted, however, that whatever may be the position in hire purchase or consumer contracts, 'premium' or 'penalty' clauses

---

12 [1961] 1 QB 445, CA.
13 Four of the Law Lords agreed with the ruling of the Court of Appeal.
14 See p 75 above.
15 [1988] 1 All ER 348 at 358, CA, where his Lordship referred to the possibility of 'a disguised penalty clause'. Dillon LJ also thought that a sum payable on an extension of the rental period in respect of certain photographic transparencies might have been void as a 'penalty' even though the sum was payable on an extension rather than a breach. The case is best explained on the basis that the payment was in fact required to be made on the occurrence of a breach, since no express power was conferred to extend the rental period by the terms of the agreement.

in international syndicated loan agreements should not be the subject of judicial attack on the basis that they are 'disguised' penalty clauses because: (a) the clause is negotiated as between parties dealing on an arm's length basis with access to legal and financial resources, and (b) the borrowers who have access to the international market-place usually have a choice of the syndicates they deal with and are capable of negotiating the content of such clauses with each prospective syndicate prior to the grant of a mandate.

4 Funding mechanisms in the international market: need for special clauses

The transnational banks active in the international syndicated loans market do not necessarily have deposits in the currencies in which they agree to lend to a borrower under a syndicated loan agreement. Thus US and Japanese banks in a syndicate may agree to lend Deutschmarks, or alternatively German, Japanese and British banks may agree to lend US dollars to a borrower. In practice this causes no problem due to the availability of a vast pool of deposits in London's international markets in the various international currencies. Consequently, members of a syndicate of banks who are lending funds in a particular currency will obtain the funding for the syndicated loan from the inter-bank market in London.

However, in practice, banks will only lend funds to each other in the inter-bank market for a period of nine, six or three months or fourteen seven days or overnight; whereas the syndicated loan is made for a long period of time, sometimes up to forty years, and a bank which is a member of a syndicate must disburse funds to a borrower without expecting to be repaid in the usual course of things until maturity of the loan at a much later date. This creates a difficulty since the inter-bank loan must be repaid to its lender in the inter-bank market within a very short space of time, while the syndicated loan made from funds so borrowed will not be repaid for a much longer period of time.

This difficulty is overcome because the syndicate bank can repay borrowings to its lender (in the inter-bank market) by borrowing again in the inter-bank market from another bank in the market. The syndicate member will continue this process until the final maturity of the loan when the borrower repays the loan to the syndicate member. This process means that the cost of funding a syndicated loan depends on the rates payable from time to time in the inter-bank markets of London. The cost of obtaining funds in the London inter-bank market is at a floating or variable rate and is referred to as the London Inter-Bank Offered Rate or LIBOR rate.[16]

Since the cost to the syndicate of funding a loan is dependent on the LIBOR rate, a borrower in the international syndicated loans market is required to pay a floating rate of interest determined in accordance with the LIBOR rate prevailing from time to time. The cost to the syndicate of borrowing in the inter-bank markets at the LIBOR rate is thus transferred to the borrower. In addition, the banks will receive a 'spread' or profit

---

16 The term has been adapted by much smaller centres such as Paris – PIBOR – and Singapore – SIBOR – to refer to rates prevalent in the loan markets for 'Euro' currencies (including yen for this purpose!).

margin, say, of $\frac{1}{2}$% over the LIBOR rate payable by the borrower. The spread is fixed at the outset by the terms of the loan agreement. The LIBOR rate is fixed from time to time on the basis of an interest rate clause, which requires the borrower to fix the rate for a period of nine, six or three months on the first date on which the funds are disbursed and thereafter on the expiry of each interest period chosen by him. For instance, if the borrower chooses a three month period he must refix the interest rate period at the end of those three months and this process continues until final maturity of the loan. It must be noted that the successive periods for which the LIBOR rate is calculated during the life of the loan is determined at the option of the borrower. The interest rate period which the borrower chooses from time to time will usually (but not always) determine the period for which syndicate banks will themselves borrow from the inter-bank markets. The LIBOR rate payable by the borrower for the chosen interest rate period is determined by reference to the median rate at which three to four named banks (called the 'reference banks') will be offering deposits in the same currency for the same period of time in the inter-bank markets.

The need to obtain the funding necessary for syndicated lending from the inter-bank market in London raises another consideration for syndicate banks. After the funds have been disbursed to the borrower under the syndicated loan agreement, deposits in the currency of the loan may become unavailable or available only in insufficient amounts in the inter-bank market. The syndicate banks may be unable to fund themselves and consequently may not be able to comply with their legal obligation to provide an interest rate quotation to the borrower under the syndicated loan agreement when required to do so. As a matter of common law it is not at all clear whether such an event would result in the frustration of the contract between the syndicate banks and the borrower. The general approach of the English courts has been to restrict to a minimum the circumstances in which a contract would be so frustrated.[17] The nearest analogy to this type of case (though by no means on all fours) are cases where the subject matter of a contract of sale was to be obtained from a particular source to the knowledge of both parties to the contract and this source dries up wholly or partially. In such situations, it has been held in at least one case that the contract was frustrated to the extent of the failure of the contemplated source of supply: *Re Badische Co*[18] while in another case the court seems to have conceded obiter that frustration would occur: *Lipton Ltd v Ford*.[19]

Given the uncertainty at common law, it is usual and necessary to include a clause which specifically deals with the problem. It is usually drafted in a form which provides that in the event that the syndicate banks are unable to provide an interest rate quotation for any particular period chosen by the borrower under the interest rate fixing clause due to any political, economic or other reason which affects the ability of the syndicate bank to fix the interest rate, the syndicate banks are conferred a right to quote to the borrower a LIBOR rate in a different currency. In effect this confers on the syndicate the ability to fund the loan to the borrower in an alternative currency obtainable in the inter-bank market. This right may be conferred

---

17 See, for example, *Tsakiroglou & Co Ltd v Noblee Thorl GmbH* [1962] AC 93, HL.
18 [1921] 2 Ch 331.
19 [1917] 2 KB 647.

for the remaining duration of the loan or until deposits in the currency of the loan (and therefore interest rate quotation in the currency of the loan) are available on the inter-bank markets. Where the right conferred on the banks in such an eventuality is a right to continue to quote interest rates for the periods chosen by the borrower in an alternative currency during the remaining duration of the loan, the borrower in effect has to accept substitution of an alternative currency for the currency of the loan. Repayment of the loan in such an eventuality could also be required in the alternative currency chosen by the syndicate banks.[20] Such a clause is referred to as the Euromarket Disaster Clause and should be drafted in the widest possible terms to provide the syndicate banks with the necessary protection in the event of the absence or insufficiency of deposits in the inter-bank markets in the currency of the loan.

The mechanics of funding are explained in the diagram overleaf.

Where the syndicated loan is a 'revolving',[1] 'multi-currency'[2] facility, it will be recalled that the borrower has a right to borrow, repay and re-borrow in a number of different currencies over the period of the loan which may be up to as long as forty years. The syndicate may not be able to obtain funding in a particular currency which a borrower may request under the facility some time during the period of the loan. To cover such an eventuality, such agreements should provide for lending in an alternative currency if the currency requested by the borrower is not available or is available only in insufficient amounts.

5 Interest payments and withholding tax

A borrower is usually required to make payments of interest to the banks free of any 'withhold'. The reason for this requirement is that in many jurisdictions interest payments made by a debtor to a creditor are required to be made subject to a deduction or a 'withhold' for tax purposes usually at the basic rate of tax payable in that jurisdiction. Such tax withholds are enacted in many jurisdictions to facilitate the collection of tax revenues.

Where there is no such clause requiring payment of interest without a 'withhold', what effect will be given by English law to a law of the borrower's home state which requires a tax withhold to be made in respect of interest payments by the borrower? The position in English law is not absolutely clear. Certain propositions may be advanced on the basis of existing case law.

First, where the governing law of a syndicated loan agreement is English law, an English court will not enforce the revenue laws of a foreign state.[3] This rule, however, applies only to cases where direct or indirect enforcement of the revenue laws of a foreign state are sought before an English court. Secondly, recognition as distinct from enforcement of the revenue laws of a foreign state is, however, permissible under the English governing law.[4]

---

20 See on the currency of repayment p 73 above.
1 See pp 47 and 75 above.
2 See p 47 above.
3 See *Sydney Municipal Council v Bull* [1909] 1 KB 7; *Indian and General Investment Trust Ltd v Borax Consolidated Ltd* [1920] 1 KB 539; see also *Dicey and Morris* r 3 at p 100.
4 See *Re Emery's Investment Trusts* [1959] Ch 410.

Funding Mechanisms in the London Interbank Market

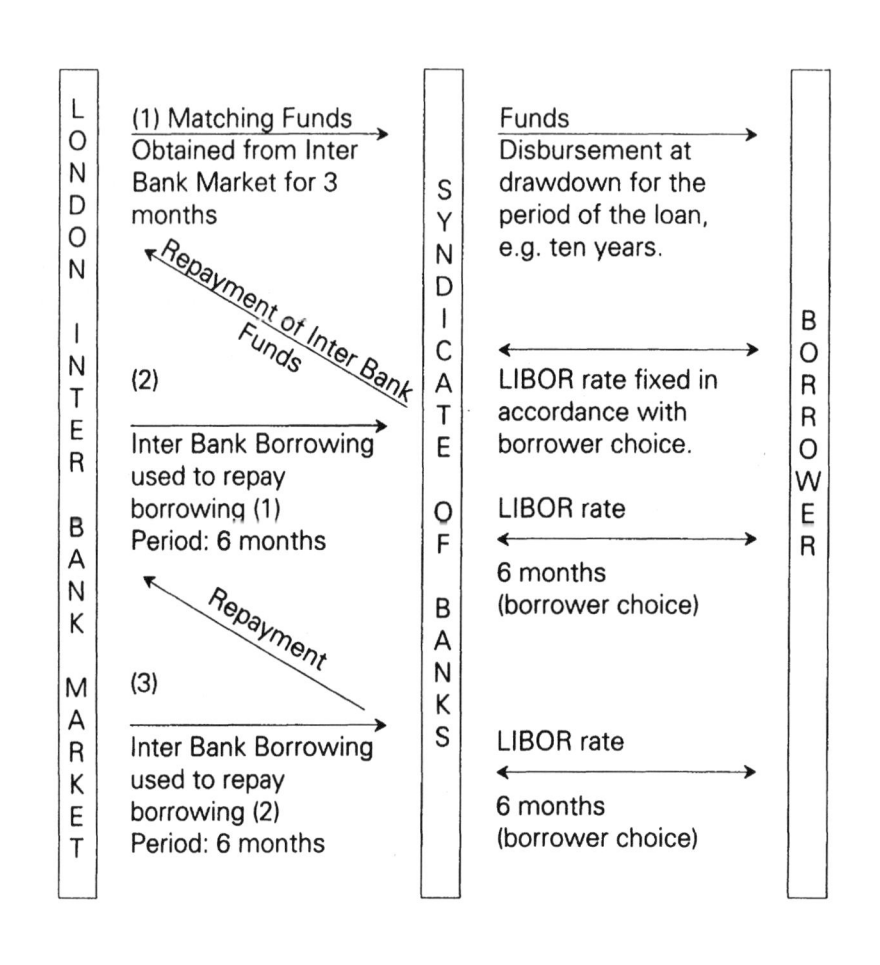

LONDON INTERBANK MARKET

(1) Matching Funds Obtained from Inter Bank Market for 3 months

← Repayment of Inter Bank Funds

(2) Inter Bank Borrowing used to repay borrowing (1) Period: 6 months

← Repayment

(3) Inter Bank Borrowing used to repay borrowing (2) Period: 6 months

SYNDICATE OF BANKS

Funds Disbursement at drawdown for the period of the loan, e.g. ten years.

LIBOR rate fixed in accordance with borrower choice.

LIBOR rate
←→
6 months
(borrower choice)

LIBOR rate
←→
6 months
(borrower choice)

BORROWER

In *Re Lord Cable*[5] the court took the view that where trustees of an estate in England had paid sums out of their own personal accounts to satisfy the demands of a foreign estate duty law, the claim by the trustees to be reimbursed from the estate in respect of such sums would be upheld by the English courts – this was mere recognition as distinct from enforcement. However, if this same estate duty was claimed by the government of the foreign state in an action against the trustees in England, an English court would hold that the estate duty was not recoverable at the instance of the foreign government: *Re Visser*.[6]

On the basis of *Re Lord Cable* the position seems to be that if a borrower pays a withholding tax prior to the transfer of interest to the syndicate banks the court may recognise the foreign tax law in so far as it is necessary to decide the extent of the borrower's obligation to make interest payments to the syndicate. Consequently, in the absence of an express clause, it is likely that a court would hold that payment of interest subject to a withhold was the extent of the borrower's obligation under the syndicated loan agreement.

In order to avoid any uncertainty in the matter, a specific clause requires that in the event that a borrower is required to make a withhold for tax purposes in respect of interest payments to the syndicate banks, the borrower shall gross up the interest payment so that the syndicate banks receive the amount of interest which they would have received otherwise than for the withholding tax. The borrower is however conferred a right to prepay the loan in such an eventuality.[7]

6 Funding and increased costs

Borrowers are usually required to make additional payments in the event that the cost to any syndicate bank in funding the loan becomes financially more onerous due to regulatory requirements in the home state of the syndicate bank in question. The usual reason why a bank would incur additional costs in respect of funding an international syndicated loan is because the central bank, to whose monetary jurisdiction it is subject, imposes or increases reserve requirements in respect of deposits taken by that bank. Such a regulation is exemplified by Regulation D[8] of the US Federal Reserve Bank which was discussed by Staughton J in *Libyan Arab Bank v Bankers Trust*[9] and by Hirst J in *Libyan Arab Foreign Bank v Manufacturers Hanover Trust Co (No 2)*.[10] Regulation D imposed a reserve requirement equal to 3% of net transaction accounts from $0–$40.5m and 12% of net transaction accounts over $40.5m, held by banks in the US. The reserve was required to be held either in the form of vault cash or as an interest-free deposit with a federal reserve bank. The result of such a regulation is that it increases the cost of lending to borrowers in that currency. However, Regulation D does not apply to 'any deposit that is payable only

---

5 [1977] 1 WLR 7.
6 [1928] Ch 877.
7 See on prepayment p 75 above.
8 12 CFR 204.2.
9 [1988] 1 Lloyd's Ref 259 at 267; see p 32 above.
10 [1989] 1 Lloyd's Rep 608 at 623.

at an office located outside the United States'.[11] Consequently Regulation D and similar reserve requirements in other countries generally have no effect on deposit-taking activity outside the home state of the central bank imposing it, for instance, in London's inter-bank market.[12]

Despite such exemptions from reserve requirements which may generally be conferred on banks in respect of deposits taken in the London inter-bank markets, the increased costs clause is an invariable feature of international syndicated loans; it provides an additional measure of protection to syndicate banks from the potential erosion of their interest rate spread.

IV   COVENANTS

The covenants and other terms of a syndicated loan agreement have as their primary objective the protection of the investment of the syndicate banks which consist of their loan to the borrower. Generally speaking, such covenants are influenced by two features in international syndicated lending. First, syndicated loans are usually for long periods of time which may extend even up to forty years. Secondly (unlike in domestic lending), in the vast majority of cases such loans are not secured by any security over assets.[13] The syndicate therefore lends on the basis of an expectation to be repaid from the cash flow generated by the borrowing entity from its business operations and those of its subsidiaries rather than from the liquidation of assets.

Because of these features, the covenants and other terms in a syndicated loan agreement attempt to achieve a number of objectives:

(a)   Financial covenants.   It is necessary to require that the borrowing entity maintains a specified level of financial performance to ensure that it will be able to meet payments of interest and repayments of principal as and when they fall due. These levels of performance are embodied in the

---

11   S 204.1(c)(5).
12   A passage from the memorandum of law submitted by the Federal Reserve Bank of New York as *amicus curiae* in *Wells Fargo Asia Ltd v Citibank SA* and quoted by Staughton J in the *Libyan Arab Bank* case ([1981] 1 Lloyd's Rep 259 at 267) explains how Regulation D, s 204(c)(5) was perceived to operate by the Federal Reserve Bank itself:

'The location where the depositor has legal right to demand payment is a distinct concept from the location where the deposit is settled. The fact that settlement of United States dollar deposit liabilities takes place in the United States between United States domiciliaries is not determinative of where the deposit is legally payable. Virtually all United States large dollar transactions between parties located outside the United States must be settled in the United States. The Clearing House Inter-bank Payment System or CHIPS operated by the New York Clearing House Association for some 140 banks handles at least 400 billion dollars in transfers each day, and it is assumed that perhaps 90% of these payments are in settlement of off-shore transactions. If that fact alone were relevant to where a deposit is legally payable the exemption in Regulation D would almost never apply to foreign branch deposits denominated in United States dollars. Clearly, the exemption is not limited to deposits denominated in a foreign currency and is available to foreign branches of United States banks that book deposits denominated in United States dollars.'

13   Sometimes guarantees of a parent company are given where the nominal legal borrower is an under-capitalised subsidiary, or shell company or other group company which cannot support the credit on the basis of its own financial strength.

financial ratio covenants.[14] Banks active in the syndicated loans markets consider these to be vital to the protection of their investment constituted by the loan to the borrower. These minimum levels of financial performance represent the level at which the borrower should have no difficulty in meeting its interest and principal payments. They also function as early warning signals to the syndicate that if the borrower fails to meet the requirements of these covenants it is likely that the borrower may soon get into difficulties with regard to the payment of interest and principal on their outstanding loans.

(b) Financial information covenants. In order to monitor compliance with the financial ratio covenants it is necessary to obtain a substantial amount of financial information from the borrower. Consequently, there are covenants designed to ensure the maximum level of disclosure of financial information to the syndicate which would enable the syndicate not only to determine compliance with the financial ratio covenants, but also generally monitor the borrower's financial and business position.

(c) Asset disposal covenants. In order to ensure proper and adequate financial performance by the corporate entity, banks usually consider that it is necessary to preserve the borrower's asset base both in terms of quantity and quality. This objective gives rise to covenants which control the substantial disposal of revenue generating assets and it may also consist of controls on the amount of dividends which may be distributed by a borrower.[15]

(d) Negative pledge. Since the syndicate banks are unsecured lenders to the borrowing entity, it becomes necessary to ensure that all future lenders to that entity are also equally unsecured. Covenants are necessary to prevent other lenders from obtaining a preferred position in a bankruptcy or insolvency of the borrower. A subsequent lender who takes a charge over the borrowing entity's assets would generally speaking have a prior claim under the bankruptcy laws applicable to the borrower's bankruptcy or insolvency. This objective is achieved by the 'negative pledge' covenant.[16]

(e) Events of default. In the event that the borrowing entity's financial performance fails to meet the minimum acceptable levels contained in the financial ratio covenants or where there has been a breach of some other covenants, such as the negative pledge, the syndicate must have the legal ability, if they so wish, to demand immediate repayment of the loan prior to its stated maturity. There must be an immediate and unqualified right to 'accelerate' on the occurrence of such an event. This is provided

---

14 See p 84 below.
15 See p 86 below.
16 See p 89 below.

for by specifying a number of events which constitute 'an event of default'[17] and which would give the syndicate banks the unqualified right to demand immediate repayment of the loan prior to its maturity.[18]

(f) Cross default. It is also necessary that syndicate banks should be able to accelerate their loans in the event that other syndicates who have made loans to the borrower are capable of accelerating their loan outstandings. In the absence of such a right, the syndicate banks may be compelled to stand by and watch other syndicates accelerating or (more likely in practice) renegotiating their loans with the borrower or obtaining repayment. The syndicate banks would not be able to participate in the process of renegotiation or repayment. This clause is referred as the 'cross default' clause.[19]

1 Financial covenants

There are a number of covenants which may be used in a syndicated loan agreement in order to ensure that a borrower meets basic financial performance criteria. The following are common in syndicated loans to corporate borrowers.

i *The debt to equity ratio*

This is perhaps the most important ratio used in the syndicated loans markets. It requires that the debt of the borrowing entity should not at any time exceed a certain multiple of its equity as represented by its share capital and accumulated profits or reserves. This ratio is designed to control the future borrowings of the borrower within prudent parameters so that the borrower will not expand its business activities by over-borrowing; it is designed to ensure that the financial growth of the borrowing entity is fuelled not only by borrowings but also by equity and profits in prudent proportions. It also prevents the erosion of the net asset base of the borrower to a level where there might be insufficient assets to meet repayment of syndicated loans when they fall due for payment.

In drafting the covenant, two accounting concepts require careful legal definition: 'debt' and 'equity'. Usually debt would cover all long-term borrowings of the borrowing entity, but a tighter ratio would encompass in the definition of debt all liabilities to banks, or all liabilities appearing on a balance sheet of a corporate entity except equity and reserves. The definition of equity would usually take into account only such capital and reserves which are represented by tangible net assets. In other words, capital and reserves are defined to exclude the value of all intangible assets such as goodwill and capitalised research and development costs.

---

17 See p 98 below.
18 Such a clause is, of course, not a 'covenant' in the usual sense of that word, though it is dealt with under this head.
19 See p 98 below.

ii *Minimum net worth*

This ratio is complementary to the debt to equity ratio. It requires that the value of tangible assets less all outstanding liabilities should be maintained above a specified threshold level.

The objective of this covenant is also considered to prevent the liquidation of revenue-generating assets for the purposes of reducing the level of borrowings on a corporate entity's balance sheet, at a time when the entity is incurring revenue losses. The reduction of outstanding borrowings by such asset liquidation could be used by a borrower to prevent a breach of the debt to equity ratio covenant even though net equity and reserves have been shrinking due to successive revenue losses. A separate minimum net worth covenant becomes necessary to prevent such asset liquidation.

Example
A debt to equity covenant of 2.5:1 is imposed on a borrowing entity. The borrower has assets of $600m, liabilities of $400m and equity of $200m which gives a debt to equity ratio of 2:1. The entity suffers an annual revenue loss totalling $50m. Equity would shrink to $150m resulting in a debt to equity ratio of 2.6:1, placing the borrower in breach of the debt to equity covenant. If the borrower now sells off $200m of assets and pays off bank borrowings of $200m, liabilities would stand at $200m. Equity would stand at $150m giving a debt to equity ratio of 1.3:1. This would mean that the borrower is in compliance with its debt to equity ratio.
Suppose now that a net tangible asset requirement of $160m had been imposed on the borrower. The borrower could not have effected the transaction without a breach of the minimum net worth covenant.

iii *Current ratio*

This ratio requires that a borrower should maintain a certain ratio between its current assets and current liabilities on its balance sheet. The objective is to ensure that there are sufficient liquid assets on the borrower's balance sheet to enable it to make payments of interest and principal, if necessary by liquidating such assets, for purposes of interest or principal payments.

iv *Minimum working capital*

This is a covenant allied to the current ratio covenant to preserve corporate liquidity.

It requires the borrower to keep a minimum level of liquid assets in excess of its current liabilities which fall due for payment within the next 12 months.

v *Debt service ratio*

This ratio requires that a borrowing entity's annual interest payments and loan repayments do not exceed a particular ratio in relation to that entity's annual profits prior to payment of tax and interest.

2 The financial information covenant

This covenant is sometimes drafted widely. It ought to enable the syndicate banks not only to obtain financial information about the borrower which is publicly available, but also other financial information as the syndicate banks consider to be reasonably necessary to enable them to monitor the performance of the borrower. Such information as is required to be submitted to the syndicate is usually tendered to the agent bank in a syndicated loan.[20]

3 Asset disposal covenant

This covenant seeks to preserve the asset quantity and asset quality of the borrower in the sense that it seeks to prohibit large scale disposals of revenue-generating assets of the borrower. It would usually provide that the borrower may not, and will procure that its subsidiaries will not, dispose of assets which in aggregate exceed a certain specified amount except 'in the ordinary course of its business'. The clause would usually seek to cover in its ambit not only a single disposal of assets at or above the specified amount, but also a series of related disposals which in aggregate exceed the specified threshold. The exception for ordinary course of business permits the borrower to sell its products and inventory in the ordinary course of commercial operations without breaching the covenant. It would therefore permit a borrower which is a car manufacturer to sell $100m worth of cars but not its manufacturing plant which may also be worth $100m.

The covenant on disposal of assets would also 'bite' not only when a holding company sells off an operating subsidiary as a business, but also when it disposes of its shareholding in a subsidiary company. Such a disposal would not generally be regarded as being in the ordinary course of business of the parent company.

The asset disposal covenant would also cover disposals in pursuance of a plan to merge the borrower with another entity whereby the borrower transfers all its assets and liabilities to a newly formed vehicle company into which both parties to a proposed merger would usually transfer their assets and liabilities.

4 Merger control covenants

It is usually the practice to include clauses which prohibit the borrower from 'merging' with another corporate entity without the consent of the syndicate banks. Sometimes the prohibition against 'merger' is restricted to cases where the merger results in the cessation of the existence of the borrower as a legal entity and the creation of a new successor entity.

The commercial purpose of the clause seems to be an attempt to preserve the legal identity of the borrowing entity.

The question as to which law determines whether the borrower has 'merged' with another entity, or whether the borrower has merged in circumstances where it has ceased to exist, or whether the borrower has ceased

---

20 See on agent banks ch 4 above.

to exist was considered previously.[1] This question is of particular importance since the vast majority of borrowers in London's markets are corporate entities incorporated outside the UK.[2] It was submitted that in this type of case a distinction needs to be drawn between the meaning of the word 'merger', which is an issue governed by the proper law, and the legal nature or legal incidents of the transaction in question, which is a matter for the law of the place of incorporation consistent with the ruling of the House of Lords in *National Bank of Greece and Athens SA v Metliss*.[3]

Under English law a distinction is made between a 'takeover' and an 'amalgamation' while 'merger' is not strictly speaking a term with a precise meaning in English law.

The concept of 'takeover' is to be found in the definition of 'takeover offer' in s 428 of the Companies Act[4] and in Section 14 of the Company Securities (Insider Dealing) Act 1985.

Section 428 of the Companies Act 1985 is as follows:

'(1) In this Part of this Act "takeover offer" means an offer to acquire all the shares, or all the shares of any class or classes, in a company (other than shares which at the date of the offer are already held by the offeror), being an offer on terms which are the same in relation to all the shares to which the offer relates or, where those shares include shares of different classes, in relation to all the shares of each class.'

Section 14 of the Company Securities (Insider Dealing) Act 1985 states:

'In this Act, "take-over offer for a company" means an offer made to all the holders (or all the holders other than the person making the offer and his nominees) of the shares in the company to acquire those shares or a specified proportion of them, or to all the holders (or all the holders other than the person making the offer and his nominees) of a particular class of those shares to acquire the shares of that class or a specified proportion of them.'

An 'arrangement' or 'amalgamation' arises under ss 425–427A in Part XIII of the Companies Act 1985. All such arrangements and amalgamations under Part XIII of that Act require court sanction.[5] Section 425 deals with an 'arrangement' between a company and its creditors or shareholders. Section 427 contemplates an 'arrangement' for the purposes of amalgamating two or more companies or reconstructing two or more companies. Section 427A deals with three cases, which are as follows:

'*Case 1*
Where under the scheme the undertaking, property and liabilities of the company in respect of which the compromise or arrangement in question is proposed

---

1 See p 41 above.
2 See Euromoney 20th Anniversary Supplement (June 1989) table 'Syndicated Loans: Country Borrowing'.
3 [1957] 3 All ER 608, especially per Lord Tucker at 615.
4 Inserted by s 172(1) of the Financial Services Act 1986.
5 This is in contrast to the 'notarial' merger of two companies which may occur under certain continental European legal systems.

are to be transferred to another public company, other than one formed for the purpose of, or in connection with, the scheme.

Case 2
Where under the scheme the undertaking, property and liabilities of each of two or more public companies concerned in the scheme, including the company in respect of which the compromise or arrangement in question is proposed, are to be transferred to a company (whether or not a public company) formed for the purpose of, or in connection with, the scheme.

Case 3
Where under the scheme the undertaking, property and liabilities of the company in respect of which the compromise or arrangement in question is proposed are to be divided among and transferred to two or more companies each of which is either –
(a) a public company, or
(b) a company (whether or not a public company) formed for the purposes of, or in connection with, the scheme.'
and in each case "the consideration for the transfer or each of the transfers envisaged in the Case in question is to be shares in the transferee company or any of the transferee companies receivable by members of the transferor company or transferor companies, with or without any case payment to members."

The word 'merger' does not have a precise meaning in English law and therefore an agreement drafted under English law should define precisely what is sought to be prohibited by an 'anti-merger' clause.

The second question is what practical and commercial objective is accomplished by the clause.

In cases where corporation A, the borrower, seeks to 'merge' (using that term in a commercial sense) with corporation B (otherwise than in the context of a takeover) the 'merger' structures commonly used in developed economies would in most cases result in a transfer of all of the assets and liabilities of corporation A to a new vehicle company or to its merger partner, corporation B.[6] Consequently, any such proposed merger would involve a breach of the clause against substantial disposal of assets. The prohibition against merger would in effect be unnecessary in this type of case. However, suppose the borrower, corporation A, takes a transfer of all assets and liabilities of corporation B; shares in corporation A are issued to shareholders of corporation B and thereafter corporation B is dissolved as a legal entity. The borrower in such a case would not be in breach of an asset disposal covenant but may be in breach of an 'anti-merger' covenant if such a transaction is specified as a prohibited transaction within the language of such a clause. In this type of case, therefore, the anti-merger covenant has a practical impact on the borrower's ability to effect certain types of corporate transactions. It will be seen that if an anti-merger clause prohibited mergers only in cases where the borrower ceases to exist as a legal entity such a clause would not prohibit the hypothetical transaction above.

---

6 See Weinberger and Blank *Takeovers and Amalgamations* (1980).

5 The pari passu covenant

Under this covenant the borrower warrants that its obligations under the syndicated loan agreement will rank equally with the rights of the borrower's other unsecured creditors.

In practice, the general format of the clause would require the borrower to warrant that his obligations to the syndicate are unsecured general and unconditional obligations of the borrower and rank pari passu and equally with all other unsecured obligations of the borrower. The primary objective of the clause is to ensure that the borrower has not conferred priority to any other unsecured creditor at the time the syndicated loan agreement is agreed.

It is, however, doubtful whether this clause is effective to prevent other *unsecured* creditors obtaining a prior or preferred position over the claims of the syndicate in the event of insolvency or bankruptcy of the borrower. In the event of an insolvency or bankruptcy of the borrower, the law governing that bankruptcy or insolvency may confer priority on other unsecured obligations of the borrower. In such an event it is difficult to see how a contractual provision in a syndicated loan agreement governed by English law or other foreign law will be held to override the law of the jurisdiction governing the bankruptcy or insolvency.

Nevertheless, in so far as it becomes known prior to a bankruptcy or insolvency of the borrower that its obligations to the syndicate under the syndicated loan agreement would not be afforded equal ranking in a bankruptcy or insolvency, such discovery should confer on the syndicate a right to terminate the loan agreement and accelerate all outstandings. The practical problem, however, is that it is extremely unlikely that before the occurrence of a bankruptcy or insolvency of the borrower, such a breach of the pari passu covenant will come to light.

6 Negative pledge[7]

Wood[8] has stated that 'by far the most pervasive covenant in international loans is the negative pledge'; it is also the covenant whose practical utility is most doubtful due to the weakness of the mechanisms available to enforce it.

The essential commercial and financial purpose of the clause is not difficult to determine. Since most syndicated lending in the international markets is unsecured it is of vital importance to ensure that the borrower does not give security over its assets to subsequent lenders. The reason is that under most systems of law secured assets would not be available to the unsecured creditors in the event of a liquidation or bankruptcy of the borrower. The covenant also has another commercial purpose, namely, to prevent the

---

[7] See Wood *Law and Practice of International Finance* (Sweet and Maxwell, 1980) pp 146–152; Professor Roy Goode *Legal Problems of Credit of Security* (Sweet and Maxwell, 2nd edn 1988) pp 17–23; Gabriel *Legal Aspects of Syndicated Loans* (Butterworths) pp 82–97; Boardman and Crosthwaite 'Whither the Negative Pledge' (1986) 3 JIBL 162; Penn, Shea and Arora *Law and Practice of International Banking* pp 110–115.

[8] *Law and Practice of International Finance* (International Business and Law Series, Clarke Boardman, New York 1981) vol 2, s 6.02(1).

borrower from obtaining financing by giving security over assets in circumstances where its financial performance has deteriorated to a level where it is unable to obtain funds from lenders on an unsecured basis.

The core prohibition in a negative pledge would be in a form similar to:

> 'The borrower shall not and shall procure that none of its subsidiaries, present or future, creates or permits to subsist any *mortgage, charge, pledge, hypothecation, lien* or other *security interest* or *encumbrance* on the whole or any part of their respective present or future assets.'[9]

The prohibition cannot, however, be imposed without a number of exceptions and qualifications. On the one hand, it is too wide: it would result in the borrower being in breach of the prohibition in circumstances where the syndicate would have no practical objection to the creation of security interests by the borrower. On the other hand, it is too narrow since it is restricted to a prohibition on transactions which create a security interest or similar encumbrance recognised in law, but does not expressly prohibit transactions which have a similar commercial effect although they do not create a security interest as a matter of technical law.

An example of the former is provided by liens arising by operation of law. Thus, under s 39 of the UK Sale of Goods Act 1979 an unpaid seller of goods has a lien on the goods arising by implication of law for the price. Similar rights are conferred on a repairer of chattels under legal systems which have adopted the common law. Thus, for instance, an unpaid bill for $30 in respect of repairs to a car would confer a lien or security interest on the repairer.[10] A syndicate of banks would hardly be concerned with the fact that a major multinational corporation has failed to pay a $30 bill in respect of the repair of one of its company cars due to a clerical error and that a repairer's lien has arisen in respect of that bill; nevertheless, unless a specific exemption is provided to the negative pledge clause the multinational corporation would be in breach of his negative pledge clause and might become liable to repay a $500m syndicated loan. Similarly, there are many commercial operations which give rise to the taking of security in the ordinary course of business. Thus, in international sales, which are financed by letters of credit issued by international banks, the bank would usually take a charge over the shipping documents until the bank is paid by the buyer.[11] Consequently, it is necessary to frame exemptions from the prohibition in the negative pledge clause to cover such cases and to prevent the borrower from being placed constantly in breach of the negative pledge clause in circumstances which would really not concern the syndicate banks.

The clause may also be too wide for other reasons. First, it may cover in its ambit security interests or encumbrances which already exist at the

---

9   See for a definition in English law of each of the italicised words: Goode *Legal Problems of Credit and Security* (Sweet and Maxwell, 2nd edn, 1988) pp 10–17.
10 See *The Sophie* (1842) 1 Wm Rob 368 for an early example of a repairer's lien.
11 See *Guaranty Trust Co of New York v Hannay & Co* [1918] 2 KB 623, CA, especially Scrutton LJ at 659; and *United City Merchants (Investment) Ltd v Royal Bank of Canada* [1982] 2 All ER 720 at 725, HL per Lord Diplock; for a discussion of security interests created under letters of credit see Penn, Shea and Arora *The Law of Practical International Banking* pp 347–361; Gutteridge and Megrah *Bankers Documentary Credits* ch 9.

time of the syndicated loan. Secondly, it could prevent the borrower from purchasing a company which may already be subject to encumbrances or security interests over its assets. These types of security interests would need to be exempted from the prohibition contained in the negative pledge covenant. However, the syndicate would need to place a 'cap' or ceiling on borrowings so that there is a maximum limit on borrowings which may be secured by such existing security. If an exemption from the prohibition in the negative pledge was given to a borrower without such a 'cap' it is always possible for the borrower to increase the amount of borrowing secured on that asset without breaching the negative pledge covenant.

The negative pledge covenant in the form set out above may, on the other hand, be too narrow. There may be many transactions which have the commercial effect of giving security over assets to a lender of funds but which cannot be classified as a 'mortgage' or 'charge' or 'pledge' etc or as creating a 'security interest' under English law.[12] Thus, for instance, a company requiring financing may enter into a sale and leaseback of an asset or a sale and repurchase of an asset in order to obtain financing. In a sale and repurchase a prospective borrower will sell an asset and transfer ownership to a finance house or bank for a sum equivalent to the total financing required; the company will simultaneously agree to repurchase the asset from the finance house or bank at the end of a given period at a premium which would reflect the interest charge for the period. The same effect could be achieved by the prospective borrower selling the asset to the finance house or bank in return for a sum representing the finance required and immediately obtaining a leaseback of that asset for a specified period of time; during this period the company will pay 'hire payments' for the asset which in effect would be the interest payable on the sum advanced; at the end of the period of the lease, the company would be given an option to buy back the asset for a nominal consideration. Even though the lender has obtained title to the assets and thus obtained security (at least in a commercial sense) in respect of funds advanced in both cases, such transactions would not constitute the creation of a charge or mortgage or other security interest under English law: *McEntire v Crossley Bros Ltd*.[13] This was a case which held that a hire purchase agreement fell outside the Bills of Sale Acts of 1878 and 1882 because a charge was not created due to the structure of the hire purchase contract which is essentially similar in legal structure to the sale and leaseback transaction described above.[14]

It has sometimes been suggested that such a transaction would be struck down as a 'sham' and the courts would analyse the real objective of the parties and hold that such transactions would constitute a loan of money subject to security over assets.[15] However, the weight of authority is to give effect to the form of the legal structure created by the parties and this view is expressed in the judgment of Diplock LJ in *Snook v London and West Riding Investments Ltd*.[16]

---

12 For definition see Goode *Legal Problems of Credit and Security.*
13 [1895] AC 457, HL.
14 See also *Helby v Matthews* [1895] AC 471, HL.
15 See Winn LJ in *Kingsley v Stirling Industrial Securities Ltd* [1967] 2 QB 747, at 780, CA.
16 [1967] 2 QB 786, at 802, CA; see also *Stoneleigh Finance Ltd v Phillips* [1965] 2 QB 537, CA; *Kingsley v Stirling Industrial Securities Ltd* [1967] 2 QB 747, CA.

Given the absence of judicial unanimity on the subject it is necessary as a matter of practice to control the ability of a borrower to enter into such transactions by specifically drafted clauses. Such a clause would need to prohibit the borrowing entity from selling its assets in circumstances where it is under an obligation to repurchase at a premium or to take a lease subject to the payment of lease rental.

i *'Borrowings' and 'indebtedness'*

The format for the negative pledge clause set out above has no reference to the mortgage charge encumbrance etc being created in respect of 'borrowings' or 'indebtedness'. The reason for this practice is that if the negative pledge prohibited the grant of security over assets only in respect of 'indebtedness or borrowings', the covenant would probably not cover a number of cases where security is in effect granted over assets. A good example of such a case is as follows:

Example
A syndicated loan is made to the parent company of a group subject to a negative pledge in respect of 'borrowings or indebtedness' of the parent and its subsidiaries; subsequently, a loan is made to a subsidiary of the same parent company (or to a specially set up financing vehicle by another lender) subject to a guarantee of the parent company; the guarantee (as distinct from the loan) is secured by the grant of a charge or other security interest over the assets of the parent company. It is arguable that a negative pledge covenant which prohibits the giving of security in respect of 'borrowings' or 'indebtedness' would probably not cover the giving of security to secure the performance of the parent company's obligations under the *guarantee*.

ii *Applicable law*

Thus far it has been assumed that English law determines whether or not a transaction constitutes a charge etc or 'a security interest' for purposes of the negative pledge. The position, however, is somewhat more complicated since borrowers, who have access to the international syndicated loans market in London, are usually located outside the UK and have subsidiaries and operations in many different countries. Consequently, the assets over which a security interest might be created would be located in a number of different countries.

Suppose a borrower has assets in Ruritania and enters into a sale and leaseback transaction in Ruritania. The loan agreement is governed by English law. The sale and leaseback transaction would not be classified under English law as creating a security interest as discussed above; suppose, however, that under Ruritanian law it is classified as a security interest in respect of assets located in Ruritania, where the transaction is effected. Would this constitute a breach of the negative pledge covenant?

In this type of situation it seems that there are in fact two questions. The first question is the meaning of the words 'a security interest' in the negative pledge covenant. The second question relates to the legal nature and effect of the transaction in respect of the assets which are the subject of the transaction.

It is submitted that the first question concerns the true meaning and interpretation of words in a contract governed by English law, and this is a matter for the proper law of the contract under English conflicts rules.[17]

The second question, however, may not be governed by the proper law of the syndicated loan agreement.[18]

In answering the second question it is necessary to distinguish between fixed assets and others. It is submitted that in the case of fixed assets this question should generally be governed by the location of the assets or the *lex situs*. While there does not seem to be any direct English authority to this effect, at least in the case of fixed assets, the commercial reality of the situation strongly supports this conclusion. The reason is that if by the law of the place where the fixed assets are located those assets are considered by the *lex situs* to be subject to a charge or security interest it would be commercially unrealistic to require lenders to regard those assets as being unencumbered, on the basis of English law as the proper law of the loan agreement. The reason is that those fixed assets would be within the jurisdictional authority of the courts of a legal system which regards the assets as encumbered. Consequently, it is submitted that if according to the *lex situs* of the assets, those assets are subject to a security interest or encumbrance, a security interest has been created within the meaning of the words in an English contract. It does not seem to be necessary for a security interest to arise in English law on the same facts. Consequently, in such a case, there would be a breach of the negative pledge clause.

Conversely, where a transaction occurring in Ruritania in respect of fixed assets located in Ruritania does not result in the creation of a charge or security interest under Ruritanian law there should be no breach of the negative pledge covenant even if under English law the same transaction would result in the creation of a security interest. This conclusion too is consonant with commercial reality, since the syndicate banks would not be concerned if such assets are regarded as being free of any security by the law of the place in which assets are located; the fact that a similar transaction in respect of those assets would give rise to a security interest under English law would be a matter of no concern to the syndicate banks.

The conclusion therefore, it is submitted, is that the *lex situs* of fixed assets should determine whether a security interest has been created for purposes of determining whether a breach of the negative pledge covenant has occurred in an agreement governed by English law.

Should the *lex situs* govern the question whether a security interest has been created in respect of assets other than fixed assets and immovable property?

First, as regards 'ambulatory' assets such as ships and aircraft application of the *lex situs* is not practicable. Dicey and Morris[19] have pointed out that in the case of ships and aircraft legal issues should be referred to the law of the flag. Consequently, at least prima facie, the question whether a ship is subject to a mortgage should be referred to the law of the flag. Suppose, however, that under a mortgage instrument created under, say, Greek law, a ship would be regarded as being subject to a mortgage which

---

17 See Dicey and Morris *Conflict of Laws* (11th edn) rr 150 and 151.
18 On proper law see ch 2 above.
19 *The Conflict of Laws* (11th edn).

will be enforced by a Greek court applying Greek law irrespective of whether a valid mortgage has been created by reference to the law of the flag. It is submitted that the English proper law of the syndicated loan should regard that a security interest has been created, if the security interest is valid and enforceable by a court which has the jurisdictional power to enforce it.

Secondly, with regard to intangible movables such as bonds or bank deposits, receivables, or rights under contracts, a different rule is perhaps applicable. It is submitted that if a security interest is created in respect of such an asset which is enforceable against that asset under the *lex situs* or under the proper law of a legal document creating the security interest, English law as the proper law of the syndicated loan should recognise that a security interest has been created and consequently that a breach of the negative pledge has occurred. It should be immaterial in such a case that the transaction would not give rise to a security interest under English law. A good example of such a case is where a person who places money on deposit with a bank seeks to give a security interest over the deposit to the bank which holds the deposit. Under English law it was held by Millet J in *Re Charge Card Services*[20] that it was a 'logical absurdity' for a security interest to arise in these circumstances. However, it is perfectly possible under foreign systems of law that such an interest may arise. Consequently, if the borrower has deposits in Japan with a Japanese bank and creates a security interest over that bank deposit enforceable under Japanese law, it is submitted that there would be a breach of a negative pledge clause in a syndicated loan agreement governed by English law, even though English law would regard it a logical absurdity for a depositor to give security over that deposit to the bank which holds such deposit.[1]

In the final analysis the key question is whether a transaction or instrument seeking to create a security interest in respect of an asset is recognised as creating such an interest by the courts of a legal system which have the jurisdictional power to enforce the security interest against that asset. If the answer to the question is 'yes', it is submitted that English law should consider that a security interest has been created which breaches the negative pledge covenant in a syndicated loan agreement governed by English law.

iii Enforcement of the negative pledge covenant

It may be thought that the obvious remedy for breach of negative pledge is that the syndicate banks should have a right to call default and accelerate their loan outstandings. Syndicated loan agreements almost invariably provide that a breach of the negative pledge constitutes an event of default giving rise to a right in the syndicate to accelerate the loan. However, there is a serious practical difficulty with enforcing the negative pledge by termination of the loan agreement and acceleration of loan outstandings. A breach of a negative pledge by a borrower in respect of one loan agreement would in practice trigger the 'cross default' clauses[2] in all syndicated loan agreements to which the borrower is a party. The consequence of this is that

---

20 [1987] Ch 150.
1 *Re Charge Card Services Ltd* [1987] Ch 150.
2 See p 98 below on cross default.

all banks who have advanced funds to the borrower subject to such cross default clauses could demand immediate repayment of all loan outstandings. The result of a declaration of default by one syndicate in practice would be to trigger a similar declaration by all banks who are lenders of the borrower with the consequence that the borrower becomes insolvent. In the event of a bankruptcy or insolvency it is extremely likely that the secured creditors would have preference over unsecured creditors although this would be determined by the law governing or applicable to the bankruptcy. Consequently, a syndicate which called default is more likely than not to precipitate the very event which the negative pledge was designed to prevent, namely a secured creditor obtaining a preferred position in a bankruptcy. Consequently, calling default and demanding immediate repayment may not be a viable enforcement mechanism in practice.

What other means exist to enforce the negative pledge covenant?

Under English law it is always possible to obtain an injunction to prevent a breach of a negative stipulation in a contract.[3] While an injunction is theoretically an available remedy, the practical difficulty is that it is unlikely that a syndicate will become aware that a borrower is proposing to breach a negative pledge sufficiently in advance to enable the syndicate to obtain an injunction in good time.

In order to overcome these deficiencies, the practice has developed to include in the negative pledge clause one of three alternative mechanisms. For the sake of convenience they may be termed 'equal security', 'same security', and 'automatic security'.

An 'equal security' clause requires that if the borrower does grant security to other lenders, the borrower is required to grant security which is equal in value to that granted to another lender. Such a clause could be enforced under English law by a decree of specific performance.[4] While this remedy is available as a matter of law, in practice it would be of use only in circumstances where the borrower has not given security over the whole or the majority of his assets in terms of financial value. Where the borrower has given security over all or the majority in value of his assets it would be impossible for the borrower to give equal security. Subject to this reservation the equal security clause is an effective mechanism to enforce the borrower's obligation under a negative pledge.[5]

The 'same security' clause requires that in the event of a borrower giving a security interest to another lender, the borrower will procure that the same asset will equally secure the syndicate's loans pari passu with the other lender to whom security over assets has been granted.

Once again, while this stipulation may be enforced by a decree of specific performance, it may be that after a security interest has been created it will be impossible to erode that security interest and create another security

---

3 See *Warner Bros Pictures Inc v Nelson* [1937] 1 KB 209; *Page One Records Ltd v Britton* [1968] 1 WLR 157.
4 For the circumstances in which an English court would grant a decree of specific performance to enforce a contractual stipulation see *Chitty on Contracts* (26th edn, 1989) ch 27, paras 1861–1902.
5 Goode in *Legal Problems of Credit and Security* p 19 considers the question whether a security interest is created by such a clause under English law and concludes that it is not.

interest which ranks equally in the event of a bankruptcy. An English court would need to consider whether the *lex situs* in the case of land or immovables and the legal system which has jurisdiction over the asset will recognise and give effect to such an order of specific performance. It is clear that 'the court does not compel a person to do what is impossible'.[6]

In the case of the equal security clause and the same security clause, the borrower is required to take positive action to give security to the syndicate banks. The 'automatic security' clause seeks to create a security interest simply by virtue of the operation of a contractual clause without more. Such clauses are generally speaking rare in practice in the international markets. The clause would, usually, provide that in the event that the borrower creates a charge pledge etc, or security interest over an asset, that same asset will 'immediately and automatically' secure the borrowings under the particular loan agreement in question. It is extremely doubtful whether a legal system would regard a contractual provision in an agreement governed by English law as being capable of creating a security interest in respect of an asset ranking equally with a security interest perfected by reference to all the formalities required by that law. Goode[7] has stated (and it is submitted accurately) that the first creditor obtains 'nothing at all beyond a mere contractual right'. It has been suggested that some form of equitable interest may arise in the hands of the syndicate due to the operation of the automatic security clause.[8] Even if this were the case under English law, it seems extremely unlikely that such an equitable interest would be of practical value to a syndicate. The courts of the *lex situs* (if fixed assets are sought to be 'automatically' secured) or the courts having jurisdictional power over movables or intangibles (where such assets are sought to be 'automatically secured') are extremely unlikely to give effect to such an equitable lien arising under English law, in a manner which erodes the security interest perfected in compliance with all formalities required by that law.

It has also been suggested that if a subsequent lender took security with full knowledge of the existence of the negative pledge clause this might in some circumstances give rise to injunctive relief against a subsequent lender. Such a cause of action might have been based on the principle laid down in *De Mattos v Gibson*[9] where Knight Bruce LJ said that where a person acquires an asset from another with knowledge of the existence of a previous contract in respect of that asset a court could interfere to ensure that the acquirer of the property shall not use the property in a manner inconsistent with the contractual stipulations of which he is aware. The precise ambit of this rule is extremely unclear except in cases of leases: *Tulk v Moxhay*[10] and charter party contracts: *Port Line Ltd v Ben Line Steamers Ltd*.[11] It is submitted that in the context of the comments of Diplock J in the *Port Line* case it is unlikely that the broad general principle

---

6 *Forrer v Nash* (1865) 35 Beaver 167 at 171; *Locobil International Finance Ltd v Agroexport, (The Sea Hawk)* [1986] 1 WLR 657, CA.
7 *Legal Problems of Credit and Security* p 20.
8 See the discussion in Penn, Shea and Arora *The Law and Practice of International Banking* (1987) pp 113–114; Gabriel *Legal Aspects of Syndicated Loans* pp 84–90.
9 (1859) 4 De G & J 276.
10 (1848) 2 Ph 774.
11 [1958] 2 QB 146.

laid down by Knight Bruce LJ in *De Mattos v Gibson* could be used by an English court to interfere with the rights of a lender who has taken security over an asset with knowledge that the borrower is acting in breach of an existing negative pledge covenant when he gave that security.[12]

There is one other basis on which a syndicate may proceed against a subsequent lender who has taken security over assets with knowledge of the existence of a negative pledge clause: the English law tort of inducing a breach of a subsisting contract.[13] It seems clear, however, that to sustain such a cause of action mere knowledge of the subsistence of the contract is by itself insufficient; there has to be some inducement or persuasion on the part of the defendant: *Emerald Construction Co v Lowthian*.[14] Knowledge would be imputed if the existence of the contractual obligation was well known in the trade: *Merkur Island Shipping Corpn v Laughton*.[15]

Where a company incorporated in the UK is subject to a negative pledge which combines an automatic, equal or same security clause, the question arises as to whether such a clause would require registration under s 395 of the Companies Act 1985[16] as a charge over the company's assets. Gough[17] takes the view that a promise to give security in the future does not require registration as a charge;[18] whereas a clause which confers security over an asset on a future date would require registration even if it relates to future assets.[19] On this analysis it seems clear that the equal and same security clauses do not create a security interest which requires to be registered.[20] Nevertheless, an automatic security clause imposed on a UK company may be caught by the registration provisions of the Companies Act 1985. Goode, however, persuasively argues that no security interest of any kind is created by the clause and that it creates merely contractual rights. Further, except in the case of a floating charge (and perhaps a charge over book debts) a charge cannot be created in English law unless the asset to which the charge relates is identified. In an automatic security clause the asset over which the clause will have effect is unknown. Consequently, it would seem that the clause may not require registration as creating a charge over corporate assets.

In the final analysis, therefore, the negative pledge covenant seems to represent more of a hope on the part of the syndicate banks than a clearly enforceable legal obligation on the part of the borrower. Nevertheless, the importance of the negative pledge clause should not be minimised in the face of the legal difficulties of enforcement since the majority of borrowers would wish to comply with what they perceive to be their legal obligations even though, as a matter of law, remedial action in the event of breach may be weak.

---

12 See also *Swiss Bank Corpn v Lloyds Bank Ltd* [1979] Ch 548 per Browne-Wilkinson J and the Court of Appeal in [1982] 2 AC 584.
13 See *Lumley v Wagner* (1852) 1 De G.M & G 604.
14 [1966] 1 WLR 691, CA.
15 [1983] 2 AC 570.
16 S 93 of the Companies Act 1989 replaces the provisions of s 395 of the Companies Act 1985 with a new s 396. For overseas companies, see s 105 of the Companies Act 1989.
17 Company Charges p 229, Butterworths (1978) citing *Re Jackson and Basford* [1906] 2 Ch 467 at 476.
18 *Re Gregory Love & Co* [1916] 1 Ch 203; *Re Jackson and Basford Ltd* [1906] 2 Ch 467.
19 *Independent Automatic Sales Ltd v Knowles and Foster* [1962] 1 WLR 974.
20 Goode *Legal Problems of Credit and Security* pp 17–23 is of the same view.

7 Default and cross default

The default clauses in a syndicated loan agreement seek to define the various events on the occurrence of which the syndicate banks will have an unqualified right to accelerate the loan and call for repayment of loan outstandings prior to their stated maturity. It is important to remember that while it may appear to a lawyer that default is the primary legal remedy in the event of a breach by a borrower of its obligations under a syndicated loan agreement, the perception of international bankers is quite different. To the international banking community the remedy of acceleration is the ultimate sanction due to the fact that the calling of default by one syndicate would result in all other syndicates also calling default on the basis of cross default clauses (a sort of nuclear button resulting in Armageddon for the borrower). Most bankers would not immediately contemplate accelerating a loan as his first course of action on the occurrence of an event of default, and bankers are more likely to see it as an occasion to consider what remedial action should be demanded of the borrower. The legal right to accelerate provides the syndicate with a bargaining lever to demand such remedial action. It is also a potent sanction which may be threatened against a recalcitrant borrower who refuses to take the necessary remedial action. This perspective is important to appreciate in drafting the events of default clause.[1]

The events of default clause is also the lynchpin which supports the network of rights and liabilities contained in the syndicated loan agreement. All covenants, representations and warranties should be locked into the default mechanisms contained in the events of default clause so as to give the syndicate banks a right to accelerate on the occurrence of a breach of covenant or of the representations and warranties of the loan agreement.

The three principal occurrences in respect of which an event of default should occur are:

(a) failure to pay interest or a principal repayment when they fall due;
(b) non compliance with any covenant of the loan agreement;
(c) breach of any representation or warranty.

It is the ability of English law to provide syndicate banks with an unqualified right to accelerate on such an occurrence without subsequent interference by a court that has been one of the major reasons for the choice of English law as the proper law to govern such international agreements.[2]

In addition, there will be clauses which make the following occurrences an event of default: the levying of any distress or other execution on the property of the borrower (or guarantor, if there is one); the insolvency of the borrower (or the guarantor); the appointment of a receiver in respect of the assets of the borrower (or a guarantor); the passing of a resolution for the liquidation, winding-up or dissolution of the borrower (or the guarantor) or any of the subsidiaries of the borrower (or guarantor); any other event which has substantially the same effect as any of the previous occurring under the laws of any applicable jurisdiction in respect of the borrower or the guarantor or any of their respective subsidiaries. While it is necessary

---

1 See the excellent article by Richard Youard 'Default' in (1985) *Current Issues of International Financial Law.*
2 See ch 2 above.

to include these clauses, they are not of much commercial value, since by the time such an event occurs the ability of the syndicate to recover their loans by calling default is rather poor.

It is also essential that none of these events be qualified by such words as 'material' or 'substantial'. The syndicate must have an unqualified right to accelerate without the necessity to make value judgments. Such judgments would inevitably lead to disputes about the materiality of the occurrence of one of such events which in the final analysis can only be resolved by a court, often after the lapse of a substantial amount of time. It has been observed by Youard[3] that the desire of borrowers to introduce some element of materiality is sometimes accommodated by a clause on the following lines:

> 'In respect of any such breach or omission which is capable of being remedied, such action as the Agent Bank may reasonably require has not been taken within 15 days of the Agent Bank despatching notice to the borrower advising it of such default and of such required action'

or a clause which reads:

> 'in the case of a default which is capable of being remedied, such default continues unremedied for a period of more than (10)/(21)/(30) days'.

The problem with this type of approach, as Youard himself points out, is that it is open to the objection that a remedy period allows other creditors by quick action to seize the remaining assets. The result is that if the remedy period expires without the required action being taken, the lenders are left with no alternative but to accelerate, only to find that other creditors have taken all the assets.

It is also sometimes the practice to include a clause which makes it an event of default that 'an extraordinary situation shall occur which situation gives reasonable grounds to conclude that a material adverse change in the financial condition of the borrower has occurred'.[4] While the objective of such a clause is clear the circumstances in which such a clause can be activated is a matter of uncertainty. Consequently, it is of little value in conferring on the syndicate a clear and immediate right to accelerate the loan.

The cross default clause

The purpose of this clause is to give the syndicate a right to call default in the event that any other lender acquires a right under his loan agreement to accelerate that loan. A typical clause would confer a right to call default when:

> 'any indebtedness to the borrower shall not be paid when due for payment or shall be found not to have been so paid or becomes capable of being declared due

---

3 Fn 1 above, at 298.
4 See Youard, above at 305.

100 *Structure and contents of a syndicated loan agreement*

prior to its stated date of payment or if payable on demand shall not be paid when demanded'.[5]

It is fair to say that every borrowing made on the international syndicated loans markets will be linked together by such a cross default clause with the result that if the borrower is in breach of any covenant in any international syndicated loan agreement, each and every one of the borrower's syndicated loans is capable of being accelerated because the cross default clause in such agreements would be triggered. To that extent the cross default clause is perhaps the most important clause in international lending agreements.

It is important to note that it is not only when a loan or borrowings have in fact been accelerated that the cross default clause is triggered. The key words are that when any borrowings 'become capable of being declared due prior to its stated date of payment' a default is triggered. Consequently, even if on the occurrence of a breach of covenant under a particular loan agreement the lenders do not take action by way of acceleration, such a breach would nevertheless give other lenders in other syndicated loan agreements a right to call their loans on the basis of the cross default clause.[6] In practice, objection is sometimes taken to the drafting of the default clause in this broad fashion on the following basis: if an event of default occurs under a loan agreement with Syndicate B, and Syndicate B decides not to accelerate, then it is unreasonable and unfair on the borrower that Syndicate A should be entitled to accelerate its loans on the basis of a breach of a covenant in the loan agreement with Syndicate B. The answer to this objection is that the decision of Syndicate B not to accelerate may be based on the fact that they might have been a secured creditor, or they concluded, perhaps wrongly, that the borrower will get over his present financial difficulties, or that there might be so short a period left until the loan by Syndicate B matures, that he will be paid out before the borrower's financial structure finally collapses.[7]

8 Sharing clauses and relationship between syndicate banks inter se

Syndicated loan agreements are drafted on the basis that they represent a number of loans granted by each member of the syndicate of banks to the borrower which are conveniently located in one document subject to the same terms and conditions. The obligation of each member of the syndicate to the borrower is expressly stated to be several and not joint. This is further clarified by clauses which state 'the failure of a bank to carry out its obligations hereunder shall not relieve any other bank party of any of its obligations under this loan agreement'. Further it is provided 'no bank shall be responsible for the obligations of any other bank'. The result of these two clauses is that in the event that a particular bank fails to make available its portion of the loan, first, the other syndicate banks are not relieved of any of their obligations; more importantly, the other members of the syndicate are not required to make up the difference. This result

---

5 Youard, above at 300.
6 In the case of sovereign debt reschedulings, the form of the cross default clause is different due to different considerations. See the discussion in Youard, above, at 301–302.
7 See Youard, above, at 301.

would ensue even if at the outset the lead manager of the syndicate had given a firmly underwritten offer of finance to a borrower in order to obtain the mandate.[8]

The separate and independent nature of each bank's relationship with the borrower is also buttressed by another clause which provides that each bank may separately enforce its rights under the syndicated loan agreement for interest and principal. It must be remembered, however, that this clause must be read in the context of the clauses in respect of the agent bank[9] whereby the agent bank is given the power to call default on behalf of the syndicate at the agent bank's discretion. The agent bank may also be required to call default on the request of a majority of the syndicate banks.[10] These clauses, however, do not affect the right of each bank in the syndicate to enforce its rights to interest and principal where this right is expressly preserved by a clause in the syndicated loan agreement.

On the face of such clauses it would be extremely difficult to classify the syndicated loan agreement as 'a joint venture' as was done by the Supreme Court of New York in *Crédit Français International, SA v Sociedad Financiera de Comerco SA*.[11]

Sharing clauses

One instance in which the concept of independent and several lenders does not hold is the case of the so-called 'sharing clause'. The sharing clause usually requires that all payments of interest and/or principal paid by the borrower should be paid only to the agent bank and not to each individual member of the syndicate. It also requires the agent bank to distribute the payments of interest and/or principal to the members of the syndicate pro rata in accordance with each member's loan to the borrower. It also requires that if any member of the syndicate is repaid wholly or partially by the borrower in respect of his loan outstandings, such member is required to share any such receipt from the borrower with all members of the syndicate on a pro rata basis.

Problems may, however, arise with regard to the sharing clause where a syndicate member exercises a right of 'set-off' in respect of a deposit held by such member from the borrower. It may not be clear whether the bank which sets off the deposit against its loan outstandings against the borrower could refuse to share the deposit pro rata with the other members of the syndicate. It is therefore usual to provide for an express clause stating that in the event that a syndicate member sets off a deposit of the borrower against that member's loan outstandings, such syndicate member is required to share the deposit pro rata with other members of the syndicate. In some cases lead managers have been able to exclude from the sharing clause any deposits which they are capable of setting off as against the loan outstandings of a defaulting borrower as happened in the case of syndicated loans lead

---

8 Provided that the offer in the term sheet was clearly specified to be a statement of intention 'subject to contract'. See ch 3 above.
9 See ch 4 above.
10 See ch 4 above.
11 490 NYS 2d 670 (1985).

managed by Chase Manhattan to the government of Iran.[12] A more difficult question arises where a syndicate member holds a deposit of a borrower which is larger in amount then its own loan outstandings to the borrower. May such a bank set-off the whole of that deposit as against a defaulting borrower not only in respect of its loan outstandings but also all loan outstandings of the syndicate as a whole, so as to enable pro rata sharing of the deposit as between the members of the syndicate? In the absence of specific contractual provision the answer to the question is to be found in the law relating to set-off which is outside the scope of this work.[13] The more practical course of action is to include a specific clause permitting the member of a syndicate to set-off such a deposit for the benefit of all syndicate members so that reliance on the general principles of set-off would not be necessary. However, the efficacy of such a clause depends, first, on whether it is regarded as creating a charge; and secondly, in the event that the borrowing entity becomes insolvent or bankrupt immediately after the set-off, whether the law governing the bankruptcy or insolvency of the borrower will give effect to the contractually established right of set-off.

---

12 See Brown 'Sharing Strains on Euromarket Syndicates' IFLR, June 1982.
13 See Philip Wood's masterly work *English and International Set-Off* (Sweet & Maxwell, 1989) Part 1, s 5, pp 143-233.

CHAPTER 6
Sales of loan assets and securitisation: legal structures and mechanisms[1]

The subject of loan asset 'sales' by banks is not strictly speaking a technique of raising finance in the international markets.[2] It is usually an inter-bank transaction which enables a bank to transfer an asset on its balance sheet consisting of its participation in a syndicated loan. The reasons for such 'sales' discussed below do not include the objective of raising finance or capital. The subject is nevertheless covered in this work so as to provide a wider perspective of international finance. The volume of such 'sales' or transfers of loan assets has created a market which is analogous to the secondary market trading in bonds or shares. The market is largely an inter-bank market but other financial institutions are also participants.

I PURPOSES OF LOAN 'SALES'

Banks will seek to 'sell' loans for one or more of the following reasons.

The principal reason why a bank would sell a 'loan' asset is regulatory. In the aftermath of the third world debt crisis, the Basle Convergence Agreement of December 1987[3] has generated a need for the reduction of risk assets on a bank's balance sheet. Under the Basle Convergence Agreement if the amount of assets on a bank's balance sheet carries a high risk weighting, that bank would be required to maintain a greater level of capital adequacy than a bank whose asset profile was low risk. A bank which had loan assets with a high risk weighting could reduce its capital requirements by selling

---

1 For some discussions of the subject, see Carver 'The Development of the Market in Participations in Syndicated Loans and Acceptance Credits: Some Legal Pitfalls and their Solution' in *Current Issues in International Financial Law* (Malaya Law Review and Butterworths, 1985; Bray, 'Developing a Secondary Market in Loan Assets' IFLR, October 1984; Norton 'Selling Loan Assets under English Law: A Basic Guide' IFLR, May 1986; Hughes and Palache 'Loan Participations – Some English Law Considerations' IFLR, November 1984; Hughes 'Transferability of Loans and Loan Participations' (1987) JIBL. See also Cresswell, Blair, Hill and Wood, *Encyclopaedia of Banking Law*, (Butterworths) F5460.
2 To that extent it may be regarded as somewhat outside the strict parameters of this work.
3 See 'International Convergence of Capital Measurement and Capital Standards' July 1988, issued by the Committee on Banking Regulation and Supervision Practices, Bank of International Settlements publication.

off such assets to banks which did not have a concentration on their balance sheets of assets which carried a high risk weighting.

The Bank of England has sought to implement the Basle Convergence Agreement by its Notice to Institutions authorised under the Banking Act 1987 dated October 1988.[4] In its paper, 'Loan Transfers and Securitisations',[5] the Bank of England recognised that loan asset 'sales' could be used to improve the position of a bank's risk-weighted assets and consequently a bank's risk asset ratio.[6]

The second reason for such loan sales is the improvement of profitability ratios of the bank in question. One measure of a bank's profitability is the ratio of profits (ie margin less cost of funds) to assets on its balance sheet. Where a bank has a large amount of loan assets which are generating low revenues or none at all (eg due to the imposition of a moratorium by a debtor country) such assets may be sold to a purchaser in order to improve profitability ratios.

Profitability ratios may also be improved where a bank sells off a revenue-generating loan asset to a buyer but retains a right to receive a portion of the interest income. The bank's profits to assets ratio is thus improved since it continues to receive revenues on an asset which is no longer on its balance sheet.

A third reason is that a bank may be able to reduce its exposure to default by borrowers in a particular country, region, industry or currency by 'selling' a certain portion of loans in that country, region, industry or currency. Central banks of various countries will usually have either formal or informal guidelines as to the percentage of loans on a bank's balance sheet which may be concentrated in one industrial, geographical or currency sector. Compliance with such guidelines would also generate a need to sell off a certain amount of loans.

II TYPES OF ASSET SALES

Banks 'sell' three types of rights and obligations which are perceived by the banking community as assets:

1 Loan 'sales'

These involve the 'sale' of an existing loan in respect of which all funds due under the loan have been disbursed to the borrower. In financial terms the 'sale' relates to the bank's right to repayment of interest and principal.

2 'Sales' of a loan facility

In the case of a revolving facility the bank may seek to sell not only its right to interest and principal on funds already disbursed to a borrower but also its obligations to lend funds in the future.[7]

---

4 BSD/1988/3.
5 Which took the form of a Notice to Institutions authorised under the Banking Act 1987 dated February 1989 (BSD/1989/1).
6 See the discussion at p 115 below.
7 On revolving facilities see pp 43, 78 above.

Even in the case of a non-revolving loan, a bank may seek to sell its rights to interest and principal as well as its obligation to lend where, for instance, it has disbursed only part of the funds under a loan agreement.

A bank may also seek to 'sell' its participation in a committed loan facility which has not been utilised. In effect the bank is 'selling' its obligation to lend.

3 'Risk participations'

Here the bank will 'sell' a part of its liability under a documentary letter of credit used in the finance of trade or 'sell' part of its liability under a performance bond issued usually in the context of construction contracts.[8] The discussion which follows below does not include this category, since performance bonds and letters of credit are aspects of traditional trade finance, a subject which is outside the scope of this work.

III TECHNIQUES OF 'SELLING' BANK ASSETS

In the case of a fully drawndown loan the asset which is 'sold' by a bank is the right to interest and principal on the loan. In English law this right constitutes a chose in action.[9] Such a chose in action is a form of intangible property which cannot be 'sold' in the same way that chattels and goods can be sold under English law. The Sale of Goods Act 1979 thus excludes 'money' and choses in action from its definition of 'goods' which are subject to the provisions of that Act.[10]

Under English law there are three traditional[11] methods which have been used in practice to 'sell' banking 'assets'. They are:

(a) assignment;
(b) novation;
(c) sub-participation.[12]

These traditional methods have also been the basis for the development of more complex techniques such as Transferable Loan Certificates ('TLCs'), Transferable Participation Certificates ('TPCs') and Transferable

---

8 The bank's risk under a performance bond materialises if the party on whose behalf the performance bond is issued fails to place the bank in funds after the performance bond is called on by the beneficiary of the bond. Performance bonds are in essence bank guarantees payable on first demand without proof of conditions. See *Edward Owen Engineering Ltd v Barclays Bank International Ltd* [1978] 1 All ER 976, CA.
9 *Torkington v Magee* [1902] 2 KB 427; revsd [1903] 1 KB 644, CA.
10 See s 61 of the Sale of Goods Act 1979. See, however, art 1689 ff of the French Civil Code which deals with assignment of debts in the law of sales.
11 See Bray 'Developing a Secondary Market in Loan Assets' IFLR, October 1984.
12 Wood *Law and Practice of International Finance* (Clark Boardman edn) s 11.04 lists eight methods which may be used under English law to transfer loan assets.

Loan Instruments ('TLIs') designed to effect the transfer of banking assets in a more flexible and effective manner.[13]

In the discussion which follows, the bank transferring a banking asset is referred to as a 'selling bank' and the bank purchasing the asset is referred to as the 'buying bank' in conformity with the terminology in the banking markets.

IV THE TRADITIONAL METHODS

In practice, assignment and sub-participation are the favoured techniques of the traditional methods used for the transfer of loan assets. Novation, although perhaps the most legally effective method, creates certain practical difficulties and is not generally used.

1 Assignment

In the case of an assignment, the selling bank transfers the loan to the buying bank by assigning its rights against the borrower to the buying bank. Under English law, the buying bank would then be able to recover interest and principal from the borrower since contractual rights to such interest and principal would have been transferred by the assignment. Such an assignment may either be effected under the provisions of s 136(1) of the Law of Property Act 1925 (referred to as a 'legal assignment') or in equity (referred to as an 'equitable assignment'). The basic difference is that equitable assignment is not subject to the preconditions of a legal assignment for its efficacy and validity. However, subject to the discussion below, an equitable assignment is generally as effective as a legal assignment in English law.[14]

Section 136(1) of the Law of Property Act 1925 provides as follows:

> '136(1) Any absolute assignment by writing under the hand of the assignor (not purporting to be by way of charge only) of any debt or other legal thing in action, of which express notice in writing has been given to the debtor, trustee or other person from whom the assignor would have been entitled to claim such debt or thing in action, is effectual in law (subject to equities having priority over the right of the assignee) to pass and transfer from the date of such notice –
> (a) the legal right to such debt or thing in action;
> (b) all legal and other remedies for the same; and
> (c) the power to give a good discharge for the same without the concurrence of the assignor.'

Before an assignment is effective under s 136(1) it is necessary that:

---

13 See Bray, fn 11 above, who suggests that these techniques were developed in the mid 1980s.
14 See *Chitty on Contracts* (26th edn) para 1393.

(a) the assignment be in writing under the hand of the assignor;[15]
(b) the assignment is 'absolute'; assignment of part of a debt does not fall within s 136(1): *Forster v Baker*;[16] and
(c) express notice in writing has been given to the debtor.[17]

While the first requirement above does not create difficulties, the requirements in (b) and (c) above render a legal assignment unattractive in practice. A selling bank may not wish the borrower to know that the right to interest and principal has been assigned to another bank. Consequently, it may require of the assignee that notice of assignment is not given to the borrower. Secondly, a bank may not wish to assign the entirety of the debt owed by the borrower; it may wish to transfer only a part of the debt owed. For instance where a loan is repayable in instalments a lender may wish to transfer its rights to some repayment instalments but not others.

Consequently, legal assignment cannot be used as the mechanism of transfer where a 'no notice' transfer (or 'silent assignment') of debt is desired or only part of a debt is sought to be assigned. An equitable assignment, on the other hand, is effective without notice in writing or otherwise being given to the debtor.[18] It may also be possible to transfer a part of a debt by an equitable assignment.[19] Notice to the debtor although unnecessary for the purpose of the validity of the assignment is nevertheless important because of the rule in *Dearle v Hall*.[20] This provides that where a creditor has made a number of assignments of the same debt, priority of assignments is determined not by priority in time of each assignment but by the priority in time of notice, ie priority being given to assignees who have given prior notice to the debtor.

2 Novation

As regards a novation, English law permits substitution of creditors by novation of contractual rights and obligations with the consent of all parties to a contract. In a syndicated loan it is perfectly possible in theory to substitute one syndicate bank with another as creditor of the borrower through a novation. The practical difficulty is that this would require the concurrence not only of the borrower but of all the banks to the syndicated loan agreement, since the loan agreement creates rights and obligations not only between the borrower and each syndicate bank but also as between banks inter se (for instance, in the case of the pro rata sharing clause).[1] For this reason novation has been used only rarely in practice as a method for the transfer of loan assets. However, as will be discussed below, more complex forms of loan sales such as TLCs and TPCs have been based on the concept of novation.

---

15 *Re Westerton* [1919] 2 Ch 104.
16 [1910] 2 KB 636; *Re Steel Wing Co Ltd* [1921] 1 Ch 349.
17 *Van Lynn Developments Ltd v Pelias Construction Co Ltd* [1969] 1 QB 607, CA.
18 *Gorringe v Irwell India Rubber and Gutta Percha Works* (1886) 34 Ch D. 128, CA; *Re Westerton* [1919] 2 Ch 104.
19 See the discussion in *Chitty on Contracts* (26th edn, 1989) p 869, para 1397.
20 (1823) 3 Russ 1 and *Chitty on Contracts* para 1425.
1 On pro rata sharing clauses see p 101.

3 Sub-participation

The third traditional method of transfer of loan assets used in practice is referred to as sub-participation although it does not in law constitute a transfer of the rights and obligations of the original loan agreement. A syndicate member which wishes to sell its loan asset will simply enter into a second loan agreement with the buying bank whereby the buying bank is required to transfer a deposit to the selling bank in an amount equivalent to the selling bank's participation in the primary loan. The buying bank agrees with the selling bank to maintain the deposit for the period of the primary syndicated loan. It further agrees that the right to repayment of the deposit and the interest payable in respect thereof is wholly conditional upon the extent of payment of interest and principal by the borrower to the selling bank. If the borrower defaults wholly or partially in the payment of interest or principal the buying bank would not receive payment to the extent of such default. The risk of non-payment is thus transferred from the selling bank to the buying bank as well as the entitlement to interest and principal.

It will be seen that as a matter of legal analysis, a wholly independent loan (or deposit) agreement is entered into between the selling bank and buying bank, which is legally distinct from the original loan agreement between the borrower and the selling bank. The legal structure is that of a back-to-back loan which provides the selling bank with a non-recourse funding arrangement and looks as follows:

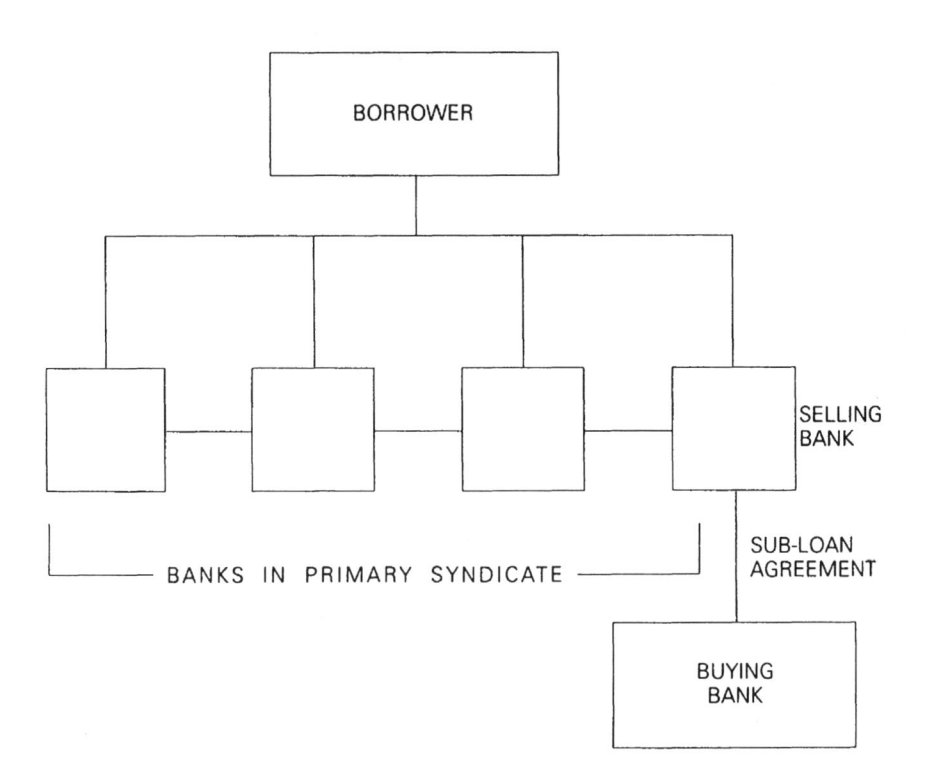

4 Comparison of assignment and sub-participation methods

A comparison between the assignment mechanism and the sub-participation structure is instructive.

i *Risk of default*

In the case of an assignment the buying bank (assignee) acquires direct contractual rights of action against the borrower by virtue of the assignment, and consequently may sue the borrower for interest and principal.[2]

In the case of a sub-participation the buying bank is not party to a contract with the borrower and may not sue the borrower for interest and principal. This right remains in the hands of the selling bank. The buying bank's contractual rights to interest and principal are against the selling bank although the right to recovery is limited to the extent that the selling bank is paid by the borrower.

In consequence of the above, the buying bank in a sub-participation not only takes the risk of default by the borrower but also that of default by the selling bank. In the case of an assignment the assignee buying bank takes only the risk of default by the borrower.

ii *'Selling' the obligation to lend*

In an assignment only the rights of the selling bank to interest and principal can be transferred to the buying bank. Any obligations of the selling bank remain with the selling bank. This follows from the general rule recognised in *Tolhurst v Associated Portland Cement Manufacturers (1900) Ltd*[3] where Collins MR, said that while contractual rights may be assigned, contractual obligations cannot be assigned under English law.

This means that assignment cannot be used where the selling bank wishes to transfer a banking 'asset' in the form of the obligation to lend under a syndicated loan agreement. Equally, where a loan has been partially drawn down by the borrower, the obligation to lend the remaining amount on the loan facility cannot be assigned, although the right to interest and principal on that part of the loan which has been disbursed may be assigned. Further, in the case of a 'revolving'[4] syndicated loan, where the borrower has a right to borrow, repay and reborrow, a selling bank cannot assign its obligations to lend funds in the future. However, in such a case, it is possible to effect a transfer by way of an assignment of future rights to interest and principal, if and when they arise, although the obligation to lend in the future when so required by the borrower remains with the

---

2 A statutory assignee can sue the debtor without joining the assignor as a party to the action (*Torkington v Magee* [1902] 2 KB 427) but an equitable assignee must join the assignor as party to an action (*William Brandts Sons & Co v Dunlop Rubber Co Ltd* [1905] AC 454, HL).
3 [1902] 2 KB 660, 668 CA. See also Tito v Waddell (No 2) [1977] Ch 106, 290.
4 See pp 43, 78 above on multicurrency loans, where again a 'revolving' feature may be provided.

assignor.[5] A mere expectancy or spes cannot be assigned although it can be the subject of an agreement to assign for valuable consideration.[6]

These problems do not arise where the sub-loan method is used. The buying bank can be obliged to provide deposits as and when required by the selling bank. Consequently, as a matter of economic reality the obligation to lend can be transferred to the buying bank.

In addition to the fact that the obligations of the assignor cannot be assigned, an assignment may not be capable of transferring the benefit of certain clauses in a syndicated loan agreement, due to the rule that an assignment may not increase the burden of the obligations of a debtor.[7] Thus the benefit of the increased costs clause[8] which requires the borrower to make increased payments in the event that a lender is subject to increased funding costs may not be capable of a valid assignment.[9]

In the case of a sub-participation, since a buying bank is not a party to the original syndicated loan agreement, only the selling bank and not the buying bank would have the benefit of such a clause vis-à-vis the borrower. In the event of a buying bank incurring an increase in the costs of funding its deposit to the selling bank, its right to terminate funding will turn entirely on the terms of the sub-participation agreement and will only be exercisable against the selling bank.

iii *Notice to borrower*

In a sub-participation there is no legal need for the buying bank to give notice to the borrower as to the existence of the sub-participation. In the case of an equitable assignment, notice of the assignment to the borrower is unnecessary for purposes of validity; however, due to the rule in *Dearle v Hall*[10] an assignee who fails to give notice runs the risk of losing priority in respect of the debt if a later assignee of the same debt gives prior notice of assignment to the debtor.

In the case of legal assignment notice of assignment to the borrower is a necessary precondition to its legal validity. In the case of an equitable assignment a selling bank which seeks to prevent the borrower from acquiring knowledge of the assignment will need to prohibit the assignee (buying bank) from giving such notice to the borrower by including appropriate contractual clauses in the assignment.

Where no notice of the assignment has been given to the borrower, payment of interest and principal to the selling bank discharges the borrower

---

5   See on assignments of future interests: *Hughes v Pump House Hotel Co* [1902] 2 KB 190, CA where it was held that sums payable to a builder under a building contract could be assigned even though it was not certain whether the builder would perform. See also *Walker v Bradford Old Bank Ltd* (1884) 12 QBD 511.
6   See *Glegg v Bromley* [1912] 3 KB 474, CA and *Tailby v Official Receiver* (1888) 13 App Cas 523, CA.
7   *Durham Bros v Robertson* [1898] 1 QB 765 at 775, CA.
8   See p 81 above.
9   See also the views of Bray in IFLR, October 1984.
10 See footnote 20 p 107.

from his obligations and he is no longer liable to the assignee in respect of such payments.[11]

In a sub-participation the borrower cannot pay the buying bank directly due to the absence of contractual privity, unless of course the selling bank has consented.

iv *Limitations on assignee's rights*

In an assignment, the assignee only acquires such rights as the assignor possesses at the time of the assignment. Consequently, if the loan agreement is void, illegal or unenforceable against the borrower, the assignee cannot sue the borrower on the basis of the assignment.[12]

It may be that an action may lie against the assignor (or selling bank) either on the basis of an implied term that enforceable rights are being transferred or on the basis of negligence. However, in practice clauses will be inserted which displace any implied term or representation as to the validity, legality and enforceability of the underlying loan.

v *Confidentiality*

Both an assignment and a sub-participation raise difficulties with regard to the rule of confidentiality under English law laid down in *Tournier v National Provincial and Union Bank of England*.[13] The Court of Appeal in that case clearly held that a bank may not reveal information obtained from a client to any third party without the client's consent. A wide range of information is covered by the *Tournier* ruling. Any information concerning the business affairs of the client, including information which came into the bank's possession prior to the establishment of the client relationship, would be within the ambit of the *Tournier* ruling. If information is disclosed by a selling bank in breach of the *Tournier* rule, and a borrower suffers loss in consequence, he will be able to recover damages for such loss.[14] In practice, when a traditional assignment is used to transfer a loan asset, a specific clause permits disclosure of information to a potential assignee of the benefit of the agreement.[15] However, such a clause permitting disclosure to an assignee would not cover disclosure to a sub-participant.

It is, however, submitted that it is questionable whether the rule in *Tournier* should be applied without qualification to transactions in the international markets where the borrowers are large transnational corporations, sovereign states and state corporations, so as to inhibit the growth of an international loan sales market.[15A]

---

11 *Stocks v Dobson* (1853) 4 De GM & G11; where notice of assignment has been given, payment to the assignor does not discharge the debtor and he remains liable to the assignee: *Brice v Bannister* (1878) 3 QBD 569, CA.
12 See Cresswell, Blair, Hill and Wood *Encyclopaedia of Banking Law* at F5480.
13 [1924] 1 KB 461.
14 See, for the type of factual situation in which a borrower may suffer loss, Carver 'The Development of the Market in Participation in Syndicated Loans and Acceptance Credits: Some Legal Pitfalls and their Solution' in *Current Issues in International Financial Law* (Malaya Law Review and Butterworths, 1985).
15 See section vii below for a sample clause.
15A See also Bank of Tokyo v Karoon [1987] AC 45, and XAG v An American Bank [1983] 2 All ER 464.

112 *Sales of loan assets and securitisation: legal structures and mechanisms*

vi   *Bar on assignment*

An assignment may not be practicable if the syndicated loan agreement contains a prohibition against assignment of contractual rights since in such a case the assignment is invalid as against the borrower.[16]

vii   *Benefit of agreement clauses*

Traditional assignment was also severely inhibited by the 'benefit of agreement' clauses found in most syndicated loan agreements. The following is an example provided by Hughes:[17]

> '*Benefit of Agreement*
>
> (A)   This Agreement shall be binding upon and inure to the benefit of each party hereto and its successors and assigns.
>
> (B)   The borrower may not assign or transfer all or any of its rights, benefits and obligations hereunder.
>
> (C)   Any Bank may at any time with the prior written consent of the borrower (which consent shall not be required in the case of an assignment to (i) a company which is a subsidiary of such Bank or (ii) a company of which such Bank is a subsidiary or any other subsidiary of that company and shall not be unreasonably withheld in any other case) assign to any one or more banks or other lending institutions all or any part of such Bank's rights and benefits hereunder and in that event the assignee shall have the same rights against the borrower as it would have had if it had been a party hereto.
>
> (D)   Unless and until an assignee has agreed with the Agent, the Managers and the Banks that it shall be under the same obligations towards each of them as it would have been under if it had been a party hereto, neither the Agent, the Managers nor the Banks shall be obliged to recognise such assignee as having the rights against them which it would have had if it had been a party hereto.
>
> (E)   Any Bank may disclose to a potential assignee or to any person who may otherwise enter into contractual relations with such Bank in relation to this Agreement such information about the borrower as such Bank shall consider appropriate.'

In effect an assignment of the benefit of the loan required the written consent of the borrower as well as of the agent bank and other syndicate banks.

---

16   *United Dominions (Commercial) Trust Ltd v Parkway Motors Ltd* [1955] 1 WLR 719. It has been stated that the assignment may not be valid even as between assignor and assignee in some cases: *Spellman v Spellman* [1961] 1 WLR 921, CA. See also Goode (1979) 42 MLR 553 and the views of the editors of *Chitty on Contracts* (26th edn) para 1413 where they suggest that a distinction needs to be drawn between the proprietary and contractual aspects of assignment. They suggest that a prohibition against assignment in an agreement would prevent the debtor under that agreement from being liable to an assignee whereas between assignor and assignee the assignee would have a claim in damages against the assignor.

17   'Transferability of Loans and Loan Participations' [1987] 1 JIBL 5.

Sub-participation however was not so inhibited by clauses in the primary loan agreement.

viii *Rescheduling*

In the event of a rescheduling or renegotiations of the original syndicated loan agreement the position of the buying bank varies depending on whether the buying bank is an assignee or party to a sub-participation agreement.[18] A buying bank which is a party to a sub-participation agreement would be entirely dependent on the terms and conditions of the sub-participation agreement as regards its rights in the event that the primary syndicated loan is renegotiated or rescheduled. Ordinarily, in the absence of express clauses, it would have no right to be consulted with regard to the calling of default or grant of a waiver or the renegotiation of terms in respect of the original syndicated loan.

In the event of rescheduling of the syndicated loan it may have no right to be repaid on the date of the original maturity of the original syndicated loan. In the absence of express clauses, the buying bank's right to repayment in the event of rescheduling will turn on the question whether the selling bank has been repaid by the borrower (as observed earlier, the buying bank's right to repayment from the selling bank is entirely dependent, under the sub-participation agreement, on the extent to which – if any – the selling bank is repaid).[19]

Whether a syndicate bank has been repaid for these purposes will depend on the legal nature of the rescheduling. Where the rescheduling takes the form of a waiver of the maturity date of an existing loan by an extension of time to repay, there is no 'repayment' of outstanding debt. Consequently, in such a case a buying bank will not acquire a right to be repaid. Similarly, where the rescheduling – as in the case of Romania in 1982[20] – takes the form of a 'release' of the borrower from its existing repayment obligations in consideration of his accepting new terms and conditions under a fresh agreement, there is no 'repayment' of debt. In a number of such reschedulings various syndicates of banks who were creditors of a single borrower released the borrower from its debt repayment obligation in consideration of a consolidation and rescheduling of all outstanding debt in one agreement. Banks which had bought loans from such syndicate banks under sub-participation agreements in such cases would not have been able to demand repayment of their deposit/loan since no repayment had occurred.

However, if as is commonly the case[1] a rescheduling is effected by the repayment of a borrower's debts owed to several syndicates of banks by a new syndicate of banks, the position is different. A bank which was a party to a sub-participation agreement with a member of one of the syndicates which had been repaid could validly claim that a repayment of the borrower's debt had occurred and, consequently, that under the sub-participation agree-

---

18 See the discussion in Carver, fn 14 above, at 314–318.
19 See the dispute in *Michigan National Bank of Detroit v Citibank NA*, in 1983, concerning the syndication to Petroleos Mexicanoscited which is cited by Bucheit *The State of the Loan Sub-Participation* p 160.
20 See Carver, fn 14 above, at 317.
1 See Carver, fn 14 above, at 316.

ment the buying bank was entitled to be repaid.[2] In current practice sub-participation agreements will usually contain express clauses dealing with the selling bank's right to reschedule defaults and renegotiate terms in respect of the primary syndicated loan agreement without the need for formal consent of or prior consultation with the buying bank.

Where the assignment method had been used the assignee's right to be consulted in respect of waiver, default and renegotiation by virtue of the assignment would turn on the clauses in the syndicated loan agreement dealing with the benefits of the agreement. The usual clause referred to above[3] would enable syndicate banks to refuse to recognise an assignee or consult with it on waiver, default and renegotiation.

ix Maturity stripping

'Maturity stripping' may not be possible in the case of an assignment. Maturity stripping occurs where a loan is repayable in several instalments and a syndicate bank seeks to sell its right to each instalment separately as an independent asset. While it seems possible to transfer rights to part of a debt under an equitable assignment, the Court in *Durham Bros v Robertson*[4] said that transfers of parts of a debt could not be effected if it would result in an increase of the burden on the debtor by multiplying the causes of action against him. No such difficulty would arise if sub-participations are used so as to transfer repayment instalments to several transferees.

x Set-off

The position with regard to set-off is also different depending on which method of transfer has been used. While set-off is a complex subject outside the scope of this work, a few basic points may be made.[5]

Where the transfer is effected by way of a sub-participation, the selling bank may set off a deposit of the borrower held by it; the buying bank may not set off a borrower's deposit. This follows from the fact that the debt is owed by the borrower to the selling bank and not to the buying bank; there is no contractual privity between the borrower and the buying bank. In the case of an assignment, a buying bank as assignee may set off a deposit of the borrower held by it as against the assigned debt once notice has been given; but an assignor may not exercise the right of set-off, since payment is owed only to the assignee.[6]

Where no notice has been given the position is by no means clear. Since a debtor may be discharged from his obligation by payment to an assignor where the debtor has received no notice of an assignment,[7] it seems to follow that until notice of assignment is given an assignee may not set off a deposit of the borrower against the assigned debt.

---

2 See the discussion in Carver, fn 14, above.
3 See p 112.
4 [1898] 1 QB 765, CA.
5 See, for a comprehensive treatment, Wood *English and International Set-Off* (Sweet and Maxwell, 1989).
6 *Brice v Bannister* (1878) 3 QBD 569, CA.
7 *Stocks v Dobson* (1853) 4 De GM & G11.

V SUPERVISORY TREATMENT

For the purposes of giving effect to the provisions of the Basle Convergence Agreement, the Bank of England has stated in its Notice of February 1989, *Loan Transfers and Securitisation*[8] that, for purposes of calculating risk asset ratios of banks, the following guidelines will apply:

(a) A loan which is transferred by novation will be excluded from the seller's risk asset ratio and included in that of the buyer's. This is because a transfer effected by novation will be regarded as a 'clean transfer' except in the case of packaging loans and selling them as a pool.

(b) A transfer by way of an assignment with notice to the borrower is also regarded as a clean transfer unless the assignor has retained rights of set-off by contract.

(c) A transfer by way of a 'no notice' or silent assignment will also be treated as a 'clean transfer' by the Bank of England with the consequence that the loan will be included in the calculation of the assignee's risk asset ratio and not the assignor's. However, the Bank of England may disregard a 'no notice' assignment if the volume of loans subject to such 'no notice' assignments is regarded as being substantial.

(d) The Bank of England has also stated that in the case of transfers by loan sub-participations the Bank will recognise the transfer of the credit risk by excluding the amount transferred from the selling bank's risk asset ratio and including it in the sub-participant's risk asset ratio as an economic claim against the the original borrower.

(e) Where a bank transfers undrawn commitments to lend, such commitment will be excluded from the selling bank's risk asset ratio in all cases when the transfer is by way of novation. A transfer by way of a 'no notice' assignment or by way of a sub-participation will not result in the exclusion of the commitment from the selling bank's risk asset ratio.

A number of conditions must be satisfied before the Bank of England gives effect to this policy. These are set out in the Notice referred to above as follows:[9]

'(i) The transfer does not contravene the terms and conditions of the underlying loan agreement and all the necessary consents have been obtained;

(ii) the seller has no residual beneficial interest in the principal amount of the loan (or that part which has been transferred) and the buyer has no formal recourse to the seller for losses;

(iii) the seller has no obligation to repurchase the loan, or any part of it, at any time (although he may retain an option to do so provided the loan remains fully-performing);

(iv) the seller can demonstrate, to the satisfaction of the Bank, that it has given notice to the buyer that it is under no obligation to repurchase the loan nor support any losses suffered by the buyer and that the buyer has acknowledged the absence of obligation;

---

8 See Notice to Institutions authorised under the Banking Act 1987 BSD/1989/1.
9 Different conditions apply where there is pooling. See the Bank of England's Notice BSD/1989/1.

(v) the documented terms of the transfer are such that, if the loan is rescheduled or renegotiated, the buyer and not the seller would be subject to the rescheduled or renegotiated terms;

(vi) where payments are routed through the seller, he is under no obligation to remit funds to the buyer unless and until they are received from the borrower. Payments voluntarily made by the seller to the buyer in anticipation of payments from the borrower must be made on terms under which they can be recovered from the buyer if the borrower fails to perform.'

The requirement that the seller has no obligation to repurchase the loan in (iii) and (iv) above does not apply to sub-participations. The requirement in (iii) above applies except where it arises from warranties given in respect of the loan at the time of its transfer, provided that these are not in respect of the future creditworthiness of the borrower.

VI NEW METHODS OF TRANSFER: TLCs AND TLIs

Due to the difficulties of using traditional assignment or novation, which were discussed above, new techniques were developed in the mid 1980s to transfer loan assets.[10]

1 The TLC

The first of these was the Transferable Loan Certificate ('TLC'). The TLC enabled a novation to be effected between a buying bank or transferee of a loan participation and all parties to the original syndicated loan agreement. The TLC is a document issued by the agent bank[11] on behalf of the borrower and the syndicated banks, which contains an offer by the borrower, the agent and other syndicate banks to any transferee of the TLC that the transferee will be accepted by all parties to the syndicated loan as a party to the syndicated loan agreement in substitution for the transferor of the TLC. The TLC would contain a statement on its face which states:

'Delivery of this Certificate by the Holder to the Transferee constitutes an irrevocable offer by the borrower, the Holder, the agents and the other Banks to accept the Transferee as a bank party to the agreement with a participation of the amount and type for which this certificate is issued.'

Provision is made for the issue of such TLCs in the primary syndicated loan agreement.

The offer contained in the TLC may be accepted by the method stated on the face of the TLC, namely by delivery of the TLC by the transferee to the agent bank duly completed both by the transferor (referred to as the 'Holder' on the face of the TLC) and the transferee together with a registration fee.

---

10 See Hughes 'Transferability of Loans and Loan Participations' (1987) JIBL and Bray in IFLR, October 1984.
11 See on agent bank ch 4 above.

Once the offer is accepted a novation of the syndicated loan agreement by substitution of parties is thus effected, without need, at the time of the loan sale, of obtaining consent of all participants; consent to the loan sale is in effect conferred by all parties at the outset in the syndicated loan agreement if the mechanics specified in the TLC are complied with.

The legal basis of the mechanics of TLCs is that under English law it is perfectly possible to make an offer to the public at large – a general offer – which may be accepted by any person who performs the act specified in the offer as constituting acceptance. This rule was laid down in the celebrated case of *Carlill v Carbolic Smoke Ball Co*,[12] familiar to all first year students of English contract law.

2 Issue and transfer mechanics

The framework for the issue of, and the nature and effect of, TLCs is specified in the original syndicated loan agreement as follows.

First, all parties need to give their irrevocable authority for the issue of such TLCs containing a general offer to novate the syndicated loan by completion and delivery of the TLC by a transferee.

The agent bank[13] will be required to issue a series of TLCs to each participant bank in the original syndicated loan. Since syndicated loans are in practice usually repaid in instalments the series will consist of one TLC for each repayment date in respect of the loan. Each TLC will therefore be expressed to relate to a specific principal amount maturing on a specified repayment date. Where the loan has been drawdown in different currencies the TLC will also specify the currency of maturity.

Sometimes provision is made which enables a syndicate bank to request the issue of TLCs in amounts which are subdivisions of the amounts due to that bank on maturity.

Each TLC is signed by the borrower and agent bank on behalf of all the syndicate banks though in fact a facsimile signature is used.

A bank wishing to transfer its participation in the syndicated loan is required to enter the name of the transferee (buying bank) and the date on which the transfer is effective, sign the TLC and deliver it to the transferee. The transferee is required to fill in the details about itself and deliver it to the agent bank. The agent bank in receipt of the duly completed TLC will obtain fax confirmation of the transfer from both transferor and transferee, endorse the TLC and cancel it.

The agent bank will maintain a register on which all such transfers of TLCs, including the name and other relevant details of transferees, are maintained.

The details of the transfer are then entered on the transfer register maintained by the agent, and subsequently notified to the borrower, the transferor and transferee. The agent bank will then despatch a TLC to the transferee to enable the transferee, if it so wishes, to transfer his loan.

The delivery of the duly completed TLC followed by registration is expressly stated to result in the transferor being substituted in place of the

---

12 [1892] 2 QB 484, affd [1893] 1 QB 256, CA.
13 See ch 4 above.

transferee in respect of all rights and obligations arising under the original syndicated loan agreement.

Protective clauses are included in the syndicated loan agreement for the benefit of the original parties to that agreement stating that none of the syndicate banks, including the agent bank, is responsible for:

(a) the legality, validity, enforceability and adequacy of the syndicated loan agreement;
(b) the creditworthiness of the borrower, or its financial or economic condition;
(c) the due performance by the borrower of its obligations; and
(d) the accuracy or completeness of any information supplied to the transferee by the transferor.

The borrower also requires protection in respect of payments of interest and principal to a transferee whose name appears in the register. Consequently, provision is usually made that payment of interest or principal by the borrower to any person whose name appears on the register of participants and transferees constitutes a discharge of its obligations.

In the event of repayment of an instalment by the borrower on a repayment date in accordance with the repayment schedule in the syndicated loan agreement, each syndicate bank is under a duty to surrender to the agent bank such TLCs as relate to that repayment. In the event of repayment of all loan outstandings all outstanding TLCs are declared void; and in the event that there is partial prepayment such TLCs as relate to the prepayment are declared void. In each case syndicate banks come under an obligation to surrender such TLCs to the agent bank.

Difficult questions are likely to arise if a TLC is transferred for value to a bona fide transferee after a prepayment has been made by the borrower to the transferor which is attributable to the repayment date and amount to which that TLC relates. It would seem that the provision in the loan agreement declaring the TLC 'void' may not be effective as against the transferee without notice. The borrower and syndicate banks which have clothed the transferor with ostensible authority to make the offer may not be able to rely on the provisions of the syndicated loan agreement against a third party without notice.[14] If the original parties to the syndicated loan agreement refuse to recognise a transferee in such a case as a substituted party, the syndicate banks and the borrower may be liable in damages for a breach of warranty of authority. This potential liability would be a real exposure in practice where the transferee (buying bank) is unable to recover the amount transferred to the transferor (selling bank).

There is one limitation imposed in practice as to who may accept the general offer contained in the TLC. The offer is usually restricted to institutions whose ordinary business consists of making Eurocurrency loans or participating in such loans. This restriction is usually contained in the syndicated loan agreement. The TLC requires any transferee who wishes to be registered to represent and warrant that it is such an institution. If an entity which is not within that definition obtains registration, it would be open to the borrower or any other party to obtain rescission of the novation

---

14 On ostensible authority, see ch 4 above.

on the ground of misrepresentation.[15] It may also be the case that the novation is void ab initio on a different ground: the party accepting the offer was not a person to whom the offer was made.[16]

3 The TLI

There are two disadvantages in adopting novation as the method of transfer of a loan through the mechanism of the TLC. First, where exchange control permission for the loan is granted to a borrower by monetary authorities in its country of incorporation, such permission may lapse where the loan agreement is novated. Under English law novation would have resulted in the termination of the existing loan agreement in respect of which exchange control permission was conferred.

Secondly, where a guarantee or other security is given in respect of the original loan the termination of the agreement would result in the release of the guarantor and any other security.[17]

These difficulties were sought to be overcome by an instrument termed a Transferable Loan Instrument ('TLI'). In essence, the TLI is a debt instrument or debenture as understood in English law[18] which acknowledges the indebtedness of the issuer of the TLI to the 'registered holder', and contains an unconditional promise by the borrower (ie the borrower in the original syndicated loan agreement) to pay a sum specified on the face of the TLI to any 'registered holder' thereof on surrender of the TLI. The sum specified represents a repayment instalment due to a syndicate participant under the original syndicated loan agreement.

The TLI enables a lender which is a participant in a syndicated loan to transfer its participation in the syndicated loan agreement to a transferee by transferring the TLI without the necessity to novate an existing syndicated loan.

Its nature as a debenture is stated on its face in language similar to:

> 'For value received [the borrower] hereby unconditionally promises to pay the registered holder for the time being of this Transferable Loan Instrument against surrender of this instrument on .... or on such earlier date as the principal sum mentioned herein may become repayable in accordance with the term and conditions endorsed on this instrument, the sum of US Dollars ....
> Interest is payable on such principal sum subject to and in accordance with the terms and conditions endorsed on this instrument.'

The instrument is signed in facsimile by the borrower (the issuer of the TLI) and by a specially appointed registrar.

---

15 See *Chitty on Contracts* (26th edn, 1989) para 458 and *Johnson v Agnew* [1980] AC 367, HL.
16 See *Boulton v Jones* (1857) 2 H & N 564; *Cundy v Lindsay* (1878) 3 App Cas 459, HL; *Chitty on Contracts* para 356.
17 See, on the effect of novation, *Chitty on Contracts* paras 1436 and 1598.
18 See p 125 below for a discussion as to the meaning of debenture.

4 Issue and transfer mechanics

A TLI is not automatically issued like a TLC to each bank in a syndicate. Typically, a specific request must be made for the issue of a TLI by a syndicate participant in accordance with the terms of the syndicated loan agreement. The issue is made by a specially appointed registrar who must authenticate, date, and release the instrument. In the absence of such authentication the instrument is stated ex facie not to be valid. The registrar is authorised by the borrower to perform this function on its behalf. The TLI may only be required to be issued in respect of the whole of a repayment instalment which is due to a syndicate bank in accordance with the repayment terms of the original syndicated loan agreement.

Once a TLI is issued to a syndicate bank the effect of such an issue is that the syndicate bank has no right thereafter to receive interest or principal under the terms of the original syndicated loan agreement for the repayment instalment(s) represented by the TLI. Such rights are converted or transformed into the TLI. The borrower's obligation thereafter in respect of such repayment instalment is to comply with the obligations as expressed in the TLI.

The registrar is required by the loan agreement to keep a register of TLIs issued including the serial number of each TLI and the name and other details of the bank to which it is issued.

The bank to which the TLI is issued (called the 'holder')[19] may then transfer the TLI to a bank which 'buys' the holder's rights under the TLI.

The transfer of the TLI is, usually, not effective under its terms unless the transfer is registered with the specially appointed registrar. Indeed, as observed earlier, the terms enfaced on the TLI expressly state that the borrower's promise to pay the sum specified with interest is made only to the registered holder. Registration is effected through the means of another document issued at the same time as a TLI, and sometimes confusingly referred to as a Transferable Loan Certificate. This certificate is usually no more than a registration form. It is issued by the registrar along with the TLI to the bank which requests the issue of the TLI. The TLI will not be registered in the name of the transferee until the certificate is completed and signed by the transferor and transferee of the TLI and delivered to the registrar. Once registered the transferee obtains all rights and interests contained in the TLI.

When the TLI is effectively transferred by completion of registration by the registrar, the contractual rights embodied in the TLI are transferred to the buying bank by way of assignment. The rights contained in the TLI, however, include the benefit of the tax withholding gross-up clause and the increased costs clause.[20]

As observed earlier it may not be possible in law to transfer the benefit of such clauses by way of assignment. Inclusion of such covenants in a document containing a promise to the holder does not seem to alter the non-assignability in law of such covenants, unless of course the document is a negotiable instrument, which is capable of transferring all rights and

---

19 Although it is far from clear whether the instrument is a negotiable instrument – see the discussion at ch 9.
20 See on these clauses the discussion at pp 79 and 81 above.

obligations contained in the instrument in a manner that a mere assignment (legal or equitable) cannot.[1] However, a TLI may not as yet be regarded a negotiable instrument under English law.[2]

Consequently, the syndicated loan agreement itself expressly provides for recognition and acknowledgment of the transferee's rights in substitution for those of the first holder of the TLI once the registration is complete. In effect this constitutes consent on the part of the borrower to the transfer of the benefit of such clauses.

Registration also serves the purpose of protecting the buyer against paying interest or principal to the wrong person. An express clause in the syndicated loan would provide that payment of interest and principal to the entity named in the register as the registered holder of the TLI discharges the borrower from its obligations. Similarly, the agent bank and other syndicate banks are given power to recognise only the registered holder as having title to the TLI.

The TLI also overcomes the difficulty discussed above, when novation is used as a medium for transfers of loan assets. It was observed that termination of the existing loan agreement is a necessary precondition to novation with the consequence that exchange control permissions and guarantees may lapse since they are given in respect of a particular loan. When the TLI structure is used, the original loan agreement is neither terminated nor extinguished if, the terms of the TLI are drafted in a manner which excludes novation. Consequently, exchange control permissions should continue to subsist in respect of the original loan. As regards guarantees and other securities there is the authority of Sir John Romilly in *Morley v Morley*[3] that such guarantees and security enure for the benefit of the assignee of contractual rights.[4]

Problems may, however, arise due to the fact that some TLIs tend to provide that all obligations of the transferor under the original syndicated loan agreement are transferred automatically to a transferee by virtue of and upon registration as holder of the TLI. If all rights and obligations under the syndicated loan agreement are automatically transferred to the registered holder of a TLI and this is accepted by all parties to the original syndicated loan agreement it may be that a novation has occurred with the result that the TLI suffers from the same difficulties as a TLC with respect to exchange control and guarantees. The obligations which are sought to be imposed on the transferee of a TLI must therefore be carefully specified in order to avoid this result.

Certain additional clauses are necessary to protect the position of a transferee of a TLI. Thus it is necessary to prevent the issuer (the original borrower) from prepaying any repayment instalment which falls due after the relevant instalment represented by the TLI. This will ensure that the holder of the TLI is not prejudiced by being prepaid before other lenders. Secondly,

---

1 See ch 9 below on the nature of negotiability.
2 See ch 9 below on negotiability.
3 (1858) 25 Beav 253.
4 Carver in 'The Development of the Market in Participations in Syndicated Loans and Acceptance Credits: Some Legal Pitfalls and their Solution' in *Current Issues in International Financial Law* at p 312 has pointed out that the reasoning in *Morley v Morley* would not apply to a floating charge.

it is necessary to provide that in the event that it becomes unlawful for the holder of the TLI to permit the funds to be outstanding, the borrower will be required to repay the amount due.

5 The nature of a TLI

Since it creates and acknowledges indebtedness a TLI falls within the conventional description of a debenture adopted by Chitty J in *Levy v Abercorris Slate and Slab Co*.[5] As such it will be regulated by the Financial Services Act 1986 as an investment falling within para 2 or 3 of Sch 1 to that Act. This aspect is discussed below.[6]

In addition, the question arises whether it is a negotiable instrument, rather than an instrument which is merely transferable or capable of assignment.

As discussed below[7] an instrument becomes negotiable under English law either because it is an instrument which falls within the statutory framework of the Bills of Exchange Act 1882 or because of recognition as a negotiable instrument by the law merchant.

It would seem that a TLI would not qualify as a promissory note under the Bills of Exchange Act 1882. In order to qualify as a promissory note, under that Act it is necessary that the instrument contain an 'unconditional' promise to pay.[8] The promise to the holder of the TLI though expressed to be 'unconditional' on the face of the TLI is nevertheless conditional on closer analysis. First, a TLI may only be transferred to certain specified entities, namely financial institutions; secondly, in order to comply with applicable regulatory law it is conditional on the fact that the transfer was not effected within the US.[9]

Further, the Bills of Exchange Act 1882 requires that 'a sum certain' be payable by the promisor.[10] Due to the tax gross-up and increased costs clauses contained in TLIs the instrument cannot be considered to contain such a promise as required by the Bills of Exchange Act 1882.

Nevertheless, if mercantile custom were to recognise a TLI as a negotiable instrument there is no doubt that under English law a TLI would constitute a negotiable instrument. The cases and authorities on this issue are discussed below in the context of Eurobonds. It is also submitted below that the law expressly chosen and enfaced on the instrument to govern the rights and liabilities of all parties to an instrument should also govern the question whether the instrument itself is negotiable. In practice TLIs used in London's international markets are subject to an express English choice of law and, consequently, as a matter of English conflicts rules English law should govern the issue.[11]

---

5 (1887) 37 Ch D 260 at 264 and see the discussion below at p 125.
6 See ch 15.
7 See ch 9.
8 See ch 9 below.
9 See below Part V for a full discussion.
10 See ch 22 below.
11 See on choice of law the discussion at ch 2 above.

VII TPCs

Transferable Participation Certificates ('TPCs') are a form of TLC which utilises the novation method to enable the transfer of the rights of a buying bank in a sub-participation agreement. A bank seeking to sell a loan asset will enter into a sub-participation agreement as described above but, additionally, will provide in that agreement for the issue of a TPC to the buying bank. The TPC will contain an offer to eligible institutions (usually banks) to novate the sub-participation agreement by completing the transfer form in the TPC and delivering the completed TPC to the selling bank exactly as in the case of a TLC. The transfer must be countersigned both by the transferor and transferee. Once the duly completed TPC is delivered to the original selling bank, the sub-participation agreement is novated so that the transferee is substituted as the buying bank in the sub-participation agreement. Such sub-participation agreements containing provision for the issue of TPCs are referred to as Transferable Participation Agreements. The clauses included in such agreements with regard to the issue of TPCs, and the protective clauses concerning the validity and enforceability of the original syndicated loan agreement, mirror those found in syndicated loan agreements which provide for the issue of TLIs. The reader is consequently referred to the discussion above. The use of TPCs is diagramatically explained below: –

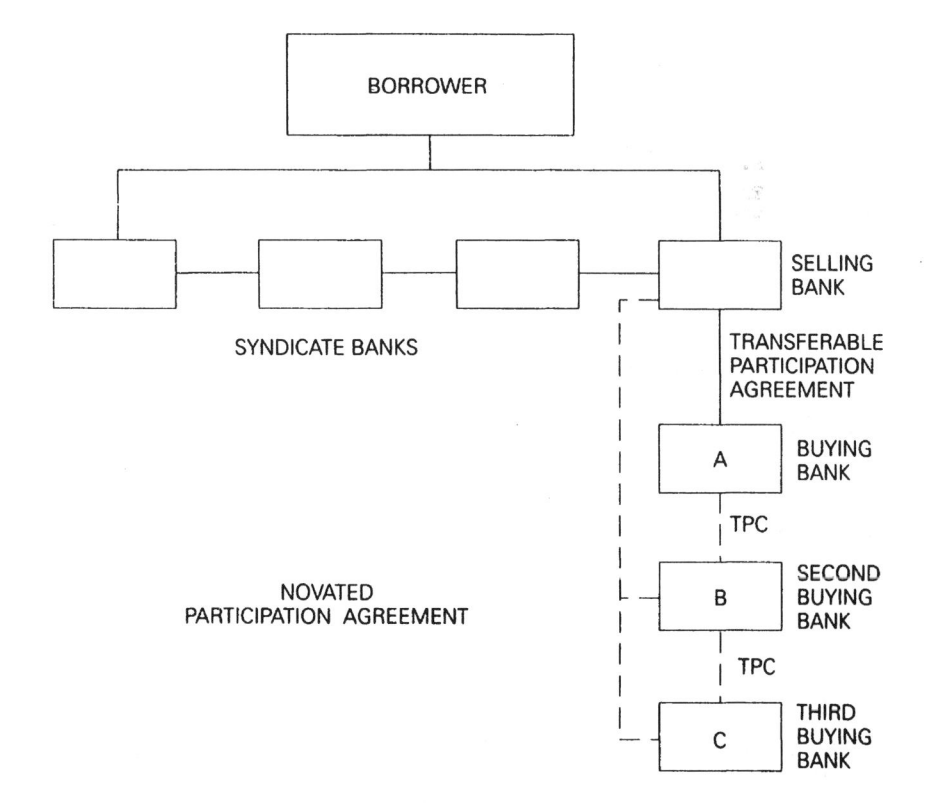

CHAPTER 7
The impact of UK and US regulation on syndicated loans and loan sales

I SYNDICATED LOANS AND THE UK FINANCIAL SERVICES ACT 1986

The UK Financial Services Act 1986 ('FSA') and its impact on Eurobond issues and Euro commercial paper issues is discussed in Part IV and chapter 23. An attempt is made in this chapter to assess the impact, if any, on syndicated loans. The reader is, however, referred to the general discussion of the framework of regulation introduced by the FSA in Part IV before embarking on this chapter.

The regime of regulation introduced by the FSA seeks to regulate the carrying on of 'investment business' within the UK.[1] Investment business consists of engaging in activities specified in Part II of Sch 1 in respect of 'investments' as defined in FSA Sch 1 Part I. Before a syndicated loan can be subject to regulation under the FSA, there must first be an 'investment' falling within Part I of Sch 1, which is either created or constituted by the syndicated loan.

1 Is a syndicated loan a para 2 or para 3 'investment'?

While a *loan* does not fall within any of the paragraphs in Part I of Sch 1 defining 'investments' it has been suggested[2] that a *loan agreement* including a syndicated loan agreement could fall within paras 2 or 3 of FSA Sch 1 Part I and consequently falls within the regime of regulation under the FSA. Under paras 2 or 3 of FSA Sch 1 Part I, an investment includes 'debentures' and 'other instruments creating or acknowledging indebtedness'. The question arises whether a syndicated loan agreement falls within the words 'debenture' or 'other instruments, etc' in paras 2 and 3 of Sch 1.

A conventional syndicated loan agreement neither 'creates' nor 'acknowledges' indebtedness. It contains a promise by the syndicate to advance a sum of money and a promise by the borrower to repay such funds as are advanced at a specified date(s). The syndicated loan agreement does not

---
1 See FSA Sch 1 as to activities constituting 'investment business', and FSA s 1.
2 By Berg IFLR, January 1991.

create the 'indebtedness'; the indebtedness is created by the disbursement of funds not *by* the loan agreement. It does not acknowledge indebtedness, because at the time of the agreement there is no debt which is capable of acknowledgement.

i   *Does a syndicated loan constitute a 'debenture'?*

The FSA does not define the word 'debenture'. The definition in the Companies Act 1985 is not exhaustive and states (unhelpfully) that 'debenture' 'includes debenture stock bonds and any other securities of a company whether constituting a charge on the assets of the company or not'. Consequently, guidance needs to be obtained from the cases.

A series of cases decided under the Bills of Sale Act (1878) Amendment Act 1882 considered the meaning of the word 'debenture' for purposes of s 17 of that Act.

The two leading cases are *Edmonds v Blaina Furnaces Co*[3] and *Levy v Abercorris Slate and Slab Co*,[4] both decided by Chitty J. In the *Blaina Furnaces* case, Chitty J came to the conclusion that the document was a debenture by considering a number of factors without laying down any particular test. Such an approach is consistent with the approach of Lawrence J in *Lemon v Austin Friars Investment Trust Ltd*[5] and Charles J in *English and Scottish Mercantile Investment Co Ltd v Brunton.*[6]

However, in *Levy*, Chitty J crystallised his view by stating: 'In my opinion a debenture means a document which either creates a debt or acknowledges it and any document which fulfils either of these conditions is a debenture.'[7] This formula has received judicial approval on many occasions.[8] Lloyd J in *NV Slavenburg's Bank v Intercontinental Natural Resources Ltd*[9] expressed reservations as to whether the word debenture was confined to documents which create or acknowledge indebtedness. In the absence of clear judicial dissent, Chitty J's formula may be regarded as representing the meaning of 'debenture' in common law.

If this is the true definition of a debenture in common law, the word 'debenture' in para 2 of FSA Sch 1 Part I is subsumed by the phrase 'instruments creating or acknowledging indebtedness' used later in that paragraph. A syndicated loan agreement could not therefore be regarded as a 'debenture' since it does not create or acknowledge indebtedness as discussed above.

Moreover, in interpreting the word 'debenture' in para 2 of FSA Sch I, it is submitted that the word must be interpreted *ejusdem generis*, particularly since there does not seem to be a crystal clear definition of the word at common law. All the other investments referred to in para 2 of Sch I are *tradable* instruments which 'create or acknowledge indebtedness'. This is consistent with the core concept of the word 'debenture' as explained

---

3   (1887) 36 Ch D 215 cited by Alan Berg in IFLR, January 1991, at 27.
4   (1887) 37 Ch D 260.
5   [1926] Ch 1 at 9.
6   [1892] 2 QB 1.
7   At 264.
8   See Rigby LJ in *City of London Brewery Co v IRC* [1899] 1 QB 121 at 139 and the court in *Clark v Balm, Hill & Co* [1908] 1 KB 667 per Phillimore J at 67, although North J in *Topham v Greenside Glazed Fire-brick Co* (1887) 37 Ch D 281 at 290 had doubts about Chitty J's formulation.
9   [1980] 1 WLR 1076 at 1100.

by Chitty J in the *Blaina Furnaces* case as being an instrument which is 'issued' in a series so that each purchaser may deal or trade in it.[10] Consequently, the word 'debenture' in para 2 of FSA Sch 1 Part I should be interpreted accordingly, so that it excludes an ordinary syndicated loan agreement which possesses neither the characteristic of tradability nor that of 'creating or acknowledging indebtedness'.

Further, it is submitted that case law on the meaning of the word 'debenture' for purposes of s 17 of the Bills of Sale Act (1878) Amendment Act 1882 should not automatically be applied to the interpretation of the word 'debenture' in para 2 of FSA Sch 1 Part I.

It must be remembered that the definition advanced by Chitty J was a departure from the established core concept of a debenture, ie an instrument issued in a series to enable persons to trade and deal with it in the markets.[11] This extension of the meaning of the word 'debenture' was for the purpose of enabling the courts to hold that a debenture issued by a company was *outside* the ambit of the Bills of Sale Act (1878) Amendment Act 1882 by virtue of s 17.[12] At the time of the cases decided by Chitty J the courts had not clearly decided that the Bills of Sale Act (1878) Amendment Act 1882 did *not* apply to companies. Cases such as the ruling of the Court of Appeal in *Re Standard Manufacturing Co*,[13] *Read v Joannon*[14] and *Clark v Balm, Hill & Co*[15] concluded that companies were outside the ambit of the Bills of Sale Act (1878) Amendment Act 1882. Rulings in cases such as the *Blaina Furnace* cases extended the concept of debenture (as is evidenced by Chitty J's judgment) so as to enable companies to take advantage of the exemption from the provision contained in s 17 of the Bills of Sale Act (1878) Amendment Act 1882 for 'any debenture issued by any mortgage loan or other incorporated company, and secured upon the capital stock or goods chattels and effects of such company'.[16] It would be mistaken (as well as ironic) to rely on these cases in order to conclude that a syndicated loan agreement constitutes a debenture for purposes of the FSA.

Further, cases decided under other statutory regimes such as the Bills of Sale Act (1878) Amendment Act 1882, the Stamp Act or taxation statutes are by no means conclusive and could be potentially misleading in determining the meaning of the word 'debenture' in the FSA. The reason is that the policy underlying such statutes and rulings is different from the policy underlying the FSA which sets up an entirely new regulatory regime.

It has also been said[17] that the statutory instruments referred to below[18]

---

10 Chitty J said that 'no doubt as a rule the instruments called debentures are issued so that each person gets his own document and can deal with it separately. He has greater facility of dealing with it in the market ...'; but then went on to say that 'it would be unreasonable to hold that because the obligation to pay and the security in favour of several persons is contained in one single document', therefore the instrument is not a debenture; and that his Lordship had 'even seen a single debenture issued to one man'. See the *Blaina Furnaces* case at 221.
11 See above.
12 See Lloyd J in NV *Slavenburg's Bank v Intercontinental Natural Resources Ltd* [1980] 1 WLR 1076.
13 [1891] 1 Ch 627.
14 (1890) 25 QBD 300.
15 [1908] 1 KB 667.
16 See Lloyd J's analysis, obiter, in the *Slavenberg* case.
17 See Berg IFLR, January 1991.
18 See p 127.

suggest that syndicated loans as such were intended to be regulated by the FSA. It was presumably to clarify any doubts which may have arisen as to whether a conventional syndicated loan was regulated by the FSA due to the old cases on the Bills of Sale Act (1878) Amendment Act 1882 that the statutory instruments were enacted.

It is submitted therefore that syndicated loan agreements cannot be classified as 'debentures' or 'other instruments creating or acknowledging indebtedness' and are therefore not regulated as such.

2 Do activities associated with a syndicated loan constitute 'investment business' under Part II of FSA Sch 1?

Clearly this question would arise only if syndicated loans constitute 'investments' within Part I of Sch 1. It has been submitted that they do not.

i *'Arranging' loans and execution of documents*

Moreover, even if one accepts the contrary view, lending activity of the syndicate banks and the arranging of the syndicated loan by the lead manager do not constitute investment business falling within Part II of Sch 1 of the FSA.[19]

This is due to the amendments introduced by the Financial Services Act 1986 (Restriction of Scope of Act) Order 1988 (SI 1988/318) and the Financial Services Act 1986 (Restriction of Scope of Act and Meaning of Collective Investment Scheme) Order 1988 (SI 1988/803).

The first of these statutory instruments removed from the ambit of para 13 of FSA Sch 1 Part II the arranging of loans, while the second of these statutory instruments removed from the ambit of para 12 of Sch 1 Part II an instrument creating or acknowledging indebtedness in respect of any loan.

The Notes to para 12 (as amended by SI 1988/803) read:

'(1) This paragraph does not apply to a person by reason of his accepting, or offering or agreeing to accept, whether as principal or as agent, an instrument creating or acknowledging indebtedness in respect of any loan, credit, guarantee or other similar financial accommodation or assurance which he or his principal has made, granted or provided or which he or his principal has offered or agreed to make, grant or provide.
(2) The references in (1) above to a person accepting, or offering or agreeing to accept, an instrument include references to a person becoming, or offering or agreeing to become, a party to an instrument otherwise than as a debtor or a surety.'

Note 4 to para 13 (as amended by SI 1988/318) reads:

'This paragraph does not apply to a person by reason of his making, or offering or agreeing to make, arrangements with a view to a person accepting, whether as principal or as agent, an instrument creating or acknowledging indebtedness in respect of any loan, credit, guarantee or other similar financial accommodation

---

19 See the FSA s 1(2).

or assurance which he or his principal has made, granted or provided or which he or his principal has offered or agreed to make, grant or provide.'

The result of these two statutory instruments is that even if a loan agreement constituted a debenture, the entry into the syndicated loan by the syndicate banks would not fall within para 12 of FSA Sch 1 Part II; the making of arrangements by the lead manager would not fall within para 13 of Sch 1 Part II.

ii *Advice*

However, giving 'advice' to other banks concerning 'buying' the loan may fall within para 15 of Sch 1 if one takes the view that a syndicated loan is a debenture. This would mean that a lead manager may be carrying on investment business.

In practice it is extremely unlikely that the lead manager will be giving advice within the meaning of para 15 to the syndicate banks. Paragraph 15 requires that the advice be given 'to investors or potential investors ... on the merits of their purchasing, selling, subscribing for, or underwriting an investment ...'. Any advice which is given by the lead manager is on the merits of making a loan to the borrower and not on the 'purchase' of the debenture, ie the syndicated loan agreement. Secondly, it is unlikely that the provision by the lead manager of information as to the terms and conditions of the loan or the transmission of an information memorandum to prospective syndicate participants constitutes giving 'advice on the merits'.

Even if a lead manager could be regarded as giving 'advice' on the merits of purchasing or selling an investment such advice probably falls within para 24 of Sch 1 and is thus exempt from regulation under the FSA.

Paragraph 24 excludes from the ambit of regulation under the FSA any advice which is given (a) in the course of carrying on any business which is not otherwise investment business, (b) as a necessary part of the services given in the course of carrying on that business. Most lead managers would usually be carrying on a 'deposit-taking' and lending business by virtue of authorisation under the Banking Act 1987. Such lending business clearly does not constitute investment business as defined in the FSA, due to Notes 1 and 2 to para 12 of Sch 1 as discussed above; nor would the arranging of a syndicated loan constitute investment business due to Note 4 of para 13 of Sch 1. Unless the lead manager is carrying on a securities dealing or investment management business, it would seem therefore that the first requirement of para 24 would be satisfied in practice. The second requirement is also satisfied since the 'advice' given to prospective syndicate participants is advice which forms a necessary part of the banking services provided by the lead manager to the borrower. Such advice would therefore be outside the ambit of Sch 1 para 15 due to Sch 1 para 24.

On either analysis it seems clear that a lead manager will not fall within the ambit of the FSA para 15.

iii *The borrower*

As far as the borrower is concerned, even if a syndicated loan is a debenture or instrument falling within para 2 or 3 of Sch 1, para 28(3) of Sch 1 excepts the issue of debentures by a person from constituting investment business.

3 Do the prohibitions on unsolicited calls (s 56) and investment advertisements (s 57) apply in respect of syndicated loans?

The prohibitions contained in s 56 and s 57 apply only if the syndicated loan agreement constitutes an investment agreement falling within s 44(9).

Section 56 (restriction on unsolicited calls) states:

'(1) Except so far as permitted by regulations made by the Secretary of State, no person shall in the course of or in consequence of an unsolicited call—
(a) made on a person in the United Kingdom; or
(b) made from the United Kingdom on a person elsewhere,
by way of business enter *into an investment agreement* with the person on whom the call is made or procure or endeavour to procure that person to enter into *such an agreement.*' [Emphasis added.]

Section 57 (restrictions on advertising) states:

'(1) Subject to section 58 below, no person other than an authorised person shall issue or cause to be issued an investment advertisement in the United Kingdom unless its contents have been approved by an authorised person.
(2) In this Act 'an investment advertisement' means any advertisement inviting persons to enter or offer to enter into *an investment agreement* or to exercise any rights conferred by an investment to acquire, dispose of, underwrite or convert an investment or containing information calculated to lead directly or indirectly to persons doing so.' [Emphasis added.]

An investment agreement is defined in s 44 (9) of the FSA as an agreement the making or performance of which involves an activity which falls within Sch 1 Part II of the FSA. Due to the amendments made to Sch 1 Part II by the two statutory instruments referred to above[21], neither the entering into a syndicated loan agreement by lenders and borrowers nor the activities associated with arranging the loan constitute activities falling within Sch 1 Part II. Neither the making nor performance of a syndicated loan agreement constitute an activity which falls within Sch 1 Part II. In consequence, the syndicated loan agreement would not constitute an 'investment agreement' under s 44(9) of the FSA.

Even if the two prohibitions in ss 57 and 56 above applied, it would seem that since the market is restricted to professional and large corporate or state entities neither prohibition would have any significant impact in practice.

This is due to the fact that, first, as regards the prohibition in s 57 (investment advertisements), art 9(3) of the Financial Services Act 1986 (Investment Advertisements) (Exemptions) Order 1988[20] (the 'Order') exempts documents (such as the information memorandum) which are circulated to banks, which are 'authorised' or 'exempt' persons under the FSA, for purposes of syndication. A breach of s 57 would therefore not be occasioned by the borrower

---

20 (SI 1988/316).
21 See page 127.

even though it is not 'authorised' under the FSA and the document is issued in its name.

The only practical consequence flowing from the conclusion that s 57 of the FSA applies to a syndicated loan agreement (although it is submitted that it does not) would be that the information memorandum would need a notice or legend. The legend would restrict transmission of the information memorandum to anyone but the addressee or recipient so that it is reasonable for an issuer to believe that the document will only reach the hands of persons falling within art 9(3) of the Order. This would enable the document to be issued by a non-authorised issuer without a potential breach of s 57.

Secondly, as regards s 56 (unsolicited calls), the Common Unsolicited Calls Regulations 1991 of the Securities and Investments Board permit cold calls by a lead manager on banks which are 'authorised' or 'exempt' under the FSA and which are potential participants in the syndicate. Further, a bank seeking a mandate would be permitted to cold call potential borrowers in the market-place, since they would undoubtedly be large multinational corporations and the Unsolicited Calls Regulations permit cold calls on a company which has a net asset value above £5 million or on a company whose parent or subsidiary has such net asset value.[1]

4 Syndicated loans as collective investment schemes

Theoretically, another basis on which the FSA can have an impact on a syndicated loan is that the syndicated loan constitutes a 'collective investment scheme' under s 75 of the FSA.

Before one can enter the realm of a collective investment scheme under FSA s 75, the following conditions must be satisfied:

(a) there must be 'arrangements' (s 75(1));
(b) with respect to 'property' of any description including money (s 75(1));
(c) the purpose or effect of which is to enable persons taking part in the arrangements to 'participate in' or 'receive profits or income arising from the acquisition holding management or disposal of the property or sums paid out of such profits or income' (s 75(1));
(d) those participating in the arrangements do not have 'day-to-day control over the management of the property in question' whether or not they have the right to be consulted or to give directions (s 75(2));
(e) 'the *contributions* of the participants and the profits or income out of which payments are to be made to them are *pooled*'; and/or
(f) 'that the property in question is managed as a whole or on behalf of the "operator of the scheme"' (s 75(3)).

On the basis of the above the first question is whether or not there is 'property' of any kind which is the subject of 'arrangements'. The property for the purposes of s 75(1) of the FSA may be constituted by the chose in action which each lending bank has against the borrower in respect

---

1 See the Common Unsolicited Calls Regulations 1991 of the Securities and Investment Board and the Securities and Futures Authority.

of the borrower's debt obligation. The funds which are advanced by the lending banks to the borrower can also constitute property which is the subject of the 'arrangements'.

On the basis that the 'property' is constituted by a chose in action it is clear that there are 'arrangements' with regard to such property which enables persons taking part in the 'arrangements' to receive 'income' (interest) arising from the 'holding' of the 'property'. Conditions (a) (b) and (c) are therefore satisfied. If, however, the 'property' is constituted by the funds which are transferred to the borrower, while it is arguable that there are 'arrangements' with regard to such funds, it is difficult to see how the persons taking part in the arrangements 'receive profits or income arising from the acquisition, holding, management or disposal of the property or sums paid out of such profits or income'. Arguably, interest is paid in consequence of the disposal of the funds. Section 75(1), however, requires that profits or income should 'arise from' the acquisition, holding, management or disposal of the property. The right to interest payments (which is the only profit or income of the syndicate banks during the life of the loan) arises on the basis that a bank holds a debt due on which interest is payable rather than from the mere disposal of the funds.

In the light of the above, it is only necessary to determine whether conditions (d) and (e) above are satisfied in respect of the choses in action held by the banks.

First, do the participants have day-to-day control over the management of the chose in action consisting of the borrower's debt obligations. In a syndicated loan, the agent bank[2] has overall supervision of the payment of interest and/or principal by the borrower arising from the debt obligation. The agent bank will also receive financial information from the borrower as is required to be transmitted by the syndicated loan agreement. Does this mean that 'day-to-day control over the management of the property' is in the hands of the agent bank and not of the syndicate? It is submitted that in relation to a chose in action consisting of a debt obligation, control and management must refer to the control and management over the right to receive interest or principal. This right is always in the hands of each syndicate bank which may at any time on the occurrence of an event or default call a default and accelerate its loan outstandings. Similarly, the syndicate as a group may also exercise that right in respect of the whole of the loan outstanding on the basis of a decision of a specified majority of syndicate banks where default and acceleration is subject to a principle of syndicate democracy. The mere fact that the agent bank received financial information from the borrower and that it generally monitors the loan and/or has a right to call default when required by a majority of banks, does not mean that day-to-day control over the management of the debt has been transferred to the agent bank or that the syndicate banks do not have such day-to-day control over the management of their choses in action.

Even if it can be argued that the agent bank in some way retains day-to-day control, it is nevertheless the position that the agent bank does so as the agent of the syndicate banks.

Secondly, is also difficult to see how the 'contributions of the participants'

---

2 See ch 4 above.

are 'pooled'. Could it be argued that if there is a pro rata sharing clause[3] in a syndicated loan agreement, this might contribute to pooling?

'Pooling' is unfortunately not defined in the FSA nor does there seem to be case law which throws light on its definition. The concept of pooling of contributions was intended to cover (and is easy to understand in the context of) ordinary unit trusts and other pooled funds. In these cases there are contributions being made by persons who will be the initial unit holders or purchasers of shares in the fund; these contributions are aggregated and placed in a fungible pool and later invested. This is hardly analogous to the position in the case of a syndicated loan which contains a pro rata sharing clause. Where there is a pro rata sharing clause the syndicate banks agree that if any syndicate bank obtains more than its proportionate share of any sum due from the borrower (including by way of set-off) such bank will share the excess repayment with the other banks. It is submitted that such an arrangement cannot constitute a pooling for the purposes of FSA s 75(3)(a). 'Pooling' does not occur where a sum of money transferred by A to B is subject to a contractual agreement between B and a number of others that B will be contractually bound to transfer a certain portion of such funds pro rata to the account of such persons.

The alternative to 'pooling' is that the 'property' is 'managed' on behalf of the 'operator of the scheme'. This formula is wholly inappropriate to the structure of a syndicated loan. The agent bank does not manage the choses in action in the manner that an investment manager would manage assets; nor can the agent bank be regarded as the 'operator of the scheme', and even if he is, there does not seem to be any person who manages the 'property' on behalf of the 'operator'.

i *Exceptions*

Even if the position was that the syndicated loan satisfied the criteria laid down by s 75 of the FSA, there are a number of exceptions provided by s 75(6) which would remove a syndicated loan from the ambit of the phrase 'collective investment scheme' in s 75 of the FSA. They are as follows.

First, if syndicated loans are to be regarded as debentures, ie investments falling within para 2, it would appear that para 35(b)(i) of Sch 1 to the FSA[4] would provide an exception for a syndicated loan. That paragraph states that:

> 'arrangements under which the rights or interests of the participants are represented by the following:
> (i) investments falling within paragraph 2 of this Schedule which are issued by a single body corporate which is not an open ended investment company or which are issued by a single issuer which is not a body corporate and are guaranteed by the Government of the United Kingdom or Northern Ireland or of any country or territory outside the the United Kingdom'

are not collective investment schemes.

---

3 See on such a clause p 100 above.
4 Previously this provision was found in the provisions of s 75(6) of the FSA and was transferred to its present position by the Financial Services Act 1986 (Restriction of Scope of Act and Meaning of Collective Investment Scheme) Order 1990, SI 1990/349, art 7.

If, on the other hand, the view which is advanced in this chapter is adopted and syndicated loans are not regarded as para 2 investments, the above exception does not apply.

Secondly, the exception contained in s 75(6)(b) may be applicable. That paragraph provides that:

'arrangements where each of the participants carries on a business other than investment business and enters into the arrangements for commercial purposes related to that business'

do not constitute a collective investment scheme. As pointed out earlier, ordinary banking business which consists of taking deposits and lending funds, is excluded from the definition of investment business. Consequently, insofar as the banks are participants in the arrangements their business falls within the requirements of s 75(6)(b). If the borrower is also considered to be a participant, it would seem that except in the case of borrowers who carry on investment business, all other ordinary commercial and industrial corporations as well as governments would fall within the formula. Where the borrower is an investment house or a securities dealer, s 76(6) would probably not apply. Similarly, where the syndicated loan is made by a group of banks at least one of whom carries on investment business (eg a universal bank from Germany) the exception would not apply. In all other cases syndicated loans would be covered by the exception.

It is submitted, however, that a better view is that a syndicated loan does not satisfy the criteria laid down in s 75(2) and (3), as discussed above, and consequently there is no necessity to rely on such exceptions.

ii *Practical consequences*

Even if a syndicated loan constituted a collective investment scheme, the practical consequences are not significant.

One consequence is that s 76 contains a prohibition on the promotion of collective investment schemes in one or two forms where the scheme is not a 'recognised' collective investment scheme.[5] Syndicated loans in practice would not be recognised collective investment schemes.

The prohibition on promotion contained in s 76 is twofold. First, it consists of a prohibition on the issue of any advertisement which invites persons to become or offer to become participants in the collective investment scheme or which contains information calculated to lead directly or indirectly to that result. Secondly, there is a prohibition on advising or procuring any person in the UK to become or offer to become a participant in such a scheme.

However, by virtue of regulations made by the Securities and Investments Board under s 76(3) of the FSA, the promotion or advice given to certain persons is exempt from the prohibitions. The Financial Services (Promotion of Unregulated Collective Investment Schemes) Regulations 1991 exempt

---

5   See s 77 on 'authorised unit trust schemes', and ss 86–89 on 'recognised schemes'.

the promotion of the scheme to 'non-private customers'[6] and any person carrying on investment business whether in the UK or elsewhere. Even on the basis that a bank which carries on banking business is not to be regarded as carrying on investment business, most if not all banks active in the syndicated loans market would qualify as 'non-private customers' within the meaning of the Financial Services (Glossary and Interpretation) Rules and Regulations 1991. So long as a syndicate participant has a called-up share capital or net assets of not less than £5,000,000, it would be possible to promote the syndicated loan by issuing information memoranda or other documents or by giving advice to prospective syndicated participants.

Equally, any advice or documents sent to a borrower by way of promotion would be exempt if the borrower satisfies the same test (which would invariably be the case in practice).

It would nevertheless be necessary to ensure that documents bear a legend stating that distribution is restricted to persons falling within the Financial Services (Promotion of Unregulated Collective Investment Schemes) Regulations 1991. This would be the only practical difference if the ultra-cautious (and it is submitted untenable) position is adopted that a syndicated loan is a collective investment scheme.

iii A caveat

While the ordinary syndicated loan would not constitute a collective investment scheme on the basis of the above analysis, more complex structures, for instance those set up in the context of project finance or property finance particularly with complex security structures, may in exceptional cases fall within the complex definition of a collective investment scheme in s 75 of the FSA.

II SALE OF LOAN ASSETS AND THE FSA

The structure and legal aspects of loan 'sales' were discussed in chapter 6 and it was observed that the traditional methods used to effect a 'sale' of loan assets were: (a) novation, (b) assignment, and (c) sub-loan or sub-participation. Novation and assignment may first be conveniently dealt with, so as to examine the impact of the FSA.

1 Novation and assignment

A novation usually consists of a release of the debtor (borrower) from all obligations under the syndicated loan by the creditor (the selling bank) in consideration of the borrower agreeing to accept the buying bank as its new creditor.

In an assignment a syndicate lender will transfer and assign his rights to interest and principal under the loan agreement (though not his obli-

---

6 As defined in the SIB's Financial Services (Glossary and Interpretation) Rules and Regulations 1991.

gations) to the buying bank. It was pointed out above that English law draws a distinction between assignment in law[7] which requires the assignment of the entirety of the debt in writing with express notice being given in writing to the debtor, and an equitable assignment where the entirety or a part of a debt may be assigned, even orally, to the buying bank.

From the perspective of the FSA the main difference between assignment and novation is that in an assignment the contractual relationship between the selling bank (assignor) and the borrower continues to subsist after the assignment, whereas in a novation the original contractual relationship between the borrower and selling bank is terminated. The selling bank (the assignor) consequently remains liable to the borrower in respect of any unperformed obligations under the original loan agreement, for example the obligation to lend any undrawn portion of the original loan.

i *Do buyers and sellers in assignments and novations carry on investment business?*

The answer to the question depends whether the selling bank as well as the buying bank are carrying on an activity falling within para 12 of FSA Sch 1, namely, are they selling or buying an investment? This in turn depends on two further questions.

First, what, if any, is the investment which is bought or sold? Secondly, if there is an investment falling within Part I of Sch 1 of the FSA, is that investment the subject of a purchase or sale when a loan sale is effected?[8]

As regards the first question, the answer turns on the nature of a syndicated loan. If the correct analysis is that a syndicated loan is not a debenture or other instrument falling within para 2 of FSA Sch 1 Part I the mere novation of a contract or the mere assignment of contractual rights does not on any analysis constitute an investment within Sch 1 Part I.

If (contrary to the submissions above) a syndicated loan is regarded as a para 2 instrument (debenture), it may either be a single debenture or a series of debentures. If the syndicated loan constitutes a single debenture or a single instrument creating or acknowledging indebtedness falling within para 2, it is submitted that the subject of the loan sale could only be an investment falling within para 11 of Sch 1. Paragraph 11 refers to 'rights to and *interests in* anything which is an investment falling within any other paragraph of this Part of this Schedule' [emphasis added].

On the other hand, a syndicated loan consists of a number of separate loans by several banks to a single borrower; and these loans are contained in one legal document for the sake of convenience. Consequently, a syndicated loan can be analysed as a series of individual debentures or instruments. If so, the 'investment' which is capable of being the subject of a 'sale' is a debenture, ie a para 2 investment. It is, however, difficult to regard a syndicated loan agreement as a series of debentures or instruments creating or acknowledging indebtedness since there is in fact only *one legal instrument* which can constitute the debenture or instrument. Consequently, a syndicated loan constitutes a single debenture or other instrument creating or

---

7 Under the Law of Property Act 1925 s 136(1).
8 Berg's analysis in IFLR, January 1991, deals with the second question but does not seem to deal with the first.

acknowledging indebtedness, and the investment which is the subject of a loan 'sale' is a para 11 investment.

The next question is whether there is a sale or purchase of the para 11 or para 2 investment.

FSA Sch 1 para 28 contains a non-exclusive definition of 'buying and selling' as including references to 'any acquisition or disposal for valuable consideration'. A 'disposal' is again defined non-exclusively as including 'in the case of an investment consisting of rights under a contract, surrendering, assigning or converting those rights' (para 28(2)(c)).

If a participant's rights under the syndicated loan agreement are para 11 investments, both a novation and an assignment would fall within Sch 1 para 28(2)(c) and thus constitute para 12 activity: buying or selling an investment. It is nevertheless submitted that the phrase in para 28(2)(c), 'surrendering' rights under a contract, cannot apply to the novation of a syndicated loan since the syndicated loan is not an investment 'consisting of rights under a contract'.[9] However, despite this, if a loan sale involves an 'investment' a court should not find it difficult to hold that there is an 'acquisition or disposal before valuable considerations' within para 28(1) and accordingly a 'buying' and 'selling' within para 12. A court would look to the substance and the commercial reality of the situation and hold that there is 'disposal' regardless of the legal form for purposes of giving effect to the regulating policy underlying the FSA.

In a tax case, *Wale v IRC*,[10] the court approached the question in the same way. Kelley CB held that there had been a 'transfer' of a mortgage for tax purposes in the case of a novation on the following analysis:

'The ground on which the Crown claims the higher duty is that the instrument is not a "transfer" of a mortgage. I asked who possessed that mortgage the day before the instrument in question was executed, and who possessed it just after the execution? Mrs Ingram and her trustee had it just before the execution and immediately after the execution Sutton had it. How did Sutton become the possessor of that mortgage, unless in substance Mrs Ingram and her trustee transferred the mortgage to her? The particular mode and form in which the change or transfer was carried out do not affect the question. In substance the effect of the whole transaction was a transfer of the mortgage from Mrs Ingram to her trustee to Sutton.'

Pollock B dealt with the question in a similar way:

'But let us look at the substance of the thing. It is true that the first mortgage is paid off, and that there is not an actual transfer of the debt of £350, but practically so far as the mortgagor is concerned, and looking at the ordinary use of ... by conveyances, one would say that the mortgagee held, not an entirely new mortgage, but a transfer of the old mortgage for £350.'

Although tax cases are not necessarily a useful guide to interpreting regulatory law (due to differences in underlying policy), it is submitted that a court construing the concept of 'acquisition or disposal for valuable consideration' would adopt a similar approach.

---

9 Berg in IFLR, January 1991, does not take this view.
10 (1879) 4 Ex D 270.

Assuming that both the buying and selling banks are carrying on a para 12 activity in a loan sale it is necessary to consider whether the activity falls within an exception contained in para 17 of the FSA Sch 1 before concluding that it constitutes investment business. The relevant exception is contained in para 17(1) of Sch 1 Part III. Paragraph 17(1) reads as follows:

'Paragraph 12 above applies to a transaction which is to be entered into by a person as principal only if—
(a) he holds himself out as willing to enter into transactions of that kind at prices determined by him generally and continuously rather than in respect of each particular transaction; or
(b) he holds himself out as engaging in the business of buying investments with a view to selling them and those investments are or include investments of the kind to which the transaction relates; or
(c) he regularly solicits members of the public for the purpose of inducing them to enter as principals or agents into transactions to which that paragraph applies and the transaction is or is to be entered into as a result of his having solicited members of the public in that manner.'

Since para 12 applies if any one of the limbs of para 17 is satisfied, each one of these limbs needs to be negatived for the to exception apply. It is not difficult to fall outside limb (c) of para 17(1) since there is no solicitation of 'members of the public' by sellers and buyers of loan assets, since the market in sales of loan assets is restricted to professionals who are authorised persons or exempt persons as defined in the FSA. Paragraph 17(2) provides that for the purposes of deciding whether a person 'regularly solicits members of the public', the solicitation of authorised persons and/or exempt persons are to be ignored.

The paragraphs which are difficult to negative are paras 17(1)(a) and (b). Paragraph 17(1)(a) would apply where a bank is making a market and quoting prices on loan assets either on electronic screens or otherwise. Thus, for instance, in the case of sovereign debt, where such a market sometimes exists, it will not be possible to rely on this exception.

Even in the absence of such 'market-making', if a selling bank or a buying bank is perceived in the markets as being a regular buyer and seller of loan assets, that bank will be regarded as holding himself out under limb (b) and the para 17 exception will not apply. In deciding whether the holding out is in respect of 'investments of the kind to which the transaction relates' within the meaning of para 17(1)(b), a distinction cannot be drawn, for instance, between dollar loan assets and DM loan assets or between sovereign loan assets and corporate loan assets. If a person holds himself out to the markets as being willing to buy and sell loan assets (of any type) the exception in para 17 does not apply.

Consequently, a bank which otherwise does not require authorisation under the FSA may fall within the ambit of the FSA if it holds itself out as being in the business of buying and selling loan assets whether corporate or sovereign in whatever currency.

2 Sub-participations

As explained in chapter 6, a sub-participation is no more than a back-to-back loan whereby the buying bank provides funding to the seller of the loan.

138　*The impact of UK and US regulations on syndicated loans and loan sales*

The buying bank in effect promises to provide the funds which are to be or have been advanced to the borrower by the selling bank and it agrees to continue to provide that funding until the maturity of the loan. There is no direct legal relationship or privity of contract as between the buying bank and the original borrower. The buying bank also agrees that it will not be paid interest or principal until and unless the borrower pays the selling bank.

If it is assumed that a loan instrument constitutes a debenture it would therefore seem that there is an issue, sale and purchase of a fresh debenture as between the selling bank and the buying bank.[11]

3　Conclusions on loan sales by traditional methods

The conclusion from the above analysis is that *if it is conceded that a syndicated loan is a debenture or other instrument creating or acknowledging indebtedness*, it seems to follow that the transfer of a loan asset by means of a novation or by means of an assignment would constitute the selling or buying of an investment falling within para 12; that such activity constitutes investment business within the meaning of the FSA; that para 17 of Sch 1 would not apply in practice to exempt such investment business. A transfer by way of a sub-loan or sub-participation would also be caught by para 12 in the same way that an ordinary loan agreement falls within the FSA on the assumption that it is a debenture or other instrument creating or acknowledging indebtedness.

4　The FSA and the use of TLCs, TLIs and TPCs

It was observed in Chapter 6 that TLCs and TPCs are simply documents which contain an offer to novate an existing contract and consequently cannot be regarded as debentures or instruments creating or acknowledging indebtedness. On the other hand a TLI does in fact acknowledge indebtedness and consequently is an instrument falling within para 2 of FSA Sch 1.

However, the transfer of loan assets by the means of a TLI falls outside the activities regulated by the FSA due to Notes 1 and 2 to para 12 and Note 4 to para 13 of Sch 1.[12] Consequently, neither a 'sale' of a TLI nor the arranging of a sale or issue of a TLI can constitute investment business. The issue of TLIs by the borrower also does not constitute investment business due to the exception in para 28(3) of Sch 1 to the FSA discussed above.

In consequence of the fact that activities associated with the issue, acceptance and arrangements for the issue of TLCs do not constitute investment activity falling within Part II of Sch 1, an agreement for the sale or purchase of TLIs does not constitute an 'investment agreement' falling within s 44(9) of the FSA. Consequently, as discussed above[13] neither the prohibition

---

11　It is difficult to see how Berg (IFLR, January 1991) on the one hand concludes that a syndicated loan agreement is a debenture and on the other that a loan instrument evidencing a sub-participation is not. Compare his analysis at 27–28 with his analysis at 30.
12　See p 127 above.
13　At pp 129–130.

on investment advertisements in FSA s 57 nor that on unsolicited calls in FSA s 56 apply in respect of TLIs.

III US SECURITIES REGULATION[14]

The framework of US securities regulation and its impact on the international capital markets in London is assessed in some detail in Part V. US securities regulation may have an impact on the syndicated loans market as well.

While US securities legislation contained in the US Securities Act 1933 and the Securities Exchange Act 1934 applies in relation to securities, the definition of the term 'security' in the statutes is extremely wide and may cover in its ambit a syndicated loan and at least some forms of loan sale.

Section 2(1) of the Securities Act 1933 provides that 'unless the context otherwise requires', the term 'security' means:

> 'Any *note* stock, treasury stock, bond, debenture, *evidence of indebtedness*, certificate of interest or participation in any profit sharing agreement, collateral trust certificate, pre-organisation certificate or subscription, transferable share, investment contract, voting trust certificate, certificate of deposit for a security, fractional undivided interest in oil, gas or other mineral rights ... or, in general, any interest or instrument commonly known as a "security", *or any certificate of interest or participation in* temporary or interim certificates for, receipt for, guarantee of, or warrant to or rights to subscribe to or purchase, *any of the foregoing*.' (Emphasis added.)[15]

The question whether a syndicated loan or participation falls within this definition is explored in a number of US cases, but the analysis in the cases may not be of much value due to the practice in the US domestic markets of taking a 'loan note' from a borrower as evidence of indebtedness.[16]

The US courts have applied three tests to decide whether syndicated loans which are evidenced by 'loan notes' constitute a 'security' for the purposes of securities law.

The first is the so-called 'investment commercial test'[17] which seeks to ask whether the transaction is an investment or is a commercial loan.[18] It is submitted that such a test is of little or no value since a loan is an 'investment' from the bank's perspective.[19]

---

14 See two excellent treatments of the subject by Bucheit 'The State of the Loan Sub-Participation' (1986) 8 Jo of Comparative Business and Capital Market Law 149–168 (Elsevier Science Publishers BV, North Holland); Reade Ryan *International Bank Loan Syndications and Participations*, ch 2, International Financial Law (Euromoney, 1985, Rendell edn).
15 See also the definition of security in s 3(a)(10) of the Securities Exchange Act 15 USC section 78C.
16 See *Williamson v Tucker* 645 F 2nd 404 (5th Cir) cert denied 454 US 897 (1981); *United American Bank v Gunter* 620 F 2d 1108 (5th Cir 1980); *National Bank of Commerce v All American Assurance Co* 583 F2d 1295 (5th Cir 1978); *CNS Enterprises Inc v G & G Enterprises Inc* 508 F2d 1354 (7th Cir) cert denied 423 US 825 (1975).
17 See Reade Ryan, fn 14 above.
18 See, for instance, *Williamson v Tucker* 645 F2d 404 (5th Cir) cert denied 454 US 897 (1981); *CNS Enterprises Inc v G & G Enterprises Inc* 508 F2d 1354 (7th Cir) cert denied 423 US 825 (1975).
19 See also the view of Reade Ryan, fn 14 above, at p 16.

The second test adopted by the US courts is the so-called 'risk–capital' test which attempts to draw a distinction between investing risk capital and making a loan, even a risky one.[20] This, too, is somewhat unhelpful since the conclusion will depend on the circumstances of each case.

Judge Friendly in *Exchange National Bank v Touche Ross & Co*[1] focused on the words 'unless the context otherwise requires' in section 2(1) of the Securities Act and pointed out that there were many 'notes' which did not constitute a security, and consequently, held that the question is whether a 'note' had a 'family resemblance' to those which had been held not to be a security in the past. 'Family resemblance' is the third test which has been applied by the US courts.

None of these tests is helpful in determining whether an international syndicated loan is a 'security' within the meaning of the US Securities Act 1933 where a loan note is not issued, and this is usually the practice in the international markets of London. It is submitted that since the policy objectives of US securities laws in protecting ordinary investors in the US[2] an international syndicated loan agreement (where loan notes are not issued) should not be regarded as falling within the parameters of US securities laws.

Ryan[3] has, however, pointed out that a noteless agreement could nevertheless constitute an 'investment contract' and thus constitute a 'security' within the meaning of s 2(1) of the Securities Act 1933. What constitutes an 'investment contract' was restated by the US Supreme Court in *SEC v W J Howey & Co*[4] in a manner which did not have in mind international syndicated loans developed in the 1970s: 'a contract transaction or scheme whereby a person invests his money in a common enterprise and is led to expect profits solely from the efforts of the promoter or third party'.

Due to the requirement that the person must expect profits 'solely from the efforts of a promoter or third party', it would seem that where a syndicate of banks enters into a loan agreement with a borrower the test is not satisfied in respect of a syndicated loan.[5]

In the structure sometimes used in the US domestic markets for syndication, the loan agreement is between the lead bank and the borrower. Other banks become indirect participants in the syndication by buying a participation. In such cases the position is not clear cut. In this type of structure some US cases have held that the sale of participations by the lead bank constituted the sale of a security in the form of an investment contract,[6] while others have held that it did not.[7]

As regards the sale of loan assets by participants in a syndicated loan

---

20 *Amfac Manufacturing Corpn v Arizona Malle of Temple* 583 F2d 426 (9th Cir 1978); *United California Bank v THC Financial Corpn* 557 F2d 1351 (9th Cir 1977).
1 544 F2d 1126 2d Cir 1976.
2 See Release 4708 of July 1964 of the SEC (17 CFR 231–470).
3 In *International Bank Loan Syndications and Participations* ch 2, International Financial Law (Euromoney, 1985, Rendell edn).
4 328 US 293 (1946).
5 See *Union Planters National Bank of Memphis v Commercial Credit Business Loans Inc* 651 F2d 1174 (6th Cir) cert denied 454 US 1124 (1981).
6 *Commercial Discount Corpn v Lincoln Trust Commercial Corpn* 445 F Supp 1263 (SDNY 1978).
7 *Union Planters National Bank v Commercial Credit Business Loans Inc* 651 F2d 1174 (6th Cir) cert denied 454 US 1124 (1981); *United American Bank v Gunter* 620 F2d 1108 (5th Cir 1980).

agreement, if the original syndicated loan itself was not a security within the meaning of the Securities Act 1933, it would follow that none of the traditional methods of transferring a loan would constitute a security. Where, however, the original syndicated loan evidenced by a note was a 'security', in *Lehigh Valley Trust Co v Central National Bank of Jacksonville*,[8] a Federal Court of Appeal held that the sub-participation agreement was itself a security, since it was a participation or interest in a security.

TLIs, TLCs and TCPs raise difficult questions of US securities law. It is submitted that a TLI is clearly a security within the meaning of s 2 of the Securities Act 1933 and s 3 of the Securities Exchange Act 1934 since it evidences indebtedness and is a debt instrument which has a 'family resemblance'[9] with the securities listed in s 2(1) of the 1933 Act. It may therefore be sold only in reliance of Regulation S discussed below[10] or on the basis of a private placement under s 4(2) of the Securities Act 1933.[11] In practice it is usual to restrict sales of TLIs to sales outside the US and to exclude US banks (except their London offices) from purchasing a TLI, so that it would be possible to rely on the foreign transactions exemption which was in Release 4708 of July 1964, and is now found in Regulation S which superceded it.[12] As regards TLCs and TPCs where the syndicated loan agreement is evidenced by a 'note' it would seem that TLCs and TPCs would fall within the definition of a security since they would constitute interests or participations in an existing security: *Lehigh Valley Trust Co v Central National Bank of Jacksonville.*[13] Where no 'note' is issued, the more logical and commonsense conclusion is that a document constituting an offer to novate a contract, which is itself not a security, cannot constitute a security. The position is, however, not free from doubt.

1 The Glass Steagall Act

Sections 16, 20, 21 and 32 of the US Banking Act 1933 are referred to as the 'Glass Steagall Act'.[14] Dealings in any instrument which constitutes a 'security' under that Act may create a difficulty under s 16 of the Act for any US commercial bank. A TLI may constitute such a security. Section 16 of the Banking Act 1933[15] contains a prohibition on a commercial bank whose activities are regulated by that Act from 'dealing in securities' unless it is limited to purchasing and selling such securities without recourse as agent for one of its customers.[16]

However, the non-banking subsidiary of a US bank holding company

---

8 409 F2d (5th Cir 1969).
9 Per Judge Friendly in *Exchange National Bank v Touche Ross & Co*, note 1 above.
10 See ch 21.
11 The SEC in Securities Act Release no 4552 'Announcement of Statement Regarding Availability of Non-Public Offering Exemption from Registration Statement' (6 November 1962) has stated that s 4(2) of the Securities Act 1933 contained the traditional exemption for bank loans. See below for a discussion of this requirement.
12 For a detailed discussion of these provisions see chs 20 and 21.
13 See note 8 above.
14 See Pollard et al *Banking Law in the United States* (Butterworths, 1988) chs 12 and 13.
15 12 USC 24.
16 Underwriting of securities issues is equally prohibited by s 16 of the Banking Act 1933.

(a 'BHC') may engage in such securities dealing *overseas* under Regulation K of the Board of the Federal Reserve Bank.[17] The structure and impact of the Glass Steagall Act and the Bank Holding Company Act 1956[18] are discussed in chapter 22.

---

17 12 CFR 211.
18 12 USC 1841 ff.

Part III

International or 'Euro' bonds

CHAPTER 8
Background and issue procedures

I BACKGROUND

The issue of Eurobonds or, more accurately, international bonds is one of the most important mechanisms for raising long-term finance in the international capital markets. It is used by transnational corporations, sovereign states, state corporations and transnational banks as an alternative to borrowing from a syndicate of banks through the medium of a conventional international syndicated loan.[1] In essence it is a method of borrowing money, though a sophisticated and complex method.

Financing by means of the issue of Eurobonds increased immensely in the 1980s so that Eurobonds came to constitute a major financing vehicle for international finance, rivaling the traditional international syndicated loan. In 1980 the total volume of Eurobonds issued amounted to US $18.8 bn in value; in 1988 the volume had reached US $175.7 bn in value,[2] and in 1990 reached US $263.3 bn in value.[3]

In a Eurobond issue an entity which requires long-term financing issues a large number of debt securities which in aggregate equals the total amount of finance required by the issuer of the bonds. The debt securities which are issued are denominated in small multiples, and in a US dollar denominated issue would traditionally be issued with a face value of US $5,000 in respect of each bond. The debt securities in the form of bonds are sold or 'placed' on behalf of the issuer by a syndicate of investment banks in the hands of a multitude of investors. The investors who purchase the bonds include insurance companies, central banks of sovereign states, commercial banks, the corporate treasury divisions of large multinationals, and to some extent wealthy private individuals.

1 The issuer's perspective

From the issuer's perspective, the decision to issue Eurobonds as a means of obtaining long-term finance rather than an issue of shares or an

---

1 On syndicated loans, see Part II.
2 See *Euromoney Special 20th Anniversary Supplement*, 'Euromarket in Figures' (June 1989).
3 See the Bank of England Quarterly Bulletin, May 1991 at p 238.

146 *Background and issue procedures*

international syndicated loan, depends largely on a number of factors such as the overall cost, tax considerations and, in the case of some issuers, whether or not they can access the international bond markets. Access to the international bond markets is, generally speaking, restricted to corporations and other entities which have at least a single A assigned to their credit rating by credit-rating agencies such as Standard & Poor's and Moody's. In 1988, 713 Eurobond issues with a total US dollars value of 91.83 bn were rated, representing 52.24% of all bonds issued in the international markets.[4] It is outside the scope of this work to consider the financial and commercial advantages and disadvantages of the different types of financing mechanisms from the point of view of a corporate entity seeking long-term funds.

2 The investor's perspective

The purchasers of bonds are referred to as 'investors' because their behaviour resembles that of investors in shares or gold or other commodities rather than of a creditor who lends funds such as a commercial bank. Under English and other systems of law, the purchaser of a Eurobond becomes a creditor of the issuer of the bonds since the investor will have a right to be repaid the principal amount of the bond which the investor has paid to purchase the bond. The investor obtains a return on his investment first in the form of interest on the bond either at a fixed rate or at a floating rate or by way of a discount on the face value of the bond in the case of deep discount bonds.[5] Secondly, the investor will look to capital appreciation of the bond. A bond though it has a redemption value at maturity nevertheless fluctuates in value in the course of trading in the international bond markets, in a manner similar to that in which share values fluctuate when traded on a stock exchange, though not with as great a volatility. Consequently, investors will purchase bonds not necessarily to hold them until their redemption on maturity date by the issuer, but for the purposes of sale in the markets to other investors with a view to realising a capital gain.

3 The investment bank's perspective

The investment banks play a central role in the issue of Eurobonds by international issuers. A syndicate of investment banks will agree with the issuer that they will sell or 'place' the bonds in the hands of investors and further they promise to the issuer that they themselves will purchase the bonds or any portion of the total aggregate amount which they have failed to place with investors. The investment banks therefore not only arrange for but also 'underwrite' the placing of the bonds. The role of the syndicate of underwriting banks is to procure that investors will purchase the bonds

---

4 *Euromoney 20th Anniversary Supplement* (June 1989).
5 For a discussion of deep discount bonds, see p 214.

and in effect lend the funds required by an issuer. Their role is not to lend funds to the issuer of bonds in the same way that a syndicate of banks will lend funds to a borrower in a syndicated loan agreement. If the investment banks are successful in selling all the bonds which are issued for purposes of the financing they are generally under no further contractual liability to the issuer, nor are they exposed to the financial risk of non-payment or default in repayment of the bonds by the issuer. The issuer's obligation to repay the funds borrowed through a Eurobond issue is owed to the holders of the Eurobonds and therefore the exposure to the risk of default, insolvency or non-payment is that of the holder of the Eurobond. In a syndicated loan the obligation of the borrower to repay on the syndicated loan is owed to the syndicate of banks and, consequently, the risk of exposure to non-payment, insolvency or default is with the syndicate of banks who advanced the funds. The role and position of the investment bank in a Eurobond issue is therefore strikingly different from that of a commercial bank involved in an international syndicated loan.

The investment banks are paid various fees for the performance of their obligation to place the issuer's bonds in the hands of investors and for arranging the issue.[6]

4 The international or 'Euro' bond issue, the 'foreign' bond issue and the 'domestic' bond issue

The international or 'Euro' bond issue must be distinguished from two other types of bond issues which are not primarily the object of discussion here. These are domestic bond issues and the so-called 'foreign' bond issue.

A domestic bond issue is one where the bonds are denominated in the domestic currency of the place of issue and are issued by an issuer which is an entity incorporated in the country where the issue is being made and where the intended purchasers of the bonds are investors who are resident in the country in which the issue is being effected. In such a case the bonds are regarded as being issued by a domestic issuer in the domestic capital markets of a given country. Thus, for instance, a US dollar bond issue by International Business Machines Corporation (IBM) in New York which is aimed at American investors in the US capital markets will be a domestic issue.

A 'foreign' issue of bonds is one where the entity which is issuing the bonds is not incorporated in the country in which the bonds are being issued but nevertheless the bonds are denominated in the currency of the country of issue and the issue is aimed at domestic investors in the capital markets of the country where the issue is being made. The only difference here is that the issuer is a foreign entity in respect of the capital market. Thus a US dollar denominated bond issue made in New York by the Mitsubishi Corporation of Japan and aimed at US investors would be a 'foreign' issue. Most economists and investment bankers would regard these two types of

---

6 On fees and commissions, see ch 8.

transactions as essentially transactions effected in the domestic capital markets and not on the international markets.[7]

The hallmarks of an international bond issue are, first, that the bonds are issued in a currency which is different from the currency of the country of the place of issue and, secondly, that the bonds are sold internationally to corporate and private investors in different countries across the world rather than to investors in the capital markets of the place of issue. These two characteristics distinguish the true international issue in London from 'foreign' issues which occur in the domestic capital markets of New York and Tokyo. In addition, it is common for the issuers of bonds to be largely corporations and entities which are not resident in the country of the place of issue of the bonds and that the underwriting syndicates which sell the bonds consist of investment banks from different countries.

The Prospectus Directive of the European Community 89/298/EEC uses the term 'Euro-securities' which are defined as:

> 'transferable securities which:
> – are to be underwritten and distributed by a syndicate at least two of the members of which have their registered offices in different states, and
> – are offered on a significant scale in one or more member states other than that of the issuer's registered office, and
> – may be subscribed for or initially acquired only through a credit institution or other financial institution.'

This definition does not coincide with the conventional perception of a Eurobond or international bond. Thus a US dollar issue in London of bonds by a Japanese company which is underwritten by US, Japanese, Swiss, German and Korean banks would not be a 'Euro-security' but would generally be regarded as a Eurobond or international bond.

The International Primary Markets Association (or IPMA) has, however, adopted the definition in the Prospectus Directive for the purposes of some of its Recommendations.[8]

The concept of 'Euro-securities' used in EC Directive 89/298/EEC[9] must also be distinguished from the concept of international securities in s 152(6) of the Financial Services Act 1986 ('FSA'). Section 152(6) defines such a security as a bond or other debt security which is 'likely to be dealt in by bodies incorporated in or persons resident in a country or territory outside the United Kingdom, is denominated in a currency other than sterling or is otherwise connected with such a country or territory'. This definition is nearer the market's perception of the true international issue from London. However, the FSA seems to contemplate that the bonds would be dealt in 'a country or territory' rather than 'countries or territories' outside the UK. In practice there would be few issues targeted *only* at one country

---

7   See, for instance, Dufey and Giddy *The International Money Market*, (Prentice Hall, 1978) pp 19–20; see also Professor Marcia Stigum *The Money Market* ch 1. Such foreign issues in the major capital markets have been given interesting names; for instance, a US dollar issue in New York is referred to as a 'Yankee' issue, an issue in sterling in London as a 'Bulldog' issue, an issue in yen in Tokyo as a 'Samurai' issue and a peseta issue in Spain as a 'Matador' issue.
8   See s 1 of IPMA Recommendations.
9   OJ L124/8, 5.5.89.

outside the UK. It is submitted that s 152(6) of the FSA should be interpreted to mean any country or territory outside the UK so that Eurobonds which are targeted at investors worldwide (except the US) should fall within the definition. Otherwise s 152(6) is likely to be a dead letter.

Issuers raise finance through bond issues denominated in US dollars, Japanese yen, German deutschmarks, Swiss francs, French francs, Australian dollars, New Zealand dollars, and other currencies using London as the place of issue. Neither New York nor Tokyo rival London as such an international centre.[10] Issues in those centres are either domestic or foreign issues. Issues in New York and Tokyo are essentially issues in domestic capital markets.

The term 'Eurobond' issue is in fact misleading because the sale of the bonds is not restricted to European investors and they are sold to investors worldwide (excluding the US for reasons explained below); the issuers are not restricted to European corporations; the currencies are not restricted to European currencies and indeed the vast majority of bonds are denominated in US dollars; and finally, the investment banks which lead manage and underwrite international bond issues are not restricted to European banks — according to Euromoney the leading investment banks which have lead managed international bond issues for 1987, 1988 and 1989 have been Japanese.[11] Nevertheless the term 'Eurobond' issue is used to refer to such a truly international bond issue.[12]

II ISSUE PROCEDURES IN THE INTERNATIONAL BOND MARKETS

Issue procedures in the international bond markets have changed rapidly in the past few years in response to the demands of the market-place and increased competition. The one distinctive feature about issue procedures which has remained constant is the pivotal and central role played by the investment bank chosen by the issuer to 'lead manage' the bond issue. The lead manager has always been responsible for arranging the entire issue and sale of the bonds and the co-ordination of administrative procedures and legal documentation.[13]

The lead manager's functions in organising and placing the issuer's bond commences from the granting of 'a mandate' by the issuer to place the issuer's bonds up to an aggregate amount specified in the mandate. In the

---

10 See 'Developments in International Banking and Capital Markets' Bank of England Quarterly Bulletin, May 1991, p 234; Hayes and Hubbard 'Investment Banking, A Tale of Three Cities', ch 14 (Harvard Business School, 1990).
11 See the *Euromoney 20th Anniversary Supplement* (June 1989).
12 It is submitted that the epithet, whatever its historical origins, is a misnomer. It also reflects a US perception of world markets as being divided into US, European and Far Eastern.
13 At present it appears that the favourite banks in the international markets to lead manage international bond issues are the Japanese houses, in particular Nomura Securities (see *Euromoney 20th Anniversary Supplement*), though over a period of ten years it appears that the London-based Credit Suisse First Boston has lead managed more issues.

past, lead managers tended to adopt either a UK style issue structure or a US style issue structure.[14] The so-called UK style structure involved the formation by the lead manager of a primary underwriting group of investment banks as well as a sub-underwriting group of banks for the purpose of placing the bonds. The sub-underwriting group were subject to underwriting obligations similar to those of the primary underwriting group. If the bonds were not placed either wholly or partially with investors, the two underwriting groups were obliged to purchase the unplaced bonds themselves in agreed proportions. In addition there was a further group of securities dealers called the 'selling group' who participated in the new issue by purchasing bonds themselves although in fact on behalf of their clients. This group undertook no underwriting obligations. Members of the two underwriting groups would also be members of the selling group in practice. The members of the selling group were not subject to any legal obligation to purchase or sell the bonds even though they entered into a 'selling group agreement' with the managers of the issue.

In the so-called US style issue structure there was only one group of investment banks who agreed to underwrite the bond issue. This would be the managing group of underwriters. There would not usually be a sub-underwriting group. A selling group would also usually be used in the US style structure.

In the modern structure which evolved in the mid 1980s, the lead manager formed a single managing group of underwriters who would agree with the issuer to place the bonds with investors or to purchase the bonds themselves. This agreement is contained in the 'subscription agreement' (discussed below)[15] entered into between the issuer and the managing group of underwriters. The sub-underwriting group is invariably dispensed with and in most cases even the selling group is dispensed with.

The second feature which evolved in the middle of the 1980s in the international bond markets was the demise of what used to be termed the 'open priced' deal. In the 1970s it was common for lead managers when taking on a mandate from an issuer to place bonds with investors to retain a discretion as to the pricing of the bonds. This meant that the lead manager would not give the issuer a firm quotation as to the interest rate or coupon or the price at which the bonds would be sold to the issuer at the time the mandate was awarded.[16] The open priced deal has now all but completely been replaced by the 'pre-priced deal'.

In a pre-priced deal the lead manager will agree all the pricing terms with the issuer at the time the issuer gives the lead manager a mandate to place its bonds in the market with investors. Rule 10.01 of chapter III s 1 of the Financial Regulations of The Securities and Futures Authority ('SFA') (formerly The Securities Association or TSA) defined a pre-priced deal as 'an International Offering, other than a Bought Deal, all the pricing terms of which have been fixed'. The terms which are fixed at the time of the giving of the mandate are usually the amount, currency, maturity, offering price, rate of or means of calculating interest and the redemption

---

14 See Fisher *International Bonds* ch 2.
15 See ch 10.
16 See *Fisher* ch 2.

price.[17] Whether or not the lead manager is legally bound to these pricing terms from the moment of the grant of a mandate depends on whether or not the lead manager has agreed to these terms 'subject to contract'.[18] Generally speaking, a lead manager who has obtained legal advice would wish to retain the flexibility, at least in law, to change the price and terms of a bond issue, until the signing of the legal documents (see below) which define the arrangements and the rights and obligations of parties to the issue of the bond. However, it must be remembered that even if the freedom to change the price and terms has been retained as a matter of law, nevertheless as a matter of market practice it would be extremely difficult for a lead manager who had agreed the price and terms to change any one of them after accepting the mandate but before the signing of the legal documents, except in the most unusual of circumstances.

A variation of the pre-price deal is the 'bought deal'. In this type of case the lead manager gives an outright commitment to a prospective issuer that the lead manager himself will purchase the entire aggregate value of bonds to be issued by the issuer. A bought deal is in a sense a pre-price deal with the difference that the lead manager is thought to be 'committed' to purchase all the bonds himself rather than to place the bonds in the market-place on pre-price terms through a syndicate of banks. Rule 10.01 of chapter III s 1 of SFA's Financial Regulations defines a bought deal as 'an International Offering where a firm on its own gives an outright commitment to the issuer or seller to purchase or subscribe for the securities to be offered'. The question whether a lead manager who enters into a bought deal becomes subject to immediate and binding legal obligations depends on the circumstances and terms of the agreement between the issuer and the lead manager. The perception in the markets is that a lead manager who enters into a bought deal has given an outright and *legally* binding commitment to purchase all the bonds himself on the pricing terms agreed as between issuer and lead manager. However, it seems that if the lead manager's offer is nevertheless made 'subject to contract' it would be more than probable that the lead manager would not be subject to legal liabilities until the signing of the appropriate legal documents giving effect to the issue.[19] The effect of using the subject to contract formula is to create a strong presumption that no legal obligations were intended until the signing of the formal legal documents. Nevertheless, if a contrary intention can be shown to exist by reference to circumstances it is possible that a court may impose legal obligations as from the moment that the commitment is given.

Even where the lead manager enters into a bought deal he would in practice form a group of managing underwriters through whom the bonds would be placed in the markets. The issue procedure and the legal structure would be virtually identical with a pre-price deal.

---

17 Rule 10.01 of chapter III of SFA's Financial Regulations defines pricing terms as 'in relation to an offering the amount, currency, maturity, offering price, rate of or means of calculating interest and any prices at which the securities may be redeemed or converted or exchanged into other securities'.
18 See p 46 above.
19 See on the legal impact of the 'subject to contract' formula p 46 below.

With this background in mind, the stages through which a new issue proceeds may be considered.

1 Mandate

The Eurobond issue process commences with the grant of a mandate by a prospective issuer of Eurobonds to a lead manager, and sometimes two or more (co-lead) managers. A lead manager will often obtain a mandate from an issuer to place its bonds in the market after a period of negotiation between the lead manager and the issuer. The lead manager would normally have made a number of presentations to a prospective issuer in order to explain to the issuer the market conditions and the terms on which a lead manager could place the issuer's bonds. By the time the mandate is given to a lead manager most of the important terms and conditions relating to the bond and the issue would have been determined as between the issuer and the lead manager. As observed above, most mandates in practice are given on a 'pre-priced' basis. If the lead manager's offer which results in a mandate is made subject to contract[20] these terms and conditions might be varied at least as a matter of legal theory, until the time formal legal documents are signed.[1]

2 Launch

Once a lead manager has obtained a mandate, it will launch the issue by a public announcement to the markets. The lead manager will announce the issue by contacting other investment banks and securities dealers by telephone or through screen communication systems in order to obtain statements of interest from investment banks in forming the managing group who will underwrite the issue of the bonds in the market. If a selling group is to be formed the lead manager will also contact prospective selling group members with a view to forming that group. Generally speaking, if bonds are to be sold at least partially to retail investors (fondly referred to in the Euro markets as 'Belgian dentists') a selling group would be formed, because members of the selling group would place the bonds not only with corporate and institutional clients, but also with such wealthy individuals.

Once indications of interest have been received by the lead manager from prospective members of the managing group of underwriters and/or prospective selling group members a more formal '*invitation telex*' will be sent to such investment banks and securities dealers offering them a position in the management group or the selling group as the case may be. The invitation telex is generally drafted carefully and is reviewed by lawyers of the lead manager. The invitation telex itself is not regarded as a legally binding offer since it is generally made subject to the signing of formal documents by the lead manager and issuer. Nevertheless, it is regarded as an extremely important document containing all the terms and conditions relating to the issue of the bonds. The contents of the invitation telex have been standardised

---

20 See above ch 3.
1 See p 156 below.

by the Recommendations of the International Primary Markets Association ('IPMA'). The recommendations of IPMA are not binding on their members but have strong persuasive force and are generally followed carefully in practice by market participants. The invitation telex is subject to careful drafting because it is market practice that the formal legal documents will be drafted strictly in accordance with the terms of the invitation telex though there is technically no legal obligation to do so. IPMA Recommendation 1.1 provides:

> 'the invitation telex should be considered as the basis of the syndicate's commitment subject to the signed syndicated agreement. The lead manager should however advise all invited parties by screen or telephone at the earliest possible moment of the basic commercial and non-commercial terms of an issue. In the case of screen displays the telephone conversation may be limited to the invitation.'

The relationship between the screen or telephone invitation and the invitation telex is also a matter of market practice, but IPMA Recommendation 1.1(3) provides:

> 'an early positive response to a screen or telephone invitation may be reversed upon receipt of the invitation telex only if there are changes in or additions to the basic commercial or non-commercial terms of the issue.'

Consequently, it is also necessary to be certain as to the terms and conditions which are communicated by telephone or by electronic communication systems. However, once the invitation telex has been sent out there seems to be a market commitment on the part of both the lead manager and prospective members of the management group and/or selling group members and neither party is expected to withdraw unless 'there are subsequent material changes in or additions to the invitation telex (whether in the agreements or otherwise)'.[2]

Despite the strength that these Recommendations carry, it is submitted that, provided the invitation telex is made 'subject to contract', it seems likely that no legal obligations of an enforceable nature arise until the signing of the formal legal agreements.[3]

The terms and conditions in relation to the bond issue which are contained in the invitation telex must in addition contain a number of matters which Recommendation 1.1(2) of IPMA specifies. These include: whether or not guarantees are to be provided for the issue of the bonds; the ratings assigned to the bonds by rating agencies such as Standard & Poor's or Moody's; whether or not the issue is to be subordinated or secured; whether or not there are negative pledge provisions;[4] whether or not there are to be early redemption provisions; whether or not there are to be restrictions on sales of the bonds in the US or UK due to securities laws in those jurisdictions;[5] whether or not 'stabilisation' will be effected;[6] whether or not cross-default

---

2 See IPMA Recommendation 1.1(3).
3 See cases cited above.
4 See p 89 above.
5 See Section D, below.
6 See ch 18 below.

154 *Background and issue procedures*

provisions will be included;[7] and whether or not 'force majeure' provisions will be included.[8]

Apart from these items of information, the invitation telex will contain a general description of the issuer, a general description of the terms and conditions of the bonds, and a timetable as to the arrangements made with regard to the issue of the bonds. IPMA Recommendations also require that the invitation telex set out the various tax provisions applicable to the issue. Further, the invitation telex must also specify the various expenses which the lead manager will incur in respect of the issue including legal costs and the cost of printing the various documents which need to be prepared for the purposes of the bond issue.[9]

After launch and before the signing of the formal legal documents the lead manager will prepare in draft form all the legal documents which provide for the marketing of the issue and the administration of the bonds after they have been sold to investors. In addition the lead manager would also prepare the *'offering circular'* or *'prospectus'* containing all material information with regard to the issuer and the bonds. This draft offering circular and the draft legal agreements are forwarded to those investment banks who have agreed to join the managing group of underwriters and/or the selling group as the case may be.

The offering circular even in draft form is an extremely important document since its purpose is twofold. First, it will provide information to the prospective members of the managing group [and/or the selling group] about the issuer and the bonds; secondly, where the bonds are to be listed on The London Stock Exchange or the Luxembourg Stock Exchange, the offering circular will also constitute the *'listing particulars'* which are submitted to the Stock Exchange on which the bonds are to be listed. Consequently, the contents of the offering circular will depend on the requirements of the London or the Luxembourg Stock Exchange with regard to the contents of listing particulars which should be submitted for purposes of listing.[10] Where the bonds are to be listed in London the offering circular must contain all the information concerning the issuer necessary to enable investors to make an informed investment decision.[11] The offering circular will, generally speaking, contain the following:

(a) the terms and conditions of the bonds;
(b) a description of the history of the issuer and the current business activities of the issuer, usually broken down by product and geographical area;
(c) financial information with regard to the borrower;
(d) a summary of the legal documents including the subscription agreement and the selling group agreement if it is used, including a statement of the selling restrictions applicable to the sale of the bonds;
(e) a confirmation by the issuer that the information in the offering circular

---

7 See 99 above.
8 See on 'force majeure' ch 5 above.
9 See Appendix A and C of the IPMA Recommendations.
10 See on listing of bonds Ch 17 below.
11 See s 146 of FSA 1986 and Ch 17 below.

is complete and accurate and that information outside the offering circular should not be relied on;

(f) the front cover of the offering circular will contain the essential information with regard to the issue, namely the name of the issuer and the managers, the title of the bonds, the issue price of the bonds, interest rate (or coupon), the date of redemption, the place of listing;

(g) the offering circular will also contain in the inside back cover the names of the legal advisers, auditors, the listing agents, the paying agents and the trustee (if any) to the issue.[12]

While the offering circular for an issuer who is new to the London Stock Exchange tends to be extremely exhaustive and detailed, where the issuer of the bonds already has listed securities on The London Stock Exchange and up-to-date financial information about the issuer is available, the offering circular takes the form of a short statement which contains little more than the terms and conditions of the bonds themselves.

The use of offering circulars gives rise to complex regulatory issues which are discussed below.[13]

Since the bonds would usually be listed either on The London Stock Exchange or the Luxembourg Stock Exchange, a formal application for listing would be made to the exchange chosen by the issuer. Listing applications would be handled in London by a 'listing agent' or sponsoring broker who needs to be a member of the London Stock Exchange.

3 Stabilisation[14]

From the moment of launch, while there are no securities in existence, the securities dealers active in the markets will commence buying and selling the bonds which will be issued at a later stage. This sort of trading in the bonds to be issued in the future is referred to as '*grey market*' trading and may cause problems for the lead manager. The reason why grey market trading can cause difficulties for the lead manager is that securities dealers may take the view that the price or interest rate of the bonds is not attractive and, consequently, may commence selling the bonds 'short' in the hope that the bond price will fall further so that they can buy at a lower price than their sale price and make a profit. If the market price for the bonds falls in the grey market as a result of such 'short selling' it becomes difficult for the lead manager to place the bonds at the announced issue price.

This difficulty becomes even more exacerbated if one or more of the members of the prospective managing group of underwriters and/or the selling group also commence selling bonds at a discount to the issue price, in effect 'dumping' the bonds on the market. The reason why prospective members of the management group and/or selling group members will commence selling bonds at a discount is that in market practice they would have indicated the amount of bonds that they would be interested in purchasing in the offering well in advance of the signing; the lead

---

12 These parties are referred to in the markets as 'the football team'.
13 See ch 16.
14 See ch 18 on regulation of stabilisation.

156 *Background and issue procedures*

manager would have informally agreed to an allotment of bonds to prospective members of the managing group of underwriters and/or the selling group members; such persons who would have been informally allotted bonds may feel that they may not be able to place the bonds at the issue price of the bonds and consequently commence selling the bonds at a discount from the issue price. Sales of bonds to members of the managing group of underwriters and/or the selling group are generally made net of the commission which they will be paid for placing bonds with investors. Thus, for instance, if the face value of the bonds is $100 and a member of the managing group is to be paid a selling commission of $2.00 he will be able to purchase the bonds at $98.00. Such a dealer would not make a loss on the sale of a bond unless the market price of the bond falls below $98.00. Consequently, what such dealers may do is to attempt to sell the bonds at a discount below the $100 face value but which is at a price above $98.00 which is the purchase price that such a dealer would have to pay the issuer for the bond.

To prevent a downward price spiral caused by short selling or dumping of the bonds the lead manager will effect 'stabilising transactions' which in effect support the price of the bonds in the markets. Stabilisation is a complex process but in effect it involves placing bids for the bonds or offers to purchase at a price higher than would otherwise prevail in the marketplace. This is done in order to prevent a fall in the price of the bonds. Stabilisation is now regulated under s 48(7) of the Financial Services Act 1986 and is discussed below.[15]

More recently, new syndication techniques have been developed to counter the practice of dumping by members of the underwriting syndicate. This technique is referred to as the '*fixed price re-offer*' mechanism. Under a fixed price re-offer, the lead manager fixes the price at which syndicate participants may re-sell bonds which are allocated to them.

4 Signing

There is a period of roughly seven to fourteen days which elapses between the launch or announcement of the bond issue to the markets and the formal signing of legal documents. The signing is a very important date since it is a date on which legal obligations arise for the managing underwriters.

At the signing the *offering circular* or *prospectus* in final form will be made available.

The documents which are signed on signing day are the two documents (sometimes three) which provide the legal framework for the marketing and placing of the bonds.

(a) The subscription agreement. This is the pivotal agreement which is signed as between the issuer of the bonds and the managing group of underwriters including the lead manager. This agreement contains the all important underwriting obligation which is given by the managing group to the issuer.[16]

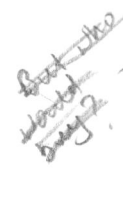

---

15 See ch 18 above.
16 For a full discussion, see ch 10 below.

(b) The agreement between managers. This will allocate the amount of bonds that each manager will take up or underwrite in respect of the issue as a whole. The reason for this agreement is that in the subscription agreement each of the managers undertakes an underwriting obligation in respect of the whole of the bond issue. Consequently, the agreement among managers seeks to cushion this obligation by specifying what proportion of unsold bonds each manager will be prepared to take up. It simply lays down the terms and conditions on which selling group members will be sold bonds if they take up their allotment.[17]

(c) The selling group agreement. A selling group is not frequently formed in current Eurobond practice. However, where such a group is formed to place bonds, this agreement regulates the terms and conditions on which selling group members may purchase and on-sell bonds purchased. It does not place any obligation to buy or sell the bonds. The real purpose of the agreement is to place restrictions on sales to nationals of the US and sometimes of the UK for the purpose of avoiding breaches of the securities laws of either or both countries.[18]

It has also been the practice in the past when UK style syndicate structures were used to have a separate sub-underwriting agreement in addition to the above documents. However, the sub-underwriting agreement is now virtually a thing of the past. There are also a number of other documents which are signed in respect of an Eurobond issue but the signing of these documents occurs only on the closing day of the issue.[19]

5 Allotment

After the signing of the legal documents a formal *allotment telex* will make offers to various investment banks and securities dealers who have informally expressed an interest in taking up a certain amount of the bonds. This is the formal or legally binding offer to sell bonds on behalf of the issuer. In practice the amount of the allotment would have been decided in advance of this telex. In the case of pre-priced offerings which are syndicated only among the managing group of underwriters, IPMA Recommendation 1.2 requires that final allotment should be made within the next business day following the launch of the issue or as soon as practicable after the management group is formed, if that is earlier. As a matter of English contract law the offer contained in the allotment telex is 'accepted' when the banks and dealers to whom allotments are made transfer funds to the lead manager on 'closing day' (see below).

Due to the lapse of time between the time when informal indications of allotment are made and the time when the formal allotment telex is sent, it is possible for a lead manager to adopt punitive measures against those securities dealers who have been dumping their contemplated allotment of bonds in the markets at a discount. Thus, for instance, if dealers sell a

---

17 For a full discussion, see ch 10 above.
18 See chs 16 and 21 below.
19 See chs 10, 12 and 13 below.

158 *Background and issue procedures*

large portion of the issue of bonds prior to the formal allotment such dealers are in a position where they have established a 'short' position and they must look to the lead manager to allot them sufficient bonds to satisfy the sales into which they have entered. It is now perfectly possible for the lead manager in the face of the short selling and dumping of the bonds by dealers who have expressed an interest in taking up a portion of the bond issue to refuse to allot any bonds to such dealers or allot a number of bonds which is insufficient to enable them to satisfy their sale contracts. Such dealers are then compelled to offer to purchase bonds from the lead manager at a large premium. Such activity is referred to as a 'short squeeze'.[20] This ability is now limited due to IPMA Recommendation 1.2 which requires that, at least in pre-priced offerings where no selling group is involved, the lead manager must make final allotments of bonds to the managing group within the next business day following the launch of the issue.

Short squeezes of this type are also now inhibited by the requirements of IPMA Recommendation 1.3 which provides for 'protection'. Once again this applies in pre-priced offerings which are syndicated among the managing group only. IPMA Recommendation 1.3 requires lead managers to grant pre-allotments of not less than 50% of the finalised or expected minimum underwriting commitments if so required by management group members at the time of their acceptance of the syndicate invitations. If the Recommendation is followed by a lead manager it would mean that members of the management group have a guarantee that they will be allotted at least 50% of their intended underwriting commitment so that they may enter into sale contracts in respect of that guaranteed portion without fear of a subsequent refusal by the lead manager to allot sufficient bonds to satisfy their sale contracts.

6 The closing

Once the bonds have been placed successfully in the hands of investors the closing of the bond issue takes place. This would usually occur approximately a week or so after the signing of the subscription agreement.

At the closing a number of documents are signed which establish the regime for the administration of the bond during its lifetime. The most important document which will be signed on the closing date is the *trust deed* if a trustee is being appointed. In a large number of bond issues the bonds are issued subject to a trust deed which is a long and complex document.[1] In addition a *paying agency agreement* is signed. The latter simply appoints a large number of paying agents who will handle the payment of principal and interest on the bonds. Where a trust deed is not being used a *fiscal agency agreement*[2] is used instead, but the legal nature of a fiscal agent is very different from that of a trustee. In essence the trustee operates as an agent of the bond holders whereas the fiscal agent is no

---

20 The *Financial Times* of 20 February 1989 reported that Credit Suisse First Boston had effected such a short squeeze in respect of the Ecu denominated issue of Eurobonds by Toyota Motor Credit Corporation.
1 See ch 13.
2 See ch 12 below.

more than a paying agent with administrative duties who acts on behalf of the issuer.[3]

On closing day the subscribers to the bonds, who would usually be the managers and/or members of the selling group, will transfer funds to the lead manager's account. In practice, of course, the managers and the selling group members would have sold the bonds to investors and, consequently, would have obtained funds from such end investors for the bonds. The lead manager will transfer the funds by same day transfer to the issuer's account. Before the funds are transferred to the issuer, the lead manager will deduct from the proceeds any commissions and other expenses which are payable under the terms of the issue to the lead manager and the managers. In return for the funds the issuer will transfer to the lead manager not the actual or 'definitive' Eurobond but a temporary global bond, which will be a substitute for the definitive bonds until the latter are printed.[4] The temporary global bond is transferred by the lead manager for the benefit of the subscribers of the bonds to the two clearing houses which are at the centre of the secondary market trading in the bonds after the bond issue has been successfully terminated. These two clearing houses are Euroclear[5] in Brussels, and Cedel[6] in Luxembourg. In practice, however, the temporary global bond is not transferred to Euroclear or Cedel physically. It will be transferred to a bank nominated by Euroclear and/or Cedel as the case may be and held by this bank as a sub-custodian of Euroclear and/or Cedel. The sub-custodian is referred to as 'a common depository'.[7]

7 The 'lock-up' period

In the case of many Eurobond issues there is usually a 40-day[8] period commencing from closing day during which the actual or definitive bonds are not made available to investors who have purchased bonds during the offer period. During this period the rights of the bond holders are represented by the temporary global bond which is delivered to the common depository of Euroclear and/or Cedel. During this period the actual or definitive bonds will be printed and handed over by the issuer to the trustee appointed under a trust deed (if there is one) or to the fiscal agent appointed under a fiscal agency agreement where this is used. It is a duty of the trustee or fiscal agent to hand over the definitive or actual bonds at the end of the 40-day

---

3   See for a discussion of the fiscal agency agreement ch 12 below.
4   See the discussion below on the relationship between the temporary global bond and the definitive bond, p 175. The definitive bonds are security printed while the temporary global bond is on ordinary paper.
5   Euroclear Clearance System Société Coopérative is a Belgian company operated by Morgan Guaranty Trust Company of New York (Brussels Office). The Euroclear system was created in 1968 by Morgan Guaranty Trust Company of New York. In 1972 the ownership of the Euroclear systems was acquired by an English company, Euroclear Clearance System Ltd. This company licensed the Belgian company to operate the system in 1987. See 'An Introduction to the Euroclear System', s 1 of the *Operating Procedures of the Euroclear System*, 1 November 1990.
6   Centrale de Livraison de Valeurs Mobilières founded in 1970 and incorporated under Luxembourg law.
7   See ss 5 and 10 of the *Operating Procedures for the Euroclear System*, 1 November 1990.
8   It was previously 90 days until the enactment in 1990 of Regulation S under the US Securities Act of 1933.

period to the clearing houses when the latter certify that all bonds held on their books are in the beneficial ownership of persons who are not US nationals or residents. This procedure is made necessary in order to avoid a breach of US securities regulations and tax laws by the issue of Eurobonds.[9]

---

9 See Part V below.

CHAPTER 9
Negotiability and governing law

In the conventional Eurobond issue a large number of legal instruments referred to as the 'definitive bonds' or 'definitive notes' are issued which in aggregate total the amount of finance required by the issuer. The term Eurobond is used to refer to these definitives, and must be distinguished from the 'temporary global bond' which is usually issued at the end of the selling period in a Eurobond issue pending the delivery of the definitives to bond purchasers.[1]

The terms and conditions contained in the definitive bond instruments are discussed in chapter 11. In this chapter, the nature and characteristic of the Eurobond will be examined as well as certain issues in the conflict of laws.

The 'definitive' bond possesses the following characteristics in practice:

(a) It is a debt instrument in bearer form which seeks to enable the holder to possess direct legal rights as against the issuer.
(b) It contains the promise of the issuer that a sum specified on the face of the bond, called the 'principal amount', (which is the redemption or 'face' value of the bond), will be paid to the 'holder' of the bond on a specified maturity date or, in certain circumstances, at an earlier redemption date.
(c) It also contains a promise that the issuer will pay interest to the holder of the bond on the principal amount during the 'life' of the bond until final maturity or earlier redemption, at a fixed or 'floating' rate of interest.[2]

There are exceptions to this standard format in the case of 'perpetual' bonds which have no maturity date. In a perpetual bond there is no obligation on the part of the issuer of the bond to pay the face value of the bond except on the occurrence of an event of default.[3] The bond simply carries an obligation on the part of the issuer to pay interest.[4] In the case of deep discount or 'zero coupon' bonds, the bond does not contain a promise by the issuer to pay interest.[5]

---
1 See p 159 above.
2 See pp 193–195 above on 'fixed' rate bonds and 'floating' rate bonds.
3 On perpetual bonds see p 215 below.
4 See on perpetuals p 215 below.
5 See on zero coupons p 214 below.

(d) Bonds are bought and sold on a secondary market by investors and are, therefore, regarded as transferable by the international financial and investment community. Trading in the secondary markets after issue is effected under the supervision of the Association of International Bond Dealers ('AIBD', soon to be re-named the International Securities Markets Association or ISMA) which is an association consisting of members who are active in bond trading.[6]

(e) The bonds contain a statement on their face that 'title to the notes passes on delivery'.

Where the bonds are to be listed on The London Stock Exchange the physical size and format of the definitives is laid down by Section 9 chapter 4 of the listing rules of The London Stock Exchange.[7] However, where Eurobonds are issued by a corporate entity in the European Community the Stock Exchange will accept definitives printed in accordance with the official requirements of that state and certified as such.[8]

The Stock Exchange's listing rules[9] further require that the definitive be security printed and issued with serial numbers. A number of matters must also appear on the face of the bond including:

(a) the authority under which the issuer is constituted and the country of incorporation;
(b) the authority under which the bond is issued;
(c) the dates when fixed interest is due;

while a number of other matters must appear on the face or back of the instrument including all conditions as to redemption, conversion (in the case of a convertible),[10] meetings and voting rights.[11]

It is necessary in the light of the above to consider the legal nature of the Eurobond, in particular whether or not it is a negotiable instrument.

I NEGOTIABILITY OF THE EUROBOND

An instrument which is regarded as 'negotiable' under English law possesses a number of characteristics which makes it a unique chose in action.

The title to and property in the instrument and all rights under it pass to a bona fide holder for value by physical delivery in the case of a bearer instrument (or by endorsement and delivery in the case of an instrument transferable by endorsement). This feature distinguishes a negotiable instrument from a mere assignment of a debt in law or in equity. Notice to the debtor is unnecessary for the purpose of perfecting title to the instru-

---

6 The activities of the Association have a special exempt status under the regulatory regime introduced by the Financial Services Act 1986 by virtue of para 25A of Sch 1 to the Act. See ch 15 below.
7 See the *Admission of Securities to Listing*.
8 See s 9, ch 4.
9 S 9, ch 4.
10 See on convertibles ch 14 below.
11 See s 9, ch 4 of the Stock Exchange's *Admission of Securities for Listing*.

ment, and the rule in *Dearle v Hall*[12] on priority of notice to the debtor does not apply to negotiable instruments: *Bence v Shearman*.[13]

A bona fide transferee for value acquires a good title free of any defects in the title or defences available against the claims of any transferor or holder.[14] This characteristic distinguishes a truly negotiable instrument from an assignment of a debt by a creditor or an instrument which is merely 'transferable' by virtue of trade custom such as a bill of lading. Transferees of a transferable instrument obtain only such title which the transferor himself possessed.[15] Similarly, assignees of debts take 'subject to equities'[16] so that as against an assignee, the debtor may set up any debt due from a creditor as cancelling or diminishing the amount which the assignee may claim by virtue of the assignment.[17] This rule does not apply where a right to a debt due is transferred by the medium of a negotiable instrument.[18]

In legal theory such negotiability is important only in relation to sales of bonds in the secondary markets. In practice the issue of Eurobonds in the international markets would be made difficult unless the international investment community had no doubts as to the negotiable character of the Eurobond. Consequently, negotiability of the Eurobond is a legal issue which is also of interest to the primary markets.

Doors to negotiability

How does an instrument become 'negotiable' in English law? Although Eurobonds always contain a statement ex facie that 'title to the bonds passes on delivery', the purpose of which is to confer negotiability, it seems clear that the parties to an instrument cannot confer negotiability on the instrument simply by stating that the instrument will be a negotiable instrument.[19]

It has been repeatedly pointed out that the only bases on which an instrument acquires the characteristic of negotiability under English law are:

(a) it comes within the definition of a bill of exchange or a promissory note in the Bills of Exchange Act of 1882;
(b) by virtue of 'mercantile custom'; or
(c) judicial precedent.[20]

---

12 (1823) 3 Russ 1.
13 [1898] 2 Ch 582.
14 *Goodwin v Robarts* (1875) LR 10 Exch 337 at 344, affd (1876) 1 App Case 476; *Bechuanaland Exploration Co v London Trading Bank Ltd* [1898] 2 QB 658.
15 *Gurney v Behrend* (1854) 3 E & B 622, per Lord Campbell CJ, at p 634; see also Benjamin *Sale of Goods* Sweet and Maxwell (3rd edn, 1987), para 1450, p 907.
16 *Mangles v Dixon* (1852) 3 HLCas 702; *Business Computers Ltd v Anglo-African Leasing Ltd* [1977] 1 WLR 578.
17 *Newfoundland Government v Newfoundland Rly Co* (1883) 13 App Cas 199.
18 On negotiability see generally Halsbury's Laws, (4th edn) vol 4, paras 302–303; *Chitty on Contracts* (26th edn) ch 19, paras 1435, 1428; Dicey and Morris *Conflict of Laws* (11th edn) r 195.
19 See Kennedy J in *Bechuanaland Exploration Co v London Trading Bank Ltd* [1898] 2 QB 658.
20 See the statements of Lord Esher MR and Bowen LJ in *Picker v London and County Banking Co* (1887) 18 QBD 515 at 518 and 519; Kennedy J in *Bechuanaland Exploration Co v London Trading Bank Ltd* [1898] 2 QB 658 at 666 and 671; Bigham J in *Edelstein v Schuler & Co* [1902] 2 KB 144 at 154–155.

It seems quite clear that an international bond or Eurobond does not qualify either as a bill of exchange or a promissory note under s 3 of the UK Bills of Exchange Act of 1882.[1] The reason why the Eurobond does not qualify as a bill of exchange is because the Bills of Exchange Act 1882 requires that such a bill of exchange must contain an unconditional order to pay: s 3(1). The Eurobond contains no such *order* to pay but a *promise* to pay.

The characteristics of a promissory note under s 83 of the Bills of Exchange Act 1882 are as follows:

> 'A promissory note is an unconditional promise in writing made by one person to another signed by the maker, engaging to pay, on demand or at a fixed or determinable future time, a sum certain in money, to, or to the order of, a specified person or to bearer.'

A Eurobond does not qualify as a promissory note on the above definition, first because Eurobonds do not contain an unconditional promise to pay. The promise to pay in a Eurobond is confined by the prohibition on sales to US persons (as defined), and consequently the promise is conditional on the holder not being such a US person. Secondly, a Eurobond does not contain a promise to pay 'a sum certain'. This is because in all Eurobond issues the issuer is required to pay additional sums by way of interest in the event of a withholding tax being imposed on the issuer in respect of interest payments to bond holders (called a withholding tax 'gross-up' provision).[2] It would seem, however, that a sum payable with interest at a fixed or variable rate does not render the sum payable uncertain.[3] Similarly, the requirement in s 83 of 'fixed or determinable future time' in respect of payment is also unaffected by the fact that the instrument contains either a promise to pay in instalments or a promise to pay prior to maturity on the occurrence of an event of default or both.[4]

Despite the fact that Eurobonds fall outside the range of negotiable instruments within the statutory framework of the Bills of Exchange Act 1882, they may be regarded as negotiable either due to judicial precedent or mercantile custom.

There is ample judicial authority to the effect that bearer bonds, whether English or foreign, are to be regarded as negotiable instruments if they are so recognised in the trading markets. The clearest statement to this effect is to be found in the judgment of Bigham J in *Edelstein v Schuler & Co*[5] where his Lordship states:

> 'In my opinion the time has passed where the negotiability of bearer bonds whether government bonds or trading bonds foreign or English can be called in question in our courts. The existence of the usage has been so often proved and its convenience is so obvious that it must be taken now to be part of the law; the very expression "bearer bond" connotes the idea of negotiability so

---

1 See the definition of a bill of exchange and of a promissory note in s 3 of that Act.
2 See p 79 above.
3 See s 9(1)(a) of the Bills of Exchange Act 1882 which is considered to codify the common law: see *Bank of England v Vagliano Bros* [1891] AC 107.
4 See s 9(1)(b) and (c) of the Bills of Exchange Act 1882 which seems to codify the common law on negotiable instruments: see *Bank of England v Vagliano Bros* [1891] AC 107.
5 [1902] 2 KB 144, at 155.

that the moment such bonds are issued to the public, they rank themselves among the class of negotiable securities.'[6]

The policy rationale underlying this recognition of negotiability of bearer bonds of all kinds was stated by Justice Bigham in terms equally applicable to the modern Eurobond:

'It would be a great misfortune if it were otherwise for it is well known that such bonds are treated in all foreign markets as deliverable from hand to hand; the attribute not only enhances their value by making them easy of transfer but it qualifies them to serve as a kind of international currency; and it will be very odd and a great injury to our trade if these advantages were not accorded to them in this country.'

If it could be argued that these cases are distinguishable on the basis that they referred to a more simple form of bearer bond when compared to the modern Eurobond with its complex terms and conditions. It is nevertheless submitted that it is beyond question that the modern Eurobond should be regarded as a negotiable instrument by reference to mercantile custom. Bigham J in *Edelstein v Schuler & Co* (above) recognised that two factors must be considered. First, the number of transactions entered into in respect of such instruments, and secondly, the time over which such transactions are spread. His Lordship considered the volume of transactions as a far more important criterion than the time period over which such transactions were entered into. In other words, it is submitted that there is no need to show a long usage or custom provided the volume of transactions is such that it is clear that mercantile customs, ie the markets, recognise the instrument as negotiable. The international bond in its modern form has probably been recognised as negotiable for nearly thirty years from the inception of the international bond markets[7] and the volume of trading is enormous: in 1990 the value of trading amounted to US $6.2trn.[8] It may, however, be the case that extremely novel forms of Eurobonds when issued for the first time may not satisfy this test.

It must be noted that it is the custom of merchants in England which is the test. Thus in *Picker v London and County Banking Co*[9] the Court of Appeal held that while bonds without coupons may have been negotiable in Prussia such bonds were not recognised as negotiable by mercantile custom in England and that consequently the bonds were not negotiable instruments in England.

II CONFLICTS OF LAWS AND EUROBONDS

In practice it may be the case that an issuer of Eurobonds is a Japanese or US multinational while the purchaser of bonds is a Swiss securities dealer.

---

6 See also to the same effect Kennedy J in *Bechuanaland Exploration Co v London Trading Bank* [1898] 2 QB 658 and *Goodwin v Robarts* (1875) LR 10 Exch 337.
7 See Kerr *A History of the Eurobond Market*.
8 See the article by John Langton, Chief Executive of the Association of International Bond Dealers in the London *Observer*, 14 July 1991.
9 (1887) 18 QBD 515.

166 *Negotiability and governing law*

The latter may sell the bonds to a German bank or the Central Bank of a sovereign state or to a pension fund resident in the Cayman Islands. It is in the context of such a truly international transactional framework that the question of applicable law arises.

The issues which may involve a conflict of laws are as follows:

(a) Which law determines the formal and essential validity of a Eurobond at the time it is issued?
(b) Which law determines the rights and liabilities as between the issuer and the 'holder' of the Eurobond? In particular, what law determines whether terms in trust deeds[10] and fiscal agency agreements[11] are part of the legal regime regulating the rights and liabilities of issuer and 'holder'?
(c) Which law determines whether a person is a 'holder' or 'holder for value' or whether a person is a 'bona fide holder for value'?
(d) Which law determines whether a holder obtains a title from a transferor and how title is to be transferred?
(e) Which law determines whether the transferee obtains title subject to or free from any defects in title of the transferor?

The UK Contracts (Applicable Law) Act 1990[12] which enacts the Rome Convention is not applicable to decide any of these questions since art 1(2) of the Convention disapplies the Convention to 'obligations arising under ... promissory notes and other negotiable instruments to the extent that the obligations under such other negotiable instruments arise out of their negotiable character'.[13] The Giuliano and Lagarde Report which accompanied the text seems to suggest that the *lex fori* (including its conflicts rules) should determine whether an instrument is negotiable.[14] A court in the UK may consider this report in applying the Convention.[15]

The approach in the Bills of Exchange Act 1882 to such questions is to adopt what has been termed by Falconbridge[16] the 'several laws' approach rather than the 'single law' approach. Section 72 of the Act deals with the question of formal validity, interpretation and perhaps essential validity.[17] The Act does not deal with the proprietory (as distinct from contractual) aspects of bills of exchange or promissory notes governed by it. (The proprietary aspects are those raised by questions (c) and (d) above.)

As observed earlier, the Bills of Exchange Act 1882 does not apply to Eurobonds since they are neither bills of exchange nor promissory notes as defined in that Act.[18] Nevertheless, the conflicts rules in the Act may

---

10 See ch 13 below.
11 See ch 12 below.
12 See the earlier discussion at in ch 2 above.
13 See art 1(2)(c) of the Rome Convention in Sch I of the Contracts (Applicable Law) Act 1990.
14 See OJ C 282, 31.10.80.
15 See s 3(3) of the Act.
16 *Essays on the Conflict of Laws* (2nd edn, 1954) p 340.
17 See Romer J in *Alcock v Smith* [1892] 1 Ch 238, but cf Vaughan Williams LJ in *Embiricos v Anglo-Austrian Bank* [1905] 1 KB 677 at 685.
18 See pp 163–164 above.

be considered to represent common law conflicts rules applicable to negotiable instruments in general.[19]

However, it is submitted that neither the Bills of Exchange Act 1882 nor the cases preceding the Act prevent parties choosing a single proper law *expressed on the face of the instrument* to govern at least the contractual elements of a bond instrument. This would mean that at least (a) to (c) above may be controlled for purposes of certainty by reference to a single chosen system of law. Dicey and Morris seem to accept this proposition[20] but seem to assert that the choice is restricted to the *lex loci contractus* or *lex loci solutionis*. It is submitted that in the absence of judicial authority there is no reason why an English court should not recognise an express choice of English law as governing at least the contractual aspects of the bonds even though England is not the *lex loci contractus* of the bonds, eg in an issue of Ecu bonds effected in Paris subject to an English proper law clause.

It is submitted therefore that a chosen proper law specified on the face of the bond instrument should control at least the contractual aspects of the bonds under English conflicts rules. Above all, such a rule would enable predictability and certainty of legal rights and liabilities arising on the instruments at the time of its issue.[1]

This leaves open the question as to which law governs the proprietary aspects of the bonds instrument, ie items (d) and (e) above, which includes the essence of negotiability.

Dicey and Morris states:

'in the conflict of laws negotiable instruments are therefore treated as chattels, ie, as tangible moveables. Whether they are "negotiable" is a question to be determined by the law of the country where the alleged transfer by way of "negotiation" takes place, and this is, in the nature of things, the country in which the instrument is situated at the time of delivery.'[2]

This would require the application of the *lex situs* to the proprietary issues. It is, however, submitted that this approach is difficult to apply in practice.

As observed earlier[3] definitive Eurobonds are usually warehoused with a 'common depository' for the two clearance systems Euroclear and Cedel. Euroclear and Cedel hold the bonds for the account of their respective securities account holders in each clearance system; where a transfer takes place it always takes place between one account holder of the clearance system and another; consequently, all transfers are effected by an electronic book entry system without any movement of the physical definitive Eurobonds. If a 'delivery' occurs for the purposes of the rule stated in *Dicey and Morris*

---

19 See *Dicey and Morris* p 1310, commentary to r 196.
20 See p 1311, commentary to r 196.
1 It must, however, be remembered that if repayment of principal or interest subsequently becomes unlawful, either by the proper law or the place specified for payment, the obligation to pay contained in the instrument will be incapable of performance in accordance with the principles discussed previously. See ch 2.
2 At p 1306, in the commentary to r 195. See also at pp 1322-1325 in the commentary to r 197. See to the same effect Wood *Law and Practice of International Finance* (ed Clark Boardman) ch IX.
3 See p 159.

168 *Negotiability and governing law*

it can only be a constructive delivery. It may be that the approach in the cases cited by *Dicey and Morris* can be adapted to apply to a system of transfer based on a clearance system such as Euroclear or Cedel. The question then arises as to whether the 'constructive' transfers of the bonds occur in the country in which the bonds are physically warehoused or where the electronic 'books' of the clearance systems are located. It is submitted the former location is to be preferred. In the large majority of cases the bank chosen as common depository for an international issue will warehouse the physical bonds in London, and consequently constructive delivery would occur in England. Negotiability of the Eurobond would thus be referred to the English *lex situs* by English conflicts rules or other conflicts rules which apply the *lex situs*.

The second problem is that the principle laid down in *Dicey and Morris* does not adequately distinguish between the relationship of issuer and transferee on the one side and the relationship between transferor and transferee on the other. Why should the relationship between the holder of the bearer instrument and the issuer be referred to a system of law where a 'delivery' fortuitously takes place, particularly if this in fact depends on where bonds happen to be physically warehoused?

It is submitted that a fresh approach is necessary. In practice all Eurobonds contain a choice of law clause which expressly subjects the bond to a specific identified system of law for purposes of determining all rights and obligations arising on the bond. Usually this system is English law. It is submitted that this express choice of law clause should govern the negotiability of the bond regardless of the place of transfer. This express choice of law, it is submitted, should govern not only the relationship between transferor and transferee and successive transferees, but also the rights of a transferee as against the issuer of the Eurobond. This approach is not inconsistent with art 1(2) of the Rome Convention discussed above, and the views of Professors Giuliano and Lagarde expressed in their Report on the Rome Convention.[4]

Such an approach is also not inconsistent with the cases relied on by the editors of *Dicey and Morris* as supporting the *lex situs* of delivery or transfer as the governing law. The two cases *Alcock v Smith*[5] and *Embiricos v Anglo-Austrian Bank*[6] were both cases where the bond instrument did not contain an express choice of law clause. In the absence of an express choice of law clause the Court of Appeal in both cases applied the law of the place of delivery to determine negotiability. These cases are therefore no authority against the proposition advanced above.

Such an approach is also extremely desirable from a practical point of view because it creates certainty in a complex financial transaction which involves innumerable parties from a large number of countries with different systems of law. In particular, it would enable the terms and conditions of the bond instrument to be tested for validity by a system of law chosen to govern the matter at the time of the issue of the instrument and by reference to which the terms and conditions may be drafted.

Further, such an approach is consistent with the doctrine of party auton-

---

4 See the Official Journal of the Communities, OJ C282, 31.12.80.
5 [1892] 1 Ch 238.
6 [1905] 1 KB 677.

omy which has traditionally been applied by the English courts in relation to commercial contracts.[7]

It may be that in many cases it is academic whether the *lex situs* or the express choice controls, due to the fact that the bank which acts as the common depository physically holds the bonds in London, so that the *lex situs* of delivery and negotiation as well as the chosen law is English.

III NEGOTIABILITY AND THE EUROCLEAR/CEDEL CLEARANCE SYSTEMS[8]

1 Mechanics of transfer in the international clearance systems

An allied question which may be considered conveniently at this point is whether the mechanics of transfer used in the international markets by the two clearing houses Euroclear and Cedel affect the traditional legal consequences attributed to negotiability under English law. Market practice in respect of the transfer of Eurobonds may be described as follows:

(a) Eurobonds are usually sold to subscribers in the primary markets who have securities accounts[9] with the two clearance systems Euroclear and Cedel. At the close of a bond issue, the lead manager will credit such securities accounts of account holders with the aggregate amount of bonds purchased in return for cash which is transferred into the lead manager's account at Euroclear or Cedel. Physical instruments or 'definitive' bonds do not exist at this stage. In effect purchase of Eurobonds in the primary markets is therefore confined to accountholders at Euroclear or Cedel. There is provision however for temporary accounts to be opened.[10]

(b) Purchases and sales of Eurobonds are effected as between account holders even before the definitive or actual bonds are delivered to the common depository of Euroclear or Cedel.

(c) Even after the definitive or actual bonds are delivered to the common depository, account holders at Euroclear or Cedel will continue trading Eurobonds without any physical movement of the bonds, which are usually warehoused with the common depository.

(d) Bonds are not sold by reference to serial numbers which identify the particular bond of the series which is issued. They are in effect sold generically (for example, a sale of $1,000,000 in aggregate value of

---

7 See especially the decision in *Vita Food Products Inc v Unus Shipping Co Ltd* [1939] AC 277; and *Miller & Partners Ltd v Whitworth Street Estates (Manchester) Ltd* [1970] AC 583, HL.

8 The Euroclear system is described extremely well in Euroclear's publications which include *Distribution of New Issues: A Guide for Lead Managers* (1985); *Lawyers' Guide to New Issues* (1987); *The Operating Procedures of the Euroclear Clearance System* (1990); as well as Euroclear's *Terms and Conditions Governing Use of Euroclear* (1982). The reader is referred to these publications for a detailed understanding of the system.

9 In Euroclear these are referred to as Securities Clearance Accounts. See ss 2 and 10 of the *Operating Procedures of the Euroclear Clearance System*, November 1990.

10 See Euroclear *Distribution of New Issues – a Guide for Lead Managers* (1985) pp 12–13.

a 6% 1997 IBM US dollar bond). One reason for this is that the clearing systems do not always provide for a system whereby bonds could be sold by reference to any specific serial number[11] even though bonds do have serial numbers allocated to them.[12]

(e) Under both the Euroclear and Cedel systems the participants in the system who hold securities accounts seem to have a right against Euroclear and Cedel to demand physical delivery of bonds equivalent to the amount credited to an account holder.[13]

(f) When a dealer or bank which is a participant in the clearing system purchases bonds from another participant in the system, they buy and sell a fungible amount of a particular class of bond. This transfer is recorded as a book entry in the accounts at Euroclear (or Cedel) for the two dealers; so that if $250,000 of IBM 1997 6% bonds are sold by dealer A to dealer B, A's account is debited and B's account is credited at Euroclear.[14]

(g) Where an investor, say the proverbial 'Belgian Dentist', who is not a participant in the system wishes to purchase a bond, he would purchase it from a dealer. The investor also purchases only an aggregate amount of bonds identified by class, eg $20,000 of 6% IBM 1997 bonds. Such an investor would operate on the basis of a securities account which he has established with the dealer. Not being a participant within the system such an investor has no direct contractual rights against Euroclear or Cedel. Consequently, when such an investor purchases a bond, what would happen in practice is that the investor's account with the dealer would be credited with the aggregate sum of bonds bought and his cash account debited. If the dealer sold the bonds to the investor from its own portfolio of bonds no change would occur as a matter of book entry in the Euroclear/Cedel system. If, however, the dealer purchased the bond from another dealer, who was a participant in the system, then a book entry would be made in Euroclear (or Cedel as the case may be) to reflect the change in the aggregate holds of each dealer with Euroclear (or Cedel) as happened in (f) above.

(h) Where the non-participant purchaser in (g) above wishes to resell, the dealer will either repurchase himself or sell to another investor who has an account with him, or will sell to another dealer the aggregate financial amount of the bonds. The mechanics are the converse of the purchase transaction. As observed earlier, a dealer has a right as against the clearing house to have physical bonds delivered to himself on demand. Consequently, an investor may demand that the dealer delivers the physical instrument to the investor. The market's perception of the existence of a negotiable instrument which is traded probably rests on this ability to demand delivery of the actual bond.

---

11 See art 4 of the *Terms and Conditions Governing the Use of Euroclear* (December 1982) and see s 3, especially 3.1 and 3.10 of the *Operating Procedures of the Euroclear Clearance System*, November 1990.
12 It is understood that Cedel apparently does provide an option to operate an account where the bonds are held by reference to specified serial numbers.
13 See for Euroclear art 4 of the *Terms and Conditions Governing the Use of Euroclear*, December 1982.
14 See again, art 4 of Euroclear's *Terms and Conditions* cited above.

Expressed diagramatically:

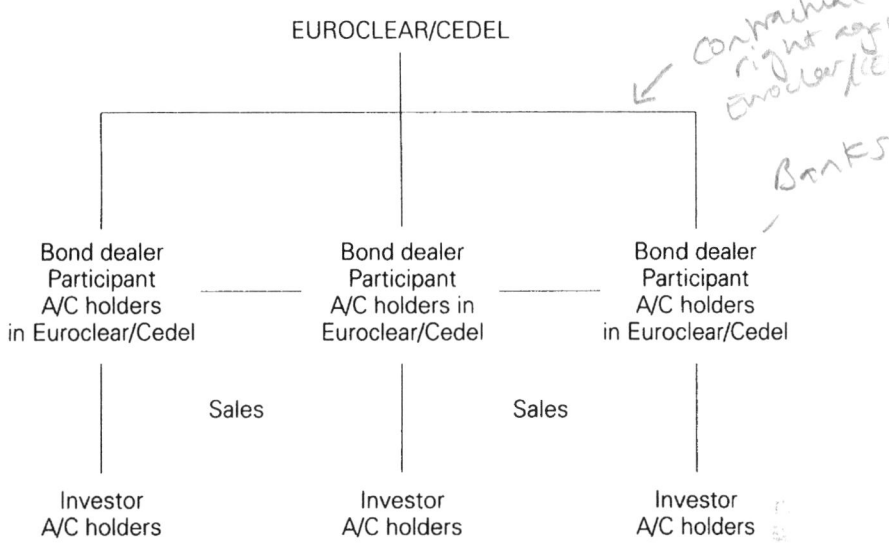

```
                    EUROCLEAR/CEDEL
        ┌──────────────────┼──────────────────┐
   Bond dealer         Bond dealer         Bond dealer
   Participant         Participant         Participant
   A/C holders    ─── A/C holders in ───   A/C holders
  in Euroclear/Cedel   Euroclear/Cedel    in Euroclear/Cedel
        │       Sales      │      Sales       │
     Investor           Investor           Investor
    A/C holders        A/C holders        A/C holders
```

2 Legal issues

Despite the fact that the Eurobond is a negotiable instrument under English law[15] a number of difficult legal questions arise in consequence of the warehousing and transfer mechanics applicable to Eurobonds:

(a) Who is to be regarded as the holder of the bearer bonds purchased? This would determine who may exercise the rights contained in the Eurobond as against the issuer.

(b) What rights do successive transferees of the bonds acquire from their transferors? Do they acquire mere contractual rights by assignment or do they acquire proprietary rights?

The answers to these questions must remain a matter of conjecture under English law in the absence of a coherent statutory system as is found in art 8 of the US Uniform Commercial Code. Article 8 provides expressly for the rights and liabilities of parties to securities in bearer form which are lodged with central depository systems. In effect they provide that even in the absence of a physical delivery of instruments as between transferor and transferee the effect of a transfer which is recorded on the books of the clearance system is exactly the same as a physical delivery of the instrument by transferor to the transferee. Consequently, proprietary rights as distinct from contractual rights in respect of the bare instrument are transmitted by the electronic or other book-entry system operated by the clearance system.[16]

The position in the international markets is complicated even further by the fact that the rights and liabilities of parties to the Euroclear clearance

---

15 See p 162 above.
16 See US Uniform Commercial Code arts 8–320.

system is governed by Belgian law, in particular by the Belgian Royal Decree no 62[17] and any contractual provisions as between Euroclear and its account holders contained in the *Standard Terms and Conditions Governing Use of Euroclear* [18] which is also subject to Belgian law. The position is similar in the case of Cedel which is subject to the law of Luxembourg. Given these difficulties a number of possibilities may be explored.

As a matter of English law, the first approach to the problem is to regard the clearance system itself as the holder of Eurobonds and as the only party who may exercise rights as against the issuer of the bonds. This approach is based on the traditional approach to bearer bonds, namely that the person in physical possession of bearer bonds is to be deemed the 'holder' with the right to exercise all rights contained in the bonds as against the issuer.[19] If this approach is correct then purchasers of bonds would have no rights as against the issuer unless they obtain transfer of the physical bond from the clearance system by virtue of contractual rights to delivery which an account holder would possess as against the clearance system. The position of a purchaser of bonds who is not a participant of the Euroclear or Cedel clearance system would also rest on such person's ability to compel his seller, usually a securities dealer, to deliver the physical instrument, but until then such a purchaser would have no rights as against an issuer. If this approach is adopted then only the clearance system has proprietary rights in respect of Eurobonds and the rights of all other purchasers would depend on the contractual arrangements as between transferor and transferee.[20] This approach is, however, open to the following objections.

First, it is contrary to the intention of the issuers of Eurobonds and the purchasers of Eurobonds in the primary markets. The structure and mechanics set up by the financial community in the form of the clearance systems were simply to enable efficient trading and effective clearance of the bonds. The intention and purpose of the structure was not to constitute the warehouse the 'holder' of the bonds. An intention to transfer seems to be necessary in addition to the mere physical movement of a negotiable instrument before a person is to be regarded as the holder of a bearer negotiable instrument.[1] Secondly, it would be a somewhat unsettling conclusion for the community of Eurobond investors that the clearing houses rather than they, the purchasers, were in fact the holders of Eurobonds. Thirdly, if the clearing houses are to be regarded as holders of Eurobonds it is extremely difficult to determine what rights are actually being transferred when sales and purchases are made of Eurobonds, not only as between account holders within the Euroclear or Cedel system, but also where sales are made to end investors in Eurobonds. It may be possible to suggest that all Eurobond trading activity is no more than a series of contractual assignments whose incidents need to be determined by the law governing the contractual assignment. Alternati-

---

17 Dated 10 November 1967.
18 December 1982.
19 See p 162 above.
20 It may also mean that in the event of a bankruptcy of the clearance system purchasers of Eurobonds may be in a position where they may not be able to obtain the Eurobond so as to proceed as against the issuer. The latter issue would presumably be determined by the rules applicable in the bankruptcy of Euroclear under Belgian law and of Cedel under the law of Luxembourg.
1   See the Canadian case of *McKenty v Van Horenback* (1911) 21 Man R 360.

vely, it may be suggested that the clearance system holds the bonds in trust for account holders who trade in the beneficial interests of bonds. The latter hypothesis would, however, be extremely difficult to sustain, given the fact that an English law trust may not exist under Belgian or Luxembourg law in the context of the clearance system.

Another difficulty is that under the Belgian Royal Decree no 62[2] Euroclear it seems occupies a position similar to that of a bailee in English law. Its assets are owned in common by its account holders in accordance with the amounts credited to each such account holder.[3] The status of bailee is not consistent with that of a 'holder'. Article 4 of the Euroclear Standard Terms also suggests that the holder of a Securities Clearance Account rather than Euroclear is the holder of the bonds.

The second approach is to regard the clearance systems as no more than bailees with constructive possession of the Eurobonds and the account holders of Euroclear and Cedel as the true holders of the Eurobonds. Even if this approach is consonant with the intention of the parties to a Eurobond issue and consistent with the perception of the investing community, it is not itself free from difficulty. The question whether the clearing house holds bonds as a bailee and a mere custodian for the purchaser of a Eurobond will depend on the contractual arrangements between Euroclear or Cedel on the one hand and the primary purchasers of Eurobonds on the other. In order to establish that the account holders of Euroclear or Cedel have constructive possession of bonds which they purchase and which are held physically by the clearing houses it must be established that at least under English common law, each account holder has a right to possess a specific chattel and not merely a generic quantity of a commodity.[4] The problem under the clearance systems is that account holders do not generally have a right to possess any specific Eurobond which is in the custody of the clearance systems. Article 4 of the *Terms and Conditions Governing the Use of Euroclear* provides: 'No participant or holder of a securities clearance account shall have any right to any specific securities certificates but each participant and each holder will be entitled ... to deliver or to repossess ...an amount of securities of any issue equivalent to the amount credited to any securities clearance account in its name'. The right of each account holder who purchases bonds is therefore a right to a fungible amount of Eurobonds held within the clearance system. In the face of this it is difficult to argue that the purchasers of Eurobonds who have accounts with clearance systems have constructive possession of the bonds under English common law.[5]

A third possibility is that the 'holder' of the Eurobond is the bank which

---

2 Dated 10 November 1967.
3 See Professor Goode 'Ownership and Obligation in Transactions' (1987) 103 LQR 433.
4 See Pollock and Wright *An Essay on Possession in the Common Law* (Clarendon Press, Oxford, 1888, 2nd edn.)
5 In sales of goods where a buyer purchases an unascertained portion of a larger bulk of goods lying in a warehouse, for example, a sale of 10,000 tonnes of wheat of a 100,000 tonne cargo lying in a warehouse, it is clear under English law that the purchaser who purchases such generic goods or an unascertained portion of a bulk does not obtain title to his goods until the goods become 'specific' by severance of the portion purchased from the bulk. (See s 16 of the Sale of Goods Act 1979; *The Elafi* [1982] 1 All ER 208; *Waite and James v Midland Bank* (1926) 31 Com Cas 172.

acts as common depositary for Euroclear and Cedel and which is in actual physical possession of the bonds.

No concluded view can be taken of the true position as to who is to be regarded as the holder of the Eurobond.

In practice this uncertainty may make no difference since any purchaser who wishes to exercise his rights in respect of an Eurobond which he has purchased would invariably have a contractual right as against a dealer or in the case of a dealer against the clearance system to demand physical delivery of the Eurobond. Consequently, a purchaser would be able to exercise rights contained in the bond as against the issuer. The only situations in which it becomes important to decide who is the holder are, first, where an account holder at Euroclear or Cedel or an end-purchaser of bonds from such an account holder wishes to grant security over a portfolio of bonds to a bank in order to raise finance; and secondly, in the event that the clearance system becomes bankrupt. Goode[6] has, however, pointed out that at least in the event of the bankruptcy of the Euroclear system, the securities within the system will not be available to the creditors of the clearance system. These issues are outside the scope of this work.

IV THE TEMPORARY GLOBAL BOND

It was pointed out earlier that prior to the delivery of definitive bonds to the Euroclear or Cedel system, a temporary global bond is delivered by the issuer to a common depositary at the closing of the bond issue. The temporary global bond ('TGB') is to be held by the common depositary until it is exchanged for the definitive bonds.

What is the nature of this TGB and what rights are transmitted through this instrument? In practice, the TGB is in bearer form and contains on its face a promise by the issuer to pay to the 'holder' the entire principal sum due on the bond issue together with interest. Usually it further states, 'until the entire principal amount of this Global Bond has been exchanged the holder of this Global Bond shall in all respects be entitled to the same rights and benefits as if such holder were the holder of the definitive bonds and coupons'. This statement is usually qualified by the formula that 'the holder of this Global Bond shall not be entitled to payment of principal and interest on this Global Bond unless upon due presentation of this Global Bond for exchange, delivery of the appropriate number of Definitive Bonds is improperly withheld or refused'.

By the terms appearing on its face, the TGB is exchangeable either wholly or partially at the request of the holder for definitive bonds and the TGB is reduced in value in proportion to the value of definitives issued in exchange. It is usually provided in the TGB that when an exchange of definitive bonds is made for a part of the aggregate principal amount of the TGB, this transaction is to be endorsed on a schedule attached to the TGB and that notation is to be made by the fiscal agent or trustee of the issue. Once the total

---

6 (1987) 103 LQR 433 at 453.

principal amount of the TGB is thus exchanged, the TGB is cancelled by the trustee or fiscal agent and returned to the issuer.

The reasons for the use of the TGB are largely to be found in the necessity to avoid breaches of US securities laws and US tax laws.[7] Eurobonds are sometimes subject to a 'lock-up' period of 40 days (previously 90 days), during which definitive bonds are not made available to purchasers. The TGB simply represents the issuer's obligation to all purchasers of Eurobonds during this period. In practice, definitive bonds will be delivered in exchange only if, and to the extent that, Euroclear and Cedel certify that the purchasers of Eurobonds whose securities accounts have been credited have each lodged with Euroclear and Cedel certifications that the bonds are not beneficially owned by 'US persons' as defined.

The instrument referred to as the TGB which Euromarket lawyers have created is unique. The terms on the face of the TGB suggest that it is a negotiable instrument and not an instrument which is simply evidence of debt. Thus, it is said to be a bearer instrument, there are a number of references to a 'holder' on the face of the TGB and a consistent attempt to confer on the 'holder' all the rights of the future holders of the definitive bonds. In addition, it is said to be subject to the trust deed (or fiscal agency agreement as the case may be) in the same way as the definitive Eurobonds. The notion that the TGB has the same qualities as the definitives is further enhanced in some TGB formats by the addition of the formulae that the TGB 'represents the definitives' and further that 'the holder of the TGB is the holder of the definitives'.

However, as observed earlier,[8] it is quite clear that the TGB cannot be made a negotiable instrument under English law by appropriate drafting or by agreement of the parties.[9] The only methods by which the TGB can become a negotiable instrument under English law is by virtue of the Bills of Exchange Act 1882, or through mercantile custom.[10]

Is there a mercantile custom, ie recognition in the Euromarket, that the TGB is a negotiable instrument? This is a difficult question to answer because neither the TGB nor an instrument similar to it has ever been traded in the markets between Eurobond dealers, unlike in the case of definitive bonds. The TGB also does not have on its face the express assertion of negotiability found on the face of definitives, namely that 'title to the Bonds/Notes shall pass by delivery'. Further, if it were a negotiable instrument it would be a very peculiar instrument because it gives a right to principal and interest as against the issuer only to the extent that the definitive bonds are improperly withheld.

It is submitted that the TGB is a *sui generis* debt instrument created by mercantile custom and should be recognised as such in accordance with the terms contained on its face. It should therefore be enforceable in English law as such an instrument. It is a debt instrument which represents the aggregate financial liability of an issuer of Eurobonds for a period of 40 (or 90) days from the close of an issue until the delivery of the definitive Eurobond instruments to Euroclear or Cedel. Its characteristics are that

---

7 See ch 21 below.
8 See p 163.
9 See p 163 above.
10 See Kennedy J in *Bechuanaland Exploration Co v London Trading Bank Ltd* [1898] 2 QB 658.

176   *Negotiability and governing law*

the person in possession of the physical instrument has direct rights as against the issuer as to principal and interest, exactly in the same way as a 'holder' of a true negotiable instrument payable to bearer. The rights against the issuer are enforceable on the occurrence of the event specified therein, namely improper and unlawful failure of the issuer to deliver definitives. It is enforceable either for the full amount of the TGB or any smaller amount represented by the financial value of definitives which the issuer has failed to deliver. The chose in action represented by the TGB is reduced in financial value to the extent that the issuer delivers the definitive Eurobonds to the clearance system Euroclear or Cedel.

Taking this logic to its necessary conclusion it means that whoever is to be regarded as the holder of this instrument would have the right to call default and accelerate payment on the TGB (subject to the provisions of the trust deed or fiscal agency agreement, the terms of which are incorporated into the TGB).

Once again one is faced with the difficult question, 'who is the "holder" of the TGB?' This question is significant only in reference to two rights: the right to call default during the 'lock-up' period prior to the delivery of definitives and the right to sue for principal and interest in the event the issuer wrongfully refuses delivery of all or some of the definitive bonds. One view is that the clearance system Euroclear or Cedel or their common depository is to be regarded as the holder for these purposes. This view is satisfactory if the contractual arrangements between the account holders of Euroclear and Cedel are such that the purchasers of Eurobonds may compel the clearance systems to take action in accordance with the terms of the TGB.

CHAPTER 10
Legal framework of marketing and distribution

The marketing and distribution of Eurobonds by investment banks and securities dealers is regulated by (a) UK statute and statutory instruments, (b) US securities statutes and SEC regulation, and (c) the contractual regime created by the legal documents which control marketing.

The regulatory framework referred to in (a) and (b) is discussed in Parts IV and V. This section is concerned with the contractual regime.

The objective of these documents is to provide a legal framework which ensures that:

(a) the investment banks give a legally enforceable promise to the effect that an aggregate amount of the issuer's bonds will be sold to or placed with investors or that the investment banks will purchase the bonds themselves;
(b) the underwriting risk which the investment banks undertake does not expose them to unrestricted liability and that adequate safeguards be provided to the investment banks;
(c) provision is made to ensure that all parties to the marketing exercise do not transgress applicable statutory prohibitions and comply with statutory obligations, in particular, the requirements of the UK Financial Services Act 1986 ('FSA')[1] and the securities laws of the US, as well as certain provisions of US tax laws.[2]
(d) the lead manager possesses the maximum control over the manner of marketing and distribution of the issue.

I THE DOCUMENTS

There are a number of documents which may be used to provide a legal framework for a Eurobond issue. They are:

(a) the Subscription Agreement;
(b) the Agreement between Managers;

and in some cases

---

1 See Part IV above.
2 See Part V above.

(c) the Underwriting Agreement;
(d) the Selling Group Agreement.

In modern Eurobond issue practice the underwriting agreement and selling group agreement are not used in the large majority of issues.

In the past, two groups of underwriters were used to provide a guarantee to the issuer that any bonds not purchased by investors would be subscribed by the underwriters. The primary underwriters were parties to the subscription agreement while the sub-underwriters who agreed to take a percentage of the underwriting risk from the primary underwriters were parties to a sub-underwriting agreement (formally termed the 'underwriting agreement'). The sub-underwriters received only an underwriting fee, while the managing underwriters received a management fee as well as an underwriting fee.

The purpose of the selling group was to establish a group of securities dealers who would agree to sell bonds on a best efforts basis without any legal obligation to do so. Selling group members received only a selling commission in respect of bonds sold by them.

This type of structure is not used in current practice except in complex or difficult issues. Generally, the entire issue is placed by the managing group of underwriters, and consequently a subscription agreement and an agreement between managers are used to market bonds. Nevertheless, the discussion below covers all four agreements.

1 The subscription agreement

The centrepiece of the legal framework for the marketing and distribution is the *subscription agreement* which is entered into between the issuer and the managing group of underwriters.

The primary obligations in this document owed by the managers to the issuer are:

(a) to offer the bonds for sale to investors or if there is a selling group to the dealers and brokers who are members of the selling group on the terms laid down in the selling group agreement; and
(b) to the extent that the bonds are not wholly subscribed and paid for on the closing date to subscribe and pay for all such bonds as are unsubscribed or unpaid for.

This latter obligation is the underwriting obligation undertaken by the investment banks who form the managing group and forms the lynchpin and driving force of the entire marketing operation. It is for this undertaking and the risk inherent in that obligation that managers are highly remunerated by way of management and underwriting commissions of around 3%–4% of the face value of the bonds. The skill and expertise of the investment banks is the ability to procure investors or dealers and brokers to subscribe to all the bonds of the issuer, leaving no residue of unsold bonds[3] and a consequential residual obligation on the underwriters to purchase unsold bonds.

---

3 Called a 'rump'.

A number of points need to be noted with regard to the subscription agreement.

First, in the Eurobond market the managers offer the bonds as agent for the issuer. This means that when an investor or a dealer who is a member of the selling group purchases a bond by subscription, he purchases directly from the issuer. In the US the practice is that the managers will purchase the bonds, as principal, from the issuer and then onsell the bonds to the selling group.

Secondly, where a selling group is formed the obligation of the managers is to offer the bonds to the selling group at the subscription price of the bonds and not the face value or redemption value of the bonds. The subscription price is the issue price of the bond less the selling commission, payable to members of the selling group.[4]

Thirdly, it must be noted that the underwriting obligation crystallises only on the closing date when it will be known whether any portion of the bonds issue remains unsold.

Fourthly, the managers' obligation to underwrite is usually joint and several. This means that each manager undertakes the full underwriting obligation, as to the aggregate amount of the subscription price of all the bonds.[5] If the issue fails wholly or partially the issuer has a legal right to require one manager to take up and pay for the subscription price of all unsold bonds and not simply a pro rata share. The impact of this obligation is mitigated by the agreement among managers[6] and the underwriting agreement.[7] The agreement among managers would provide that if one of the managers is called on by the issuer to subscribe for the aggregate amount he could call on other managers to take up a pro rata share of the issue.[8]

Under the subscription agreement the managers are also obliged on the 'closing date' to transfer to the issuer the funds representing the total subscription price of the bonds underwritten by the management group. The closing date is a date specified in the subscription agreement as marking the end of the primary distribution period for the issue. If there is delay in transferring funds after closing date, for instance because selling group members who have purchased bonds have not transferred funds to the managers, the managers are usually obliged to pay interest on any amount so delayed at an interest rate equivalent to that appearing on the face of the bonds.

The manager's obligation to transfer subscription monies on closing date is synchronised with the issuer's concurrent obligation to make delivery of a temporary global bond[9] representing the bonds, in a format usually specified in the trust deed or fiscal agency agreement. The delivery of the temporary global bond is made to a bank which is a common depository of the two clearance systems, Euroclear and Cedel, and not to the lead manager.

---

4 Thus if the issue price is $1,000 and the selling commission payable to the selling group member is 1.5%, the subscription price would be $985.
5 On joint and several liability see cases cited in Treitel *Law of Contract* ch 4.
6 See p 184 below.
7 See p 184 below.
8 See pp 184–189 below.
9 See previous discussion at p 174.

180 *Legal framework of marketing and distribution*

The manager's exposure to the underwriting obligations is always subject to a number of 'conditions' which must be satisfied prior to closing date. In the event that any of these conditions are not satisfied the subscription agreement is capable of being terminated at the option of the managers. The usual conditions are as follows:

(a) That the latest financial statements of the issuer have been prepared in accordance with the regulations of law and standard accounting principles either in the issuer's country of incorporation or some other country, eg according to US standard accounting rules; furthermore, that they are a fair and accurate view of the financial condition of the company.

(b) That there has been no material adverse change in the financial position of the borrower since the date of the accounts.

(c) That the offering circular[10] contains all the material information with respect to the issuer and, further, that all statements contained therein and to the use of proceeds are in every material particular true and accurate and not misleading.

(d) That the listing particulars published in accordance with the rules of the stock exchange on which bonds are to be listed contain all the necessary information to enable investors and their advisers to make an informed assessment of the issuer and comply with the rules of the relevant stock exchange. Where listing particulars are submitted to the London Stock Exchange the obligation of disclosure is specified in ss 146 and 147 of the Financial Services Act 1986.[11]

(e) That the issue of the bonds and the execution of the subscription agreement constitutes a valid and legally binding obligation of the issuer. This condition is similar to that found in a syndicated loan agreement.[12]

(f) That the issue of the bonds and the execution of the subscription agreement and other documents do not contravene any regulatory laws. The obligation to comply with all applicable regulatory law in the course of the bond issue is also imposed on the managers, although not as a condition of the managers' obligation to underwrite.

(g) That the issuer is not involved in litigation or arbitration where the amounts involved are material to the issue of the bonds and that such litigation or arbitration is not threatened or contemplated.

(h) That all necessary consents, authorisations and permissions from any applicable regulatory body required for the issue and distribution of bonds are obtained.

(i) That disclosure will be made of any material adverse change which has occurred at any time after the signing of the subscription agreement and the making of payment on closing date.

If there is a guarantor of the bonds these conditions are imposed in addition on the guarantor.

The purpose of these conditions is twofold. First, they should be made capable of conferring on the manager a right to terminate the marketing

---

10 See ch 8 above.
11 See ch 17 below.
12 See ch 5 above.

and distribution of the bonds at any time prior to closing date in the event that any one such condition is not satisfied. Secondly, they should provide a basis for the recovery of any loss or damage suffered or expenses incurred by the managers in the event that any one of such conditions is not satisfied.

Legal opinions will be required in practice to ensure that a foreign corporation has capacity to issue bonds or that the issue has been duly authorised by internal authorisation procedures or that external regulatory requirements have been complied with. Similarly, accountants' certificates become necessary to verify the issuer's financial statements. Consequently, the delivery of such opinions and reports prior to or on closing date are made a 'condition', in the sense of conditions precedent,[13] of the subscription agreement and the obligations of the underwriters.

In addition, the underwriting obligation is made conditional on (a) the bonds being listed on a specified Stock Exchange, and (b) the execution of the trust deed or fiscal agency agreement and the paying agency agreement. These requirements would also operate as conditions precedent to the managers' underwriting obligation.

In addition to the above, the managers require protection from major market disruptions which would make the issue of the bonds impracticable. To achieve this end a Euromarket disaster clause which operates as a force majeure clause is included in every subscription agreement. It would be drafted in the widest possible terms and a sample clause would be in the following terms.

> 'Notwithstanding anything in this agreement, the lead manager on behalf of the managers may by notice to the company terminate this agreement at any time before the time on the closing date when payment would otherwise be due hereunder to the company in respect of the bonds if *in the opinion* of the managers there shall have been such a change in national or international financial, political or economic conditions or currency exchange rates or exchange controls, as would *in their view* be likely to prejudice materially the success of the offering and distribution of the bonds or dealings in the bonds in the secondary market and upon such notice being given the parties hereto shall be released and discharged from their respective obligations hereunder.'

The International Primary Markets Association ('IPMA') recommends the use of one of two standard forms of force majeure clauses which were recommended in the wake of the Gulf war in January 1991. One of the recommended forms of the clause is similar to the above.[14] The sample format clause (above) was widely used in practice even prior to the IPMA recommendation. The reason for the recommendation was that there was no uniformity in practice and in the context of the Gulf war doubts were expressed as to whether force majeure clauses which had been drafted with reference to 'unforeseen events' could be relied on as giving rise to force majeure. In the case of the Gulf war, Iraq had been given an ultimatum by the United Nations to leave Kuwait by 15 January 1991 and it was thought that war was a foreseeable event in December or January. Consequently it was argued

---

13 See pp 68–71 above for a discussion of the distinction in the context of syndicated loans.
14 See IPMA's Recommendation dated 19 March 1991 for issues launched after 8 April 1991.

that the Gulf war could not be regarded as an unforeseen event in December and January.

The wide-ranging nature of this clause needs to be noted. First, it is a matter of subjective judgment of the managers whether the alleged change has occurred. Under a conventional agreement between managers the lead manager is authorised to exercise all powers conferred on the managers in the subscription agreement.[15] It is interesting to ask to what extent a court would give effect to this clause if the lead manager were to exercise this power capriciously. It is submitted that a court is likely to hold that there must be some grounds for the managers to exercise their power. The court need not necessarily consider the exercise of the power to be reasonable but it must not be wholly unreasonable and it must be bona fide.

Secondly, the clause covers not only events which affect the issue and distribution, but also the subsequent trading of the bonds.

Thirdly, since the lead manager is required to exercise the power to terminate the issue as agent for the other managing underwriters as well as the lead manager it would mean that the lead manager owes a duty of due care, skill and diligence in the exercise of the power to terminate the issue. The lead manager must, as an agent, act in the interest of the management group as a whole and may not act having regard only to his own position.

Despite the width of the language, the clause is rarely relied on in practice, since reliance on the clause by a lead manager except in wholly exceptional circumstances would seriously damage its market reputation. The safeguard against capricious use of the clause by a lead manager is consequently commercial rather than legal. The potential sanctions in the markets are in reality a greater safeguard than the potentiality for judicial redress.

The effect of activating the Euromarket disaster clause is of course to terminate the bond issue and the agreement, but the issuer will be under a residual liability to reimburse the managers for all expenses incurred.

Some subscription agreements also confer on the managers the power to increase the amount of the issue in the event that the managers consider that the issue is oversubscribed. This power is also controlled by the lead manager due to the provision in the agreement between managers.[16]

Compliance with applicable regulatory laws

The subscription agreement will also need to include a number of clauses which seek to ensure compliance with the securities laws of the UK and the US and other applicable systems.

The regulatory law in the UK and the US is discussed in detail in Parts IV and V, entitled 'The regulation of the international capital markets'.

As far as UK law is concerned clauses are necessary requiring the managers to the issue to comply with all applicable provisions of the Financial Services Act 1986 ('FSA') (and with Part III of the Companies Act 1985 until Part

---

15 See p 184 below.
16 See p 184 below.

V of the FSA is brought into force) particularly in respect of the marketing and distribution of the bonds. Essentially this is to ensure:

(a) that all participants in the issue are 'authorised' persons under the FSA or may carry out their activities within applicable exceptions to the prohibition in s 3 of the FSA on unauthorised persons 'carrying on investment business in the UK';[17]
(b) that all participants comply with the rules regulating the issue of publicity material including the offering circular and other advertisements in the course of marketing and distribution of the bonds;[18]
(c) that all telephone and oral marketing is carried out in compliance with the regulations on unsolicited calls framed under FSA s 56;[19]
(d) that stabilising activity is carried out by the lead manager in compliance with the Stabilisation Rules of the Securities and Investment Board.[20]

For purposes of US securities laws which are discussed in detail below in Part V, the agreement will *at least* include:[1]

(a) a warranty on the part of an issuer which is a 'foreign issuer' as defined in Regulation S[2] that it is such;
(b) if such an issuer claims that there is no 'substantial US market interest'[3] in its debt securities a warranty to that effect;
(c) in all cases that no 'directed selling efforts' have been made in the US as defined in Regulation S;[4]
(d) that no offers or sales are made in the US or to or for the account of 'US persons' as defined (differently) in Regulation S (if applicable),[5] and US tax laws, either during the offering period or during the 'restricted period' as defined in Regulation S and US tax laws;[6]
(e) that all 'offering restrictions' as defined in Regulation S will be implemented, if applicable.[7] This would include ensuring that all offering materials and documents contain a legend that the securities have not been registered under the Securities Act 1933 and may not be sold in the US or to 'US persons' (other than the managers) as required by r 903 (c)(2); this requirement is applicable under Regulation S in all *international* bond issues other than in the case of a governmental issuer or a 'foreign issuer' which reasonably believes at the commencement of the offering that there is 'no substantial US market interest' in its debt securities;[8]
(f) that the managers warrant that 'confirmation notices' be sent to purchasers notifying them of restrictions on sales as required by Regulation

---

17 This aspect is discussed in detail in ch 15.
18 This aspect is dealt with in ch 16.
19 This is dealt with in ch 16.
20 This is dealt with in detail in ch 18.
1 This is not intended to be a drafting guide and should not be relied on as such. Compliance with US securities and tax laws should always be confirmed by US lawyers.
2 See ch 21 below.
3 As defined in Regulation S, see discussion at ch 21, p 300 below.
4 See p 395 below.
5 See p 405 below.
6 See discussion in ch 21.
7 See p 404 below.
8 See Regulation S r 903(c) and detailed discussion in ch 21 below.

184 *Legal framework of marketing and distribution*

S; this warranty would be necessary in the case of an issuer which is a US or foreign 'reporting issuer' as defined in Regulation S, or a foreign non-reporting issuer who cannot warrant that there is 'no substantial US market interest' in the class of securities to be offered or sold;

(g) in the case of an issuer which falls within r 903(c)(3) of Regulation S that the debt securities will be represented only by a global bond which is not exchangeable for definitives until the expiry of a 40-day period from the close of the issue until certification of non-US beneficial ownership of the bonds;[9]

(h) in all cases a warranty requiring a certification of non-US beneficial ownership as defined in US tax laws prior to delivery of definitives during a 40-day restricted period, as required by TEFRA 'D' Regulations.[10]

Such clauses, which are designed to ensure compliance with US securities and tax laws, are usually drafted or confirmed as sufficient by US lawyers due to the extreme sanctions which attach for non-compliance.

2 The agreement between managers and the underwriting agreement

The agreement between managers is invariably used in practice, but the 'underwriting agreement' is rarely used in modern Eurobond issues.

The agreement between managers and the underwriting agreement (if used) achieve three further objectives:

(a) the redistribution of the primary underwriting obligation contained in the subscription agreement which is owed by each manager to the issuer;

(b) they strengthen the lead manager's complete control over the marketing and distribution of a Eurobond issue;

(c) they ensure compliance with applicable securities laws of the UK, the US and any other applicable jurisdiction.

i *The redistribution of the primary underwriting obligation*

The managers agree *as between themselves* that their obligations are only to take up and subscribe for bonds up to a specified maximum. The issuer who is not a party to this agreement is not prevented by these provisions from calling on any of the managers to subscribe unsold bonds up to the aggregate amount of the issue. Nevertheless, a manager called on by the issuer may then require other managers to subscribe in accordance with the terms of the agreement between managers.

However, if a group of banks and dealers is set up as a separate sub-underwriting group under an agreement called 'the underwriting agreement', the provisions for redistribution in the agreement between managers becomes different. Where there is such a separate underwriting group of banks, there

---

9   See ch 21 below.
10 See p 413 below.

is in effect a 'sell down' of a portion of the aggregate underwriting commitment of the managing group. This is achieved by the lead manager entering into an agreement as agent of the managing underwriters with a group of underwriting banks whereby they agree to underwrite a portion of the aggregate subscription price of bonds. This underwriting commitment is not subject to or protected by any conditions precedent save that if the subscription agreement is terminated on or before closing date, such termination automatically terminates the underwriting agreement.

Consequently, the sub-underwriters are dependent on the managers for protection by way of termination of the issue in the event of market disruption by unforeseeable events. They do not have an independent right to terminate the issue.

If the underwriting group is to be directly liable to the issuer under the underwriting agreement, say up to 30% or 40% of the aggregate subscription price of the bonds, this would leave 70% or 60% of the aggregate value of the bonds to be underwritten by the managing group. If this is to be the case, the agreement between managers will provide for a 'primary underwriting commitment' of each manager and a 'secondary underwriting commitment' of each manager, reflecting his position before and after the 'sell down' of a portion of the aggregate underwriting commitment.

The liability of each member of the managing group and each member of the underwriting group (where there is one) to subscribe for bonds not taken up by the selling group[11] is sometimes, however, subject to a netting-off provision. This is because most members of the managing group and underwriting group (where there is one) would also purchase bonds themselves, particularly if they are members of the selling group (if used). Consequently, where they purchase bonds themselves as members of the selling group or otherwise, the amount of bonds so purchased can be set off in reduction of their underwriting obligation under the agreement between managers and the underwriting agreement.

If an issue has an underwriting group as well as a managing group of underwriters and the bonds are not fully subscribed the position would be as follows:

(a) The issuer could proceed against the lead manager (or any other manager of the issue) and require him to take up and subscribe for all bonds which remain.

(b) In this eventuality the lead manager can activate the provisions in the agreement between managers requiring each manager to underwrite up to a stated amount of the aggregate of bonds issued; each manager called on may have a right to set off against his underwriting commitment any bonds which that manager has already subscribed.

In the event that an issue has partially failed and, say, $60m of a $200m issue has not been subscribed, the agreement between managers should ensure that each member of the managing group is required to subscribe only a pro rata share in relation to his original underwriting commitment, and that he is not liable for any amount up to his original maximum underwriting liability. Thus, for instance, if Bank X has agreed to underwrite $20m in the above example, that

---

11 See this chapter, below.

bank should not be liable to take up and pay for a total of $20m (the equivalent of his original underwriting commitment), but liable only to take up 10% of the unsold bonds, reflecting the proportion of its original underwriting commitment to the aggregate $200m. It is submitted, however, that in the absence of express clauses a pro rata solution should be applied as a matter of law.

(c) In the event that there is a separate underwriting group in addition to the managing group, the position in practice becomes different. The lead manager may only call on members of the managing group to subscribe and pay for bonds up to the maximum of their secondary underwriting commitment. This means, in effect, that the lead manager must have recourse to the underwriting group and require each member of that group to subscribe and pay for bonds up to the maximum of their underwriting commitment, less the amount of bonds each member would have purchased as a member of the selling group (if any). It is only thereafter that the managing group member's liability becomes activated, and is crystallised in the form of the liability to subscribe for bonds up to the maximum of each member's secondary underwriting commitment.

Here too there is a problem where only a portion of the aggregate amount of bonds issued remains unsold and it needs to be addressed in drafting. Is the lead manager under an obligation to pro rate the liability of each member of the underwriting group? Sometimes express clauses are not found in Eurobond documents addressing the issue, but there may be an obligation on the part of the lead manager to act fairly and require subscription on a pro rata basis, on the basis of an implied term to that effect.

Two points need to be made in addition to the above. First, the right to call on the underwriting group to satisfy their underwriting obligations is a right which is conferred on the managers by the usual clauses of an underwriting agreement. However, by virtue of the clauses in the conventional agreement among managers, this right is transferred to the lead manager.

Secondly, in order to ensure that the management group can activate the underwriting group's underwriting obligation, care is necessary in drafting. It may not be sufficient to provide that the managers obtain the underwriting commitment from the underwriting group as agents for the issuer. It is arguable in such cases that, under ordinary rules of agency, only the issuer can activate that obligation, not the lead manager or managers. Consequently, it is necessary to provide in the subscription agreement that the issuer not only authorises the managers to obtain a sub-underwriting commitment, but, in addition, also irrevocably authorises the managers to activate it on the issuer's behalf.

ii *Provisions strengthening lead manager control of the issue*

The second purpose of the agreement among managers is to consolidate the lead manager's control over the marketing and distribution of the Eurobonds. This is achieved by a number of provisions.

(a) A general authority is conferred on the lead manager by all the managers to do all acts and perform all functions which the managers are required or entitled to do under any of the Eurobond marketing documents. Consequently, all powers conferred by the issuer on the managing group by the subscription agreement become transmitted to the lead manager, including the power to terminate on the basis of the force majeure clause discussed above. The lead manager is also conferred power to waive certain conditions imposed on an issuer by the subscription agreement.

(b) Where a selling group is to be set up, the lead manager is specifically authorised to obtain preliminary indications of interest from banks, brokers and dealers interested in becoming selling group members and subscribing for bonds, and to enter into the selling group agreement on the manager's behalf. For this purpose the selling group agreement is attached to the agreement among managers. He is further authorised to allot bonds to whichever members of the selling group and in whatever amounts that the lead manager decides in his absolute discretion. In an issue which is fully subscribed or over-subscribed, the lead manager wields immense power in the market due to the width of this clause.

(c) Where a sub-underwriting group is to be set up the lead is also authorised to set up the underwriting group so as to sell down part of the manager's underwriting commitment. The actual amount so taken up by the underwriting group is negotiated in advance and set out in the agreement between managers so that the lead manager's discretion is not unfettered.

(d) The lead manager must be appointed 'stabilising manager' and given the power to stabilise the price of the bonds during distribution in accordance with the applicable law[12] in the agreement between managers. It should also prohibit any other manager from effecting stabilising transactions. This is necessitated by the need to comply with the stabilisation rules of the UK Securities and Investment Board, so that a potential breach of s 47(2) of the FSA can be avoided.[13] In the past the lead manager was entitled to debit costs of stabilisation to a stabilisation account and the costs of such activities were borne by the managers pro rata to their underwriting commitments. IPMA Recommendation 1.7 now provides that in 'pre-priced debt issues' other than equity linked issues (ie convertibles and issues with warrants)[14] lead managers should not deduct stabilisation costs from fees paid to participants unless the lead manager has specifically reserved such a right in the invitation telex. Consequently, the IPMA recommended form of agreement among managers provides that stabilising transactions are for the lead managers' account.[15]

IPMA has also recommended that where the lead manager has reserved a right to recover stabilising costs from the managers, he should not have a right to recover an amount in excess of the underwriting commission; or where an underwriter is paid a confirmed underwriting fee and a management fee, 60% of that fee.[16]

---

12 See ch 18 below on regulation of stabilisation.
13 See for a detailed discussion ch 18 below.
14 See ch 14 below.
15 See cl 5(a) of the IPMA recommended Agreement among Managers published on 19 March 1991.
16 See IPMA Recommendations 1.8(3).

The underwriting agreement, if there is one, should also confer similar powers on the lead manager subject to similar limits on the underwriter's liability to reimburse. Once again these clauses concentrate in the hands of the lead manager a wide discretion.

Where the bond issue is terminated under the force majeure clause[17] or because conditions precedent are not satisfied, the lead manager's ability to obtain reimbursement from the managers for stabilisation costs, and/or to be reimbursed by the underwriters for such costs, will depend on the existence of express provision to that effect.

Can the managers recover stabilisation costs from the issuer? A clause in the subscription agreement would usually provide that costs of stabilisation cannot be for the account of the issuer.

However, if the bond issue is terminated due to the issuer's failure to satisfy the 'conditions' referred to above[18] the managers may be able to recover stabilisation costs from the issuer if the 'conditions' which are not complied with are drafted in the form of promissory conditions. In such cases it is arguable that the costs represent losses incurred which flow from the issuer's breach of condition. An express indemnity is a more effective technique to enable the managers to recoup their costs from the issuer in such an eventuality.

Where the lead manager terminates the issue by reference to the market disaster clause, the managers will not be able to recover their share of stabilisation costs from the issuer on the above analysis in the absence of a specific indemnity, because in such a case the issuer would not be liable in damages for breach of condition.

Could the underwriters recover their costs from the issuer in the event of a breach of promissory conditions precedent in the subscription agreement? It seems that the underwriters may not claim their costs from the issuer because the obligations of the issuer in the subscription agreement are not owed to the underwriters and, consequently, the argument available to the managers does not avail the underwriters. The underwriters' liability for stabilisation costs is not permitted to exceed each underwriter's underwriting commission.

(e) The managers are conferred authority by the underwriters in the underwriting agreement to reduce or increase the aggregate amount of the issue or the terms and conditions of the bonds, and where necessary to vary the underwriting commitment. This sort of variation becomes necessary in response to market demand for the bonds. The variation will of course require the consent of the issuer. Variations in the amount or terms of the issue or the underwriting commitments specified in the underwriting agreement require consent on the part of the underwriters.

While these powers are conferred on the managing group by the underwriting group, the agreement between managers, it must be remembered, permits the lead managers to exercise these powers on behalf of the managers.[19]

(f) The power of the managers to terminate the issue under the subscription agreement in the event of force majeure is exercisable by the lead manager

---

17 See p 181 above.
18 See p 180.
19 See this chapter, above.

under the terms of the conventional agreement between managers. Sometimes this power is restricted to cases where there is no unanimity among the managers. This restriction does not operate as a control on the lead manager in practice. In effect such clauses confer on the lead manager the power to terminate the issue for force majeure even where a majority of the managing group do not wish to terminate the issue. As observed earlier, the lead manager must exercise the power fairly vis-à-vis the managers since he acts as the agent for the managing group of underwriters.

(g) All expenses and the costs incurred by the lead managers in the marketing and distribution process are recoverable from the issuer under the subscription agreement but, where he is not so reimbursed, there is usually provision in the agreement between managers and the underwriting agreement which gives the lead manager the right to recover such costs from the managers and/or the underwriters pro rata their commitments to subscribe for the bonds. IPMA's recommended form of Agreement Among Managers, however, imposes a limit on the amount which can be recovered from the managers by the lead manager.

The manager's and underwriter's liability to reimburse continues even after termination of the issue due to force majeure or where the issuer fails to satisfy conditions precedent. Once again it seems that the managers may be able to recover their expenses from the issuer if the termination results from the issuer's failure to satisfy promissory conditions.

iii *Compliance with requirements of regulatory law*

All warranties given for the purpose of ensuring compliance with applicable regulatory laws by the managers to the issuers in the subscription agreement will need to be repeated in the agreement between managers[20] by each manager for the benefit of all other managers mutatis mutandis.

3 The selling group agreement

Where a selling group is set up, usually consisting of banks and securities dealers, the primary purchasers of Eurobonds are the members of the selling group. As pointed out earlier, members of the managing group and members of the underwriting group (if there is one) are, generally speaking, also members of the selling group. The selling group agreement is made between members of the selling group and the managers as agents for the issuer of the bonds.

The selling group agreement is in fact misleadingly named, because it is not a sale or purchase agreement at all. It is in effect the standard terms and conditions of sale of bonds in the primary market. The actual offer for sale of bonds is made by the lead manager on behalf of the issuer in the allotment telex sent to members of the selling group after the signing of the subscription agreement. The allotment telex will make the formal offer of sale on the basis of the terms set out in the invitation telex and

---

20 See this chapter, above.

190 *Legal framework of marketing and distribution*

subject to the conditions of the selling group agreement which would have been sent to selling group members previously. The allotment telex will set out the number and price of the bonds offered ('allotted') to each member of the selling group and each member will be required to confirm acceptance of his allotment. The acceptance of the offer contained in the allotment telex concludes the purchase contract in respect of the bonds. It must be remembered that in some issues the allotment is made prior to the signing of the subscription agreement, in which case the allotment (ie the sale contract) is made conditional on the signing of the subscription agreement.

Any obligation of the issuer and the managers to sell bonds to members of the selling group is made subject to a condition subsequent. Thus if the subscription agreement is terminated by the lead manager for force majeure or if the subscription agreement is subject to termination due to a failure by the issuer to satisfy a condition, the selling group agreement terminates any sale contract which selling group members might have by reason of the allotment telex. However, the termination clause in the selling group agreement keeps alive any liability of a selling group member to the managers and the issuer in respect of breaches of selling group obligations which had been committed prior to such termination. This is an important reservation in the light of selling restrictions imposed on selling group members to ensure compliance with applicable regulatory laws which are discussed below.

The primary obligation of each member of the selling group is to make payment for the bonds allotted to him at the subscription price and this obligation must be carried out at the latest by, and in practice on, the closing date by funds transfer to a designated account. Failure to do so results in a liability to pay interest. The selling group members have a right to delivery of bonds from the issuer which is concurrent with payment on the closing date, but the selling group agreement usually requires selling group members to accept a temporary global bond in return for subscription funds. Further, the lead manager is authorised by selling group members to take delivery on their behalf of this temporary global bond. The right to definitive bonds may be postponed for 40 days (previously 90 days) and is conditional on certification of beneficial ownership by non-US persons (as defined) due to the requirements of US tax laws.[1]

The major objective of the selling group agreement, when used, is the imposition of selling restrictions and this is perhaps the major function performed by that agreement. The selling restrictions are imposed in order to avoid infringement of securities regulations in different countries, primarily the US and UK, due to the fact that Eurobonds are offered in the vast majority of cases without complying with registration requirements under US law[2] and sometimes the prospectus requirements of UK law.[3]

The prohibitions required for the purposes of compliance with US securities laws in the selling group agreement will mirror those which the managers would have given the issuer in the subscription agreement and the reader is referred to the discussion above.[4]

---

1 See ch 21 below.
2 See chs 8 and 19.
3 See ch 16 below.
4 See p 182.

In some cases this would include a provision which requires selling group members to send notices to purchasers for purposes of Regulation S.[5] Such notices required by Regulation S[6] prohibit sales to 'US persons' during the 40-day restricted period.

Suppose, however, that a sub-purchaser from a selling group member did breach the selling restrictions despite the fact it received such a notice, and suppose the breaches were sufficiently serious for the SEC to threaten action, and the issue was terminated in consequence. What remedy would the issuer and the lead manager have? They could not recover from the selling group member if he had carried out his obligation under the selling group agreement to serve a contractual notice on sub-purchasers as required by the selling group agreement. Could they recover from the sub-purchaser who breached the selling restrictions of which he had notice? If English law were to govern, it is arguable that a purchaser in breach of the provisions of a notice is liable for the loss in negligence since the loss is foreseeable and results from circumstances giving rise to a relationship of 'proximity' between lead manager, issuer and managers on the one hand and the defendant sub-purchaser on the other.[7] It is submitted that the 'proximity' required in addition to foreseeability by rulings such as *Murphy*[8] and *Caparo*[9] is supplied by the existence of the chain of notices.

In addition, the selling group agreement will impose obligations on selling group members designed to ensure compliance with the provisions of the FSA. The impact of the FSA is dealt with in detail in Part IV. Some of the prohibitions would vary depending on whether the bonds are listed on the London Stock Exchange or not, and will mirror those in the subscription agreement and agreement between managers.

The second objective of the selling group agreement is to restrict the information disseminated in the market in respect of the bonds to that which is contained in the final offering circular. The selling group is prohibited from giving any information or making any representation in connection with the issue subscription or sale of the bonds other than the information contained in the final offering circular. The final form of the offering circular will usually reach the selling group before the allotment telex is received by them. However, selling group members who do not wish to purchase bonds for their own account but who wish to resell to sub-purchasers would already have transmitted information about the issuer and the bonds to prospective purchasers. Such information would usually be based on the information contained in the preliminary offering circular, which is in practice despatched soon after the invitation telexes are sent when the issue is launched.

The obligation of the selling group is to ensure that all representations they make and information they disseminate in respect of the bonds is contained in the final offering circular and if, for instance, information previously

---

5 See detailed discussion of Regulation S in ch 21.
6 R 903(c)(2)(iv).
7 See *Murphy v Brentwood District Council* [1990] 2 All ER 908, cf *Caparo Industries plc v Dickman* [1990] 2 AC 605, HL and *Morgan Crucible Co plc v Hill Samuel Bank Ltd* [1991] 1 All ER 148, CA which related to negligent misstatements rather than negligence.
8 Above, note 7.
9 Above, note 7.

disseminated is not accurate by reference to the final offering circular, they must rectify the representation or misinformation.

The reason for such restrictions is that the lead manager, the managers and/or the issuer may be exposed to liability for any oral misrepresentation made to a potential purchaser of bonds by a selling group member, on the basis that they were acting as agents of the managers and/or the issuer in the distribution of the bonds. The clause attempts to eliminate any authority in the selling group member, by expressly providing that selling group members have no authority to make representations save those in the final offering circular. Such a clause has been held to be sufficient to eliminate a principal's liability in English law for misrepresentation by an agent, and further that it is not subject to a test of reasonableness under s 3 of the Misrepresentation Act 1967: *Overbrook Estates Ltd v Glencombe Properties Ltd*[10] which was approved by Bridge LJ in *Cremdean Properties v Nash*.[11] Secondly, the clause provides for an indemnity to be given by each selling group member to the managers and the issuer against any loss, damages, claims, actions or expenses which such persons may incur in consequence of a breach by the selling group member of his obligations.

Any inaccurate or misleading statement which is dishonestly or recklessly made in the UK, or the dishonest concealment of facts for the purpose of effecting a sale of bonds, in any event runs the potential risk of a breach of the criminal provisions of s 47(1) of the FSA.

---

10 [1974] 3 All ER 511, [1974] 1 WLR 135.
11 [1977] 244 Estates Gazette 547 at 549.

CHAPTER 11
The bond instrument: the legal relationship between issuer and Eurobond holder

In this section the rights and obligations as between the issuer of Eurobonds and the 'holders' of Eurobonds will be examined.[1]

I RIGHTS AND OBLIGATIONS ARISING ON THE BOND INSTRUMENT

Since the Eurobond is a bearer negotiable instrument,[2] it is capable under English law[3] of creating a direct legal nexus between each successive bondholder[4] and the original issuer, and of transmitting to each successive holder the rights and obligations contained in the bond instrument, as well as any restrictions and exemptions.

These rights and obligations are specified or summarised on the face of the bond instrument. Many clauses in the trust deed or fiscal agency agreement are in practice incorporated by reference into the bond instrument and only summaries of such clauses appear on the face of the bond. These rights and obligations are discussed below.

1 Payment of interest and principal

The primary obligation of the issuer to each bondholder is to make periodic payments of interest specified on the face of the bond.[5] Secondly, the issuer is obliged to pay the principal amount due on the bond on maturity, or at an earlier redemption date where such early redemption is required or permitted by the terms of the bond.[6]

Interest is payable at a fixed rate if the bond is a fixed rate bond and at a variable rate if the bond is a 'floating rate note' ('FRN'). Interest is

---

1 See p 171 above as to who is the 'holder' of Eurobonds.
2 See p 162 above.
3 See p 167 above as to applicability of English law.
4 See p 171 above as to who is the Eurobond holder.
5 There is no such obligation in the case of 'zero coupon' or deep discount bonds. See p 214 below.
6 In the case of 'perpetual' bonds (see p 215) there is no maturity date and consequently no obligation to repay principal except in the event of default.

usually payable on a semi-annual basis in the case of FRNs or on an annual basis in the case of rate bonds, and in both cases interest payments must continue until final maturity or redemption of the bond, whichever is earlier.

Interest and principal payments are made by the issuer to bondholders through a network of paying agents appointed for that purpose. Payment of principal or interest is made only at the offices of such paying agents upon surrender of the bond (in the case of principal) or the relevant coupon (in the case of interest). Bondholders' rights to interest or principal are conditional on such surrender.

In the case of an FRN the interest rate payable is usually determined by reference to a bench mark rate such as the London Interbank Offered Rate (LIBOR)[7] plus a margin which the issuer has agreed to pay to bondholders. The rate of interest payable on an FRN is determined by a bank specially appointed for the purpose by a process similar to that used in syndicated loans.[8] Two business days prior to a semi-annual or annual interest fixing date the agent bank will request each of four reference banks for their interest rate quotations for inter-bank deposits in London which are denominated in the currency of the bonds. The agent bank will then determine an arithmetical mean between these rates, and this calculation will constitute the LIBOR rate in question. The agent bank is usually authorised to decide the rate by reference to less than four banks if quotations are not forthcoming from all four reference banks. Where no quotations are available the agent bank is authorised to decide the interest rate by reference to the interest rate paid on the previous interest period. The agent bank's determination of interest is usually made conclusive as to the rate payable to bondholders.

Sometimes there is a specified minimum or 'floor' level of interest payable on an FRN. This level represents the minimum interest rate to which a bondholder will be entitled in the event of a downward spiral of interest rates applicable to the currency of the bond.

In the case of some bonds such minimum level of interest becomes fixed if the LIBOR for, say, six-month deposits in the currency of the bonds, falls below the 'floor' level specified in the bond. In this type of case, the FRN converts automatically into a fixed rate bond until maturity, if the LIBOR falls to the specified minimum level. This type of legal mechanism produces a bond referred to as a 'drop-lock' bond.[9] In such a case, if the LIBOR rate subsequently moves above the level at which the FRN converted into a fixed rate bond, the holder of such a bond is at a disadvantage. The fixed rate bond in the drop-lock format does not reconvert into a floating rate note to give the bondholder the benefit of the upward movement in interest rates.

Consequently, a more flexible structure provides for a minimum 'floor' level interest rate which must be paid to a bondholder in the event that the LIBOR or other bench mark interest rate falls below that floor level. In this type of structure the floating rate bond does not convert into a fixed rate bond. If the LIBOR (or other bench mark interest) rate moves

---

7 Or the London Interbank Bid Rate (LIBID) or, a mean between the two, LIMEAN.
8 See ch 5 above.
9 See Fisher *International Bonds* p 145; Ugeux *Floating Rate Notes* (Euromoney Publications) p 112; Watkins 'Types of Bonds' in Current Issues of International Finance Law p 115.

upwards to a rate above the 'floor' level the holder is entitled to interest payments at that rate. Consequently the holder is not subject to the disadvantage inherent in drop-lock structures when interest rates move upwards after the drop-lock clause has converted the floating rate bond into a fixed rate bond.

2 Repayment of principal and early redemption provisions

The right to payment of the principal or face value of the bond accrues on the maturity date of the bond, unless early redemption is permissible under the terms of the bond. Generally, the repayment of the principal amount is required to be made in one single payment.[10] Redemption on maturity is usually made to coincide with an interest payment date. However, it is also invariably the case that an issuer has a right under the bond instrument to repay the principal amount due on the bonds in the event that there is a change in the tax laws or regulations in the issuer's state of incorporation which requires the issuer to subject all interest payments to a withholding tax.[11] It is the practice to distinguish between different bonds of the issuer by referring to the maturity date (as well as the interest rate).[12]

Certain types of bonds provide for early redemption prior to maturity independently of redemption for tax reasons. Such early redemption may either be optional or mandatory.

i Bonds with optional early redemption

(a) Bonds with 'call' options. These provide the issuer with an option to redeem or 'call' the bonds usually within the last 12 or 24 months (and in some cases at an earlier date) prior to final maturity[13] by giving a redemption notice to bondholders of not more than 60 days and not less than 30 days of such a redemption. The right to redeem is usually a right to redeem the bond at face value or 'at par', ie by paying the principal amount specified on the face of the bonds. This right, however, can work to the bondholders' prejudice if the bonds are trading at a premium in the markets, that is to say, above their face value.[14] This is because the bondholder is compelled by a legal duty to tender his bond to the issuer for repayment at the face value or principal amount of the bond, though he could have sold the bond on the markets for a higher amount. Consequently, some bond instruments provide for redemption at a certain premium if the redemption right is exercised between certain specified periods, eg 2% premium if the right is exercised within four years to maturity. Once again the redemption can only be effected on an interest payment date as specified in the redemption notice.

(b) Bonds with 'put' options. In these bonds each bondholder is given an option to require the issuer to redeem his bond during a certain period

---

10 This is referred to as a 'bullet' maturity.
11 See ch 13 below for the role of the trustee in such an event.
12 This practice is traceable to the requirement in s 7, ch 2 of The Stock Exchange listing rules which requires specification of maturity date in the title.
13 See *Fisher* p 165.
14 See ch 9, p 161 above.

in the life of the bond. The bondholder is required to give notice to the issuer of the exercise of this right (the 'put') by delivering the bonds with a put notice to a paying agent.[15]

ii   *Mandatory early redemption*[16]

Some bonds are issued subject to mandatory early redemption provisions by way of amortisation of the principal amount in instalments. The result is that the issuer is obliged to repay a specified portion of the principal amount due on the whole of the bond issue at times specified in the bond.

This type of redemption by instalments is capable of being structured in two ways.

The first is to require the issuer to redeem a certain number of bonds which add up to a certain percentage of the total value of bonds issued. Thus, if the aggregate value of an issue was $100m, an issuer would be required to redeem 10% of the aggregate value in one year, 20% in the next year and so on. This would result in some bondholders being repaid before others.

(a) Serial notes.   The second is to require instalments repayment in relation to each bond issued, each instalment representing a percentage of the value of each bond. The latter variety are referred to as 'serial notes'[17] because each bond is amortised according to a predetermined schedule so that all bondholders are paid off in instalments at the same time. Each instalment of principal repayable is represented by a repayment coupon which must be surrendered by the bondholder to a paying agent in order to claim repayment of the instalment of the principal amount.

(b)   Bonds with sinking fund.   Where the first structure is adopted, ie the total principal amount of a bond issue is subject to amortisation over a period of time, the instalment repayments are required to be effected by the issuer in one of two ways. The first method is that the bonds are subject to a 'sinking fund' provision. In this type of structure the issuer is required to redeem a certain amount (eg $50m of a $200y, by redeeming bonds chosen by drawing lots ($50m on each instalment in the above example). Bondholders whose serial numbers are drawn are under a duty and have a correlative right to have their bonds redeemed. In practice, since bonds are held by Euroclear and Cedel as fungibles[18] this requirement is effected by Euroclear and Cedel.[19] The usual legal requirement in such cases is that the serial

---

15 See as to paying agents ch 12 below.
16 See Watkins 'Types of Bonds' in Current Issues in International Financial Law (1985) Malaya Law Review and Butterworths.
17 See *Fisher* p 146.
18 Ie in aggregate amounts credited to the accounts of members of those clearing systems, and not in specie by reference to serial numbers (see p 169 above).
19 See as regards Euroclear s 5.9 of the *Operating Procedures of the Euroclear System*, which describes the computerised lottery system operated in respect of securities clearance accounts.

numbers of the bonds which have been selected for redemption must be notified to bondholders a number of weeks prior to the date of redemption in newspaper advertisements.

(c) Bonds with purchase fund. The second method is the 'purchase fund', which requires the issuer to appoint a purchase agent who is required to purchase a certain aggregate amount of bonds in the markets, during specified periods. He is given a discretion as to the price at which he purchases the bonds with an upper limit of the redemption or face value of the bonds. In some bond issues this obligation is triggered only where the market price of the bond falls below a certain threshold level. It is important to note that bondholders are not under any obligation to redeem their bonds by sale to the purchase agent. This is the fundamental difference between a sinking fund and a purchase fund.

If the bonds, which are subject to a purchase fund, are listed on The London Stock Exchange there is a requirement in s 5 of the listing rules of The International Stock Exchange[20] that purchases of listed corporate bonds should be notified to The Stock Exchange when an aggregate of 10% of the initial nominal amount of the securities has been purchased and thereafter when 5% of the initial nominal amount is purchased.

Where the purchase fund is set up to operate in the early life of the bond by way of stabilisation as a price support mechanism[1] it may contravene s 47(2) of the Financial Services Act 1986 ('FSA'), since it may result in the creation of a 'false or misleading impression as to the market in or the price or value of' the bonds.[2] Since the purchases are not effected by the stabilising manager during the stabilisation period in accordance with the stabilisation rules of the Securities and Instruments Board[3] but by a specially appointed purchase agent, such activity would not have the benefit of the exemption in s 48(7) of the FSA.[4]

Where Eurobonds are listed on The London Stock Exchange the provisions in section 9, chapter 2 of the listing rules need to be complied with when bonds are subject to redemption. In particular, if purchases are to be made by tender, they must be made to all bondholders alike. In the case of domestic bonds where redemption is being effected by market purchases the repurchase price cannot exceed 5% of the average middle market quote for ten days previous. This rule does not, however, apply to Eurobonds.[5]

iii Extendable and retractable bonds

In the case of some bonds the maturity date of the bonds can be extended or retracted at the option of the holder of the bond. The option to extend or retract maturity must be exercised during a specified period, usually in the last years during the life of the bond. The retraction or extension is usually for two or three years. It is usual for such a retraction option to

---

20 See *Admission of Securities to Listing* s 5 ch 2 para 17.4.
1 See Watkins, fn 16 above, at 113.
2 See Ch 18 on s 47(2) of the FSA and stabilisation.
3 See above.
4 See on stabilisation and s 47(2) Ch 18.
5 See s 2, ch 1, para 10 of *Admission of Securities to Listing*.

carry a provision for the payment of fees to the holder if the retraction option is not exercised.[6]

Can bonds which are redeemed or purchased prior to maturity be resold by the issuer? At common law there is the authority of Lord Ellenborough to the effect that payment by the maker or issuer of a negotiable instrument prior to its stated maturity does not extinguish the bill and that it may be reissued.[7] As regards companies incorporated under the UK Companies Act 1985, the company has power to reissue debentures which it has redeemed unless provision to the contrary is found in the company's articles of association or in a relevant contract or unless a resolution to that effect has been passed.[8] However, in modern Eurobond instruments, bonds redeemed prior to maturity or purchased prior to maturity are usually subject to cancellation clauses which require the issuer to cancel the bonds and not reissue or resell them.

Redemption or purchase prior to maturity is also subject to an obligation on the part of the bondholder to surrender all unmatured coupons. Where an unmatured coupon is missing the holder is not deprived of his right to have his bond redeemed, but in practice issuers of fixed rate bonds are usually conferred the right to deduct the amount of the missing coupon from the principal amount due when making payment to the Eurobondholder. If the missing coupon can be located prior to the date of prescription[9] the bond holder will be entitled to payment of the amount deducted. No such deduction for missing coupons is possible in the case of an FRN because it is impossible to quantify the amount of interest payable in the future. Consequently, a deduction provision is not provided but instead the issuer is given the right to ask for an indemnity from the bondholder presenting the FRN for redemption with missing coupons, in respect of any loss which the issuer may incur as a result of such payment without surrender of coupons.

3 Taxation and payments of interest and principal

It is invariably the practice that all payments of interest and principal in respect of the bonds are required to be made free and clear of any withhold or deduction by way of taxes or other levies. In the event of such a tax being imposed on the issuer, he is required to pay the interest payable on the bond on a grossed-up basis. However, the issuer would usually be given a right to redeem the bonds in such an eventuality.

4 Covenants in the bond instrument

There are two major covenants usually contained in the Eurobond instrument. First, there is the pari passu covenant and the second is the negative pledge.

---

6 See further *Fisher* p 162; Watkins, fn 16 above, at p 114.
7 *Burbridge v Manners* (1812) 3 Camp 193 at 195; see also *Attenborough v Mackenzie* (1856) 25 LJ Ex 244. The Bills of Exchange Act 1882 also permits reissue under s 59(2) of bills governed by the Act.
8 See s 194 of the Companies Act 1985.
9 See p 203 below.

Rights and obligations arising on the bond instrument 199

i *The pari passu covenant*

This is to the effect that:

> 'The bonds and coupons constitute direct and unsecured obligations of the Issuer and shall at all times rank pari passu and without any preference amongst themselves. The payment obligations of the issuer under the bonds and coupons shall at all times rank at least equally with all its present and future unsecured and unsubordinated obligations.'

The effect of the first limb of the clause is that the issuer may not repay principal amounts due on the bonds to some of the bondholders but not others prior to maturity, unless it is expressly provided for in the bond instruments as in the case where there is a sinking fund or purchase fund;[10] nor may the issuer do so when the bonds mature. The obligation is to treat all bondholders equally. The effect of the latter half of such a clause in a Eurobond needs to be considered. In the case of a corporate entity at least, it seems that the purpose of this part of the pari passu clause is to ensure that on an insolvency or a composition of creditors, all unsecured creditors will be treated equally and ratably. However, in many jurisdictions such a result may not be possible due to applicable tax laws or corporate laws of insolvency which give priority to various unsecured creditors.[11] Consequently, if the law applicable to the insolvency is a law which does recognise different treatment of different types of unsecured creditors, it does not seem possible to override the law applicable in the insolvency by a contractual rule contained in an instrument governed by English law.[12] Further, if an English court were to take jurisdiction in respect of a foreign registered company under s 221(5) of the Insolvency Act 1986, it is likely that an English court would apply English rules on the priority of creditors.[13]

However, the result of the clause seems to be that if for any reason any unsecured creditor does in fact obtain priority over other unsecured bondholders under the law of any applicable jurisdiction, the issuer is in breach of his obligations. It also seems clear that such a clause cannot prevent early repayment by the borrower of other unsecured creditors under other bond issues.

ii *The negative pledge covenant*

The next major covenant is the negative pledge clause. A detailed discussion of this clause is to be found in chapter 5. The purpose of the clause is the prevention of the creation or subsistence of any security interest in or over any assets of the issuer or its subsidiaries (if it is a corporation), so that the assets will be available to all unsecured creditors in the event of liquidation or other 'work-out' situation. This is sought to be achieved by a prohibition in a form similar to:

---

10 See pp 196–197 above.
11 Such an instance is the priority claim of the Inland Revenue in UK tax law: see ss 175 and 386 and Sch 6 of the Insolvency Act 1986.
12 See comments in respect of pari passu clauses in syndicated loan agreements.
13 Priority rules are, however, outside the scope of the work.

'the Issuer will not create or permit to subsist any mortgage pledge lien hypothecation security interest or other charge or encumbrance in or over the whole or part of its undertaking or assets present or future to secure any of its indebtedness or guarantees.'

In addition the issuer is required, in the case of corporate entities, to procure that none of its subsidiaries will commit any of the above prohibited acts. The clause usually goes on to require that if the issuer or one or more of its subsidiaries wishes to create any such security, the issuer must ensure that the bonds are equally and ratably secured by such security, or alternatively that the issuer provides security of equal value for the bonds.[14]

While the negative pledge is common to both bond instruments and syndicated loan agreements the negative pledge covenant in a bond issue is usually not as extensive as it is in syndicated loans.[15] Thus it is common to find in practice that the negative pledge clause in bond instruments prohibits the giving of security by the issuer or any of its subsidiaries, only in respect of 'international bond issues', or in respect of 'public indebtedness'. Such restrictions are not usually incorporated in syndicated loans. In syndicated loans the negative pledge would usually prohibit the giving or creation of any form of security interest in respect of all forms of borrowing and indebtedness, and would not be restricted in the manner that the negative pledge clause is limited in an international bond issue. The format of the negative pledge when restricted to international bond issues would not prohibit the giving of security in respect of bank borrowings, even if the security consisted of a charge as comprehensive as a floating charge under English law.[16] Consequently, the clause in this form which is to be found in bond instruments is of little value to the bondholders. The real protection against the eventuality that an issuer may grant security over its assets to banks or other commercial lenders to the prejudice of a bondholder is, however, not legal but commercial. Only the highest rated transnational corporations and entities have access to the international bond markets and therefore it is unlikely that such entities would need to give security over assets for the purpose of obtaining bank financing.

Bondholders do not, in practice, have any additional covenant protection which is substantial. The position of banks in a syndicated loan bears comparison with that of the bondholders in an international bond issue in this respect. In a syndicated loan, the banks would at least have, in addition to a negative pledge and pari passu clause, covenant protection in the form of:

(a) financial ratio covenants, eg a minimum debt to equity ratio, a minimum net worth, a minimum current asset ratio, a minimum working capital and so on;[17]

---

14 See ch 5 above as to the analysis of this clause and the drafting problems in relation to the clause.
15 See on negative pledge in syndicated loans ch 5 above.
16 See on floating charges Gough *Company Charges* Part Two.
17 See ch 5 above.

(b) covenants prohibiting substantial disposal of corporate assets;[18]
(c) covenants seeking to control a merger of the borrowing entity with other entities.[19]

Such covenant protection is not usually found in international bond issues although financial ratio covenants have been used in many long-dated issues. There is no reason in law or in commercial practice why such covenant protection should not be provided to bondholders.

One reason for the absence of wide-ranging covenant protection for bondholders is said to be the much greater financial and commercial stature of the entities who can raise finance through international bond issues as compared with the financial and commercial stature of borrowers in the international syndicated loans markets.

Another reason is that the legal structure of a bond issue is such that the financial risk of the investment banks who arrange the bond issue is limited to the risk that the bonds cannot be successfully sold to investors and this risk terminates within a short period of time from launch. Once the bonds have been placed with investors the credit risk of the issuer's insolvency is with the bondholders until maturity of the bonds; the risk is not with the investment banks. By contrast, in a syndicated bank loan the credit risk of borrower insolvency is always with the banks until repayment. Further, in a bond issue the real lenders, namely the bondholders, have no part in negotiating the covenants to which the issuer will be subject, whereas in a syndicated loan the real lenders, ie the banks, determine the nature and extent of the covenants necessary for the protection of their loan assets. However, where a trustee is to be appointed he may be under a duty to future bondholders to insist on proper covenant protection.[20] As far as the investment banks in an international bond issue are concerned the level of bondholder protection which must be secured through covenants is largely determined by what potential investors in the market would expect and, secondly, by what issuers are prepared to accept. If the investment banks considered that bond purchasers would demand greater protection by way of covenants there is no doubt that such covenants would be included as are necessary to enable the bonds to be successfully sold to investors.

The level of covenant protection in an international bond issue is therefore partially a result of a marketing and sales decision and is taken in respect of an extremely 'high quality borrower' in terms of long-term credit risk; whereas the level of covenant protection in a syndicated loan is the result of a credit risk decision by commercial bank lenders in respect of borrowers who may not have the same level of quality as long-term credit risks.

It is also the case that nearly all bonds are subject to a cross-default clause.[1] Consequently, the bonds would have the benefit of any default occasioned by a breach of the much more stringent covenants in syndicated loan agreements.[2]

---

18 See ch 5 above.
19 See on covenants in syndicated loan agreements ch 5 above.
20 See on trustees ch 13 and ch 11, pp 204–213 below.
1 For syndicated loans see p 98 above.
2 See ch 5 below.

5 Events of default

Bond instruments usually specify a number of instances on the occurrence of which the issuer may be required to repay the sums due on the bonds prior to maturity. These are the events of default and, in practice, are very similar to events of default in a loan agreement.[3]

They are usually as follows:

(a) Failure by the issuer to pay interest or principal on any of the bonds when due; a grace period of seven days is usually permitted.

(b) Failure by the issuer to perform any of its obligations in the bond instruments (or the trust deed where there is one). There is usually a grace period of two weeks or one month after the issuer receives notification of default. This permits the issuer to remedy the default within that period without becoming liable to make immediate repayment on bonds.

(c) A cross-default provision which would usually put the issuer in default if any other indebtedness of the issuer (or the guarantor, if any, or any of their subsidiaries) becomes due and payable prior to its stated maturity. The clause is sometimes widened as in the case of syndicated loans to include situations where such indebtedness is 'capable of being declared due and payable prior to its stated maturity'. The latter form of draft is more stringent and would create an event of default enabling the bonds to be accelerated, even if the other indebtedness which is capable of being accelerated is not in fact accelerated by the other creditor because the latter may have decided to waive the default. The more stringent form of the clause is frequently used in practice.[4]

This clause is vitally important in practice given the absence of wide-ranging covenant protection for bondholders. It enables the issuer's repayment obligation to be accelerated whenever any other unsecured bank lender or creditor is capable of accelerating his loans or indebtedness of the issuer for breach of covenant. The bondholders are thus capable of getting the benefit of covenants imposed on the issuer in other financings effected by him, particularly covenants in syndicated loans which are more tightly drafted.

The cross-default clause can also be made flexible by specifying a minimum amount of indebtedness which must become due and payable before an event of default occurs. Specification of such minimum thresholds is common in practice.

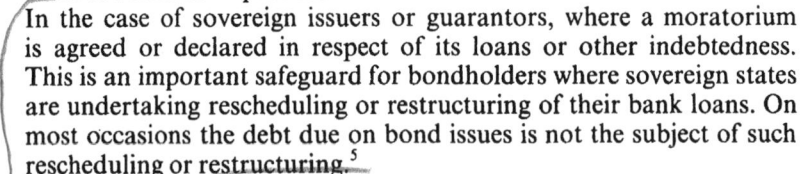

(d) In the case of sovereign issuers or guarantors, where a moratorium is agreed or declared in respect of its loans or other indebtedness. This is an important safeguard for bondholders where sovereign states are undertaking rescheduling or restructuring of their bank loans. On most occasions the debt due on bond issues is not the subject of such rescheduling or restructuring.[5]

---

3 See on events of default in syndicated loan agreements p 98.
4 See on cross-default the discussion at p 98.
5 See Walker & Bucheit 'Legal Issues in the Restructuring of Commercial Bank Loans to Sovereign Borrowers' in *Sovereign Lending: Managing Legal Risk* (Euromoney, Gruson and Reisner edn) ch 12.

Consequently, some protection is necessary for the bondholder and since the rescheduling exercise typically commences with the announcement of a moratorium on the sovereign's external debt, the default mechanism in the bond instrument is locked in to this declaration.[6]

(e) Where authorisation or consent or approval of a governmental or other agency is necessary for the issuer to comply with its obligations, including repayment under the bond instrument, the failure to obtain such authorisation or consent or approval or the withdrawal thereof is made an event of default.

Exchange control authorisations in the case of some issuers, or consent of the Ministry of Finance in the case of Japanese issuers, would come within such an event. The clause is also capable of being expanded to include the fulfilment of any precondition or the obtaining of any licence or registration by the issuer in respect of the issue of the bonds or in order to comply with obligations arising under the bond instrument.

These are the principal events of default which are important in practice. However, bond instruments contain a further host of events on the occurrence of which the issuer may technically be declared in default. These include:

(f) Insolvency of the issuer or guarantor of the bonds. This usually includes the appointment of a liquidator or receiver in respect of the issuer or guarantor or any of their subsidiaries or in respect of any part of their assets, undertakings or revenues; the taking of any proceedings to defer any obligation to make payment; entry into a composition with creditors; ceasing or threatening to cease its business; the making of a general assignment of assets or an arrangement with creditors.
(g) The making of a winding-up order by a court of competent jurisdiction or the passing of a resolution to wind up the issuer, guarantor or any of their subsidiaries.
(h) The levying or enforcement of any distress or execution.
(i) Appointment of a receiver in respect of part or the whole of the property assets revenues or undertaking of the issuer guarantor or any of its subsidiaries.
(j) Any occurrence having an effect similar to those mentioned in (f) to (i).

6 Limitation period

Market practice has resulted in issuers granting bondholders a ten-year limitation period for purposes of bringing actions on the bond in respect of principal. The period is calculated from the date it falls due for payment. A five-year period is provided in respect of interest from the date it falls

---

6 As to declaration of moratoria in the sovereign debt restructuring process, see Walker and Bucheit, above; Clark and Hughes 'Approaches to the Restructuring of Sovereign Debt' in *Sovereign Lending: Managing Legal Risk* (Euromoney, Gruson and Reisner edn) ch 11.

due. The limitation period agreed between issuer and bondholders is longer than the statutory limitation period which may be applicable.[7]

II DEFAULT, ACCELERATION AND ENFORCEMENT

The rights of bondholders to call default, accelerate the bonds and take action in court are different depending on whether the Eurobonds are issued subject to a trust deed or fiscal agency agreement.[8]

Where a trust deed is used the above rights of *individual* bondholders are conferred in the first instance on a trustee who may exercise them on behalf of bondholders as a group; individual bondholders are, however, conferred secondary rights of enforcement. The trustee in effect is empowered to act on behalf of the bondholders as a group. This is not the case when a fiscal agent rather than a trustee is appointed in pursuance of a fiscal agency agreement. The fiscal agent is little more than a paying agent of the issuer and has no duties or powers comparable to those of a trustee.[9]

The impact of the trustee and trust deed on bondholder rights is as follows:

(a) Only the trustee is conferred a power by the bond instrument to accelerate the bonds on the occurrence of an event of default. Individual bondholders are not permitted to call default or demand acceleration of bonds.

(b) The trustee is not under a duty to bondholders to accelerate the bonds and demand repayment on the occurrence of an event of default; he is merely conferred the power to do so.

(c) No express restrictions, conditions or qualifications are placed on the trustee's power to accelerate; it is usually declared to be 'absolute and unconditional'.

(d) Bondholders (and coupon holders, where coupons are detached from the host bond and sold separately from the bonds) are prohibited from taking any action in a court of law to enforce their rights to principal and interest; only the trustee has a primary right to do so. Bondholders (and coupon holders) acquire rights to proceed in a court of law only where (i) the trustee has become bound to proceed against the issuer, and (ii) the trustee has failed to bring proceedings in court within a reasonable time. Such clauses are referred to as 'no action' clauses.[10]

(e) Some trust deeds provide that an event which may constitute an event of default only becomes such if the trustee certifies in writing that such an event is 'materially prejudicial in the trustee's opinion to the interest of bondholders'. Until such certification no event of default has occurred. Failure to pay interest or principal is not subject to certification of material prejudice by the trustee; the occurrence of

---

7 See pp 204–213 above.
8 On trust deeds see ch 13 below and on fiscal agency agreement see ch 12 below.
9 See ch 12 below.
10 The term is used by US courts. See *Watts v Missouri-Kansas Texas Railroad Co* 383 Fzd 57 5 Cir (1967).

either a failure to pay interest or principal is ipso facto an event of default. A trustee's determination as to whether there is material prejudice or not is made final and conclusive vis-à-vis the bondholders.

1 Enforceability of trust deed provisions restricting individual bondholder rights

The first question which arises is the legal basis on which an individual bondholder's rights may be restricted by the terms and provisions of a trust deed.

It was submitted previously[11] that the regime of rights and liabilities created by the bond should be governed by the proper law of the bond as specified by an express clause on the face of the bond. Most international bonds are subject to an express choice of English law, and consequently, the question is considered under English law.

Under English law there are two legal bases on which the trust deed provisions may be binding on successive bondholders. The first is the doctrine of incorporation by reference and the second is that there is a valid trust affecting the rights of bondholders.

First, it is expressly provided on the face of the bond instrument that the bonds are subject to all the terms and conditions of the trust deed. Consequently, the English doctrine of incorporation of a document by reference should apply,[12] although the cases on the subject do not deal with negotiable instruments. However, the terms of the trust deed become part of the bond instrument by virtue of the doctrine of incorporation only if the trust deed is referred to in the bond instrument as an existing document.[13] In practice this is usually the case.

There seems to be no legal objection to the use of such incorporation by reference, in the light of the fact that (a) the bonds state that the trust deed is available for inspection by any bondholder at the principal office of the trustee, and (b) summaries of the provisions contained in the trust deed are contained in the bond instrument itself. In practice, purchasers of bonds rarely examine the provisions of a trust deed and have no detailed knowledge of its provisions.

Secondly, there is a valid trust created by the trust deed. The nature of the trust created by a Eurobond trust deed is discussed later.[14] It is perhaps on this basis that some early English cases on trust deeds, such as *Rogers & Co v British and Colonial Colliery Supply Association*[15] assume that trust deeds are binding on successive bondholders.

US case law also quite clearly recognises the ability of an issuer to incorporate the terms and conditions of trust deeds or 'indentures' into the terms of a bond instrument though they seek to restrict bond holder rights.[16]

---

11 See ch 9.
12 On incorporation by reference see *Smith v South Wales Switchgear Ltd* [1978] 1 WLR 165 which related to the incorporation in a commercial contract of the terms of a trade association's standard terms; Gorrell Barnes P in *Re Bonis Smart* [1902] P 238 especially at 240 for the application of the principle in testamentary cases.
13 See the two cases cited in the previous footnote.
14 See ch 13 below.
15 (1898) 68 LJ QB 14.
16 *Guardian Depositors Corpn v David Stott Flour Mills Inc* (1939) 291 Mich at 180, 188 per Butzel CJ; *Cunningham v Pressed Steel Car Co* 238 App Div 624, 265 NYS 256 aff'd (1934) 263 NY 671 (1933); *Watts v Missouri-Kansas-Texas Railroad Co* 383 Fed 571 where Judge Goldberg approved Butzel CJ's formulation in *Guardian Depositors* (above); *Noble v European Mortgage Investment Co* (1933) 165 A 157 19 Del Ch 216.

Some doubt may arise in respect of incorporation of the trust deed due to the approach of the courts in cases relating to the incorporation by reference of the terms of a charterparty into a transferable bill of lading. In *SIAT di del Ferro v Tradax*[17] the court held that since successive purchasers of the bills must know as a matter of commercial reality precisely what their rights are immediately prior to payment on tender of the bill, the charterparty should be attached to the bill of lading and tendered to the purchaser; incorporation by reference was ineffective unless the charterparty was attached. It is arguable that there is little commercial difference as between the purchaser of a bill of lading and the purchaser of a Eurobond, and consequently that the case should apply by analogy to Eurobonds.

It is submitted that the logic underlying the ruling in cases such as *SIAT di del Ferro v Tradax*[18] does not apply to displace the ordinary rule of incorporation by reference applicable to the incorporation of trust deed provisions into a Eurobond. The *SIAT* ruling is based on the logic that when shipping documents including a transferable bill of lading are tendered to a buyer under a c.i.f. or f.o.b. contract he must take up and pay for it or reject the documents immediately. For this purpose he (or his bank) must be able to decide immediately whether or not the shipping documents comply with the requirements of the c.i.f. or f.o.b. contract pursuant to which the seller will tender the bill of lading. If the bill of lading refers to another document, eg a charterparty, and the law permitted the seller to incorporate by reference, the buyer who is required to pay immediately would not be able to determine whether the seller has complied with his contractual obligation when the buyer makes payment. It was for this reason that the court refused to permit incorporation by reference. In the case of a Eurobond an intending purchaser has the necessary time to examine the trust deed before he decides to purchase the bond. Consequently, it is submitted that the *SIAT* ruling should not be applied to Eurobonds.

Assuming that trust deed provisions are binding on successive bondholders, it may be asked, on what basis the trustee has rights vis-à-vis the issuer to sue on behalf of bondholders and enforce the rights contained in the bond instrument.

The trustee's right to accelerate the bonds on the occurrence of an event of default and his right to bring actions on behalf of the bond holders is achieved by the following mechanism:

(a) the issuer promises in the trust deed to make payments of interest and principal on the bonds to the trustee; this promise is in addition to a similar promise made to bondholders which is contained in the bond instrument;

(b) it is provided in the trust deed that payment of interest or principal to the bondholders through the paying agents is pro tanto satisfaction of the issuer's obligations to the trustee;

(c) the trustee's right to interest and principal is held on trust by the trustee for the benefit of the bondholders;

(d) the trustee has a right to call for immediate repayment of outstanding

---

17 [1980] 1 Lloyd's Rep 53, CA.
18 Above.

principal on the occurrence of an event of default including a failure to pay interest or principal when due.

It is submitted that the true analysis of this structure under English law is that while the bond instrument itself is not the subject of a trust, the Eurobond trustee is indeed the trustee of the chose in action consisting of the right to enforce payment of interest and principal and the trustee may enforce it as against the issuer on behalf of the Eurobondholder. The nature of the trust and trust assets are discussed in detail below.[19] The validity and enforceability of such a trust and a trust-based structure outside the UK courts is a matter which is not capable of a clear-cut answer. Where arts 6 and 8 of the Hague 'Convention on the Law applicable to Trusts and on their Recognition' apply, the courts of state parties to the Convention will apply the law expressly chosen by the settlor of the trust to the question of validity and enforceability of the trust and recognition of the trust will be afforded by the courts of state parties to the Convention under art 11.[20]

The result of this structure is that although there are two parallel covenants to pay interest and principal (one to the trustee and the other to bondholders) each covenant is individually satisfied by one payment of interest and of principal to the designated paying agent. The issuer is not liable to pay interest and principal twice over, once to the trustee and once to the bondholders. However, on the occurrence of a failure by the issuer to pay either interest or principal to the bondholders, the trustee's right to demand immediate payment or 'acceleration' of all principal amounts is activated; whereas individual bond holders do not have similar acceleration rights by the terms of the bond instrument. The trustee also has a right to accelerate and demand immediate repayment of the principal outstanding on the occurrence of other events of default such as a breach of the negative pledge covenant. This power is necessary to protect the trust asset, ie the right to interest and principal, which the trustee holds for the benefit of the bondholders.

2 Bondholder control of trustee powers

Two further questions arise in this respect. First, do bondholders have any rights to interfere or control the trustee's exercise of discretion if they consider, for instance, that a decision not to accelerate on default is unfair or unreasonable? Secondly, is the trustee's exercise of discretion capable of being subject to review by the courts?

The bond instrument itself generally confers on 20% or more of bondholders of the total principal amount of bonds outstanding, a power to compel the trustee to accelerate on the occurrence of an event of default. In addition, bondholders may require the trustee to accelerate by virtue of an 'extraordinary resolution' passed in accordance with the terms of the trust deed.

If the aggrieved bondholder is an individual, the problem with these provisions is that in practice he would find it difficult to use them. First, it is difficult for individual bondholders to locate 20% of bondholders

---

19 See below Ch 13 especially pp 225–228.
20 The Convention is operative in the UK by virtue of the Recognition of Trusts Act 1987.

in aggregate amount of bonds outstanding due to the anonymity of the holders of Eurobonds which are invariably in bearer form.[1] Even if it were possible to muster such a percentage by advertising, say, in the *Financial Times*, there is a practical problem for the bondholder who wishes to get repaid on his bond. If an event of default has occurred on the bonds, it is inevitable that cross-default clauses in syndicated loan agreements[2] would have been activated and that the issuer would also be in default under its loan agreements. In this situation bank lenders would accelerate their loans long before the bondholders muster themselves so as to proceed against the issuer.

With regard to passing an 'extraordinary resolution', first, it is necessary once again to convene a meeting of bondholders. This cannot easily be achieved in practice since Eurobond instruments subject to trust deeds usually require a notice to that effect to be given by at least 10% of bondholders to the trustee or to the issuer. This requirement in itself may operate as a 'brake' on the extraordinary resolution procedure, again, because it is difficult in practice to locate 10% of bond holders in principal amount due to their anonymity. Where the meeting can be summoned an extraordinary resolution cannot be passed unless two or more persons holding or representing a clear majority of the aggregate principal amount of the bonds are present at the meeting to form a quorum. If there is no such quorum usually the bondholder meeting must be adjourned.

The resulting position is that in practice the ability of even a substantial proportion of bondholders to require the trustee to accelerate is limited.

Further, in some bond instruments the ability of bondholders to compel the trustee by using either the extraordinary resolution procedure or the 20% demand procedure to accelerate payment on the bonds is also curtailed. Bondholders can use these procedures only on the occurrence of an event of default and some bond instruments will provide that an event of default does not occur until (a) a specified event occurs, eg breach of negative pledge, and (b) the trustee certifies in writing that such an event is 'materially prejudicial in the trustee's opinion to the interest of bondholders'. In effect this means that the occurrence of an event of default becomes dependent on the exercise of the trustee's discretion in the same way that acceleration is itself subject to the trustee's discretion.

There is also no duty imposed by trust deeds on the trustee to consult bondholders. General principles of equity applicable to trustees do not seem to take the matter much further in favour of bondholders where a discretion is conferred on the trustee in such wide terms as is common in Eurobond trust deeds. Beneficiaries of ordinary trusts need not be consulted by the trustee as to the exercise of a discretion[3] nor indeed are they entitled to be given reasons as to why the trustee exercised his decision to accelerate or not to accelerate.[4]

Nevertheless, in practice, these mechanisms work well. Eurobond trustees

---

1 See p 161 above.
2 see p 201 above.
3 See *Hawksley v May* [1956] 1 QB 304.
4 *Re Beloved Wilkes Charity* (1851) 3 Mac & G 440; Harman LJ in *Re Londonderry's Settlement* [1965] Ch 918 at 928; though if the trustee did give reasons a court will look into the question of their sufficiency: *Klug v Klug* [1918] 2 Ch 67.

are likely to call a meeting of bondholders and obtain confirmation of the course of action the trustee proposes to take when an event of default occurs. Such a course of action reduces the risk of any action by aggrieved bondholders. Consequently, in practice bondholders generally participate, if they so wish, in the trustee's decision-making process.

The next question is whether exercise or failure to exercise his power to accelerate can be subject to review by the courts at the request of an aggrieved bondholder.

A Eurobond trustee has a very wide discretion whether or not to accelerate on default, and it is not subject to any guidelines or principles as to its exercise under the terms of Eurobond trust deeds; there is also no indication in trust deeds in practice of the factors which the trustee should take into account in exercising his discretion, including whether a failure to accelerate will be materially prejudicial to the bondholders. Eurobond trust deeds generally provide that the trustee's discretion in all situations is 'absolute and uncontrolled'. The ability of a court to review the exercise of discretion is very limited indeed in such circumstances.

It seems, however, the Eurobond trustee must at least consider whether to exercise his discretion to accelerate[5] but once he has done so the courts will be most reluctant to interfere.

There is authority, however, to the effect that the court will interfere if the exercise of the discretion amounts to misconduct or is 'capricious'[6] but not otherwise. Arguably, a court may be able to interfere if the exercise of the discretion is wholly unrealistic or wholly unreasonable but there seems to be no direct authority in point. In *Gisborne v Gisborne*[7] the House of Lords held that in relation to a discretion which was said to be absolute and uncontrolled, the discretion had to be exercised 'bona fide', and it may be that this is the only fetter on a trustee's discretion.

It is submitted, however, that if a Eurobond trustee exercises his discretion in a manner which is wholly commercially unrealistic or wholly unreasonable it may be regarded as not being bona fide and as being capricious and thus subject to review by a court.[8] A trustee must exercise his powers fairly if he is to avoid the risk of action by bond holders.[9]

Could a Eurobond trustee's determination as to material prejudice which is declared to be final and conclusive be subject to review by the courts at the instance of aggrieved bond holders?[10]

It seems that while the courts may interfere, they will not interfere on the basis that the trustee's determination was simply unreasonable. More is required before a court sets aside a trustee's determination in the face of such a final and conclusive determination clause. Lord Denning, in *Re Tuck's Settlement Trusts*[11] was prepared to interfere only where the trustee had 'misconducted himself or come to a decision which is wholly unreasonable', while

---

5 *Tempest v Lord Camoys* (1882) 21 Ch D 571.
6 See *Re Manisty's Settlement* [1974] Ch 17.
7 (1877) 2 App Cas 300.
8 See also Underhill and Hayton *The Law of Trusts and Trustees* p 186.
9 The writer has not found any cases where bondholders did in fact seek review by the courts of trustee action, nor has the writer been able to locate cases where bondholders had been publicly critical of action taken in the case of a bond issue.
10 The issue is also discussed later at p 210.
11 [1978] Ch 49.

the House of Lords in *Dundee General Hospitals Board of Management v Walker*[12] thought that such a conclusive determination could be impugned not only on the basis of bad faith but also on the basis of a failure to appreciate the issue.

In the final analysis the controls on arbitrary or unreasonable behaviour by a Eurobond trustee are non-legal. Trustees active in the Eurobond markets such as Law Debenture Corporation plc, Deutsche Bank and Bankers Trustee Co Ltd[13] are highly reputed companies and the highest standards of market conduct are necessary to maintain such reputation and goodwill in the markets.

3 Efficacy of the 'no action' clause

As observed earlier, bondholders and coupon holders are expressly prohibited by bond instruments from taking any proceedings against the issuer unless two conditions are satisfied:

(a) the trustee has become bound to proceed against the issuer; and
(b) the trustee has failed to do so within a reasonable time.

It is important to note, however, that condition (a) above is not satisfied merely because there is an occurrence of an event of default or indeed even if the trustee is actually aware of the occurrence. He is 'bound to proceed' only if he does accelerate the bonds, demands repayment and does not receive payment from the issuer. Since, as observed earlier, the bond instrument in practice never imposes a duty on the trustee to accelerate but merely confers a power on the trustee to accelerate on the occurrence of an event of default at his discretion, the only other occasion on which he will be bound to proceed against the issuer is where either (a) 20% of bondholders in aggregate principal amount require him to accelerate or (b) an extraordinary resolution of bondholders requires the trustee to accelerate, and he does not do so within a reasonable time.

The question arises whether such clauses which in effect deprive bondholders of their common law right to sue on their rights as creditors is enforceable.

Early English case law proceeds on the basis that such clauses are valid and enforceable, even when they restrict the rights of bondholders to sue for interest or principal.[14] Leading English commentators like Wood[15] have not expressed any view on the validity of such clauses. It is submitted that the early English cases should be applicable to the modern Eurobond trust deed 'no action' clause, on the basis of the policy rationale underlying such clauses, which is discussed below.

It is nevertheless submitted that the limitation on bondholder rights imposed by such clauses should appear on the face of the bond instrument. In the absence of such specification on the face of the bond instrument, it would run the risk of being struck down by a court. US case law discussed below points to such a result.

---

12 [1952] 1 All ER 896.
13 See an article by Carr in IFLR, March 1987, at 16.
14 See *Rogers & Co v British and Colonial Colliery Supply Association* (1898) 68 LJ QBD 14; *Pethybridge v Unibifocal Co Ltd* [1918] WN 278.
15 See *Laws and Practice of International Finance* (1980) Sweet and Maxwell Chs 8 and 9.

The US cases decided in the context of domestic (rather than Euro) bond instruments, draw a distinction between 'no action' clauses which restrict or prevent bondholders from enforcing their rights in respect of interest payments and right to principal on maturity on the one side, and 'no action' clauses which restrict or prevent bondholders from enforcing other rights as bondholders.[16]

The courts in the US have been more than willing to uphold the validity of 'no action' clauses of the latter type provided adequate and clear notice is given to the bondholders in the bond instrument, ie the restriction must be brought to their attention with clarity on the face of the instrument.[17]

In *Friedman v Airlift International Inc.*[18] the court refused to uphold a 'no action' clause in a trust indenture even though the bond referred to the indenture twenty-nine times because the actual restriction on the right of action of the bondholder did not appear on the face of the bond. The line of US authority commencing with *Noble*,[19] requiring clarity of notice of the restriction on bondholder rights to sue, cannot, however, be of assistance in attacking Eurobond 'no action' clauses because the 'no action' clause in a Eurobond is clearly spelt out on the bond instrument.

The policy underlying the recognition of the validity of such clauses in the US has been first, that such clauses protect both the issuer and bondholders in general from rash and precipitate action by one or few bondholders in respect of technical breaches which can be cured with ease and without delay; and secondly, that they increase the saleability of the bonds.[20]

It may, however, be the case that where coupons are split from their host bond and are traded separately, a coupon holder might be able to avail himself of the approach adopted in the US cases on the basis that he did not have clear and express notice of the 'no action' clause. The bond instrument attempts to impose on such a coupon holder the obligations contained in the trust deed by a clause in the bond instrument. However, it is unlikely that this would bind a coupon holder who had no notice of either the restrictive terms in the bond instrument or the trust deed, if the approach of the court in *Friedman v Airlift International Inc* is adopted; nor does it seem likely that simply because the bond instrument states that the bonds are 'constituted' by a trust deed, the coupon holder is necessarily bound by such no action clauses.

US case law does not deal with the issue of whether a 'no action' clause which seeks to restrict the rights of a bondholder in respect of rights to principal on maturity or rights to interest is valid, because the US Trust Indenture Act of 1939[1] makes such a clause void save in exceptional cases.[2]

---

16 See especially *Watts v Missouri–Kansas–Texas Railroad Co* 383 F2d 57 (1967) (5th Cir) and cases cited.
17 *Noble v European Mortgage & Investment Co* (1933) 165 A 157 19 Del Ch 216; *Halle v Van Sweringen Corpn* 37 Del 491; *Japha v Delaware Valley Utilities Co* (1940) 15 A2d 432.
18 355 NYS 2d 613 (1974).
19 Above.
20 See *Japha v Delaware Valley Utilities Co* (1940) 15 A2d 432 at 434 and *Watts v Missouri–Kansas–Texas Railroad Co* 383 F2d 571.
1 See on rationale for this Act pp 249–250 below and on the applicability of this statute to Eurobonds p 378 below.
2 See the Trust Indenture Act 1939, 15 USC s 77 ppp(b) and s 77 ddd(a).

Dicta in the cases, however, suggest that the courts would not uphold such a clause, in the absence of the Trust Indenture Act 1939, even if the clause was explicitly and clearly stated on the face of the bond. The reason given for this conclusion in the US case law is that it would violate common law principles as to the rights of creditors or on the basis that such a clause if effective would make the instrument non-negotiable.[3] In *Watts v Missouri–Kansas–Texas Railroad Co*[4] the US court of appeals for the Fifth Circuit said in 1967:

> 'It is common for indentures to restrict suit by bondholders unless conditions similar to those in section 6.06 (of the indenture) are met. These restrictions are justified where they prevent rash, precipitate or harassing suits by bondholders who disrupt corporate affairs by seeking to reach and deal with the security underlying the bond obligations. No such justification exists where a bondholder seeks merely to collect the interest or principal due and owing him under the bond. Courts have recognised this distinction and have limited "no action clauses" (as the provisions setting forth the restrictions on suit are often called) so that they do not restrict suits by individual bondholders for interest or principal due and owing.'

It is submitted that the distinction drawn in the US cases is inapplicable in English law, in the absence of statutory provisions similar to the Trust Indenture Act of 1939.[5]

4 Rationale for trustee control over acceleration and enforcement[6]

The commercial logic which underlies the above structure regarding acceleration and enforcement action may be explained by reference to two concepts. First, there is the spectre of what Herbert[7] calls the 'mad bondholder' and, secondly, there is what Wood[8] terms the 'race to the courthouse door'.[8]

If there were no trustee vested with discretion to be flexible on the occurrence of a technical default it would be open to one 'mad bondholder' to accelerate his bond and precipitate a series of accelerations and activate cross-default clauses giving rise to the possibility of a liquidation of the issuer. The absence of a trustee who is in control of acceleration on default would also prevent a commercial compromise which would be advantageous to all creditors and which would stave off a liquidation. The 'no action' clause is justified on the basis that if bondholders could sue in court on their bonds upon acceleration, bondholders who were first off the mark would reach the doors of a court earlier and obtain payment on their bonds prior to those bondholders who were less astute or knowledgeable. The interposition of a trustee eliminates this race to the courthouse door and enables the trustee to obtain enforcement for all bondholders at the same time.

---

3 See especially dicta of the court in *Watts v Missouri–Kansas–Texas Railroad Co* 383 F2d 571 and Steur J in *Friedman v Airlift International* 355 NYS 2d 613.
4 383 F 2d 571.
5 See for a discussion of this Act and the rationale p 378 and pp 249–250 below.
6 See also for a wider discussion on the advantages of trustees in general pp 246–248 below.
7 1987 (1) JIBL 48.
8 'Law and Practice of International Finance' in *Clark Boardman's International Business Law* vol 2, ss 9 and 12 [1][b].

The trustee is also under a duty by virtue of express clauses in the Eurobond to hold all monies he recovers on trust for all bondholders ratably if he recovers funds by way of court action or otherwise.

The problems which according to Carr[9] arose in the case of the Canadian multinational Dome Petroleum, where a Swiss franc issue was subject only to a fiscal agency agreement but not a trust deed, best illustrate the need for, and constitute the most powerful argument in favour of, the appointment of a trustee who may operate with the benefit of a 'no action' clause. It appears that Dome with balance sheet debt of C$6.1bn had negotiated waivers from its creditors but a holder of SFr 50,000 bonds insisted on being paid and bringing proceedings for repayment. The waivers were subject to a requirement that no proceedings being brought by any bondholder to enforce payment. The Swiss franc bonds had been drafted by reference to Swiss law and there was consequently no trustee with the benefit of a 'no action' clause who could negotiate a settlement binding on all bondholders for everyone's benefit.

III TYPES OF BONDS

In the discussion of the legal rights and liabilities of bondholders, references were made to a variety of bonds such as FRNs and 'drop-lock' bonds. This section is intended as a focus on the different types of bonds which have been issued in the international bond markets.[10]

The traditional bond, referred to as a 'straight vanilla' or 'straight', is issued with a fixed coupon or fixed interest rate, with a fixed maturity date on which the principal amount becomes payable.

Variations on these basic characteristics have been made in the following areas:

(a) interest rate;
(b) maturity and redemption provisions;
(c) linkage with equities and other securities;
(d) drawdown period.[11]

1 Interest rate

i *FRNs*[12]

The most important variation was the introduction of the Floating Rate Note or FRN. The FRN is a bond which contains a promise to pay interest

---

9   See the account by Josephine Carr in IFLR, March 1987, at 15.
10 Although it is impossible to describe all varieties which have appeared in the markets in order to do justice to the ingenuity of the investment banks.
11 See *Fisher* for a full discussion and Watkins 'Types of Bonds' in *Current Issues of International Financial Law* (Malaya Law Review and Butterworths, 1985).
12 See Georges Ugeux *FRNs* (Euromoney, 2nd edn 1985); Fisher *International Bonds* (Euromoney).

at a rate which varies according to a reference or benchmark rate, usually the London Inter Bank Offered Rate ('LIBOR').

The LIBOR rate payable is the six-month rate prevailing at an interest rate fixing date. Interest is calculated at six-monthly intervals by reference to the six-month LIBOR rate. The reference rate specified in FRNs is sometimes three-month LIBOR and sometimes the six-month US Treasury bill rate in the case of US dollar issues. Fisher[13] has pointed out that by 1983 FRN issues accounted for 37% of all Eurobond issues, most of them being issued by banks for purposes of capital adequacy.[14]

The holder, however, does not have an option to fix the LIBOR rate applicable to such bonds in the way that a borrower has in a syndicated loan.[15] Many FRNs were issued with protection against a substantial fall in the LIBOR rate, in that there was a minimum interest rate which was payable on the bond. The rate payable 'floated' and varied only above this floor level.

The rights of an FRN holder in other respects would be the same as those of a holder of a straight bond.[16]

ii Drop-lock FRNs

These were FRNs issued with the feature that if interest rate payable by reference to the six-month LIBOR rate fell below a certain threshold, the FRNs automatically converted into fixed rate bonds.[17]

The legal and financial aspects of these bonds were discussed previously.[18]

iii Floating to fixed rate convertibles

These were essentially FRNs where the bondholder was given an option to convert the FRN into a fixed rate bond. The option was exercisable within a time specified in the bond.

iv Zero coupon bonds

These are bonds which have no coupon or interest rate but are issued at a deep discount from their face value. The holder receives his income from capital appreciation of the bond instrument as time goes by. Watkins[19] has pointed out that holders of such bonds have tax advantages in some tax jurisdictions in that the income is taxed at a lower rate as capital gains rather than as 'income' liable to higher rate income tax.

---

13 *International Bonds* (Euromoney).
14 See Georges Ugeux *FRNs* (Euromoney) p 68.
15 See pp 77–79 above.
16 See also discussion at pp 193–213 above. Average maturities were between 5 and 8 years although Fisher (above) has pointed out that Sweden issued an FRN for 40 years in February 1984.
17 See *Fisher* p 145; Ugeux, fn 141 above, p 112.
18 See p 193.
19 'Types of Bonds' *Current Issues of International Financial Law* p 116.

v *RRNs*

These are little more than FRNs except that the interest payable is calculated on a 30-day basis although payable on a six-monthly basis by reference to six-month LIBOR. The interest accruing on a 30-day basis is added to the capital and the payment every six months of interest is calculated later on the aggregated amount.

2 Maturity and redemption

i *The perpetual bond*

These are bonds issued with no maturity date, and consequently may be outstanding perpetually. The principal amount is nevertheless capable of being subject to immediate acceleration on the occurrence of an event of default.

Watkins[20] has pointed out that these were in the main issued by banks, the first of its kind being by National Westminster Bank in 1984. The motivation for the issue was that these bonds were capable of being regarded as quasi-equity, if subordinated to all other debt, and consequently assisted in improving the capital ratios of banks for purposes of the capital adequacy requirements of many central bank regulators. The market for these bonds, however, diminished in the mid 1980s.[1] To that extent the perpetual had the advantage to the issuing bank of equity, but unlike equity the cost of raising capital through a perpetual bond, ie the interest payable, was capable of being set off against the issuers' tax liability in many jurisdictions; dividend payments, on the other hand, would not usually be capable of being offset against tax.

Section 193 of the Companies Act 1985 removes any doubts concerning the validity under English law of perpetual bonds. It provides that:

> 'A condition contained in debentures ... is not invalid by reason only that the debentures are thereby made irredeemable or redeemable only on the happening of a contingency (however remote), or on the expiration of a period (however long), any rule of equity to the contrary notwithstanding.'[2]

ii *'Flip-Flop' bonds*

These were bonds which were issued as perpetuals but where the issuer had an option to convert the bond into a bond with a maturity date; and a second option to reconvert the bond into a perpetual at a later time. These options were exercisable by the issuer during a specified period.

---

20 Above.
1 See Fisher *International Bonds* (Euromoney); Georges Ugeux FRNs (Euromoney).
2 The section is retroactive in operation. See s 193.

iii Extendable bonds

Such bonds conferred on the holder an option to extend the maturity date of the bond for a further period of time, usually two or three years. The option was exercisable in most cases in the last year prior to the original maturity date.

iv Retractable bonds

These were the converse of extendables in that they gave an option to the holder to shorten the life of the bond by bringing forward the original maturity date.[3]

v Bonds subject to a 'sinking fund'

These were discussed previously.[4]

vi Bonds subject to a 'purchase fund'

These were discussed previously.[5]

vii Serial notes

These too were considered previously.[6]

viii Bonds with 'call options'

These confer on the issuer an option to redeem the bonds prior to their stated maturity, usually within the last year or two, prior to their original maturity date. Such a call option is exercisable at par, ie the bondholder is paid only the face value of the bond and not the market price of the bond.

Call options are usually made available to an issuer in the event that a withholding tax is imposed on the issuer triggering a tax gross-up clause, discussed previously.[7]

ix Bonds with 'put options'

These permit the holder at his option to redeem his bonds prior to maturity (this is the 'put'). The option is exercisable during a specified period.

---

3 See p 197.
4 At p 196.
5 See p 197.
6 See p 196.
7 See p 195.

3 Bonds linked to equity and other assets

i *Equity convertibles*

These are bonds which may be converted into or exchanged for shares in the issuer of the convertible or in some cases its guarantor and are discussed in detail in chapter 14.[8]

ii *Bonds with equity warrants*

This is not an issue of one instrument but of two; the warrant is attached to the host bond but the investor is sold the warrant for the price of the bond. The warrant entitles the investor to subscribe equity in the issuer and in some cases its guarantor. These are discussed in detail in chapter 14.[9]

iii *Commodity linked bonds*

The holder of such a bond is paid the face value of the bonds or the market price of a specified amount of a particular commodity calculated at the date of maturity.[10]

---

8   See also *Fisher*.
9   See also *Fisher* ch 8.
10 *Fisher* p 153 has given the example of the 15-year bonds issued by Sunshine Mining Company which were redeemable at par on maturity at $1,000 per bond or the market price of 50 ounces of silver, whichever was higher at the time of issue; 50 ounces of silver at $16 an ounce was $800.

CHAPTER 12
The role of fiscal agents in a Eurobond issue

I GENERAL

The fundamental difference between the role of a Eurobond trustee and that of the fiscal agent is said to be that a trustee is the representative of the bondholders and that the fiscal agent is the representative and agent for the issuer and not of the bondholders.[1]

Under Eurobond trust deeds most of the legal rights which would usually be in the hands of bondholders are transferred to the trustee so that in effect only the trustee may exercise such rights against the issuer. The trustee is conferred a wide discretion as to whether and how he should exercise such rights. Some aspects of the trustee's powers were discussed in chapter 11. Generally speaking, the trustee exercises complete supervisory control over the issuer's liabilities and bondholder's rights during the life of the bond for the overall benefit of the bondholders as a group. To perform his duties and exercise his discretions in a manner which individual bondholders may sometimes find unacceptable the trustee is also conferred wide immunity from legal actions by bondholders. These aspects of the Eurobond trustee are discussed in chapter 13.

A fiscal agent has no such role. He is appointed under a fiscal agency agreement and is little more than the principal paying agent for the issuer. He does not possess anything similar to the great degree of control which a Eurobond trustee possesses under a trust deed over the regime of rights and liabilities created by the bonds; nor does he possess anything like the vast array of powers, discretions and immunities which a trustee enjoys and, in particular, the fiscal agent has no control over the rights of bondholders.

It is important to note that in practice a fiscal agent is not appointed in cases where a trustee is appointed.

II THE ROLE OF THE FISCAL AGENT

The main functions of a fiscal agent may be summarised as follows.

---

1 There is a substantial volume of learning on the subject. See Wood *Law and Practice of International Finance* (Sweet & Maxwell, 1980) p 216, 9.4(1); Herbert 'Why have a Trustee for a Eurobond Issue' (1987) JIBL 48; Pergam 'Eurobonds: Trustees, Fiscal Agents and the Treatment of Default' in *Studies in Transnational Economic Law* (Horn, ed) vol III, p 337; Smart 'Fiscal Agency or Trust Deed' (1982) IFL Rev, December, at 18; Marsden 'The Case for the Eurobond Trust Deed' Euromoney, April 1983, at 145.

1 Delivery of bonds

Where a temporary global bond is being used, it is the fiscal agent's duty to exchange the definitive bonds for the global bond. The issuer is required to deliver the definitive to the fiscal agent for this purpose. He would owe a duty in practice to ensure that the clearing systems Euroclear and Cedel provide the necessary certificate to establish that the bonds credited to accounts within the clearing systems are not beneficially owned by US persons (as defined by TEFRA 'D' Regulations: see chapter 21). Any failure to ensure that such a certificate is submitted may result in liability of the issuer to action by the US Securities and Exchange Commission[2] and if the issuer suffers loss in consequence, the fiscal agent would be liable to the issuer under the ordinary law of agency to make good that loss.

2 Principal paying agent

In order to facilitate payment of interest and principal in a Eurobond issue paying agents are usually appointed in financial centres. The fiscal agent is the issuer's primary paying agent. Funds are transferred by the issuer to the fiscal agent who in turn transfers funds to the other paying agents for the purposes of making payments of interest and/or principal. In practice, the paying agents pay out funds from their own accounts and are in turn entitled to reimbursement from the fiscal agent under the fiscal agency agreement. The paying agents are themselves authorised in the fiscal agency agreement by the issuer to make payments of interest or principal on due dates to bondholders or coupon holders and obtain reimbursement from the fiscal agent who is obliged by the fiscal agency agreement to so reimburse.

The fiscal agent is potentially exposed to the risk that an issuer may default in payment after the fiscal agent has disbursed funds, and is consequently provided protection against this eventuality by a number of provisions in the fiscal agency agreement.

First, the issuer is required to put the fiscal agent in funds in respect of interest or principal two business days prior to each date on which any payment in respect of the bonds becomes due, and secondly, the issuer is required to confirm to the fiscal agent the day before the above funds transfer that irrevocable instructions have been issued for payment of funds to the fiscal agent. The fiscal agent is, thirdly, conferred a right to telex the paying agents that he has not received any particular payment in respect of the bonds on its due date, and on receipt of such notification the paying agents' authority to pay interest or principal on the bonds is suspended.

Some fiscal agency agreements also provide that funds held by the fiscal agent will be held on trust for the bondholders and coupon holders. The object of this clause is to protect funds from the creditors of a fiscal agent in the event of his liquidation after receipt of funds from the issuer. It is also designed to protect the funds from claims by the liquidator or receiver of the issuer in the event that the issuer goes into receivership or liquidation. The logic underlying the clause is that the funds will be imprinted with

---

2   See Part IV, ch 19.

an English law trust so that the funds will not be available to the creditors of the fiscal agent or the issuer (whichever entity goes into liquidation).

There are, however, a number of difficulties with such a clause. First, the usual Eurobond fiscal agency clause permits commingling of the fiscal agent's funds with the funds received from the issuer for purposes of payment to bondholders and coupon holders. Segregation of funds is dispensed with by an express clause. It is clear from the leading case of *Re Hallett's Estate*[3] that where a trustee in breach of trust commingles in a bank account his funds with those of the trust fund equity will permit the beneficiaries to trace into the fund. It is also clear that where there is commingling in breach of trust the beneficiaries have a first charge over the mixed funds.[4] What is far from clear is whether the same results would follow in the event of a liquidation or insolvency of a trustee, particularly where commingling is permitted by the legal agreement imposing the trust obligation. The second problem is that while these results may follow liquidation governed by English law, a Eurobond issuer or fiscal agent's insolvency may be governed by a system of law which may not recognise the English trust concept.

3 Redemption of bonds

Where bonds are to be redeemed prior to maturity, the fiscal agent is required to publish redemption notices. If only some of the bonds are to be redeemed prior to maturity, the fiscal agent will be required to make drawings of bonds for purposes of such redemption.

Where early redemption is at the option of bondholders the fiscal agent is required to keep redemption notices which bondholders may demand of him so as to exercise their right to early redemption of bonds. It is also his function to make payments in respect of bonds so redeemed.

The fiscal agent is obliged under fiscal agency provisions to cancel all bonds redeemed prior to maturity so that they cannot be reissued. If bonds are redeemed at maturity by the issuer or his paying agents they are required to cancel the bonds so redeemed and return the cancelled bonds to the fiscal agent.

He is also required to keep account of the aggregate number of bonds redeemed and the aggregate amount of coupons which have been paid and cancelled. All cancelled bonds and coupons must be destroyed.

He must also keep a record of the aggregate amount of bonds outstanding. This is crucial for purposes of determining rights of bondholders at bondholder meetings where certain quora and majorities are required.[5]

4 Replacement of bonds

The fiscal agent is also obliged to replace, at the request of a bondholder, any bond which is lost, destroyed or defaced, and cancel any mutilated or defaced bonds for which he has issued replacement bonds.

For the above purpose the fiscal agent is authorised to treat any bond-

---

3   (1880) 13 Ch D 696.
4   *Re Tilley's Will Trusts* [1967] Ch 1179 at 1182; *Re Oatway* [1903] 2 Ch 356.
5   See pp 222–223 below.

holder as the true owner thereof and to treat every bond presented to him in the usual form as being genuine.

He is also usually authorised to purchase or hold bonds of the issuer or its guarantor for his own account without any breach of fiduciary duties owed in his capacity as agent, to the issuer (or guarantor).[6] The fiscal agent is also authorised to make profits by doing business with any subsidiary or holding company of the issuer (or guarantor) without being liable to account for such profits for breach of fiduciary duty under the rule laid down in cases such as *Phipps v Boardman*.[7]

5 The position of bondholders

Where a fiscal agent as distinct from a trustee is appointed, individual bondholders are entitled to exercise their usual rights as creditors without any qualification or restriction. The fiscal agent has no control or influence on their actions:

(a) they can accelerate the bond for a failure to pay interest or principal or for breach of covenant; and
(b) they may sue to recover interest or principal due to them.

The other side of the coin is that each bondholder must himself monitor compliance with any covenants in the bond. This is particularly difficult in the case of a negative pledge or cross-default. It has been suggested by Pergam[8] that an issuer could be required to issue a 'no default' certificate to a specified paying agent to overcome the problem. However, this suggestion does not seem to have generally been acted on in practice.

There is also no right to financial information about the issuer or guarantor except that which is publicly available.

From an issuer's point of view the use of a fiscal agent has major disadvantages:

(a) each bondholder could put the issuer in default for any technical breach of the terms of the bond including late payment of interest;
(b) there is no ability of the issuer to negotiate a compromise by dealing with one entity who can act according to the best interests of all the bondholders together;
(c) there is no ability to modify the terms of the bonds or negotiate a rescheduling except through meetings of bond holders.[9]

Where a fiscal agent is used, therefore, it is imperative that provision be made for bondholder meetings and that matters relating to the bonds be subject to the majority decision of the bondholders. Failure to include such a clause may result in the problems which arose in the case of the Canadian multinational Dome Petroleum. In Dome's case one of its Eurobond issues was subject to Swiss law and subject to a fiscal agency agreement with no provision for majority bond holder decision. It appears that one holder of SFr50,000 note refused to waive a technical default and thus vir-

---

6 See on this duty pp 64–67 above.
7 See pp 64–67 above.
8 IFLR, September 1988.
9 See ch 13 below.

tually placed Dome at risk of being in default of its Canadian $6.1bn debts by reason of cross-default clauses.[10]

6 Bondholder meetings

Where a fiscal agent is used in respect of a bond issue there is invariably provision for bondholder meetings to prevent the type of occurrence reported in respect of the Swiss franc issue by Dome. There are similar provisions for bondholder meetings in the case of bond issues subject to trust deeds although in the case of bond issues with trust deeds the matters which are within the powers of bondholder meetings are more restricted. Further such meetings of bondholders operate as a supervisory mechanism over the trustee's actions, rather than the primary source of decision-making which is in the hands of the trustee.

Fiscal agency agreements usually provide that an extraordinary resolution of bondholders at a properly convened meeting with a specified quorum may take decisions in respect of certain specified matters which are binding on all bondholders. Such provisions in fiscal agency agreements are binding on all bondholders under English law because the bond instruments are made subject to, and incorporate by reference, the terms and conditions of fiscal agency agreements in the same way that trust deeds are incorporated by reference.[11]

The matters which are subject to such extraordinary resolution procedure and which are binding on all bondholders once an extraordinary resolution has been passed are:

(a) any compromise of or arrangement in respect of bondholders' and coupon holders' rights against the issuer;
(b) any variation, modification or abrogation of bondholders' or coupon holders' rights against the issuer;
(c) any alteration to the terms of the bonds or of the trust deed or fiscal agency agreement;
(d) any exchange or substitutions of the bonds for bonds or other obligations of the issuer or guarantor or other substitute debtor;
(e) to appoint a committee to represent bondholders and to give such committee the powers of the bondholders acting by way of extraordinary resolution;
(f) postponing the maturity date of the bonds or the dates on which interest is payable;
(g) changing the currency of the bonds;
(h) reducing or cancelling the principal amount or the interest payable on the bonds;
(i) changing the procedure and quorum for an extraordinary resolution.

Where Eurobonds are listed on The London Stock Exchange, the rules in *Admission of Securities to Listings*[12] require that for an extraordinary

---

10 See IFLR, March 1987, 15.
11 See p 205 above as to incorporation.
12 S 9, ch 2 para 3.3.

resolution there must be a quorum of two or more persons holding or representing a clear majority in principal amount of the bonds outstanding. In respect of items (f) to (i) inclusive, a quorum of two or more persons representing in aggregate not less than three-quarters in principal amount of the bonds outstanding at that time is usually made necessary in practice. Where the bonds are listed in London, it is a necessary condition under the listing rules of The International Stock Exchange that an extraordinary resolution may not be passed even at a meeting with the necessary quorum unless at least three-fourths of persons voting are in favour of the resolution (each holder of securities being entitled to one vote for each security).[13]

The issuer or guarantor or trustee (where there is one) may at any time convene such a meeting. Under The London Stock Exchange rules for listing the trust deed must contain provision that the trustee is obliged to convene a meeting, if a request in writing is made by bondholders representing 10% in aggregate value of bonds outstanding at the time a bondholder meeting must be convened.[14]

It will be noticed that where a fiscal agency agreement is used, provisions for convening bondholder meetings are vitally important because they give the issuer the ability to require waiver of technical breaches, or negotiate a compromise in respect of breaches or reschedule the maturity of the bonds or negotiate a modification of terms.

It also means that even where there is no trustee, breach can be waived by the requisite majority of bondholders and a satisfactory compromise arrived at which is binding on a recalcitrant minority of bondholders since the waiver would operate on behalf of all bondholders. This would prevent a minority from accelerating and/or suing on individual bonds. The problem for the issuer where there is no trustee is of course to secure a quorum and then the required majority. In the case of a trust deed most of these matters may be decided on by the trustee without convening meetings of bondholders.

Proper notice must be given to bondholders of such meetings and fiscal agency agreements (as well as trust deeds) usually provide for 21 days notice to be given to bondholders as to the meeting and the nature of the resolution to be considered. Provision is also made to enable bondholders to vote by proxy by requiring a paying agent to issue 'block voting instructions'. The latter is done by depositing the bondholders' bonds with a paying agent and requiring the paying agent to issue a document stating that a certain number of bonds have been deposited with such paying agent and that he has been required to vote in a particular way in respect of the resolutions to be considered at the meeting. The bonds subject to such block voting instructions must be specified by serial number in such instructions.

Where the specified quorum is not present the meeting must be adjourned for at least 14 days. At the adjourned meeting there is no specific quorum requirement except in relation to any resolution in respect of matters referred to in (f) to (i) above in which case a quorum representing 25% in principal amount of all bonds outstanding at the time must be present or represented.

---

13 See s 9, ch 2, para 3.4 and 3.5.
14 See the Yellow Book, s 9, ch 2, para 3.2.

CHAPTER 13
Trustees under Eurobond trust deeds

I PRELIMINARY

Trustees are usually appointed to safeguard the interests of bondholders and act on behalf of bondholders. There is no mandatory rule of English law that a trustee should be appointed in respect of an issue of bonds. The listing rules of the London Stock Exchange require that a trustee(s) be appointed in respect of domestic bond issues, but this requirement does not apply to an issue of Eurobonds listed on the London Stock Exchange.[1] The listing rules[2] require that when a single trustee is appointed it, must be a trust corporation.[3]

If a trustee is to be appointed the choice of trustee is made in practice by the lead manager, the issuer and their lawyers. The contents of trust deeds are also determined by the same parties. Bondholders do not have any direct control over the initial appointment of a trustee or the contents of the trust deed. Nevertheless, the lead manager of an international bond issue is acutely sensitive to the expectations of the sophisticated investment community who are potential investors and purchasers of Eurobonds. The expectations of this investment community have a large influence on both the choice of trustee and the contents of the trust deed. A Eurobond issue with a trustee or trust deed which is not entirely acceptable to the investment community in the international markets would be more difficult to place successfully, and consequently the trustees usually appointed in Eurobond issues have high commercial reputations for integrity and professionalism.

While a trustee is primarily the representative of the bondholders, it will be seen that the appointment of a trustee confers great advantages to an issuer.

---

1 See s 9, ch 2 of *Admission of Securities to Listing* (the 'Yellow Book').
2 See s 9, ch 2 and s 7, ch 1 of the Yellow Book and ch 17, below.
3 According to an article in the *Financial Times* of 15 May 1990, Law Debenture Corporation is trustee for over 1,800 debt issues and is a major force in the market. Law Debenture Corporation was incorporated in 1889. Bankers Trustee Co Ltd was mentioned as another leading participant. Sometimes banks may act as trustees. It has been reported in the *Financial Times*, 15 May 1990, that a trustee in an unsecured issue will receive a fee in the region of £2,500.

It was stated previously[4] that the terms and provisions of the trust deed are binding on Eurobond holders due to the fact that the trust deed is incorporated by reference into each bond instrument under the English law doctrine of incorporation. The validity and enforceability of a trust will be determined by reference to the Hague Convention on the *Law Applicable to Trusts and on their Recognition* where that Convention has been given effect to. Article 8 provides that 'the validity of the trust, its construction, its effects' will be governed by the rules of the Convention and art 6 provides that 'a trust shall be governed by the law chosen by the settlor'. In respect of Eurobond trust deeds, as a matter of general market practice trust deeds will be governed by English law and foreign courts which are bound by the Hague Convention Rules will consequently give effect to the English chosen law under art 6. The UK has given effect to the Convention by the Recognition of Trusts Act 1987.[5]

II NATURE OF THE TRUST

Under English law the question arises whether a Eurobond trustee is, in law, a trustee. This turns on whether a valid and binding trust has been created and constituted under English law.

The valid creation of an express private trust in English law depends on whether three certainties exist: certainty of the trust property; certainty as to the intention to create a trust on the part of the settlor in respect of such property; and certainty as to the beneficiaries: Lord Langdale MR in *Knight v Knight*.[6] Further, there must be a proper transfer of trust property for the trust to be validly constituted.[7]

Where bond issues are secured on corporate assets, as in the case of many domestic issues, the trustee holds such corporate assets on trust for the bondholders. However, where, as in most international issues, security over corporate assets is not given the question arises as to what are the assets which are subject to a trust.

The bond instruments themselves are not in any sense trust assets; the legal title to bonds is not vested in the trustee. The bondholders 'hold' the bonds as legal owners of the instruments and not as beneficial or equitable owners.[8]

The bond instrument usually provides that the 'Bonds are constituted by a Trust Deed dated ...' but, it is submitted, this is insufficient to vest legal title in the bonds in the bond trustee without clear words to that effect.[9] The purpose of these words seems to be to facilitate the incorporation of the terms of the trust deed into the bond instrument.[10]

---

4   See ch 11, pp 204–207.
5   See, on the Convention, Hayton (1987) 36 ICLQ 260.
6   (1840) 3 Beav 148.
7   See the locus classicus of Turner LJ in *Milroy v Lord* (1862) 4 De GF & J 264 at 274; and Hanbury and Maudsley *Modern Equity* 116.
8   As to the distinction between legal and equitable ownership see Underhill and Hayton *Law of Trusts and Trustees* (14th edn, 1987) art 2; Hanbury and Maudsley *Modern Equity* (12th edn, 1985) pp 17–22.
9   See the discussion in Underhill and Hayton (above) ch 2, art 8.
10 See p 205 above.

If the bonds were trust assets, the trustee would have legal title to the bonds; the bondholders would only have a beneficial or equitable interest in the bonds. The negotiability of such an instrument which would be capable of transferring only an equitable interest to a purchaser would be doubtful under English law, and certainly under civil law systems.[11] Such a construction also seems to run counter to the usual clause in every Eurobond instrument that 'Title to the Bonds and Coupons passes on delivery'. Title cannot be taken to refer to equitable title, in the context of an instrument which is sold internationally and purchased by persons in jurisdictions which do not recognise the English law distinction between equitable and legal title. It is also unlikely in the context of the tradability of a Eurobond in the markets that what is sought to be transferred is some form of equitable and beneficial title recognised only under English law.

Under English law, the covenants given in the trust deed by the issuer to the trustee for the benefit of bondholders are, on the other hand, capable of being the asset which is the subject of the trust.[12] This includes the promise to pay interest and principal due on the bonds. It was pointed out earlier[13] that the issuer usually gives a direct covenant to the trustee to pay interest and principal on the bonds which is parallel to that given to bondholders. Payment to the bondholders of interest and principal duly discharges the issuer's obligation to the trustee. The covenants given to the trustee in the trust deed are consequently capable of being trust assets under the principle stated above.

The difficulty, however, is that the issuer's covenants, including the promise to pay interest and principal, can constitute an asset or a chose in action *only in the hands of the Eurobond trustee*. Consequently, it is only the trustee who may declare a trust and not the issuer; the issuer being the debtor or obligor under the covenants has no asset over which he can declare a trust. In so far as the promise to pay is concerned, a trust over a debt can only be declared by the creditor and not the debtor.[14] Nevertheless, in *Fletcher v Fletcher*[15] Wigram V-C found no difficulty in holding that the promisor or obligor could make the declaration of trust. The American Restatement[16] takes the same view as Wigram V-C when it provides that 'the promisor is the creator of the trust and if he manifests an intention that the promisee's rights under the promise shall be held in trust, the promisee immediately becomes the trustee of his rights under the promise'.[17] If the courts were to adopt this view, and it is submitted they should, the declaration of trust by the issuer that the trustee should hold the issuer's promise should suffice as a proper declaration of a trust over the issuer's own promise. There is on this basis a due constitution of the trust of the promise. The ordinary rule requiring

---

11 The matter would fall outside the scope of the Rome Convention on the Law Applicable to Contracts (see p 166 above) as well as the Hague Convention on the Law Applicable to Trusts and on their Recognition (see the discussion at p 207 above).
12 *Tomlinson v Gill* (1756) Amb 330; *Lloyd's v Harper* (1880) 16 Ch D 290; *Les Affréteurs Réunis SA v Leopold Walford (London) Ltd* [1919] AC 801.
13 See p 206 above.
14 See *Vandepitte v Preferred Accident Insurance Corpn of New York* [1933] AC 70.
15 (1844) 4 Hare 67; 14 LJ Ch 424.
16 *The Restatement of Trusts* (2nd edn) para 26.
17 Hanbury and Maudsley. *Modern Equity* at p 131 also seem to support such an approach.

the transfer of a chose by assignment[18] has perhaps no application if *Fletcher v Fletcher*[19] is good law. It may, however, be preferable to have a declaration of trust by the trustee declaring himself trustee over the chose he holds for the benefit of bondholders, a device recognised in the ordinary law of trusts.[20]

Finally, there remains the question whether the trust is in favour of beneficiaries who are certain. The beneficiaries are quite clearly bondholders. Whether the bondholders for this purpose are to be regarded as the successive purchasers of the bonds in the secondary market or whether Euroclear and Cedel are to be regarded as the bondholder[1] it is at least clear that the beneficiaries are ascertained or ascertainable.[2]

It may be due to these conceptual difficulties that Wood[3] asserts that 'the Anglo-American Eurobond trustee turns out to be more like a fiduciary representative than a trustee. This is because the trustee of an unsecured Eurobond issue does not actually hold assets in trust for the bondholders as beneficiaries in the normal sense'. However, on the above analysis it is submitted with respect that a modern Eurobond trustee is a trustee of a validly created and duly constituted trust in the traditional English law sense of the word.

If the Eurobond 'trustee' was no more than a fiduciary representative or agent of the bondholders an individual bondholder could terminate the agent's authority to act on his behalf in the absence of express provision supported by consideration conferring irrevocable authority on the agent. If the 'trustee' were a mere agent whose authority was revocable, the trustee's power to accelerate on the occurrence of an event of default on behalf of the bondholders[4] could equally be terminated by an individual bondholder in respect of his bond. The bondholder may be liable in damages because he is in breach of the terms of the 'trust deed' upon such termination of authority, but the fiduciary agent's or trustee's authority would nevertheless be effectively terminated vis-à-vis third parties including the issuer. The trustee on such termination would be *hors de combat*. This would follow from ordinary principles of agency law.[5] Individual bondholders could thus accelerate and indeed sue on their bonds without trustee intervention. A 'no action clause' of the type discussed above[6] will be ineffective against the bondholder after the termination of the 'trustee' agent's authority to act on behalf of that bondholder. The 'trustee' agent could no longer sue on that bondholder's behalf and a court would be compelled to hold that the no action clause was inoperative. It is therefore vital to the structure

---

18 *William Brandts Sons and Co v Dunlop Rubber Co Ltd* [1905] AC 454 at 462.
19 See p 171 above.
20 See *Jones v Lock* (1865) 1 Ch App 25; and *Richards v Delbridge* (1874) LR18 Eq 11 where, however, the court held that there was insufficient evidence on the facts as to the declaration of trust; *Middleton v Pollock* (1876) 2 Ch D 104.
1 See ch 9 above.
2 See the tests laid down by the House of Lords in *McPhail v Doulton* [1971] AC 424 for fixed trusts, although *McPhail* was itself concerned with a discretionary trust.
3 In his *Law and Practice of International Finance* (Clark Boardman edn, 1981, at 9.12[3][b]).
4 See p 206 below.
5 See, for example, *Martin-Baker Aircraft Co Ltd v Canadian Flight Equipment Ltd* [1955] 2 QB 556; *Denmark Productions Ltd v Boscobel Productions Ltd* [1969] 1 QB 699.
6 At p 210.

adopted in Eurobond issues subject to trust deeds that there is a validly constituted trust in the conventional sense.

III FUNCTIONS AND POWERS OF THE EUROBOND TRUSTEE

The role of the Eurobond trustee is characterised by the following:[7]

(1) Only the trustee may accelerate the bonds on the occurrence of an event of default; the bondholders have a right to require acceleration on the occurrence of an event of default, if a substantial percentage of bondholders require the trustee to do so.[8]

(2) The trustee has a very wide discretion as to whether or not to accelerate.[9] Such discretion is in practice declared to be 'absolute and uncontrolled'.

(3) Sometimes even the occurrence of an event of default is made dependent on the trustee's discretion, ie whether the trustee considers that specified events, eg breach of negative pledge, are 'materially prejudicial' to the interests of bondholders. In such cases the bondholders cannot require the trustee to accelerate until the trustee has determined that an event of default is materially prejudicial.[10] Trust deeds provide that the trustee is not deemed to have knowledge of an event of default unless he has been notified expressly of the occurrence of an event of default.

(4) On the occurrence of an event of default the trustee has power to require all paying agents to make all payments in respect of the bonds to the trustee and require them to hold all money, bonds and coupons on the trustee's behalf.

(5) The trustee alone has power to bring enforcement proceedings against the issuer; individual bondholders may not.[11]

(6) The trustee is not under a duty to bondholders to act as a policeman and make reasonable enquiries with a view to ascertaining whether an event of default has occurred. Although he receives financial information from the issuer and although he has a power to ask for information (see 8 (a) and (b) below), he is generally empowered by the trust deed to assume that no such event of default has occurred unless he has 'actual knowledge' or has 'express notice' of the occurrence.[12] His duty is to examine the information provided him by the issuer to ensure compliance with the covenants of the bond instrument and trust deed. Under the trust deed clauses he need not go further and make investigation. However, a court may require a professional trustee such as a bank or trust corporation to act with due care, skill and diligence in the exercise of his powers to call default[13] and

---

7 Some of these have already been discussed in ch 11, pp 204–213.
8 See p 207 above.
9 See p 209 above.
10 See p 209 above.
11 See p 210 above.
12 See pp 238–243 below.
13 See pp 238–243 below.

a trustee is therefore well advised to examine financial and other information available to him.

(7) If the trustee receives any payments from the issuer as to interest or principal on the bonds on an acceleration or after action in court or otherwise, he must hold all such funds on trust for the bondholders pro rata after recovering his costs and expenses.

(8) All covenants of the issuer in the trust deed are given solely to the trustees by the issuer and not to the bondholders. The major exceptions in practice, are the covenant to pay interest and principal and the negative pledge covenant, each of which is also given to the bondholders in the bond instrument. A trustee could by virtue of the terms of the trust deed waive any breach of covenant.

The covenants in the trust deed which are given exclusively to the trustee are given to him in his capacity as bondholder representative and, therefore given for the benefit of bondholders. He must ensure that the issuer is in compliance with such covenants as part of his obligations qua trustee to the bondholders. However, this duty of the trustee may not be capable of direct enforcement by bondholders due to the trustee's powers to waive breaches of covenant[14] and his wide immunities.[15]

The usual covenants given only to the trustee by the issuer largely concern the obligation of the issuer to give financial and other information about the issuer and are as follows.

(a) The issuer is required to send to the trustee audited year-end balance sheets, audited profit and loss statements, financial and other reports which are issued by the issuer or any holding company of the issuer, usually not more than 180 days after year end; this covenant is usually drafted in a form which requires the issuer to transmit to the trustee all financial and other information sent to the shareholders and creditors of an issuer (or its group holding company) as is required by statute or by contractual obligation.

(b) The obligation in (a) is buttressed by a further obligation on the issuer to give to the trustee 'such information as it reasonably requires for the performance of its functions'.

These financial information covenants will be much more useful if trust deeds imposed financial controls on the issuer by way of financial ratio covenants similar to those found in syndicated loan agreements, such as debt to equity ratios, minimum net worth requirements and so on.[16] However, it is not common in Eurobond trust deeds to encounter such controls. Financial information covenants are nevertheless regarded as necessary since they give the ability to a trustee to pursue any line of enquiry which may appear necessary to the trustee, for instance, where the financial statements reveal a weakening performance or strength of the issuer or where there are adverse press or industry reports on the issuer, even in the absence of financial ratio covenants. It is for this reason that commentators like Wood[17] and Herbert[18]

---

14 See (9) below.
15 See pp 239-243 below.
16 See ch 5.
17 *Law and Practice of International Finance* (Clark Boardman) 9.12 (1)(b)f.
18 (1987) JIBL 48.

have extolled the advantages to bondholders of having a sophisticated institution to monitor compliance and which will examine financial information received from the issuer.

The issuer is also obliged to send at specified times, usually at the same time as year-end audited financial statements are sent to the trustee, a certificate from the auditors listing the principal operating subsidiaries of the issuer (and of the guarantor if there is one).

(c) The issuer is obliged to keep proper books of account and permit the trustee to have access to such books of account at all reasonable times where the trustee 'has reasonable grounds to believe' that any event of default has occurred and where the issue is guaranteed the obligation is imposed on the issuer and the guarantor; in all cases the obligation extends to giving access to the books of account of the subsidiaries of the issuer and the guarantor.

This covenant is of potentially great use if the trustee believes there is a possible breach of negative pledge or the non-payment of sums due in respect of other indebtedness.[19]

(d) The issuer is obliged to give notice to the trustee in writing immediately upon becoming aware of the occurrence of an event of default or the occurrence of any event which may potentially be an event of default; the issuer's obligation to give notice of a potential event of default is designed to cover cases where an event constitutes an event of default only on the expiration of a number of days, eg a failure to pay interest, or where there is a requirement as to the giving of a notice or certificate by the trustee that it is materially prejudicial to the interests of bondholders.

(e) The above obligation is usually strengthened by an obligation imposed on the issuer to send to the trustee, within 14 days of the publication of the annual audited balance sheet and accounts, a certificate signed by any two of its directors that to the best of their knowledge and belief no event of default (or potential event of default) has occurred as at the date of the certificate; the directors must also state that they have made all reasonable enquiries. This is in fact a powerful covenant because the potential exposure of individual directors to liability for negligent or fraudulent misstatement provides a powerful incentive to individual directors to be absolutely accurate. This in effect means that the directors must police the compliance by the issuer of its obligations under the bond instrument and trust deed. The covenant also has the practical effect that it assists the trustee in policing the covenants of the issuer.

(f) The issuer is obliged to maintain the listing of the bonds on the Stock Exchange in London or Luxembourg, whichever was chosen when the bonds were issued; the trustee, however, has power to agree to the substitution of an alternative exchange for listing if (i) the trustee agrees that the maintenance of the listing is onerous, and (ii) the trustee is satisfied that such substitution is not materially prejudicial to the interests of the bondholders.

(g) The issuer is also obliged to send to the trustee on request a certificate

---

19 See p 204 above on default.

stating the number of bonds which are held by the issuer, the guarantor (if any) and their subsidiaries as at the date of the certificate.

(9) The trustee has power to waive breaches of covenant committed by the issuer if in his opinion such breach is not materially prejudicial to the interest of bondholders. Such a waiver is stated to be conclusive and binding on the bondholders. The bondholders nevertheless have a power to require the trustee not to waive, by passing an extraordinary resolution. This power may be theoretical, given the time constraints on convening a meeting of bondholders: a trustee could easily waive such a breach, and once it has been waived, the waiver is made binding on the bondholders by the terms of the trust deed. In practice, most Eurobond trustees are likely to ask the issuer to convene a bondholder meeting if they are in any doubt as to the propriety of a waiver, since otherwise a trustee may be exposed to actions by aggrieved bondholders for breach of trust.

(10) Eurobond trustees are also given a power to modify the terms of the trust deed without the consent of the bondholders but with the agreement of the issuer. This may encompass the terms and conditions of the bond instruments since the bonds are said to be 'constituted by' the trust deed.[20]

The protection afforded in practice to bondholders in respect of unilateral modification by the trustee in practice is twofold. First, certain provisions of the trust deed are immune from modification under the trustee's power of modification. Secondly, it cannot be exercised in circumstances where the modification would be 'materially prejudicial to the interests of the bondholders in the opinion of the trustee'.

It is therefore provided that the trustee cannot modify the trust deed so as to have the effect of:

(a) altering the date on which interest is payable; or
(b) postponing the maturity date of the bonds; or
(c) reducing or cancelling the interest payable on the bonds; or
(d) reducing or cancelling the principal amount payable on the bonds; or
(e) reducing or cancelling the minimum interest rate payable on the bonds where a 'floor' interest rate is payable in case of a floating rate note.

As a matter of legal principle there seems to be no reason why a trustee should not be vested with the power of unilaterally modifying the terms of the trust deed.[1] In the absence of such an express power, the only basis on which a properly constituted trust could be amended is under the rule in *Saunders v Vautier*[2] or where the beneficiaries are unascertained under the Variation of Trusts Act 1958. The limitations inherent in these rules of law are inapplicable to a case where a trustee is given an express power to vary the terms of a trust.

The second restriction is that a trustee may not modify the terms of the trust deed if in the trustee's opinion such modification would be materially

---

20 See p 225 above.
1 See also Trustee Act 1925 s 69(2).
2 (1841) Cr & Ph 240; see also Hanbury and Maudsley *Modern Equity* ch 21.

prejudicial to the interests of the bondholders. In practice trust deeds usually require that material prejudice need only exist in the opinion of the trustee.

The significance of this is that a trustee's decision to modify could only be challenged if he could not have honestly held the opinion that there was no material prejudice; the mere fact that bondholders were materially prejudiced would by itself not suffice to expose the trustee to liability. In addition, the Eurobond trust deeds sometimes provide that the opinion of the trustee as to material prejudice or the absence of it shall be final and conclusive and binding on all bondholders.

It is submitted, however, that this clause is unlikely to be construed by an English court to confer an unfettered discretion in the trustee to determine the existence or non-existence of material prejudice.[3] A court is likely to look for some evidence which could give rise to the trustee's opinion, although it seems that so long as there was some supportable (even if mistaken) basis for the opinion a court is unlikely to interfere with the trustee's decision even where the court disagreed with the trustee's views. Indeed, as observed earlier, Lord Denning in *Re Tuck's Settlement Trusts*[4] said that a court would not interfere with such a 'conclusive' determination only 'so long as he does not misconduct himself or come to a decision which is wholly unreasonable'[5] and the House of Lords in *Dundee General Hospitals Board of Management v Walker*[6] obiter said that a conclusive determination could be impugned not only on the ground of bad faith but also on the basis of a failure to appreciate the issue.[7]

In practice a trustee is well advised to seek bondholder approval to any substantial modification of the terms of the trust deed or the bonds. It is also submitted that a trustee is under an inherent duty to act fairly.

It is interesting to consider to what extent a trustee may modify the trust deed and bond instruments (in so far as the terms of the bond may be regarded as part of the trust deed). It must be noted that the issue here is not a retrospective waiver of breach but the limits of the power of prospectant alteration of the regime of rights and liabilities.

The following would generally not be permissible modifications in the exercise of a trustee's power in the absence of special circumstances.

(a) Any alteration of the bearer nature of a Eurobond which would impair its negotiability.
(b) Any substantial alteration of the pari passu or negative pledge covenant; thus, if the negative pledge were drafted to prohibit the giving of security in respect of indebtedness of the issuer, a variation which permitted the issuer to grant security in respect of bank borrowings would prima facie be materially prejudicial, though special circum-

---

3 See also on this subject pp 209–210 above.
4 [1978] Ch 49.
5 See ibid p 62.
6 [1952] 1 All ER 896.
7 See especially Lord Reid, ibid at 905. See also pp 209–210 above.

stances may exist where this may be justified as, for instance, where the alternative might be a disastrous liquidation of the issuer.
(c) Any modification of the issuer's obligations to pay interest free of withholding tax or other deduction.
(d) Any change in the cross-default provision which would place the bondholders in a less advantageous position as, for example, a deletion of a clause which triggered an event of default when other borrowings or indebtedness 'becomes capable of being declared due and payable prior to its stated maturity'.
(e) Any modification of the right of bondholders to compel the trustee to accelerate on the occurrence of an event of default. Thus, if a trustee were to modify a trust deed, so as to increase the percentage of bondholders who are required to make the demand to accelerate, such a modification may not be within the trustee's powers. Similarly, suppose that a trustee were to modify a trust deed so as to transform an event of default framed in objective terms (eg failure to pay interest on a due date which is not cured within seven business days) into one where that event does not amount to an event of default unless the trustee certifies that it is detrimental to bondholders. It is submitted that in the absence of special facts such a modification could not be regarded by a trustee as not being materially prejudicial because it deprives or at least substantially impairs the stipulated percentage of bondholders from compelling the trustee to accelerate, due to the introduction of the subjective element into the occurrence of an event of default.
(f) Any modification in the power of bondholders by extraordinary resolution to compel the trustee to institute proceedings on the bonds against the issuer.
(g) Any change of the chosen governing law and a substitution of a different governing law. This is because of the prejudicial effect which a change of governing law would have on bondholders due to the uncertainty created in legal rights resulting from a change in governing law. A trustee who wishes to do so may be able to protect his decision from attack by obtaining legal opinion from lawyers of the country whose system of law is being substituted.

There is also a more difficult question here. Can a third party be given a power under English law to alter the chosen proper law of a negotiable instrument? There is no authority on this point, though there is authority which suggests that both parties to a contract may agree to change the proper law of a contract.[8]
(h) Alterations which release the issuer from maintaining a listing on a stock exchange, since such a modification may affect the commercial saleability of the bonds.
(i) Any modification of the clause which makes the trustee liable to bond-

---

8 Per Lord Reid in *James Miller & Partners v Whitworth Street Estates (Manchester) Ltd* [1970] AC 583 at 603. Lord Reid in *Whitworth* probably had in mind cases of express alteration virtually in the form of a novation, as was in the case of *Kremezi v Ridgway* [1949] 1 All ER 662. See further Briggs (1986) LMC LQ 508. This is not the position with regard to unilateral modification by the trustee. See also *Armar Shipping Co Ltd v Caisse Algérienne d'Assurance* [1981] 1 WLR 207 on the need for an ascertainable proper law when the contract is concluded.

holders for his negligence in the performance of his duties. Such a modification would in any event be subject to the restrictions contained in s 192 of the Companies Act 1985.[9]

(j) Any modification of the provision that the trustee may be removed by extraordinary resolution of bondholders or that the appointment of a new trustee requires the approval of bondholders by an extraordinary resolution.[10]

(11) Eurobond trustees are also sometimes given a power to substitute another corporate entity as the debtor or obligor in place of the issuer. Once again, the power does not require the consent of the bondholders for its exercise and is not subject to control by an extraordinary resolution of bondholders or otherwise. This is really a power to novate by substitution of debtors.[11]

The power is, however, subject to limitations in practice. First, the trustee is usually permitted to accept a substituted debtor who is either a successor in business to the issuer or a subsidiary of the issuer and in the latter case only if the issuer guarantees the subsidiary's obligations under the trust deed and bond instruments. Secondly, the trustee is required to ensure that the substituted debtor undertakes all obligations of the trust deed and bonds. In cases where there is a guarantee a similar power is usually conferred to accept a substitute guarantor of the issuer, subject to the same safeguards. It must be remembered that modifications may be necessary to the trust deed and bonds to effect such a substitution and, for this purpose, the trustee would be capable of exercising its powers of modification as discussed above.[12]

The first restriction placed by trust deeds as to the entities who may be accepted as substituted debtors indicates the rationale for this power, namely to facilitate a corporate restructuring or amalgamation or merger in respect of the issuer. However, in acceding to a request for substitution of debtors the trustee is exposed to legal liability. Since the Eurobond trustee, like any other paid trustee, is required in equity to exercise a high degree of due diligence in respect of the financial condition of the substituted debtor,[13] the trustee may be liable to an action for damages if the substituted debtor later becomes incapable of paying interest and principal on the bonds and this fact was discoverable by the trustee by a proper analysis of the substituted debtor's financial statements and reports.[14] To overcome this problem the trustee is permitted to rely on the written statements of the directors of the substituted debtor that the latter is financially solvent, and the trust deed expressly absolves the trustee from having regard to the financial condition, profits or financial future of the substituted entity or from comparing

---

9 See p 237 below.
10 See p 208 regarding extraordinary resolution.
11 See on novation by substitution of debtors at common law: *Miller's case* (1876) 3 Ch D 391.
12 See p 231 above.
13 See p 237 below.
14 See on the standard of care expected of professional trustee corporations *Bartlett* v *Barclay's Bank Trust Co Ltd* [1980] Ch 515 at 534 per Brightman J.

such information about the substituted entity with that of the issuer. It will be noticed that the trustee is thus absolved from making a credit decision but this is probably justified in the circumstances due to the fact that the trustee can only accept a corporate successor to the issuer's business or a subsidiary of the issuer which is guaranteed by the issuer as a substitute debtor.

(12) Under some trust deeds, Eurobond trustees are also given a power to determine conclusively any question as to the interpretation of the trust deed. The effect of this if taken literally is that the trustee can do as he pleases, interpreting the document in any way he wishes. It would amount to summarising the trust deed in one line: it is what the trustee says it is, and the trustee's powers are what he says they are, and the rights of bondholders are what the trustee says they are! The jurisdiction of the court to determine the effect of a particular clause in the trust deed as a matter of law would be completely ousted.[15] In cases such as *Lee v Showman's Guild of Great Britain* and *Baker v Jones*[16] the courts have held that the construction of the clauses in the rules of an association which purported to give a committee exclusive jurisdiction to construe the rules were void because the construction of the rules was a question of law and any attempt to deprive the court of jurisdiction would be void. In cases such as *Re Tuck's Settlement Trusts*[17] and *Re Coxen*[18] the courts allowed clauses which permitted a factual determination by a trustee to be conclusive by reference to a clause making a trustee's determination conclusive. Neither case, however, involved an ouster clause.

Consequently, it is submitted that such clauses should be construed so as not to oust the jurisdiction of the courts. A court would in any event require a trustee to place a reasonable interpretation on trust deed clauses.

(13) The Eurobond trustee can only be removed under trust deeds by an extraordinary resolution of Eurobond holders. Eurobond trust deeds in practice do not, however, contain any specified grounds on which a trustee may be removed.

The issuer has power, however, to appoint new trustees in addition to or in substitution for an existing trustee but such an appointment requires the approval of the bondholders by extraordinary resolution. It is interesting to note that the bondholders do not have any power to appoint a new trustee.

The removal of an existing trustee is not effective until the appointment of a new trustee.

Could bondholders invoke the Trustee Act 1925 so as to remove trustees and appoint new trustees, for instance in cases where they feel that the trustee has not exercised his discretion fairly?

There are two provisions in the Trustee Act 1925 which are relevant, namely s 36 and s 41, both of which deal with the appointment of new trustees in substitution for, or in addition to, an existing trustee. It is clear that the bondholders could not proceed under s 36(1), because under that section only the person or persons nominated for the purpose of appointing

---

15 *Anctil v Manufacturers Life Insurance Co* [1899] AC 604.
16 [1952] 2 QB 329 and [1954] 1 WLR 1005 respectively.
17 [1976] Ch 99.
18 [1948] Ch 747.

new trustees by the instrument or, where such person is not willing to act, the continuing trustee, may appoint new trustees. The Eurobond trust deed in practice confers the power of appointment of new trustees only on the issuer and not on the bondholders.

Under s 36(2) 'where a trustee has been removed under a power contained in the instrument' a new trustee may be appointed. However, even under s 36(2) only the issuer will be able to appoint a new trustee, because appointments under that subsection are also subject to the provision of s 36(1). Consequently, only the person with the power to appoint under the instrument may do so. The bondholders do not have the ability to use the s 36 procedure because the Eurobond trust deed confers the power to appoint new trustees on the issuer.

Under s 46, however, the court is given power to 'make an order appointing a new trustee or new trustees either in substitution for or in addition to any existing trustee ...'. Such an order may be made on the application inter alia of any person beneficially interested in a chose in action subject to a trust under s 58 of the Act. Consequently, a bondholder may make an application under this provision, but such an order to appoint new trustees can be made under the terms of s 41(1) only where 'it is found inexpedient, difficult or unpracticable so to do without the assistance of the court'. The circumstances in which a court will exercise this power in the case of a Eurobond trustee are extremely difficult to predict. There is authority that a court will not appoint a trustee even where the trustee is guilty of breach of trust unless there is 'something which induces the court to think either that the trust property will not be safe, or that the trust will not properly be executed in the interests of the beneficiaries'.[19]

IV EUROBOND TRUSTEE'S IMMUNITIES, DUTIES AND LIABILITIES

Under English law, Eurobond trustees, like all other trustees, and persons subject to fiduciary obligations, must act in compliance with a very strict regime of duties and obligations imposed on them by equity. It is outside the scope of this work to describe all these duties and obligations of an ordinary trustee under English law.[20] However, it is important first to consider the impact of equitable doctrines on the role of the Eurobond trustee so as to evaluate his exposure to claims by bondholders and, secondly, to consider how Eurobond trust deeds deal with this potential exposure. In practice it will be seen that the Eurobond trustee's exposure is usually minimised by an array of protective clauses contained in Eurobond trust deeds, to such an extent that it is difficult to state with certainty in what circumstances he is exposed to liability, or indeed to what duties he is subject.

---

19 *Re Wrightson* [1908] 1 Ch 789 at 803. See also *Re Pauling's Settlement Trust No 2* [1963] Ch 576.
20 See on the duties of trustees: Underhill and Hayton *Law of Trusts and Trustees* ch 11; Hanbury and Maudsley *Modern Equity* Part III.

1 Duty to act with due skill and diligence

The most important and overriding duty of a trustee is to show due care, skill and diligence in carrying out the management of the trust. Eurobond trustees are invariably paid trustees or professional trustee corporations and as such would ordinarily owe much higher standards of care and conduct than ordinary trustees in equity. In an oft cited passage Brightman J said in *Bartlett v Barclay's Bank Trust Co Ltd*:[1]

> 'a trust corporation holds itself out in its advertising literature as being above ordinary mortals. With a specialist staff with ready access to financial information and professional advice, dealing with and solving trust problems day after day, the trust corporation holds itself out as capable of providing an expertise which it would be unrealistic to expect and unjust to demand from the ordinary man or woman who accepts probably unpaid and sometimes reluctantly from a sense of family duty, the burden of trusteeship ... I think that a professional corporate trustee is liable for breach of trust if loss is caused to the trust fund because it neglects to use the special care and skill it professes to have.'[2]

Any attempt at derogation from this fundamental duty of due care, skill and diligence by way of an exemption clause in the trust deed seems to be declared void by s 192 of the Companies Act 1985. That provision applies to every trust deed governed by English law for securing an issue of 'debentures' or any contract with the holders of debentures secured by a trust deed. Since, in practice, Eurobond trust deeds are invariably subject to English law, s 192[3] would apply to virtually all Eurobond trust deeds. Section 192 (1) provides as follows:

> 'Subject to this section any provision contained –
> (a) in a trust deed for securing an issue of debentures, or
> (b) in any contract with the holders of debentures secured by a trust deed,
> is void in so far as it would have the effect of exempting a trustee of the deed from or indemnifying him against liability for breach of trust where he fails to show the degree of care and diligence required of him as trustee, having regard to the provisions of the trust deed conferring on him any powers, authorities or discretions.'

Two initial points need to be made in respect of this provision. First, this provision is not confined to debentures issued by UK companies even though it is found in the UK Companies Act 1985. Secondly, the provision would apply to all trust deeds governed by English law in respect of an issue of bonds since the word 'debenture' in s 192 includes bonds by virtue of s 744 of the Companies Act 1985.

The impact of s 192, however, is not easy to determine.

One interpretation of s 192 is that 'any provision in a trust deed securing

---

1 [1980] Ch 515 at 534.
2 See to similar effect Harman J in *Re Waterman's Will Trusts* [1952] 2 All ER 1054; see on the duty owed by unpaid trustees *Re Lucking's Will Trusts* [1967] 3 All ER 726 at 733 *Cowan v Scargill* [1985] Ch 270 at 288 per Megarry V-C.
3 Its predecessor was s 88 of the Companies Act 1948 and was based on the recommendation of the Cohen Committee (1945, Cmnd 6659).

debentures or in a contract with debenture holders is void so far as it could have the effect of exempting a trustee from or indemnifying him against liability for breach of trust where he fails to show the degree of care and diligence required of him as trustee'.[4] This view, it is submitted with respect, seems to ignore the impact of the last limb of s 192 which provides that regard must be had to the provisions of the trust deed conferring on him any powers, authorities or discretions.

In the context of the last limb of s 192, an alternative interpretation would be that in determining the level of due care and diligence required a court may have regard 'to the provisions of the trust deed conferring on him any powers, authorities or discretions'. This interpretation leads to the conclusion that if the functions of the trustee are expressed in a trust deed purely in the form of discretions and powers and the trustee is given an uncontrolled and absolute discretion in the exercise of such powers, s 192 requires that this fact must be taken into account in determining whether the trustee is in breach of trust. In other words, while s 192 regulates trust deed provisions exempting the liability of trustees for breach of trust and failure to show due care etc, it does not regulate the provisions of the trust deed conferring powers and discretions on the trustee. Trust deed provisions conferring powers and discretions on the trustee cannot be struck down under s 192, however wide they may be. The standard texts on company law unfortunately do not deal with this analysis.[5]

Eurobond trust deeds seem to be drafted on the basis of the latter and, it is submitted, the better, interpretation of s 192. It is a striking feature of Eurobond trust deeds that the trustee is rarely subject to any express duties or obligations in the performance of his functions. As pointed out previously, he is conferred wide-ranging powers and discretions to carry out necessary functions.[6] These powers and discretions are then expressed to be 'absolute and uncontrolled' and further the trustee is declared 'not liable for any loss, damage, cost, claim or action which may result from their exercise or non exercise'. Some trust deeds then provide that the trustee will be liable for a failure to show good faith in the exercise of his functions and powers. The question remains whether this technique is effective to eliminate any duty of due care, skill and diligence on the part of a Eurobond trustee in the exercise of his powers and discretions.

Before this issue is considered it is useful to consider whether, and if so to what extent, Eurobond trust deeds reduce the scope of the duty of skill, care and diligence which a trustee would ordinarily owe under the general law.

(a) *Policing the covenants of the bonds and trust deed* It may be thought that the trustee would be under a specific duty to monitor the covenants in the bonds and trust deeds for the benefit of bondholders in order to determine whether an event of default has occurred, but an express clause in the trust deed negatives such a duty. Eurobond trust deeds provide that a trustee is under no duty to take steps to ascertain whether an event of default has occurred and further confer a power on the trustee to assume that the

---

4 See, for instance, *Palmer's Company Law* (Schmitthoff, edn, 1987) p 230.
5 See *Palmer's Company Law* ch 45, p 729 and *Gore-Brown on Companies* (Boyle & Sykes, 44th edn) Part III, ch 17.
6 See discussion at pp 228–236.

issuer is complying with all its obligations and that no such event of default has occurred until the trustee has 'actual knowledge' of the occurrence or the trustee has been given 'express notice' that an event of default has occurred. It is arguable that he is entitled, under these clauses, to bury his head in the sand until he is informed or actually becomes aware of the default. It is submitted, however, that if the trustee fails to examine the financial information submitted to him by an issuer, and fails to become aware of a potential default on the basis of such information or fails to follow up on a line of enquiry which was apparent on the face of such information he may be in breach of a trustee's duty to exercise his *powers* with due care, skill and diligence. Any clause seeking to exempt him from such liability would probably be struck down by a court under s 192 of the Companies Act 1985.

It must also be remembered that the trustee receives or may demand from the issuer a certificate signed by its directors stating that no event of default has occurred, or that the issuer has effected a transaction or taken remedial steps in respect of a default. The trustee is then empowered to act solely on the basis of such certificate and is placed under no further duty of enquiry. Despite his unqualified and uncontrolled discretion in the matter he must exercise due diligence or reasonable care in examining this certificate and deciding to take action or not as the case may be. An exemption clause which seeks to exempt the trustee's liability for a breach of that duty may be caught by s 192.

(b) *Breach of covenant and default* Even where a breach of covenant has occurred or an event of default has occurred, the Eurobond trust deed imposes no duties on the trustee to take action.[7]

First, where a breach of covenant has occurred the trustee has a power to waive the breach provided that in certain cases the trustee is of the opinion the breach is not materially prejudicial to the interests of bondholders. Once again the general discretion is made absolute under trust deed provisions and the trustee's determination as to material prejudice is made conclusive and binding on the bondholders, issuer and guarantor. It may be the case that the trustee must have some factual basis for his determination or opinion, ie it must not be capricious or wholly unreasonable[8] and arguably only a determination or opinion which has such a factual basis is binding on bondholders.[9] However, it is submitted that a court probably will create a *duty* of due care and diligence in relation to the *exercise of the power* to waive breach of covenant. Secondly, as observed earlier,[10] even on the occurrence of default – even one consisting of a failure to pay interest and principal – there is no duty to accelerate the bonds and demand repayment; the trustee has an 'absolute and uncontrolled' discretion subject only to a duty to accelerate if so required by the appropriate percentage of bondholders or by extraordinary resolution. Once again, while a strict duty of due care, skill and diligence is inapplicable it is submitted there may be liability for the negligent exercise of a *power*.

(c) Even where the trustee decides to accelerate the bonds there is no duty on the trustee to take enforcement proceedings against the issuer; that,

---

7 See p 204 above.
8 See p 232 above.
9 See p 232 above.
10 See p 204 above.

too, is at the discretion of the trustee and there is no duty to act unless the trustee is required by the specified percentage of bondholders or an extraordinary resolution to take proceedings. If the trustee is not so required he is under no duty to act. This is in a contrast to the mandatory duty imposed on trustees by equity not only to demand repayment of debts due but also to enforce payment by taking legal proceedings promptly: *Re Brogden*.[11] However, it is submitted that a failure to exercise the *power* with due care, skill and diligence would give rise to liability and any exemption of such liability would be void under s 192 of the Companies Act 1985.

(d) In the event that payments for bonds made by initial purchasers of bonds do not reach the issuer and are misdirected, it is possible that the trustee may in equity be responsible to the bondholders on the basis that it was his duty to ensure that payments reached the issuer. Eurobond trust deeds negative any such duty which may arguably arise. Similarly, it is expressly provided that he owes no duty to ensure that the global bond is in fact exchanged for definitives or that definitives reach the hands of those who are entitled thereto.

(e) The trustee has access to financial information from the issuer and indeed has a power to demand information from the issuer.

Stemming from the power there may be duty arising in equity to keep bondholders informed of the financial performance of the issuer, particularly where it appears to the trustee that the financial performance of the issuer has been deteriorating continuously; equity imposes a general duty to keep beneficiaries informed of matters affecting the trust: *Re Londonderry's Settlement*.[12] However, an express provision in the trust deed provides that the trustee is under no duty to disclose any confidential information, financial or otherwise, about the issuer and consequently no duty of due diligence can arise here.

It is submitted[13] that a negligent failure to exercise this power to call for information and follow a line of enquiry would expose a trustee to an action for negligent breach of trust and any exemption from such liability would be void under s 192 of the Companies Act 1985.

(f) It will be remembered that the trustee is required on a number of important occasions to comply with resolutions of bondholders, eg acceleration, bringing enforcement proceedings. It may be thought a duty of due care and diligence would exist here to ensure that, before the trustee acted, he ought to ensure that proper procedures had been followed and that the requisite percentage had voted. However, no duty of diligence is owed by the trustee to determine the constitutionality or procedural regularity of such a resolution; the only duty is one of good faith. If he has minutes of a meeting which are signed purporting to be from a meeting of bondholders he is empowered to act without further enquiry.

(g) When a trustee agrees to a modification of the terms of the trust deed with the issuer, it was pointed out earlier[14] that he acts under wide powers and he has only a duty to consider whether bondholders will be materially prejudiced. Provided he has considered the issue his deter-

---

11 (1888) 38 Ch D 546.
12 [1965] Ch 918.
13 See also (b) and (e) above.
14 See the discussion at pp 231–234 above.

mination is made final and conclusive in respect of bondholders. It is submitted that here, too, a court would impose a duty of reasonable care in respect of the exercise of the power.

(h) In all cases where the trustee must consider whether material prejudice would result to bondholders his determination is made final and conclusive for all purposes. The courts have, as observed earlier, upheld such conclusive determination clauses in *Re Coxen*[15] and in *Re Tuck's Settlement Trusts*[16] and have recognised that a strict duty of due care, skill and diligence does not exist in such cases. It must be remembered, however, that Lord Denning in *Re Tuck's Settlement Trusts* added that in arriving at the determination the trustee must not 'misconduct himself or come to a decision which is wholly unreasonable' while Lord Reid in *Dundee General Hospitals v Walker*[17] thought the determination was open to review on grounds of bad faith and a failure to appreciate the issue. These dicta lend support to the view that some elements of reasonableness must exist in respect of any determination made by the trustee.

(i) The trustee is empowered to obtain advice or information from professionals and experts in the performance of his functions and there is a wide exemption clause which provides that the trustee is not to be responsible for acting on such advice or information. In many cases a trustee corporation is not in a position to evaluate the advice or information, eg advice from an overseas lawyer, or investment adviser, and the clause serves a justifiable purpose in excluding liability. However, trust deeds also attempt to exclude any duty to seek out a professional with reasonable skill and diligence by conferring a power rather than imposing a duty to choose a professional to obtain advice or information.[18] It is submitted, however, that a court would find it easy to imply a duty of care in the exercise of the power.

(j) The trustee is also under no duty to make enquiry whether bonds presented for payment (interest or principal) are genuine or forged or to enquire whether a holder is in fact the owner. This clause reverses the rule laid down by Lord Nottingham in *Ashby v Blackwell* in 1765.[19]

(k) Where the trustee is in possession of funds to be held for bondholders, for instance after he has directed paying agents to make payments to him, it would usually be the case that the trustee must show due skill and diligence in handling such funds and investing them. However, the Eurobond trustee is given complete power to invest such funds in any investments anywhere or place such funds on deposit whether or not they produce income. Here again due to the wide nature of the power it seems that it may be difficult to imply a duty of due diligence. It is submitted, however, that if the trustee exercises this power negligently or incompetently so that the trust incurs a substantial capital loss or receives no income the trustee would be in breach of his duty to exercise his powers with due care.

There is a further power which permits the trustee to vary or substitute investments without any restriction and without liability for loss resulting

---

15 [1948] Ch 747.
16 [1978] Ch 49.
17 [1952] 1 All ER 896.
18 See also the discussion as to the trustee's power to delegate the performance of various functions to professionals, p 245 below.
19 (1765) 2 Eden 299.

from fluctuations in capital value or currency rates. The analysis above would equally apply in respect of this power.

It is nevertheless usual for Eurobond trust deeds to provide in a clause that the trustee will be liable in negligence for a failure to show due care, skill and diligence which the trustee is required to show as trustee. The clause is in a form similar to

> 'none of the provisions of this trust deed shall in any case in which the trustee has failed to show the degree of care and diligence required of it having regard to the provisions of the trust deed conferring on the trustee any duties, powers, authorities and discretions relieve the trustee from liabilities which by any rule of law would otherwise attach to it in respect of any negligence default breach of duty or breach of trust of which it may be guilty in relation to its duties under this deed.'

The purpose of such a clause is presumably to indicate that there is no derogation from the provisions of s 192 of the Companies Act 1985 which the clause virtually reproduces. It is submitted that this clause would apply in the event of a negligent exercise of any of the powers of the Eurobond trustees.

However, a literal reading of the express clauses of a Eurobond trust deed may lead to the conclusion that the Eurobond trustee has hardly any duties to be performed for the benefit of all bondholders; all his functions are exercisable by way of 'absolute and uncontrolled' discretions and powers in respect of which he is not accountable to bondholders (except in some cases, where he can be compelled by extraordinary resolution or by a specified percentage of bondholders); he is sought to be made liable only in the event he acts in bad faith but otherwise he is not to be liable for carelessness or negligence, subject to the overriding provision of s 192 of the Companies Act 1985.

It is submitted, however, that neither the specific elimination of duties nor the transformation of what are usually trustee's duties into absolute discretions and powers has that effect. First, the courts as a matter of judicial policy are unlikely to permit a paid professional trustee or a trust corporation to be careless and negligent even if they act bona fide. It is difficult to see how English courts will accept such wide exemption in respect of a paid trustee to a point where the duties they owe are well below those imposed by law on ordinary trustees in family trusts. The current policy of the courts is encapsulated in the quotation from Brightman J in *Bartlett* cited above[20] and it is probable that as a matter of policy paid trustees will be held at least to the level of reasonable care and due diligence which the courts require even the family trustee to satisfy. Secondly, it seems that the provisions of s 61 of the Trustee Act 1925 represent the minimum level of conduct which may be expected of any trustee, namely that he acted 'honestly *and reasonably*'.[1] Thirdly, as Pergam has pointed out citing Kennedy,[2] if the trust deed is a 'complete whitewash' it would be unacceptable to the investing

---

20 See p 237.
1 See also on this point the views of John Kennedy cited in Pergam's article 'Eurobonds: Trustees, Fiscal Agents and Default' Studies in Transnational Economic Law vol 3.
2 Above.

community, and it is more than likely that the courts would take this into consideration. Finally, there is little justification in general legal principle or commercial sense to require anything less than due care, skill and diligence from a professional trustee or trustee corporation who undoubtedly conform to these standards in practice in any event.

To achieve this objective a court can easily hold as submitted above that while a Eurobond trustee is under no express duties and may act through powers, *such powers must be exercised reasonably and with due care.*

Could the provisions of the Unfair Contract Terms Act 1977 be invoked in respect of clauses in trust deeds which seek to reduce or eliminate the duty to exercise due care, skill and diligence?

Section 2 of the Unfair Contract Terms Act probably has no application to the question of liability for negligence of a Eurobond trustee, due to the fact that by s 1(1) negligence means any duty arising by virtue of a contract or by reference to a 'common law duty to take reasonable care or exercise reasonable skill'. A trustee's duty arises in equity and is probably outside the ambit of s 2(2). If, however, the position is that the trustee's duties under a trust deed arise by virtue of contract there is recent Court of Appeal authority in *Phillips Products Ltd v Hyland*[3] that a clause negativing a duty as well as an exemption of liability clause was caught by s 2(2) of the Unfair Contract Terms Act 1977. Slade LJ delivering the judgment of the court, held that the law looks at the effect and substance of clauses and not the structure and form. If this analysis is correct then Eurobond trust deed clauses which negative trustees' duties are liable to attack on this basis and are liable to a test of 'fair and reasonable' as a precondition to validity. A court may hold that a clause conferring a power on a trustee to act in his 'absolute discretion' and one which states that the exercise of the power is conclusive and binding are exemption clauses in disguise.

2 Duty of trustee not to allow his duty as trustee to conflict with his own interests[4]

This duty, like the previous duty, is capable of elasticity in application and can cover a host of circumstances.[5] It is also inextricably interwoven with two other duties:

(a) Duty not to traffic in trust property or purchase trust property.[6]

The rule is absolute and is not dependent on the trustee obtaining an advantage or making a profit at the expense of beneficiaries or paying an inadequate price; though there is some latitude in special cases as the Court of Appeal recognised in *Holder v Holder*.[7]

(b) Duty not to make incidental or secret profits by virtue of his fiduciary position. This rule was affirmed in all its rigidity in the leading case

---

3 [1987] 2 All ER 620; cf Nourse LJ in *Harris v Wyre Forest District Council* [1988] 1 All ER 691.
4 See Lord Upjohn in *Boardman v Phipps* [1967] 2 AC 46 at 123.
5 See discussion in *Boardman v Phipps*, above.
6 See *Campbell v Walker* (1800) 5 Ves 678; *Holder v Holder* [1968] Ch 353.
7 See [1968] Ch 353.

of *Boardman v Phipps*[8] by Wilberforce J, the Court of Appeal and a majority of the House of Lords. They held that the duty which lay on a fiduciary in this respect was absolute and if he had made incidental profits by virtue of his position as a fiduciary he was in breach of duty, and he must account for the profit to the beneficiaries. Indeed, the House went as far as to hold that even though the Phipps trust had not suffered any loss of capital or income, and even though the trust itself had been greatly benefited financially by the fiduciary's activities, and despite the fact the fiduciary had acted bona fide at all times, nevertheless he was in breach of his duty. Formulated in this way, it appears that a fiduciary is in breach of duty not to make incidental profits, both in cases where he does so in conflict with his duties to beneficiaries and also where there is, in fact, no conflict.

Cases such as *Boardman v Phipps* are cases where the fiduciary used trust property to make the profit. A breach of fiduciary duty can arise even where trust property is not used to make incidental profits but profits are made by the use of information obtained qua fiduciary: *Aas v Benham*.[9]

In the context of the Eurobond trustee these rules would probably have a number of consequences. First, while the bonds are not trust property,[10] nevertheless since the covenants of the bond instrument are trust property the trustee may be regarded as trafficking in trust property if he buys and sells the bonds to which the trust deed relates. In any event, given the Eurobond trustee's access to financial information from the issuer a purchase or sale of the issuer's bonds would be caught by the rule against making incidental profits.[11]

Similarly, the wide ruling in *Phipps v Boardman* would also prevent the trustee from purchasing and selling shares in the issuer or guarantor or any subsidiary or associated company at a profit. So, too, any commission fee or revenue obtained from any other business, eg acting as a trustee for the issuer in another issue of bonds, would be caught by the incidental profits rule. Further, any contract, transaction or business with the issuer or the guarantor (if any) or any subsidiary or associate would put the trustee in breach of his duty not to place himself in a position of conflict with his fiduciary duties.

Consequently, Eurobond trust deeds eliminate these duties and permit the trustee to buy and sell shares or bonds of the issuer; they permit the trustee to enter into any contract, transaction or business with the issuer and permit the trustee to make profits or fees or commissions or to obtain any revenue without any duty to account to bondholders. Such permission is extended to cover on the one hand the trustee corporations, subsidiaries, associate companies and holding companies and on the other to any guarantor of the issuer and any subsidiary holding company, or associated company of the issuer or guarantor.

Difficult questions of conflict of duty with duty (as distinct from conflict

---

8 [1967] 2 AC 46.
9 [1891] 2 Ch 244, approved in *Phipps v Boardman*, above.
10 See p 225 above.
11 *Phipps v Boardman*, above.

of interest with duty) may arise where one professional trustee has been appointed trustee in respect of a number of different bond issues by the same issuer. Thus in the British and Commonwealth Holdings restructuring it was reported[12] that the interests of convertible bondholders might have been different from ordinary bondholders in respect of the restructuring although the two groups of bondholders were represented by the same trustee.

It is important to note that permissions in the trust deed can only affect the trustee's duties qua fiduciary. They cannot eliminate duties imposed by other rules of law. For instance, supposing that an employee of the trustee has access to unpublished price-sensitive information about a corporate issuer, which the trustee obtained due to its powers under the trust deed; and suppose that the employee purchases shares in the issuer on behalf of the trustee while in possession of such information. It is beyond doubt that the employee may be guilty of committing the criminal offence of insider trading in breach of s 1 of the Company Securities (Insider Dealing) Act 1985.

3 Duty of trustees to provide information about matters affecting the trust

As pointed out earlier,[13] this duty is expressly negated by a clause which releases the trustee from a duty to disclose any confidential or financial or any other information made available to the trustee by the issuer in connection with the trusts. Some trust deeds expressly add that bondholders have no right to ask for such information. However, under the terms of the bond instrument the trust deed is made available to the bondholders at the principal office of the trustee and the offices of paying agents whose addresses are provided in the bond instrument.[14]

4 Duty not to delegate the trustee's duties or powers

The old rule in equity was 'revolutionised' by s 23 of the Trustee Act 1925[15] which permits trustees to employ and pay agents including solicitors, bankers, stockbrokers or other persons 'to transact any business or do any act required to be transacted or done in the execution of the trust' and further renders them immune from liability 'for the default of any such agent if employed in good faith'.[16]

Similarly, s 23(2) permits trustees to appoint any persons to act as their agents and permits the delegation of 'discretions' and 'powers' to agents,

---

12 See the *Financial Times*, 21 May 1990, p 26.
13 See p 208 above.
14 This public availability is essential to its incorporation in the bond instrument (see p 205 above) and in order to ensure that successive bondholders are bound by its terms given the significant restriction on the exercise of rights by individual bondholders under the trust deed both in their capacity as creditors (eg right to sue) and as beneficiaries of a trust (eg right to a high degree of professional skill and diligence). How far a court would extend the doctrine of incorporation by reference to such a wide range of exemptions is a difficult question to answer.
15 See per Maugham J in *Re Vickery* [1931] 1 Ch 572.
16 S 23(1)

but only in so far as trust property is situated outside the UK. The liability of the trustee under s 23(2) is eliminated in respect of any loss arising 'by reason only of their having made any such appointment'. Quite clearly s 23(1) would apply to Eurobond trustees but s 23(2) requires closer scrutiny. It applies if the trust property is outside the UK and if the trust property is a chose in action against the issuer on a debt.[17] If payment is due at the offices of paying agents outside the UK, the trust asset would be regarded as being outside the UK since a chose in respect of a debt is located where the debt is payable.[18] The benefit of s 23(2) would thus be available to a Eurobond trustee.

Nevertheless, it is clear that these sections do not go so far as to state that so long as the trustee acts in good faith he is not liable for the acts and defaults of his agents. Maugham J in *Re Vickery*[19] thought that s 23(1) at least did not exclude a duty to act with ordinary prudence in selecting an agent and indeed supervising his activities[20] and the protection provided a trustee under s 23(2) is much narrower in respect of the delegation of powers and discretions, since it is confined to any loss arising merely 'by reason only of their having made such appointment'. Consequently, the trustee would owe a duty to supervise with due care[1] and there would probably be liability for negligence in selection, on the basis that s 23 deals only with vicarious liability of the trustee and not his primary liability. This distinction has been recognised by the court in *Re Lucking's Will Trusts*.[2]

Eurobond trust deeds seek to eliminate any duty to supervise and any liability for the default of an agent. The problem with such clauses is that they attempt indirectly to eliminate any duty to act prudently in selecting an agent; and any duty of reasonable supervision of an agent. It is submitted that in the light of *Re Vickery* and *Re Lucking's Will Trusts* it is probable that a court may not permit such an elimination of fiduciary duty to a point that a trustee may act carelessly though in good faith.[3]

5 Rationale for trustee in a Eurobond issue

It remains to consider advantages to bondholders and issuers in having a trustee clothed with such powers and immunities. The advantages of a trustee in the event of default have already been discussed previously.[4]

Wood[5] lists eight advantages to a bondholder, of which the following require closer consideration.

---

17 See p 226 above.
18 See Dicey and Morris *Conflict of Laws* r 115; *New York Life Insurance Co v Public Trustee* [1924] 2 Ch 101 at 109; and the recent case of *Libyan Arab Foreign Bank v Manufacturers Hanover Trust Co* (No 2) [1989] 1 Lloyd's Rep 608.
19 See p 245 above.
20 See also the views of text writers to similar effect Hayton and Marshall *Cases and Commentary on the Law of Trusts* (Stevens and Sons, 8th edn, 1986), pp 550–551, Hanbury and Maudsley *Modern Equity* pp 546–548.
1   See *Speight v Gaunt* (1884) 9 App Cas 1, HL and *Mathew v Brise* (1845) 10 Jur 105.
2   [1968] 1 WLR 866.
3   See also p 242 above on the duty to act with due skill and diligence.
4   See p 212.
5   *Law and Practice of International Finance* (Clark Boardman, International Business Law, vol 2) s 9.12(1)(b).

(a) 'Unified suit': the advantage is that individual bondholders are not left with the difficulty of costly enforcement action in England or elsewhere in an unfamiliar jurisdiction, but have the advantage of a professional trustee who can act on their behalf. As pointed out earlier,[6] the trustee has absolute discretion in this respect and only a large percentage of bondholders or an extraordinary resolution can compel a trustee to act.

(b) 'Default compromise': it is said that a disastrous liquidation can be avoided on the occurrence of an event of default because the trustee can effect a compromise by effecting a grant of security, or by an amalgamation of the issuer. If there were no trustee, all the bondholders would have to agree to any compromise, which would be practically impossible.

(c) Cases where security needs to be taken in the event of a breach of negative pledge[7] would create insuperable difficulties if there were no trustee to accept security; since it would be practically difficult to give security to each bondholder.

(d) The presence of the 'no action' clause prevents what Wood has referred to as a 'race to the courthouse door' by bondholders so that only those who are quick off the mark get paid. The trustee is able to act on behalf of all bondholders and distribute the proceeds ratably. A trustee may, however, choose to take no action upon acceleration by way of enforcement since it is within his uncontrolled discretion and power whether to act, although it is likely that he would be exposed to an action on the basis of an unreasonable exercise of powers.[8]

(e) Monitoring compliance: it is said that the bond holders have the benefit of a sophisticated professional trustee to monitor compliance with covenants and to evaluate financial information.

There are limitations to this. The financial information made available to a Eurobond trustee[9] is obviously of greater practical value to bondholders where financial controls are imposed on the issuer by way of financial ratio covenants and in the majority of cases this is not the case. It must also be remembered that there are express clauses in the trust deed which negative any duty of monitoring compliance. Eurobond trust deeds contain what Wood[10] terms an 'ostrich' clause, which provides that the trustee is under no duty to ascertain whether the issuer is complying with covenants or whether an event of default has occurred until he has actual knowledge of such or has been given express notice of such. However, where the trustee is conferred a power to obtain information by the trust deed he will be under a duty to follow up any leads and make enquiry for the benefit of bond holders.

---

6 See p 207 above.
7 See pp 89 et seq above.
8 See p 232 above.
9 See pp 229–230 above.
10 *Law and Practice of International Finance* s 9.12(13). See also p 239 above.

248   *Trustees under Eurobond trust deeds*

The advantages to the issuer are also numerous.

(a) Herbert[11] has pointed out the appointment of a trustee provides the issuer with flexibility on the occurrence of a default. The issuer can negotiate with one professional rather than a multitude of bondholders. The issuer has flexibility in coming to a compromise solution to any difficulties which have arisen. He can be assured that technical defaults would be waived if they are not materially prejudicial to the interests of bondholders.

(b) Modification of terms: the issuer need not have to deal with a multitude of bondholders if he wishes to alter the terms of the bonds (except his obligation to pay interest and principal and his obligation to redeem the bonds on maturity). He can deal with a sophisticated professional trustee.

(c) Wood has pointed out that events of default can be framed in a somewhat imprecise manner, eg materially prejudicial so as to provide flexibility; this would be impossible in the absence of a trustee.

(d) In the event that litigation ensues the issuer need only deal with one action rather than a host of actions possibly in different jurisdictions.

(e) Rescheduling: while the trustee cannot unilaterally change the date on which the bonds mature it is useful in practice to negotiate terms in advance with a trustee who can then call a meeting of the bondholders to approve a rescheduling.

(f) The 'no action' clause prevents ill-advised and precipitous litigation at the instance of a small minority of bondholders.[12] Time for negotiation and arriving at a solution on default is preserved.

It also prevents such a minority precipitating an insolvency of the issuer by taking court action and triggering cross-default clauses in other bond instruments as well as syndicated loans.

In the final analysis, the balance of factors is strongly in favour of the appointment of a trustee in international bond issues.

6   Regulation of the contents of trust deeds

As observed earlier, English law neither requires the appointment of a trustee nor regulates comprehensively the contents of a trust deed in respect of international bonds. However, as observed at the beginning of this chapter bonds which are to be listed on The London Stock Exchange must be issued subject to a trust deed. Trust deeds are also subject to the prohibition on the exclusion of a trustee's liability in negligence under s 192 of the Companies Act 1985.

The position is different in the US where trust deeds (indentures) are required (subject to certain exceptions) by the Trust Indenture Act of 1939 to contain certain provisions before such a deed qualifies as a qualifying trust indenture. Penalties are imposed by the Act for a failure to comply.[13]

The question arises whether a similar regime is appropriate for the interna-

---

11   See note 18 at p 229.
12   See the events concerning Dome discussed at p 222.
13   See 15 USC ss 77eee and 77fff.

tional bond markets. The logic underlining the enactment of the US Trust Indenture Act is set out in the preamble to the main provisions of the Act and they are worthy of consideration. They are set out below.[14]

'*Necessity for Regulation*
(a) Upon the basis of facts disclosed by the reports of the Securities and Exchange Commission made to the Congress pursuant to s 78jj of this title and otherwise disclosed and ascertained, it is hereby declared that the national public interest and the interest of investors in notes, bonds, debentures, evidences of indebtedness, and certificates of interest or participation therein, which are offered to the public, are adversely affected—
  (1) when the obligor fails to provide a trustee to protect and enforce the rights and to represent the interests of such investors, notwithstanding the fact that (A) individual action by such investors for the purpose of protecting and enforcing their rights is rendered impracticable by reason of the disproportionate expense of taking such action, and (B) concerted action by such investors in their common interest through representatives of their own selection is impeded by reason of the wide dispersion of such investors through many States, and by reason of the fact that information as to the names and addresses of such investors generally is not available to such investors;
  (2) when the trustee does not have adequate rights and powers, or adequate duties and responsibilities, in connection with matters relating to the protection and enforcement of the rights of such investors; when, notwithstanding the obstacles to concerted action by such investors, and the general and reasonable assumption by such investors that the trustee is under an affirmative duty to take action for the protection and enforcement of their rights, trust indentures (A) generally provide that the trustee shall be under no duty to take any such action, even in the event of default, unless it receives notice of default, demand for action, and indemnity, from the holders of substantial percentages of the securities outstanding thereunder, and (B) generally relieve the trustee from liability even for its own negligent action or failure to act;
  (3) when the trustee does not have resources commensurate with its responsibilities, or has any relationship to or connection with the obligor or any underwriter of any securities of the obligor, or holds, beneficially or otherwise, any interest in the obligor or any such underwriter, which relationship, connection or interest involves a material conflict with the interest of such investors;
  (4) when the obligor is not obligated to furnish to the trustee under the indenture and to such investors adequate current information as to its financial condition, and as to the performance of its obligations with respect to the securities outstanding under such indenture; or when the communication of such information to such investors is impeded by the fact that information as to the names and addresses of such investors generally is not available to the trustee and to such investors;
  (5) when the indenture contains provisions which are misleading or deceptive, or when full and fair disclosure is not made to prospective investors of the effect of important indenture provisions; or
  (6) when, by reason of the fact that trust indentures are commonly prepared by the obligor or underwriter in advance of the public offering

---

14 See 15 USC s 77bbb.

of the securities to be issued thereunder, such investors are unable to participate in the preparation thereof, and, by reason of their lack of understanding of the situation, such investors would in any event be unable to procure the correction of the defects enumerated in this subsection.

(b) Practices of the character above enumerated have existed to such an extent that, unless regulated, the public offering of notes, bonds, debentures, evidences of indebtedness, and certificates of interest of participation therein, by the use of means and instruments of transportation and communication in interstate commerce and of the mails, is injurious to the capital markets, to investors, and to the general public; and it is hereby declared to be the policy of this subchapter, in accordance with which policy all the provisions of this subchapter shall be interpreted, to meet the problems and eliminate the practices, enumerated in this section, connected with such public offerings.'

It is submitted that the experience in the international or Eurobond markets does not seem to necessitate such regulation.

CHAPTER 14
Convertible Eurobonds and bonds with warrants

I INTRODUCTION

The previous chapters of Part III have been concerned with bonds which are purely debt instruments. Convertible bonds and bonds with warrants are linked to equity and have special features. Consequently, they raise legal issues which require additional discussion to that in the previous chapters.

The convertible bond is a debt instrument which confers an option on the holder to exchange the debt instrument for another security, representing either debt or equity (usually an equity security) issued by the issuer of the bond or its guarantor. Less frequently, a convertible is exchangeable for a security issued by an entity other than the issuer of the convertible or its guarantor.

A bond with a warrant, on the other hand, is a bond issued with a second instrument attached to it which confers a right to subscribe or acquire equity or debt. The more common form of warrant issued with Eurobonds is a warrant which confers on the holder a right to subscribe the common stock or ordinary shares of the issuer of the bonds (or of its guarantor). Less frequently, Eurobonds are issued with warrants to subscribe debt securities; and infrequently, Eurobonds are issued with warrants to acquire securities issued by an entity which is neither the issuer or the guarantor of the bonds, nor an entity which is a member of the same corporate group as the issuer.

The warrant instruments are nearly always detachable from the bond with which they are issued (the 'host bond') and are traded separately in the practice of the international capital markets. Consequently, a Eurobond issued with warrants is capable of being traded in one of three ways:

(a) the bond with warrants;
(b) the bond ex warrants;
(c) the warrants on their own.

A convertible or warrant which confers a right to *subscribe* equity or debt must be distinguished from one which confers a right to *acquire* equity or debt. An instrument which confers a right to subscribe confers a right which entitles the holder to require the issuer of the convertible or warrant (or sometimes the guarantor) to issue new equity or debt securities to the holder of the convertible or the warrant. A convertible or warrant containing a right to acquire does not entitle the holder to so subscribe new equity or debt in exchange for the convertible (or for cash in the case of a warrant); it confers a right to demand delivery or transfer of a specified amount of debt or equity securities already in existence, usually of an entity which has no corporate relationship with the issuer of the convertible or warrant.

A warrant entitling the holder to subscribe equity or debt is an instrument which falls within para 4 of Sch 1 to the FSA, while a warrant to acquire securities probably falls within para 7 or para 5(c) of Sch 1 to the FSA.[1]

Convertibles and warrants are similar in one sense in that each instrument confers an option on the holder either to subscribe for or acquire equity or debt. The fundamental difference, however, is that the convertible confers an option on the holder to subscribe for other securities by exchanging or converting the bond instrument for that other security at a specified price *without providing any further cash or consideration*; whereas the holder's option contained in a warrant is to subscribe for other securities *by providing additional consideration by way of cash* at the price specified in the warrant.

Consequently, in a convertible the original convertible bond and the security into which it can be exchanged can never subsist simultaneously in the holder's hands; they are mutually exclusive and the exercise of the conversion option results in the cancellation of the bond as a debt instrument. In a Eurobond issue with warrants, the warrants are cancelled when the securities to which they confer rights of subscription come into existence. The host bond, however, can subsist in law after the issue of shares or other securities in consequence of the exercise of the option, although in practice contrary provision is usually made.[2]

In both cases the holder is conferred an *option* to subscribe or acquire other securities from the issuer; he is under no obligation to do so.[3]

In the international capital markets of London (unlike in the US or Japanese domestic market), another feature of such equity convertibles is that the currency of the bond may, and usually is, different from the currency of the stock or shares into which the bond is convertible. For instance, a US dollar dominated bond may be convertible into the shares of a Japanese company denominated in yen. Consequently, they are also referred to as 'currency convertibles'. In the case of Eurobonds issued with warrants, a substantial amount of such warrants confer rights to subscribe equity which is denominated in a currency different from the currency of the host bond.

The following discussion is concerned with bonds which possess an equity element, ie which are convertible into equity or are issued with equity warrants; first, because these types of instruments constitute a large segment

---

1 See also the discussion at ch 15 below.
2 See ch 15 below.
3 Though in a convertible the issuer in certain circumstances may in effect force a conversion, see p 256 below.

of the international capital markets, whereas bonds which are convertible into other bonds, and warrants conferring rights to subscribe bonds are infrequently issued in practice; and secondly, because such Eurobond issues create special legal considerations.

II EQUITY CONVERTIBLES

1 Financial features of equity convertibles

It is necessary to discuss the financial characteristics of an equity convertible bond prior to considering the legal structure and legal issues in respect of such bonds.

The main characteristics are as follows:

(a) Low coupon and conversion privilege An equity convertible bond is usually issued with a low 'coupon'. This means that the rate of interest payable on the convertible is lower than that payable on a comparable 'straight' bond of the same issuer in the same currency. An investor who purchases such a bond is prepared to accept a lower interest rate in consideration of the option contained in the bond to convert the bond into the issuer's (or guarantor's) equity. This right is called the 'conversion privilege' or conversion option and is regarded as the 'sweetener' which induces the investor to purchase a bond paying a coupon lower than market rates. The attractiveness to an investor of the convertible feature is dependent on investor perception that the value of the shares into which the bond may be converted will rise due to the future commercial and financial performance of the corporate entity in question, and the general upward trend of share values in the stock markets where the shares are traded. The coupon or interest rate payable on the bond is, however, fixed at a premium over the current dividend yield of the underlying shares so as to make the convertible an attractive investment when compared with purchasing the underlying equity.

(b) Conversion price and conversion premium The price at which the convertible bondholder may subscribe to shares in the issuer or guarantor (called the 'conversion price') is usually a price which is higher than the prevailing market price for the shares at the date of the bond issue. This 'conversion premium' is usually around 5% to 15% above current share value.[4]

Thus, for instance, ABC Corpn may issue a convertible bond in London at a time when its stock price in Tokyo may be yen 2,000. The conversion price will be fixed at around yen 2,100 to 2,300. This premium reflects the expectation that stock prices will rise.

(c) Currency conversion Where the convertible bond is also a currency convertible the conversion price will usually be linked to the prevailing exchange rate in respect of the currency of the bond and the currency of

---

[4] See Fisher *International Bonds* p 15. Katzin in 'Financial and Legal Problems in the use of Convertible Securities' Business Lawyer, January 1969, says that in the US domestic market the premium was around 10% to 20%; McCormick and Creamer, *Hybrid Corporate Securities* (Sweet and Maxwell) at p 47 place the premium between 5% and 25% in the international markets in London.

the equity. Thus if ABC Corpn issued Deutschmark denominated bonds, say in April 1988, there will an exchange rate of around US $1 = DM 1.88, so that the number of dollar shares which the holder of, say, a 5,000 DM denominated bond may obtain by exchange can be determined by dividing the face value of the bond by the exchange rate and then dividing the resulting figure by the conversion price.

(d) Conversion period The period during which a bondholder may exercise his conversion privilege usually commences at the end of the 40-day period after completion of distribution and continues until about a week prior to final redemption of the bonds.[5] In practice, however, a bondholder would not wish to convert his bond into equity until the market price of the shares has exceeded the conversion price specified in the bond instrument, otherwise he would be subscribing shares at a price higher than the market price of the shares.

(e) Call option A 'call option' is usually conferred on the issuer in convertible bonds, giving it a right to redeem the bonds prior to the final maturity date.[6] An issuer would usually wish to redeem if interest rates moved significantly below the rate payable on the convertible.

Such a right of redemption is also a mechanism whereby an issuer can force the bondholder to convert and exercise the conversion privilege, since the redemption of the bonds results in the extinction of the conversion privilege.[7] Ideally the issuer would wish bondholders to convert soon after the market price for the issuer's ordinary shares or conversion stock is at a level above the conversion price specified in the bond instrument.

2 Attractions of convertibles

i To issuers

(a) A convertible offers the issuer an opportunity to raise capital at interest rates lower than those prevailing in the markets for borrowers such as the issuer.[8] The conversion privilege is the 'sweetener' to the investor which enables the issuer to raise capital at such rates.

(b) The second reason is that the issuer obtains 'deferred equity financing'.[9] The underlying logic of this is as follows: the management of the issuer wishes to raise equity capital but considers that the market price for the issuer's equity is too low; consequently, convertible bonds are issued with a conversion price which management feels is the share price which accurately reflects the value of corporate assets and per-

---

5 See Wood 'International Convertible Bond Issues' [1986] 2 JIBL 69 who refers to a period ending a fortnight prior to final redemption.
6 See p 257 below on call protection for the bondholder.
7 See p 256 below.
8 See Pilcher *Raising Capital with Convertible Securities* (1955) pp 84–85, but see Klein 'The Convertible Bond: A Peculiar Package' 123 Univ of Pennsylvania LR 547.
9 See American Bar Foundation, Corporate Debt Financing Project, Commentaries on Model Indenture Provisions 524 (1971).

formance.[10] In effect this enables management to place stock at a premium above current market price. Looked at differently, it enables management to raise capital by issuing 10% to 15% fewer shares (depending on the percentage of the conversion premium) than the company would otherwise have to issue at the share price prevailing at the time of the bond issue.

(c) It is said that the cost in relation to the capital raised is lower in a convertible bond financing than in respect of a public share issue.[11]

(d) A convertible enables a company to place its equity in markets where its name is not well known.

(e) Convertibles can also be used to form part of the consideration offered in connection with 'takeover' bids. The shareholders in the target company may find the higher return on the debt instrument an added attraction to accept the offer of the bidder.[12]

ii *To investors*

The value to investors of convertibles may be difficult to analyse comprehensively,[13] but the attraction to an investor of an equity convertible bond[14] is that the investor has the advantage of a debt security containing a conversion option which permits him to take advantage of the rise in the issuer's share price, while at the same time it offers him the security of a debt instrument which guarantees payment of regular interest and return of principal, in the event that the share price does not rise sufficiently to justify conversion.

The bondholder's investment in a fixed rate convertible bond is also protected against an upward movement in interest rates which would usually depress bond value, due to the equity cushion in the form of the conversion privilege. Even if interest rates rise well above the rate payable on the convertible, the value of a convertible may not fall or fall as much as ordinary bonds, because investors would regard the convertible feature as adequate compensation for lower interest rates. The investor stands to lose only where interest rates rise well above the convertible coupon and at the same time the stock price of the issuer does not rise above the conversion price. Of course, the optimal gain to an investor would occur if the issuer's stock price rises well above the conversion price specified in the bond at a time prior to final redemption. A windfall of this nature is, however, unlikely because, as pointed out earlier, the convertible usually contains a call option which entitles the issuer to redeem the bond about the time that the share

---

10 See, however, Klein's rejection of this analysis in 'The Convertible Bond: A Peculiar Package' referred to in fn 8, p 254.
11 See Loosemore p 129 and Bratton *Economics and Jurisprudence of Convertible Bonds* p 673.
12 See Katzin, fn 4 above, 360 and also McCormick and Creamer, fn 4 above, p 47.
13 See Brennan and Schwartz 'Analysing Convertible Bonds' (1980) 15 Jo of Financial and Quantitative Analysis 907; and Brennan and Schwartz 'Convertible Bonds: Valuation Operational Strategies for Call and Conversion' (1977) 32 Jo of Finance 1699, but see Klein's response in 'The Convertible Bond: A Peculiar Package' (see fn 8 above).
14 See Katzin 'Convertibles – The Two-Way Play' in *The Strategy of Corporate Financing* (1971) pp 260, 271.

price begins to move above the conversion price. Klein[15] has also pointed out that another reason is that some institutional investors who are prohibited from investing in options and warrants on common stock may nevertheless invest in convertibles of the same corporation because a convertible is regarded as a bond and not an option or warrant, though it does in fact contain an option to purchase equity.[16]

3 The conversion privilege

i Conflicting objectives of issuer and bondholder

It will be seen from the above that there are a number of potential conflicts of objectives between an investor who wishes to purchase a convertible bond and the issuer of such a bond. It will also be seen that the conflict of objectives revolves around the 'conversion privilege' or conversion option, which is the raison d'être for the purchase of a convertible.

The investor's objective is to preserve and maximise the value of the conversion privilege and he has an interest in deterring any action by the issuer which would devalue or destroy that privilege. The issuer is not concerned with the value of the conversion privilege after the bonds have been placed with investors, although he has an interest as regards the timing of the conversion.

The first area of potential conflict between issuer and bond investor concerns the timing of the conversion. In a rising market for the underlying shares the investor would like to postpone conversion as long as possible to a point just prior to final maturity of the bond. This would enable the investor to maximise the gain on the exchange of the bond for shares. From the issuer's viewpoint the sooner he can compel the bondholders to convert the bonds into the underlying shares the more advantageous it is for him. An issuer may also wish to redeem the convertibles to prevent a continuing equity 'overhang', ie the contingent obligation to issue further equity on conversion.

The timing conflict is resolved by conferring on the issuer a call option or early redemption option, in respect of the convertible, which enables him to redeem all or some of the bonds from time to time prior to maturity during a specified period in the life of the bond. This call option in effect enables the issuer to force the convertible bondholder to exercise his conversion option. This is because on the exercise of the issuer's option of redemption prior to conversion, the bond instrument must by its terms be tendered by the holder to the issuer for payment and cannot thereafter be converted by the bondholder. If the bondholder wishes to derive any benefit from the conversion privilege he must exercise the conversion option prior to redemption of the bonds by the issuer. Nevertheless, the conversion privilege will be of little value to the bondholder if the redemption option can be exercised by the issuer prior to a time at which the market price of the shares exceeds the conversion price for the underlying shares.

---

15 Fn 8, above.
16 This seems to arise from regulations or law similar to the 'Prudent Investor' rule in US law. See 'The Regulation of Risky Investments' (1970) 83 Harvard LR 603.

Consequently, legal structures have been developed both in the US and the international markets which enable the issuer to force conversion, but which preserve the value of the conversion privilege. They are as follows.

First, an issuer is not permitted to make a call until at least three years after issue.[17] Alternatively, the issuer is prohibited from calling the bond until the average market price for the underlying shares over a given period exceeds the conversion price, usually by about 30% but sometimes by up to 50%. Such a provision is usually applicable in the three-year period immediately after issue of the bond.

Secondly, there is a 'call premium' payable by the issuer. This is an amount in excess of the principal or face value of the bond which must be paid by the issuer to the holder if the issuer exercises his call option. This premium is usually on a sliding scale, the premium being at its highest in the first year when call is permissible (that is, at the end of the three-year period), and diminishing as time lapses.

Thirdly, in any event an issuer must give notice of redemption to convertible bondholders. A notice period is usually a minimum of 45 days and not more than 60 days but this may vary in practice. This enables the bondholders to exercise the conversion option prior to the actual redemption of bonds after the call has been published.[18] The issuer is usually required to specify the conversion price and the current stock market price of the shares.

Fourthly, when the issuer exercises a call option by giving notice, bondholders will usually exercise their option to convert. In order to ensure that some bondholders may not be prejudiced by a failure to exercise their conversion option, trust deeds used in practice usually confer a power on trustees (within a certain number of days after the date for redemption) to subscribe shares on behalf of such bondholders. This power is operative only where the trustee is satisfied that such shares could be sold on the open market during the subscription period at a price which would exceed the principal and interest on the bonds. If the trustee decides to exercise this power, he is then under a duty to sell the shares which are allotted in respect of the unpresented bonds and credit the net proceeds to an account for the benefit of such bondholders. The paying agent for the issue is then required to distribute the proceeds pro rata to all bondholders who are entitled. The usual rule is that bondholders will be entitled to the proceeds if they present their bonds to the paying agent with all unmatured coupons. This clause is referred to as the 'widows and orphans' clause and is intended to protect the interests of those bondholders who may not be as vigilant as others in exercising their rights of conversion.

Such a clause is also of benefit to the issuer. The purpose of the exercise of the call option is to force bondholders to convert their bonds into the equity of the issuer (or guarantor), and is not meant to trigger the payment obligations of the issuer in respect of bonds which are being redeemed or called by the issuer. Consequently, it is undesirable from the issuer's

---

17 In the US the period seems to be two years, see Bratton *Economics and Jurisprudence of Convertible Bonds* p 678 citing a survey in the *New York Times* 6 March 1983; and see also Wood *Law and Practice of International Finance* (Clark Boardman ed) s 9.07(8).
18 Katzin in Business Lawyer, January 1969, at 366.

point of view if some recalcitrant bondholders refuse to convert and do not present bonds by the date fixed for redemption. This is because, while a bond cannot be converted under its terms after redemption date, the bond survives as a debt obligation of the issuer and must be redeemed by the issuer by payment in full of the principal value. This payment is of course undesirable from the issuer's point of view since it makes an unnecessary demand on its cash flow and available funds. This problem may be overcome by the so-called 'widows and orphans' clause.

ii The conversion privilege and corporate action of the issuer

The second aspect of conflict arises, on the one hand, from the issuer's need to retain complete freedom of corporate action and, on the other, from the desire of bondholders to preserve the value of the conversion option which may be adversely affected or 'diluted' or even completely destroyed by certain forms of corporate action. The forms of corporate action which may have this effect are numerous and vary with the corporate law to which the issuer is subject.

The principal forms are as follows.[19]

(a) Subdivision by a company of its shares into shares of smaller amounts.[20] In such a share division, the company splits or divides its shares originally worth, say, £10 into, say, two shares worth £5; now suppose a convertible bondholder had a right to convert his $5,000 bond at a conversion price of £15 per share at a currency ratio of £1 = $2, the bondholder's conversion privilege has been diluted because the value of the underlying shares has been halved, and consequently the bondholder's ability to convert at a profit has been diminished.[1]

(b) The issue of further shares by the issuer (or guarantor if the bonds are convertible into the guarantor's shares) An increase in the number of shares in the market would generally depress share values and thus prejudice the value of the conversion option.[2]

---

19 The power of a corporation to take certain forms of corporate action (as well as the true legal nature and effects of such corporate action) will be referred, if English law governs, to the law of the place of incorporation. See ch 2 above and *National Bank of Greece and Athens SA v Metliss* [1958] AC 509 and *Adams v National Bank of Greece SA* [1961] AC 255.
20 A company incorporated under the UK Companies Act 1985 with a share capital may do so by ordinary resolution if authorised by its articles to alter the memorandum of the company: see s 121 of the Companies Act 1985. In the US these are called 'stock splits'.
1 See, for instance, *Re Lissberger* 71 NYS 2d 585 (1947) aff'd 78 NYS 2d 199 (1948).
2 Under the provisions of ss 89–96 of the UK Companies Act 1985 such equity securities must usually be issued to existing shareholders. See, however, the exception in s 95. The position is similar under the laws of New York and most American states. See the New York Business Corporations Law s 622 and the comments of Hallows J in *Fuller v Krogh* 15 Wis 2d 412 1962 where he said: 'A pre-emptive right of a shareholder in a corporation is recognised so universally as to have become axiomatic in corporation law.' Although the doctrine of pre-emptive rights was not known to English common law, it has been known to American law at least since 1807 after *Gray v Portland Bank* 3 Mass 364 (1807). See Gower 'Some Contrasts between British and American Corporation Law' 69 Harvard LR 1369 (1956).

(c) Issue of shares at a price below the conversion price For similar reasons as in (b) above there is a dilution of the value of the conversion privilege.[3]

(d) The issue of other convertible bonds with a lower conversion price than the conversion price of the issue in question

(e) Unusually large dividend distributions or other distribution of corporate assets[4] In the case of a UK incorporated company, dividends can be made only out of profits under s 263(1) of the Companies Act 1985. This, however, does not prevent a UK incorporated company from declaring dividends out of its accumulated realised profit and such action can dilute the conversion privilege. In the case of a UK public company, under s 264 of the Companies Act 1985 such a dividend cannot be distributed unless, first, the amount of its net assets is not less than the aggregate of its called-up share capital plus its undistributable reserves, and secondly, provided that the distribution does not reduce the amount of net assets to an amount less than the stated aggregate. The position is similar in the US.[5]

(f) The merger of the corporate entity which issued the convertibles, with another corporate entity This could also completely destroy the value of the conversion privilege. The reason is that depending on the structure, nature and effect of the merger permissible under the law of the country in which the issuer is incorporated[6] the market for the underlying shares of the issuer might cease to exist.[7] Three types of transactions referred to as mergersmay be considered here.

First, suppose there is a merger whereby the issuer of the convertibles, company A, and another company, B, transfer all their assets and liabilities to company C; companies A and B are then liquidated and the shareholders in companies A and B are given shares in company C. If convertible bondholders of company A have not converted prior to the merger (for instance, because the share price of company A was below the conversion price), what is the legal position of the conversion privilege? Given the international nature of the Eurobond market, the issuer is more than likely to be a foreign incorporated entity rather than a company incorporated in the UK under the Companies Acts. Consequently, the nature and effect of the merger will be

---

3   See, however, Professor Ratner in 33 Univ of Chicago LR who argues persuasively that this event has no dilutory effect.
4   See on this: Berle 'Corporate Devices for Diluting Stock Participations' 31 Columbia LR 1239 (1931); Hills 'Convertible Securities Legal Aspects and Draftsmanship' 79 California LR (1930); Kaplan 'Piercing the Corporate Boilerplate: Anti-Dilution Clauses in Convertible Securities' 33 Univ of Chicago LR (1965); Klein 'The Convertible Bond: A Peculiar Package' 123 Univ of Pennsylvania LR 547, 565 argues that even ordinary dividend policy may have this effect.
5   See the Model Business Corporations Act s 40 and s 2; Ballantine and Hills 'Corporate Capital and Restrictions upon Dividends under Modern Corporations Laws' 23 California LR 229 (1935); see also the Virginia Corporations Law of 1956 s 43 which prohibited the so-called 'nimble dividend', ie the payment of dividends from current earnings while there is no accrued revenue surplus.
6   See on applicable law the discussion at ch 2 above and *National Bank of Greece and Athens SA v Metliss* [1958] AC 509, HL.
7   Since the typical issuer of Eurobonds is a non-UK entity there seems to be little value in considering UK law on mergers and restructuring of corporate entities.

determined by an English court by reference to the law of incorporation of the old corporate entity as well as the new entity. This was the conclusion of the House of Lords in the two cases concerning Greek bonds: *National Bank of Greece and Athens SA v Metliss*[8] and *Adams v National Bank of Greece and Athens SA*.[9] It follows therefore that whether company C is an universal successor or not is governed by the relevant foreign law. The liability in respect of the bonds of company C as the universal successor, would be governed by the proper law of the bond instruments, which would be English law in the practice of the international markets.

Since company A no longer exists, one answer is that the conversion privilege contained in the bond instrument is destroyed by supervening impossibility and frustration. The second answer is that company C is in breach of the obligation contained in the bond to the convertible bondholder and is under a duty to mitigate damages by offering the convertible bondholder an opportunity to convert the bonds into the shares of the new company C.

In a second type of merger, company A transfers all its assets and liabilities to another company, B, the shareholders of company A exchange their shares for shares or other securities in company B, and then company A is dissolved. Once again, if the market price of company A shares (at the time of the merger) was below the conversion price specified in the convertible and consequently bondholders did not wish to convert, they may lose their conversion privilege in consequence of the merger.[10]

The third type of transaction regarded as a merger is where company A transfers all its assets (but not its liabilities) to company B in consideration of shares in company B or cash. This is really not a merger of two companies but an asset transfer. In this situation, company A is legally capable of giving effect to the conversion but the conversion privilege will be of little value. This is due to the fact that the transaction would probably cause downward pressure on the market price of the shares of company A, and consequently make it unattractive for convertible bondholders to convert. It may even be the case that the market price of the shares of company A would never reach conversion price. Consequently, the convertible bondholders' conversion right is practically valueless.

Another possibility, given the international dimension of the Eurobond market, is that an issuer of convertible bonds could be merged or amalgamated with another entity by a specific decree or legislation of the government of the country of its incorporation. The decree could itself destroy the conversion privilege but permit the bonds as straight debt securities to survive as obligations into the new merged entity. The rights of a convertible bondholder, in such a case, assuming the bonds are governed by English law, depend largely on how one classifies the issue. If the rights of the bondholders including the rights of conversion are classified as matters for the proper law of the contract, the right survives. This was the analysis of the

---

8 [1958] AC 509, HL.
9 [1961] AC 255.
10 See also the form of merger which gave rise to actions by convertible bondholders in the US case of *Gardner and Florence Call Cowles Fund v Empire Inc* 589 F Supp 669 (1984).

House of Lords in the second of the two Greek bond cases, *Adams v National Bank of Greece and Athens SA*.[11] If the issue is classified as one relating to the nature of the merger or amalgamation, then the result is that the bonds survive but company C need not permit conversion and the conversion rights are destroyed. It is still arguable on the basis of Lord Denning's judgement in *Adams'* case that even if the survival of the conversion right was a matter for the law governing the merger, an English court would not recognise the law governing the merger or amalgamation unless it gave effect to universal succession rather than selective succession.[12]

(g) The takeover of the issuer[13] (or guarantor) by a hostile takeover bid (in UK practice) or tender offer (in US practice). This would have the result that the conversion right would be destroyed for all practical purposes. The reason is that after the takeover becomes effective, there will be no market in the shares of the issuer (which would usually have become a subsidiary of the bidder under the company law of most developed countries).[14] In conse-quence, it is also more than likely that the shares will cease to be listed on major stock exchanges and this would in effect mean the absence of a public market for the shares where price appreciation can occur. The consequence of this would be that while the convertible bondholders would have a theoretical legal right to convert, this right will be of little value because a bondholder converting at the conversion price has little chance of recovering the price paid by a sale of the shares issued.[15]

Given this vulnerability to dilution and destruction the question arises whether the conversion privilege is accorded any special protection at law. There does not seem to be authority in the common law of England which confers a special status to a convertible bondholder and he is treated in the same way as a holder of a straight bond. Consequently, unless special protection is afforded under the terms of the bond instrument and the trust deed[16] the convertible bondholder is exposed to the dilution or destruction of the value of the conversion option or privilege.

Academic writers in the US such as Bratton[17] have criticised the classification as debt of convertible bonds, and have argued that there ought to be recognition of their hybrid nature as quasi-equity, and consequently that convertible bondholders must be afforded better protection on the basis that they are holders of quasi-equity. The US courts have also been

---

11 Fn 9, above.
12 See [1961] AC 255 at 289.
13 A 'takeover offer' is defined in s 428 of the UK Companies Act 1985 (inserted by the FSA 1986 s 172(1) and Sch 12) as 'an offer to acquire all the shares, or all the shares of any class or classes, in a company, (other than shares which at the date of the offer are already held by the offeror), being an offer on terms which are the same in relation to all the shares to which the offer relates or, where those shares include shares of different classes, in relation to all the shares of each class'; cf the definition of 'takeover offer' in s 14 of the Company Securities (Insider Dealing) Act 1985.
14 In the UK, see the Companies Act 1985 ss 736 and 736A (substituted by the Companies Act 1989 s 144(1)) which defines 'subsidiary', 'wholly-owned subsidiary' and 'holding company'.
15 See the US case of *Kessler v General Cable Corpn* App 155, Cal Rptr 94, especially at 98.
16 See chs 11 and 13 on trust deeds.
17 Economics and Jurisprudence of Convertible Bonds.

pressed with the argument that convertible bondholders are owed fiduciary duties by corporate management and further that corporate management is under fiduciary duties to preserve the conversion privilege and not dilute or destroy it by corporate action. Although these arguments found favour in a few US cases,[18] they were decisively rejected in later US cases such as *Broad v Rockwell International Corpn*,[19] *Harff v Kerkorian*[20] and *Kessler v General Cable Corpn*.[1]

The use of such fiduciary concepts to protect convertible bondholders would in any event be possible only in jurisdictions adopting English common law.

4 Protecting the conversion privilege

Given the fragile nature of the conversion privilege, protection needs to be afforded through specific contractual provisions in the bond instrument and trust deed.

In *Broad v Rockwell International Corpn*[2] the full court of the US Court of Appeal, Fifth Circuit, after a full review concluded that there were in fact three contractual techniques which can be used in practice to guard against the conversion privilege being diluted or destroyed.

(a) Outright prohibition of certain types of voluntary conduct which would dilute or destroy the conversion privilege, eg an absolute prohibition on mergers. This approach, as the court observed, erodes flexibility in corporate management and, consequently, issuers resist the imposition of such clauses in practice. It may also be the case that under the law of the place of incorporation a fetter on corporate power by such contractual provisions is void.

(b) Adjustment of the conversion price in the event of certain types of corporate conduct which dilute the market value of the underlying equity and the conversion privilege. The type of event which can be covered by this type of clause includes rights issues or stock splits (division of shares). However, this type of clause cannot protect against complete destruction of the conversion privilege by a merger of the issuer where the ordinary shares or common stock of the issuer cease to exist altogether.[3]

(c) Requirements as to notice to convertible bondholders which would enable them to exercise the conversion privilege prior to the occurrence of a particular event such as a merger or reconstruction of a company.

---

18 See *Van Gemert v Boeing Co* 520 F2d 1373 (2nd Cir) cert denied 423 US 947 (1975); see also two cases concerning convertible stock: *Zahn v Transamerica Corpn* 162 F2d 36 (3rd Cir 1947) and *Speed v Transamerica Corpn* 235 F2d 369 (3rd Cir 1956).
19 454 US 965 (1981).
20 324 A2d 215 (Del Ch 1974) rev'd 347 A2d 133 (Del 1975).
1 155 Cal Rptr 94, 103 US Court of Appeals 2nd Cir; see also *Simons v Cogan* 542 A2d 785 (Del Ch 1987) and *Gardner and Florence Call Cowles Fund v Empire Inc* 589 F Supp 669 (1984) especially Allen J at 786.
2 642 F2d 929 (1981).
3 See *Broad v Rockwell* itself, above, at 945 and American Bar Foundation Commentaries on Indentures (1971) at 528.

The two latter techniques are used widely in international issues in the London market as well as in the US domestic market.[4]

These practical techniques are discussed below.

i *Adjustment of conversion price*

The technique is that express clauses require the conversion price to be adjusted on the occurrence of certain events so that the value of the privilege of conversion is not diminished. The price adjustment is made effective as of the record date in respect of the event triggering the price adjustment. The adjustment is made on the basis of a mathematical formula, based on either the so-called 'conversion price' formula or 'market price' formula. In the international markets the market price formula is more common.[5]

No attempt is made here to explain in detail the financial mechanics or the precise mathematical formulae used to calculate the adjustment to the conversion price.[6] An adjustment based on the market price formula occurs whenever share issues are made by the issuer below the current market price of its shares, regardless of whether the issue is made above or below the conversion price, whereas the 'conversion price' formula seeks to adjust the conversion price whenever a share issue is made below the conversion price.

The conversion price is to be adjusted usually on the occurrence of each one of the following events:

(a) The issue of ordinary shares wholly for cash at less than the current market price for a unit of the issuer's ordinary shares on the dealing day preceding the announcement of the share issue. A dealing day is usually defined as being a day on which a particular stock exchange is open for business. This provision usually does not apply to an issue of shares occurring on conversion. Rights issues are also not subject to this provision and are dealt with separately since a different price adjustment is usually necessary. Employee share issues under an employee share scheme are also generally excepted.

(b) Issues of securities, including bonds and preferred shares, either of which is convertible into the ordinary shares of the company at a price which is less than the current market price for an ordinary share on the business day preceding the announcement of the issue.

(c) An issue of shares to the holders of ordinary shares of the issuer, by way of a capitalisation issue, ie by a distribution of accrued profits to shareholders.

(d) An issue of shares in lieu of a cash dividend for the current financial year of the issuer.

---

4 See *Broad v Rockwell International*, above as regards US practice.
5 This seems to be the case in the US domestic market also according to a survey of convertible bond issues effected between October 1981 and October 1982. See Bratton, loc cit, p 261 fn 17.
6 See the discussion in Kaplan 'Piercing the Corporate Boilerplate: Anti-dilution Clauses in Convertible Securities' 33 Univ of Chicago LR 1 (1965); and Ratner 'Dilution and Anti-dilution: A Reply to Professor Kaplan' in the same issue of the Chicago LR at 494.

(e) A rights issue made to ordinary shareholders of the company.[7]
(f) An issue of share options or warrants to subscribe shares or other subscription rights to ordinary shareholders, at a price less than the current market price for the issuer's shares on the business day preceding the announcement of the terms of the issue.
(g) The issue of any securities to ordinary shareholders by way of rights, or the grant of options or warrants to subscribe for or purchase any securities by way of rights.
(h) Any alteration in the nominal value of the ordinary shares by virtue of a consolidation or subdivision (ie a stock split).
(i) Any capital distribution to ordinary shareholders of the company other than by way of a capitalisation issue.
(j) Any alteration or modification of rights of conversion or exchange or subscription attaching to any securities issued by the issuer, which results in the conversion (or exchange or subscription) price being less than the market price of the ordinary shares of the issuer on the last dealing day preceding the date of announcement of the alteration or modification.

It must be emphasised that the nature and number of events on which the conversion price requires adjustment depends entirely on the nature of company law in the jurisdiction in which the issuer (or other entity into whose shares the bonds may be converted) is incorporated.[8] The types of corporate conduct which are permissible under that law must necessarily determine the anti-dilution provisions and in some cases it may be that anti-dilution protection is not as wide as under Anglo-American systems.

ii *Notice provisions*

While the above clauses offer some protection against dilution, conversion price adjustments do not offer any protection against takeovers, mergers, amalgamations and reconstructions.

The technique adopted here is to require the issuer to give specific notice to convertible bondholders after the public announcement of an impending takeover,[9] merger, amalgamation or reconstruction, so that convertible bondholders may exercise their conversion option, if they so wish. The clauses are structured so that in the event of an occurrence similar to a UK takeover or a US tender offer, bondholders are given notice during the offer period. Notification prior to the announcement of such an event may breach provisions in applicable insider dealing laws such as the UK's Company Securities (Insider Dealing) Act 1985 and the comparable rules in the US developed under r 10b-5 of the US Securities Exchange Act 1934.

In the case of an occurrence similar to a takeover offer or tender offer, notice provisions are usually linked to an obligation on the part of the issuer of the convertible to procure that a like offer is extended to the holder of any ordinary shares allotted or issued to convertible bondholders who exercise their conversion rights during the period of such offer. This obli-

---

7 In the case of UK incorporated companies see also ss 89–96 of the Companies Act 1985.
8 See the discussion on applicable law in Part I ch 1, above.
9 For the definition in UK law see s 428 of the Companies Act 1985 and p 261 fn 13 above.

gation would be owed primarily to the trustee of the bond issue if there is a trust deed and would in practice be contained in the trust deed.

In the case of amalgamations, mergers and reconstructions,[10] which result in the issuer ceasing to exist as an entity, the notice provisions are linked to a clause which imposes on the issuer an obligation to procure that the corporation which results or survives from the merger executes legal instruments or documents legally necessary to ensure that each convertible bondholder is not prejudiced by the merger, amalgamation or reconstruction. This is achieved by requiring the issuer to ensure that convertible bondholders shall have rights of convertibility into the amount of shares or other securities or property which a convertible bondholder would have received had he converted prior to the amalgamation, merger or reconstruction.

It will be clear that these provisions are of benefit to the convertible bondholder only when the market price of the shares of the issuer as at the date of the announcement of the takeover, amalgamation or merger is at or above the conversion price. If the market price is below the conversion price the consequences to the convertible bondholder would be highly disadvantageous even with the benefit of the clauses. The facts of the US case of *Broad v Rockwell International Corpn*[11] are a classic illustration of the exposure of the convertible bondholder even with the benefit of these clauses. In that case Collins, a radio company incorporated in the State of Iowa, issued $40m aggregate principal amount of convertible bonds maturing in 1987 at a low coupon rate. Collins' stock was trading around $60 per share at the time of the issue, and the conversion price of the bonds was fixed at $72.50 per share. In 1971, however, the share price had fallen to $21 per share and had on occasion fallen to $9.75 per share during that year. Collins then entered into an agreement with Rockwell International Corporation whereby Rockwell invested $35 million in Collins in return for preferred loan stock in Collins which was convertible into common stock and which gave Rockwell management control of the company. Two years later Rockwell made a tender offer for Collins' common stock at $25 per share tendered. Rockwell were able to purchase 75% of Collins common stock on this transaction. Rockwell then proposed that Collins be merged so that each holder of the remaining common stock would receive $25 per share and this was approved by the Board of Collins and by two-thirds of Collins stockholders as required by Iowa law and Collins was merged with Rockwell in consequence. The Collins trust deed in respect of certain convertible bonds provided that:[12]

> 'In case of any consolidation of [Collins] with or merger of [Collins] into any other corporation [Collins] or the corporation formed by such consolidation into which [Collins] shall have been merged shall execute and deliver to the [Trust Company] a supplemental indenture providing that the holder of each Debenture then outstanding shall have the right (until the expiration of the conversion right of such Debenture) to convert such Debenture into the kind and amount of shares of stock and other securities and property receivable

---

10 See pp 259–261 above for a description of the different types of transaction commonly called a 'merger'.
11 See p 262 above.
12 642 F2d 929 at 949.

upon such consolidation [or] merger ...by a holder of the number of shares of common stock of [Collins] into which such Debentures might have been converted immediately prior to such consolidation or merger....'

The notice provisions were of little value to the convertible bondholder in this case because there was little purpose in converting the bonds either on the tender offer or at the time of the proposed merger since the bondholder would have converted at $72.50 but could only sell to Rockwell at $25. Furthermore, even if the issuer of the convertible had procured the issue of the number of shares or other securities to convertible bondholders (which they would have been entitled to if they had converted prior to the takeover or merger) the convertible bondholders would nevertheless have suffered a loss.[13] The court was also of the opinion that no rule of law required that the convertible bondholders be offered shares in the corporation into which Collins had been merged. They were entitled only to such shares, cash or other property which the trust deed provided for.

It is submitted that the position would be the same in English law. It would be impossible under English law by appropriate clauses in a convertible bond instrument or trust deed to impose direct obligations on a bidder in a takeover offer for the issuer of the convertible, which would oblige the bidder to issue its shares to convertible bondholders in the target company, due to the absence of contractual privity. For this reason the bond instrument and the trust deed impose obligations only on the issuer and the trustee when the issuer is the subject of a takeover bid.

iii *Other cases*

There may, however, be many corporate devices which dilute the conversion privilege which are not caught by the anti-dilution provisions or by the notice provisions. The two most difficult forms to control are, first, ordinary dividend policy and, secondly, the so-called 'spin-off' of the assets of subsidiaries. Ordinary payments of dividends which are within the statutory constraints placed on a company by the law of the issuer's incorporation[14] may nevertheless erode the conversion privilege.[15] If dividend policy is such that, after the issue of the convertible, the rate of dividend payments is increased so that the conversion privilege is diluted due to a much slower increase in the appreciation of the market value of the underlying shares, the result is similar to a subdivision of shares (or stock split). Provisions usually seen in practice in bond instruments and trust deeds in the international markets do not seek to control this type of dilution.

The method of control would be a clause which restricts dividend payments to a particular percentage of net corporate revenues and an adjustment of

---

13 In the *Rockwell* case the convertible bondholders were lawfully offered only $25 per share on conversion.
14 Eg limits on the distribution of the accrued profits of a company found in the UK Companies Act 1985 ss 263 and 264. See p 259 above.
15 See Klein (p 254, fn 8) p 566.

the conversion price on the occurrence of such an event. Courts in the US applying ordinary English common law principles have refused to interfere with corporate dividend policy in the absence of express clauses in the bond instrument or trust deed and in the absence of fraud. Thus, in the leading case of *Harff v Kerkorian*[16] the court refused to interfere at the instance of convertible bondholders even though the cash dividend was unusually large in the context of dividend policy in the previous years. The court's intervention was sought on the basis of a breach of fiduciary duty, given the absence of any fraud or any contractual provision controlling dividend policy. Some commentators have nevertheless pointed out that the *Harff* ruling does not rule out interpreting the concept of 'fraud' as meaning a duty of good faith towards convertible bondholders.[17] Such an interpretation would give the courts a power to intervene on behalf of convertible bondholders in the face of acceleration in the size and/or frequency of dividend distributions.

Similarly, the transfer of assets of the issuer and/or its subsidiaries could virtually destroy the value of the conversion privilege. The transfer may be made for cash or shares in the purchaser company. In either event the value of the issuer's shares is likely to diminish or at least not increase. This type of occurrence is usually the result of corporate restructuring or is a prelude to a merger. The problem may be handled by a clause which requires that, if a substantial asset transfer is effected by the issuer of convertibles, the holder of convertibles will be given shares or other property which a bondholder would have received, had he converted prior to the asset sale. Alternatively, a clause may be inserted requiring the issuer to procure that the ability is conferred on the convertible bondholder to convert into the common stock or ordinary shares of the company purchasing the issuer's assets.

The first form of clause is of little use except in cases where the ordinary shareholders of the issuer are given rights to convert their shareholdings into the shares of the purchasing company. If this does not occur the convertible bondholder is without remedy. In the second type of case it seems that the bondholder has protection only where the issuer who sells off assets receives a shareholding in the purchasing corporation as consideration. In the US case of *BSF Co v Philadelphia National Bank*[18] the issuer of convertibles transferred 75% of all its assets for cash. The trust indenture contained the usual provision that the convertible bondholder would be entitled to common stock in the corporation which made substantial purchases of the issuer's assets. The court held that the clause did not apply in the event of a cash transfer but applied only where stock of the purchaser was exchanged for assets in the seller. The court's reasoning was influenced by the notion that the convertible bondholders could still convert the bonds into the stock of the issuer. This, however, ignores the dilutory effect of such a substantial asset transfer for a cash consideration, since cash is a non-performing asset in a company's balance sheet and does not facilitate stock appreciation by profit generation.

---

16 324 A2d 215 (Del Ch 1974) rev'd 347 A2d 133 (Del 1975).
17 See Bratton (p 261 fn 17) p 695 n 113.
18 42 Del Ch 106, 204 A2d 746 (Sup Ct 1964).

iv *Additional notice provisions*

Two other types of notice are usually required to be given for the benefit of convertible bondholders. These are in practice required by the trust deed to be given to the trustee.

The first is one which requires the issuer (or the guarantor as the case may be) to give notice to the trustee by issuing a certificate stating that a particular event which gives rise to the adjustment has occurred; the date on which such adjustment takes effect; and any other information required by the trustee. In addition, the issuer (or the guarantor) is required within a specified time (usually 14 days) after the notice is given to the trustee to give a second notice through a financial newspaper[19] to the bondholders informing them of the event and the adjustment of the conversion price.

This covenant, however, does not protect the conversion rights of a bondholder who may have exercised his conversion option during the 14-day period prior to notice being given to bondholders. The trustee may be under a fiduciary obligation to notify bondholders immediately so that some bondholders would not expose themselves to incurring losses by converting their bonds prior to the adjustment date.[20] This need for advance notice to bondholders is dealt with in a separate clause, but only in respect of certain adjustment events.

Secondly, certain types of events giving rise to adjustments of the conversion price require the issuer (or the guarantor as the case may be) to give notice to the bondholders through a publication in a specified financial newspaper[1] advising them of the date on which the adjustment will take effect and furthermore as to the effect of exercising the conversion right prior to that date. This type of notice is usually required in the event of:

(a) an issue of shares for cash (other than shares issued on conversion of the bonds in question); or
(b) an issue of convertibles or warrants for cash where the conversion or subscription price is less than the current market price for the underlying shares prevailing at the time of issue; or
(c) where the conversion or subscription price of securities already in issue is altered so that it is less than the market price for the underlying shares prevailing at the time of the alteration; or
(d) rights issues or the issue of any other securities (eg warrants to subscribe) to holders of ordinary shares of the issuer, is made at a subscription price below current market price of the shares.

Considered from the point of view of a vigilant bondholder this type of clause is extremely useful. It provides additional protection to that provided by a notice given to the trustee, since the sooner a convertible bondholder becomes aware of the probability of an adjustment in the conversion price, the more likely it will be that he will refrain from exercising his conversion right prior to such an adjustment. In many instances, for example, where a capitalisation issue is contemplated or where a capital distribution is contemplated, the first notice must be given to the trustee, and it is only after

---

19 Usually at least the *Financial Times*.
20 See ch 13 above on the obligations of bond trustees.
1   Usually the *Financial Times*.

some 14 days thereafter that convertible bondholders are required to be notified.

v *Other protective mechanisms*

(a) Distributions to shareholders prior to conversion – equal rights Where distributions are made to shareholders by way of capitalisation issues or capital distributions or where a rights issue or securities issue by way of rights is made to existing shareholders, the question arises whether bondholders who convert immediately prior to such events would be given the same rights to receive such distributions. As a matter of strict law since they are not shareholders as of the record date of the distribution they would not receive the benefit of the distribution.

However, provision is usually made in the trust deed to permit bondholders who exercise their conversion rights immediately after the record date for such distribution or issue to have the same rights to the distribution or issue possessed by existing shareholders. In such an event, while no adjustment to the conversion price is to be made, the convertible bondholder acquires rights to the distribution or issue which will be commensurate with the amount of shares he would have received if an adjustment had been made to the conversion price immediately after the record date of the distribution. The converting bondholder does not, however, get the additional benefit which would accrue from a conversion price adjustment.

(b) Acceleration notices What happens where an event of default occurs and the bonds become due and payable or are declared to be so by a trustee? Quite clearly, if as a result of the events causing the default the shares to which the conversion right relates are not of much value, a bondholder would have no interest in conversion. However, there may be many cases where the bonds could be declared immediately due and payable by a trustee on the occurrence of an event of default, but nevertheless the shares of the company retain their value so that bondholders may prefer to convert rather than be repaid on the bonds.

Consequently, in cases of acceleration the trustee is required to give notice immediately to the bondholders. The bondholders are permitted a specified period (usually six weeks) from the date of the notice to exercise their conversion rights. Subject to this ability, acceleration by the trustee results in the termination of the conversion right by the express provisions of the convertible bond.

(c) Maintenance of listing It is also important to the value of the conversion right that the underlying shares and the shares which are issued on conversion are listed and remain listed on a stock exchange. In the absence of such a listing due to suspension or otherwise of the shares, the liquidity and tradability of the shares is seriously affected. Consequently, the issuer is required in the trust deed to covenant that it will maintain a listing for its existing shares, and obtain and maintain listing for the shares issued on conversion.

(d) Certain prohibitions The issuer of the bonds (or the guarantor, if the shares are to be issued by that entity) is usually required on conversion:

(a) not to make any reduction of share capital, share premium account or capital redemption reserve, which involves any repayment of money to ordinary shareholders, although repayment to holders of preferred shares is generally excepted;

(b) not to reduce the amount of uncalled capital;

unless in either case an adjustment to the conversion price is made;

(c) not to issue any securities by way of capitalisation of profits or reserves, except by the issue of ordinary shares to ordinary shareholders or by the issue of ordinary shares by way of a cash dividend and credited as fully paid out of distributable profits. The latter permission applies only if the amount payable for each ordinary share is not less than the current market price of each ordinary share on the day before the date of announcement of such dividend;

(d) not to modify in any way the rights attaching to the ordinary shares as such and, more importantly, not to create or issue any other class of equity share capital of the issuer (or guarantor as the case may be) carrying any right which is more favourable than the rights attaching to the ordinary shares of the issuer (or guarantor as the case may be);[2]

(e) to procure that no securities in issue shall be converted into equity share capital of the issuer (or the guarantor as the case may be) unless they were so convertible at issue;

(f) that at no time shall there be in issue ordinary shares of differing nominal values;[3]

(g) not to make any issue of shares or distribution of shares or take any other action if the effect would be that on the exercise of any conversion right the issuer would be required to issue ordinary shares at a discount.[4]

(e) Availability of authorised unissued capital It is important that the issuer of the bonds[5] should keep available for issue a number of ordinary shares out of its authorised but unissued capital.[6]

How much capital is authorised would depend on the constitutional docu-

---

2 Such a prohibition usually exempts from its ambit certain issues such as (a) the issue of any equity share capital pursuant to any employee share scheme; or (b) any consolidation or subdivision of the ordinary shares; or (c) any shares issued to give effect to the conversion.

3 This is to prevent confusion as to the type of share into which conversion can occur.

4 Such a clause is necessary in respect of a company incorporated under the UK Companies Acts because under the provisions of s 100(2) of the Companies Act 1985 if shares are issued on conversion at a discount the allottee becomes liable to pay the company an amount equal to the amount of the discount plus accrued interest.

5 Or its guarantor, whichever is to issue shares on conversion.

6 The Second Directive on Company Law of the EEC requires a public company to have a minimum authorised capital of 25,000 European Units of Account, but under UK law the Companies Act 1985 by s 118(1) requires an authorised minimum of £50,000. Under s 117(1) of the Companies Act 1985 a company registered as a public company on its original incorporation cannot do business or borrow unless the Registrar of Companies has certified that the minimum capital requirement has been met.

ments of the company. Authorised capital represents the maximum amount of shares which can be issued or allotted in respect of that company without alteration of its constitutional documents.[7] Each time shares are allotted or issued such allotment or issue uses up the amount of authorised capital of the company.[8]

Consequently it is important to ensure that the company issuing convertibles:

(a) has the ability under the law of its incorporation to allot all necessary shares on conversion without reaching or exceeding the ceiling on authorised capital; and
(b) maintains that ability during the conversion period.

Both these requirements need to be dealt with by appropriate clauses.

The first is usually dealt with in practice by a representation and warranty given to the manager in the subscription agreement, while the latter is dealt with by a warranty in the trust deed enforceable by the trustee.

If the issuer is unable to issue shares on conversion due to restrictions on the maximum authorised capital, the issuer would be liable in damages for breach of warranty under an English governing law. It needs to be recalled here that even if the issuer's obligation to issue shares on conversion is governed by English law, its capacity as a corporate entity to issue shares is a matter for the law of the place of incorporation of the issuer.[9] Consequently, it is arguable that the contractual obligation in an agreement governed by English law to issue shares is void if at the time of the issue of the convertible, the company did not have the legal capacity to issue shares in satisfaction of its conversion obligation. A representation as to capacity may, however, give rise to an action for damages or an estoppel under English law.[10]

However, if at the time it issued the convertibles the issuer did have the necessary constitutional power to issue all necessary shares on conversion, but had subsequently made it practically impossible to issue shares to convertible bond holders on conversion, the position is different. It would seem that since the inability is subsequent to the issue, the agreement cannot be void ab initio. However, since the inability is self-induced, English law would not regard the obligation as being terminated by impossibility or frustration.[11]

(f) Issues at discount Under English company law, shares may not be

---

7 See also s 118 of the UK Companies Act 1985 as to the authorised minimum capital for public companies.
8 Under English company law shares may be allotted but need not be paid up in full but in respect of a public company at least one-quarter of the nominal value and the whole of any share premium must be paid up. See s 101 of the Companies Act 1985.
9 See ch 2 above.
10 See the more detailed discussion in ch 2 above.
11 See *Joseph Constantine SS Line Ltd v Imperial Smelting Corpn Ltd* [1942] AC 154; *Maritime National Fish Ltd v Ocean Trawlers Ltd* [1935] AC 524; *The Eugenia* [1964] 2 QB 226.

issued at a discount from their nominal value.[12] This doctrine of capital maintenance is also embodied in the second EEC Directive on Company Law.[13] Consequently, it is important to ensure that the issue of convertibles does not contravene a rule of this type which is a part of the law of incorporation of most issuers in the international markets. In practice this rule creates no difficulty, since it is highly unlikely as a matter of commercial reality that a convertible bond will be issued with a conversion price below the nominal value of the shares.

(g) Pre-emption rights It is also important to ensure that the allotment of shares is not subject to the rules on pre-emption under the corporate law of the issuer comparable to s 89 of the UK Companies Act 1985. That section prohibits the allotment of 'equity securities' by a company unless it has made an offer of a proportion of those 'equity securities' to each ordinary shareholder in proportion to his shareholding. The proportion is calculated by reference to the nominal value of his shareholding in relation to the aggregate nominal value of shares in the company. A breach of a pre-emption rule under UK law would result in the company and its directors being liable to compensate any shareholder, to whom an offer should have been made, for any loss which such shareholder has sustained.[14] Under English company law, due to s 94, the issue of a convertible itself is caught by the rules on pre-emption, though not the subsequent allotment of shares pursuant to the exercise of the conversion right.[15]

It is necessary to ensure that the issue of the convertibles not caught by pre-emptive provisions in the corporate law of the issuer similar to those discussed above, either by ensuring that pre-emption rights do not apply because of the memorandum and articles of association or due to specific corporate resolutions. Consequently, the issuer is required to covenant in the trust deed that he is able to issue the shares free of pre-emptive rights. The reason is that if there is a breach of pre-emptive rights it is possible that either the convertible issue or the subsequent issue of shares could be terminated by injunctive action in the issuer's country of incorporation.

5 Conditions precedent to conversion and conversion procedure

Conversion can only be effected during the conversion period which, in accordance with provisions common in practice, commences 40 days from the completion of distribution (ie closing date), and ends seven days prior to final maturity.

Where an issuer seeks to redeem the bonds prior to maturity by exercising a right of redemption, he is required to give notice to bondholders. Conversion is usually permitted even after notice of redemption is given by the issuer to the bondholders.

Conversion is sometimes permitted of a part of the bond rather than the whole of the aggregate principal amount. However, if this flexibility

---

12 See s 100 of the Companies Act 1985 and *Ooregum Gold Mining Co of India v Roper* [1892] AC 125, HL.
13 OJ 1977 L26/1.
14 See the Companies Act 1985 s 92.
15 See s 94(3).

is conferred by the bond, it is usually restricted to conversion in multiples of US $1,000 for purposes of administrative convenience.

In practice, the procedure for conversion is that a bondholder is required to deposit the definitive bond together with an appropriate conversion notice duly signed at the office of the conversion agent, specially appointed for that purpose. The day subsequent to the deposit of these documents is usually made the conversion date in Eurobond market practice, and is important for purposes of interest on the bonds and dividends on shares.[16] The bond must be deposited with all unmatured coupons. If all such coupons are not delivered the conversion agent is given a right to demand a payment of an amount equal to the face value of such coupons.

The bondholder is given a right to claim reimbursement on delivery of the unmatured coupons within a specified time, usually six years. The conversion agent will then transmit share certificates to the converting bondholder within a given period of time.

The procedure for the issue of shares and the corporate formalities necessary will be governed by the law of incorporation of the entity in question.[17]

6 Right to interest and dividends on conversion

This is a difficult area in practice due to certain clauses which are usually found in convertibles. No interest is payable on the bond for the period from the last interest payment date on the bond to the date of conversion. Shares are allotted to the converting bondholder only 28 days after the conversion date. These shares are declared to be fungible and rank pari passu with other ordinary shares of the issuer. However, the shares being issued on conversion are not entitled to any dividends or distribution (eg shares issued by way of dividend) paid or made in respect of the period ending prior to the conversion date.

Secondly, it is also the case that the shares do not carry a right to dividends and distributions in respect of the financial period during which the conversion date falls, if an interest payment date has fallen in such financial period prior to the conversion date. The result achieved by such clauses has been criticised as disadvantageous to the convertible bondholder, and operates as follows.[18]

Suppose an interest payment date on a convertible bond falls on 30 March 1990. Suppose a dividend has been declared by the issuer on 1 March 1990 for the year January 1989 to January 1990. Suppose a bondholder converts his bonds as of 30 May, the conversion date.

He will not be entitled to

(a) interest between 30 March and 30 May on the bond;
(b) the dividend declared on 30 January;
(c) the dividend which may be declared for the year from 30 January 1990 to 30 January 1991.

Such clauses may further provide that even if a dividend or distribution is declared after the conversion date, but the record date for such a distribu-

---

16 See below (6).
17 See ch 2 above.
18 Such clauses have been attacked as a 'con-trick'. See 'The Conversion Con-trick' Corporate Finance, January 1988, at p 25.

tion is fixed by the company, on a date prior to the conversion date, the converting bondholder is not entitled to that dividend or distribution. It may be that pressure from institutional and other investors may result in issuers being forced to modify the clause.

III BONDS WITH EQUITY WARRANTS

1 The equity warrant

As observed earlier,[19] the equity warrant confers on the holder an option to subscribe the underlying equity of the issuer (or guarantor, as the case may be). The warrant, unlike its host bond, is not a debt instrument, but an instrument which contains an option.

In the international markets of London, an equity warrant is usually, if not always, issued in bearer form. It usually carries a legend on its face that it is a negotiable instrument the title to which passes on delivery.[20] This is to facilitate the tradability of the warrants as separate instruments from the host bond. In a Eurobond issue with warrants, if the bonds are subject to English law, the warrants too would be subject in practice to English law. Consequently, the question whether the equity warrant when detached from a host bond is a negotiable instrument is governed by the same principles discussed previously with regard to the negotiability of the bond.[1] It is submitted that the negotiability of bearer equity warrants should now be regarded as being beyond doubt under English law, since market recognition is the test of negotiability.[2]

In practice, a warrant does not have an issue price which is separately attributable to it, although the host bond has an issue price. Nevertheless, since the warrants are detachable from the bonds and in practice always are so detached and traded separately, a market price develops swiftly for the warrants. This price depends, first, on the market's perception of the value of the underlying equity to which the warrants relate and, secondly, on the exercise price specified in the warrant. The exercise price is the price at which a warrantholder who exercises the option contained in the warrant may subscribe for equity. The warrant will specify this exercise price, and also the maximum amount in value of shares which a warrantholder may subscribe.

The warrant is therefore issued nil paid, together with the host bond to provide an incentive or 'sweetener' to the investor to purchase the bond. The reason for this attractive incentive is that the host bond (as in the case of a convertible)[3] carries a coupon rate which is substantially lower than market rates prevailing at the time for issues of comparable bonds of a comparable issuer. The underlying commercial logic of a bond issue

---

19 See p 251.
20 On negotiability, and the ability of such a clause to confer negotiability on an instrument under English law, see ch 9.
1 See p 164.
2 See on market tradability 'Warrant Fever' Euromoney, November 1985; 'The Wonderful World of Warrants' Euromoney, August 1987.
3 See p 253 above.

with warrants is therefore extremely similar to that underlying the issue of a convertible.

Consequently, most of the motivations to invest in an equity convertible Eurobond equally apply to investing in a Eurobond with equity warrants attached. The investor accepts a low coupon rate on the bond in return for the opportunity to subscribe equity in the issuer at a price (the exercise price of the warrant) which will be lower than the market price of a unit of the issuer's shares or stock (or guarantor's, as the case may be) at the date on which the subscription right is exercised by the holder. From the issuer's viewpoint the essence of his motivation is the lower coupon rate and the equity financing he will receive if the share price rises as anticipated.

From the issuer's viewpoint the issuer obtains equity finance when the holder of the warrant exercises his option to subscribe shares for cash. This is in contrast to a convertible which does not provide additional finance to the issuer when the bond is exchanged for shares.

2 The subscription right

The subscription right embodied in the warrant consequently possesses a financial value to the warrantholder which is the same as the value of the conversion privilege to a holder of a convertible Eurobond.

The subscription right is generally stated in warrant instruments to subsist as from the closing of the bond issue. Technically, this may not be completely accurate. The right to subscribe comes into existence only when the option contained in the warrant is exercised by the warrantholder according to the procedure for exercise specified in the warrant. Until then the issuer of the warrant is under no legal obligation to issue shares. Nevertheless, in practice, since the option can be exercised immediately on issue of the warrants, for all practical purposes a subscription right does exist from the time when the warrants are issued.

Unlike in the case of a convertible, since the warrant is a separate negotiable instrument from the host bond, the maturity or earlier redemption of the bond has no legal effect on the continued validity and existence of the warrant. However, in practice, a specific clause in the warrant terminates the validity of the warrant on the date when the host bonds are redeemed at or prior to maturity. Additionally, it is usually provided that in the event that the bonds are accelerated due to a default by the issuer, the subscription right terminates on such date as the bonds become due and payable. Warrantholders are conferred protection in that they are entitled to notice of such acceleration, usually from a bond trustee, in order to enable them to exercise their rights to subscribe, if they so wish.

As pointed out earlier, the value of this subscription right is dependent on the value of the shares to which it relates. Consequently, any occurrence which dilutes share value or causes substantial impairment or destroys it completely, would inevitably result in diminution or loss in value of the subscription right. The events which can cause such dilution, impairment or destruction are identical with those which can cause a similar impact on the conversion privilege in a Eurobond convertible. Consequently, protective devices, as in the case of convertibles, consist of anti-dilution provisions and notice provisions.

First, there are a number of events which trigger adjustments of the subscription price exactly in the same way as in convertibles. Once again complex mathematical formulae are used.

Secondly, notice needs to be given to warrantholders of the occurrence of such events, of the date on which the subscription price adjustment will occur and of the adjusted subscription price. If warrantholders are to be adequately protected, once again it is also necessary to give notice to them of the impending occurrence of a diluting event which would trigger a subscription price adjustment. If no such notice is given it is always possible that warrantholders would exercise their warrant subscription right immediately prior to the occurrence of the event which triggers the subscription price adjustment. Clauses used in warrant instruments usually require notice to be given around 14 days prior to the record date in respect of such an event.

From a warrantholder's point of view, a notice is necessary as soon as the diluting event is publicly announced by the issuer. This would usually be when a board resolution has been passed to issue shares or to merge the issuer with another entity or effect some other transaction which will trigger an adjustment of the subscription price as of the record date. Such a notice will make it evident to warrantholders that if they exercise their warrants before the date on which the subscription price adjustment occurs they will suffer a loss.

3 The deed poll

Where a Eurobond issue with warrants is subject to English law these price adjustment provisions and notice clauses are contained in a 'deed poll' instrument to which the warrant instrument is expressly made subject. A deed poll must be distinguished from a deed inter partes or an indenture.

Unlike an indenture or deed inter partes a deed poll is a form of deed under English law which is capable of conferring rights on third parties who are not named as parties to the deed.[4] By common law a party may not take a benefit under an indenture or deed unless he was named therein as a party.[5] Section 56(1) of the Law of Property Act 1925 does permit, however, a deed to be used to confer benefits on third parties but this provision unfortunately does not apply to personal property[6] and, consequently, the benefit of covenants cannot be conferred on persons who are not parties to a deed under s 56.

The party (or parties) indicated in a deed poll, though not named, may enforce any obligation thereby undertaken in his favour. His rights are subject only to the proviso that he has complied with any preconditions to the liability of the maker of the deed specified in the deed poll.[7] Rights may thus be conferred on unnamed and unascertained warrantholders.

---

4   See Halsbury Laws (4th edn) vol 12, paras 1303, 1357.
5   *Harmer v Armstrong* [1934] Ch 65 at 86; *Re Sinclair's Life Policy* [1938] Ch 799; *White v Bijou Mansions Ltd* [1938] Ch 351.
6   See *Beswick v Beswick* [1968] AC 58.
7   See *McDonald v Law Union Insurance Co* (1874) LR 9 QB 328.

Consequently, in practice the benefit of anti-dilution clauses is conferred on holders of the warrants by the deed poll mechanism.

It may be the case, however, that if the negotiability of the warrants is regarded as being beyond doubt, under English law[8] there is no technical necessity for the deed poll because the provisions can be included in the warrant instrument itself. This would be sufficient to transfer rights and impose obligations on the warrantholders.

4 Conditions precedent to and procedure for exercise of the subscription right

The warrantholder is required by the terms and conditions of the warrant instrument and deed poll to deposit the warrants which he wishes to exercise together with an 'Exercise Notice' in specified form with a specifically appointed warrant agent, and pay all taxes and fees arising on the exercise of warrants in accordance with the law of the place in which the warrants are deposited for exercise. Secondly, the warrantholder must make payment in respect of subscription money to a specially appointed bank for the credit of a special account. In the event that subscription conditions are not satisfied after the giving of the exercise notice, such funds credited to the account, are held by the bank for the account of the issuer usually for two weeks, and if the subscription conditions remain unfulfilled, are then returned to the party remitting such funds.

5 Issue of shares

Once the above conditions are satisfied, the issuer is required to ensure the issue of shares and share certificates in accordance with the legal requirements of the law of the domicile of the issuer. Under English conflicts rules, this will be the law of the place of incorporation of the entity issuing the shares.[9] The law to be complied with is, however, specified in the warrant instrument for purposes of clarity.

What would happen if the law of the place of incorporation of the issuer made it unlawful for the issuer to issue shares or share certificates as required in the warrant instrument? One line of analysis is that by analogy of the ruling of the House of Lords in the second of the Greek bond cases, *Adams v National Bank of Greece SA*,[10] the issuer would be in breach of his obligation contained in the warrant which is governed by English law. While *Adams* can admittedly be distinguished due to its special facts, the principle in the case must apply to the question whether the subsequent incapacity of the issuer to perform a contract governed by English law discharges that contract. The difficulty with this analysis is that, assuming the issuer is liable under a contract governed by English law to issue shares, the problem is that the performance of the contractual obligation (ie the issue of shares) must occur in the country of incorporation of the issuer. This would render the performance of the contractual obligation unlawful

---

8   See p 274 above.
9   *Risdon Iron and Locomotive Works v Furniss* [1906] 1 KB 49.
10 [1960] 1 QB 64.

even under English conflicts rules, because the performance of the obligation is unlawful by the law of the place of performance.[11] It was submitted previously[12] that this rule is still good law even after the Rome Convention was given effect to in the UK by the Contracts (Applicable Law) Act 1990. In any event the issue of shares may necessarily involve doing an act within the country of incorporation which is unlawful by that law, eg the issue of share certificates, the holding of shareholder meetings or the making of Board resolutions, which again would render performance unlawful under English law under English conflicts rules.[13]

In addition, even if it could be argued that the place of performance was outside the place of incorporation and therefore that English proper law governed performance, it is difficult to see how an English court would enforce performance. It is hardly likely that a decree of specific performance will be granted by an English court when damages would be a perfectly adequate remedy. Warrant instruments usually recognise this in practice, and provide by an express clause that in the event that the issue of shares or the delivery of share certificates becomes unlawful by the law of the issuer's incorporation, substitute performance becomes permissible. The entity which is required under the warrant instrument to issue shares is obliged instead to pay to a warrantholder, who exercises his subscription right and satisfies the conditions precedent,[14] the market value of the shares to which he would have been entitled. The market price of the shares is calculated by reference to the date on which the shares ought to have been issued.

A Paying and Warrant Agency Agreement ('The Agency Agreement') entered into by the issuer formally appoints a number of warrant agents to facilitate the exercise of the subscription right by the warrantholders, by accepting the deposit of warrant instruments together with a warrant exercise notice. The issuer also appoints a bank to handle payments in respect of subscription moneys by warrantholders exercising warrants. The warrantholder exercising a warrant is required by the warrant instrument to make payment to such specially appointed bank, which is required by the Agency Agreement to credit all such sums paid on exercise to a special account for the benefit of the company which issues the shares. Under the Agency Agreement, a custodian is appointed to whom the issuing company will deliver the share certificates. The warrant agent and the bank receiving subscription moneys are required in practice to communicate with each other when exercise notices and/or subscription moneys are received to ensure that warrantholders have duly exercised their subscription rights.

The warrant agents also act as paying agents in respect of the host bonds. It must be noted, however, that all these agents are agents of the issuer of the bonds and owe no contractual duties to the warrantholders. The issuer therefore has a right to terminate their appointments but he is generally under a contractual obligation to warrantholders to maintain warrant agents in a specified location, usually London and/or Luxembourg.

---

11   See *Libyan Arab Foreign Bank v Bankers Trust Co* [1988] 1 Lloyd's Rep 259 at 268; *Kleinwort, Sons & Co v Ungarische Baumwolle Industrie Akt* [1939] 2 KB 678 and ch 2.
12   See ch 2.
13   See the *Libyan Arab Bank* case above.
14   See p 277 above.

Part IV

Regulation of the international capital markets:
(A) Regulation of international bond issues under UK laws

Introduction

There is no comprehensive or systematic legal framework which seeks to regulate the international bond markets. A patchwork of national securities laws nevertheless needs to be considered and complied with in respect of a Eurobond issue from London. Since the large majority of issues are 'launched' and effected from London, securities laws of the UK need to be complied with, virtually as the 'domestic' law of the international market. US laws on securities regulations have also traditionally been an important source of potential regulation, and Eurobond market practice has evolved in response to the shape and structure of US securities laws. In addition, administrative regulation by the Ministry of Finance in Japan needs to be considered in respect of issues denominated in yen or by Japanese issuers. Increasingly, regulation by the various regulatory bodies being established on the continent of Europe, eg CONSOB (Commissione Nazionale per le Societa e la Borsa) in Italy, may have an impact on a Eurobond issue. While it is not possible to cover all such regulatory laws, an attempt is made in Parts IV and V to deal, first, with the UK system of regulation, as the law of the home state of the international bond markets in so far as it affects new issues in that market and, secondly, with those provisions of US securities regulations which directly affect the operations in the international markets.

As far as the law in the UK is concerned Eurobond issues must comply with the provisions of the new regime regulating 'investments' which was introduced by the Financial Services Act 1986 ('FSA').[1] The purpose of the FSA was to provide a framework of investor protection in the UK rather than a comprehensive regulatory framework for the vast international securities market which is based in London. Nevertheless, the FSA has had some impact on the operations of this international market. However, liberal exceptions have been provided in respect of many of the rules of the FSA in order to enable the international markets to carry on business with the maximum possible flexibility. Consequently, the practical effect of the FSA regime on the Eurobond new issue market has not been substantial.[2]

---

1 Most of the provisions of the FSA were in effect on 29 April 1988. See the FSA 1986 (Commencement) (No 8) Order 1988.
2 For a brief overview of the new regulatory regime and its key features see Tennekoon 'Regulation of London's Financial Markets under the Financial Services Act 1986' (1989) 32 German Yearbook of International Law 362–381.

282 *Introduction*

The impact of the FSA on Eurobond issues will be discussed under the following headings:

(a) The requirement of 'authorisation' to carry on 'investment business' (chapter 15).
(b) The regulation of advertising and marketing of Eurobonds (chapter 16).
(c) The requirements as to listing of securities under FSA Part IV (chapter 17).
(d) The requirements as to stabilisation (chapter 18).

CHAPTER 15
The requirement of 'authorisation' under the Financial Services Act 1986

I AUTHORISATION TO CARRY ON INVESTMENT BUSINESS IN THE UK

The cornerstone of the new regime introduced by the FSA is the rule that 'no person shall carry on or purport to carry on investment business in the UK unless he is an authorised person ... or an exempt person ...'.[1]

A breach of the prohibition in FSA s 3 carries severe penalties including criminal sanctions under s 4.[2]

Further, under s 5, agreements entered into in the course of carrying on unauthorised investment business are unenforceable in the circumstances specified in FSA s 5. Section 5 states:

> '(1) Subject to subsection (3) below, any agreement to which this subsection applies:
> (a) which is entered into by a person in the course of carrying on investment business in contravention of section 3 above; or
> (b) which is entered into:
> (i) by a person who is an authorised person or an exempted person in respect of the investment business in the course of which he enters into the agreement; but
> (ii) in consequence of anything said or done by a person in the course of carrying on investment business in contravention of that section,
> shall be unenforceable against the other party; and that party shall be entitled to recover any money or other property paid or transferred by him under the agreement, together with compensation for any loss sustained by him as a result of having parted with it.'[3]

It will be seen from the analysis which follows that it is extremely difficult

---

1 FSA s 3.
2 It is a defence for a person charged to prove that he took all reasonable precautions and exercised all due diligence to avoid the commission of the offence: s 4(2).
3 The agreements to which s 5 applies are specified in s 5(7) as being agreements 'the making or performance of which' by the person seeking to enforce it constitutes carrying on of investment business as defined by Sch 1 Part II and not excepted by Parts III and IV. Similar agreements are called 'investment agreements' by s 44(9) but there are technical differences between 'investment agreements' under s 44(9) and agreements to which s 5 applies. It must be noted that for the purposes of s 5(7) there is no requirement that the carrying on of investment business should be in the UK.

for any entity to participate in an issue of Eurobonds in the international markets unless it is an 'authorised person' under the FSA. Consequently, in practice, almost all participants in Eurobond issues effected from London have become 'authorised' persons under the FSA. In any event, most of these participants are investment banks, transnational commercial banks and securities dealers which carry on such a wide range of business that it is impossible in practice for them to carry on such business activities in the UK without authorisation or exemption. Authorisation has been conferred in practice by the mechanism provided by s 7 of the FSA, namely, membership of a self-regulating organisation ('SRO') set up under the FSA. In the case of investment banks and securities dealers the SRO of which they have to become members is the Securities and Futures Authority ('SFA').

It is nevertheless necessary to consider whether a non-authorised entity seeking to participate in a Eurobond issue needs to be authorised simply because of its participation in effecting a Eurobond issue. This depends on whether the participant 'carries on investment business' in the UK by undertaking one or more of the activities associated with a Eurobond issue.

1 'Investment business'

What activities associated with a Eurobond issue constitute 'investment business'?

An entity which engages in certain business activities specified in FSA Sch 1 Part II in respect of 'investments' is regarded as carrying on investment business unless it can fall within one of the exceptions contained in FSA Sch 1 Part III or IV.[4]

An 'investment' is 'any asset, right or interest falling within any Paragraph in Part I of Sch 1 to this Act',[5] and includes shares, bonds, options, futures and swaps.[6] All conventional Eurobonds would constitute 'investments' which fall within paras 2 or 3 of FSA Sch 1. Paragraph 2 covers 'Debentures including ... bonds ... and other instruments creating or acknowledging indebtedness ... '. Paragraph 3 covers 'bonds and other instruments creating or acknowledging indebtedness issued by or on behalf of a government, local authority or public authority'. The phrase 'a government, local authority or public authority', is defined in the statutory note to mean the government of a country or territory anywhere, including the UK, local authorities in the UK or elsewhere, any international organisation the members of which include the UK or any member state of the European Community.

Convertible Eurobonds also fall within para 2. They may also fall within para 5(b) of Sch 1 Part I. Warrants (issued with Eurobonds) to subscribe equity or debt would fall within para 4.[7]

---

4 S 1(2) provides that 'in this Act investment business means the business of engaging in one or more of the activities which fall within the Paragraphs in Part II of that Schedule [1] and are not excluded by Part III of that Schedule [1]'.
5 S 1(1),
6 See Sch 1 Part I.
7 If, however, the bonds have warrants to acquire equity (as distinct from a right to subscribe (see p 274 above for a discussion of Eurobonds with warrants) the warrants would fall within para 5(c) which refers to 'certificates or other instruments which confer— ... (c) a contractual right (other than an option) to acquire any such investment otherwise than by subscription', although it seems that the words in brackets 'other than an option' may exclude such warrants from falling within para 5(c).

The activities which may potentially constitute the carrying on of investment business for purposes of the FSA are specified in Part II of FSA Sch 1. So far as a Eurobond issue is concerned the following paragraphs are relevant.

(a) Paragraph 12

'Buying, selling, subscribing for or underwriting investments or offering or agreeing to do so either as a principal or as an agent.'[8]

(b) Paragraph 13

'Making or offering or agreeing to make—
(a) arrangements with a view to another person buying, selling, subscribing for or underwriting a particular investment; or
(b) arrangements with a view to a person who participates in the arrangements buying, selling, subscribing for or underwriting investments.'

It appears from the statutory note to para 13 that where the person making the arrangements becomes a party to the transaction as principal the paragraph does not apply; nor does it apply where the person making the arrangements proposes to be a party to the transaction as agent for one of the parties to the transaction. Further, in respect of sub-paragraph (a) above, the arrangements must be such that they 'bring about or would bring about the transaction in question'. Passive participation in arrangements made by others would probably be insufficient.

(c) Paragraph 15

'Giving or offering or agreeing to give to persons in their capacity as investors or potential investors advice on the merits of their purchasing, selling, subscribing for or underwriting any right conferred by an investment to acquire, dispose of or underwrite or convert an investment.'

It will be seen from the above that most of the activities engaged in by parties to a Eurobond issue are potentially within these definitions unless an exception applies.

First, the activities of the lead manager in arranging the issue would fall within para 13 of Sch 1 above. The activities of each member of the underwriting syndicate in respect of underwriting the bonds would fall within para 12 of Sch 1.

Secondly, the activities of the members of the underwriting group or selling group (if any) in buying and selling Eurobonds would fall within para 12 of Sch 1. Equally, the purchases of Eurobonds by investors during the issue period is also potentially within para 12, but purchases by ordinary investors are likely to fall outside para 12 due to the principal transactions exception contained in para 17. Paragraph 17 is an important provision in this respect and provides as follows:

'(1) Paragraph 12 above applies to a transaction which is or is to be entered into by a person as principal only if—

---

[8] Para 28(1)(c) of FSA Sch 1 extends the meaning of the word 'offering' to include 'invitations to treat'.

(a) he holds himself out as willing to enter into transactions of that kind at prices determined by him generally and continuously rather than in respect of each particular transaction; or

(b) he holds himself out as engaging in the business of buying investments with a view to selling them and those investments are or include investments of the kind to which the transaction relates; or

(c) he regularly solicits members of the public for the purpose of inducing them to enter as principals or agents into transactions to which that paragraph applies and the transaction is or is to be entered into as a result of his having solicited members of the public in that manner.'

However, no sale or purchase by a member of the selling group or underwriting group could fall within the exception in para 17 because it does not apply where the person 'holds himself out as engaging in the business of buying investments with a view to selling them and those investments are or include investments of the kind to which the transaction relates'.[9] In practice, securities dealers would hold themselves out as buying Eurobonds with a view to selling them. Another reason why a securities dealer involved in the placing of bonds in the primary markets cannot rely on para 17 is that it does not apply where the person 'holds himself out as willing to enter into transactions of that kind at prices determined by him generally and continuously rather than in respect of each particular transaction'.[10] In practice, securities dealers would be providing price quotations on price display screens as well as by telephone. Consequently, they would be regarded as 'holding out' and would not be able to rely on the exception in para 17.

Difficult questions arise when this exception is sought to be relied on by large institutional investors or by corporate treasury divisions who purchase and sell securities, including Eurobonds, in large volumes. The key question is whether on the facts such investors in securities can be said to be 'holding out' as being in the business of buying securities with a view to selling them. If they may be so regarded such investors may not be able to rely on the principal transactions exception in para 17 of FSA Sch 1.

Thirdly, does the 'issue' of Eurobonds by the issuer constitute carrying on of investment business? In practice this will be an important question because most issuers of Eurobonds will be overseas entities who are neither authorised nor exempt, and who would not wish to go through authorisation procedures purely for the purpose of effecting an issue of bonds in London's international markets.

While para 12 of Sch 1 states that selling bonds constitutes an activity which may fall within the phrase 'carrying on investment business', para 28(1)(d) of Sch 1 says that 'references to buying and selling off include references to any acquisition or disposal for valuable consideration', and para 28(2)(b) says that 'disposal' includes 'issuing or creating the investment . . .'. If the matter were left here issuers would fall within para 12. However, para 28(3) provides that 'a person shall not by reason of issuing his own debentures or debenture warrants be regarded for the purposes of this Schedule as disposing of them . . .'. Consequently, since Eurobonds would consti-

---

9 Para 12(1)(b).
10 Para 17(1)(a).

tute debentures under English law,[11] the issuer is not caught by para 12. Equally, where the issue of Eurobonds is made with share warrants attached, para 28(3) expressly excludes not only the issue of bonds from falling within para 12, but also the issue of equity warrants.[12]

It may also be argued that the arrangements which an issuer makes to effect the issue constitutes the

'making or offering or agreeing to make –
(a) arrangements with a view to another person buying, selling, subscribing for or underwriting a particular investment; or
(b) arrangements with a view to a person who participates in the arrangements buying, selling, subscribing for or underwriting investments'

and is thus within para 13 of Sch 1. However, para 28(3) of Sch 1 provides that a person shall not by reason of anything done for the purpose of issuing bonds, bond warrants or equity warrants 'be regarded as making arrangements with a view to a person subscribing for or otherwise acquiring them or underwriting them'.

Fourthly, could the provision of mechanisms to list, trade and clear Eurobonds come within the broad formula of making arrangements?

Since a listing on a stock exchange[13] facilitates the buying and selling of Eurobonds, an exchange making such provision may be said to be carrying on investment business. Thus The London Stock Exchange or the Luxembourg Stock Exchange or the Tokyo Stock Exchange may fall within para 13 of FSA Sch 1. The London Stock Exchange is a Recognised Investment Exchange under FSA s 36, and consequently its activities as such are exempt under s 36(1). As regards overseas stock exchanges, if such 'arrangements' are made outside the UK, as would be the case in practice, the arrangements would fall outside the prohibition in s 3 of the FSA due to the fact that the arrangements must be made in the UK before the prohibition in FSA s 3 has any effect.[14]

The provision of facilities for trading in Eurobonds, such as those provided by the Association of International Bond Dealers ('AIBD') may also potentially constitute the making of arrangements.[15] The same may also be true of Euroclear and CEDEL, the two main clearing systems for Eurobonds, since they too may be regarded as making arrangements 'with a view to another person buying, selling . . . ' Eurobonds.

However, para 25B of FSA Sch 1, which was enacted by statutory instrument,[16] excludes from the definition of investment business all activity falling within para 13 of Sch 1 (ie making arrangements for deals in investments) which is carried out by an 'international securities self-regulating organisation' ('ISRO') or by any person acting on its behalf. The exception, however, applies only to making arrangements in respect of 'international securities business'

---

11 See chs 7 and 8 for a discussion on the meaning of 'debenture' and the legal nature of the Eurobond.
12 See para 28(3) of FSA Sch 1.
13 See on listing of Eurobonds ch 17 below.
14 See below as regards territoriality and FSA s 1(3) and s 3.
15 The AIBD is to be renamed the International Securities Market Association from January 1992: see an article by John Langton, Chief Executive of AIBD, in the *Observer*, Sunday, July 14 1991.
16 See the FSA 1986 (Restriction of Scope of Act) Order 1988, SI 1988/318 which became effective on 27 February 1988.

by such an organisation. These provisions seek to exclude the activities of the AIBD from being regulated under the provisions of the FSA.

The phrase 'international securities business' is defined in para 25B(2) in a manner which makes it directly applicable to Eurobonds, as follows:

> 'International securities business' means the business of buying, selling, subscribing for or underwriting investments (or offering or agreeing to do so, either as principal or agent) which fall within any of the paragraphs in Part I above other than paragraph 10 and, so far as relevant to paragraph 10, paragraph 11 and which, by their nature and the manner in which the business is conducted may be expected normally to be bought or dealt in by persons sufficiently expert to understand any risks involved, where either the transaction is international or each of the parties may be expected to be indifferent to the location of the other, and, for the purposes of this definition, the fact that the investments may ultimately be bought otherwise than in the course of international securities business by persons not so expert shall be disregarded.'

An ISRO is defined in para 25B(2) as follows:

> 'international securities self-regulating organisation' means a body corporate or unincorporated association which
> (a) does not have its head office in the United Kingdom;
> (b) is not eligible for recognition under s 37 or s 39 of this Act on the ground that (whether or not it has applied, and whether or not it would be eligible on other grounds) it is unable to satisfy the requirements of s 40(2)(a) or (c) of this Act;
> (c) has a membership composed of persons falling within any of the following categories, that is to say, authorised persons, exempted persons, persons holding a permission under paragraph 23 above and persons whose head offices are outside the United Kingdom and whose ordinary business is such as is mentioned in para 17(2)(e) above; and
> (d) which facilitates and regulates the activity of its members in the conduct of international securities business.'

The Secretary of State has power under para 25B(3) to approve any body or association which appears to fall within the above definition of ISRO simply by giving notice in writing. See para 25(B)(4).

Euroclear, CEDEL and Reuters applied to the SIB for authorisation prior to the appointed day, 27 February 1988, and the SIB has exempted all three entities from complying with nearly all the rules and regulations of the SIB, including the Conduct of Business Rules (1987), the Financial Resources Rules (1987), the Clients Money Regulations (1987) and the Financial Records Rules (1987). See the Financial Services (Interim)(Service Companies) Rules and Regulations 1988.[17]

Finally, one has to ask whether the agreements made by paying agents, fiscal agents, and trustees are similarly within the ambit of para 13. In the case of all these functionaries since all these arrangements are made in practice by the lead manager, it may be the case that their activities in respect of a Eurobond issue do not fall within para 13. However, this remains a question of fact in each case.

---

17 Issued by the SIB in April 1988 in SIB Release no 20.

Consequently, most of the activities associated with a Eurobond issue constitute 'investment business' within FSA Sch 1 Part II and will be caught by the prohibition in s 3 if a participant may be said to be carrying on such business *in the UK*.

2 Investment business carried on in the UK

When can it be said that such investment business is carried on *in the UK*?

The FSA states that a person carries on investment business in the UK if one of two criteria is satisfied. First, where he carries it on from a permanent place of business in the UK; and secondly, if he engages in activities in the UK which constitute investment business even though he does not have an office or place of business in the UK.

Section 1(3) provides as follows:

> 'For the purposes of this Act a person carries on investment business in the UK if he—
> (a) carries on investment business from a permanent place of business maintained by him in the UK; *or*
> (b) engages in the UK in one or more of the activities which fall within the paragraphs in Part II of that Schedule and are not excluded by Part III or IV of that Schedule and his doing so constitutes the carrying on by him of a business in the UK.'

The first basis specified in s 1(3)(a) is not difficult to apply. There is little difficulty in deciding whether an underwriter or selling group member carries on his Eurobond business from a permanent place of business. The maintenance of an office in the UK with ordinary business facilities would be sufficient if the Eurobond investment business is carried on from that office. In practice most Eurobond market participants would come within this limb of s 1(3).

However, there may be difficult cases. What would be the case if, say, a selling group member carries on its Eurobond business such as underwriting or sales from its Geneva office, but maintains a representative office or an office which does no investment business of any kind in London? It would seem that the entity is not carrying on investment business *from* the place of business in the UK and would consequently fall outside s 1(3)(a), although it may fall within s 1(3)(b).[18]

In practice, most participants in a Eurobond issue will have a permanent place of business in the form of an office or branch in London from which its Eurobond new issue work is carried on and, consequently, would require authorisation under chapter III of the FSA.

---

18 If the London office carried on any investment business (though not Eurobond business) such as arranging swaps (para 9 read with paras 12 and 13 of Sch 1) buying and selling certificates of deposit (para 2 read with paras 12 and 13 of Sch 2) it may be carrying on investment business in the UK and would fall within s 1(3)(a) and thus require authorisation or exemption due to such activity.

II OFFSHORE ENTITIES: THE 'OVERSEAS PERSON'

Where a participant does not have a permanent place of business in the UK, such a person is termed an 'overseas person' by the FSA.[19] As observed earlier, it is possible for such an entity to be regarded by the FSA as carrying on investment business 'in the UK' if he 'engages in the UK' in one or more of the activities constituting investment business under Sch 1 Part II and 'his doing so constitutes the carrying on by him of a business in the UK'. Such persons, however, have the benefit of special exceptions in Part IV of Sch 1.

Where there are 'off-shore' participants in a Eurobond issue, in particular an underwriter or a lead manager, these provisions would apply to such entities and need to be considered.

The first question is whether the overseas person may be said to be engaging in the UK in any FSA regulated activity such as underwriting, selling or buying securities. Assuming that English law is to be applied, at least the following activities of an 'overseas person' may trigger the provisions of s 1(3)(b) on the basis that he 'engages in the UK' in activities classified as investment business in FSA Sch 1 Part II:

(a) an offer telex sent from 'offshore' to London (or elsewhere in the UK);[20]
(b) any offer made by an overseas underwriter to underwrite an issue or any offer to purchase or sell bonds made by a prospective selling group member who is an overseas person, where such offers are received in the UK;[1]
(c) the sending of an invitation telex by a lead manager who is an overseas person to prospective underwriters and selling group members who receive such a telex in London;[2]
(d) the execution of subscription or underwriting agreements in London to which an overseas person is a party as an underwriter;
(e) the receipt in London of an allotment telex sent by an overseas lead manager since the allotment telex constitutes an offer made in London by the lead manager.[3]

Difficult questions arise if ordinary principles of English private international law or conflict of laws are applied to determine whether a particular activity occurs in the UK for purposes of FSA s 1(3).

Suppose a Eurobond issue is lead managed by an investment bank in Switzerland, Hong Kong or Korea which has no place of business in the UK. Suppose the documents governing the issue, such as the subscription agreement, are subject to a foreign governing law and are entered into outside the UK.[4] Which law governs the issue which arises under the FSA, namely, whether certain activities were engaged in within the UK? If English conflicts

---

19 See FSA para 26(1) Sch 1 and s 1(3).
20 Under Sch 1 para 12.
1   Under Sch 1 para 12.
2   Under Sch 1 para 12 read with para 28(7)(c).
3   Under Sch 1 para 12.
4   On governing law see ch 2 above.

rules embodied in the Contracts (Applicable Law) Act 1990 were applied many such issues would be referred to the chosen proper law of the contractual agreements.[5]

If this were the case, it may equally be possible by reference to the chosen proper law to state in the contractual documents that all offers, acceptances, the making of arrangements in respect of the issue and all other conduct with legal consequences are deemed to occur outside the UK, in Switzerland, Hong Kong or Korea, as the case may be. This approach would enable such activity to be deemed to occur outside the UK.

Another approach is to state that as far as a UK court is concerned, the FSA 1986 represents the mandatory law of the forum, and must be applied in accordance with art 7(2) of the Rome Convention. Consequently, the question whether a person 'engages in' investment activity in the UK must always be determined by reference to the FSA itself, irrespective of the existence of a chosen proper law in the issue documentation.[6]

It is submitted that this approach is to be preferred. In any event, in practice in a large number of Eurobond issues English law is expressly made the governing law of the legal agreements and the FSA would apply as part of that law. However, it is submitted that the applicability of the FSA should not depend on whether English law is chosen as the proper law of the transaction; it should be applied as mandatory law of the forum.[7]

Assuming that the offshore participant's activities (in underwriting the issue or offering to do so or buying or selling bonds) are regarded as being 'engaged in' in the UK, there are two exceptions contained in paras 26 and 27 of FSA, Sch 1 Part IV which may be relied on by such entities.[8]

1 Exception for transactions 'with or through' certain persons

The first exception is that the 'overseas person' may transact business '*with or through*' authorised or exempt persons: FSA Sch 1 Part IV para 26. In relation to dealing and underwriting in investments para 26 provides:

> 'Paragraph 12 above does not apply to any transaction by a person not falling within s 1(3)(a) of this Act ('an overseas person') with or through:

---

5 See art 3 para 1 of the Rome Convention which is now part of English law due to the Contracts (Applicable Law) Act 1990, and the discussion in ch 2 above.
6 See art 7(2) of the Rome Convention which provides for the applicability of mandatory law of the forum. S 7(1) permits the application of other systems of law as mandatory, but due to s 2(2) of the Contracts (Applicable Law) Act 1990, art 7(1) does not apply as part of English law. See, for an instance where the English courts applied a statute as mandatory law: *The Hollandia* [1983] 1 AC 565. See also Cheshire and North *Private International Law* (11th edn, 1987) p 466.
7 The Securities and Investments Board in a Consultative Paper, published in March 1989, Paper no 19, has itself stated that it will adopt a 'transaction-based' approach to the enforcement of the FSA in this respect.
8 It must be remembered, however, that to fall within Part IV of Sch 1 and to avoid a breach of the prohibition in FSA s 3 against carrying on an unauthorised investment business in the UK, the overseas person must establish that *all* its business activities in the UK, which are within the definition of investment business, are covered by one or more of the exceptions contained in Sch 1. It is not sufficient that its Eurobond activities can be fitted within the exceptions contained in Part IV, unless of course, the overseas person only carried on business which is associated with Eurobond issues in the UK.

(a) an authorised person; or
(b) an exempted person acting in the course of business in respect of which he is exempt.'

In relation to 'arranging deals in investments' para 26 provides:

'Paragraph 13 above does not apply if:
(a) the arrangements are made by an overseas person *with*, or the offer or agreement to make them is made by him to or with, an authorised person or an exempted person and, in the case of an exempted person, the arrangements are with a view to his entering into a transaction in respect of which he is exempt; or
(b) the transactions with a view to which the arrangements are made are, as respects transactions in the United Kingdom, confined to transactions by authorised persons and transactions by exempted persons in respect of which they are exempt.'

These provisions enable the overseas person to deal in investments (Sch 1 para 12 transactions) and to arrange deals in investments (Sch 1 para 13 transactions) if they deal '*with*' an authorised or exempt person; and they further enable the overseas person to deal in investments (para 12 activity) '*through*' an authorised or exempt person.[9] Schedule 1 para 26(2) explains what dealing 'through' means, namely, that the exempt or authorised person may act as agent. The 'with or through' formula therefore means that the authorised person or exempt person may act as principal or agent in the transaction or act as an arranger of the para 12 transaction.[10]

This means that, so long as the overseas person agrees or offers[11] to underwrite, subscribe or sell Eurobonds with or through an authorised or exempt person who is acting as principal or as agent in the UK, the overseas person will not be in breach of s 3. Thus, for instance, it would be possible to include a Swiss underwriter or selling group member with no office in the UK and whose offices are in Zurich as part of the underwriting group or selling group, though the person is neither exempt nor authorised, provided he is engaging in the underwriting or the subscription and purchase of bonds with or through an authorised lead manager.

In practice this exception is not of great value since the offshore entity will need to share fees or commissions with the UK authorised entity and this may not be commercially acceptable.

---

9 Note that para 26(2)(a) unlike para 26(1) is confined to making arrangements *with* an authorised or exempt person but does not go so far as arrangements made *through* an authorised person or exempt person.
10 Para 26(2)(b) is curiously drafted, but seems to provide that (a) even if the overseas person makes arrangements in investments, in a manner which constitutes doing investment business in the UK, but (b) does not make the arrangements with an authorised person or exempt person, nevertheless authorisation is unnecessary, provided (c) that the transaction (which is the subject of the arrangements) in so far as it is transacted in the UK is entered into by authorised persons.

Note also that the exception for overseas persons dealing with authorised or exempt persons is confined to para 12 or para 13 activity. It does not extend to other forms of investment business such as giving investment advice (para 15 activity).
11 Including an invitation to treat: Sch 1 para 28(1)(c).

2 Paragraph 27, Schedule 1 exception

The second exception is one relating to (a) unsolicited transactions by overseas persons, or (b) to transactions solicited by overseas persons in compliance with FSA rules on advertising and unsolicited calls.[12]

Paragraph 27 reads as follows:

'(1) Paragraph 12 above does not apply to any transaction entered into by an overseas person as principal with, or as agent for, a person in the United Kingdom, paragraphs 13, 14 and 15 above do not apply to any offer made by an overseas person or to agreement made by him with a person in the United Kingdom and paragraph 15 above does not apply to any advice given by an overseas person to a person in the United Kingdom if the transaction, offer, agreement or advice is the result of:
  (a) an approach to the overseas person by or on behalf of the person in the United Kingdom which either has not been in any way solicited by the overseas person or has been solicited by him in a way which has not contravened section 56 or 57 of this Act; or
  (b) an approach made by the overseas person which has not contravened either of those sections.

(2) Where the transaction is entered into by the overseas person as agent for a person in the United Kingdom, sub-paragraph (1) above applies only if:
  (a) the other party is outside the United Kingdom; or
  (b) the other party is in the United Kingdom and the transaction is the result of such an approach by the other party as is mentioned in sub-paragraph (1)(a) above or of such an approach as is mentioned in sub-paragraph (1)(b) above.'

This exception covers all forms of investment business activity in the UK connected with a Eurobond issue but does not seem to apply to the *making of arrangements* under para 13, as distinct from offering to or agreeing to make such arrangements. Consequently, it would seem that it would not be possible for an overseas entity to lead manage a Eurobond issue on the basis of this exception, because in practice it would invariably involve making arrangements in the UK in respect of the issue.

Paragraph 27 allows an unauthorised overseas person to carry on certain kinds of activities in the UK associated with a Eurobond issue through a number of routes.

First, where investment agreements are entered into with a person in the UK by the overseas person on a completely unsolicited basis, ie as a result of an approach made to the overseas person by a person in the UK. This limb of the exception, however, is perhaps not of great practical value because it does not permit the overseas person to market its services in the UK or to persons in the UK.

Secondly, para 27 permits the overseas person to do business with UK customers where he has solicited them 'in a way which has not contravened s 56 or 57 of this Act'.[13] One interpretation of this limb of para 27 is that so long as the overseas person complies with *either* s 57 (the prohibition on unapproved 'investment advertisements') or s 56, (prohibition on unsolicited calls), he may do business in the UK. The alternative analysis is that the overseas person must comply with *both* s 56 and s 57, ie advertising

---

12 See ch 16.
13 For a detailed discussion of the impact of s 57 and s 56 on the marketing of Eurobonds, see ch 16.

rules and unsolicited calls rules. In other words, the word 'or' in the last line of para 27(1)(a) has to be read conjunctively.

If the former view is adopted, then para 27 would permit the following. Suppose a securities dealer, A, in Switzerland has a subsidiary, B Ltd, in the UK which is authorised. Suppose A issues advertisements in the UK which are 'approved' by B Ltd (the authorised person),[14] and in consequence of such advertising A is successful in carrying on investment business in the UK, it would seem A falls within para 27 even if he has breached s 56 (ie the prohibition against unsolicited calls by cold calling the person in the UK). The reason is that due to the 'approval' of the advertising by the authorised person the advertisement does not breach FSA s 57 and in consequence the solicitation and the investment activity in the UK which results in business for A is within para 27.

It is submitted that the policy objective of investor protection requires that there should be no breach of both s 56 and s 57 in order to enable an overseas person to rely on this exception. Compliance with ss 56 and 57 of the FSA, however, does not create too much difficulty in practice in the context of the international bond markets due to the professional character of the investing community. The reason is that the regulations framed under s 57 (prohibition on investment advertisements)[15] and s 56 (prohibition on unsolicited calls)[16] are such that an overseas person may market the Eurobond issue to professionals and certain specified persons and consequently may engage in investment business associated with a Eurobond issue within the 'safe harbour' provided by para 27 of FSA Sch 1.

Thus an overseas person may comply with the prohibition on the issue of investment advertisements in the UK contained in s 57 by confining their issue in the UK to persons falling within art 9(3) of the FSA 1986 (Investment Advertisements)(Exemptions) Order 1988. Article 9 permits the issue of investment advertisements (which would include Eurobond marketing material)[17] to authorised persons, exempt persons and, more importantly, companies which have a net asset value of £5m or more or have a parent or subsidiary with such a net asset value. This means that the unauthorised overseas person may, by virtue of para 27, advertise to such corporate entities in the UK and do business with them without the need for authorisation. Equally, as regards s 56, unsolicited calls may be made on 'non-private customers'[18] who may be cold called under the Common Unsolicited Calls Regulations of the Securities and Investments Board.[19] Prior to the enactment of these common rules, the Unsolicited Calls Regulations 1987 of the SIB[20] and

---

14 Such 'approval' is now subject to the constraints of Core rule 6 of the SIB: see Release no 94 of the SIB of 30 January 1991 which applies to all authorised persons under s 63A of the FSA.
15 See p 297 below.
16 See p 310 below.
17 See ch 16 below.
18 As defined in the *Financial Services Glossary 1991* (2nd edn). See Release no 101 of the SIB of 27 June 1991.
19 Made on 20 June 1991 and effective from 1 September 1991 for some purposes, and generally from 1 January 1992. These Regulations apply to all members of Self-Regulating Organisations by virtue of s 63A of the FSA. See especially Part I of the Regulations.
20 See the Financial Services (Unsolicited Calls) Regulations 1987, reissued text incorporating amendments made up to 21 April 1989 in Release no 53 of the SIB.

those of the Securities and Futures Authority[1] permitted cold calls on authorised persons, exempt persons and corporate entities which had a net asset value of £5m or more or which had a parent or subsidiary with such a net asset value. This impact of ss 56 and 57 on Eurobond issues is dealt with in more detail below.

The ability of an 'overseas person' to engage in investment business in the UK and thus participate in a Eurobond issue under para 27 of FSA Sch 1 however, seems to have been narrowed by the Securities and Investments Board under Part III of its new Common Unsolicited Calls Regulations.[2] The ability of an 'overseas person' to cold call even 'non-private customers'[3] is confined by the fact that any 'marketing' must be effected through an exempt or authorised person or the investment agreement which results from cold calling such a customer must be entered into through an authorised or exempted person. This restriction was absent under the previous Unsolicited Calls Regulations of 1987 of the SIB[4] and, it is understood, will be deleted in the near future.

The major limitation to the use of para 27 of FSA Sch 1 as a means of carrying on Eurobond new issue activity under para 27, however, seems to be that due to the language of para 27 a lead manager may not make arrangements within the safe harbour of para 27 in the UK.

The provisions concerning the requirement of authorisation will be modified when the provisions of the draft Investment Services Directive[5] and the Second Banking Coordination Directive[6] become part of UK law. The objective of these directives is to provide for a 'single passport' within the European Community, enabling an institution authorised to carry on investment business or banking business in a member state of the Community to carry on such business in all other member states of the Community.[7] Machinery already exists within the framework of the FSA in s 31 to confer authorisation in the UK on persons authorised to carry on investment business in other member states of the Community.[8] Once the Investment Services Directive is enacted into the laws of the member states it will be possible for entities authorised in a member state[9] to become authorised in the UK under the provisions of FSA ss 31 and 32 simply by giving notice of commencement of business to the Secretary of State under s 32. However, such persons must be authorised by the regulatory body in the member state in which that person has his head office, before the EC entity can obtain authorisation under s 31. The language of s 31 is as follows:

'(1) A person carrying on investment business in the United Kingdom is an authorised person if—
(a) he is established in a member State other than the United Kingdom;
(b) the law of *that* State recognises him as a national of that or another member State; and

---

1 Previously The Securities Association.
2 Release no 101 of 27 June 1991.
3 As defined in the SIB's *Glossary 1991*; see discussion below in chapter 16, p 310.
4 See Release no 53 of the SIB.
5 The latest available text was published in February 1990 (OJ C42/7).
6 89/646 EC adopted on 6 December 1989.
7 See the UK Department of Trade and Industry's Consultative Document of July 1990: *EC Investment Services Directive*.
8 See FSA s 31.
9 See s 31(3)(b).

(c) he is for the time being authorised under *that* law to carry on investment business or investment business of any particular kind.

(2) For the purposes of this Act a person is established in a member State other than the UK if his head office is situated in that State and he does not transact investment business from a permanent place of business maintained by him in the United Kingdom.' (Emphasis added.)

CHAPTER 16
The regulation in the UK of advertising and marketing of Eurobond issues

The Financial Services Act 1986 ('FSA') seeks to regulate the marketing of investments and investment services, first, by rules governing advertising, and secondly, by rules governing 'cold calling'. These provisions will need to be considered in the context of the marketing of a Eurobond issue. The regulation of advertising is dealt with first.

I REGULATION OF ADVERTISEMENTS

The FSA contains two basic prohibitions on advertising which are relevant to a Eurobond issue.

First, s 57 contains a prohibition on the issue of an 'investment advertisement' in the UK unless it is issued or 'approved' by an authorised person.

Secondly, s 160 contains another type of prohibition relating to the issue in the UK of an advertisement 'offering any securities', where the advertisement constitutes 'a primary or secondary offer' of any securities.

The word 'advertisement' is not defined in the FSA although s 207(2) provides that an advertisement includes any form or manner of advertising through any medium of communication.

Section 207(2) states:

'In this Act "advertisement" includes every form of advertising, whether in a publication, by the display of notices, signs, labels or showcards, by means of circulars, catalogues, price lists or other documents, by an exhibition of pictures or photographic or cinematographic films, by way of sound broadcasting or television, by the distribution of recordings, or in any other manner: and references to the issue of an advertisement shall be construed accordingly.'

The ordinary dictionary meaning of the word 'advertisement' is 'a public notice or announcement' and this meaning would presumably be applied by a court.[1]

---

1 See the *Concise Oxford Dictionary of Current English* (Clarendon Press, Oxford, 8th edn, 1990) p 18.

1 The prohibition in FSA s 57

Section 57(1) states:

> 'Subject to section 58 below, no person other than an authorised person shall issue or cause to be issued an investment advertisement in the United Kingdom unless its contents have been approved by an authorised person.'

Breach of this provision has serious consequences: first, under s 57(3) breach is a criminal offence; secondly, under s 57(5) the party in breach is denied the ability to enforce 'any agreement to which the advertisement related and which was entered into after the issue of the advertisement' and further, 'the other party shall be entitled to recover any money or other property paid or transferred by him under the agreement together with compensation for any loss sustained by him as a result of having parted with it'. There is also potential liability to injunctive action by the Securities and Investments Board ('SIB') if 'there is a reasonable likelihood of a contravention'; or where there has already been a contravention, the SIB may obtain an order requiring the taking of remedial steps. See s 61(1). Under s 61(3) and (4) the SIB may also have an action for the recovery of profits made as a result of the contravention. These need not be restricted to the profits which have accrued to the party contravening the section. Further, the court may under these subsections also make an award for the recovery of compensation for any loss or 'adverse effect' suffered by any person in consequence of the breach. See s 61 (3) and (4) which are set out below:

> '(3) The court may, on the application of the Secretary of State, make an order under subsection (4) below or, in relation to Scotland, under subsection (5) below if satisfied—
> (a) that profits have accrued to any person as a result of his contravention of any provision or condition mentioned in subsection (1)(a) above; or
> (b) that one or more investors have suffered loss or been otherwise adversely affected as a result of that contravention.
> (4) The court may under this subsection order the person concerned to pay into court, or appoint a receiver to recover from him, such sum as appears to the court to be just having regard—
> (a) in a case within paragraph (a) of subsection (3) above, to the profits appearing to the court to have accrued;
> (b) in a case within paragraph (b) of that subsection, to the extent of the loss or other adverse effect; or
> (c) in a case within both paragraphs (a) and (b) of that subsection, to the profits and to the extent of the loss or other adverse effect.'

i *'Investment advertisements' which are 'issued in the UK'*

It will be noticed that s 57 governs the issue of 'investment advertisements'. The definition of an investment advertisement is to be found in s 57(2) which states:

> 'In this Act "an investment advertisement" means any advertisement inviting persons to enter or offer to enter into an investment agreement or to exercise any rights conferred by an investment to acquire, dispose of, underwrite or convert an investment or containing information calculated to lead directly or indirectly to persons doing so.'

Consequently, if a publication is an advertisement, it must possess one of two characteristics specified in s 57(2) before it is regarded as an investment advertisement falling within s 57(2), namely that either:

(a) it invites persons to enter into or offer to enter into an investment agreement or to exercise certain rights conferred by an investment; or
(b) it contains information 'calculated to lead' directly or indirectly to persons entering into an investment agreement or to exercise certain rights conferred by an investment.

It is clear therefore that even an advertisement which does not contain an invitation to enter into an investment agreement may constitute an investment advertisement, provided it contains information 'calculated to lead' to result in persons entering into an investment agreement or exercise rights conferred by an investment.

The phrase 'calculated to' has been interpreted consistently by the English courts (in the context of other statutes) to mean 'likely' or 'reasonably likely'. Thus Viscount Cave LC in the leading case of *McDowell v Standard Oil Company (New Jersey)* [1927] AC 632 held that 'calculated to deceive' did not mean intended to deceive but 'likely (or reasonably likely) to deceive'.[2] It is submitted that the words in s 57(2) will also be interpreted by the courts in a like manner. The test is an objective one rather than subjective, and any advertisement which is likely or reasonably likely to result in one of the consequences mentioned in s 57(2) would fall within it. It is submitted that the concept of likely or reasonably likely means that the advertisement must, first, possess the causative potential to result in an investment agreement and, secondly, that such consequence is reasonably foreseeable. In other words, the mere fact that an advertisement may in some remote circumstances result in someone entering into an investment agreement or exercising rights etc is insufficient. Such consequences must be foreseeable by a reasonable man as proximate or direct result.

An 'investment agreement' for these purposes (and generally for the purposes of the FSA) is defined in s 44(9):

'(9) In this Act "investment agreement" means any agreement the making or performance of which by either party constitutes an activity which falls within any paragraph of Part II of Schedule 1 to this Act or would do so apart from Parts III and IV of that Schedule' [ie any of the activities of buying, selling, underwriting, arranging, advising, managing which were discussed previously].[3]

It must be noted that in determining whether an activity which falls within Part II of FSA Sch 1 may give rise to an investment agreement for the purposes of s 44(9) one is required to ignore all exceptions in Part III or

---

2 The ruling in this case was followed by Parker CJ in *Collett v Co-Operative Wholesale Society Ltd* [1970] 1 WLR 250 in respect of s 24(2) of the Weights and Measures Act 1963; see also Parker J in *British Vacuum Cleaner Co Ltd v New Vacuum Cleaner Co Ltd* [1907] 2 Ch 312; and *Turner v Shearer* [1972] 1 WLR 1387 which concerned the phrase 'calculated to deceive' in s 20 of the Companies Act 1862.
3 See pp 284–289 above.

IV.[4] Consequently, an advertisement may be regarded as an investment advertisement even though the agreement which is likely to result from it does not constitute the carrying on of investment business because an exception in Part III or Part IV applies to it; all that is necessary is that the investment agreement constitutes activity falling within Part II of Sch 1 in the making or performance thereof.

The concept of investment agreement is thus sufficiently wide to catch every agreement entered into in the course of an issue of Eurobonds and would include the subscription agreement, the underwriting agreement (if any), any agreement to buy or sell bonds, as well as a sale or purchase of bonds, any agreement to allot bonds, the trust deed, the fiscal agency agreement and the paying agency agreement.[5]

On this basis, 'the advertisements' which are within s 57 either because they contain an invitation to enter into an 'investment agreement' or exercise rights in respect of an investment or contain information likely to lead to such a result are as follows:

(a) the offering circular in draft and final form;
(b) the invitation telex sent out by the lead manager to prospective underwriters and selling group members in the market-place;
(c) Reuter screen and other electronic announcements of the bond issue to the markets;
(d) any advertisement issued by selling group members to prospective investors in Eurobonds.

An offer telex to a prospective issuer on the other hand would not come within the prohibition due to the absence of the essential quality of an advertisement as being a public notice or announcement.

Assuming that the document or publication is an 'investment advertisement', s 57 applies only if it is 'issued in the UK'.

The phrase 'issued in the UK' is not defined by the FSA, but it is submitted that it would cover a case where the advertisement is distributed in the UK, as well as a case where a document is prepared, printed and distributed from (though not in) a place of business in the UK. Section 207(3) widens the concept of issued in the 'UK' to include an advertisement issued 'outside the UK' but 'directed to persons in the UK' by whatever means, eg an electronic communications system. Again, even if such an advertisement is not directed to persons in the UK, yet if it is 'made available' to persons in the UK, the FSA deems the advertisement to have been issued in the UK, unless it is 'made available in a newspaper, journal, magazine or other periodical publication published and circulating principally outside the UK or in a sound or television broadcast transmitted principally for reception outside the UK'.

This extension is obviously significant to an offshore participant in a Eurobond issue. Thus, for instance, if an offshore non-authorised selling group member were to solicit UK companies and investors by means of advertise-

---

4 See on these ch 15 above.
5 Note that it is sufficient for purposes of s 44(9) if one (not necessarily both) of the parties to an agreement is engaging in an activity falling within Part II.

ments from an overseas office, s 57 would apply to such advertising due to the extension embodied in s 207(3).

Section 207(3) is as follows:

'For the purposes of this Act an advertisement or other information issued outside the United Kingdom shall be treated as issued in the United Kingdom if it is directed to persons in the United Kingdom or is made available to them otherwise than in a newspaper, journal, magazine or other periodical publication published and circulating principally outside the United Kingdom or in a sound or television broadcast transmitted principally for reception outside the United Kingdom.'

If the investment advertisement is regarded as being issued or caused to have been issued in the UK by an unauthorised person, it must be 'approved' by an authorised person, unless it can fall within one of the numerous exceptions to s 57 contained in the FSA or the statutory instruments framed under FSA s 58(3).[6]

The invitation telex and Reuter screen announcements are issued by the lead manager, who is in practice most likely to be an authorised person. Consequently, no difficulty should arise in practice in respect of such advertisements.[7]

On the other hand, in practice, the offering circular or bond prospectus in preliminary and final form is issued in the name of the issuer who is usually a non-authorised person.

Consequently, it would need to be approved by an authorised person unless an exception to s 57 is applicable and there are two exceptions which can and are in practice relied on.

ii *Exceptions to s 57*

The first, s 58(1)(d)(ii), contains a major exception in respect of Eurobond issues listed in London:

'(d) any advertisement which – [. . .]
    (ii) consists of or any part of listing particulars, supplementary listing particulars or any other document required or permitted to be published by listing rules under Part IV of this Act or by an approved exchange under Part V of this Act'

is outside the scope of the prohibition in s 57.

If the bonds are to be the subject of a listing application to The London International Stock Exchange the draft offering circular will consist of draft listing particulars submitted to that stock exchange under FSA Part IV,

---

6 See p 302 below.
7 On one reading of s 57 if the advertisements are issued by an authorised person, this is an end to the matter. On the other hand, s 57 may be read as meaning that if an unauthorised person 'causes' it to be issued the advertisement requires approval by an authorised person even if the advertisement is issued by an authorised person. Arguably, the issuer of the bonds 'causes' all these advertisements to be issued. This latter reading of the section leads to the absurd result that the authorised person issuing an advertisement must approve his own advertisements, because it has been 'caused to be issued' by a non-authorised person. Consequently, it is submitted that, if an advertisement is issued by an authorised person, s 57 does not operate.

while the final offering circular will consist of the listing particulars in final form.

Consequently, the final offering circular would be exempt under s 58(1)(d)(ii) if the bonds are to be listed on The London International Stock Exchange on the basis that the final offering circular 'consists of ... listing particulars' submitted under FSA Part IV to The London International Stock Exchange. The draft offering circular may be distributed in the form of draft listing particulars as 'any other document required or permitted to be published by listing rules' framed under FSA Part IV by The London International Stock Exchange, since the listing rules made under FSA Part IV (the 'Yellow Book' or *Admission of Securities to Listing*) [8] permit the distribution of draft listing particulars 'for the purposes of arranging syndication, underwriting and selective marketing of Eurocurrency debt securities'.[9]

If, however, the bonds are not to be listed in London but are to be listed in Luxembourg, this exception would not apply because a listing in Luxembourg is not a listing under Part IV of the FSA.[10] The London Stock Exchange was recognised on 28 April 1988 under FSA ss 36 and 37 as a Recognised Investment Exchange.

Advertisements which do not fall within s 58(1)(d)(ii), such as an offering circular in a Luxembourg listed issue (or any other investment advertisement such as an invitation telex and screen announcements by non-authorised persons) may nevertheless be issued without occasioning a breach of s 57 within the provisions of art 9 of the Financial Services Act 1986 (Investment Advertisements) (Exemptions) Order 1988[11] framed under FSA s 58(3). Approval by an authorised person would not be necessary in such a case. Where the advertisement takes the form of a document, art 9 creates a 'safe harbour' where the document is issued to persons in the UK whom the non-authorised person reasonably believes to be within one of the categories of persons specified in art 9(3); and in cases where the advertisement is issued by other means, such as Reuter screens or electronic communication systems, where the issuer reasonably believes that the means by which the advertisement is issued are such that it will not generally be made available in the UK except to persons specified in art 9(3). The persons specified in art 9(3) are essentially professionals in the Eurobond markets and include authorised or exempted persons, governments, public authorities, local authorities, international organisations of which an EEC state is a member, and institutions or corporate entities with a specified minimum net asset value. The provisions of art 9 are extremely important in the case of a non-London listed issue since it enables the marketing of the Eurobonds and the issue and distribution of the draft (and final) offering circular without occasioning a breach of s 57. The persons falling within art 9(3) of that Order are as follows:

'(3) A person falls within this paragraph if he is either—
    (a) an authorised person; or
    (b) an exempted person; or
    (c) a person who is acting in the course of a business or employment

---

8 Issued by the Council of the Stock Exchange, November 1984 edn, containing amendments up to April 1991.
9 Yellow Book s 7, ch 1, para 5.4.
10 See FSA Part IV s 142.
11 SI 1988/316.

which involves the dissemination of information concerning investments or activities of the kind described in Part II of Schedule 1 to the Act through newspapers, journals, magazines or other periodical publications or by way of sound broadcasting or television; or
(d) a government, local authority or public authority within the meaning of Note 1 to paragraph 3 of Schedule 1 to the Act;[12]
(e) a body corporate or an unincorporated association which either—
   (i) if it is a body corporate and has more than 20 members or is the subsidiary of a holding company which has more than 20 members, it, or any of its holding companies or subsidiaries, has a called up share capital or net assets of not less than £500,000; or
   (ii) if it is a body corporate other than one described in sub-paragraph (e)(i) above, it or any of its holding companies or subsidiaries has a called up share capital or net assets of not less than £5 million; or
   (iii) if it is an unincorporated association, it has net assets of not less than £5 million; or
(f) a person who holds a permission granted under paragraph 23 of Schedule 1 to the Act; or
(g) a person acting in his capacity as a director, officer or employee of a person of a kind described above in this paragraph being a person whose responsibilities, when acting in that capacity, involve him engaging in activities which fall within Part II of Schedule 1 to the Act or which would fall within that Part were it not for the provisions of Part III of that Schedule.'

A Reuter screen or other electronic screen announcement may not, however, come within art 9 if its pages can be accessed by private individuals in the UK who are not art 9(3) persons.

As far as advertising by selling group members (where there is a selling group) is concerned, in so far as the advertisement is not issued to private investors or small companies in the UK, it should be possible in practice to fall within the provisions of art 9(3) and avoid a breach of s 57.[13]

Further, exceptions to s 57 are to be found in s 58(1) which exempts the following:

'(a) any advertisement issued or caused to be issued by, and relating only to, investments issued by –
   (i) the government of the United Kingdom, of Northern Ireland or of any country or territory outside the United Kingdom;
   (ii) a local authority in the United Kingdom or elsewhere;
   (iii) the Bank of England or the central bank of any country or territory outside the United Kingdom; or
   (iv) any international organisation the members of which include the United Kingdom or another member State;

---

12 Note 1 to para 3 makes it clear that this covers governments, local authorities or public authorities anywhere, and any international organisation the members of which include the UK or another member state of the European Community.
13 The ability to issue investment advertisements to persons within art 9(3) without breaching s 57 enables a selling group member who is an overseas person to solicit art 9 investors within the UK through advertisements and carry on investment business under Sch 1 para 27 without breaching s 3 of the FSA. See discussion on p 290 above.

(b) any advertisement issued or caused to be issued by a person who is exempt under section 36, 38, 42, 44 or 45 above, or by virtue of an order under section 46 above, if the advertisement relates to a matter in respect of which he is exempt;
(c) any advertisement which is issued or caused to be issued by a national of a member State other than the United Kingdom in the course of investment business lawfully carried on by him in such a State and which conforms with any rules made under section 48(2)(e) above.'

As regards an exempt person (such as a bank which is on the Bank of England's list of Listed Institutions under FSA s 43) it is only an advertisement in respect of exempt business which is covered by s 58(1)(b). In the case of a Listed Institution, therefore, it must be an activity falling with FSA Sch 5. In the case of an entity authorised in an EC member state, s 58(1)(c) requires compliance with the SIB rules on advertising made under s 48, and which are contained in rr 5 to 13 (inclusive) of the SIB's *Core Conduct of Business Rules*.[14]

Supposing, however, that an advertisement is not within an exception to s 57, and is issued by an unauthorised person, eg a Swiss selling group member who is an overseas person seeking to place bonds by advertising to private investors resident in the UK. Such an advertisement cannot be issued unless it is 'approved' by an authorised person. The question arises as to how approval must be given and what legal obligations are owed by the authorised person in approving the advertisements. The FSA is silent on both these issues. Rule 5 of the SIB's *Core Conduct of Business Rules*[15] provides that the authorised firm should not approve the advertisement unless it has 'appropriate expertise' and it has 'reasonable grounds' to believe that the advertisement is 'fair and not misleading'. Core r 6 further requires the authorised person not to approve a 'specific investment advertisement'[16] for an unauthorised overseas entity if it would lead to a private investor in the UK entering into an investment agreement, unless (a) the advertisement contains prescribed disclosures, and (b) the firm has no reason to doubt that the overseas person will deal with UK investors 'in an honest and reliable way'.

In practice, documents issued in respect of Eurobond issues which constitute investment advertisements hardly, if ever, require to be 'approved'. The reason is that most advertisements, such as invitation telexes and Reuter screen announcements, are issued by authorised persons; while the offering circular in final and draft form (which is in practice the only document likely to be issued by a non-authorised person), falls within the safe harbour of FSA s 58(1)(d)(ii) in the case of a London listed issue of Eurobonds; or, in cases where the bonds are to be listed outside London, the bonds will only be issued to persons falling within art 9(3) of the Investment Advertisements (Exemptions) Order 1988.

---

14 See Release no 94 dated 30 January 1991.
15 See Release no 94 issued 30 January 1991 and SFA's Board Notice no 2 of 15 April 1991.
16 See definition in *The Financial Services Glossary 1991* (2nd edn) which states that it is one 'which identifies and promotes a particular investment or a particular investment service'.

2 FSA s 160 prohibition on advertisements

There are two further prohibitions on advertising contained in ss 159 and 160 of FSA Part V, which is not as yet in force at the time of writing.[17] A number of points need to be made in respect of the prohibitions in Part V.

First, these prohibitions will only apply to Eurobond issues which will not be listed on The London International Stock Exchange in accordance with Part IV of the FSA. Section 158(1) provides that Part V 'applies to any investment (a) which is not listed or the subject of an application for listing in accordance with Part IV of this Act'; and s 161(1) states that 'Sections 159 and 160 above do not apply to any advertisement offering securities if the offer is conditional on their admission to listing in accordance with Part IV of this Act ...'. Consequently, once a listing application has been made under Part IV of the FSA to the London Stock Exchange or if the offer in the advertisement is made conditional on such listing, the prohibitions in Part V have no application.

The exemption from the prohibition in s 160 in respect of securities which are the subject of a listing application under FSA Part IV includes, under s 161(2), all advertisements falling within FSA s 58(2). This includes 'advertisements which consist of or any part of, listing particulars, supplementary listing particulars' and further 'any other document required or permitted to be published by listing rules under Part IV of the Act ...'. As discussed previously, this would exempt the draft offering circular due to the permission contained in s 7 of the Yellow Book,[18] as well as the final offering circular.

Secondly, these prohibitions apply whether or not the advertisement is issued by an authorised or exempt person.

Thirdly, it must be noted that the prohibitions in Part V of the FSA including that in s 160 apply only to securities which fall within paras 1, 2, 4 or 5 of Sch 1 of the FSA. A notable exception is an investment falling within para 3 of Sch 1. Consequently the prohibition does not affect issues by:

(a) any government of any country;
(b) any local authority;
(c) any international organisation the members of which include any member state of the European Community.

Eurobond issues by such entities may, however, be listed under Part IV of the FSA due to s 142(1) and (2).[19]

Fourthly, it is probably the case that the prohibition in s 159 will be of no relevance in practice to marketing documents used in Eurobond issues, such as the offering circular. Section 159 prohibits the issue in the UK of 'an advertisement offering any securities on the occasion of their admission to dealings on an approved exchange' unless a 'prospectus' containing information about the securities has been submitted to and approved by the

---

17 On 1 July 1991.
18 See s 7, ch 1 para 5.4 and the discussion of this at ch 17 above.
19 Issues by member states of the European Community or a local authority of such a state are not covered by Part V or Part IV of the FSA. Curiously, warrants to subscribe for bonds or debentures are caught by the Part V prohibitions, but it seems that while they can be listed they cannot be listed 'in accordance with Part IV'. This is the result of s 142(3)(c) read with s 142(1) and (2).

exchange and delivered for registration to the registrar of companies. Section 159 applies only if the bonds are to be admitted to dealings on an 'approved exchange'. An 'approved exchange' is an investment exchange recognised in accordance with s 37(1) of the FSA and 'approved for purposes of Part V: section 158(6)'. In practice, Eurobonds are either listed on The London International Stock Exchange in which case Part IV applies and s 159 is consequently inapplicable; alternatively, the bonds are listed on the Luxembourg Stock Exchange which is not a recognised investment exchange and consequently s 159 is once again inapplicable.

i *FSA s 160*

Section 160, however, contains prohibitions which are potentially applicable to Eurobond issues. Section 160 prohibits the issue of 'an advertisement offering securities' containing or constituting 'a primary offer or secondary offer' of securities unless a prospectus has been delivered for registration to the registrar of companies.[20]

The phrase 'advertisement offering securities' has a wide meaning and is not confined to advertisements containing an express offer to subscribe or underwrite securities. Section 158(4) states:

'(4) For the purposes of this Part of this Act an advertisement offers securities if—
   (a) it invites a person to enter into an agreement for or with a view to subscribing for or otherwise acquiring or underwriting any securities; or
   (b) it contains information calculated to lead directly or indirectly to a person entering into such an agreement.'

Securities are defined for these purposes by s 158(1)(b) as meaning investments specified in Sch 1 paras 1, 2, 4 and 5 to the FSA, and would therefore include all forms of Eurobonds.[1]

The formula is extremely similar to that in s 57 of the FSA, except that the invitation or information must relate to an agreement for or with a view to the subscription, acquisition or underwriting of securities, whereas the language of s 57 is not so confined.[2]

A 'primary offer' is defined by s 160(2) as:

'(2) For the purposes of this section a primary offer is an advertisement issued otherwise than as mentioned in section 159(1) above inviting persons to enter into an agreement for or with a view to subscribing (whether or not in cash) for or underwriting the securities to which it relates or containing information calculated to lead directly or indirectly to their doing so.'

It will be noticed that an invitation telex to prospective underwriters or selling group members, as well as a preliminary offering circular, would be caught by the formula used to describe a primary offer.

A 'secondary offer' is defined in s 160(3) as follows:

'(3) For the purposes of this section a secondary offer is any other advertisement

---

20 See s 160(1).
1   On types of Eurobonds, see pp 213–217 above.
2   See p 298 above.

issued otherwise than as mentioned in section 159(1) above inviting persons to enter into an agreement for or with a view to acquiring the securities to which it relates or containing information calculated to lead directly or indirectly to their doing so, being an advertisement issued or caused to be issued by—
- (a) a person who has acquired the securities from the issuer with a view to issuing such an advertisement in respect of them;
- (b) a person who, with a view to issuing such an advertisement in respect of them, has acquired the securities otherwise than from the issuer but without their having been admitted to dealings on an approved exchange or held by a person who acquired them as an investment and without any intention that such an advertisement should be issued in respect of them; or
- (c) a person who is a controller of the issuer or has been such a controller in the previous twelve months and who is acting with the consent or participation of the issuer in issuing the advertisement.'

It will be noticed from the above that the provisions in s 160(3), particularly (3)(a), are of relevance only to secondary sales of Eurobonds and not to the primary market for Eurobonds.[3]

A contravention of s 160 has serious consequences. If the breach is by an authorised person he will be treated as having contravened the rules of the SRO regulating his business.[4] The consequence is that he is liable to an action in damages the suit of any 'private investor'[5] who suffers loss in consequence.[6] He is also exposed to other consequences of a breach of SRO rules. Further, action may be taken by the SIB under s 61(3) and (4) for the recovery of profits obtained as a result of the contravention of s 160, or the recovery of compensation for any loss sustained by any person as a result of the contravention.

If the breach is by a non-authorised person (this includes a breach by a non-authorised but exempt person), that person is liable to criminal prosecution (s 171(3)) subject to a defence of reasonable belief that there is no such contravention, which is available to a person who 'issues an advertisement to the order of another person' 'in the ordinary course of business other than an investment business'. The defence is hardly applicable to any selling group member, underwriter or lead manager, nor to the issuer.

In addition *any* person who is in breach of s 160 will be liable to an action for damages for any loss suffered by any person as a result of the contravention (s 171(6)). In the case of an authorised person this means that the exposure is not restricted to actions by private investors, as is the case with actions under FSA s 62.[7]

---

3 It must be noted that s 160(4) contains a presumption on the question whether securities have been acquired with a view to issuing an advertisement:

'(4) For the purposes of subsection (3)(a) above it shall be presumed in the absence of evidence to the contrary that a person has acquired securities with a view to issuing an advertisement offering the securities if he issues it or causes it to be issued

- (a) within six months after the issue of the securities; or
- (b) before the consideration due from him for their acquisition is received by the person from whom he acquired them.'

4 S 171.
5 As defined by reg 2 of the Financial Services Act 1986 (Restriction of Right of Action) Regulations 1991.
6 FSA s 62(2) and s 62A read with s 171(1).
7 FSA s 62A.

In practice, Part V will need to be complied with (when it is brought into force) only in cases where a bond issue is not subject to a London listing. Even then, it is unlikely that a Eurobond offering circular would need to comply with the contents requirements of a Part V prospectus due to the regulations expected to be framed under s 160A of the FSA.[8] Section 160A of the FSA provides as follows:

'(1) The Secretary of State may by order exempt from sections 159 and 160 when issued in such circumstances as may be specified in the order –
  (a) advertisements appearing to him to have a private character, whether by reason of a connection between the person issuing them and those to whom they are addressed or otherwise;
  (b) advertisements appearing to him to deal with investments only incidentally;
  (c) advertisments issued to persons appearing to him to be sufficiently expert to understand any risks involved;
  (d) such other classes of advertisements as he thinks fit.
(2) The Secretary of State may by order exempt from sections 159 and 160 an advertisment issued in whatever circumstances which relates to securities appearing to him to be of a kind that can be expected normally to be bought or dealt in only by persons sufficiently expert to understand any risks involved.'

Provision is expected to be made by statutory instrument under the above provision which will permit the issue of advertisements to professionals as defined in such statutory regulations. The regulations are widely expected to permit the distribution of offering circulars to market professionals and large institutional and corporate investors. No significant impact is therefore expected on Eurobond marketing practices in consequence of FSA Part V being brought into effect, in particular on the range of persons to whom the distribution of the offering circular is made in current market practice even in a non-London listed issue.

Until Part V is brought into force, however, Part III of the Companies Act 1985 will apply to any document by which an 'offer to the public' is made of shares or debentures of a company incorporated in the UK or overseas, unless such securities are subject to an application for listing to The London International Stock Exchange under FSA Part IV. The regulatory framework of a London listing and the regulatory advantages of a London listing in the context are discussed in the next section.

3 Provisions in the Companies Act 1985 Part III (to be repealed)

Until Part V (and with it, s 160) of the FSA comes into force, there are prohibitions in Part III of the Companies Act 1985 which are operative in respect of the distribution of marketing documents in a Eurobond issue, in particular the offering circular in draft and final form. The Companies Act 1985 contains prohibitions on the issue of a 'prospectus' in the UK, unless the prospectus complies with the requirements laid down in the Companies Act 1985. A prospectus is widely defined in s 58(1) in the following way: 'If a company allots or agrees to allot its shares or deben-

---

[8] Which was introduced by s 198(1) of the Companies Act 1989 replacing the old s 160(6)-(9): see s 198(4) of the Companies Act 1989.

tures with a view to all or any of them being offered for sale to the public any document by which the offer for sale to the public is made is deemed for all purposes a prospectus.'

The prohibition on the issue of such a prospectus which does not comply with the requirements of the Companies Act is imposed by s 56(1) and (2) of the Act in respect of bonds (and shares) of a UK company and by ss 72, 75 and 77 of the Companies Act in respect of companies incorporated outside Great Britain. These prohibitions would therefore be potentially applicable to Eurobond marketing documents such as the invitation telex, allotment telex, offer telex and the offering circular.

These prohibitions will, however, be repealed by s 212(3) of the FSA when that provision is fully implemented. Section 212(3) was partially brought into effect by the Financial Services Act 1986 (Commencement No 3) Order 1986.[9] Article 5 and Sch 4 of that Commencement Order limit the repeal of Part III of the Companies Act 1985 only 'to the extent to which they would apply in relation to any investment which is listed or the subject of an application for listing in accordance with Part IV of the Act'. Consequently, at present where a formal listing application has not been made to The London Stock Exchange for the listing of the bonds Part III prohibitions apply.

Even where a London listing is being sought there are a number of points to note. First, any document issued prior to the making of the formal application to list the bonds would be caught by the prohibition in the Companies Act if it constitutes a prospectus within the meaning of s 58(1) of the Companies Act 1985. Secondly, this result would ensue even if the offer in the document is said to be conditional on admission to listing.

Consequently, in practice contractual restrictions need to be imposed in the subscription agreement on each of the managers that they will not sell or offer to sell the bonds by means of any document prior to the formal application for listing in accordance with Part IV of the FSA, unless the offer does not constitute an 'offer to the public' within the meaning of Part III of the Companies Act 1985. Similar language is necessary in the offering circular and in the selling group agreement where it is used.

Where listing is to be made in Luxembourg (and not in London) the prohibitions in Part II and III of the Companies Act 1985 will therefore apply. However, a company which is not incorporated in Great Britain can escape the prohibition on the issue of a non-complying prospectus (in ss 72, 75, 77 of the Companies Act 1985) by relying on the exception contained in s 79(2), namely that the bonds are placed with persons 'whose ordinary business it is to buy or sell shares or debentures (whether as principal or agent)'. This is because such an offer to professionals does not constitute an 'offer to the public' by virtue of s 79(2) and consequently any document by which the offer is made is not regarded as a prospectus under s 58. The prohibitions in Part III Chapter II of the Companies Act 1985 do not therefore apply.

A company incorporated in Great Britain is, however, not entitled to rely on the exemption contained in s 79(2) of the Companies Act 1985 except in respect of an issue of debt securities with a maturity of under five years: FSA s 195.[10] Consequently, as far as a UK company is concerned the only

---

9 SI 1986/2246.
10 As amended by s 202 of the Companies Act 1989.

alternative to an application for listing in London is the registration of a complying prospectus in accordance with Part III of the Companies Act 1985, if it wishes to offer bonds with a maturity of five years or more by the use of an offering circular.

The exception in s 79(2) of the Companies Act 1985 must, however, be approached with caution in practice. While it is clear that Eurobond dealing houses and banks would come within the category of persons, it is by no means clear whether an offer to persons such as pension funds or insurance companies or the treasury divisions of large companies by means of a prospectus falls within the 'safe harbour' of s 79(2). It is questionable whether or not it is the 'ordinary business' of such entities to buy or sell shares. As a matter of practice, in order to enable an overseas incorporated company to take advantage of the safe harbour in s 79(2) in respect of a non-London listed Eurobond issue, it is necessary to include appropriate clauses in the Eurobond prospectus and subscription agreements. Such clauses should impose restrictions on the sale of bonds to any person in Great Britain who is not within the class of persons designated in s 79(2).

II REGULATION OF COLD CALLING

The FSA 1986 introduced a new regulatory requirement in s 56 that:

'no person shall in the course of or in consequence of an unsolicited call—
 (a) made on a person in the United Kingdom; or
 (b) made from the United Kingdom on a person elsewhere,
by way of business enter into an investment agreement with the person on whom the call is made or procure or endeavour to procure that person to enter into such an agreement.'

An unsolicited call is defined in the Act as a 'personal visit or oral communication made without express invitation'.[11]

The prohibition covers both an unsolicited call made:

(a) on a person in the UK from anywhere; and
(b) from the UK on a person elsewhere.[12]

It will be noticed that[13] there are in fact two prohibitions contained in s 56. The first is the restriction on marketing (ie cold calling to procure or endeavour to procure an investment agreement) and, secondly, the dealing prohibition (ie entering into an investment agreement which is made in the course of or in consequence of an unsolicited call).[14]

A breach of this prohibition has the consequence that an investment agreement entered into in consequence is unenforceable against the person on whom the call is made and he is entitled to recover any money or property

---

11 S 56(8).
12 S 56(1)(a) and (b).
13 See SIB's Consultative Paper 44 of October 1990 'The Proposed Common Regulations on Unsolicited Calls'.
14 The former deals with a case where the caller does not enter into a resulting investment agreement.

transferred under the agreement as well as recover compensation for any loss sustained by him as a result of such transfer of funds or property.[15] It is also to be noticed that it is not only the person who made the unsolicited call who is prevented from enforcing the resulting agreement; the unenforceability of the agreement entered into in consequence of the unsolicited call extends to any person seeking to enforce it against the person cold called. A court is, however, given a power to permit the enforcement of such an agreement in limited circumstances.[16]

In practice Eurobonds are sold by cold calling and on many occasions agreements such as the subscription agreement are entered into in consequence of cold calling.

If the rule in s 56 were applied in this situation, managing underwriters and selling group members who are called on by a lead manager on the telephone in order to invite them to be parties to the subscription agreement and selling group agreement respectively would be able to rely on s 56, to plead unenforceability of such agreements. Similarly, if selling group members telephone institutional investors and pension fund trustees, cold called for the purpose of placing bonds, they could equally be met with a defence of unenforceability. Section 56, however, permits regulations to be framed by the SIB which create exceptions to this prohibition in order to permit the continuance of ordinary market practice. Wide-ranging exceptions have in fact been created so as to confine the protection afforded by the rule largely to the protection of private investors. Unsolicited calls made in accordance with these regulations will not breach s 56.

The Common Unsolicited Calls Regulations of the Securities and Investments Board[17] which are effective from 1 January 1992 in respect of members of all SROs seek to simplify the existing regime.[18]

The Common Unsolicited Calls Regulations[19] lift the prohibitions contained in s 56 in respect of unsolicited calls on 'non-private investors' (as well as unsolicited calls where the investment agreement which results from the call is entered into by a 'non-private investor'), unless the unsolicited call is 'an overseas person call'.[20] Where the unsolicited call is made by an overseas person, the prohibitions in s 56 are lifted to the extent that the call is made on a 'non-private customer' (or where the investment agreement which results from the unsolicited call is entered into by a 'non-private customer') subject to reg 14.[1]

An 'overseas person' is defined in the SIB's *Financial Services Glossary 1991*[2] as a person who carries on investment business 'but who does not do so from a permanent place of business maintained by him in the UK'.[3]

---

15 S 56(2).
16 S 56(4).
17 Issued on 20 June 1991.
18 See Release no 101 of the SIB and Board Notice 23 of 25 July 1991 of the Securities and Futures Authority. The Regulations are made under s 56 and Sch 11 para 20 to the FSA and apply to all members of SROs by virtue of 'designation' under s 63A and Sch 11 para 22B of the FSA. The Regulations are effective for some purposes from 1 September 1991.
19 'CUCRs'.
20 See CUCRs Part 1 reg 1.
1 Discussed below.
2 2nd edn published in Release no 101 by the SIB.
3 This formula is co-extensive with the concept of overseas person used in para 26 of FSA Sch 1 Part IV.

An 'overseas person call' is defined as a 'call made by or on behalf of an overseas person and with a view to the provision of investment services: (a) to a person in the UK; and (b) by an overseas person who is not an authorised person in relation to those sources'. This means that it is only a non-authorised overseas person whose cold calling is restricted to non-private investors and is consequently prohibited from cold calling a private investor. Authorised 'overseas persons', and authorised persons with a place of business in the UK (from where it carries on investment business) as well as other entities are prohibited from cold calling 'private customers'. The concept of 'private investor' is different from 'private customer' and the former is a narrower category than the latter.

A private customer is defined by the SIB's *Financial Services Glossary 1991*[4] (the '*Glossary*') as:

'(a) a customer who is an *individual* and who is not acting in the course of carrying on investment business; or
(b) a customer who is a *small business investor* unless he is reasonably believed to be an 'ordinary business investor'.

Small business investors are defined as a company partnership or trust which does not fall within the definition of ordinary business investor.

Non-private customers will therefore comprise largely (though not exclusively) of those persons falling within the definition of 'ordinary business investor'. The definition in the *Glossary* is sufficiently wide to enable lead managers and underwriters (and selling group members, if any) to cold call potential Eurobond investors within the UK. Ordinary business investors are defined in the *Glossary* as:

'(a) a government, local authority or public authority within the meaning of Schedule 1 to the Act;
(b) a company or partnership which satisfies any of the following size requirements:
   (i) that it is a body corporate which has more than 20 members (or is the subsidiary of a company which has more than 20 members) and it (or any of its holding companies or subsidiaries) has a called up share capital or net assets of £500,000 or more;
   (ii) that it is a body corporate and it (or any of its holding companies or subsidiaries) has a called up share capital or net assets of £5 million or more; or
   (iii) if it is not a body corporate, it has net assets of £5 million or more; or
(c) a trustee of a trust which satisfies either of the following size requirements:
   (i) that the aggregate value of the cash and investments which form part of the trust's assets (before deducting the amount of its liabilities) is £10 million or more; or
   (ii) that that aggregate value has been £10 million or more at any time during the previous two years.'

It will also be noticed that there is no restriction on cold calling market professionals or 'market counterparties' as defined in the *Glossary* since 'they are not classified as '*customers*'. Consequently cold calls on market

---

4 2nd edn, see Release no 101 of the SIB.

counterparties, ie entities carrying on investment business of the same description as the party marking the unsolicited call, are not prohibited.

'Overseas person calls' are, however, restricted to 'non-private investors'. While there is no definition of 'private investor' in the *Financial Services Glossary 1991* a definition is to be found in the Financial Services Act 1986 (Restriction of Right of Action) Regulations 1991[5] framed under s 62A of the FSA.[6] This definition may presumably be used in interpreting the CUCRs of the SIB. A 'private investor' under reg 2 in the case of an individual is any natural person[7] acting otherwise than in the course of carrying on investment business and in the case of any other person acting otherwise than in the course of carrying on business of any kind. A government local authority or public authority is by definition excluded from being classified as a 'private investor'.[8]

The key difference between a 'private customer' and 'private investor' is that a company which does not have net assets of £5m or more (while acting in the course of its business) is a 'private customer' but is not a 'private investor'.

The overseas person is further limited in his ability to cold call even non-private customers by reg 14. This proviso requires either that the cold call must be made through an authorised or exempted person or, if it is made directly by the overseas person, the resulting investment agreement must be entered into by the investor with an authorised or exempted person. (It is understood, however, that this restriction is to be removed.)

The cumulative effect of the CUCR is that, except for the restrictions on marketing by 'overseas persons' who are not authorised, an authorised person may market Eurobonds to all corporate and institutional entities as well as pension fund trustees within the UK which satisfy the size criteria laid down in the Regulations.

The Unsolicited Calls Regulations 1987 of the SIB,[9] which remained in force until 1 September 1991, permitted the making of unsolicited calls on the following categories of persons in the context of the marketing of Eurobonds.

(a) Market counterparties[10] A market counterparty was defined by SIB's Financial Services (Glossary and Interpretation) Rules and Regulations 1990 (the '1990 Glossary') as a person who carries on investment business of the same description as that carried on by the party making the unsolicited call and in the course of carrying on such business he acts as counterparty to the transaction which is effected in consequence of the unsolicited call.

This exception would cover a lead manager cold calling prospective underwriters, managers and selling group members.

(b) Business investors[11] The 1990 Glossary provided that a 'business investor' means:

---

5 SI 1991/489.
6 Which was inserted into the FSA by s 193 of the Companies Act 1989.
7 Ie non-corporate or non-artificial person.
8 Reg 2(1) of SI 1991/489.
9 Release no 53 of the SIB amended to 21 April 1989.
10 Reg 4(1)(e).
11 Reg 4(1)(e).

(a) a government, local authority or public authority within the meaning of note 1 to Sch 1 para 3 of the Act or any body whose functions are confined to acting on behalf of any such government, local authority or public authority; or
(b) a company which carries on a business which is not investment business or which, if it is investment business, may under the Act be lawfully carried on by a person who is not an authorised person being a company which satisfies the following criteria:
  (i) if the company is a body corporate which has more than 20 members or which, being a subsidiary, has a holding company which has more than 20 members, the company or any of its holding companies or any of its subsidiaries has a called-up share capital or net assets of not less than £500,000; or
  (ii) if the company is a body corporate other than one described in (i), the company or any of its holding companies or any of its subsidiaries has a called up share capital or net assets of not less than £5m; or
  (iii) if the company is not a body corporate, the company has net assets of not less than £5m;[12] or
(c) a trustee of a trust where the aggregate value of the cash and investments which form a part of the trust's assets (before deducting the amount of its liabilities) is £10m or more or has been £10m or more at any time during the previous two years.

This category of exception permitted selling group members to make unsolicited calls on a large range of companies and institutions.

(c) Professional investors These are entities or persons carrying on investment business.

III MISLEADING STATEMENTS

FSA s 47(1) also creates a criminal offence in respect of an oral or documentary statement which is false or misleading or which dishonestly conceals material facts. This too must be considered in the context of the regulation of marketing.

Section 47(1) states as follows:

'Any person who –
  (a) makes a statement, promise or forecast which he knows to be misleading, false or deceptive or dishonestly conceals any material facts; or
  (b) recklessly makes (dishonestly or otherwise) a statement, promise or forecast which is misleading, false or deceptive,
is guilty of an offence if he makes the statement, promise or forecast or conceals the facts for the purpose of inducing, or is reckless as to whether it may induce, another person (whether or not the person to whom the statement, promise or forecast is made or from whom the facts are concealed) to enter or offer

---

12 Net assets are to be computed by reference to the formula in s 264 of the Companies Act 1985 if the company is a UK company. (See Practice Note to r 1.05 of the SIB's Financial Services (Conduct of Business) Rules 1987 which were replaced by the 1990 Rules.)

to enter into, or to refrain from entering or offering to enter into, an investment agreement or to exercise, or refrain from exercising, any rights conferred by an investment.'

This offence is relevant and needs to be considered in the context of statements forecasts and projections made by an issuer of bonds, particularly in the prospectus. Clearly it is of fundamental importance that all information emanating from the issuer be as accurate and complete as due diligence can make it. In so far as false statements are contained in listing particulars delivered to The Stock Exchange under Part IV[13] civil consequences follow which are discussed in the next chapter.[14] For the offence in s 47(1) to be committed there must be the actus of:

(a) the making of a statement, promise or forecast which is misleading, false or deceptive (the 'making'); or
(b) the concealing of material facts ('concealing').

Secondly, there must be two levels of mens rea:

(i) in respect of (a) above the making must be misleading etc to the knowledge of the maker or alternatively it must be made 'recklessly';[15] in respect of (b) above, the concealing must be dishonest;
(ii) at the second level the 'making' or 'concealing' must either be for the 'purpose of' inducing another person to enter into (or offer to enter into or to refrain from entering into or to offer to refrain from entering into) an investment agreement or to exercise or refrain from exercising any rights conferred by an investment; alternatively absent such a purpose, the maker of the statement (or person concealing material facts) must be reckless as to such consequences.

It is also important to note that the offence has extraterritorial ramifications.[16] First, if conduct occurs in the UK there is liability regardless of whether the party who may have been induced to enter into an investment agreement etc was resident outside the UK.

Secondly, even if the conduct capable of constituting the offence occurred entirely outside the UK, nevertheless, if the person who may have been induced to enter into an investment agreement etc is in the UK, the offence may be committed in the UK.

Thirdly, even if all the conduct constituting the offence occurred outside the UK, and the person who is likely to have entered into an investment agreement etc in consequence is outside the UK, nevertheless if the investment agreement is or would be entered into in the UK (or rights were to be exercised under it in the UK), the offence could be committed in the UK.

Thus, for instance, if a false statement is contained in a prospectus issued

---

13 Or in a prospectus issued under Part V.
14 See ss 150 and 152, 153 in respect of listing particulars and ss 166 and 168 in respect of a Part V prospectus.
15 As to what constitutes 'recklessness' in the criminal law see Smith and Hogan *Criminal Law* (Butterworths, 6th edn, 1988) pp 61–63 and 63–69; *R v Cunningham* [1957] 2 All ER 412; *R v Caldwell* [1982] AC 341; *R v Lawrence* [1982] AC 510.
16 See s 47(4).

in London and, subsequently, it is delivered by a selling group member resident in Switzerland to an end investor in Switzerland, an offence could be committed in the UK. It is also extremely important to appreciate the requirement as to disclosure of material facts. In respect of a bond issue which is London listed compliance with listing requirements should usually eliminate any danger of exposure to liability under s 47(1) on the basis of a failure to disclose material facts.

However, where there is a failure to disclose material facts and the non-disclosure was 'dishonest',[17] the issuer would nearly always be liable under s 47 (even if the issuer is a foreign entity) since all the operative investment agreements are usually entered into in London,[18] or because banks and dealers from whom material facts are concealed and who are the persons likely to be induced to enter into investment agreements as a result of concealment, are in the UK.[19]

Section 47(1) is also potentially applicable to the statements of forecasts of lead managers, underwriters and selling group members.

Thus, any statements by the lead manager to prospective underwriters or selling group members as to the likely demand for the issuer's bonds, or the likely yield on the bonds, are potentially within s 47 if recklessly made (or with knowledge of falsity). Similarly, statements made by selling group members to end investors as to these matters are also within s 47, again if made recklessly (or with knowledge as to their falsity).

---

17 See Smith and Hogan *Criminal Law* pp 555, 556 and 573 for a discussion of the meaning of dishonesty.
18 S 47(4)(c).
19 S 47(4)(b).

CHAPTER 17
The listing of Eurobonds[1]

Eurobonds are usually listed on either the International Stock Exchange in London (referred to in this chapter as 'The London Stock Exchange')[2] or the Luxembourg Stock Exchange.

1 WHY ARE EUROBONDS LISTED?

There is no positive legal requirement under English law that bonds must be listed before they are sold. The reasons for listing are largely commercial. English regulatory law moreover confers certain advantages on Eurobond issues which are listed on The London Stock Exchange.

Usually an investor is more likely to buy securities when they are issued if he knows that there is a liquid secondary market where he can subsequently sell those securities at a good price. A stock exchange will generally result in the availability of such a market where securities can be sold to purchasers. It will also provide a mechanism whereby the best price for the shares can be determined by bringing intending sellers into contact with intending purchasers of shares. Most stock exchanges restrict the securities which may be traded there to those which are listed on that stock exchange. Consequently, a listing becomes desirable since it enables an issuer of securities to obtain the advantages of the liquid trading market provided by a stock exchange.

However, this is not why Eurobonds are listed, as the secondary market for trading in Eurobonds is not The London Stock Exchange or the Luxembourg Stock Exchange where Eurobonds are listed, but an 'over the counter' ('OTC') market where transactions are effected as between professional

---

1 See generally: *Euro Currency Debt Securities, Guide to Listing*, published by The Stock Exchange, January 1989 (called the 'Blue Guide'); *A Practitioner's Guide to the Stock Exchange Yellow Book* (Westminster Management Consultants) especially chs 2 and 8; Fisher *International Bonds* (Euromoney Publications) ch 6 (hereafter *Fisher*).
2 The formal title of The London Stock Exchange is The International Stock Exchange of the United Kingdom and the Republic of Ireland Ltd.
    In respect of Deutschmark denominated issues a listing is usually obtained in Frankfurt, sometimes in addition to London or Luxembourg. A similar practice exists in respect of Swiss franc denominated issues (which are listed on Swiss stock exchanges) as well as in respect of yen denominated issues (which are listed in Tokyo).

dealers who are members of the Association of International Bond Dealers (the 'AIBD'), which is soon to be renamed the International Securities Markets Association. The stock exchange on which bonds are listed usually obtains the price quotations from AIBD members.[3]

The reason for obtaining a listing for Eurobonds must therefore be looked for elsewhere. The primary reason seems to be that in many countries major institutional as well as private investors are prevented by local law from purchasing bonds which are not listed on a stock exchange, and sometimes even if laws do not prevent the purchase of unlisted securities it seems that in practice institutional investors such as pension funds have a policy of not purchasing unlisted bonds.[4] There is also an advantage to bondholders in having a daily price quoted in the financial press which reflects the official stock exchange price for their investments. Further, it is thought the publication of an official price list for listed securities in the financial press is an attraction for corporate issuers who regard it as an advertising and publicity medium.[5]

To the intending purchaser of bonds the major advantage of listing is that detailed disclosure and publication of information about the securities and the issuer is required by the relevant stock exchange as a precondition to listing. Both London and Luxembourg have disclosure requirements based on the European Community Admissions Directive[6] and the European Community Directive on Listing Particulars.[7] First, there is the initial disclosure required to be submitted and published in the form of 'listing particulars', prior to the admission of securities to dealing on a stock exchange. Secondly, both stock exchanges require continuing disclosure of information during the time a listing is maintained for the bonds, in compliance with the requirements of the Admissions Directive of the European Community.

II REGULATORY BACKGROUND TO A LONDON LISTING

The vast majority of Eurobond issues are effected from London, and there are provisions of English securities law which make a London listing desirable though not mandatory. The importance of a listing on The London Stock Exchange from a regulatory standpoint is that it enables the bonds to be marketed and sold to a much wider range of investors in the UK than would otherwise be possible. This is due to the fact that prohibitions contained in UK securities regulation which prevent the issue of advertisements including an offering circular or prospectus in respect of a securities issue cease to apply when an application for listing is made.

---

3 Stock exchanges are, however, used for some smaller 'odd lot' transactions. See *Fisher* ch 6 at 96.
4 See *Fisher* p 96.
5 *Fisher* p 96.
6 (EEC) 79/279 of 5 March 1979.
7 (EEC) 80/390 of 17 March 1990.

1 Provisions of FSA 1986

As discussed previously, FSA s 160[8] and s 57 contain prohibitions on the issue of certain types of advertisements.

i Section 160

Section 160 states that:

> '(1) No person shall issue or cause to be issued in the United Kingdom an advertisement offering any securities which is a primary or secondary offer within the meaning of this section unless—
> (a) he has delivered for registration to the registrar of companies a prospectus relating to the securities and expressed to be in respect of the offer;
> ...'

It was also pointed out[9] that due to FSA s 158(1), s 160 (when brought into force) will not apply where securities are listed under Part IV of FSA or are 'the subject of an application for listing in accordance with Part IV of this Act'. Further, s 161(1) provides that s 160 will not apply to any 'advertisement offering securities if the offer is conditional on their admission to listing in accordance with Part IV of this Act'.

In the absence of listing, s 160 would prevent the distribution of the Eurobond offering circular (in draft or final form) unless a prospectus complying with the requirements of FSA Part V had been delivered for registration to the registrar of companies; alternatively, as discussed previously, the distribution of the offering circular is confined to persons specified by statutory instrument by the Secretary of State under s 160A(1)(c) and 160A(2),[10] namely, persons sufficiently expert to understand any risks involved.

As pointed out earlier, until such time as FSA Part V (including s 160) is brought into force, Part III of the Companies Act 1985 will continue to apply to distribution of the offering circular in draft and final form. Again, a London listing or an application for such a listing disapplies Part III of the Companies Act 1985.

ii Section 57

Section 57 of the FSA contains the wider prohibition on the issue of 'investment advertisements' by persons who are not 'authorised' under the provisions of the FSA unless it is 'approved' by an authorised person, as discussed in the previous chapter. Issuers of Eurobonds are generally not 'authorised' persons under the FSA regime whereas the issuer's offering circular (in draft and final form) constitutes an 'investment advertisement'. These documents are not 'approved' in practice by an authorised person. Consequently, s 57 would prohibit the issue of the offering circular unless an exemption applied. Section 58(1)(d)(ii) of the FSA exempts from the prohibition in s 57 of that Act 'any advertisement which consists of or any part of listing particu-

---

8 When it is brought into force.
9 See ch 16, pp 305 et seq.
10 These provisions were inserted by s 198(1) of the Companies Act 1989.

lars or any other document required or permitted to be published by listing rules under Part IV of this Act'. An application for listing to The London Stock Exchange under FSA Part IV requires the submission of draft listing particulars and in practice would consist of the draft offering circular and, as pointed out earlier, The London Stock Exchange permits the circulation of the draft listing particulars for the purposes of underwriting and selective marketing.[11]

Consequently, a listing has the added advantage that it provides an exception to the prohibition in s 57 as regards the issue of the offering circular.

III LISTING RULES: THE LEGAL BASIS

A listing of bonds on The London Stock Exchange must be effected in accordance with listing rules contained in The London Stock Exchange *Admission of Securities to Listing*,[12] referred to as the 'Yellow Book'.

The legal status of these rules governing listing now rest on the statutory framework provided by Part IV of the FSA 1986.[13]

Part IV was intended to give effect to three European Community Directives:

(a) the Admissions Directive (Council Directive no 79/279/EEC);
(b) the Listing Particulars Directive (Council Directive no 80/390/EEC); and
(c) the Interim Reports Directive (Council Directive no 82/121/EEC).

These directives represent the minimum requirements as to the conditions for listing and admission to dealing on European Community stock exchanges. The regulatory framework in the UK, which gives effect to these directives, is Part IV of the FSA. Under Part IV, the Council of The London Stock Exchange is made 'the competent authority' to make listing rules (s 142(6)). The London Stock Exchange's rules, in *Admission of Securities to Listing* (the 'Yellow Book'), contain the body of regulations which meet the standards laid down in the directives referred to above. While there is no express obligation on the part of The London Stock Exchange to comply with the requirements of the directives, the Secretary of State has a power under s 192 to give directions to the Council of The London Stock Exchange where it appears to him that the regulations do not meet with minimum criteria laid down by the directives or indeed any other aspect of European Community law.

A listing in accordance with rules laid down in the Yellow Book is thus a listing 'in accordance with Part IV'. Part IV confers specific powers on the competent authority as to the rules which may be enacted.

(a) Section 143(1) provides that the Council may make rules as to the manner in which an application for listing is to be made. No application for listing can be made except in accordance with such rules.

---

11 See the Yellow Book s 7, ch 1, para 5.4 and the discussion at pp 301–302 above.
12 Published by The Stock Exchange, loose-leaf edn, 1984 as amended to June 1991.
13 As to the history of regulation see *Practitioner's Guide to the Stock Exchange Yellow Book* ch 2.

(b) Section 144(2) empowers the Council to require the submission and approval of 'listing particulars' in a form and manner specified by the rules as a precondition to listing.
(c) Section 144(2) empowers the Council to make rules which require the publication of such listing particulars as a precondition to listing.
(d) Section 144(3) gives the Council power to refuse an application if it considers that the admission of the securities would be 'detrimental to the interests of investors' or where the securities are listed outside Great Britain that the issuer 'has failed to comply with any obligations to which he is subject by virtue of that listing'.
(e) Section 153 empowers the Council to make rules laying down requirements as to listed securities, ie it may impose obligations on the issuer of listed securities. These could cover requirements as to the continuing disclosure of information as to the issuer.
(f) Section 145(2) confers a power on the Council to suspend listing temporarily in accordance with the rules. A power of permanent discontinuance of listing is conferred by s 142(3).

IV THE REQUIREMENTS FOR LISTING

1 Basic requirements[14]

These require that:

(a) in the case of a corporate issuer, it must be duly incorporated and must be acting in accordance with the law of the place of incorporation and its memorandum and articles of association;
(b) the securities for which listing is sought must be issued in conformity with the law of the place of incorporation of the issuer;
(c) there is a minimum aggregate value for the bonds but that figure is only £200,000 and it is of no importance in practice; 'tapstock' issues are exempted;
(d) the securities must be transferable; in practice The London Stock Exchange usually also requires that bonds be denominated in small amounts, eg US $5,000 for purposes of tradeability;
(e) the issuer should have published or filed accounts covering the two years preceding application for listing, though this requirement may be waived by the Council;
(f) if the bonds are convertible Eurobonds then they can be listed only if the underlying shares into which the bonds can be converted are themselves listed on The London Stock Exchange or listed or traded on another major stock exchange or market.

2 Preconditions to a listing application

(a) an application for listing requires the appointment of a member firm of The London Stock Exchange or the Securities and Futures Authority

---

14 Yellow Book s 7, ch 1, para 2 and s 1, ch 2.

322   *The listing of Eurobonds*

to 'sponsor' the listing application and to lodge the necessary documents with the Quotations Department;[15]

(b) a paying agent in respect of the bonds must be appointed with an office in the City of London.

3 Requirements as to time and documents

(a) Draft listing particulars and a number of other documents must be submitted at least 14 days prior to the intended date of publication which in a Eurobond issue is the signing date.[16] In the case of states, public international bodies and local authorities this requirement is modified to require submission two days prior to the determination of the listing application.

(b) The 48-hour rule: under s 7, ch 1, para 4 the requirements of the '48-hour' rule applicable in domestic issues[17] are modified in the case of Eurobonds. However, this provision requires that at least two days prior to the hearing of the listing application a number of documents must be lodged with the appropriate committee. These documents include the following:

  (i) four copies of the listing particulars (or equivalent offer document in the case of states and regional or local authorities) in final form dated and signed by a duly authorised officer of the issuer;
  (ii) an application form (Form AFA) for admission to listing of securities signed by a duly authorised officer of the issuer; it is this formal application which activates Part IV of the FSA and results in the disapplication of Part III of the Companies Act 1985;
  (iii) a copy of the executed trust deed, or fiscal agency agreement unless the issuer is a state or regional or local authority (this requirement may be satisfied by submission of the trust deed or fiscal agency agreement in draft form);[18]
  (iv) necessary board resolutions from the issuer;
  (v) letter and application by the sponsoring firm;
  (vi) the temporary global bond or the definitive bond.

The listing particulars are then approved by The London Stock Exchange.

4 Registration and publication of listing particulars

After approval of the listing particulars these must be published as required by the Yellow Book.[19] However, it is a mandatory requirement under s 149(1) of the FSA that on or before the date on which listing particulars are published as required by the listing rules a copy of the listing

---

15 See s 1, ch 1, para 1.4.
16 See s 2, ch 1, para 2.1 and s 7, ch 1, para 4.3.
17 S 2, ch 1, para 5.
18 See s 2, ch 1, para 5.8.
19 S 7, ch 1, para 5.

particulars must be delivered to the Registrar of Companies for registration and a statement that a copy has been delivered to him must be included in the particulars. Failure to deliver a copy of the listing particulars prior to publication is a criminal offence under s 149(3) (the Yellow Book makes no mention of the requirement).

After delivery of a copy of the listing particulars for registration, listing particulars must be published before the Eurobonds are formally admitted to listing on The London Stock Exchange. Publication consists in sufficient copies of the listing particulars being made available free of charge at the office of the paying agent and the registered office of the issuer for 14 days from the day on which the bonds are admitted to listing.[20] Publication follows immediately after approval of the listing particulars in final form by the Committee of the Quotations Department.

It has been pointed out above[1] that it is a condition precedent in the subscription agreement that the issuer obtains a listing of the bonds by closing date. For this purpose a letter is obtained from The London Stock Exchange confirming the grant of listing subject only to the issue of documents of title.

The Yellow Book requires a formal notice of the listing to be published in the Official List of The London Stock Exchange which appears in a daily newspaper, if the bonds are those of an issuer who does not already have its shares listed on The London Stock Exchange.[2] However, para 6 of the Blue Guide (*The Euro Currency Debt Securities, Guide to Listing*) states that The London Stock Exchange itself will arrange for this formal notice that application has been made for listing to be included in The London Stock Exchange's Official List.[3]

5 Determining the contents of listing particulars

The purpose of listing particulars is to provide maximum disclosure to investors and their professional advisers of information concerning the issuer and the securities in question.

The contents of listing particulars, however, vary significantly depending on:

(a) the type of issuer, that is, whether it is a company, sovereign state or international organisation;
(b) the type of bond, that is, whether the bonds are straight debt securities or have an equity element (ie are they convertibles or bonds with equity warrants?);
(c) whether the issuer is already listed or whether it is a new applicant; The London Stock Exchange treats issuers who have a listing on a major international stock exchange on the same footing as an issuer who is listed in London.[4]

---

20 See s 7, ch 1, para 5 and s 2, ch 3, para 7 of the Yellow Book.
1 See ch 10 above.
2 See s 2, ch 3, para 3 of the Yellow Book.
3 As for contents of the formal notice see para 6.1 of the *Guide to Listing of Eurocurrency Debt Securities* and para 3.6 of s 2 ch 3 of the Yellow Guide.
4 See para 5.2 of the Blue Guide.

6 FSA section 146

Independently of the specific requirements of disclosure contained in the listing particulars of the Yellow Book, there is an overriding duty of disclosure contained in s 146 of the FSA, derived from art 4(1) of the Listing Particulars Directive.[5] The duty is to disclose 'all such information as investors and their professional advisers would reasonably require, and reasonably expect to find there for the purpose of making an informed assessment of:

> '(a) the assets and liabilities, financial position, profits and losses and prospects of the issuer of the securities; and
> (b) the rights attaching to the securities.'

The obligation is imposed on the 'persons responsible' for listing particulars under s 152 of the FSA and extends to the disclosure of all such matters that are 'within the knowledge of any person responsible for the listing particulars or which it would be reasonable for him to obtain by making enquiries'. The obligation therefore is much wider than a duty to disclose that which is within a person's actual knowledge; there is a duty of due enquiry.

The London Stock Exchange is, however, given a power of derogation under s 148 which provides that they may authorise omissions from listing particulars or supplementary listing particulars of any information which would otherwise require disclosure under s 146:

(a) if disclosure would be contrary to the public interest; or
(b) on the ground that its disclosure would be seriously detrimental to the issuer unless non disclosure would mislead an investor (ss 148(1)(b) and 148(2)); or
(c) on the ground that disclosure is unnecessary for the type of persons who may be expected to purchase securities. (This particular derogation is available only in respect of bonds or debentures.)

Consequently, even where a disclosure would be required under s 146, disclosure may be dispensed with under s 148 by The London Stock Exchange.[6]

7 Section 7 of the Yellow Book

Much of the Yellow Book is concerned with issues of securities to the public at large. Eurobonds are offered in a manner which precludes the average member of the public from participating directly in the primary distribution and purchase of bonds. Such distributions are referred to in the Yellow Book as 'selective marketing', since the bonds are 'normally bought and traded in by a limited number of investors who are particularly knowledgeable in investment matters'.[7] Consequently, the requirements of the Yellow Book applicable to ordinary public offering of securities are considered inap-

---

5 (EEC) 80/390 of 17 March 1980.
6 See also Sch 6 to The London Stock Exchange's *Guide to Listing of Euro Currency Debt Securities* (the 'Blue Guide').
7 See s 7, ch 1, para 1.

propriate for Eurobonds by The London Stock Exchange[28] and a large number of exemptions are therefore granted in the case of Eurobonds (referred to as 'Eurocurrency securities') in s 7 of the Yellow Book.[9]

It must be noted, however, that the special exemptions apply only if the issue of bonds is effected by means of a marketing structure which is regarded by The London Stock Exchange as a 'Eurocurrency selective marketing' within the meaning of s 7, ch 1 of the Yellow Book.[10]

8 Requirements of disclosure: contents of listing particulars

The more important categories of information which are required to be disclosed in listing particulars under the Yellow Book in the case of a listed corporate issuer are as follows:

(a) Details relating to the name, registered office, place of incorporation of the issuer, followed by a corporate declaration of responsibility for the accuracy and completeness of the listing particulars in a form specified in the Yellow Book.[11]
(b) Information about the bonds including aggregate nominal amount, number and denomination, summary of rights conferred on bondholders, whether bearer or registered, issue and redemption price, currency of the bonds, interest rates and due dates for interest, tax on the bonds in particular withholding and arrangements for the transfer of securities including any restrictions on transfer.[12] If there is a trustee, or a subordination clause, or a guarantee, details of such must also be given.
(c) Financial and corporate information about the issuer and its management.

This last will include a brief description of the corporate group to which the issuer belongs, a consolidated capitalisation table and indebtedness statement for the issuer (and any guarantor), a statement that year-end financial statements have been audited and that no significant change has occurred since the end of the last audited financial statement. The indebtedness statement is an important feature of this section of the listing particulars and the statement must distinguish between different types of debt, for instance between loan capital and term loans, guaranteed and unguaranteed debt, secured and unsecured debt, mortgages and contingent liabilities. The audited accounts of the issuer (or guarantor) or the consolidated group audited accounts for each of the two years previous must be made available at a place specified in the listing particulars though they need not be included

---

8   See s 7, ch 1, para 1 of the Yellow Book.
9   The Stock Exchange has also published in January 1989 a *Guide to Listing of Euro-currency Debt Securities* (the Blue Guide), but it does not replace the Yellow Book rules.
10 In practice all matters concerned with the Yellow Book are dealt with by the Committee of the Quotations Department of The London Stock Exchange rather than the Council which is the administrative governing body of The London Stock Exchange.
11 S 3, ch 2, Part 1 of the Yellow Book and Sch 1 of the Blue Guide.
12 See Yellow Book s 3, ch 2, Parts 2 and 8.

in the listing particulars and a statement to that effect must be contained in the listing particulars.

In addition to financial statistics, information about the directors of the group and general prospects for the products, costs and sales of the group must be provided.

Disclosure is also required of legal or arbitration proceedings pending or threatened against any member of the group which may have or have had in the previous 12 months a significant effect on the group's financial position. If there is none then an appropriate negative statement must be made. This is, of course, an important safeguard for investors. A similar requirement does, however, exist in respect of material contracts which may have an adverse effect on the issuer's or guarantor's financial position in the case of domestic issues.[13] This requirement is deemed to be satisfied in the case of Eurobonds by the summary of the principal provisions of the documents in respect of the issue, such as the subscription agreement and trust deed, which must be included in the listing particulars.[14]

Where the issuer or guarantor is not listed in London or on another major international exchange additional disclosure is required. The principal items of additional information required to be disclosed in listing particulars are, first, that the group's principal activities must be itemised specifying the main products and/or services with figures and explanations demonstrating the relative importance of each business activity[15] and, secondly, audited balance sheets and revenue statements must be incorporated in the form of an accountant's statement for the preceding three years together with the latest interim financial statements.[16]

Where the Eurobond issue is guaranteed by a state entity, a number of items which the ordinary listed issuer must disclose in the listing particulars may be dispensed with. The principal matters which need not be disclosed are the capitalisation table and statement of indebtedness. These liberal disclosure provisions are also applied to corporate entities which are not state guaranteed but which are companies incorporated in a member state of the European Community.[17] The same level of disclosure is required of a number of public international bodies such as:

> The International Monetary Fund
> The International Finance Corporation
> The International Bank for Reconstruction and Development
> The European Investment Bank
> The Asian Development Bank
> The Inter-American Development Bank
> The Caribbean Development Bank
> The African Development Bank.

Convertible Eurobonds attract greater and much more stringent disclosure requirements than straight Eurobonds. Some of the additional disclosure provisions relate to the underlying shares into which the bonds can be con-

---

13 See s 3, ch 3, Part 3, para 3.16.
14 See s 7, ch 1, para 6.3(d).
15 See the Yellow Book s 3, ch 2, Part 4.
16 See the Yellow Book s 3, ch 2, Part 5.
17 See Sch 2 of the Blue Guide to Listing.

verted while others require disclosure of corporate information more relevant to a share issue than a bond issue.

The main additional disclosure provisions are that:

(a) the nature of the shares offered by way of conversion or exchange and the rights attaching to those shares; and
(b) the conditions of and procedure for conversion exchange or subscription and the circumstances in which such rights can be amended,

must be disclosed.

The contents of listing particulars for convertible Eurobonds are specified in s 7, ch 1, para 6.4(iii) of the Yellow Book and it is not proposed to reproduce them here.

9 Other requirements of listing

i *Security printing of definitive bonds*

Definitive bonds must comply with the high security printing requirements laid down by s 9, ch 4 of the Yellow Book. This requirement does not apply to issuers incorporated or established in a member state of the European Community, in which event bearer documents of title produced in compliance with standards in the home state will suffice.

Previously there were two other conditions which needed to be complied with. These are no longer applicable.

ii *Extel Cards*

In the past the Yellow Book required that arrangements must be made for particulars relating to the bonds to be circulated through the Extel Card statistical services system before the formal notice in the newspapers. The Extel system is the service maintained by Extel Financial Ltd where each issuer of securities listed on The London Stock Exchange provides details of the securities and the issuer to Extel which are then circulated to members of the system. The details included on the Extel Card need not be as extensive as those found in the listing particulars but must include the terms and conditions of the bonds and, in the case of convertible Eurobonds, the terms, conditions and procedures for conversion, and a description, of the underlying shares. The London Stock Exchange, however, announced on 16 January 1989 that this requirement will no longer be insisted on in the case of Eurobonds.

iii *Offer of participation to two market makers*

In the past, as a condition of a London listing participations had to be offered in the marketing of the bonds to two registered market makers in the type of bonds in question. This requirement has been withdrawn by The London Stock Exchange with effect from 16 January 1989.

V SUPPLEMENTARY LISTING PARTICULARS: FSA S 147

If there is a significant change of circumstances at any time after the preparation of listing particulars but before the commencement of dealings in the bonds after their admission to the Official List, the issuer is obliged under FSA s 147 to disclose these changed circumstances in 'supplementary listing particulars'. The supplementary listing particulars must also be approved and published in accordance with the Yellow Book.[18]

It is important to note the type of matter which triggers the s 147 obligation. Section 147(1)(a) refers to 'a significant change affecting any matter contained in the listing particulars whose inclusion was required by s 146' (ie the general duty of disclosure) while s 147(1)(b) refers to 'a significant new matter' arising which should have been included in the listing particulars had it existed at the time of their preparation. Section 147(2) clarifies the word 'significant' by providing that significance of a fact must be judged by reference to the question of 'making an informed assessment' of the matters referred to in s 146, namely, the financial position and future prospects of the issuer of the bonds or the rights attaching to the bonds. Thus, for instance, if a hostile takeover bid is launched for the issuer this would need to be disclosed. So too if there is a concrete merger proposal or restructuring of the group which is decided on, supplementary listing particulars may be required.

The obligation does not arise, however, unless the issuer is aware or has notice of the significant change or significant new matter (s 147(3)). 'Persons responsible for listing particulars' are, however, under an obligation to notify the issuer of any such significant change or matter if they are aware of it (s 147(3)).

The London Stock Exchange nevertheless has wide power under s 148 to authorise the omission from supplementary listing particulars of any matter requiring disclosure under s 146.[19] Nevertheless, there is an overriding requirement that non-disclosure should not be likely to mislead an investor of facts which it is essential for him to have knowledge of to make an informed assessment (s 148(2)). The balance which must be struck between these conflicting considerations is obviously a difficult one for The London Stock Exchange in deciding to exempt a fact from disclosure. It is not clear whether if The London Stock Exchange decides to waive disclosure under s 148 it may equally waive the need for supplementary listing particulars, if the only significant matter which was to be published consisted of the information which The London Stock Exchange exempted from disclosure. As a matter of common sense this must be the logical result though as a matter of language s 148(1) empowers The London Stock Exchange only to 'authorise the omission from ... supplementary listing particulars of any information ...', but does not authorise waiver of the supplementary listing particulars itself.

---

18 FSA s 147(1).
19 See p 324 above.

VI LIABILITY FOR FALSE OR MISLEADING LISTING PARTICULARS AND SUPPLEMENTARY LISTING PARTICULARS

Criminal as well as civil liability may attach to the publication of false or misleading listing particulars, or the omission of material facts from such particulars.

1 Criminal liability

While no special criminal offence is created in respect of false or misleading statements in listing particulars criminal liability can arise under the provisions of s 47(1) of the FSA. Section 47 imposes liability on any person who 'makes a statement, promise or forecast which he knows to be misleading, false or deceptive or dishonestly conceals any material facts or recklessly makes a statement promise or forecast which is false or misleading', if he does so for the purpose of inducing or being reckless as to whether it may induce another person to enter into or offer to enter into an 'investment agreement'.[20] Any sale or purchase of bonds in the market would constitute an 'investment agreement' by virtue of FSA s 44(9).[1] It should be noted that mere negligence in making the statement or forecast is not enough for the offence to be constituted. On the other hand, given the necessary mens rea, it does not matter that the person who enters or offers to enter into the investment agreement was in fact the person to whom the statement, promise or forecast was knowingly or recklessly made.

Further, even if the statement, promise or forecast is made overseas, eg because the particulars are prepared overseas, nevertheless there can be liability on the basis that either the recipient is in the UK or that the investment agreement is to be entered into in the UK. The offence therefore has extra-territorial effect.[2] Proof of loss is unnecessary.

2 Civil liability

Civil liability is imposed by FSA s 150 where a person has acquired securities and suffered loss in respect of them as a result of any untrue or misleading statement or due to *an omission* from the listing particulars of facts which ought to have been disclosed by virtue of the duty of disclosure under s 146 or s 147 of the FSA.[3] A similar liability is imposed in respect of supplementary listing particulars by s 151. A number of points need to be made.

First, liability arises provided there is a causal nexus between the false or misleading statement or omission in the listing particulars and the loss suffered by a purchaser of the securities to which the listing particulars relate. Reliance (even partial reliance) by the plaintiff on the contents of the listing particulars in deciding to acquire the securities in question is

---

20 See s 44(9) and p 299 above.
1 See FSA s 44(9) for the definition of an investment agreement.
2 See FSA s 47(3).
3 See p 324 above.

not technically a necessary precondition to the availability of the cause of action under s 150. Indeed, theoretically even a plaintiff who had not seen or was unaware of the existence of the listing particulars is capable of bringing an action under s 150. However, a plaintiff who cannot show reliance would have an exceedingly difficult task in establishing a causal nexus between the inaccuracy or omission in the listing particulars and the loss which he has suffered.

Secondly, negligence is not a precondition which needs to be proved in order to bring the action. However, under s 151 reasonable belief in the accuracy of statements or that an omission was proper is a defence in certain circumstances to an action under s 150. The reasonable belief must, however, be based on enquiry which ought reasonably to have been made. Further:

(a) the belief must have continued until the securities were acquired (presumably by the plaintiff); or
(b) the defendant may show that the bonds were acquired before it was reasonably practicable to bring a correction to the attention of persons likely to acquire the securities; or
(c) that before the securities were acquired he had taken all reasonable steps to secure that a correction was brought to the attention of persons who are likely to have bought the securities; or
(d) that he continued in the belief until commencement of dealings in the bonds following their admission to the Official List of The London Stock Exchange and that the securities were acquired after such a lapse of time that he ought in the circumstances to be excused.

Thirdly, where an obligation has arisen under s 147 to publish supplementary listing particulars liability can arise for a failure to file such supplementary listing particulars where a person has acquired securities and suffered loss in consequence of the failure.

Fourthly, the question arises as to whether liability may arise under s 150 where The London Stock Exchange authorises omission of information from the listing particulars or supplementary listing particulars under s 148, for instance, on the ground that it would be seriously detrimental to the issuer, if loss is suffered in consequence of the omission. It is submitted that there is no cause of action here, because once The London Stock Exchange has exercised its powers of derogation under s 148 there is no further duty of disclosure under s 146. Further, there would also be a defence of reasonable belief in proper omission available to the defendant under s 151(1).

Liability under s 150 attaches not only to the issuer but also to all persons 'responsible' for the listing particulars or supplementary listing particulars. Section 152 defines persons responsible as being:

(a) The issuer.
(b) All persons who accept and are stated to accept responsibility for the particulars or any part of the particulars; in effect this means all persons who are required to give the responsibility statement under s 3, ch 2, para 1.7 and 1.8 of the Yellow Book. In Eurobond issues, The Stock Exchange permits an issuer to give a corporate responsibility statement[4]

---

4   Under s 7, ch 1, para 6.3 of the Yellow Book.

and consequently the directors of the issuer need not be exposed to liability as 'persons responsible' by giving a personal responsibility statement.

(c) All other persons who have 'authorised the contents of or any part of' the particulars; the formula used here is wide and while it would certainly encompass persons such as accountants who authorise the financial figures it may also be sufficiently wide to encompass the managers of an issue whose names appear on the front of the listing particulars.

Where a person has accepted responsibility for or authorised only a part of the contents of particulars, liability attaches only in respect of that part and only in so far as it is included substantially in the form and context to which he agreed (s 152(3)).

Section 152(1) also makes the directors of the issuer liable as 'persons responsible' for listing particulars in ordinary securities issues, but s 152(5) expressly exempts such persons from being regarded as persons responsible under s 152(5) in the case of issuers of 'international securities' as defined in FSA s 152(6) and specified in the listing rules. The definition of 'international securities' is sufficiently wide to cover Eurobonds and, consequently, it is submitted that s 152(1) does not apply to directors of issuers of Eurobonds.[5] However, such directors would be regarded as 'persons responsible' under s 152(1)(d) if they are stated in the listing particulars to be persons responsible. As pointed out above, there is a specific provision for the issuer of Eurobonds to give only a corporate responsibility statement in Eurobond listing particulars thus removing the issuer's directors from the net of liability under s 152(1).[6]

VII ADVERTISEMENTS IN CONNECTION WITH LISTING PARTICULARS

Where listing particulars are or are to be published s 154(1) of the FSA contains a prohibition that:

> 'no advertisement or other information of a kind specified by listing rules shall be issued in the United Kingdom unless the contents of the advertisement or other information have been submitted to the competent authority and that authority has either—
> (a) approved those contents or
> (b) authorised the issue of the advertisement or information without such approval.'

Where a breach of this rule is committed by an authorised person, it is treated by FSA s 154(2) as a breach of the conduct of business rules of the Self-Regulating Organisation ('SRO') of which the authorised person is a member.[7] A breach of s 154 therefore would result in exposure to (a) disciplinary action by the SRO or failing which, (b) injunctive action

---

5 But see the difficulties of the definition of 'international securities' discussed at ch 8 above.
6 See the Yellow Book, s 7, ch 1, para 6.3 and Sch 1 of the Blue Guide.
7 On SROs see ch 16 above.

332 *The listing of Eurobonds*

by the SIB under s 61, and (c) civil liability under s 62 as well as s 61(3) of the FSA.

In the case of a non-authorised person (including an exempt person) a breach of the rule is a criminal offence (s 154(3)). There is a defence for persons whose ordinary business is not investment business where such a person publishes the advertisement to the order of another if the former had reasonable grounds to believe that the advertisement or information had been approved or its issue authorised by The London Stock Exchange (s 154(4)).

The London Stock Exchange in s 2, ch 1, para 9 of the Yellow Book has 'specified' the following advertisements and documents for purposes of s 154:

(a) formal notices, the publication of which is required by listing rules;[8]
(b) offer notices;[9]
(c) mini prospectuses;[10]
(d) other advertisements (excluding listing particulars) issued by or on behalf of the issuer:
   (i) for the purpose of announcing the admission of securities to listing; or
   (ii) required by the listing rules to be issued by it in order to obtain a listing.

The purpose of the 'specification' seems to be to confer authority to issue the advertisement and documents under s 154(1)(b) (although, if one reads s 154 together with para 9, it appears that these are the documents which are 'specified' for purposes of s 154 and are consequently prohibited by s 154!).

The London Stock Exchange has made it clear in that paragraph that press releases or draft listing particulars do not fall within the above categories. All documents falling within (d) above must state that listing particulars have been published and that copies may be obtained at the time and places mentioned therein as required by the listing rules.[11] Such documents must also contain a statement that the issue of the advertisement has been authorised by the Council 'without approval of its contents'.[12]

While the above are the only documents approved specifically for purposes of FSA s 154, section 7, ch 1, para 5.4 of the Yellow Book also provides that in respect of Eurobonds:

> 'Listing particulars may not be circulated or made available publicly unless they have first been published as required by these paragraphs.[13] However, the Council do not seek to place unnecessary burdens on issuers or their advisers in making arrangements for syndication underwriting and selective marketing of Eurocurrency debt securities, and therefore circulation is permitted of draft listing particulars, clearly marked as such for the purposes of arranging syndication, underwriting and selective marketing of debt securities.
>
> Similarly, circulation is also permitted of other documents of a marketing nature such as the invitation or offering telex (or their equivalent in another

---

8   See s 2, ch 3, para 3.8.
9   See s 3, ch 3, para 3.11.
10 See s 3, ch 3, para 3.11.
11 Ie s 3, ch 3, para 3.8 (vi).
12 See s 2, ch 1, para 9.
13 Ie made available at places specified by the Yellow Book.

medium) and press release, and documents which consist of or are drafts of or relate to agreements to be entered into in connection with the issue of the securities, provided that any obligation thereunder to issue, subscribe, purchase or underwrite securities are conditional on listing being granted.'

This is an extremely important provision in practice and it will be noticed that the authority granted is very wide to accommodate the practices in the international bond market in London. It is submitted that documents falling within this 'permission' will not contravene s 154, either on the basis that they are not 'specified' for purposes of s 154 by s 2, ch 1, para 9, or on the basis that their issue is 'authorised'.

VIII LISTING UNDER THE 'MUTUAL RECOGNITION' PROVISIONS OF THE ADMISSIONS DIRECTIVE

An important development for issuers of Eurobonds (as well as other securities) is contained in the Mutual Recognition provisions of section IV of the Admissions Directive.[14]

The mutual recognition provisions of the Admissions Directive seek to enable companies to effect a listing of securities on any official stock exchange within the European Community on the basis of listing particulars approved in accordance with art 24 of the Directive by another official stock exchange within the European Community. These provisions, although referred to in practice as the Mutual Recognition Directive, are in fact an integral part of the EC Admissions Directive. The London Stock Exchange has given effect to these provisions in section 8, chapter 2 of the Yellow Book.

Under the provisions of art 24(a) mutual recognition is available if:

(a) an application for listing is made simultaneously to stock exchanges *in two or more member states including the member state in which the issuer's registered office is situated*; or if not made simultaneously, within a 'short interval'; the 'mutual recognition' provisions of The London Stock Exchange's Yellow Book state that application should usually be made to The London Stock Exchange within six weeks of an application being made to another European Community stock exchange to satisfy the requirement of within a 'short interval'.[15]
(b) the listing particulars have been approved as such by a stock exchange in the member state in which the issuer of securities has its registered office (referred to here as the 'primary stock exchange');
(c) the listing particulars comply with the requirements of the Admissions Directive (in practice compliance with the requirements of The London Stock Exchange or another European Community exchange should generally suffice for this purpose).

If the above conditions are satisfied the competent authority in each mem-

---

14 (EEC) 79/279.
15 See s 8, ch 2, para 3(a)(i).

ber state (usually an official stock exchange) to which application for listing has been made is required to list the securities on the basis of listing particulars approved by the primary stock exchange situated in the member state in which the issuer is registered.

These mutual recognition provisions are also available for the benefit of companies who do not have a registered office within the Community. Such companies, eg Japanese or US companies, must choose a member state in which they will obtain a primary listing for purposes of mutual recognition under art 24(a). Once such a company has had its listing particulars approved by this stock exchange, it may obtain mutual recognition in the same way as a company registered within the European Community.

The London Stock Exchange's listing rules, however, provide that where a company is not registered in the EC it must be a listed company or 'the Council must be satisfied that it can properly be regarded as a company of international standing and repute'.[16]

Information additional to that contained in the listing particulars approved by the primary stock exchange cannot be demanded by the stock exchange to which an application for listing has been made under the Directive, except as permitted in the Directive.

The additional information which may be demanded under the Directive for purposes of recognition is stated by art 24 to be:

> 'information specific to the market of the country of admission concerning in particular the income tax system, the financial organisations retained to act as paying agents for the issuer in that country and the way in which notices to investors are published.'

These local information requirements may, of course, vary from country to country.

The London Stock Exchange's mutual recognition provisions state in section 8, chapter 2, para 3(d) that the Council of The London Stock Exchange may require additional information specific to the UK market including:

> '(i) a description of the tax treatment of UK resident holders of the securities;
> (ii) names and addresses of the registrars and paying agents for the securities in the United Kingdom;
> (iii) a statement of how notices of meetings will be given to UK resident holders of the securities.'

Where partial exemption or partial derogation from any informational requirements of listing has been granted by the primary stock exchange in accordance with the Admissions Directive, such exemption or derogation must also be recognised and given effect to by the other European Community stock exchanges to which applications for recognition have been made.

However, if the partial exemption or derogation granted is not of a type recognised by another European Community stock exchange additional information may be required by that stock exchange.[17]

The primary stock exchange which approves the listing particulars must

---

16 See s 8, ch 2, para 2 of the Yellow Book.
17 See for the provisions applicable in London s 8, ch 2, para 3(e).

provide a certificate of approval to the other European Community stock exchanges in which a listing is sought. This certificate must also specify any exemption or derogation and the reason for it.

The London Stock Exchange also requires that at least 14 days prior to the intended publication of the foreign listing particulars in the UK, the following be submitted to The London Stock Exchange:

(a) four copies of the foreign listing particulars;
(b) a certificate by the European Community exchange confirming that the document has been approved by it for the purposes of listing particulars; and
(c) the certificate giving details of any derogation granted, or exemption applied and stating the grounds on which such derogation has been granted, or exemption made.[18]

The foreign listing particulars may not be published until The London Stock Exchange confirms in writing that the document qualifies for mutual recognition.[19] Once admitted to listing, an issuer of securities must comply with The London Stock Exchange's rules on 'continuing obligations'.[20]

The ability of a company to use the mechanics provided in this Directive to obtain listings in other European Community countries will depend on the number of member states which have given effect to the Directive. All member states except Spain and Portugal should have implemented the Directive into domestic law by 1 January 1990 (Spain had time until January 1991 and Portugal until January 1991).[1]

It remains to be seen whether issuers of Eurobonds will utilise these provisions.

1 Special provisions applicable to a London listing of convertibles or equity warrants

Under the listing rules of The London Stock Exchange special rules apply where a listing is sought of a convertible Eurobond or Eurobonds with equity warrants attached.

The basic rule is that the convertible Eurobonds or the warrants, as the case may be, will not be granted a listing on The London Stock Exchange unless the securities into which the convertibles may be exchanged or in respect of which the warrants confer an option to subscribe, are themselves to be listed on The London Stock Exchange or on some other 'regulated regularly operating recognised open market'.[2] However, The London Stock Exchange has reserved the power to list convertibles or warrants even if the above condition is not satisfied, where The London Stock Exchange

---

18 See s 8, ch 2, para 4.
19 See s 8, ch 2, para 4.
20 See below.
1 The European Commission's department DG XV have said that all member states (save Greece and Spain) have (as of 1 April 1991) given effect to the mutual recognition provisions.
2 See s 1, ch 2, para 20 of the Yellow Book.

is 'satisfied that holders have the necessary information available to form an opinion concerning the value of the underlying securities'.[3]

In the case of convertibles, information which is additional to that which is required in respect of ordinary Eurobonds must be provided under s 7, ch 1[4] of the Yellow Book. In particular, an applicant for listing must provide information concerning the nature of the shares offered by way of conversion or exchange and the rights attaching to such shares, as well as the conditions of and procedures for such conversion or exchange.

There are other items of information required in a convertible issue which are not required for listing of Eurobonds which are not convertible.

Thus a summary of the provisions of the issuer's memorandum and articles of association or equivalent documents are required.[5] Similarly, disclosure is required of the names of persons who hold 3% or more of the issuer's capital together with the amount of each person's interest; names of persons who exercise directly or with others control over the voting capital of the issuer must be provided.

More information is also required as to the financial performance of an issuer of debt securities. Thus where an issuer prepares consolidated and non-consolidated accounts both sets of accounts must be included in listing particulars and must include financial statements for the previous three years; it must also include information as to profit or loss per share after tax for three years previous.[6]

IX CONTINUING OBLIGATIONS

Under the listing rules of the The London Stock Exchange (s 5), the issuer continues to be subject to 'continuing obligations' of disclosure of information after the bonds have been formally admitted to listing. The continuing obligations imposed on issuers of listed Eurobonds are contained in section 5, chapter 3 of the Yellow Book[7] although chapter 2 of section 5 would apply if the issuer has securities other than Eurobonds listed on The London Stock Exchange.[8]

The objective of continuous disclosure obligations is to 'secure immediate release of information which might reasonably be expected to have a material effect on market activity in and the price of listed securities'.[9] In the context of Eurobonds, the Yellow Book provides therefore that 'any information necessary to enable holders of the listed securities and the public to appraise the position of the issuer and to avoid the establishment of a false market in its listed securities must be notified' to the exchange.[10]

In addition to this overriding duty, there is also a requirement of equal treatment of holders of debt securities in respect of information and disclo-

---

3   See s 1, ch 2, para 20 of the Yellow Book.
4   See para 6.4.
5   See s 7, ch 1, para 6.4 (iii)(3) of the Yellow Book.
6   See the provisions of s 7, ch 1, para 6.4 of the Yellow Book.
7   See s 7, ch 1, para 7.
8   Yellow Book s 7, ch 1, para 7.
9   See Yellow Book s 5, ch 1.
10 See Yellow Book s 5, ch 3, para 1.

sure.[11] If debt securities of the issuer are listed on other stock exchanges the issuer must ensure that equivalent information is made available to the market at The London Stock Exchange and each such other exchange.[12]

As far as Eurobonds are concerned, section 5, chapters 2 and 3 of the Yellow Book contain the matters to be publicly announced by notification to the exchange as soon as possible.

In particular:

(a) The issuer must notify any major new developments in its sphere of activity which are not public knowledge and which may significantly affect its ability to meet its commitments.[13]
(b) Any decision to pass any interest payment on listed debt securities must be notified.[14]
(c) Any new issues of debt securities and any guarantee of security in respect thereof must be notified.[15]
(d) Any proposed repurchase by the issuer, or by the group of which the issuer is part, of its listed debt securities must be notified, where the proposal is to be open to all holders of that debt security by way of a general offer.[16]
(e) Independently of (d) above an announcement should be made when an aggregate of 10% of the outstanding initial nominal amount of a debt security has been acquired, redeemed or cancelled. The announcement should also state the amount of the relevant securities outstanding after such operations. A further announcement is necessary for each additional purchase of 5% in initial nominal value of a debt security which is acquired.[17]
(f) Any change in the rights attaching the listed debt securities (including any change in the rate of interest carried by a security) must be notified.[18]

Issuers are also required to perform other functions for the benefit of bondholders.[19]

(a) Annual accounts must be published at least within six months after year end.
(b) Copies of the drafts for approval of all notices to holders of listed debt securities must be forwarded to The London Stock Exchange through the issuer's sponsoring member firm in the UK. In addition, drafts of any proposed amendment to the memorandum and articles or equivalent documents which would affect the rights of holders of listed debt securities must be submitted to The London Stock

---

11 Yellow Book s 5, ch 3, para 2.
12 See s 5, ch 2, para 4(b) and s 5, ch 3, para 2 of the Yellow Book and Sch 5, paras 2 and 3 of the Blue Guide.
13 Yellow Book s 5, ch 3, para 4.
14 Yellow Book s 5, ch 3, para 5.
15 Yellow Book s 5, ch 3, para 6.
16 Yellow Book s 5, ch 3, para 7.
17 Yellow Book s 5, ch 3, para 8.
18 Yellow Book s 5, ch 3, para 9.
19 See Sch 5 of the Blue Guide and s 5, ch 2 of the Yellow Book.

338 *The listing of Eurobonds*

Exchange. Draft documents should be submitted through the issuer's sponsoring member firm and not by the issuer direct.[20]

(c) The issuer must ensure that:

'at least in each member state of the European Community in which its debt securities are listed, all the necessary facilities and information are available to enable holders of such securities to exercise their rights. In particular, it must inform holders of the holding of meetings which they are entitled to attend, enable them to exercise their right to vote, where applicable, and publish notices or distribute circulars giving details of the payment of interest in respect of such securities, the exercise of any conversion, exchange, subscription or renunciation rights and repayment of its securities.'[1]

(d) The issuer must maintain a paying agent in the UK until the date on which the securities are finally redeemed unless it performs this function itself.[2]

(e) 'If the debt securities are in bearer form, a paid advertisement must be inserted in at least one leading London daily newspaper drawing the attention of holders to:

(i) the availability of the annual report and accounts of the issuer and, if applicable, its parent company and any other company providing a guarantee for the security or into the securities of which any conversion, exchange or subscription rights are exercisable (unless that company's equity capital is itself listed or adequate information is otherwise available) immediately following the audit of the accounts;

(ii) the availability of any right in connection with an issue of securities to holders; and

(iii) the procedure for voting on any resolution affecting holders, notice of which must be set out in the advertisement, and to forward to the Department copies of such advertised notices.'[3]

(f) 'Where listed debt securities carry rights of conversion, exchange or subscription for the securities of another company, or are guaranteed by another company, issuers must ensure that adequate information is at all times available about the other company and about any changes in the rights attaching to the shares to which their conversion, exchange or subscription rights relate. This must include the publication of the annual report and accounts of the company together with its half-yearly or other interim reports and any other information necessary for a realistic valuation of listed debt securities carrying such rights to be made.'[4]

Where the issuer is a state or a regional or local authority or a public international body, the continuing obligations which are imposed are liberal

---

20 Yellow Book s 5, ch 3, para 11.
1 Yellow book s 5, ch 3, para 12.
2 Yellow Book s 5, ch 3, para 13.
3 Yellow Book s 5, ch 3, para 14.
4 Yellow Book s 5, ch 3, para 15.

Continuing obligations 339

compared with those imposed on corporate issuers.[5] They are subject to the following principal obligations.

(a) The issuer must ensure that, at least in each member state in which its securities are listed, all necessary facilities and information are available to enable holders of such securities to exercise their rights. In particular it must publish notices and distribute circulars giving details of the holding of meetings of the holders of such debt securities and the payment of interest on and the redemption of such debt securities. In addition it must appoint a registrar and/or where appropriate, a paying agent in the UK.[6]
(b) The issuer must ensure equality of treatment for all holders of its listed debt securities of the same class in respect of all rights attaching to such securities.[7]
(c) An issuer whose securities are also listed on other stock exchanges must ensure that equivalent information is made available to the market at The London Stock Exchange and each of such other stock exchanges.[8]
(d) All proposed payments of interest or the decision to pass any interest payment must be notified prior to the due date.[9]
(e) All proposed drawings must be notified in advance.[10]
(f) The amount of the security outstanding after any purchase or drawing has been made must be notified immediately.[11]

The rules with regard to announcements when it is proposed to make a general offer to repurchase securities and when aggregate repurchases, redemptions or cancellations are effected are the same as for other issuers.[12]

---

5 See Yellow Book s 5, ch 4.
6 Yellow Book s 5, ch 4, para 1.
7 Yellow Book s 5, ch 4, para 2.
8 Yellow Book s 5, ch 4, para 11.
9 Yellow Book s 5, ch 4, para 3(a).
10 Yellow Book s 5, ch 4, para 6.
11 Yellow Book s 5, ch 4, para 7.
12 Yellow Book s 5, ch 4, paras 4 and 5.

CHAPTER 18
Regulation of stabilisation

I AN INTRODUCTION TO STABILISATION[1]

Until the enactment of the FSA 1986,[2] the practice of lead managers in stabilising the price of Eurobonds during the issue period was generally regarded as a lawful activity in the Eurobond markets. Stabilisation is a complex and sophisticated transactional process and is an important function of the lead manager in ensuring that an international bond issue is a success. In essence, a lead manager will effect stabilisation by buying and selling Eurobonds in the open market for the account of the syndicate during the issue period, by placing bids on screens used by dealers in the market, in such a manner as to provide a price support mechanism for the bonds. The placing of screen bids creates upward pressure on the price of the bonds in the market and, consequently, stabilisation prevents any downward slide of the price of the bonds below issue price during the issue period. Maintaining the market price of the bonds by such stabilising activity facilitates the successful placement of the bonds.

Stabilisation can also be used to create demand in such a way as to drive up the price of the bonds well above their issue price. In the case of Eurobonds which are convertible into shares (or in the case of Eurobonds issued with warrants to subscribe shares), it is also possible to 'ramp' or drive up the price of the underlying equity securities prior to the launch of the bond issue in order to make the convertible Eurobond (or the Eurobond with warrants) an extremely attractive investment despite its low coupon.[3] An investor purchasing a convertible will expect to make a gain when he converts the bond into the underlying equity and this expectation is heightened when the price of the shares is perceived to be rising due to 'ramping'. Ramping is effected by dealers artificially bidding up the price of the shares of the company which will issue convertible Eurobonds within a short period of time.

A more common practice associated with stabilisation is that a lead manager may over-allot bonds to members of the underwriting syndicate during the issue phase, and buy back bonds to stabilise the price through the artificial demand created by 'buy back' purchases.

---

1 The reader is referred to chapter 8, especially pp 155–156 which deal with stabilisation.
2 Operative on 29 April 1988.
3 See chapter 14 on convertibles.

Another practice associated with stabilisation is termed 'squeezing the shorts'.[4] This is where a lead manager under-allots bonds to a managing underwriter (or selling group member) which has established a short position in the bonds by over-selling or dumping bonds on the market prior to allotment. The ability of a lead manager to do so in pre-priced offerings of Eurobonds syndicated among managers is now limited due to Recommendation 1.2 of the International Primary Market Association[5] which requires that final allotments should be made within the next business day following launch of the issue or as soon as practicable after the management group is formed if earlier. The lead manager cannot therefore delay allotment so that those dealers who have established short positions are compelled to close the short positions by buying in the market.

However, 'squeezing the shorts' can also be effected after allotment by purchasing bonds in the open market so as to make it expensive for short sellers to close their position.

II THE STATUTORY PROVISIONS OF FSA 1986 SECTION 47(2)

Section 47(2) of the FSA creates a new statutory offence of market manipulation which is potentially capable of making unlawful the practices associated with stabilisation.

Section 47(2) states as follows:

> 'Any person who does any act or engages in any course of conduct which creates a *false or misleading impression* as to the *market in or the price or value of any investments* is guilty of an offence if he *does so for the purpose* of creating that impression and of thereby inducing another person to acquire, dispose of, subscribe for or underwrite those investments or to refrain from doing so or to exercise, or refrain from exercising, any rights conferred by those investments.' (Emphasis added.)

It will be noticed that the essence of the offence consists of engaging in a course of conduct which creates a false or misleading impression as to the market in or price or value of any investment (including bonds).[6] This conduct must be 'purposive', ie for the purpose of creating such impression *and* thereby inducing a person to buy, sell or subscribe the investment.[7] It is also a defence under s 47(3) that the person 'reasonably believed' that his acts or conduct would not create a false or misleading impression.

The offence created by s 47(2) is also extraterritorial in application due to s 47(5). It is sufficient for the purpose of constituting the offence that *either* the false or misleading impression is created in the UK, *or* that the

---

4 See the article entitled 'Toyota issue calls stabilisation into question' in the *Financial Times*, 20 February 1989, relating to the alleged 'short squeeze' in respect of the Toyota bond issue of 30 January, and a further article in the *Financial Times* of 16 May 1988 entitled 'Regulators attempt to define "acceptable stabilisation"'.
5 Members and Recommendations, as amended up to April 1991.
6 See FSA Sch 1 Part 1 as to the meaning of 'investments'.
7 See s 47(2).

course of conduct was engaged in in the UK. Consequently, it is no defence that stabilising activity was engaged in outside the UK (say in Tokyo or in Frankfurt) if as a result of such activity a false impression was created in London. Such an impression could occur in London, for instance, because price quotations in respect of the bonds were available on Reuter screens in London.

Does stabilisation effected in respect of a Eurobond issue fall within FSA s 47(2)?

The answer to this question depends on the interpretation of the key concept of 'false or misleading impression' in s 47(2). It is arguable that there is no such thing as a 'true' price, value, or market in a security, and consequently that a 'false or misleading' price etc cannot exist in respect of a security. It is, however, submitted that it is not necessary for the purposes of s 47(2) to establish that there is some 'true' price or value of or market in a security, which must first be quantified or ascertained as a matter of certainty, before it can be established that a 'false or misleading' impression as to the price or value of or market in that security has been created. The key to the offence is that it is committed by creating an *impression* which is false or misleading; it is not necessary to establish that a price, market or value in respect of a security is false or misleading.

Consequently, if a person effects a change in the price at which securities are being quoted or traded in the market by any conduct which is not attributable to the confluence of genuine supply and demand, the impression created by the change constitutes a false or misleading impression as to the price of a security; equally, even if no change in price is effected, if a person creates the impression that there are more (or less) buyers (or sellers) in respect of a security and, consequently, creates an impression of greater (or lesser) liquidity than would otherwise exist, a false or misleading impression is created as to the market in that security.

Stabilising bids or transactions are in all cases an attempt to maintain the price of a bond at a level higher than the price which would otherwise prevail in the market by creating the impression in the market that there are more buyers than exist in fact. Consequently, such stabilising activity creates the impression of demand which is not generated by genuine buyers of bonds. It also provides a bid price in the market which is not the product of the confluence of genuine supply and demand.

Stabilising activity therefore potentially falls within the first limb of s 47(2), namely, as conduct creating a false or misleading impression as to the market in or price or value of any security.

On the other hand, it is arguable, first that if 'impression' is the key to s 47(2) every participant in the market is aware that, during an issue, stabilising activity is probably being effected and that, therefore, whatever price or market prevails for the bonds, it is at least partially the result of stabilising activity. Thus it is arguable that no 'false' or 'misleading' impression is created in the market and hence no offence is committed.

Secondly, it is arguable that the 'purposive' requirement means that the only (or at least the only dominant) purpose of such conduct must be the creation of a false impression as to the market in, or price of, the bonds before such conduct can be caught by s 47(2). Except perhaps in the case of 'ramping', it is arguable that this is not the dominant purpose of the lead manager in carrying on ordinary stabilising activity. The purpose of the lead manager is to prevent the price of a bond from falling below issue price and to facilitate a successful completion of the bond issue. Consequently, it is arguable that stabilisation does not constitute a breach of FSA s 47(2).

It is however submitted that it would be difficult to sustain this line of reasoning. As regards the first argument above, the response is that, no one in the market would know whether the price of bonds which prevails in the market at any given time is the result of stabilising activity or not. A general awareness in the market that stabilising activity may be effected is not a basis to assert that no false and misleading impression was being created in respect of the price or market in or value of any particular security.

As regards the second argument, it seems sufficient that the creation of the false or misleading impression is one of the purposes in engaging in the conduct rather than the only or dominant purpose. The word 'purpose' in s 47(2) may have a meaning in this context which is different from the 'ultimate objective' of a lead manager. Consequently, if the creation of a false impression is one of the purposes in engaging in a course of conduct, the end objective of which is the successful completion of the issue, this may suffice for purposes of s 47(2).

Apart from these difficult questions as to 'purpose' and 'impression', there are two further factors which suggest strongly that stabilisation will be regarded by a court as falling within s 47(2).

First, Parliament seems to have assumed that stabilisation was within s 47(2) because, a 'safe harbour' is provided by s 48(7) for stabilisation conducted in accordance with stabilisation rules made by the Securities and Investments Board ('SIB Rules'). Stabilisation effected in conformity with such SIB Rules on stabilisation is made lawful by s 48(7).

Secondly, the creation of demand by market techniques which would seem artificial to the ordinary person is likely to be regarded with hostility by the courts and lay juries. Consequently, it is submitted that the better view is that stabilising activity is potentially caught by s 47(2), unless it is carried out in accordance with SIB Rules. In practice, therefore, all stabilising activity should be conducted in accordance with these Rules if a breach of s 47(2) is to be clearly eliminated.

III STABILISATION AND INSIDER DEALING LEGISLATION

i *Can stabilisation constitute insider dealing?*

Stabilising activity may also constitute a breach of the Company Securities (Insider Dealing) Act 1985 ('CSIDA').[8] A lead manager's officers or employees who are effecting stabilising transactions may be in possession of information in respect of the stabilising book position (eg that bonds have been over allotted and will be subject to a buy back during the issue period) and this information may constitute 'unpublished price-sensitive information' (as defined in CSIDA s 10) in respect of the securities of the

---

8 As amended by FSA Part VII.

344 *Regulation of stabilisation*

issuer. Section 10 states that unpublished price-sensitive information in relation to securities of a company means information which:

(a) relates to specific matters;
(b) relating or of concern (directly or indirectly) to that company, and
(c) is not generally known to those persons who are accustomed or likely to deal in those securities, and
(d) which would, if it were generally known to them, be likely materially to affect the price of those securities.

The stabilising book position of a lead manager, it is submitted, would satisfy these criteria in practice. Consequently, a senior employee or officer of the lead manager effecting stabilising transactions as an individual 'connected with a company',[9] ie the lead manager, may be committing a breach of s 1(2) by dealing 'on a recognised stock exchange' (or of s 1(7) by procuring such dealing) 'in securities of *any other company*'[10] (ie the issuer's bonds), since he is in possession of unpublished price-sensitive information in relation to the securities of the issuer[11] (ie the book position in respect of the bonds) which 'relates to any transaction ...involving both the first company and that other company' (ie the issuer) or 'involving one of them and the securities of the other'.[12]

CSIDA s 1(2) is as follows:

'Subject to section 3, an individual who is, or at any time in the preceding 6 months has been, knowingly *connected with a company* shall not deal on a recognised stock exchange in *securities of any other company* if he has information which—
(a) he holds by virtue of being connected with the first company,
(b) it would be reasonable to expect a person so connected, and in the position by virtue of which he is so connected, not to disclose except for the proper performance of the functions attaching to that position,
(c) he knows is unpublished *price sensitive information in relation* to those *securities of that other company*, and
(d) relates to any *transaction* (actual or contemplated) *involving both the first company and that other company*, or *involving one of them and securities of the other*, or to the fact that any such transaction is no longer contemplated.'
(Emphasis added.)

ii *Contrary arguments*

However, there are two questions which throw some doubt on the applicability of CSIDA s 1(2).

First, does the dealing in respect of Eurobonds occur 'on a recognised stock exchange'? The London Stock Exchange is a 'recognised' exchange for the purposes of CSIDA[13] and by r 300 of the Rules of The London Stock Exchange[14] any transaction by a member firm is deemed to be 'on exchange'. It is not clear from the language of CSIDA whether the

---

9   See CSIDA s 9 for the definition of 'connected with a company'.
10 See s 1(2) CSIDA.
11 See s 1(2)(c) CSIDA.
12 See s 1(2)(d) CSIDA.
13 See CSIDA s 16(1).
14 Published May 1988 which includes amendments up to Amendment 13 of February 1991.

provisions of r 300 are conclusive for purposes of CSIDA s 1 on the question as to whether a transaction is on exchange. If that is the case transactions effected by member firms of The London Stock Exchange may potentially fall within s 1(2), but not those of a lead manager which is not a member of The London Stock Exchange. On the other hand it is also arguable that since Eurobonds are traded under the rules of the Association of International Bond Dealers ('AIBD') dealings are not 'on a recognised stock exchange' since the AIBD is not recognised for purposes of CSIDA.

Secondly, are Eurobonds 'securities' within the meaning of CSIDA s 12 for purposes of the prohibition in CSIDA s 1?

Securities are defined in s 12(a) as 'listed securities' and s 12(b) says that this means 'any securities listed on a recognised stock exchange'. Where Eurobonds are listed on The London Stock Exchange, the provisions of s 1(2) would apply from the time the bonds are actually listed but not before. Much stabilising activity occurs prior to a listing becoming effective (usually on closing date of the issue).[15] It is therefore difficult to see how s 1(2) applies prior to listing. It is equally clear for the same reason that s 1(2) can have no application if the bonds are not listed in London but in Luxembourg which is not a 'recognised stock exchange' for purposes of CSIDA.[16]

iii *Defences*

There is also a potential defence in s 3(2) to a charge under CSIDA s 1(2).
CSIDA s 3(2) states as follows.

'An individual is not, by reason only of his having information relating to any particular transaction, prohibited –
(a) by section 1(2), (4)(b), (5) or (6) from dealing on a recognised stock exchange in any securities, or
(b) by section 1(7) or (8) from doing any other thing in relation to securities which he is prohibited from dealing in by any of the provisions mentioned in paragraph (a), or
(c) by section 2 from doing anything,
if he does that thing in order to facilitate the completion or carrying out of the transaction.'

It is necessary for the applicability of s 3(2) that the information relates to 'any particular transaction' and the information on the book position of a lead manager may not be regarded as relating to any particular transaction. It is nevertheless arguable that the transaction is the stabilisation of the bond issue and, consequently, that the book position relates to that transaction.

iv *CSIDA s 4*

The alternative basis on which stabilisation may fall within CSIDA is under s 4, which covers dealing in the circumstances defined in s 1 of CSIDA, but 'otherwise than on a recognised stock exchange'.

---

15 See pp 155–156 and p 340 above.
16 It is to be noted that a 'recognised stock exchange' for purposes of CSIDA is not the same as 'a recognised investment exchange' under ss 36 or 40 of FSA 1986. Only two exchanges other than The London Stock Exchange are recognised for purposes of CSIDA s 16, namely, NASDAQ of New York (see the Financial Services, The Insider Dealing (Recognised Stock Exchange) Order 1989, SI 1989/2165) and OM London Limited (see the Financial Services, The Insider Dealing (Recognised Stock Exchange) (No 2) Order 1990, SI 1990/47).

CSIDA s 4(1) states:

'Subject to section 6, sections 1 to 3 apply in relation to—
  (a) dealing otherwise than on a recognised stock exchange in the advertised securities of any company—
    (i) through an off-market dealer who is making a market in those securities, in the knowledge that he is an off-market dealer, that he is making a market in those securities and that the securities are advertised securities, or
    (ii) as an off-market dealer who is making a market in those securities or as an officer, employee or agent of such a dealer acting in the course of the dealer's business;
  (b) counselling or procuring a person to deal in advertised securities in the knowledge or with reasonable cause to believe that he would deal in them as mentioned in paragraph (a);
  (c) communicating any information in the knowledge or with reasonable cause to believe that it would be used for such dealing or for such counselling or procuring,
as they apply in relation to dealing in securities on a recognised stock exchange and to counselling or procuring or communicating any information in connection with such dealing.'

Assuming that stabilising activity occurs under the rules of the Association of International Bond Dealers[17] which is not a recognised investment exchange under CSIDA s 16, s 4 is potentially applicable.

However, a number of other conditions need to be satisfied before an offence is constituted under CSIDA s 4.

First, Eurobonds must constitute 'advertised securities'. 'Advertised securities' according to s 12(c) means 'in relation to a particular occurrence listed securities or securities in respect of which not more than six months before that occurrence *information indicating the price at which persons have dealt or are willing to deal in those securities has been published* for the purpose of facilitating deals in those securities'. It is submitted that the bid and offer prices appearing on Reuter or Telerate screens from the commencement of stabilisation would satisfy this requirement.[18]

Secondly, for the offence in s 4 to be constituted it must be established that there is a dealing (otherwise than on a recognised stock exchange) either

'(i) through an off market dealer who is making a market in those securities, in the knowledge that he is an off market dealer, that he is making a market in those securities and that the securities are advertised securities; or
(ii) as an off market dealer who is making a market in those securities or as an officer, employee or agent of such a dealer acting in the course of the dealer's business.'

---

17 Soon to be called the International Securities Market Association.
18 S 12(c) on one reading is circular since advertised securities are said to constitute either 'listed securities' falling within s 12(b) or 'securities' which are defined in s 12(a) as referring to listed securities. However, s 16(3) provides that definitions in s 12(a) and (b), but not (c), apply unless 'the context otherwise requires' and it is submitted that the s 12(a) definition should not be used to define securities in s 12(c) due to the circularity which would result.

An 'off market dealer' is a person authorised under the FSA 1986.[19] Given the fact that, almost invariably, every lead manager of an international bond issue is an authorised person under the FSA, it is submitted that s 4 is potentially applicable to stabilising activity, and both the lead manager as well as the officer or employee is exposed to the risk of a breach of CSIDA s 4.

Parliament also seems to have assumed that stabilisation could amount to insider dealing, and provided a further 'safe harbour' in s 175 of the FSA which substituted a new s 6 in the Company Securities (Insider Dealing) Act 1985. This provides that nothing done for the purpose of stabilising the price of securities which is done in conformity with SIB Rules framed under FSA s 48(7) will constitute insider dealing. Consequently, the necessity to avoid a potential breach of s 1 or s 4 of the Company Securities (Insider Dealing) Act 1985 also makes it necessary that SIB Rules be complied with.

IV THE SIB's STABILISATION RULES

The current SIB Rules on stabilisation are contained in Part 10 of the Financial Services (Conduct of Business) Rule 1990.[20] The present rules are expected to be adopted for purposes of the proposed new Core Conduct of Business Rules of the SIB by r 29 which deals with market integrity and stabilisation.[1] The proposed *Financial Services Glossary 1991* (2nd edn) designates the current stabilisation rules as the rules applicable under the proposed Core r 29 when it comes into force.[2]

The SIB Rules seek to set down the parameters of stabilising activity which is good market practice. Since stabilising activity is effected as between market professionals, the SIB Rules seek to permit such activity within a defined set of criteria so that market efficiency is not hampered, while ensuring that there is sufficient regulation to safeguard the integrity of the markets.

The SIB Rules are discussed in detail below but, broadly speaking, the integrity of the markets is sought to be ensured by specifying permissible stabilising activity, by requiring appropriate disclosure of stabilisation, by requiring the keeping of records and by restricting the persons who may stabilise an issue.

In addition to the SIB's rules, the International Primary Markets Association[3] and The London Stock Exchange[4] have laid down additional requirements in respect of stabilisation. These, however, need not be complied with for purposes of falling within the statutory safe harbours created by FSA s 48(7) and CSIDA s 6 and thus avoiding a breach of FSA s 47(2)

---

19 S 13(3) of CSIDA, inserted by the FSA 1986, s 174(4)(b) as from 29 April 1988.
20 Release no 90 of 18 October 1990.
1 See Release no 94 of 30 January 1991 and Release no 101.
2 The expected date is some time near the end of 1991.
3 IPMA Recommendation 1.2 and 1.3. See further Recommendation 1.7.
4 See r 326.1.

and CSIDA ss 1 or 4. However, they must be complied with in so far as a lead manager is a member of either body.

The position under SIB Rules is as follows.

1 Securities which may be stabilised

The SIB Rules permit the stabilisation of the bonds which are the subject of the issue (referred to as 'relevant securities') as well as the stabilisation of any 'associated securities' provided that the relevant and/or associated securities fall within one or more of paras 1-5 of FSA Sch 1. The rule that only securities which fall within paras 1-5 are 'relevant' is laid down by FSA s 48(7) as well as SIB Rules.[5]

Associated securities are defined in the SIB r 10.07 as:

'securities of any description:
(a) which are in all respects uniform with the relevant securities, or
(b) for which the relevant securities may be exchanged or into which they may be converted, or
(c) which the holders of the relevant securities have, by virtue of their holdings of those securities, rights to acquire or to subscribe for, or
(d) which are issued or guaranteed by the issuer of the relevant securities or by any guarantor of the relevant securities and the prevailing market price of which is, by reason of similarity with the relevant securities in the terms and conditions which attach to each of them respectively, likely to have a material influence on the market price of the relevant securities.'

Items (b) and (c) above make it clear that the SIB Rules are applicable to the stabilisation of the underlying equity securities in an issue of convertible bonds, or bonds with warrants to subscribe equity.

The question arises whether all types of bonds can be the subject of stabilisation. Section 48(7) confines lawful stabilising under that section to investments which fall within paras 1-5 of FSA Sch 1. Most bonds, fixed and floating, perpetual, or deep discount[6] would fall within paras 2 and 3 of Sch 1. A convertible bond would also fall within para 2 as well as para 5(b) of Sch 1.[7] A Eurobond with warrants to subscribe is in effect two instruments: the bond falls within para 2 and the warrants to subscribe fall within para 4.

A difficulty, however, exists with warrants to acquire as distinct from warrants to subscribe. A warrant to acquire is different from a warrant to subscribe, in that the holder does not have rights against the issuer to subscribe new shares or bonds, but confers a right to the holder to acquire shares or bonds otherwise than by subscription from the issuer of the bonds. Such warrants may fall within para 5(c) (rather than para 4) as 'Certificates

---

5 See FSA s 48(7) and r 10.01(2).
6 See pp 213–217 above.
7 The SIB Rules expressly provide that for the purposes of some of the rules convertibles should be treated as a para 2 instrument. See note 4 to Table S2 of r 10.05.

or other instruments which confer ... (c) a contractual right (other than an option) to acquire any such investment otherwise than by subscription'.

However, the phrase within brackets '(other than an option)' in para 5(c) may exclude such warrants, because in effect they are contractual options. Consequently, such warrants probably fall within para 7 of Sch 1 and therefore cannot be stabilised within SIB Rules framed under s 48(7). On the other hand, it may be argued that para 5 deals with 'certificates' and 'instruments' while para 7 deals with currency options, gold options, share options which are 'traded' or 'traditional' options in the financial markets, and that para 7 is not concerned with 'instruments' or 'certificates' which may contain an option. The Stock Exchange in s 7, ch 3 of its listing rules (the Yellow Book), however, treats such warrants as para 7 instruments.[8] No concluded view can be taken on the matter, but the better view seems to be that generally such warrants do not fall within para 5(c), although in many uses the actual language of the warrant may need to be considered to arrive at a firm conclusion.

The second difficulty is that even with regard to warrants to subscribe, under SIB r 10.01(2)(a), only a new issue of relevant securities 'for cash made at a specified price' may be stabilised. Specified price seems to refer to the price at which the securities are issued since r 10.07 says that the 'issue price' 'means the specified price at which the relevant securities are issued'. This creates a problem where bonds are issued with warrants. While the bond has an issue price at the moment of issue, the warrant by itself has no issue price; the warrants usually develop a market price in trading. This has the awkward result that the warrant is not a 'relevant security' for purposes of the rules; nor does it constitute an 'associated security' as defined in SIB Rules. Consequently, while the bond can be stabilised either by itself or with the warrant, the warrant on its own may not be stabilised since it is not issued for cash at a specified price.

Further, under SIB r 10.01(2)(b), stabilising activity is not permissible unless a formal application has been made to an exchange specified in r 10.01(3) for the securities to be dealt in on that exchange or the securities can be 'dealt in on that exchange without a formal application'. Under r 10.01(3) London is a specified exchange, Luxembourg is not. Consequently, it seems that if an application has been made to deal in the bonds on The London Stock Exchange then stabilisation is permissible in respect of such bonds. Arguably, a listing application made on 'launch' comes within r 10.01. However, r 10.01(2)(b) provides that if one of the exchanges specified in r 10.01(3) permits dealings in the relevant securities without the need for a formal application, the securities may be stabilised. The Association of International Bond Dealers ('AIBD')[9] is also such a specified exchange[10] and no formal application is necessary to deal in Eurobonds through the AIBD.[11] Consequently, since in practice all Eurobondsare dealt in under the AIBD rules, the application requirements do not apply to Eurobond stabilisation.

---

8 See the Yellow Book s 7, ch 3, para 3.
9 Soon to be renamed the International Securities Markets Association.
10 See r 10.01(3).
11 See the *Rule Book* of the AIBD, September 1990.

2 The stabilising manager

Under SIB r 10.02 only the 'stabilising manager' may stabilise an issue of securities. The stabilising manager is the lead manager to the issue, and if there is more than one such lead manager, then the manager appointed as stabilising manager by the managers of the issue, is permitted to stabilise the issue.[12]

Consequently, where a purchase fund is set up to operate by way of a price support mechanism[13] stabilising purchases by a purchase agent (who is not the stabilising manager) would fall outside the safe harbour of the SIB Rules and may contravene s 47(2) of the FSA. In addition, such stabilising activity will fall outside the safe harbour of the SIB, since it will invariably occur outside the stabilising period specified in the SIB Rules.[14]

3 The stabilising period

Under r 10.02, stabilisation of any security may only be effected during the 'stabilising period'. Under r 10.07 the stabilising period commences for all types of Eurobonds when the first 'public announcement' of the issue is made. Rule 10.07 defines this phrase as 'any communication made by or on behalf of the issuer or the manager being a communication made in circumstances in which it is likely that members of the public will become aware of the communication'. While it is not clear who is envisaged as being 'members of the public', the definition of public announcement suggests that stabilisation can commence at the earliest only on the 'launch' of the issue which is the first time that the issue is announced to the financial markets and the financial press. In the case of bonds it does not matter that the issue price is not announced at launch. The position is otherwise under r 10.07 in the case of equity securities.

This has the result that pre-launch stabilisation in the event of the occurrence of a pre-launch grey market would constitute a breach of SIB Rules and is therefore unlawful under s 47(2). It also means that the pre-launch 'ramping' of underlying stock or shares in a convertible bond issue or warrant issue is equally unlawful.

It seems that due to SIB r 10.04 a different rule applies to an issue of convertible Eurobonds and Eurobonds with warrants. In such cases, the stabilising manager may not effect stabilising bids or effect transactions in the *underlying equity securities* (ie 'associated securities') until all the terms and conditions of the right to convert, exchange, subscribe for or acquire the underlying associated securities have been finally determined and publicly announced. Consequently, if the conversion price in a convertible issue or the exercise price in a warrant issue have not been fixed by the 'launch' date, stabilisation of the underlying equity securities could not commence on that date; the bonds may nevertheless be stabilised from launch. The logic of this rule is that if stabilising of the underlying shares was

---

12 See r 10.07 and the definition of 'stabilising manager' and 'manager'.
13 See Watkins 'Types of Bonds' in *Current Issues in International Financial Law*, (Malaya Law Review and Butterworths, 1985) at p 113.
14 See below.

permitted in a convertible (or warrant issue) prior to the announcement of the conversion price (or warrant exercise price) that price could be fixed favourably by reference to the upward movement in the price of the shares caused by stabilisation.[15]

Once lawfully commenced, stabilisation must terminate under SIB Rules shortly after the close of the issue. The stabilising manager is not permitted to effect any stabilising bid after the 30th day subsequent to the closing date of the issue or, the 60th day from the date of allotment, whichever is earlier.[16] In practice it will usually be the former.

The closing date of an issue is defined in r 10.07 as the date on which the issuer receives the proceeds of the issue, or in a case where the issuer is to receive the proceeds of the issue in instalments, eg in a deferred purchase bond, it is the date on which he receives the first instalment; and the date of allotment in a case where there is a preliminary allotment subject to confirmation is the date of such a preliminary allotment, otherwise it is the date when securities are finally allotted to the subscribers and purchasers.

This rule, however, does not affect transactions falling under r 10.03 as 'ancillary stabilising action' rather than primary stabilising action under r 10.02.[17]

Recommendation 1.3 of the International Primary Markets Association,[18] however, requires that stabilising activity by the lead manager for the account of the syndicate must cease on the closing date in a pre-priced issue.[19] In the case of other issues, including all equity-related issues, eg convertibles or warrant issues, stabilisation must cease 30 days following the signing date (not the closing date as specified by SIB Rules).[20]

4 Preconditions to lawful stabilisation: legends and warnings

Before stabilisation can commence the stabilising manager must observe a number of conditions and certain procedures.

The first duty of the stabilising manager is to warn the markets that stabilising activity may be taking place. It is, however, not apparent why such a warning is necessary, because the markets are well aware that stabilisation will be effected in a Eurobond issue. Two warnings (a long form and a short form) and a notification must be given by the lead manager or stabilising manager as the case may be.

Under r 10.04 the long form warning must be contained in the preliminary (or draft) offering circular and the final offering circular.[1] The short form warning must be given in any screen-based announcement, press announcement and invitation telex. The allotment telex, pricing telex or any other

---

15 See p 355 below.
16 SIB rr 10.07 and 10.02 and FSA s 48(7).
17 See p 353 below.
18 See the International Primary Market Association's Members and Recommendations (including amendments up to April 1991).
19 See pp 150–151 above on pre-priced issues.
20 See on signing date p 156 above.
1 See Table S1 or r 10.04.

352 Regulation of stabilisation

press, radio or television 'warm up' advertisement and 'tombstone' advertisements need not contain any stabilising legend or warning.[2]

The long form warning is as follows:

> 'In connection with this issue (name of stabilising manager) may over-allot or effect transactions on (name of specified exchange) which stabilise or maintain the market price of (description of relevant securities and of any associated securities) at a level which might not otherwise prevail on that exchange. Such stabilising, if commenced, may be discontinued at any time.'

The requirement that a 'specified exchange' be included in the warning is not operative until 1 January 1993, due to r 3.11 of the Financial Services (Miscellaneous Amendments) (no 17) Rules and Regulations 1991.[3]

There is, however, a problem for the lead manager. It is the lead manager's duty to ensure that from the time of the first public announcement of the issue, each 'advertisement', 'public announcement' or 'communication' *'referring to the issue'* contains such stabilisation legends and warnings as required by r 10.04. Consequently, if a selling group member or manager makes a communication or advertisement without the warning, stabilisation by the stabilising manager does not comply with SIB Rules, and there may be potential breach of s 47(2) by the stabilising manager. It is therefore necessary to include clauses in the selling group agreement and the subscription agreement to prevent such an occurrence. If such a clause is used, and if an unauthorised advertisement is issued by, say, a managing underwriter, which does not contain the appropriate legend, the stabilising manager should be able to rely on the provisions of r 10.04, which enable him to comply with that rule, if he has *reasonable grounds for believing* that the conditions of r 10.04 have been fulfilled.

In addition to these warnings the stabilising manager must inform, in writing, the principal exchange on which the bonds or associated securities are dealt in that stabilising transactions will be effected during the stabilising period.[4]

Member firms of The London Stock Exchange must also give the Stock Exchange notice under r 326 that they intend to act as or on behalf of a stabilising manager and request the council to display to the market a statement that stabilising transactions may be made by or on behalf of the member firm during the stabilisation period. This will, however, apply only to bonds listed in London which fall within r 535 of the Rules of The London Stock Exchange.

5 Pre-stabilisation ramping

Further, in respect of an issue of convertibles or bonds with warrants the stabilising manager cannot stabilise the issue if the stabilising manager ought

---

2 See Table S1 to r 10.04 and note 5 to Table S1.
3 See Release no 99 of the SIB dated 27 June 1991.
4 See r 10.04(2)(b). The requirement that the warning be given to an exchange 'specified' in the SIB Rules r 10.01(3) is, however, not operative until 1 January 1993. See Release no 99 of the SIB of 27 June 1991 and r 3.11 of the Financial Services (Miscellaneous Amendments) (No 17) Rules.

reasonably to be aware that the price of the underlying equity securities has been 'ramped' or manipulated in breach of s 47(2), and as a result the issue price of the 'relevant securities' (ie the bonds which are the subject of the issue) is higher than it would otherwise have been. Rule 10.04(2)(c) provides:

> 'where there are associated securities in existence the market price of which was, at the time the issue price of the relevant securities was determined, at a level higher than it otherwise would have been because of any act performed by, or any course of conduct engaged in by, any person which the stabilising manager knows or ought reasonably to know was a contravention of section 47(2) of the Act, the stabilising manager is satisfied that the issue price of the relevant securities is no higher than it would have been had that act not been performed or that course of conduct not been engaged in.'

6 Permitted stabilising transactions

The SIB Rules attempt to specify 'permitted stabilising action' in r 10.02 and 'ancillary stabilising action which is also permitted' under r 10.03.[5]

The guiding principle is that all permitted stabilising transactions must be effected 'in order to maintain the market price of the securities he is offering'.[6] Consequently, stabilising transactions must be effected only as a price support mechanism to maintain a floor level for the bonds; it cannot be used to artificially increase the market price. Within this primary constraint, a stabilising manager may stabilise either the bonds (the relevant securities) or any underlying associated security or both, 'by purchasing, agreeing to purchase or offering to purchase such securities' provided that these actions are with a view to maintaining or stabilising the market price of *the relevant securities*, ie the bonds.

Under r 10.03 ancillary stabilising action which is permitted is stated as follows:

> '(1) *General*. Subject to paragraphs (2) to (5) below, the stabilising manager of an issue of securities may over-allot or go short of securities, so as to facilitate his subsequently purchasing them by stabilising action; and he may buy or sell on the market or elsewhere in order to close out or liquidate positions established by stabilising action or by going short.
> (2) *Permitted ancillary action*. Subject to paragraph (3) below, the stabilising manager may:
>   (a) with a view to effecting stabilising transactions in relevant or associated securities:

---

5 This is a difficult task since it is an attempt to explain extremely complex market operations and hedging techniques in language possessing the clarity and precision required of a legal rule.
6 See r 10.02(1) of SIB Rules Part 10.

(i) make allotments of a greater number of the relevant securities than will be issued;
(ii) sell, offer to sell, or agree to sell relevant or associated securities so as to establish a short position in them;
(b) sell, offer to sell or agree to sell relevant or associated securities in order to close out or liquidate any position established by stabilising transactions whether or not those transactions were in accordance with rule 10.02 above, and
(c) purchase, offer to purchase or agree to purchase relevant or associated securities in order to close out or liquidate any position established by sub-paragraphs (a)(i) or (ii) above.

'Squeezing the shorts'[7] cannot be accommodated within r 10.02 as 'permitted stabilisation', and probably cannot be accommodated within r 10.03, as ancillary stabilising action.

Three important distinctions should be noticed as between transactions under r 10.02 and r 10.03.

First, all transactions under 10.02 in respect of relevant securities (but not associated securities) must be effected on 'specified exchanges', which are at present as follows:[8]

American Stock Exchange
Association of International Bond Dealers
The International Stock Exchange of the United Kingdom and the Republic of Ireland
National Association of Securities Dealers
New York Stock Exchange
Pacific Stock Exchange
Paris Stock Exchange
Tokyo Stock Exchange
Toronto Stock Exchange.

This requirement has, however, not as yet been brought into force. The Financial Services (Miscellaneous Amendments) (No 17) Rules and Regulations 1991[9] states the date on which it will be brought into force as 1 January 1993.

Ancillary stabilising action under r 10.03 need not be 'on a specified exchange' and may be effected either on or off specified exchanges. It will be noticed that where there is an issue of convertible bonds or bonds with warrants where the underlying equity securities are traded on an exchange which is not specified, such as the Frankfurt exchange, stabilisation of the underlying stock will be permissible on such an exchange due to r 10.02(2)(b).[10]

Secondly, price limits may apply to stabilising transactions under r 10.02 but they do not apply under r 10.03(4) to sales and underlying purchases

---

7 See p 341 and fn 4 on that page.
8 See r 10.01(3).
9 R 3.11. See Release no 99 of 27 June 1991.
10 See further on this aspect pp 353 and 340 above.

of shares which are effected to close out or liquidate 'short' positions established by stabilising transactions under r 10.03(2)(a)(i) and (ii).[11]

Thirdly, transactions covered by r 10.03 may be effected outside the stabilising period.

7 Price limits applicable to stabilisation[12]

The SIB Rules lay down the maximum price at which a purchase of securities may be made by a stabilising manager in order to effect price stabilisation. The Rules are aimed at preventing stabilising bids above issue price in respect of the securities which are issued and, in the case of associated securities, above market price. However, these price limits rules do not apply to the Eurobonds themselves.

The price limits specified in Table S2 of r 10.05 apply only to 'relevant securities' (ie those which are the subject of the issue) and to 'associated securities', provided they come within paras 1, 4 and 5 of FSA Sch 1. These are shares, warrants, ADRs and similar instruments, but not bonds, which are investments falling within paras 2 or 3 of FSA Sch 1. However, the price rules will apply to the stabilisation of underlying shares in a Eurobond issue with warrants to subscribe and in a convertible issue in accordance with Table S2 of r 10.05.

As far as the underlying equity securities (ie associated securities) in a convertible or warrant issue are concerned, stabilising bids in respect of such shares must comply with price limits laid down by Table S1 of r 10.05. First, the stabilising manager is not permitted to effect an initial stabilising bid or transaction in any associated shares or stock above the market bid price of such securities at the commencement of the stabilising period. It will be remembered that in respect of the underlying shares in a convertible or bond issue with warrants to subscribe, the commencement of the stabilising period is the time at which the first public announcement which states the issue price is made. Secondly, the stabilising manager is not permitted to effect any subsequent stabilising bids or transactions in such associated equity securities at a price higher than the market bid price for the shares at the commencement of the stabilising period or the initial stabilising bid price, whichever is the lower.

However, where the initial stabilising bid or transaction for the underlying shares was at a price lower than the market price for the shares at the commencement of the stabilising period, the stabilising manager must effect all subsequent stabilising bids or transactions at that lower price. An exception exists to this latter rule where a third party who is not acting on the manager's behalf has effected a stabilising bid or transaction on a specified exchange subsequent to the initial stabilising bid or transaction at a price higher than the initial bid or transaction price. In such a case, the stabilising manager may effect subsequent stabilising bids or transactions at a price not higher than the market bid price of that associated underlying stock at the commencement of the stabilising period.[13]

---

11 But not action taken under r 10.03(2)(b) or r 10.02.
12 R 10.05 and Table S2 of the SIB Rules Part 10.
13 See Table S2, r 10.05 B2 and B3.

356 *Regulation of stabilisation*

8 The stabilisation register

The stabilising manager must also establish a stabilising register in which he must record a number of matters specified in r 16.18 in respect of stabilising transactions. This is a precondition to the commencement of lawful stabilisation.[14]

The stabilising manager must record each stabilising transaction effected under rr 10.02 and 10.03 in the stabilisation register established under r 10.04.[15] He must do so as soon as possible and at latest by the opening of the business day next following the day on which the transaction was effected.[16]

He must record the following details in relation to each such transaction as required by SIB r 16.18:

(a) the description of the security which is the subject of the transaction;
(b) the unit price of the transaction; and where price rules apply the stabilising manager must specify the details of the transaction by reference to which the price has been determined, eg the initial stabilising bid or a subsequent market transaction effected by a third party;[17]
(c) size of the transaction;
(d) date and time of the transaction;
(e) the identity of the counterparty to the transaction;
(f) where over-allotments are made of securities in contemplation of stabilising transactions, the names of the persons to whom the securities were allotted and how much was allotted to each person.

9 SFA Rules on stabilisation

In addition to complying with SIB Rules on stabilisation the stabilising manager must, if he is an authorised person by virtue of membership of The Securities and Futures Authority ('SFA'), also comply with SFA Rules on stabilisation as part of the SRO rules applicable to a member firm.[18] The SIB Rules on stabilisation, namely Part 10 of the Financial Services (Conduct of Business) Rules 1990 which were discussed above, have been designated by SIB's Core r 29 as being applicable under FSA s 63A to all members of SROs, when such Core Rules are brought into force. Consequently, when the Core Rules are brought into force a stabilising manager need comply only with one set of rules for purposes of, first, avoiding criminal liability under s 47(2) and, secondly, for the purpose of complying with SRO Rules. However, it is important to remember the different consequences which attach to breach of SIB Rules and SRO Rules. Breach of SIB Rules on stabilisation may result in:

(a) criminal prosecution under s 47(2);
(b) injunctive action by the SIB under s 61; and
(c) SIB action to recover any profit which has accrued to any person

---

14 See r 10.04.
15 See r 10.02(3) and r 10.03(3).
16 See r 16.18 of the SIB Conduct of Business Rules.
17 See p 355 above.
18 Currently r 1110 of SFA Conduct of Business Rules ch IV.

as a result of a contravention of SIB Rules (s 61(3) read with s 61(1)(a)(i) and s 48(7)) or to recover from the party in breach any loss or the financial equivalent of any adverse effect suffered by an investor in consequence of such contravention.[19]

A breach of SFA Rules exposes a person authorised by SFA to a civil action for damages by any 'private investor' who has suffered loss in consequence.[20]

10 The extraterritorial impact of s 47(2), and international stabilisation

As observed earlier,[1] s 47(2) creates an offence which has extraterritorial impact.

There is potential liability if either a false or misleading impression is created in the UK or the conduct which results in such impression is engaged in the UK due to the provisions of s 47(5).

This creates problems in some situations. Thus in a convertible Eurobond issue where the underlying equity securities are listed and traded overseas, eg Tokyo, an overseas entity, with no presence whatsoever in the UK, which stabilises underlying equity securities on the overseas market, is exposed to a potential breach of s 47(2), if a false impression is created in respect of the price or value of the shares in the London markets. This would be the position under English law, even if the overseas entity has complied with the mandatory requirements of the overseas market. Of course, the overseas entity may avoid any liability under UK law by complying with SIB Rules on stabilisation and thus falling within s 48(7). This, however, may not be a course of action which the overseas entity, say in Tokyo, would find desirable. Further, it may not always be possible to comply with SIB Rules on stabilisation because the stabilisation rules applicable in the foreign market may be significantly different from the SIB Rules. One practical solution in these situations may be to seek a 'no action' assurance from the SIB.

Some concessions have been made in the SIB Rules in order to accommodate the needs of international stabilisation. First, more than one stabilising manager may be appointed so that there can be one manager in each foreign location or market.[2] Secondly, under r 10.04 stabilising legends necessary under that rule may be adopted or omitted in documents not to be circulated in the UK but only in an overseas market, where stabilising is to be effective in order to comply with local requirements of the overseas market. Thirdly, such legends may be adopted or omitted in all documents in order to avoid a breach of the law in the overseas market-place where stabilising transactions are being effected.[3]

These, however, do not go far enough in practice and serious problems may arise due to conflicts of stabilisation rules in different jurisdictions in cases where stabilisation is effected internationally. In the long term it

---

19 See pp 341–342 above.
20 See FSA s 62(2) and s 62A. 'Private investor' is defined in reg 2 of the Financial Services Act 1986 (Restriction of Right of Action) Regulations 1991, framed under s 62A of the FSA as amended.
1 See p 341 above.
2 See r 10.06.
3 See note 4 to Table S1 of r 10.04.

is essential that common stabilisation rules are adopted in the three major centres which are homes to the world's major capital markets – New York, London and Tokyo – as well as in other centres such as Frankfurt, Paris, Amsterdam and Hong Kong.

Part V

Regulation of the international capital markets
(B) Impact of US securities laws on international bond issues

Introduction

There are a large number of statutes in the US which seek to regulate the issue and sale of 'securities' and which are compendiously referred to as US securities laws.

The term 'securities' in the US statutes, namely the Securities Act 1933 and the Securities Exchange Act 1934, would cover ordinary Eurobonds as well as convertible bonds or warrants to subscribe equity or debt, as well as Euro Commercial Paper.[1]

It is therefore necessary to consider the potential applicability of US securities laws since in practice (a) a large number of issuers in the international markets are US corporations; (b) many of the lead managers and key underwriters of international bond issues are US investment banks; and (c) over half the international bond issues are denominated in US dollars.[2]

There are three statutes at the federal level which may have a direct impact on the issue and sale of Eurobonds in the international markets:

Securities Act 1933 ('SA 1933')
Securities Exchange Act 1934 ('SEA 1934')
Trust Indenture Act 1939 ('TIA 1939').[3]

---

1 See ch 23. S 2 of the Securities Act of 1933 defines the term 'security' as:

'Any note, stock, treasury stock, bond, debenture, evidence of indebtedness, certificate of interest or participation in any profit sharing arrangement, collateral trust certificate, pre-organisation certificate or subscription, transferable share, investment contract, voting trust certificate, certificate of deposit or a security, fractional undivided interest in oil, gas, or other mineral rights, any put, call, straddle, option, or privilege on any security, certificate of deposit, or group or index of securities (including any interest therein or based on the value thereof), or any put, call, straddle, option, or privilege entered into on a national securities exchange relating to a foreign currency, or, in general, any interest or instrument commonly known as a "security", or any certificate of interest or participation in, temporary or interim certificates for, receipt for, guarantee of, or warrant to or rights to subscribe to or purchase any of the foregoing.' There is a similar definition of a security in s 3(a)(10) of the Securities Exchange Act of 1934.

2 See *Euromoney 20th Anniversary Supplement, The Euromarket in Figures* (June 1989).

3 There are three other federal statutes which may also have an impact on the sale of securities. These are: the Investment Company Act 1940, the Investment Advisors Act 1940, and the Public Utility Holding Company Act 1935.

In addition, in each of the 52 states there are statutes similar to the federal statutes, which are called 'Blue Sky Laws'.

The Securities and Exchange Commission ('SEC') which is the statutory body set up under SEA 1934 to oversee the system of regulation has also promulgated a vast body of rules under its rule-making powers conferred by these statutes. The statutes both at federal and state level and the rules and regulations of the SEC are compendiously referred to in this work as US securities laws or US securities regulations.

US securities laws are potentially applicable to an issue of Eurobonds in the international markets in London for two reasons.

First, many of the key provisions of US securities laws are activated when the US 'mails' or 'interstate commerce' are used in the context of an activity. The phrase 'interstate commerce' is used in SA 1933 and SEA 1934, as well as in TIA 1939.

SA 1933 s 2(7) states that:

> 'the term "interstate commerce" means "trade or commerce in securities or any transportation or communication relating thereto among the several States or between the District of Columbia or any Territory capital of the United States and any States or other Territory or between any foreign country and any State, Territory or the District of Columbia, or within the District of Columbia"'.

SEA 1934 s 3(17) contains a similar definition and includes in its definition of interstate commerce any means of transportation or communication including the use of a telephone as between a foreign country and any state within the US. A telephone call made from New York to London would thus be sufficient on a literal reading to activate the provisions of US securities laws in respect of an international bond issue.[4]

Secondly, the US courts and the SEC have taken the view that US securities laws may be applied extraterritorially, although the circumstances in which this would occur is by no means clear.[5]

Consequently, it is necessary first to consider the key provisions of US securities laws which are potentially applicable to an international bond issue in London; secondly, to consider in what circumstances US courts and the SEC will apply the provisions of US securities laws extraterritorially; and thirdly, to consider the circumstances and the conditions under which international bond issues in London can be effected without breaching the provisions of US securities laws.

US laws regulating banking, particularly the four provisions of the Banking Act 1933 referred to as the Glass Steagall Act which separate commercial banking from investment banking in the US (the Glass Steagall wall), must also be considered in this context, since these provisions control the ability of US commercial banks and their subsidiaries to engage in underwriting and placing Eurobonds as well as Euro Commercial Paper. These are discussed in chapter 22.

---

4 For a discussion of the provisions relating to 'the use of the means or instrumentality of interstate commerce' in US securities laws see *Myzel v Fields*, 386 F 2d 718 (8th Cir 1967), *Loveridge v Dreagoux*, 678 F 2d 870 (10th Cir 1982) and also *Ellis v Carter*, 291 F 2d 870 (9th Cir 1961).
5 See the discussion at ch 20 below.

CHAPTER 19
The legislative framework of US securities laws[1]

I SECURITIES ACT 1933 ('SA 1933')

The Securities Act 1933 is primarily aimed at regulating the distribution of securities in the primary market when securities are first offered for sale. It is not primarily concerned with trading of securities by dealers in the secondary market which is a subject regulated by SEA 1934. Key provisions potentially applicable to international bond issues in London are considered below.

1 Section 5

The hub of SA 1933 is s 5, and it contains a number of prohibitions which are potentially applicable to a Eurobond issue.
First, s 5(a) provides that:

> 'unless a registration statement is in effect as to a security it shall be unlawful for any person, directly or indirectly ... to make use of any means or instruments of transportation or communication in interstate commerce or the mails to sell such security through the use or medium of any prospectus or otherwise.'

Secondly, s 5(c) provides that:

> 'it shall be unlawful for any person, directly or indirectly, to make use of any means or instruments of transportation or communication in interstate commerce or the mails to offer to sell or offer to buy through the use or medium of any prospectus or otherwise any security unless a registration statement has been filed as to such security ...'.

Under s 5(c) the prohibition extends to an 'offer to sell' which is defined

---

1 See generally for an introduction, Professor Louis Loss *Fundamentals of Securities Regulation* (Little, Brown, 1983) and Jennings and Marsh, *Securities Regulation, Cases and Materials* (Foundation Press, New York, 6th edn, 1987).

in s 2(3) to include 'every attempt or offer to dispose of or solicitation of an offer to buy a security or interest in a security for value'. The prohibition is sufficiently wide to cover both sales in the primary markets during an issue of Eurobonds as well as subsequent sales in the secondary markets.

If s 5 were to be given extraterritorial application, it would be unlawful under US law to distribute a Eurobond offering circular by using the US post or any other means of interstate commerce or transportation, including a fax machine, in the absence of a registration statement complying with the provisions of SA 1933. Theoretically, it will also be unlawful under US law to make a telephone call to the US or from the US with a view to selling or offering to sell a Eurobond unless a registration statement has been filed.

The fundamental purpose of s 5 is to compel adequate disclosure of information to investors by an issuer of securities so as to enable an investor to make an informed judgment. The contents of a registration statement are detailed and are governed by Sch A or B of SA 1933. Schedule A lays down the requirements for non-governmental issuers and Sch B applies to governmental issuers. Subsequent modifications to the procedure and methods of disclosure have reduced the formal requirements for foreign issuers in the US markets. Thus, Regulation S-K and Regulation S-X provide for integrated disclosure statements combining statements required both under SA 1933 and s 12 of SEA 1934.

There are a number of exceptions to the prohibition in s 5 contained in SA 1933 but these are not of much practical value in the context of a Eurobond issue. Thus, s 2(3) exempts from the prohibition in s 5(c) any 'preliminary negotiations or agreements between an issuer... and any underwriter or among underwriters who are or who are to be in privity of contract with the issuer'. This would in theory permit the formation of underwriting groups and exempts the making of 'best efforts' or 'fully committed' offers to place securities made by a lead manager or managing group. It would also exempt competitive bidding by groups of prospective managers. However, any further steps would be caught by the prohibition, such as any offer or solicitation of interest from a selling group or from corporate, institutional or individual investors who may be potential purchasers of bonds.[2]

Again, s 4(3) exempts from these provisions transactions by a dealer (including those of a broker: s 2(12)) but it does not exempt:

(a) dealers who are participants in the initial issue or distribution in relation to such securities which they had taken up from the lead manager, ie they cannot sell unregistered securities which are part of their unsold allotment or subscription;
(b) sales or transactions by dealers made within 40 days after the date of issue of the securities or 90 days from the date of issue, if securities of the issuer have not been issued previously with a registration state-

---

[2] S 4(2) exempts transactions by an issuer which do not involve a 'public offering'. While this exemption has little relevance to a public offering of bonds on the international markets in London, it is of practical significance in the context of the recently promulgated r 144A of the SEC (see ch 21 below).

ment, ie it is only after 40 or 90 days as the case may be, that a dealer who effects a transaction in respect of unregistered securities can rely on the s 4(3) dealer exemption.

Nevertheless, Eurobond offerings are routinely made in pursuance of Eurobond 'offering circulars' without the filing of a registration statement under s 5 of the SA 1933 which complies with requirements of SA 1933. The perception of issuers in the international markets is that US disclosure requirements are too detailed and onerous to comply with.

2 Consequences of breach

The consequences which may ensue from a breach of s 5 are serious.

i *SEC action*

Under s 20 the SEC can obtain injunctions from a US court to prevent the breach or the continuance of a breach of the provisions of SA 1933.

Where there is a possibility that a breach has been or is about to be committed, the SEC also has powers similar to those of a court to conduct investigations into the circumstances constituting the breach or alleged breach and, in particular, it has power to call on the party responsible for the breach or potential breach to file a statement as to all the facts and circumstances.[3]

This is a potent sanction in practice since most major investment banks which lead manage Eurobond issues would have offices in New York and, if necessary, the SEC could obtain injunctions against a lead manager in an issue out of London which has an office in New York.

ii *Criminal sanctions*

A breach of the rules of SA 1933 or its regulations gives rise to potential criminal liability to fines not exceeding US $10,000, or imprisonment for up to five years, or both (s 24).

iii *Civil sanctions*

Under s 12(1), any person who offers or sells a security in violation of s 5 is liable to the purchaser to refund the price paid for the security, together with interest. The action is available only to persons who are in privity but not otherwise. Consequently, a purchaser of a security can sue the issuer or underwriter or dealers involved in the initial distribution only if he purchased the security from them. It also seems that this action is available

---

3 On the use of injunctive actions see the SEC's 50th Annual Report (1984) and an article by Ringle 'The SEC Injunction: Recent Trends and New Approaches' in *Contemporary Issues in Securities Regulation* (Steinberg edn, Butterworths, 1987).

only to the owner of a security so that if the purchaser has resold the security and no longer 'owns' it, he may sue in damages only.[4]

There are anti-avoidance provisions in ss 14 and 15 designed to prevent evasion of liability under s 12. A condition or term contained in the security or elsewhere attempting to remove this right is made void under s 14.

Section 15 makes liable not only the party liable under s 12, but any person who by 'stock ownership or otherwise' 'controls' the party liable, unless the latter has no knowledge of or reasonable grounds to believe that a breach giving rise to s 12 liability has occurred. This would mean that where a Eurobond issue has been made, for instance, through a financing subsidiary of a major corporation, the liability under s 12(1) for breach of s 5 provisions would extend to the ultimate parent of the group.

The plaintiff must prove further that some means of US interstate commerce or the US mails was used not just in connection to the initial issue or distribution of the security but in respect of the sale to the particular plaintiff: *Aid Auto Stores Inc v Cannon*.[5]

The requisites of the action are thus:

(a) that the defendant sold a security to the plaintiff;
(b) that the US mails or other means of US interstate commerce was used;
(c) that the defendant was in breach of the registration requirements of s 5;
(d) that the plaintiff is the 'owner' of the security if he wishes to claim rescission, recovery of the price paid and interest; alternatively, that he no longer owns it and is entitled to damages.

It seems that the defendant's good faith or ignorance of the violation of s 5 is irrelevant to his liability.[6] Thus even a legal opinion from a major US law firm, that a particular issue was exempt from registration requirements, would not absolve the defendant from liability, if in fact there is a breach of s 5.[7]

The question which does not seem to have been answered in the cases is whether a plaintiff who was aware at the time of the purchase that the securities were not registered can nevertheless maintain an action. As far as Eurobonds are concerned, in practice the definitive Eurobonds bear a legend on their face that they are not registered under SA 1933 or SEA 1934 and it may be that a purchaser of Eurobonds may be precluded by this legend from bringing an action under s 5. However, since nearly all Eurobonds are warehoused with Euroclear or Cedel,[8] and are hardly ever physically delivered to investors, they may not have actual knowledge of the absence of registration at the time of purchase.

---

4 The damages to which a previous holder of a security will be entitled are to be determined by an amount which would place him in the position he would be in if he had rescinded the sale. This is the difference between the purchase price of the security and the plaintiff's resale price (if it is lower) plus interest on that differential. See on this action: *Cady v Murphy* 113 2d 988 at 991 (1st Cir 1940).
5 525 2d 468 (2nd Cir 1975).
6 *Wonneman v Stratford Securities Co* CCH Fed Sec L Rep 91 (SDNY 1961).
7 *Smith v Manausa* 385 F Supp 443 (affd 535 F 2d 353 (6th Cir 1976) on other grounds).
8 See pp 169 et seq above.

The other problem with the s 12 action as far as Eurobonds are concerned is that of ownership. It is difficult to determine whether a purchaser is to be considered as 'owner' of bonds which are purchased for purposes of the action under s 12.[9]

3 'Anti-fraud' provisions

In addition to the registration and prospectus requirements, SA 1933 also contains two provisions aimed at controlling fraud and establishing adequate standards of disclosure.

i Section 12 of SA 1933

The anti-fraud provisions contained in s 12(2) give a cause of action where a security has been sold or is offered for sale by the 'use of any means or instrument of transportation or communication in interstate commerce or of the mails' by the means of false information in a prospectus or otherwise. This provision applies whether a registration statement has been filed with the SEC or not,[10] and irrespective of whether a prospectus complying with s 10 is in existence or not. Further, this provision applies regardless of whether the false information is contained in a prospectus or similar document or is communicated orally. In effect, it applies to any dissemination of information. What amounts to false information is the same as in other provisions of SA 1933 (eg s 11), namely, it is 'an untrue statement of material fact' or the failure to disclose a material fact necessary to make other statements not misleading.[11]

The action is available, first, to the holder of a security giving him the legal right to recover the price paid on the security and, secondly, to someone who had previously been the holder of a security though he can only claim damages for any loss he might have suffered.

Once again the party liable (as in s 12(1)) is the immediate vendor of the security from whom the plaintiff purchased the security but not anyone else. Consequently, if an issuer sells securities to underwriters who in turn sell them to other dealers or members of the public the issuer cannot be directly sued by the present holder.[12]

There is no need for the plaintiff to prove 'reliance' on the untrue or misleading statement though the need for materiality of the untrue or misleading statement imports the requirement that the misleading or false material was reasonably likely to influence the prudent purchaser of a security.[13] It also seems that it need not be proved that there was a causal nexus between the misleading statement and the purchase, even though the section requires that the security be sold 'by means' of a misleading or false statement.[14]

---

9   See ch 9, p 171 above.
10 *Franklin Sav Bank v Levy* 551 F 2d 521 (2nd Cir 1977).
11 See *Dave v Rosenfeld* 229 F 2d 855 at 857 (2nd Cir 1956).
12 *Collins v Signetics* 605 F 2d 110 (3rd Cir 1979); cf *Pharo v Smith* 621 F 2d 656 (5th Cir 1980).
13 *John Hopkins University v Hutton* 422 F 2d 1124 (4th Cir 1970).
14 *Sanders v John Nuveen & Co* 619 F 2d 1222 (7th Cir 1980).

In *Sanders*[15] the court was prepared to hold that s 12(2) could be used by a person who had never seen the prospectus containing the misleading statement. 'It is enough' said the court, 'that the seller sold by means of a misleading prospectus securities of which those purchased by the plaintiff was a part'.[16]

Some aspects need to be noted. First, problems under this section can arise where there are misleading statements in the preliminary prospectus, and this is cleared up and corrected in the final prospectus. There might still be a cause of action because s 12(2) draws a distinction between 'offering' securities by means of a misleading prospectus and 'selling' securities by means of a misleading prospectus, and both these activities give rise to liability so that an offer by means of a misleading prospectus will give rise to liability even though the sale of the securities has not been made by means of the misleading prospectus.

The second aspect of s 12(2) is that so long as the misrepresentation or other misleading statement is made to the plaintiff it does not matter that interstate facilities were not used in the making of it, provided that interstate facilities were used in the offer or sale of the security to the plaintiffs. In other words, if, say, a prospectus contained a misleading or untrue statement and this was transmitted without the use of the facilities of interstate commerce, but the security sold was delivered by use of the facilities of interstate commerce, this is sufficient for purposes of a s 12(2) action.[17]

Thirdly, it appears that a party sued under s 12(2) may not simply be able to rely on the defence that it was 'expertised', ie is part of an expert report. He himself must have been diligent and must show that he could not with reasonable care have been aware of the error.[18]

ii *Section 17 of SA 1933*

The more compendious and catch-all provision is set out in s 17 which provides as follows:

'(a) It shall be unlawful for any person in the offer or sale of any securities by the use of any means or instruments of transportation or communication in interstate commerce or by the use of the mails, directly or indirectly—
   (i) to employ any device, scheme, or artifice to defraud; or
   (ii) to obtain money or property by means of any untrue statement of a material fact or any omission to state a material fact necessary in order to make the statements made, in the light of the circumstances under which they were made, not misleading; or
   (iii) to engage in any transaction, practice, or course of business which operates or would operate as a fraud or deceit upon the purchaser.
(b) It shall be unlawful for any person, by the use of any means or instruments

---

15 See fn 14, above.
16 The court's view was that the causation required under s 12(2) was 'open market causation' rather than specific causation (see also *Hill York Corp v American International Franchise Inc* 448 F 2d 680 (5th Cir 1971). However, some causal connection has been required for the activation of s 12(2) in other cases (see *Jackson v Oppenheim* 533 F 2d 826 (2nd Cir 1976) and in *Alton Box Board Co v Goldman Sachs & Co* 560 F 2d 916 (8th Cir 1977) which concerned the collapse of Penn Central Bank.
17 *Blackwell v Benstein* 203 F 2d 690 (5th Cir 1953).
18 *Gould v Tricon Inc* 272 F Supp 385 (SDNY 1967).

of transportation or communication in interstate commerce or by the use of the mails, to publish, give publicity to, or circulate any notice, circular, advertisement, newspaper, article, letter, investment service, or communication which, though not purporting to offer a security for sale, describes such security for a consideration received or to be received, directly or indirectly, from an issuer, underwriter, or dealer, without fully disclosing the receipt, whether past or prospective, of such consideration and the amount thereof.
(c) The exemptions provided in section 3 shall not apply to the provisions of this section.'

This section is enforced by the usual range of sanctions provided for in SA 1933, namely: SEC initiated injunctions (s 20(b)), SEC investigations (s 20(a)), SEC initiated prosecution (s 20(b)), and criminal penalties under s 24 (in case of wilful violation). The ramifications of s 17(a), which is essentially an anti-fraud provision, will be considered along with similar anti-fraud provisions in SEA 1934.[19]

II THE SECURITIES EXCHANGE ACT 1934 ('SEA 1934')

There are a number of key provisions which may potentially apply in respect of an issue of Eurobonds in the international markets in London.

1 Section 15: broker dealer registration

Section 15 of SEA 1934 makes it unlawful for any 'broker' or 'dealer' 'to make use of the mails or any means or instrumentality of interstate commerce to effect any transactions in, or to induce or to attempt to induce the purchase or sale of any security ... unless such a broker or dealer is registered' in accordance with the provisions of s 15.

The term 'broker' is defined in s 3(a)(4) to mean 'any person engaged in the business of effecting transactions in securities for the account of others but does not include a bank', while s 3(a)(5) defines a dealer to mean 'any person engaged in the business of buying and selling securities for his own account through a broker or otherwise but does not include a bank or any person in so far as he buys or sells securities for his own account, either individually or in some fiduciary capacity, but not as a part of a regular business'.

The phrase 'broker' or 'dealer' as defined is quite clearly capable of applying to many securities houses who would be involved in practice in issuing Eurobonds. Any user of the mails or the means or instrumentality of interstate commerce by a British, European, or Japanese broker active in the Euromarkets could therefore trigger a registration requirement under s 15 of SEA 1934. The SEC itself has consistently taken the view that the scope of these provisions is not restricted to domestic brokers and dealers within the US.[20] The SEC has pointed out that given the fundamental significance

---

19 See p 371 below.
20 See for instance Exchange Act Release no 27017, 11 July 1989 at (iii)(B).

of the policy underlying the requirement of broker dealer registration within the structure of US securities market regulation, the extension to foreign broker dealers of the registration provisions is justified in particular where the broker dealer's activities involve contacts with individuals or institutional investors within the US.

The SEC has wide powers in relation to any alleged violation of s 15 including powers of investigation under s 21(a) and a power to proceed by way of injunction to prevent any conduct which may violate s 15. In addition, under s 32 of SEA 1934 a breach of s 15 constitutes a criminal offence carrying a maximum penalty of $1,000,000 or imprisonment for up to ten years.

2 Other provisions of SEA 1934

Section 30 of SEA 1934 makes it unlawful for 'any broker or dealer' (not only brokers or dealers registered under the SEA 1934) to effect a securities transaction on an exchange not within the US (such as London or Luxembourg or Zurich) in respect of 'any security the issuer of which is a resident of, or is organised under the laws of, or has its principal place of business in a place within the United States', in contravention of the rules and regulations 'as the Commission may prescribe in the public interest'. This provision is intended to be extraterritorial and would mean that every broker or dealer who is involved in the issue or trade of Eurobonds of a US incorporated or US resident corporation may be required by SEC rules and regulations to comply with such rules and regulations under s 30 of SEA 1934. This duty of compliance is also capable of being enforced by the SEC by investigation and injunction under s 21(a) and by criminal sanctions under s 32. However, no rules or regulations have been formulated by the SEC under this section to date. Section 30 thus remains dormant until activated by SEC rules promulgated under it.

Section 12(g)(1) requires issuers of securities which have total assets exceeding $1m and whose securities are traded by the use of the US mails or any means or instrumentality of interstate commerce, to file a registration statement. Section 12(g)(3), however, permits the SEC to exempt any security of a foreign issuer if it 'is in the public interest and is consistent with the protection of investors'. The SEC in pursuance of this section has issued r 12(g)3-(2). Under this rule the SEC has exempted from the registration provisions securities of issuers who have provided the SEC with certain specified categories of information. The required information is (a) whatever information which has been made public by the issuer according to the law of the country of its domicile or organisation or required by the stock exchange of such country; or (b) whatever information has been distributed to its security holders. The SEC publishes a list of such issuers who provide such information. A US broker or dealer who 'effects any transaction' in relation to such foreign securities which are not registered but are exempt under r 12(g)3-(2) must ensure that the securities are on the SEC's list, for otherwise he could be committing a criminal offence under s 12(a) of SEA 1934. However, the SEC has stated in Release no 8066 (1967) that no action will be taken against brokers or dealers on this basis.

It is only a foreign issuer as defined who comes within r 12(g)3-(2). A corporation does not come within the r 12(g)3-(2) exemption if (a) more than 50% of the voting stock is held by residents of the US (either directly or indirectly through voting trust certificates or depository receipts); and (b) the business is carried on principally in the US or 50% of more of its board of directors are US residents.

If SEA 1934 s 12 applies to an issuer and securities must be registered under SEA 1934, s 13 imposes further regulatory requirements in the form of filing periodic and other reports with the SEC. Section 12 itself contains the detailed disclosure requirements required to be filed with the SEC to satisfy s 12. Under s 13 three reports are required to be filed: an annual report on Form 10-K, a quarterly report on Form 10-Q and a current report on Form 8-K in any month when certain events occur. The SEC has attempted to reduce this onerous reporting requirement by permitting much of the required information to be incorporated by reference to the company's annual and quarterly reports to the shareholders. In addition, in March 1982 the SEC in Release no 6383 promulgated an 'integrated disclosure system', so that reporting and disclosure under SA 1933 and SEA 1934 could be made in one document, Form S-K under Regulation S-K. Registration for new issues of securities under SA 1933 could be achieved under Forms S-2 and S-3 where the issuer was already registered under SEA 1934. These forms permit incorporation of the information in Form 10-K (under SEA 1934) into an SA 1933 registration form. Both Form S-2 and Form S-3 can only be used by issuers who have made SEA 1934 filings for at least three consecutive years previous, and there are other limitations. Section 18 contains provisions which give the holder of a security cause of action if there are any misleading or untrue statements in any of the registration documents.

3 Anti-fraud provision of SEA 1934 : r 10(b)-5[1]

The primary anti-fraud provision of SEA 1934 is s 10(b) together with the rules of the SEC issued thereunder.

S 10(b) applies to registered and unregistered securities alike but it is a section which is operative only through such rules as are made by the SEC. There are three major anti-fraud rules framed by the SEC under s 10(b): namely, r 10(b)-5, r 10(b)-6 and r 10(b)-7. Rule 10(b)-6 and r 10(b)-7 are dealt with below.

R 10(b)-5 is based on the wording of s 17(a) of SA 1933 and contains three prohibitions.

First, r 10(b)-5(a) contains a general prohibition on employing 'any device, scheme or artifice to defraud'.

Secondly, r 10(b)5-(b) contains a further prohibition on engaging 'in any act, practice or course of business which operates or would operate as a fraud or deceit' when it is engaged in the 'purchase or sale of a security'.

These two provisions are virtually on all fours with s 17(a)(1) and (3) of SA 1933, from which the SEC borrowed the formula. There is, however,

---

[1] Section 9 prohibits manipulation of the price of securities registered on national securities exchanges. While s 9 is of fundamental importance in the US it has minimal importance for the Eurobond market because, as observed earlier, Eurobond issues are not registered under SEA 1934 (nor indeed under SA 1933).

a significant change in the formula used. Section 17 applies in relation to 'the offer or sale of any security', while r 10(b)-5 applies to 'purchase or sale of any security'. The result is that the combined anti-fraud provisions of r 10(b)-5 and s 17(a) apply to 'sales', 'purchases' and 'offers' of any security.

Thirdly, r 10(b)-5(b) prohibits the making of any untrue or misleading statement directly or indirectly by the use of any means or instrumentality of interstate commerce, while s 17(a)(2) of SA 1933 prohibits the obtaining of money or property by means of any misleading or untrue statement.

As far as these anti-fraud rules are concerned there can be little doubt that they can be applied to the Eurobond markets if the US courts wish to apply them extraterritorially.

Much of the case law and jurisprudence of r 10(b)-5 is concerned with 'insider trading' but r 10(b)-5 has also been applied in the context of the dissemination of information in *SEC v Texas Gulf Sulphur Co*.[2] The court in that case held that the rule is violated whenever information is disseminated in a manner which is reasonably calculated to affect investor behaviour, for instance by way of a press release in the financial press; and if such information is false or misleading or is so incomplete as to mislead, irrespective of whether the issuance of the release was motivated by corporate officials for purposes of facilitating purchase of stock by them at a low price, the rule is violated. In that case a misleading press release was issued in respect of an ore strike made by the company in Ontario which undervalued and understated the value of the ore strike. The court held that this ipso facto amounted to a breach of r 10(b)-5. The rule is therefore capable of being applied to a Eurobond offering circular prospectus or other publicity material.

III REGULATION OF STABILISATION DURING AN ISSUE OR DISTRIBUTION OF SECURITIES: R 10(b)-6 AND R 10(b)-7

There are a number of rules seeking to regulate the market activities of underwriters, issuers and dealers, during the initial distribution period. They are s 9 and s 10(b) of SEA 1934 and r 10(b)-6, r 10(b)-7, r 15(c)-1(6) and (8) and r 17(a)-2 of the SEC issued under SEA 1934. These rules overlap with the all-embracing anti-fraud rule 10(b)-5. The policy objective of these rules is to prevent the manipulation of the price of or market in a security during the initial issue and distribution. As observed earlier, artificial demand can be created during this period to drive up the price of a security or create a misleading appearance of active trading.[3] Section 9 of SEA 1934 attacks the problem in so far as securities are registered on an exchange in the US, and is of little potential relevance to the Euromarkets since Eurobonds are hardly, if ever, registered. Rule 10(b)-6 and r 10(b)-7, however,

---

2 258 F Supp 262.
3 See ch 18 on stabilisation.

apply to all securities registered or unregistered and are potentially applicable to Eurobond issues.

Stabilising activity in particular is potentially within the prohibition in r 10(b)-6 as well as r 10(b)-7 and may need to comply with the 'safe harbour' provisions of r 10(b)-7 in order to escape sanctions under SEA 1934. Rule 10(b)-6 and r 10(b)-7 are potentially applicable where the 'means or instrumentalities of interstate commerce or the US mails or any facility of any national securities exchange' is used to effect transactions prohibited by the two rules.[4]

Rule 10(b)-6 makes it unlawful for any person who is an underwriter or prospective underwriter or who is the issuer of securities or who is a broker, dealer or other person who has agreed to participate or is participating in a 'distribution' or who is 'an affiliated purchaser'[5] to bid for or purchase for any account in which he has a beneficial interest any security which is the subject of a 'distribution' or any right to purchase any such security or to attempt to induce any person to purchase any such security or right until after 'he has completed his participation in such distribution'. This prohibition applies where the bid or purchase is 'engaged in for the purpose of creating actual or apparent active trading in or raising the price of' the securities. A distribution is defined in r 10(b)-5 (5) as meaning 'an offering of securities whether or not subject to registration under the Securities Act 1933 that is distinguished from ordinary trading transactions by the magnitude of the offering and the presence of special selling efforts and selling methods'. In other words, the rules are concerned with the large-scale offering of a class of securities by the use of the usual marketing framework, consisting of an underwriting syndicate or sole underwriter, a selling group and the transmission of offering circulars and prospectuses.

An issue of convertible Eurobonds or Eurobonds with warrants is also potentially within the prohibition in r 10(b)-6. Rule 10(b)-6(6)(b) provides that 'the distribution of a security (i) which is immediately exchangeable for or convertible into another security, or (ii) which entitles the holder thereof immediately to acquire another security, shall be deemed to include a distribution of such other security within the meaning of this rule'.

Where the security which is the subject of the distribution is a convertible, or is a security which entitles the holder to purchase another security (for example, a Eurobond with warrants to purchase stock/shares of the issuer) the prohibition in r 10(b)-6 also prevents the issuer, underwriters and dealers participating in the distribution and 'affiliated purchasers' from purchasing the underlying equity security during the distribution period: r 10(b)-6(6)b.[6]

If stabilising bids or purchases in respect of a Eurobond issue fall within the prohibition in r 10(b)-6 due to the use of the means or instrumentality of interstate commerce, it will be necessary to comply with the rules contained in r 10(b)-7, because r 10(b)-6(viii) provides that stabilising transactions effected in accordance with r 10(b)-7 do not constitute a violation of r 10(b)-6.

---

4 See rr 10(b) 6 and 7.
5 An 'affiliated purchaser' is defined in r 10(b)-6(6)(i) to include a person who is acting in concert with a participant in the distribution. See also the definition of affiliated purchaser in r 10(b)-7(6).
6 See also r 10(b)-6(a)1(4).

374 *The legislative framework of US securities laws*

Rule 10(b)-7 itself contains a prohibition on any form of stabilising activity which is not effected in accordance with the provisions of r 10(b)-7. It provides that 'it shall constitute a manipulative or deceptive device or contrivance' as used in s 10(b) of SEA 1934 for any such person directly or indirectly by the use of any means or instrumentality of interstate commerce or the mails or of any facility of any national securities exchange to effect any transaction or series of transactions prohibited by this rule.

Rule 10(b)-7 defines stabilising transactions as 'the placing of any bid, or the effecting of any purchase, for the purpose of pegging, fixing or stabilising the price of any security'. It further provides that a bid shall not constitute a stabilising bid unless or until 'it is shown in the market', though no definition is given in the rules as to what constitutes 'shown in the market'.

The stabilising rules in r 10(b)-7 cover any form of security as defined in s 3(a)(10) of SEA 1934 but do not apply to 'exempt securities' as defined in s 3(a)(12)(A) of SEA 1934. 'Exempt securities' include securities issued by the US Government or a corporation in which the US Government has a participating interest and which are designated by the Secretary of the Treasury for exemption.

A number of conditions must be satisfied before stabilising activity falls within the 'safe harbour' provisions of r 10(b)-7.

(a) Written notices must be given to any person to whom a stabilised security is sold or from whom a stabilised security is purchased. The notice must be to the effect that such security may have been the subject or may be the subject of stabilising purchases. This written notice needs to be given at or before the completion of each transaction entered into while the distribution is in progress. Compliance with this requirement would render stabilising activity virtually impossible to effect in practice, and consequently, r 10(b)-7(K) provides for an exemption whereby if the purchaser receives a prospectus, offering circular or confirmation in writing containing a legend that stabilising activity may be or has been effected the written notice requirement is deemed to be satisfied.[7]

(b) Only one stabilising bid may be made in the market at any given point in time. Unlike in the UK[8] there is no formal requirement that only the stabilising manager may post bids in compliance with the stabilising rules. However, the effect of the US rule is very much the same in practice as the UK rule. The syndicate of underwriters in practice would need to decide which of their members would place stabilising

---

7 The legend generally used in practice is one similar to the legend provided for in item 502(d) of Regulation S-K of the SEC.
8 See ch 18 above.

bids in order to prevent a multiplicity of stabilising bids in breach of r 10(b)-7(E).
(c) The person placing the stabilising bid or transmitting a stabilising bid is required to disclose the purpose of such bid to the person with whom it is placed or to whom it is transmitted.
(d) Any person placing a stabilising bid or effecting a stabilising purchase is required to grant priority to any independent bid at the same price.
(e) No stabilising bid or purchase may be made to facilitate 'any offering at the market' (r 10(b)-7(G)). An offering at the market is defined in r 10(b)-7(B)(i) to mean 'an offering in which it is contemplated that any offering price set in any calendar day will be increased more than once during such day'. The prohibition on stabilisation of such offerings means that the securities which are being distributed must have a fixed issue price. This requirement is virtually the same as the one operative in the UK[9] and operates in tandem with the rules governing the price levels at which stabilising bids may be made.
(f) No stabilising bid can be made at a price which the party stabilising knows or has reason to know is a result of activity which is fraudulent, manipulative or deceptive under SEA 1934 or the SEC rules framed thereunder. This requirement is again similar to the requirement under the UK rules.[10]
(g) The person or entity making the stabilising bids or purchases is required under r 10(b)-7(L) to keep a record of stabilising transactions and make a report to the SEC containing the information required by r 17(a)-2 even though the person stabilising is not subject to r 17(a)-2.[11]

The requirements of r 17(a)-2 are that the stabilising manager should promptly record and maintain in a separate file for a period of not less than 12 months certain items of information which include the name and class of any security being stabilised; the price, the date and the time at which the first stabilising purchase and each succeeding stabilising purchase was effected by the manager or by any participant in the syndicate or group; and the names and addresses of the members of the syndicate or group and their respective underwriting commitments. The stabilising manager must also promptly furnish to each of the members of the syndicate or group the name and class of any security being stabilised and the date and time at which the first stabilising purchase was effected by the manager of or any participant in the syndicate or group. The manager must also notify each of the members of such syndicate or group of the date and time when stabilising was terminated.[12] Rule 17a-2(b)(i) requires that the lead manager in a securities issue must be the stabilising manager.

---

9 See ch 18 above.
10 See ch 18 above.
11 R 17(a)-2 does not apply to a broker, dealer or member of a national securities exchange.
12 See r 17(a)-2(c).

Where stabilising activity has been effected by a person who is not the stabilising manager for his account or for the account of the syndicate, such person is required within three business days following such a stabilising purchase to notify the manager of the price, the date and the time at which such stabilising purchase was effected and also notify the date and time when stabilising activity was terminated by him.[13]

(h) Price limits must be observed during the course of stabilisation.

The primary rule is contained in r 10(b)-7(C) which states that 'no stabilising bid or purchase shall be made except for the purpose of preventing or retarding a decline in the open market price of a security'. Stabilising bids therefore cannot be made with the objective of driving up the price when there is no possibility of a downward movement in the price of a security which is being distributed.

Rule 10(b)-7(J) then provides that 'no person shall (a) begin to stabilise a security at a price higher than the highest current independent bid price for such security or (b) raise the price at which he is stabilising'. Given the fact that usually at the time that the first stabilising bid is posted there may not in fact be a market for the securities which are being distributed, rule 10(b)-7(J) further provides that 'if no bona fide market for the security being distributed exists at the time stabilising is initiated, stabilising may be initiated at a price not in excess of the public offering price'. In effect this would mean that the first stabilising bid would need to be made at the public offering price of the securities which are being distributed.

Where stabilising bids or purchases are made prior to the determination of the initial public offering price of securities to be distributed and this offering price is higher than the stabilising bid or purchase price, stabilising may be resumed at either the current independent bid price for the security or, if no bona fide market for the security being distributed exists, then at a price not in excess of the public offering price.[14]

1 Remedies and enforcement

The enforcement mechanisms in respect of the obligations imposed by SEA 1934 are as follows:

(a) Under s 32(a) it is a criminal offence to violate any of the provisions of SEA 1934 or SEC rules framed under it. However, for purposes of criminal liability the conduct which breaches a provision of SEA 1934 must be 'wilful'; negligence will be sufficient.[15]

---

13 See r 17(a)-2(d).
14 See r 10(b)-7(J)(iii) and (i).
15 A person convicted of a violation of SEA 1934 provisions may not be subjected to imprisonment 'if he proves he had no knowledge of such rule or regulation'. He is subject to financial penalties whether he had such knowledge or not.

(b) Under s 21(a) the SEC has power to investigate violations and where appropriate to bring an action by way of injunction under s 21(d).

It has been held by the Federal Supreme Court in *Aaron v SEC*[16] that injunctive relief is not available unless there is 'scienter' in the sense of an intention to deceive, manipulate or defraud, where the alleged violation is a violation of r 10(b)-5 or of s 17(a)1 of SA 1933.[17]

(c) Section 29(b) makes void every contract made in violation of the provisions of SEA 1934 or the rules made under it. Contracts whose performance involves a violation of such provisions and rules are also declared void. However, the contract is void not only in respect of the person who made the contract in violation of SEA 1934 or its rules, it is also void in respect of a person who is not a party to the contract, but who has knowledge of the violation.

(d) In addition where there is a violation of r 10(b)-5 it has been held that a cause of action in damages can be maintained.[18] These rulings stand unaffected by a recent trend in US case law to deny private rights of actions in damages for violations of statute, and the US Supreme Court said in 1983 in *Herman & Maclean v Huddleston*[19] that 'a private right of action under section 10(b) of the 1934 Act and rule 10(b)-5 has been consistently recognised for more than 35 years. The existence of this implied remedy is beyond peradventure'.[20]

---

16 446 US 680 (1980).
17 It has further been held that in respect of violations of s 17(a)(2) and (3) there was no need for proof of such intent, though the court said in the same breath: 'This is not to say however that scienter has no bearing at all on whether a district court should enjoin a person violating or about to violate section 17(a)(2) or section 17(a)(3)' (per Justice Stewart); though this comment seems to refer to the issue of whether the court should grant injunctive relief rather than to the issue whether there is or is about to be a violation of s 17(a)(2) or (3). Justice Stewart's conclusions that intention was unnecessary was based on the absence of any reference to intention and fraud in s 17(a)(2); and as regards s 17(a)(3) because that section was activated on an effects basis, ie 'quite plainly focuses upon the effect of particular conduct on members of the investing public rather than on the culpability of the person responsible'. In other words, if the *effect* of a transaction or course of business or practice is that it defrauds or deceives, s 17(a)(3) is violated regardless of intention to defraud or deceive. The court was capable, quite accurately, to come to a different conclusion with regard to the similarly worded provision in r 10(b)-(5)(c) because the whole of r 10(b)-5 was made within the framework of s 10(b) of SEA 1934, which in the court's view required scienter and intention to deceive and defraud.
18 *Blue Chip Stamps v Manor Drug Stores* 421 US 723 (1975) affirming *Affiliated Ute Citizens v US* 406 US S 128 (1972); *Superintendent of Insurance v Bankers Life and Casualty Co* 404 US 6 (1971).
19 103 S Ct 683, 687.
20 However, it has been held that the action under r 10(b)-5 can only be brought by a purchaser or seller of securities and a plaintiff who refrained from purchasing due to manipulative, deceptive or fraudulent activity has no right to sue: *Blue Chip Stamps v Manor Drug Stores* (above). It must also be proved that there was an intention on the part of the defendant to deceive or defraud: *Ernst & Ernst v Hochfelder* (425 US 185 (1976)). The ruling of the Federal Supreme Court in *Hochfelder* is a limitation on the efficacy and availability of actions for damages for breaches of r 10(b)-5. The Supreme Court per Justice Powell, justified reading into the language of r 10(b)-5 the requirement of scienter on the basis that r 10(b)-5 was only operative by virtue of s 10(b) of SEA 1934 and

(e) The question whether similar civil actions for damages may be brought in respect of breaches of other provisions of US securities law (ie other than r 10(b)-5 violations) is far from clear. The US courts have oscillated between a robust view that a breach of a statutory obligation should usually give rise to the implication of a private remedy by way of a civil action for damages as, for instance, in *JI Case Co v Borak*,[1] a case concerning r 14a-9, to a more cautious view that private rights action should not be easily read into statute if it does not expressly provide for such a remedy as in *Piper v Chris-Craft Industries Inc*,[2] an action based on a breach of s 14(e) of SEA 1934.[3]

More recent cases decided by the Federal Supreme Court suggest that where civil rights of action in damages have been recognised for some time the court will not 'de-recognise' their existence.[4]

IV THE TRUST INDENTURE ACT 1939 ('TIA 1939')

TIA 1939 s 306 is also a provision which, like s 5 of SA 1933, is potentially applicable to a Eurobond issue. It requires that whenever the offer or sale of debt securities involves the use of the US mails or the means or instrumentalities of interstate commerce the securities must be issued subject to a

---

'Section 10(b) makes unlawful the use or employment of "any manipulative or deceptive device or contrivance" in contravention of Commission rules. The words "manipulative or deceptive" used in conjunction with "device or contrivance" strongly suggest that section 10(b) was intended to proscribe knowing or intentional conduct.'
The damages awarded in actions under r 10(b)-5 have been assessed in accordance with the usual tort measure in Anglo-American law – the out-of-pocket measure: *Affiliated Ute Citizens of Utah v US* (406 US 128 at 154–155 (1972)). However, the courts have on occasions awarded damages on a different measure. See the *Affiliated Ute* case itself and *Osofsky v Zipf* 645 F 2d 107, 114 (2nd Cir 1981).
1 377 US 426 (1964).
2 430 US 1 (1977).
3 In *Transamerica Mortgage Advisors v Lewis* 447 US 11 (1979) the US Federal Supreme Court stated the view that private rights of action in damages will not be read into a securities statute where the statute makes certain conduct unlawful and then prescribes expressly the legal consequences of such conduct. That case involved a breach of s 206 of the Investment Advisors Act 1940 which proscribed certain conduct subject to criminal penalties and also provided SEC action by way of injunctive action to compel compliance. The court's ruling, however, did not consider statutory obligations which were backed not only by criminal sanctions and SEC action but also by a s 29 type sanction (ie all contracts entered into in violation of the statutory obligation being declared void). Arguably this case does not affect provisions of SEA 1934 covered by s 29. Indeed, the court in dealing with s 29 of SEA 1934 did not rule out the availability of civil remedies by way of damages for the breach of any of the obligations contained therein.
4 See *Merrill Lynch Pierce Fenner & Smith Inc v Curran* 102 S Ct 1825 (1982) and *Herman & Maclean v Huddleston* 103 S Ct 683 especially at 687.

'trust indenture', ie a trust deed complying with the requirements of that Act and must be 'qualified' under that Act. The need for such a 'qualified' trust deed is explained by the SEC in s 302 of TIA 1939 and is quoted at the end of chapter 13 above.

CHAPTER 20
Extraterritoriality of US securities laws[1]

I INTRODUCTION

It seems clear that US courts will apply the provisions of US securities laws extraterritorially although it is difficult to predict the circumstances in which they will do so.

A few points need to be made initially. First, there seems to be no express statutory basis for applying securities laws extraterritorially. Indeed, s 30(b) of SEA 1934 seems to suggest that at least SEA 1934 was not intended to be applied extraterritorially until the SEC formulated regulations under the section. Nevertheless, despite the fact that no such regulations have ever been framed under s 30, the court in *Schoenbaum v Firstbrook*[2] dismissed[3] the significance of s 30 in its holding that section 10b of SEA 1934 and r 10(b)-5 framed thereunder had extraterritorial application.

Secondly, the case law has held that the question whether a statute has extraterritorial application, in the absence of express provision, must be decided by reference to the 'intention of Congress' and if that intent can

---

1 The literature on the extraterritorial application of US securities laws is voluminous. The following are particularly useful. Loomis and Grant 'The US Securities and Exchange Commission, Financial Institutions Outside the US and Extraterritorial Application of the US Securities Laws' Jo of Comparative Corporate Law and Securities Regulation 1 (1978) 3-38 (North Holland Publishing Company); Murano 'Extraterritorial Application of the Antifraud Provisions of the Securities Exchange Act of 1934' International Tax and Business Lawyer vol 2, pp 298-321; Karmel 'The Extraterritorial Application of the Federal Securities Code' 7 Connecticut LR 669-709; Johnson 'Application of Federal Securities Laws to International Securities Transactions' and Pergam 'Eurocurrency Financing: Securities Considerations for US Corporate Issuers' in *Financing in the International Capital Markets* (Seventh Annual Fordham Corporate Law Institute, Sprow edn, Law and Business, Harcourt Brace Jovanovich).

See also the following: 'The Extraterritorial Application of the Federal Securities Code: A further Analysis' 9 Conn LR 67 (Fall 1976); 'Extraterritoriality in the Federal Securities Code' 20 Harvard Int'l LJ 305 (Spring 1979); 'American Adjudication of Transnational Securities Fraud' 89 Harvard LR 553 (January 1976); 'Subject Matter Jurisdiction In Transnational Securities Frauds' 3 Ohio Northern Univ LR 1305 (1976); 'Transnational Application of the Federal Securities Laws Expanded' 8 Seton Hall LR (1977).

See also ch 24 of Jennings and Marsh *Securities Regulation: Cases and Materials* (The Foundation Press, 6th edn, 1987).
2 405 F 2d 200 (2nd Cir 1968).
3 It is submitted, in a wholly unconvincing fashion.

be determined it will be upheld by the courts even if it violates the bounds of extraterritoriality laid down by public international law: *US v Aluminium Co of America*[4] and *Leasco Data Processing Equipment Corpn v Maxwell*.[5]

Thirdly, the obligation to comply with federal securities legislation is activated the moment there is 'a use of any means or instrumentality of interstate commerce or of the mails ...'[6] This phrase is repeated in the US statutes whenever obligations are imposed and conduct prohibited as the jurisdictional predicate for their application. Section 3(a)(12) of SEA 1934, which defines the phrase, states that it includes 'trade, commerce, transportation or communication between *any foreign country* and any state or between any state and *any place* or ship *outside thereof*'. Section 2(7) of SA 1933 defines interstate commerce in similar terms referring to 'trade or commerce in securities or any transportation or communication relating thereto between any foreign country and any State, Territory or the District of Columbia'.[7] The courts have consistently refused to decide whether a mere communication between the US and foreign location, eg London, would be sufficient to give rise to the extraterritorial application of US securities laws. As the 9th Circuit said in *SEC v United Financial Group Inc*:[8] 'An alternative theory of jurisdiction advanced by respondent is based solely upon appellant's use of the facilities of interstate commerce. If accepted without qualifications there would be jurisdiction in every case regardless of whether American investors were involved.' The reluctance to apply US securities laws extraterritorially on the mere user of any facilities of interstate commerce is at least sensible because, if it were otherwise, even a telephone call from London to New York would then justify the application of US securities laws to a transaction in London.[9]

Fourthly, nearly all the cases in which US courts have in fact applied US securities laws extraterritorially have been in relation to the breaches of the anti-fraud provisions of r 10(b)-5 and s 15 of SEA 1934. Whether the principles to be derived from these cases can readily be applied to other provisions is a matter of conjecture, though it is more than likely that similar results would be arrived at in relation to other anti-fraud provisions which are based on similar policy considerations.

Fifthly, the US cases have never approached the question of whether US securities law would apply to a foreign transaction on the basis of applying ordinary choice of law rules in the conflict of laws. If the US courts apply choice of law rules the outcome may be different because in practice international bond issues from London have little connection with the US. It is difficult to understand why the US courts have not considered the choice of law issue.[10]

---

4   148 F 2d 416, especially at 443 (2nd Cir 1945).
5   468 F 2d 1326 at 1334 (2nd Cir 1972).
6   See, for instance, s 5 of SA 1933 and s 10b, r 10(b)-5, s 15(c)1, 2 and 3 of SEA 1934.
7   See ch 19 above.
8   474 F 2d 354 (9th Cir 1973).
9   See dicta in *Leasco Data Processing Equipment Corpn v Maxwell* 468 F 2d 1326 especially at 1335.
10 See generally Trautman 'The Role of Conflicts Thinking in Defining the International Reach of American Regulatory Legislation' 22 Ohio St LJ 586 (1961) and also Sandberg 'The Extra-Territorial Reach of American Economic Regulation: The Case of Securities Law' 17 Harvard International LJ 315 (1976).

This leads to the difficult question which requires an answer: in what circumstances have the US courts held that US securities laws may be applied extraterritorially?[11] Jurisdiction has been asserted by the US courts in securities cases where a breach of r 10(b)-5 has occurred on the basis of two principles to be found in the Second Restatement of the Foreign Relations Law of the United States (1965): the so-called 'objective territorial principle' stated in s 18 – the 'effects doctrine' – and the 'subjective territorial principle' stated in s 17 – the 'conduct doctrine'. The objective territorial principle is concerned with asserting jurisdiction over transactions occurring outside the US but having effects in the US. The subjective territorial principle confers jurisdiction over conduct which occurs within the US but causes effects outside US territory.[12]

II THE 'EFFECTS' DOCTRINE

The two leading cases which applied US securities law extraterritorially on an objective 'effects' basis were: *Schoenbaum v Firstbrook*[13] and *Des Brisay v Goldfield Corpn*.[14]

In *Schoenbaum*, a US stockholder of a Canadian corporation sued its directors who were a Canadian company, Acquitaine, and a US corporation, Paribas Corpn, on the basis of fraud and breach of s 10(b) and r 10(b)-5 of SEA 1934. The fraudulent transactions occurred outside the US (in Canada) between non-US persons. The US court, relying on the effects doctrine, held it had jurisdiction to adjudicate on the merits for a breach of US securities law, on the basis that jurisdiction would be asserted in respect of transactions outside the US if it was 'necessary to protect American investors', such as the injured plaintiff. The scope of the decision is unclear. Arguably, if *Schoenbaum* is given a wide meaning, when Eurobonds find their way into the hands of American investors the entirety of US securities regulation is activated if it is necessary to protect an American investor. The court said: 'we believe that Congress intended the Exchange Act to have extraterritorial application in order to protect domestic investors who have purchased foreign securities on American exchanges and to protect the domestic securities market from the improper foreign transactions in American securities'.[15] The *Schoenbaum* decision, however, may not be as wide as that. In that case the stock of the Canadian corporation was listed not only in Canada but also on US stock exchanges and the court said at one point that it would assert jurisdiction '*at least when the transactions involve stock registered and listed on a national securities exchange* and are detrimental to the interest of American investors' (emphasis added).[16] Arguably the judgment is therefore restricted to cases where the transaction is

---

11 The literature on the subject is voluminous. See *Financing in the International Capital Markets* (Fordham Corporate Law Institute) Part II and the articles cited in fn 1 above.
12 See ss 17 and 18 of the Second Restatement of the Foreign Relations Laws of the United States (1965).
13 405 F 2d 200 (1968) cert denied 395 US 906 (1969).
14 549 F 2d 133 (9th Cir 1977).
15 At 206.
16 At 208.

in relation to stock or securities listed and traded on a US stock exchange. This restriction in the interpretation of *Schoenbaum* seems to have found support in the case of *Leasco Data Processing Equipment Corpn v Maxwell*,[17] where Judge Friendly said:

> 'if all the misrepresentation here alleged had occurred in England we would entertain most serious doubt whether, despite *United States v Aluminium Co of America* ... and *Schoenbaum*, s 10(b) would be applicable simply because of the adverse effect of the fraudulently induced purchases in England of securities of an English corporation not traded in an organised American securities market, upon an American corporation whose stock is listed on the New York Stock Exchange ... the language of section 10(b) of the Securities Exchange Act is much too inconclusive to lead us to believe that Congress meant to impose rules governing conduct throughout the world in every instance where an American company bought or sold a security.'

The court, however, did not disagree with *Schoenbaum* but preferred to say, 'when no fraud has been practised in this country and the purchase or sale has not been made here, we would be hard pressed to find justification for going beyond *Schoenbaum*'.

The *Leasco* judgment thus seems to restrict the applicability of the effects doctrine in *Schoenbaum* to cases where the security which is the subject of the transaction was traded on an American stock exchange. This limiting factor as one commentator has pointed out is devoid of any logical justification.[18] Another restriction on the application of the effects doctrine may be found in *Bersch v Drexel Firestone*.[19] The court commenting obiter on the effects test thought that it would only apply where the impact was 'a direct and foreseeable result of the conduct' occurring outside the US, in accordance with s 18(b)(iii) of the Restatement on Foreign Relations Law.

The restrictive interpretation of *Schoenbaum* and the restriction laid down in *Bersch* were, however, discarded in *Des Brisay v Goldfield Corpn*[20] where the court applied US securities law to a securities transaction in Canada, simply on the basis that the transaction had an adverse effect on the price of stock of a US corporation whose stock was listed on a US stock exchange, even though the transaction did not relate to these securities. The court seems to have founded its conclusion on two alternative bases: (a) adverse impact on the US market in general, and (b) adverse effect on US investors in respect of stock listed on a US stock exchange, although the transaction did not involve securities listed and traded on an American stock exchange as was the case in *Schoenbaum*. The effect on the American investors was also not direct, in the sense that they suffered loss due to the fact that the SEC suspended trading in the stock of the US corporation involved in the transaction. The case is therefore direct authority for rejecting the limitations placed on the *Schoenbaum* decision by the courts in *Leasco* and *Bersch*.

What impact do these cases have on the Eurobond market? The answer seems to be that if *Schoenbaum* is applied in the manner that the court was prepared to do in *Des Brisay*, without the limitations imposed in *Leasco*

---

17 468 F 2d 1326 (2nd Cir 1972).
18 See Johnson fn 1 above, at 70.
19 519 F 2d 974 (2nd Cir 1975).
20 549 F 2d 133 (9th Cir 1977).

and *Bersch*, issuers, underwriters and sellers of Eurobonds may find themselves exposed to SEC injunctive action and, more importantly, to civil actions brought by American purchasers of Eurobonds, on the basis of the effects doctrine. Indeed, the SEC has acted on the basis of a wider interpretation of *Schoenbaum* in other situations.[1]

III 'CONDUCT' BASED JURISDICTION

The subjective 'conduct' approach holds that where there is significant or substantial conduct within the territory of the US which violates US securities law, the US courts will apply US securities law even though part of the transaction occurred outside US territory, and even though the effects of the transactions, if any, were also outside US territory. Most of the cases in this area have been cases where a fraud or misleading information had emanated partially or wholly from the US.[2]

In asserting jurisdiction to apply US law to such transactions, the courts have held that even non-US plaintiffs may activate US securities legislation provided substantial conduct occurred within the US. In an oft-quoted passage, Judge Friendly in *ITT v Vencap* said 'we do not think Congress intended to allow the United States to be used as a base for manufacturing fraudulent security devices for export even when these are peddled only to foreigners'.

The difficult question in this category of cases is to determine how much conduct within US territory is necessary to justify the extraterritorial application of US securities laws. Judge Friendly in *ITT v Vencap* seems to have drawn a distinction between the level of conduct necessary before jurisdiction would be asserted in respect of a foreign (ie non-US) plaintiff and that required for US citizens resident abroad. In respect of the fraudulent transaction involved in *ITT v Vencap*, he said that jurisdiction will not be asserted for the benefit of foreign plaintiffs unless the perpetration of the fraudulent act itself was committed in the US; 'mere preparatory activities or the failure to prevent fraudulent acts where the bulk of the activity was performed in foreign countries' were insufficient. In that case, the deal had been set up in the Bahamas while the legal documentation was negotiated and drafted in the US. This was considered insufficient by Judge Friendly to apply US securities laws extraterritorially for the benefit of a foreign plaintiff.

In *Bersch v Drexel Firestone Inc*[3] Judge Friendly returned to this distinction and formulated it in this way:

> 'we have thus concluded that the anti-fraud provisions of the federal securities laws ... apply to losses from sales of securities to Americans resident abroad

---

1 See *SEC v Osec Petroleum* SA [1974–1975 Transfer Binder] Fed Sec L Rep (CCH) 94, 915.
2 See, for instance, *SEC v Gulf Intercontinental Finance Corpn* 223 F Supp 987 (SD Fla 1963); *SEC v United Financial Group Inc* 474 F 2d 591 (3rd Cir 1976); *Straub v Vaisman and Co Inc* 540 F 2d 591 (3rd Cir 1976); *US v Cook* 573 F 2d 281 (5th Cir) cert denied 439 US 836 (1978); *ITT v Vencap* 519 F 2d 1001 (2nd Cir 1975); *Bersch v Drexel Firestone Inc* 519 F 2d 974 (2nd Cir) cert denied 423 US 1018 (1975); *SEC v Kasser* 548 F 2d 109 (3rd Cir) cert denied 43 US 938 (1977).
3 Above.

if, but only if, *acts* (or culpable failures to act) *of material importance in the United States have significantly contributed thereto*; but ... do not apply to losses from sales of securities to foreigners outside the United States unless acts (or culpable failures to act) within the United States *directly caused* such losses.' (Emphasis added.)[4]

The distinction seems to be that before a non-resident foreigner can claim the benefit of US securities legislation it must be shown that the breach of US law (or fraud) which caused the loss occurred within the US; whereas in respect of a US citizen abroad, it is sufficient that material or substantial activity which contributed to the loss occurred in the US. In the latter case the commission of the fraud or breach need not occur within the US.

The distinction is difficult to apply in practice and consequently it is difficult to predict whether given conduct activates US securities legislation. The distinction drawn by Judge Friendly was nevertheless applied by the court in respect of a Eurodollar financing in *FOF Proprietory Funds Ltd v Arthur Young & Co.*[5] In that case debt securities issued by a Massachusetts Corporation and guaranteed by its Delaware incorporated parent had been sold outside the US by foreign dealers to the plaintiff who was a Canadian corporation. The securities were sold only to foreign investors and not to US nationals or residents as was the case in most Euro-offerings. The court held that the Canadian plaintiff could not ask the US courts to assert jurisdiction for violation of its securities laws because the actual conduct complained of which caused the plaintiff losses occurred outside the US. There was some conduct in the US, in particular the drafting of the offering circular, but the court regarded this as merely 'preparatory'.

If the *Arthur Young* judgment stood on its own, most Eurobond financings (even in respect of US-based corporations) would be immune from conduct-based jurisdiction, unless the actual fraud or the actual breach causing loss occurred entirely in the US or there had been sales of Eurobonds to US citizens resident abroad.

The ruling in *Arthur Young*, however, is put in doubt by Judge Friendly's own judgment in *ITT v Cornfeld*.[6] The court held in *Cornfeld* that the conduct in question was not merely preparatory but was such as directly to cause losses to foreigners. The significance of the case lies in what was considered by the court to go beyond the preparatory level. The plaintiff was a Luxembourg-based trust. The fraud action related partly to the purchase of convertible bonds issued by the Netherlands Antilles financing vehicle of a US corporation registered in Maine. The purchases were made in Europe. In asserting subject matter jurisdiction the 2nd Circuit relied on the following conduct:

(a) the prospectus was drafted entirely in the US;
(b) the prospectus was printed entirely in the US;
(c) the accounting work was done entirely in the US.

Cornfeld suggests that the apparent difference between the test for foreigners and that for American residents abroad is simply a matter of language

---

4 519 F 2d 974 (2nd Cir) cert denied 423 US 1018 (1975).
5 400 F Supp 1219 (SDNY 1975).
6 619 F 2d 909 (2nd Cir 1980).

and not of substance. The one significant difference between the *Cornfeld* and the *Arthur Young* cases was that the convertible Eurobond issue in *Cornfeld* was part of an overall financing which included a much larger issue of such securities in the US. In addition, there was more involvement in the underwriting of the issue by American investment banks in *Cornfeld*. Despite these differences it is difficult to disagree with the proposition that 'It would appear to be impossible for an American corporation to raise funds in the Euromarket without engaging in the activities found by Judge Friendly in *Cornfeld* to constitute a sufficient basis for subject matter jurisdiction.'[7]

Two other cases point to the conclusion that so long as there is substantial conduct within the US, the courts will assert subject matter jurisdiction over violations of US securities legislation regardless of whether the plaintiff is a foreigner or US national. In *SEC v Kasser*,[8] in relation to an alleged fraud involving an investment contract, negotiations had taken place in the US; one of the investment contracts had been executed there; US telephone and mail services had been used; and the New York office of a Swiss bank had been used to transfer funds. These were regarded by the district court as 'miscellaneous acts' and not substantial; but the Court of Appeal having observed that, in addition, corporate records had been maintained in the US and that many of the agreements were drafted in the US, though executed outside, and that funds had been transmitted to and from US territory, held that the conduct was substantial and not merely preparatory. The *Kasser* judgment seems to have relaxed the criteria as to the quantum of conduct in the US necessary for the purpose of asserting jurisdiction, when compared with those laid down in *Vencap* and *Bersch* in respect of injuries to foreigners. This relaxation has been recognised in *Continental Grain Australia Pty Ltd v Pacific Oilseeds Inc*.[9] The formula used in that case was that where the defendant's conduct was in furtherance of a fraudulent scheme then if it was 'significant with respect to its accomplishment', subject matter jurisdiction did exist.

The distinction drawn by Judge Friendly in *Bersch v Drexel Firestone Inc* between cases of injuries to foreigners and those of injuries to US nationals resident abroad therefore no longer seems to hold good, and 'substantial conduct' in the US would seem to give rise to subject matter jurisdiction for r 10(b)-5 violations.

In the final analysis, it seems that the decision to assert jurisdiction on the basis of conduct within the US is purely a matter of policy and it is impossible to draw fine distinctions. The court in *SEC v Kasser*[10] quite candidly said that their decision was based on policy;[11] the court was concerned that to deny jurisdiction would be 'to allow the United States to become a "Barbary Coast", as it were, harbouring international securities pirates', and as a corollary it wished 'to ensure high standards of conduct in securities transactions within this country in addition to protecting dom-

---

7   Johnson (fn 1, p 380) p 95.
8   584 F 2d 109 (3rd Cir) cert denied 431 US 938 (1977).
9   592 F 2d 409 (8th Cir 1979).
10 Above at 116.
11 See also the comments in *Continental Grain (Australia) Pty Ltd v Pacific Oilseeds Inc* 592 F 2d 409 at 416, where the court recognised that it was making a policy decision.

estic markets and investors from the effects of fraud'. Fine distinctions such as those drawn by Judge Friendly therefore seem inappropriate in deciding the issue.

If judicial policy as articulated by the court in *SEC v Kasser*[12] is the true basis of conduct-based jurisdiction, it is submitted that while the US courts are far more inclined to assert conduct-based jurisdiction in r 10(b)-5 fraud cases on the basis of some conduct in the US, it is likely that in relation to other breaches of US securities laws not involving r 10(b)-5 fraud, they would be less inclined to assert jurisdiction in respect of Eurobond activity, unless the violative conduct occurred entirely within the US. They would nevertheless be willing to assert jurisdiction on the effects principle in *Schoenbaum*.

IV THE SEC AND EXTRATERRITORIALITY

The applicability of US securities law to transactions in the Eurobond markets cannot, however, be considered simply as a matter of law by analysing the decisions of the US courts. The practice of the SEC is also of importance. The administrative practice of the SEC is fundamental in this area because most of the enforcement mechanisms of US securities laws are concentrated in the hands of the SEC.[13] Thus, for instance, SA 1933 s 20 provides for SEC investigations into alleged breaches or threatened or continuing breaches of SA 1933 and for the grant of injunctions against violations of SA 1933 (and rules framed thereunder) at the instance of the SEC. Section 20 also provides for the initiation of criminal prosecutions by the SEC and where successful these may attract criminal sanctions under s 24. The same is true of SEA 1934 under the provisions of ss 21 and 32.

The SEC issues Releases outlining circumstances in which certain transactions will not attract such SEC enforcement action and those Releases form an important aspect of securities law. The SEC also issues 'no action' letters on an ad hoc basis stating that in the context of a proposed transaction no enforcement action will be taken by the SEC. These Releases and 'no action' letters are an important source of administrative precedent.

Consequently, the application of US securities law to transactions occurring wholly or substantially outside the US must also be considered in the context of such Releases and 'no action' letters. Indeed, it is perhaps the case that until the enactment of Regulation S in 1990 the structure and mechanics of an international bond issue were based on SEC Release 4708 of July 1964.[14]

The SEC's position in the past with regard to extraterritoriality was summarised in 1978 by Commissioner Loomis of the SEC writing in his private capacity:[15]

'The Commission believes that in the international area, as in the domestic area, vigorous enforcement of the laws is essential to the confidence of investors

---

12 Above.
13 See ch 19 above for a discussion of this aspect.
14 See 388, below.
15 See the Jo of Comparative Corporate Law and Securities Regulation (1978) at 4.

and to the strength and efficiency of the securities markets. Nevertheless when the Commission has believed it necessary for the protection of investors and the securities markets and for fulfilment of the purposes of the US securities laws, it has not hesitated either in actions initiated by it or in private actions to urge US courts to assert broad bases of subject matter and personal jurisdiction.'

The SEC's official view in 1968 as summarised in its amicus curiae brief in *Schoenbaum v Firstbrook*[16] was to the effect that 'there are no so-called territorial limitations' and that securities legislation 'is generally applicable whenever such application is necessary and appropriate for the protection of American investors and markets'.

V SEC RELEASE 4708 OF JULY 1964

Until the promulgation of Regulation S in April 1990,[17] the Eurobond market in fact relied on the text of SEC Release 4708 of July 1964 and a number of 'no action' letters to avoid the extraterritorial application of two key provisions, namely s 5 of SA 1933 (registration provision)[18] and s 15(a) of SEA 1934 (broker dealer registration).[19] This Release formed the basis of 'no action' by the SEC in respect of two key provisions of US securities laws (SA 1933 s 5 and SEA 1934 s 15) in their application to the international bond markets for over 25 years. Consequently, the Release and the procedures developed under it will be discussed in the following pages.

However, it is important to note that it is no longer possible to rely on Release 4708 and the procedures developed under it to disapply s 5 (or other provisions of US securities laws) since the promulgation of Regulation S by Release no 33–6863[20] in the Federal Register.[1] As regards s 15 of SEA 1934 the provisions of the Release have also been superseded by r 15a-6.[2]

The remainder of this chapter is of historical interest only.

In Release no 33–4708 dated 9 July 1964, the SEC stated that it would not take action in respect of the distribution of securities outside the US under certain specified conditions even though SA 1933 s 5 (the registration provision) has not been complied with. The SEC also stated that it would not take action against foreign broker dealers who were not registered under SEA 1934 s 15(a) even though they participated as underwriters in the distribution of US securities outside the territorial limits of the US. The first part of the Release was of great importance to the Euromarkets and it enabled Eurobond issues to be made without the risk of SEC intervention, particularly in the case of US issuers.

---

16 405 F 2d 200 (2nd Cir 1986).
17 See below on Regulation S.
18 See ch 19 above.
19 See ch 19 above.
20 See ch 21.
1 See Release 33–6863 at p 2.
2 See ch 21 above.

The important provisions of the Release were as follows:
Releases 33–4708 and 34–7366, 9 July 1964[3]

'The registration requirements of the Securities Act apply to any offer or sale of a security involving interstate commerce or use of the mails unless an exemption is available. Since "interstate commerce" is defined in Section 2(7) of the Act to include "trade or commerce in securities or any transportation or communication relating thereto ... between any foreign country and any State, Territory, or the District of Columbia", this might be construed to encompass virtually any offering of securities made by a United States corporation to foreign investors. However, the Commission has traditionally taken the position that the registration requirements of Section 5 of the Act are primarily intended to protect American investors. Accordingly, the Commission has not taken any action for failure to register securities of United States corporations distributed abroad to foreign nationals, even though use of jurisdictional means may be involved in the offering. It is assumed in these situations that the *distribution is to be effected in a manner which will result in the securities coming to rest abroad*. On the other hand a distribution of securities by a United States corporation, through the facilities of Canadian Stock Exchanges may be expected to flow into the hands of American investors and may therefore be subject to registration. Similarly, a public offering specifically directed toward American nationals abroad, including servicemen, would be regarded as subject to registration. Apart from such situations, however, it is immaterial whether the offering originates from within or outside the United States, whether domestic or foreign broker-dealers are involved and whether the actual mechanics of the distribution are effected within the United States, *so long as the offering is made under circumstances reasonably designed to preclude distribution or redistribution of the securities within, or to nationals of, the United States.*

Active trading in the United States of the securities subject to the offering during or shortly after the distribution abroad may raise a question whether a portion of the distribution was in fact being made by means of such trading. However, absent such a situation, if a distribution of securities by a United States corporation is made abroad without registration reliant upon the foregoing interpretation of the Act, dealers may trade in other securities of the same class in the United States without regard to the time limitations of the dealer's exemption in section 4(1).' (Emphasis added.)

As regards application of s 15(a) of SA 1933 to foreign underwriters, brokers and dealers, the SEC stated as follows in the same Release:

'Generally speaking, section 15(a) of the Securities Exchange Act of 1934 makes it unlawful for any broker or dealer to use the mails or instrumentalities of interstate commerce, including commerce between the United States and any foreign country, to engage in securities transactions otherwise than on a national securities exchange unless he is registered with the Commission. However, if a foreign broker-dealer, participating as an underwriter in a distribution of American securities being made abroad, or being made both abroad and in the United States, limits his activities to (1) taking down securities which he sells outside the jurisdiction of the United States to persons other than American nationals, and (2) participating solely through his membership in the underwriting syndicate in activities of the syndicate in the United States such as sales to selling group members, stabilising, over-allotment, and group sales, which

---

3 29 FR 9828 17 CFR 231.4708.

activities are carried out for the syndicate by the managing underwriter or underwriters who are registered with the Commission, then the Commission will generally raise no objection if the foreign broker-dealer performs these limited functions without registration as a broker-dealer under section 15 of the Act.

If a foreign broker-dealer limits his securities activities in areas subject to the jurisdiction of the United States in the manner described above, then he could participate in any number of such distributions, assuming that he does not engage in other activities which require registration. Such other activities would include either selling securities into the United States or purchasing securities in the United States for sale to American investors abroad.'

As regards s 5 of SA 1933, the most vital aspect of the Release in respect of a Eurobond issue was that the SEC would not take action in cases where 'the distribution is to be effected in a manner which will result in the securities coming to rest abroad'. These key words gave effect to the SEC's perception of the policy underlying US securities laws, namely the protection of US investors and US securities markets. Consequently, it was stated in the Release that the SEC would not take action, where 'the offering is made under circumstances reasonably designed to preclude distribution or redistribution of the securities within or to nationals of the United States'.

The problem for the issuer, underwriters and their lawyers was to devise mechanisms which would ensure that the bonds would come to 'rest abroad'. Some discussion of the procedures developed under Release 4708 is useful, since the procedures used currently in practice in consequence of Regulation S and the US Treasury's TEFRA D Regulations,[4] are largely based on such procedures.

The technique developed in the Euromarket under Release 4708 was as follows.[5] First, legal documents prohibited the members of the underwriter's group and members of the selling group (if there was one) from selling or offering to sell any bonds of that particular issue, to which the prohibition related, to any US national (wherever resident) or to US residents.[6]

Secondly, each underwriter and selling group member agreed to deliver a notice to anyone purchasing a bond from them to the effect that the purchaser would not sell or offer to sell the securities to US residents, or US nationals, for a period of 90 days after the completion of the initial distribution of the bonds, that is 90 days after the 'all sold' telex was sent. If the purchaser was a bond dealer the notice required the dealer to confirm that he had not and would not offer or sell the securities to US residents or US nationals (wherever resident) and that the dealer was not purchasing the securities for the account of any US resident or US national (wherever resident) and that the dealer would require similar covenants from persons to whom such dealer would sell the securities.[7]

Thirdly, every underwriter and selling group member was required to con-

---

4 See ch 21(II) below.
5 See Cannell 'Selling Restrictions Under United States Securities Laws Applicable to Foreign Issues' in *Current Issues of International Financial Law* (Malaya Law Review and Butterworths, 1985).
6 See now Regulation S r 903(c)(2)(ii).
7 See now Regulation S r 903(c)(2)(iv).

firm by telex to the managing underwriter that its allotment had been sold to persons who were neither US residents nor US nationals.

Fourthly, on 'closing day' at the end of the selling period, the issuer would not deliver the actual bonds (the 'definitives') to the bond purchasers in return for the transfer of funds. The issuer would deliver only a temporary 'global bond'[8] which represented the total aggregate of bonds issued. The definitive bonds would only be delivered 90 days after closing day, and the global bond exchanged for the definitives only when the trustee or fiscal agent of the issue, who was charged with administering the bonds, received a certificate that all bonds were held beneficially by non-US persons.[9]

Two questions usually arose in practice.

First, were such 'lock-up' mechanisms necessary in every Eurobond issue including those of non-US entities, in order to avoid the possibility of SEC action?

Secondly, even if it was necessary to use the 'lock-up' mechanisms was it sufficient to use only a contractual 'lock-up' without the necessity for a global bond and the exchange of definitives for the global bond on certification of non-US beneficial ownership of bonds?

The answer to the first question was that, unless it was clear that the bonds would come to rest abroad, lock-up mechanisms had to be used. This depended largely on US investor interest in purchasing the bonds issued. If it was a US issuer, issuing US dollar denominated bonds involving US bond dealers and banks there was no question that there was a great likelihood that US residents or US nationals would wish to purchase the bonds. Even if the issue was in, say, DM or yen this would still be necessary. However, what if the issuer was non-US and the underwriting group was non-US? Once again, if the issue was dollar denominated it was likely that there might have been US investor interest, in particular, if the issuer was a household name like Fiat or had stock listed on an American stock exchange. Further, even if the issue was non-dollar denominated but the issuer was a household name, or had previously issued bonds in the US market, it was likely that the bonds would not come to rest abroad and lock-up procedures would be necessary. The answer always turned on the level and the likelihood of US investor interest.

Assuming that 'lock-up' procedures were necessary, was it always necessary to use the full procedures? Was it sufficient that only contractual lock-up provisions were used in some cases? The answer depended again on the level of investor interest in the US (or amongst US nationals) because this would determine whether the procedures were, in the eyes of the SEC, 'reasonably designed to preclude distribution or redistribution of the securities within or to nationals of the United States'. Some lawyers felt that if the issuer was a non-US issuer, issuing non-dollar denominated bonds and the issuer was not an international household name (ie not Mitsubishi or British Petroleum) there was no need for the global bond lock-up procedure. A contractual lock-up in the form of a prohibition on sale of bonds to US nationals or residents should suffice. If there was a doubt the practice was to obtain the usual 'no action' letter from the SEC.

---

8 See ch 9 for a discussion of its legal nature.
9 See now Regulation S. Such procedures are now required only under r 903(c)3 which does not apply to issuers of straight debt securities.

The detailed structure and mechanics of the global bond and the 90 day lock-up procedure under Release 4708 was as follows.[10]

(a) On closing day after all bonds had been allotted and sold the issuer would deliver a global bond in the form and manner prescribed by the trust deed (or the fiscal agency agreement, whichever was used)[11] to Euroclear or Cedel, or more usually to a common depository for the account of Euroclear or Cedel. A legal obligation was imposed on the issuer to deliver such a global bond by the trust deed (or fiscal agency agreement) and enforceable by the trustee or fiscal agent. Euroclear or Cedel took the global bond on behalf of the lead manager of the issuer under their agreements with the lead manager. The lead manager in turn was authorised by the selling group, where there was one, to take delivery of the Global bond on their behalf.

(b) Within 90 days, the issuer was also required to deliver to the fiscal agent or the trustee, as the case may be, the definitive bonds. This obligation was also imposed on the issuer by the trust deed or fiscal agency agreement.

(c) Euroclear or Cedel would receive certificates in the form specified in the trust deed or fiscal agency agreement from bond dealers or other account holders in Euroclear or Cedel stating that 'no part of the interest in the bonds held for our account is beneficially owned by a US person'. In practice, the dealers would hold a portfolio of bonds for their clients, who may be institutional or private investors, and would usually have purchased these bonds for their clients' accounts.

(d) When Euroclear or Cedel received these certificates from the dealers they in turn would issue a further certificate stating that Euroclear or Cedel had received certificates of non-US beneficial ownership of bonds from their account holders, namely the dealers. This certificate was submitted with the Global bond to the trustee or fiscal agent, in return for the definitive bond. The definitive bonds were then held by Euroclear or Cedel or by a sub-depository on their behalf. The fiscal agent or trustee was legally obliged to the issuer, under the fiscal agency agreement or trust deed respectively, to transfer the definitive notes only when it received a certificate of non-US beneficial ownership of the bonds. The dealers or other account holders in Euroclear or Cedel who had purchased the bonds for the account of their clients agreed (in the selling group agreement if there was one) with the lead manager of the issuer that selling group members had a right to the definitive bonds at the end of the 90-day period upon certification of non-US beneficial ownership of bonds.[12]

---

10 This procedure or one similar may need to be used for purposes of TEFRA D (save that the 'lock up' is only 40 days) for purposes of its certification requirements as to non-US beneficial ownership of the bonds. See ch 21(II) below.
11 See chs 11, 12 and 13 above.
12 The SEC had not formally approved 90 days as the acceptable number of days for which the bonds should be locked up, but the absence of disapproval had been regarded as indicating that the period was sufficient.

CHAPTER 21
Regulation S rule 15a-6 and other provisions

US case law[1] makes it clear that at least the anti-fraud provisions of SA 1933 and SEA 1934 may be applied extraterritorially to securities transactions occurring outside the US, in certain circumstances. The question whether other key provisions of the US securities laws[2] which could be applied extraterritorially to an issue of Eurobonds in London has never been the subject of clear judicial pronouncement. As far as s 5 of SA 1933 and s 15 of SEA 1934 were concerned, the Eurobond markets had operated for over 25 years on the basis of SEC's Release 4708 of July 1964[3] which had provided a safe harbour from any action which the SEC was capable of taking provided the issue of Eurobonds was effected in circumstances 'reasonably designed to ensure that the securities would come to rest abroad'. The compliance with the requirements of the Release was, however, no guarantee that issuers and underwriters of Eurobonds could not be sued by purchasers of Eurobonds on the basis of the various statutory provisions in SA 1933 for breaches of s 5 of that Act.[4] Recently, two sets of rules promulgated by the SEC have sought to restrict the extraterritorial impact of US securities laws: these are Regulation S and r 15a-6; another related rule, r 144A, has attempted to widen access to US markets of international securities issues. These are discussed below.

I REGULATION S

Regulation S was promulgated by Release no 33-6863 under SA 1933 and became effective in May 1990.[5]

Regulation S seeks to clarify and place on a firm statutory basis the circum-

---

1 See ch 20 above.
2 Discussed at ch 19 above.
3 See pp 388 et seq above.
4 The writer's research has, however, not brought to light any such actions in respect of a Eurobond issue in the past 25 years.
5 Regulation S was originally proposed in SEC Release no 33-6779 (53 FR 22661, 17 June 1978) and reproposed with revisions in Release no 33-6838 (54 FR 30063, 18 July 1989). The statutory basis for Regulation S is to be found in the SEC's power to make rules and regulations under ss 2, 4 and 19 of SA 1933.

stances in which s 5 of SA 1933 will not apply extraterritorially in respect of transactions occurring outside the territory of the United States. It is important to note at the outset that Regulation S relates solely to the extraterritorial application of SA 1933 s 5; it is not the basis for a general disapplication of US securities laws and does not affect the scope of the extraterritorial applications of other provisions of SA 1933 or of SEA 1934, in particular, the anti-fraud provisions of those statutes.[6]

Broadly speaking, Regulation S seeks to permit foreign issuers for whose securities there is no 'substantial US market interest' to issue securities in off-shore transactions outside the US without running the risk of a breach of SA 1933 s 5. Secondly, it also seeks to permit US corporations to issue securities in off-shore transactions without being exposed to the risk of a breach of SA 1933 s 5 provided they comply with certain conditions.

Regulation S, however, is permissive and non-mandatory. Strict compliance with Regulation S clearly results in the avoidance of the risk of a breach of SA 1933 s 5; in other words, it is a 'safe harbour'.[7] This means that it is possible, theoretically at least, for a Eurobond issue to escape a breach of SA 1933 s 5 even though it does not comply with the permissive regime of Regulation S.

Regulation S disapplies SA 1933 s 5 in respect of securities issues made in compliance with its requirements by providing in r 901 that s 5 of SA 1933 'shall be deemed not to include offers and sales that occur outside the United States', and then providing in r 903 that if the various conditions laid down in Regulation S are complied with in respect of an issue of securities such an issue 'shall be deemed to occur outside the United States within the meaning of r 901'.

Regulation S in fact creates two safe harbours. The first is the 'issuer safe harbour' and the second is the 'resale safe harbour'. The issuer safe harbour[8] is open to an issuer or 'distributor', a phrase which means 'any underwriter, dealer or other person who participates pursuant to a contractual arrangement in the distribution of the securities offered or sold in reliance on this Regulation S'.[9] The resale safe harbour[10] is open to any person other than the issuer, the distributor, or any of their respective affiliates or any person acting on behalf of any of the above. It will be seen that the issuer safe harbour is of fundamental importance to those involved in the issue of Eurobonds in the primary markets. The resale safe harbour concerns sales of securities including Eurobonds in the secondary rather than primary issue markets and is consequently, not of much importance to the legal position of those participating in the issue of the Eurobonds.[11]

The conditions attaching to the two safe harbours are different but there

---

6 Equally, Regulation S does not affect the provisions of state law relating to the offer and sale of securities.
7 However, the SEC has made it clear in the preliminary notes to Regulation S that 'In view of the objective of these rules and the policies underlying the Act, Regulation S is not available with respect to any transaction or series of transactions that, although in technical compliance with these rules, is part of a plan or scheme to evade the regulation provisions of the Act. In such cases registration under the Act is required.' See Release no 33–6779.
8 See r 903.
9 See r 902(c).
10 See r 904.
11 It is nevertheless dealt with below at p 408.

are two primary requirements which must be satisfied both under the 'issuer safe harbour' and the 'resale safe harbour' by any person who wishes to take advantage of either safe harbour. Under the 'issuer safe harbour' further conditions are imposed in addition to these two primary conditions depending on the classification of the issuer of the securities under Regulation S.

These two primary requirements reflect the basic policy requirement of Regulation S that the issue or offering of bonds or securities must be one which has minimal contacts with the US or US persons. The two primary requirements specified in r 903 and r 904 are:

(a) that no 'directed selling efforts' should be made in the US;
(b) that the transaction should be 'an off-shore transaction'.

1 The prohibition on 'directed selling efforts'

'Directed selling efforts' is defined in r 902(b) as meaning 'any activity undertaken for the purpose of, or that could reasonably be expected to have the effect of, conditioning the market in the United States for any of the securities being offered in reliance on this Regulation S'. The core requirement is that there should be no activity in terms of advertising or publicity which 'conditions' the market in the US. Rule 902(b)(1) specifically provides that the placing 'of an advertisement in a publication with a general circulation in the United States that refers to the offering of securities' would constitute a conditioning. The SEC have also indicated[12] that activities such as mailing printed material to US investors or conducting promotional seminars in the US or placing advertisements either with radio or television stations broadcasting into the US, or in publications with a general circulation in the US, which discuss the issue of securities, would fall within the concept of conditioning the market in the US. It seems that for there to be a 'conditioning' within the meaning of the provision, in respect of a Eurobond issue (as distinct from a stock/share issue), the advertisement or publication must have some reference, either directly or indirectly, to the issue of the securities in question; general advertising of a corporate nature would probably not constitute conditioning. The conditioning must relate to the securities which are being issued rather than to the corporate entity which is the issuer. Each case, it is submitted, would depend on (a) the nature of the publicity, (b) the intent with which it is published, and (c) the impact on the US investing community. There are, however, some grey areas. For instance, where a Eurobond issue is to be effected in Swiss francs by a Japanese corporation and one of the investment banks which is a member of the underwriting group issues a research publication in the US immediately prior to the issue. It recommends investment in Swiss franc denominated debt securities of Japanese corporations. This may constitute conditioning within the meaning of the prohibition.

The concept of 'directed selling efforts' under Regulation S must also be distinguished from activities which would constitute 'solicitation' in the

---

12 See Release no 33-6863 at p 29.

context of r 15a-6 of SEA 1934.[13] In Release no 27017 issued under SEA 1934 (the release was issued on 11 July 1989), the SEC stated that solicitation would include 'any affirmative effort by a broker or dealer intended to induce transactional business for the broker, dealer or its affiliate' and consequently telephone calls from a broker or dealer to a customer encouraging use of the broker or dealer to effect transactions or the transmission of information, opinions, or recommendations to specific customers or potential customers in the US would constitute solicitation. Such categories of activity would not generally constitute directed selling efforts within the meaning of Regulation S unless such communications related to the particular securities which are to be issued.[14]

The requirement that there should be no directed selling efforts in the US is one which is imposed on the issuer or 'distributor' participating in the issue[15] or any of their respective affiliates or any person acting on behalf of any of the above. Selling efforts of similar securities undertaken by independent brokers and dealers would not deprive issuers and distributors of the issuer safe harbour.

Rule 902(b)(3) provides that 'contact with persons excluded from the definition of "US person" pursuant to paragraph (o)(7) of this section or persons holding accounts excluded from the definition of "US person" pursuant to paragraph (o)(2) of this section solely in their capacities as holders of such accounts, shall not be deemed "directed selling efforts"'. There are a number of international organisations within the US, including the World Bank and its affiliates, the United Nations and its agencies[16] and, more importantly, dealers or fund managers incorporated or resident in the US, who operate discretionary accounts and similar managed accounts for persons who are not 'US persons'.[17] It is submitted that communications made with or to *overseas* branches and offices of US banks and US insurance companies carrying on a bona fide business *overseas* would not constitute directed selling efforts in the US, although such entities are not specified in r 902(b)(3), because it could not be said that such activity would have 'the effect of conditioning the market in the United States'.

There are also a number of specific exemptions in respect of certain activities. Thus, under r 902(b)(2) advertisements published in the US due to the requirements of US or foreign law under the rules or regulations of a US or foreign regulatory authority do not constitute directed selling efforts provided that the advertisement contains no more information than that legally required. Such an advertisement must, however, contain a statement to the effect that the securities have not been registered under SA 1933 and may not be offered or sold in the US (or to a US person, as defined in Regulation S) if the advertisement relates to certain offerings under r 903(c). Under r 902(b)(6) a distribution in the US of price quotations in respect of securities of a non-US broker dealer through a system owned or operated by an independent third party which distributes such quotations primarily in foreign countries would not constitute 'directed selling efforts',

---

13 See pp 416–420 below on r 15a-6.
14 See also the SEC's views expressed in SEC Release 33-6863 at p 36.
15 See above for definition, r 902(c).
16 R 902(o)(7).
17 Para 902(o)(2).

provided certain conditions were satisfied. The first is that securities transactions cannot be executed between foreign broker dealers and persons in the US through the quotation system; and secondly, that the issuer, distributors, their respective affiliates and persons acting on behalf of the above, do not initiate contact with US persons or persons within the US beyond those contacts exempted under r 15a-6 of SEA 1934.[18]

'Tombstone' advertisements published in a journal, newspaper or other publication with a general circulation in the US are exempted from the prohibition on directed selling efforts provided certain conditions are met.[19] First, the publication must have less than 20% of its aggregate circulation occurring in the US. Secondly, the advertisement must contain a legend to the effect that the securities have not been registered under SA 1933 and may not be offered or sold in the US (or to a US person if the advertisement relates to an offering under r 903(c)(2) or (3)). Thirdly, the advertisement can only contain the information specified in r 902(b)(4)(iii). This information includes the issuer's name, the amount and title of the securities being sold, a brief indication of the issuer's general type of business, the price of the securities, the yield of the securities if they are debt securities, the name and address of the person placing the advertisement and whether such person is participating in the distribution, the names of the managing underwriters and the date, if any, upon which the sales commenced and concluded.

2 Requirement of 'off-shore transaction'

The second primary requirement which must be satisfied to come within the issuer's safe harbour (as well as the resale safe harbour) is that the transaction must be 'an offshore transaction' as defined in r 902(i).

As far as a Eurobond issue is concerned, in order to satisfy the offshore transaction requirement, two conditions need to be satisfied. First, no offer should be made to a person in the US; and secondly, it must be shown that 'at the time the buy order is originated, the buyer is outside the United States, or the seller and any such person acting on its behalf reasonably believes that the buyer is outside the United States'.

The first requirement will be satisfied if the issuer and the distributors, their affiliates and persons acting on behalf of any of the above, make no offers for sale of the Eurobonds to any person in the US. There is no definition of 'person in the United States' though there is a definition of 'US person'.[20] While it is easy to decide whether an offer is made to an individual who is in the US, it is not easy to decide whether an offer is being made to a corporate entity in the US. Thus, where a corporation incorporated in the US has a branch in London, and an offer is made to the London branch, the question arises whether an offer for the sale of Eurobonds is being made to a person in the US. It seems that in such a case the offer is not being made to a person in the US, either on the basis that the offer is directed at a person at a location outside the US, or because the person to whom the offer is directed may be regarded as resident outside the US for the

---

18 See pp 416–420 below in respect of r 15a-6.
19 R 902(b)(4).
20 See r 902(o) and p 405 below for a discussion.

purposes of the offer. The point requires clarification so that it is clear that an offer made to the European branch of a US incorporated entity comes within the first limb of the off-shore transactions requirement.

Rule 902(i)(3), however, does provide that 'offers and sales of securities to persons excluded from the definition of "US person" pursuant to paragraph (o)(7) of this section or persons holding accounts excluded from the definition of "US person" pursuant to paragraph (o)(2) of this section, solely in their capacity as holders of such accounts, shall be deemed to be made in "off-shore transactions"'. In effect, this means that direct offers and sales can be made to the same persons who may be contacted as an exception to the requirement of no directed selling efforts.[1]

The second condition which must be satisfied is that at the time the 'buy order is originated' the buyer is outside the US. Once again, it is not clear how this requirement is applied to a corporate entity incorporated in the US with a branch or office located in Europe or elsewhere. Can such a corporate buyer be regarded as being outside the US despite the fact that its principal place of operation is within the US? The SEC in its Release 33–6863 states that 'when the buyer is a corporation or partnership if an authorised employee places the buy order while abroad the requirement that buyer be outside the United States will be satisfied'.[2] It is, however, difficult to understand how the SEC arrives at this conclusion. It is also not clear how one decides *when* a 'buy order is originated'. One answer to the first problem may be that for purposes of Regulation S the European branch of an entity incorporated in the US is to be regarded as a separate person for purposes of determining whether a transaction is an off-shore transaction within the meaning of Regulation S.

The other type of case which may cause difficulty is where an employee of a European or British company who is temporarily in the US places a buy order in respect of Eurobonds which are being issued in London. On a plain reading of the off-shore transactions provisions in Regulation S, it seems that the benefit of Regulation S will be lost.

Once again, the answer to these difficulties may be to make clear in a rule amendment that offers and sales to person excluded from the definition of US person are deemed to be made in an 'off-shore transaction', so that offers and sales are strictly confined to such persons; there should then be no difficulty in practice. It is submitted this is probably the position in practice under the current rule. In order to comply with these two primary requirements with regard to the prohibition of selling efforts directed at the US and the requirements of the off-shore transaction, the subscription agreement and the agreement between managers (and the selling group agreement, if any) should, first, at least contain appropriate clauses preventing offers being made to persons in the US; secondly, require that no sale ought to be made to any person unless he is originating the buy order from outside the US; and finally, that the issuer and the underwriters (and the selling group, if any) refrain from any activities which are intended or have the effect of conditioning the market in the US in respect of Eurobonds which are the subject of the issue.

---

1 See p 396 above as to such persons and see p 405 below for a detailed discussion of who is a 'US person'.
2 See p 23 of Release 33–6863.

There is an alternative to this second requirement, namely, that the transaction is to be executed 'in, on or through a physical trading floor of an established foreign securities exchange that is located outside the United States'. However, this exception is of little practical importance in the context of a Eurobond issue since the distribution does not occur on the floor of a securities exchange in the UK or elsewhere but through telephonic means or screen-based systems. It may be noted that in respect of a sale of Eurobonds in the *secondary markets* the second requirement may be satisfied if the sale is effected 'through the facilities of a designated off-shore securities market' (r 902(i)(ii))(B)(2)). The Eurobond markets as regulated by the Association of International Bond Dealers as well as The London Stock Exchange are 'designated off-shore securities markets' for these purposes: r 902(a)(1). Unfortunately, a similar exemption is not available *in the primary markets*, in respect of the 'issuer safe harbour'.

3 Issuer conditions

In addition to the two primary requirements discussed above, further conditions are imposed by Regulation S on certain categories of issuers. Issuers of securities are classified into three categories for this purpose.[3] Issuers falling within two of these categories must satisfy further conditions as a prerequisite to the availability of the safe harbour in Regulation S.

(a) A *'foreign issuer'* which reasonably believes at the commencement of the offering that there is no *'substantial US market interest'*[4] in its securities does not need to comply with any further conditions other than the two primary requirements discussed above: r 903(c)(1)(i); foreign governments also fall within this category, as do 'overseas directed offering': r 903(c)(1)(ii) and (iii).

(b) US and foreign 'reporting issuers'[5] and non-reporting 'foreign issuers' of debt securities: r 903(c)(2).

These issuers are required to comply with what the SEC has termed certain 'transactional restrictions'[6] and certain 'contractual restrictions' *in addition* to satisfying the two primary requirements with regard to off-shore transactions and directed selling efforts.

Foreign issuers of Eurobonds who are not 'reporting issuers' will fall within this category if there is a 'substantial US market interest' for the relevant securities.

(c) All other issuers who do not fall within (a) or (b) above fall within the third category and are subject to further requirements including a 40-day lock-up period in respect of the securities which are the subject of the issue: r 903(c)(3). This category essentially comprises non-reporting foreign issuers for whose equity securities there is a 'substantial US market interest'.

---

3 See r 903.
4 As defined: see p 400 below.
5 As defined, see p 403 below.
6 See SEC Release 33–6863.

In practice nearly all Eurobond issuers should fall within either category (a) or (b) above.

4 Foreign issuers with no substantial US market interest (category (a))

To come within this issuer category, it must first be shown that the issuer is a 'foreign issuer' as defined in r 902(f) and, secondly, that there is no 'substantial US market interest' with respect to the issuer's debt securities as defined in r 902(n)(2).

i 'Foreign issuer'

A foreign issuer is defined as any issuer which is a foreign government or a corporation or other organisation incorporated under the laws of a country other than the US. However, in respect of a company or corporation incorporated overseas, the foreign issuer requirement is not satisfied if: (a) more than 50% of the outstanding voting stock of such issuer is held by persons who have a US address; and (b) one of three further conditions is satisfied: that (i) the majority of the executive officers or directors of the issuer are US citizens or residents; or (ii) more than 50% of the assets of the issuer are located in the US; or (iii) the business of the issuer is administered principally in the US.[7]

ii 'Substantial US market interest'

The second key requirement of this issuer category is that there is no 'substantial US market interest' in the issuer's securities. The purpose of this requirement is to ensure that there is no serious possibility of flowback of the securities to the US even in the absence of directed selling efforts and even though the offer is made to persons outside the US.

What constitutes a substantial US market interest in the issuer's securities is defined in a complicated manner. Nevertheless the complexity of the definition is somewhat tempered by the fact that the requirement is satisfied if the issuer 'reasonably believes at the commencement of the offer' that there is no such substantial US market interest in its debt securities.[8]

In determining whether a substantial US market interest exists, Regulation S focuses on the type of security which is the subject of the issue rather than the issuer's securities in general.

Where debt securities are being issued which are neither convertible into equity nor have equity warrants attached to them (eg 'straight' Eurobonds), substantial US market interest turns on the aggregate amount of the issuer's debt securities (and certain other specified securities[9]) which are 'held of record'[10] by US persons. However, where the Eurobonds which are being

---

7 See r 902(f).
8 See r 903(c)(1)(i); for the definition of 'substantial US market interests' see r 902(n).
9 Described in r 903(c)(4)(i) and r 903(c)(4)(ii).
10 As defined in r 12(g)5–1 of SEA 1934. See r 902(g).

issued are convertible into the equity securities of the issuer, the question of substantial US market interest is determined by reference to the convertible debt security as well as in relation to the underlying equity securities into which the bond is convertible.[11] Where Eurobonds are issued with warrants, 'substantial US market interest' turns on the question whether there is such interest not only in relation to the debt security, but also in relation to the underlying equity securities which may be subscribed by the exercise of the warrants.[12]

In effect this means that in the case of a convertible Eurobond or a Eurobond issue with warrants the question of substantial US market interest needs to be determined by reference both to the issuer's debt securities and its equity securities.

Whereas in the case of debt securities, substantial US market interest turns on the aggregate amount of the issuer's debt (and other specified) securities held of record by US persons, substantial US market interest in relation to the equity securities of an issuer turns on whether securities exchanges in the US constitute the single largest market for such equity securities or whether a large volume of trading in the issuer's equity securities occurs within the US.[13]

Substantial US market interest in respect of an issuer's debt securities exists where (a) the issuer's debt securities and certain other securities[14] in the aggregate are held of record by 300 or more US persons,[15] or (b) that one billion dollars or more of the aggregate of its debt securities and other specified securities[16] are 'held of record' by US persons,[17] or (c) that 20% or more of the principal amount outstanding of debt, securities and certain other specified securities is held of record by US persons. The two types of securities which need to be aggregated for these purposes together with the issuer's debt securities are 'non-participating preferred stock'[18] and all 'asset backed securities'.[19]

---

11 See r 903(c)(1)(i)(D).
12 See r 903(c)(1)(i)(C).
13 See r 902(n)(1)(i) and (ii).
14 Specified in r 903(c)(4)(i) and (ii).
15 As defined in r 902(o).
16 Specified in r 903(c)(4)(i) and (ii).
17 As defined in r 902(o).
18 As defined in r 903(c)(4)(i).
19 As defined in r 903(c)(4)(ii). 'Non-participating preferred stock refers to non-convertible capital stock, the holders of which are entitled to a preference in payment of dividends and in distribution of assets on liquidation, dissolution, or winding-up of the issuer, but are not entitled to participate in residual earnings or assets of the issuer'; and asset-backed securities refers to 'securities of a type that either: (A) represent an ownership interest in a pool of discreet assets or certificates of interests or participation in such assets (including any rights designed to assure servicing or the receipt or timeliness of receipt by holders of such assets, or certificates of interest or participation in such assets, of amounts payable thereunder), provided that the assets are not generated or originated between the issuer of the security and its affiliates; or (B) is secured by one or more assets or certificates of interests or participation in such assets, and the securities, by their terms, provide for payments of principal and interest (if any) in relation to payments or reasonable projection of payments on assets meeting the requirements of paragraph (c)(4)(ii)(A) of this section, or certificates of interest or participations in assets meeting such requirements'. Assets for these purposes are defined in that section to mean 'securities, instalment sales, accounts receivable, notes, leases or other contracts, or other assets that by their terms convert into cash over a finite period of time'.

The test of substantial US market interest with respect to an issuer's equity securities is that, either (a) 'the securities exchanges and inter dealer quotation systems in the United States in the aggregate constituted the single largest market for such class of securities in the shorter of the issuer's prior fiscal year or the period since the issuer's incorporation'; or (b) '20 per cent or more of all trading in such class of securities took place in, on or through the facilities of securities exchanges and inter dealer quotation systems in the United States and less than 55 per cent of such trading took place in, on or through the facilities of securities markets of a single foreign country in the shorter of the issuer's prior fiscal year or the period since the issuer's incorporation'.[20]

These tests are somewhat difficult to apply in practice in the context of the international markets. In the case of debt securities, for instance, it is necessary to show that the specified amount in aggregate is not 'held of record'. Rule 902(g) provides that 'held of record' has the meaning assigned to that term in r 12(g)5-1 of SEA 1934. The rule in SEA 1934 provides that 'securities shall be deemed to be held of record by each person who is identified as the owner of such securities on records of security holders maintained by or on behalf of the issuer'. In the case of Eurobonds, which are bearer instruments, the records (if any) to which r 12(g)5-1 can be applied are the records of Euroclear and of Cedel. In respect of those two clearing systems it is by no means clear whether there is identification of the 'owner' of securities. This is due to the fact that the 'owner' of a bearer instrument is generally the 'holder' of the bearer instrument.[1] First, it is not clear which law will determine the ownership of the instrument for purposes of Regulation S read with r 12(g)5-1 of SEA 1934. Secondly, the problem with regard to who is the holder of Eurobonds resurfaces as a problem in the context of r 12(g)5-1 for the purposes of determining ownership.[2]

In addition to these difficulties, r 12(g)5-1(a)5 further states that 'each outstanding ... bearer certificate shall be included as held of record by a separate person, except to the extent that the issuer can establish that, if such securities were registered, they would be held of record, under the provisions of this rule, by a lesser number of persons'. This requirement would, however, not be too difficult to satisfy given the fact that the records of Euroclear and Cedel are capable of establishing the total number of securities held by any given account holder in Euroclear or Cedel.[3]

It is submitted that as far as a Eurobond issue is concerned, the approach of Regulation S which relies on the concept of 'held of record' contained in r 12(g)5-1 of SEA 1934, creates uncertainty in the application of the Regulation and needs to be clarified. A rule which provides that held of record refers to the aggregate amount of Eurobonds held on the books of Euroclear and/or Cedel or such other clearance system designated by the SEC would eliminate the uncertainty.

It will be seen from the above that the majority of 'foreign issuers' in the international bond markets would come within the so-called foreign issuer category although it needs to be remembered that issues by offshore

---

20 See r 902(n)(1)(i) and (ii).
1 See ch 9 above.
2 See discussion at pp 171–174 above.
3 See on this aspect pp 169–170, above.

subsidiaries of US multinationals would not qualify as foreign issuers for these purposes.

5 Reporting issuers and issuers of debt securities (category (b))

This category[4] comprises, first, all domestic US issuers which file reports pursuant to ss 12(b) or 12(g) of SEA 1934 or under s 15(d) of SEA 1934. These are reports which provide continuing disclosure of financial and business information about US issuers whose securities are traded on US exchanges.

Secondly, this category also comprises foreign reporting issuers who also file reports under those provisions, and presumably cannot establish that there is no substantial US market interest in their securities. It must be noted that foreign issuers submitting reports and information to the SEC pursuant to r 12(g)3-2(b) of SEA 1934 are not regarded as reporting issuers falling within this category.[5]

Thirdly, foreign issuers of debt securities (including Eurobonds) which do not submit reports under the relevant provisions of SEA 1934 also come within this category. Non-reporting foreign issuers of Eurobonds would need to rely on this safe harbour only if there is a substantial US market interest for their debt securities and consequently fall outside the first category (a) above. US issuers of debt securities who do not submit reports under SEA 1934 will fall within category (c) below.

In addition to the primary restrictions[6] a number of further conditions must be satisfied by issuers falling into category (b).

First, certain '*transactional restrictions*' need to be complied with;[7] and, secondly, '*offering restrictions*' must be implemented.[8]

(i) *Transactional restrictions*

These require first that any offer or sale of the Eurobonds must not be made to a 'US person' or for the account or benefit of a 'US person' during a 40-day restricted period. This requirement does not, however, preclude the offer or sale of the Eurobonds to any underwriter, dealer or other person who participates in the distribution of the securities pursuant to contractual agreements.[9] The 40-day restriction period with regard to sales to US persons is much shorter than the 90-day period which was used in practice in respect of Eurobond issues under Release 4708[10] prior to Regulation S coming into effect.

The 'restricted period' for the purposes of the transactional restrictions (and 'offering restrictions', discussed below) is a 40-day period under r 902(m) which commences on the later of the date upon which the Eurobonds are first offered to persons other than the underwriters and dealers in reliance

---

4   Dealt with in r 903(c)(2).
5   See the definition of 'reporting issuer' r 902(l).
6   See pp 395-399, above.
7   R 903(c)(2)(iii).
8   See r 903(c)(2)(ii).
9   See r 903(c)(2)(iii) read with r 902(c).
10 See p 388, above.

on Regulation S, or the date of closing of the issue. While this is the general rule, there are a number of exceptions in r 902(m). First, where a Eurobond issue is not completely allotted any sales by an underwriter or dealer of an unsold allotment or subscription are regarded as being made during the restricted period, even if made 40 days after the closing date of an issue. Further, where a non-convertible Eurobond issue is being issued in tranches, the restricted period is applied in relation to each tranche. If it were otherwise, the Eurobonds would be caught by the restrictions on sales to US persons until 40 days elapse from the issue of the last tranche of bonds.

Secondly, the transactional restrictions also require that each underwriter or dealer selling securities pursuant to contractual agreements during the 40-day restricted period must send a confirmation or other notice to the purchaser stating that the purchaser is subject to the same restrictions on offers and sales that apply to the underwriter or dealer.[11] This requirement is also quite similar to the interlocking chain of notices used previously in the Eurobond markets to prevent sales to US persons during a 90-day period from the closing date of a Eurobond issue. There is, however, an important difference between the practices prevailing in the Eurobond markets prior to Regulation S and the requirements of Regulation S. The confirmation or other notice need not create a binding agreement to abide by the restrictions as between the underwriter or dealer on the one side and the purchaser of the securities on the other. The SEC has stated that the notice could include a notice given on screen rather than on paper or a notice given on the telephone, provided that the seller has kept written records of notices given; the SEC has also stated that the screen notice may be given in summary form provided that all subscribers to the screen-based system are sent prior to first use and periodically thereafter a key that indicates what each summary notice represents and includes the full text of each notice.[12]

ii Offering restrictions

Offering restrictions[13] require, first, that all underwriters and dealers who are participating in the issue or distribution of the Eurobonds should be subject to contractual obligations that all offers and sales of securities will be made by them in accordance with the safe harbour provided by r 903. In effect this imposes on the underwriters and dealers an obligation to comply with all applicable requirements of Regulation S.

Secondly, various documents used in connection with the distribution of the Eurobonds prior to the expiration of the 40-day 'restricted period' must carry a legend to the effect that the securities have not been registered under SA 1933 s 5 and consequently, may not be offered or sold in the US or to a US person, excluding the underwriters and dealers, unless an exemption from s 5 is applicable. These legends are required on the prospectus, offering circular or any other document other than a press release used in connection with the issue.[14]

---

11 See r 903(c)(2)(iv).
12 See SEC Release 33–6863 at p 68.
13 See r 903(c)(2)(ii).
14 See r 902(h).

Finally, with regard to an issue of warrants to subscribe equity, the 40-day restricted period commences on the completion of the allotment of the warrants as determined and certified by the lead manager provided however that a number of conditions are satisfied. These are as follows:

'(1) each warrant bears a legend stating that the warrant and the securities to be issued upon its exercise have not been registered under the [SA 1933] and that the warrant may not be exercised by or on behalf of any US person unless registered under the [SA 1933] or an exemption from such registration is available;

(2) each person exercising a warrant is required to give:
  (i) written certification that it is not a US person and that the warrant is not being exercised on behalf of a US person; or
  (ii) a written opinion of counsel to the effect that the warrant and the securities delivered upon exercise thereof have been registered under the [SA 1933] or are exempt from registration thereunder; and

(3) procedures are implemented to ensure that the warrant may not be exercised within the United States and that the securities may not be delivered within the United States upon exercise other than in offerings deemed to meet the definition of "off-shore transaction" pursuant to paragraph (i)(3) of this section, unless registered under the [SA 1933] or an exemption from such registration is available.'[15]

The primary purpose of these restrictions is to prevent sales to 'US persons'[16] during the restricted period of 40 days from the close of the issue. The reason for this approach seems to be that since there is substantial interest in the Eurobonds of issuers in this category, the potential for flowback into the US of the securities issued in the offshore transaction is at its highest in the period of highest price volatility, namely during and in the immediate aftermath of the issue. Such flowback can be controlled by preventing sales during this 40-day period. The assumption is that secondary trading in such bonds after the 40-day period would not be as extensive as during the issue period and its immediate aftermath.

The definition of 'US person' in Regulation S is such as to enable certain US market professionals and sophisticated investors to participate in an issue of Eurobonds without prejudicing its off-shore transaction status under Regulation S.[17]

A *'US person'* is defined in r 902(o) to cover any natural person resident in the US and any corporation organised or incorporated under the laws of the US or any partnership organised under any laws of the US.

However, there is an extremely important exemption to the definition of a US person, namely that any agency or branch of a US bank or US insurance company located outside the US and operating in the foreign jurisdiction for a valid business reason is not regarded as a US person.[18] This enables Eurobonds to be placed with a very large and important group of investors.

Another important source of investment in Eurobonds comes from accounts managed by portfolio managers or fund managers. As far as such managed accounts are concerned, Regulation S draws a distinction between

---

15 See r 902(m).
16 As defined in Regulation S r 902(o).
17 See r 902(o) and below.
18 R 902(o)(6).

non-discretionary accounts and discretionary accounts held by a dealer or fund manager. Any non-discretionary account held by a dealer or other fiduciary fund manager for the benefit or account of a US person is deemed to be a US person; but any discretionary account or similar account which is held for the benefit or account of a non-US person by a dealer or other professional fiduciary which is organised or incorporated in the US is deemed not to be a US person.[19] This exception enables US fund managers to invest funds held by them for foreign clients in international bonds. Any other discretionary account or similar account held by a dealer or other fund manager who is a fiduciary which is incorporated in the US is, however, regarded as a US person.

A further exception is created to the definition of US person by excluding from the definition a large number of international bodies such as the International Monetary Fund, the International Bank for Reconstruction and Development, the Inter-American Development Bank, the Asian Development Bank, the African Development Bank, the United Agencies, affiliates and pension plans and 'any other similar international organisations'.[20]

It must, however, be noted that two types of entities are included in the definition of a US person even though they might otherwise be thought to be foreign entities. First, any agency or branch of a foreign entity located in the US is deemed to be a US person.[1] Secondly, any foreign partnership or corporation which is organised or incorporated under the laws of a foreign jurisdiction is regarded as a US person if it is formed by a US person principally for the purposes of investing in securities which are not registered under SA 1933, unless it is organised or incorporated and owned by 'accredited investors' as defined in r 501(A) under SA 1933.[2]

There is a key difference in the above definition of a US person in Regulation S as compared with the approach under Release 4708.[3] The exemption from the extraterritorial application of US securities laws granted in Release 4708 by the SEC was dependent on offers or sales of unregistered securities not being made to US residents or US nationals resident abroad. Offers and sales to US nationals resident abroad, however, do not constitute an offer or sale to a 'US person' under Regulation S. Nevertheless, where offers and sales of unregistered securities are 'specifically targeted at identifiable groups of US citizens abroad, such as members of the US armed forces serving overseas', the offer or sale will cease to be within the requirements of the 'off-shore transaction' under Regulation S.[4]

6 All other issuers (category (c))

Issuers not falling within category (a) and (b) above are required to comply with additional requirements laid down in r 903(c)(3). These are in addition to the primary requirements set forth in r 903(a) and (b) and the offering restrictions imposed on issuers in category (b) above. These additional

---

19 R 902(o)(2).
20 See r 902(o)(7).
1   See r 902(o)(1)(v).
2   See r 902(o)(1)(viii).
3   Release 33–4208, 9 July 1964.
4   See r 902(i)(2).

requirements are essentially the imposition of a 'lock-up' similar to that developed under Release 4708 except that the period of the 'lock-up' is 40 days rather than 90.

The transactional restrictions imposed on issuers in this category are as follows:

First, the offer or sale of the securities, if made prior to the expiry of a 40-day restricted period, cannot be made to a US person or for the account or benefit of a 'US person' other than an underwriter or dealer participating in the distribution of the securities and qualifying as a 'distributor' as defined in Regulation S.

Secondly, the debt securities must be represented on issue by a temporary global bond which is not exchangeable for definitives until the expiration of the 40-day restricted period and until certification of beneficial ownership of the securities by a non 'US person'. The certification of beneficial ownership by non US persons does not, however, apply to holdings by underwriters and dealers.

Thirdly, each underwriter and dealer participating in the distribution and sale of securities to another underwriter or dealer or a person receiving a selling commission, fee or other remuneration prior to the expiry of the 40-day restricted period is required to send a confirmation or other notice to the purchaser stating that the purchaser is subject to the same restrictions on offers and sales that apply to an underwriter or dealer participating in the distribution of the Eurobonds. Once again, it is not necessary that a confirmation or other notice sent to a purchaser constitutes a binding legal agreement.[5] In the case of equity securities, however, an underwriter or dealer selling to a purchaser who is not participating in the distribution is required to obtain the contractual agreement of such a purchaser that he would only resell such equity securities in accordance with the provisions of Regulation S.[6]

7 Effect of non-compliance with issuer safe harbour requirements

If the issuer, the underwriters and dealers participating in the distribution of Eurobonds do not comply with the requirements with regard to 'directed selling efforts' in the US and with the 'offering restrictions' as defined in Regulation S, it would seem that the safe harbour provided in r 903 is unavailable in respect of the entire offering of Eurobonds. It seems also that the non-compliance with any of the other requirements imposed by Regulation S would also have the same effect. This is, however, not the view of the SEC itself as expressed in Release 33–6863 which promulgated Regulation S. The SEC's view is that if the issuer or an underwriter or dealer (or any of their affiliates) participating in the distribution fails to comply with any other requirements of the issuer safe harbour, only the sales or offers of the Eurobonds made by the person in breach of a condition of Regulation S (other than the offering restrictions and directed selling efforts as defined) loses the benefit of Regulation S. The issuer and any distributor or dealer who is not so in breach is said to be entitled to the

---

5 See r 903(c)(3)(iv).
6 See r 903(c)(3)(iii)(2).

benefit of Regulation S.[7] It is, however, difficult to reconcile this conclusion with the language of Regulation S.

8 The resale safe harbour

This provides a safe harbour to offers or sales of securities by any person other than the issuer or an underwriter or dealer who is participating in the distribution of the securities or any person acting on behalf of such person. Such sales are also provided an exemption from the requirement of registration under SA 1933 s 5 provided the following conditions are satisfied:

(a) The offer or sale must be made in an off-shore transaction as defined above.
(b) There should be no directed selling efforts as defined above in the US by the seller, an affiliate of the seller or any person acting on their behalf.
(c) Any resale by a dealer must satisfy two further conditions:
  (i) neither the seller nor any person acting on his behalf knows that the offeree or buyer of the securities is a US person as defined; and
  (ii) if the seller or any person acting on the seller's behalf knows that the purchaser is a 'dealer'[8] or is a person receiving a selling commission or other remuneration in respect of the securities sold, the purchaser must be sent a confirmation or other notice stating that the securities may be offered and sold during the restricted period only in accordance with the provisions of Regulation S or pursuant to registration of the securities under SA 1933 or pursuant to an available exemption from the registration requirements of SA 1933.

These restrictions, however, do not seem to affect the position of the issuer, the lead manager or the syndicate of investment banks underwriting the issue nor of any other dealer participating in the issuing of the securities. A breach of the resale restrictions therefore has no effect on the availability of the issuer safe harbour to such entities.

9 Regulation S and the applicability of the Trust Indenture Act 1939

Compliance with Regulation S also has the effect that provisions in the Trust Indenture Act 1939 which would otherwise apply to a securities issue do not apply to an issue falling within Regulation S. Section 306 of the Trust Indenture Act of 1939 requires that whenever an offer or sale of debt securities involves the use of the means or instruments of interstate commerce or the US mails and such offer or sale is of debt securities not registered under SA 1933, the securities must be issued under a trust indenture which conforms to the requirements of and has been qualified under the provisions

---

7 See SEC Release 33–6863 at pp 77–78.
8 As defined in SA 1933 s 2(12).

of the Trust Indenture Act 1939, unless an exemption is available.[9] The SEC has in the past issued 'no action' letters in respect of the application of provisions of the Trust Indenture Act of 1939 whenever securities were issued in reliance and in conformity with Release 4708 of 10 July 1964. The SEC has now stated in Release 33-6863 promulgating Regulation S that 'the Commission will not take any enforcement action under the Trust Indenture Act where an offer and sale of securities is made otherwise than under a qualified indenture, if the offer and sale are made in compliance with r 903 or 904' of Regulation S.[10]

II THE INTERACTION OF REGULATION S AND US TAX LAWS

1 TEFRA D Regulations

Regulation S permits the issue of securities, including Eurobonds, without compliance with the registration requirements of SA 1933 s 5, provided certain conditions specified in Regulation S are met.

However, additional requirements are laid down by rules framed by the US Treasury under the Tax Equity and Fiscal Responsibility Act of 1982 of the United States ('TEFRA'). TEFRA[11] imposed a number of sanctions on the issuers of debt obligations in bearer form. These sanctions, referred to generally as 'issuer sanctions', are as follows.

First, there is a denial of deduction for interest on 'registration-required' debt obligations which are not in registered form[12] unless it was excluded from the definition of 'registration required' under s 163(f)(2)(B) of the US Internal Revenue Code on the basis that:

'(i) there are arrangements reasonably designed to ensure that such obligation will be sold, (or resold in connection with the original issue) only to a person who is not a United States person; and
(ii) in the case of an obligation not in registered form—
 (I) interest on such obligation is payable only outside the United States and its possessions; and
 (II) on the face of such obligation there is a statement that any United States person who holds such obligation will be subject to limitations under the United States income tax laws.'[13]

Prior to Regulation S, the arrangements referred to in s 163(f)(2)(B)(i) were satisfied if the procedures laid down by the SEC in Release 4708 of 10 July 1964 were complied with by an issuer of Eurobonds.

The second sanction is that s 4701 of the US Internal Revenue Code

---

9 See s 306 of the Trust Indenture Act of 1939 (15 USC ss 77aaaabbbb).
10 No further discussion of this Act is included in this section for this reason.
11 See also Pergam 'Legal Dimensions of Eurobond Financing' in *Prospects for International Lending and Rescheduling* (Matthew Bender, New York, 1988) s 21.03.
12 See s 163(f) of the US Internal Revenue Code.
13 See s 163(f)(2)(B).

provides that a tax would be imposed on an issuer of a debt obligation which is not issued in registered form. The tax on the person who issues the obligation is

> 'an amount equal to the product of –
> (i) one per cent of the principal amount of such obligation, multiplied by;
> (ii) the number of calendar years (or portions thereof) during the period beginning on the date of issuance of such obligation and ending on the date of maturity.'

This excise tax does not apply to bearer debt obligations which are not in registered form which comply with the requirement of s 163(f)(2)(B) of the US Internal Revenue Code as described above.

In addition to these issuer sanctions a tax advantage conferred on the payment of any 'portfolio interest' to a non-resident individual from sources within the US by s 871(h) of the US Internal Revenue Code is not available in respect of bearer debt obligations which do not satisfy the requirements of s 163(f)(2)(B) of the US Internal Revenue Code. The advantage of the concession in s 871(h) is that payments could be made to a non-resident individual from sources within the US without a 'withhold' for tax which would otherwise be imposed under s 871(a) of the Internal Revenue Code. The absence of such a withholding tax is extremely important in market practice to the marketability of Eurobonds issued by a US issuer.[14]

The US Treasury Department, on May 4th 1990, issued regulations relating to the issuance of bearer debt obligations to specify the circumstances in which such bearer debt obligations would qualify under s 163(f)(2)(B). These regulations, referred to as 'TEFRA D Regulations', specify what constitutes 'arrangements reasonably designed to ensure that the obligation will be sold (or resold in connection with the original issue) only to a person who is not a United States person' within the meaning of s 163(f)(2)(B)(i) of the US Internal Revenue Code.[15] These requirements of TEFRA D for purposes of s 163(f)(2)(B) would generally be satisfied if the arrangements developed in the international bond markets under SEC Release 4708 are complied with.[16]

The TEFRA D Regulations do not, however, affect the need to satisfy the requirements of s 163(f)(2)(B)(ii) of the Internal Revenue Code, namely, that the interest should be payable on the bearer debt obligation only outside the US, or that the instrument should bear the legend (the 'TEFRA legend') required by s 163(f)(2)(B)(ii).[17]

The TEFRA D Regulations require issuers of bearer debt obligations to satisfy three conditions before they escape the issuer sanctions described

---

14 The term 'portfolio interest' is defined in s 871(h)(2) as referring to any interest including an original issue discount which would be subject to tax under s 871(A) as interest payable by a US issuer of a debt obligation.
15 See p 409 above.
16 TEFRA D Regulations are effective in respect of bearer Eurobonds issued after 7 September 1990 and repeal Treasury Regulations referred to as the TEFRA 'A' Regulations and the TEFRA 'B' Regulations which are to be found in Treasury Regulations ss 1.163–5(c)(2)(i)(A) and (B).
17 The TEFRA D Regulations are now to be found in Regulations under s 1.163–5(c)(2)(i)(D) of the US Internal Revenue Code.

above and before interest payments payable on bearer bonds escape the withholding tax imposed by s 871 of the US Internal Revenue Code.

In summary the three requirements relate to:

(a) Restrictions on offers and sales During a 40-day 'restricted period' the issuer and distributors may not offer or sell the bearer debt securities in the US or to US persons.

(b) Restrictions on delivery With respect to delivery of obligations sold during the restricted period, neither the issuer nor any distributor may deliver the obligation in definitive form within the US or its possessions.

(c) Certification Certification is required on the earlier of the date of the first payment of interest on the obligation, or the date of delivery by the issuer of the obligation in definitive form to the effect that beneficial ownership of the bearer debt security is with non-US persons.

i *Restrictions on offers and sales*

The requirement is that neither the issuer nor any 'distributor' may offer or sell the bearer debt obligation during 'a restricted period' to a person who is either within the US or to a 'US person' as defined in the US Internal Revenue Code (rather than Regulation S).

A key distinction between the formula used in Regulation S[18] and the TEFRA D Regulations is in the definition of a US person. Under the TEFRA D Regulations, any citizen of the US wherever resident, as well as any resident of the US is regarded as a US person, whereas under Regulation S only persons resident in the US come within the formula of 'US person'. In addition, any corporation, partnership or other entity created or organised in or under the laws of the US falls within the definition of a US person under s 7701(a)(30) of the Internal Revenue Code.

A distributor for this purpose is defined as:

(a) 'a person that offers or sells the obligation during the restricted period pursuant to a written agreement with the issuer';
(b) 'any person that offers or sells the obligation during the restricted period pursuant to a written contract' with a person described in (a) above; and
(c) any 'affiliate' of a distributor who acquires the debt obligation for the purpose of offering or selling that obligation during the restricted period provided the affiliate obtains the debt obligation from the issuer or a distributor.[19]

The distributor of a bearer debt obligation is deemed not to have offered or sold the bearer debt obligation during the restricted period within the US or to a US person if certain conditions are satisfied.

---

18 See p 405 above.
19 'Affiliate' is defined in s 150.4(a) of the US Internal Revenue Code but without regard to the exceptions contained in s 150.4(b) of that Code and substituting '50%' for '80%' in those sections. See s 1.163–5(c)(2)(i)(D)(4) of the US Internal Revenue Code.

These are first that the distributor covenants that it will not offer or sell the obligation during the restricted period to a person who is within the US or to a US person; and that, secondly, the distributor of the obligation has in connection with the offer and sale of the obligation during the restricted period, established procedures reasonably designed to ensure that its employees or agents who are directly engaged in the selling of the obligation are aware that the obligation cannot be offered or sold during the restricted period to a person who is within the US or is a US person.[20]

Certain offers or sales of bearer debt obligations will not be treated as made to a person within the US or to a US person. These are offers or sales to 'an exempt distributor'; certain international organisations;[1] a foreign central bank;[2] the foreign branch of a US financial institution including a foreign branch of a US bank, broker or dealer in securities and a foreign branch of an insurance company.[3] An exempt distributor is defined[4] as referring to a distributor which has entered into the covenant not to offer or sell the bearer debt obligation during the restricted period to a person who is within the US or to a US person.

An important exception to the requirement of no offers and sales to US persons is contained in TEFRA D Regulation 163(c)(2)(i)(D)(1)(iii)(C) which states that a sale of an obligation will not be treated as made to a person within the US or to a US person if the person to whom the sale is made is a US person who acquired the obligation through the foreign branch of a US financial institution and who holds the bearer debt obligation through such financial institutions when it provides the certificate required under TEFRA D Regulations discussed in (3) below.

ii *Restrictions on delivery*

The second requirement contained in TEFRA D Regulations is that in connection with the sale of the bearer debt obligation during the restricted period, neither the issuer nor a distributor may deliver the 'bearer debt obligation in definitive form' within the US.[5] A temporary global bond is excluded from the definition of a 'bearer debt obligation in definitive form' for these purposes.[6]

iii *Certification*

On the earlier of the date of the first actual payment of interest by the issuer of the bearer debt obligation or the date of delivery by the issuer

---

20 See s 1.163–5(c)(2)(i)(D)(1)(ii)(D) of TEFRA D Regulations.
1   As defined in s 770.1(a)(18) of the US Internal Revenue Code.
2   As defined in s 895 of the US Internal Revenue Code and regulations framed thereunder.
3   The term 'financial institution' is defined by US Treasury Regulation s 1.165–12(c)(1)(v) to mean a bank, broker or dealer in securities, an insurance company, an investment adviser, a mutual fund and a pension plan, amongst others; it also covers an entity of which more than 50% of the total combined voting power of all classes of voting stock is owned by such a bank etc.
4   In s 1.163–5(c)(2)(i)(D)(5) of US Federal Tax Regulations.
5   See s 1.163–5(c)(2)(i)(D)(2) of US Federal Tax Regulations.
6   See s 1.163–5(c)(2)(i)(D)(3)(i)(C).

of the bearer debt obligation in definitive form, a certificate must be provided to the issuer stating that on such date:

(a) the obligation is 'owned' by a person who is not a US person; or
(b) the obligation is 'owned' by a US person which is a foreign branch of a US financial institution purchasing for its own account or for resale; or
(c) the obligation is 'owned' by a US person who has acquired the obligation through the foreign branch of a US financial institution and who holds the obligation through an account held overseas by such financial institution on the date of the certificate; or
(d) the obligation is 'owned' by a financial institution for purposes of resale during the restricted period and such financial institution certifies in addition that it has not acquired the obligation for purposes of resale directly or indirectly to a US person or to a person within the US.

Two points need to be noted with regard to the certificate which must be provided to the issuer of the bearer debt obligations. First, if the certificate is issued stating that the obligation is owned by a person who is not a US person under (a) above or that the obligation is owned by a US person falling within (b) or (c) above, it must be shown that the bearer debt obligation is not owned by a financial institution for purposes of resale during the restricted period.

Secondly, the certificate which is to be provided to the issuer may be provided by a clearing organisation such as Euroclear or Cedel and it may also be provided electronically.[7] Electronic certification is permissible only if the person providing the electronic certificate maintains adequate records for the four-year period of retention and provided there is a written agreement entered into prior to the time of certification which provides that the electronic certificate has the effect of a signed certificate. The written membership rules of the clearing organisation have the same effect as a written agreement for these purposes. These rules would enable Euroclear or Cedel to provide the certificate required under the TEFRA D Regulations.[8]

2 Impact of TEFRA D on Regulation S[9]

It will be noticed that TEFRA D does not distinguish between categories of issuers and imposes its requirements on any issuer of a bearer debt security. Its requirement of certification of non-US beneficial ownership by a custodian would in practice result in a 40-day 'lock-up' for bearer Eurobonds issued by an entity potentially liable to TEFRA. This type of 'lock-up' would

---

7 See US Treasury Regulation s 1.163–5(c)(2)(i)(D)(3)(C).
8 There are exemptions which are intended to apply to DM and Swiss franc denominated Eurobond issues where the certification requirement is not applicable; see s 1.163(c)(2)(i)-(D)(3)(iii).
9 See Braverman and Pergam 'Redrafting Eurodocumentation after US Initiatives' IFLR, July 1990.

have been necessary under Regulation S only in respect of issuers falling into the third category (c) discussed above.[10]

The impact of Regulation S and TEFRA D seems to be as follows on issues of Eurobonds:

US corporations
(including corporations controlled by US persons as described in 902(f) of Regulation S)

Restriction applicable	Source
(a) Off-shore transaction	Regulation S
(b) No directed selling efforts	Regulation S
(c) Offering restrictions	Regulation S
(d) Notices of selling restrictions	Regulation S
(e) Certification of non-US ownership	TEFRA D (Regulation S as well, for issuers falling within category (c))
(f) 'Lock-up'/temporary global bond	Regulation S for issuers falling within category (c) above TEFRA D certification would require lock-up in practice
(g) 40-day restriction on offers to US persons	Regulation S; TEFRA D

Foreign issuers

Restrictions applicable	Source
(a) Offshore transaction	Regulation S
(b) No directed selling efforts	Regulation S
(c) Offering restrictions	Only if 'substantial market interest exists': Regulation S
(d) Notices of selling restrictions	Only if 'substantial US market interest': Regulation S
(e) Certification of non-US beneficial ownership	TEFRA D
(f) 'Lock-up'/temporary global bond	TEFRA D makes it necessary in practice
(g) 40-day restriction on offers to US persons	TEFRA D

The much more stringent requirements of the TEFRA D Regulations seem to have been considered necessary by the US Treasury Department due to the fact that tax policies underlying the various tax sanctions in respect of bearer debt securities, are different from the regulatory policies underlying Regulation S and s 5 of SA 1933. In particular, it seems to have

---

10 See p 406 above.

been assumed that bearer debt securities can be used for tax avoidance and the absence of certification might result in a tendency towards tax avoidance.

3 TEFRA C Regulations

As far as foreign issuers are concerned, it may be possible to issue bearer debt obligations within the safe harbour provided by US Treasury Regulation s 1.163.5(c)(2)(C) ('TEFRA C' Regulations) which provides a safe harbour where the bearer debt obligation (a) is issued only outside the US and its possessions, and (b) is issued by an issuer which does not 'significantly engage in interstate commerce with respect to the issuance of such obligation either directly or through its agent, an underwriter or a member of the selling group'. The TEFRA C Regulations provide that an issuer will not be considered to engage significantly in interstate commerce with respect to the issue of a bearer debt obligation if the only activities with respect to which the issuer uses the means or instrumentalities of interstate commerce are activities of 'a preparatory or auxiliary character that do not involve communication between a prospective purchaser or an issuer, his agent, an underwriter, or member of the selling group if either is inside the United States or its possessions'. TEFRA C also provides a non-exhaustive description of what constitutes activities of preparatory or auxiliary character as including the following:

(a) negotiations between the issuer and underwriters as to the terms and pricing of an issue;
(b) transfer of funds to an office of an issuer in the US or its possessions by a foreign branch or to a US shareholder by a foreign corporation;
(c) consultation by an issuer with accountants and lawyers or other financial advisers in the US or its possessions regarding the issue of the bearer debt obligation;
(d) document drafting and printing;
(e) provision of payment or delivery instructions to members of the selling group by an issuer's office or underwriters which are located in the US or its possessions.

On the other hand, certain activities are designated as not being preparatory or auxiliary in character:

(a) negotiation or communications between a prospective purchaser and an issuer, an underwriter or member of the selling group concerning the sale of the bearer debt obligation if either is within the US or its possessions;
(b) involvement of an issuer's office, its agent, an underwriter or a member of the selling group in the US or its possessions in the offer or sale of a particular bearer debt obligation either directly with the prospective purchaser or through the issuer in a foreign country;
(c) the delivery of the bearer debt obligation in the US or its possessions;
(d) advertising or otherwise promoting the bearer debt obligation in the US or its possessions.

A foreign issuer hoping to rely on this exemption which is in the TEFRA C Regulations needs to be extremely careful in order to fall within the four corners of this exemption. In practice it is likely that even foreign issuers may opt as a matter of caution to rely on the requirements of the US Treasury's TEFRA D Regulations rather than the TEFRA C Regulations. Consequently, despite the more liberal regime introduced by Regulation S for issuers of international bonds, the requirements of TEFRA D would need to be complied with if issuer sanctions are to be avoided. The resulting position for issuers on the international bond markets is extremely complex and unsatisfactory and there is a strong case for a uniform set of regulations acceptable both to the SEC and the US Treasury to clarify the position.[11]

III SEA 1934 R 15a-6

Despite the assumption of the SEC that s 15 (which seeks to regulate broker dealers) applies extraterritorially, it nevertheless recognised recently that the accelerating pace of internationalisation in securities markets required a different approach. The legal rules applicable to the activities of non-US broker dealers when they transact business overseas, in circumstances where they might use the US 'mails or any means or instrumentality of interstate commerce', were far from clear and there was a risk of a breach of the registration provisions of SEA 1934 s 15.[12]

The US Securities and Exchange Commission in July 1989 adopted r 15a-6 which seeks to provide exemptions from the broker dealer registration provisions of SEA 1934 s 15 for foreign broker dealers engaged in certain activities involving US investors and securities markets.[13] Rule 15(a)-6[14] provides exemptions to foreign broker dealers who use US mails or the means or instrumentality of interstate commerce in certain circumstances.[15]

The exemptions contained in r 15(a)-6 apply to any entity which is not resident within the US including any US incorporated entity which is engaged in business wholly outside the US as a broker or dealer.

Where a broker dealer has an office or branch in the US, such an entity would not qualify as a foreign broker dealer under r 15(a)-6.[16] This is the position even where the broker dealer is incorporated outside the US but has a branch or office within the US.

The exemptions provided to foreign broker dealers under r 15(a)-6 are generally speaking somewhat restricted in nature. There are basically four categories of activities which the foreign broker dealer may carry on without breaching the provisions of s 15 of SEA 1934.

These are:

---

11 See also on TEFRA D Regulations: James A Duncan and Lawrence Silverstein 'Tighter US Rules for International Debt Offerings' International Tax Review, July/August 1990, 8; and Braverman and Pergam 'New SEC and IRS Initiatives Mean Euromarket Opportunities' IFLR, June 1990, 17.
12 See Release 27017 of 11 July 1989 under SEA 1934.
13 See Release 27017 of 11 July 1989 under SEA 1934.
14 Which became effective on 15 August 1989.
15 See Release 27017.
16 See r 15(a)-6(b)(3).

(a) unsolicited transactions;
(b) the provision of research reports to 'major US institutional investors' and effecting transactions in securities for such 'major US institutional investors';
(c) inducing or attempting to induce the purchase or sale of any security by 'a major US institutional investor' or by a 'US institutional investor' but effecting the resulting transaction through a registered broker dealer;
(d) inducing or effecting transactions in securities for persons outside the US or with or for registered brokers and dealers and other specified persons.

Many of these categories are also restricted by a large number of conditions which must be satisfied before the foreign broker dealer's activities can fall within one of these categories.

1 Unsolicited transactions

Rule 15(a)-6(a)(1) provides that where a foreign broker or dealer effects transactions in securities with or for persons which had not been 'solicited' by the foreign broker or dealer, such transactions do not trigger the registration provisions of SEA 1934. There is no definition of soliciting or solicitation in r 15(a)-6. The SEC has stated[17] that the question of solicitation will be addressed by them on a case-by-case basis, consistent with certain principles discussed in Release 27017.[18]

According to the statement of principles in Release 27017 the dissemination in the US of a broker dealer's quotations for a security would constitute solicitation if the dissemination is effected by that broker dealer. However, the distribution in the US of foreign broker dealers' quotations by systems operated by foreign market-places, such as stock exchanges, or by private vendors which distribute such quotations primarily in foreign countries, would not constitute solicitation on the part of the broker dealer whose quotations appear in the third party systems.

The SEC has nevertheless pointed out in Release 27017 that the dissemination through third party systems would not constitute solicitation, only where the third party system did not allow securities transactions to be executed between the foreign broker dealer and persons in the US through such systems. The SEC has also indicated that the direct dissemination of foreign market makers' quotations to US investors through a private quote system controlled by the foreign broker dealer would constitute solicitation.

2 Furnishing of research reports

Furnishing of research reports to 'major US institutional investors' and effecting transactions in the securities discussed in the research reports with

---

17 In Exchange Act Release 27017.
18 Of 11 July 1989, issued under SEA 1934.

or for those major US institutional investors is permissible under r 15(a)-6(a)(2) subject to certain conditions.

The provision of research to such institutions would, according to the SEC[19] constitute solicitation and would fall outside the unsolicited transactions exception discussed in (1) above. It is for this reason that a special exception is created in respect of the distribution of such research.

For the purposes of this exception, a 'major US institutional investor' is defined as a person which has or has under management, total assets in excess of $100,000,000 and investment advisers registered with the SEC under s 203 of the Investment Advisors Act of 1940 which has total assets under management in excess of $100,000,000.

Even where the foreign broker dealer is dealing with such a major US institutional investor, a number of conditions must be satisfied by the foreign broker dealer:

(a) the research reports should not recommend the use of the foreign broker or dealer to effect trades in any security;
(b) the foreign broker or dealer should not initiate contact with those major US institutional investors to follow up on the research reports and should not otherwise induce or attempt to induce the purchase or sale of any security by those major US institutional investors;
(c) if the foreign broker or dealer has a relationship with the registered broker or dealer, transactions with the foreign broker or dealer in securities discussed in the research reports must only be effected through that registered broker or dealer; and
(d) the foreign broker or dealer must not provide research to US persons pursuant to any expressed or implied understanding that those US persons will directly commission income to the foreign broker or dealer.

It would seem from the above that even with regard to dealings with major US institutional investors, the foreign broker dealer can do no more than send research reports, and that too, without making any recommendation as to the use of the foreign broker dealer; and then he must wait for the major US institutional investor to contact him before executing any transaction for such a major US institutional investor.[20]

Where research is to be made available to major institutional investors it appears that the requirements of Release 34–25801 under SEA 1934 need to be followed: namely, that the research reports must be distributed to US institutional investors only through a registered broker dealer and that broker dealer must prominently state on the research report that it accepts responsibility for its content and that any US persons receiving the research and wishing to effect any transactions in any security discussed in the report should do so with the registered broker dealer and not with the foreign broker dealer.

---

19 See Release 27017.
20 It appears from the text of Release 27017 that many commentators thought that the restrictions were unnecessary when a foreign broker dealer was dealing with a major US institutional investor with the sophistication and resources to manage investments of $100,000,000 or more, but the SEC took a different view.

3 Inducing or attempting to induce transactions with major US institutional investors or US institutional investors including banks, savings and loan associations and insurance companies[1]

This category of activity is severely restricted by a number of conditions. The primary condition which must be satisfied by any foreign broker dealer inducing or attempting to induce the purchase or sale of a security by any US institutional investor is that any resulting transaction with or for the US institutional investor or major US institutional investor must be effected through a registered broker or dealer. The registered broker dealer is then required by r 15(a)-6(a)(3)(iii) to comply with all regulatory requirements applicable to registered broker dealers in respect of that transaction. In addition, the foreign broker dealer must provide the SEC on request or pursuant to an agreement with foreign securities authorities with any information or document or other evidence within the control of the foreign broker or dealer. Thirdly, any employee of the foreign broker dealer who effects transactions with the US institutional investor or the major US institutional investor must conduct all securities activities from outside the US, though he may visit the investors in the US accompanied by an employee of a registered broker or dealer which accepts responsibility for the foreign associated person's communications with US investors. If transactions are to be effected in consequence of such communications or visits, they must once again be effected through the registered broker or dealer.[2]

4 Effecting transactions in securities with certain other specified persons

A foreign broker dealer is permitted under r 15(a)-6(a)(4) to induce or attempt to induce the purchase or sale of any security by the following persons:

(a) a registered broker or dealer whether the registered broker or dealer is acting as principal for its own account or as agent for others;
(b) a bank acting in the capacity of a broker or dealer as permitted by US law;
(c) the African Development Bank, the Asian Development Bank, the Inter-American Development Bank, the International Bank for Reconstruction and Development, the International Monetary Fund, the United Nations and their Agencies, Affiliates and Pension Funds;
(d) a foreign person temporarily present in the US but with whom the foreign broker dealer has a bona fide 'pre-existing relationship' before the foreign person entered the US;
(e) any agency or branch of a US person permanently located outside the US; in this case, however, the transaction must be effected outside the US;
(f) US citizens resident outside the US, provided that the securities transaction is effected outside the US; where, however, a foreign broker or dealer targets its selling efforts towards an 'identifiable group' of US

---

1 See for the definition of 'US institutional investor' r 15(a)-6(b)(7).
2 See for other requirements r 15(a)-6(a)(3)(i)(ii)(iii).

citizens resident abroad, such as personnel of the US Armed Forces, the exemption will not apply.

5 Interaction of r 15a-6 with Regulation S

While the categories of exempt activity are limited, r 15(a)-6 permits Eurobond houses operating in London to contact US investment companies and US banks within the US as well as agencies or branches of US persons which are located outside the US subject to the conditions discussed above without occasioning a breach of SEA 1934 s 15.

However, it is extremely important to appreciate that activity which is permissible under r 15(a)-6 in respect of persons within the US may nevertheless take the Eurobond issue outside the safe harbour of Regulation S[3] and thus trigger the registration provisions of SA 1933 s 5. Consequently, the provisions of r 15(a)-6 need to be used in conjunction with the requirements of Regulation S in the context of an issue of Eurobonds. Rule 15(a)-6 would then provide a safe harbour to foreign broker dealers, particularly those with US affiliated companies (as distinct from branches), who may need to use the US mails or the means or instrumentalities of interstate commerce during the course of a Eurobond issue which is effected under the provisions of Regulation S.

6 Exemptions for 'comparably regulated' foreign broker dealers

Release 34-27018, which was issued by the SEC simultaneously with r 15(a)-6, contains a proposal to permit foreign broker dealers who are subject to regulation in a foreign country which is comparable with the regulation of US broker dealers to carry on limited business with 'major US institutions' (as defined) from a location outside the US. The proposal, however, limits the proposed exemption to foreign broker dealers whose business is predominantly foreign and who do not have affiliates which are registered broker dealers within the US. The proposal is also premised on the existence of 'memoranda of understanding' or comparable treaties between the SEC and the regulatory authorities of the foreign state.

IV SUMMARY: US SECURITIES LAWS AND TEFRA

The position with regard to US securities legislation may be summarised as follows:
1. US securities laws are capable of being and are applied extraterritorially on the basis of 'conduct' or 'effects' in the US.
2. The registration provisions in SA 1933 s 5 may be applicable on the basis of 'conduct' or 'effects' in the US but, if the requirements laid down in Regulation S are complied with, there should be no need to comply with

---

3 See above pp 395–397.

SA 1933 s 5; s 5 would otherwise require the registration of a prospectus complying with SA 1933, whenever the US mails or the means or instrumentalities of interstate commerce are used to sell or offer to sell Eurobonds.

3. Brokers and dealers (including investment/merchant banks and bond dealers) who are not registered with the SEC and who participate in a distribution of Eurobonds in London which involves the use of US 'mails or instrumentalities of interstate commerce', would not be in breach of the requirements as to registration in s 15 of SEA 1934, if the brokers and dealers offer and sell the securities in accordance with r 15(a)-6.[4] Care must be taken to comply with the requirements of Regulation S in addition to r 15(a)-6.

4. The anti-fraud provisions of SA 1933 s 12(2) as well as the anti-fraud provisions of r 10b-5 of SA will apply to the dissemination of false or misleading information in a Eurobond offering circular or any other information. However once again it would have to be shown either that there was sufficient 'conduct' in the US, for instance because the prospectus was prepared in the US,[5] or that there were 'effects' in the US.

5. With regard to stabilisation rules and the prohibitions contained in r 10b-6, since stabilisation occurs in the London market it is unlikely that US securities laws will be activated on the basis of non-compliance with r 10b-7 unless there is 'conduct' within the US.[6]

6. In consequence of the US Treasury's TEFRA D Regulations compliance with the requirements in Regulation S are insufficient if tax sanctions on an issuer are to be avoided. Most issuers would need to comply with certification and 'lock-up' provisions required by TEFRA D Regulations, even though similar procedures are unnecessary under Regulation S.

7. A number of representations and warranties are probably necessary as a minimum in the issue documents, to comply with the combined effect of Regulation S and the TEFRA D Regulations.

(a) The invitation telex would need to contain selling restrictions which would enable compliance with Regulation S and TEFRA D Regulations.

(b) The offering circular would need to contain restrictions with regard to subscription and sale of the Eurobonds which enable compliance with the requirements of Regulation S and TEFRA D Regulations.

(c) The subscription agreement, the agreement between managers and the selling agreement (if used) should impose obligations restricting offers or sales except in compliance with Regulation S and TEFRA D Regulations.

Those agreements in (c) above should also contain a representation and warranty that neither the members of the underwriting syndicate nor the issuer have engaged in any directed selling efforts with regard to the Eurobonds.

---

[4] See p 416 above.
[5] As in *Cornfeld*, see ch 20 above.
[6] The possibility of breaches of r 10b-6 and 10b-7 were envisaged in the two British Petroleum offerings of shares in 1977 and 1979 and the SEC issued no action letters in both cases: see Howard T Sprow (ed) *Financing in the International Capital Markets* ch 17.

There would also need to be clauses requiring the sending of notices under r 903 of Regulation S to dealers purchasing during the restricted period.

Clauses which ensure compliance with the requirements of the TEFRA D Regulations would also be necessary; in particular, that during the restricted period there will be no offers or sales to US persons or within the US and that there will be procedures reasonably designed to ensure that the employees and agents of the underwriters or other brokers and dealers who are engaged in the distribution do not offer or sell securities within the US or to US persons.

There would also need to be a clause which requires an issuer to covenant that there is no substantial US market interest for his debt securities as defined in Regulation S, where the issuer is relying on that condition in r 903 of Regulation S.

In practice these types of clauses would need to be drafted or confirmed by, and the procedures confirmed as being in compliance with Regulation S and TEFRA D, by US law firms.

V R 144A, PORTAL AND PRIVATE PLACEMENTS

No discussion of US securities laws which have an impact on the international bond markets would be complete without a discussion of r 144A framed under SA 1933.[7]

Rule 144A deals with the ability of a person, other than an issuer, to resell securities which are not registered in accordance with the provisions of SA 1933 s 5 in the US. Consequently, it may seem at first glance that this rule has little to do with international bond issues. Nevertheless, r 144A has implications for the manner in which international bonds are issued. The background to r 144A is as follows.

While public offerings of bonds in the international markets may be made without encountering the risk of a breach of US securities laws[8] by complying with the conditions of Regulation S, there are also two other avenues which may be available to an issuer of international bonds to avoid a breach of SA 1933 s 5.

One such avenue is to be found in SA 1933 s 4(2), which provides that the provisions of s 5 shall not apply to 'transactions by an issuer not involving any public offering'. This avenue has been utilised to place securities including bonds in what are termed 'private placements' with a few large institutional investors in the US. However, this route was severely inhibited by the requirements of r 144 of the SEC.[9] Rule 144 required that any person who sells securities which have been acquired from an issuer in a transaction not involving a public offering ('restricted securities': by r 144(a)(3)) could

---

7 R 144A was adopted by the SEC in Release 33–6862 and 34–27928 on 19 April 1990, at the same time as the adoption of Regulation S which was discussed previously. Rule 144A became effective on 30 April 1990. (R 144A was originally proposed in October 1988 by Release 33–6806 and reproposed in July 1989 in Release 33–6839. The rule was adopted in substantially the form of the reproposal.)
8 Though not tax laws: see pp 409 et seq above.
9 Made under SA 1933.

not onsell the securities to any third party until a minimum of two years had lapsed between the date of the acquisition of the securities from the issuer. In addition, a number of other conditions had to be fulfilled. Thus the issuer in question should have been filing reports under s 13 or s 15(d) of SEA 1934 or ensured that information concerning the issuer specified in r 15(c)(2)-11 of SEA 1934 is publicly available.[10] There are also limitations on the number of securities which can be sold under r 144.[11]

R 144A permits resales of securities by dealers and others who purchase securities from an issuer to resell those securities to certain 'qualified institutional buyers' within the US without breaching SA 1933 s 5 due to the fact that the securities are unregistered. It will be remembered that SA 1933 s 5 applies both to initial offers of securities in the primary markets as well as resales in the secondary markets. Rule 144A, however, does not actually permit an issuer to make a public or private offering of securities within the US or to US persons. However, if an issuer is able to rely on some other exemption to the prohibition in s 5 in respect of the issue of unregistered securities in the US or to US persons, the resale of those securities will be permissible under r 144A and the conditions laid down therein. Thus, if an issuer can rely on the private placement exemption in SA 1933 s 4(2), dealers purchasing such securities in a private placement may resell those securities before the end of the two-year period laid down in r 144(d) by utilising the safe harbour provided by r 144A.

The resale of the securities which are privately placed by an issuer is confined to 'qualified institutional buyers' who are essentially large US institutions who would have the necessary sophistication and resources to enable them to 'fend for themselves' and who do not require the full protection of the entire range of US securities laws. A 'qualified institutional buyer' is an entity which, acting for its own account or the accounts of other qualified institutional buyers, in the aggregate owns and invests on a discretionary basis, at least $100m in securities of issuers which are not affiliated with that institution. This test is not applied to securities dealers, who qualify as a 'qualified institutional buyer' if they have assets of $10m or more.

Qualified institutional buyers include the following:

(a) insurance companies[12] which own and invest $100m;
(b) any investment company[13] or any investment adviser[14] which owns and invests $100m;
(c) any securities dealer registered under SEA 1934 s 15 acting either for its own account or the accounts of other qualified institutional buyers, who in the aggregate owns and invests on a discretionary basis at least $100m of securities of issuers which are not affiliated with that dealer;[15] or any dealer registered under SEA 1934 s 15 acting on behalf

---

10 See r 144(c)(1) and (2).
11 See r 144(e).
12 As defined in SA 1933 s 2(13).
13 Registered under the Investment Company Act 1940.
14 Registered under the Investment Advisors Act 1940.
15 There is an exception that securities constituting the whole or a part of an unsold allotment or subscription by a dealer as a participant in a public offering is not taken into account in determining the value of securities owned by that dealer.

of a qualified institutional buyer regardless of such dealer's ownership of assets;
(d) any bank as defined in SA 1933 s 3(a)(2), any savings and loan association or other institution referred to in SA 1933 s 3(a)(5)(A), or any foreign bank or savings and loan association or equivalent institution acting for its own account or the accounts of other qualified institutional buyers, provided such bank or savings and loan association in aggregate owns and invests on a discretionary basis at least $100m of securities of issuers which are not affiliated with it and which has an audited net worth of at least $25m as demonstrated in its latest annual financial statements.[16]

There is an important limitation to the securities which may be resold under r 144A: they cannot be 'fungible' securities; that is to say, they cannot be of the same class of securities as those listed on a national securities exchange in the US or quoted in a US 'automated interdealer quotation system' including NASDAQ.[17] The question as to whether or not the security for which the benefit of r 144A is required is of the same class as securities listed or quoted in the US is to be determined at the time of the issue of the securities for which the benefit of r 144A is claimed. In other words, a subsequent listing on a US securities exchange or quotation on an interdealer quotation system such as NASDAQ does not deprive the securities sold on the basis of r 144A of the protection from the registration requirements of SA 1933 s 5. However, in order to prevent issuers of stock who have their stock listed or quoted in the US from circumventing the above requirement by the issue of convertible securities or American depository receipts (which are convertible or exchangeable into listed stock or quoted stock but which would not ordinarily be regarded as being of the same class), r 144A provides that American depository receipts and convertibles will be regarded as of the same class as those securities into which they are convertible or exchangeable; in other words, American depository receipts and convertible securities are regarded as fungible with the underlying securities to which they relate for the purposes of determining whether the r 144A safe harbour applies to the issue of the American depository receipt or the convertible.[18]

In addition, r 144A requires that the issuer of the securities to be resold under r 144A should either be an issuer which provides information under s 13 or s 15(d) of SEA 1934 or a foreign issuer which provides information pursuant to r 12(g)(3)-2(b) of SEA 1934 to the SEC. Alternatively, an issuer is required to furnish to the SEC certain information specified under r 144A. This information is 'a very brief statement of the nature of the business of the issuer and the product and services it offers; and the issuer's most recent balance sheet and profit and loss and retained earnings statements, and similar financial statements for such part of the two preceding fiscal years as the issuer has been in operation (the financial statement should

---

16 See r 144A(a)(1). See r 144A(a)(2), (3) and (4) for rules governing how the aggregate amount of securities owned and invested by such persons is to be calculated.
17 The National Association of Securities Dealers Automated Quotations System. See r 144A(d)(3)(i).
18 See r 144A(d)(3)(i).

be audited to the extent reasonably available)'.[19] It is thought that issuers hoping to place securities through the avenue opened by r 144A and who are required to provide information to the SEC in the form of the 'very brief statement' may nevertheless be subject to a requirement to update such information in order to avoid any liability under the anti-fraud provisions of SA 1933. It is also thought that this would be a disincentive to foreign issuers who do not submit information under r 12(g)(3)-2(b) from using the avenue opened by r 144A to place securities, including international bonds, in the US.

1 Interaction of Regulation S, TEFRA D and r 144A

Rule 144A would permit resales of unregistered securities which have not been the subject of a public offering as noted above; it will also be possible to resell securities which have been publicly offered without registration in an overseas offering under Regulation S. Consequently, securities sold under Regulation S could be resold in the US under r 144A without a breach of SA 1933 s 5. However, while a foreign dealer may use this route for purposes of reselling the securities to qualified institutional buyers under r 144A, it seems to be the case that a US dealer participating in an international bond issue in London may not always be able to do so due to the provisions of SA 1933 s 4(3)(a), which provide that s 5 shall not apply to transactions by a dealer, including an underwriter, provided that the transaction takes place after the expiry of 40 days after the first date upon which the security was offered to the public by the issuer or by an underwriter on his behalf. Consequently, a placement by a US dealer relying on r 144A would only be possible after the 40-day restricted period in Regulation S and the period in SA 1933 s 4(3)(a) had ended.

The ability of r 144A to encourage both US and non-US issuers to raise capital in the US domestic capital markets rather than the international bond markets is also seriously restricted due to the requirements of TEFRA D. An issuer wishing to offer bearer debt obligations in the US or to US persons, as defined in the Internal Revenue Code, will need to comply with the certification and other requirements if the issuer is to avoid the issuer sanctions under the US Internal Revenue Code. In effect this makes the r 144A route unattractive to issuers of bearer debt obligations in the form of Eurobonds.

2 The PORTAL system and r 144A

In order to facilitate the trading in securities placed with qualified institutional buyers under r 144A, the National Association of Securities Dealers of the US ('NASD') have also set up an automated market system entitled 'Private Offerings, Resales and Trading through Automated Linkages' popularly referred to by its acronym, PORTAL. The SEC in its Release 34–27956 of 1 May 1990 approved the rules of NASD which implement the PORTAL trading system. The PORTAL system provides for a market which will use

---

19   See r 144A(d)(4)(i).

computerised communications systems to effect the dissemination of price quotations as well as clearance and settlements of securities traded through PORTAL. The PORTAL system has its own PORTAL brokers and POR-TAL dealers who will provide price quotations on securities traded in POR-TAL. Transactions through the PORTAL system may be effected only as between 'PORTAL qualified investors', 'PORTAL brokers', and 'PORTAL dealers'. All transactions, however, must be effected through a PORTAL broker or dealer and no investor may deal directly with another PORTAL qualified investor. To be entitled to participate in the PORTAL system as a PORTAL qualified investor, the institution must be a qualified institutional buyer under r 144A and continue to meet the definition of a qualified institutional buyer so long as it remains a member of PORTAL. An international security within the PORTAL system must be deposited with Cedel SA of Luxembourg before it can qualify as a PORTAL security.[20]

While resales by qualified institutional buyers to other qualified institutional buyers or to dealers is thus made possible through the PORTAL system, the resales must nevertheless qualify within the safe harbour provisions of r 144A if SA 1933 s 5 is not to be breached. In other words, each seller of a r 144A security within the PORTAL system must ensure or have reasonable grounds to believe that the purchaser is a qualified institutional buyer. While the rules of the PORTAL system seek to ensure that each participant within the PORTAL system is a qualified institutional buyer within r 144A, it seems that the obligation to ensure that a reasonable belief that the purchaser is a qualified institutional buyer is necessary if a breach of SA 1933 s 5 is to be avoided.

The PORTAL system, together with the legal framework of r 144A, provides issuers with access to the vast private placement market in the US capital markets. The PORTAL system provides liquidity to this market by providing a trading system and a quotation system for privately placed securities under r 144A. The development of this market is seriously affected in respect of bearer debt securities due to the requirements of US tax regulations under TEFRA D, discussed above. Its value at present is as an alternative to the international equity markets rather than the international bond markets.

---

20 In the case of domestic US securities, the securities must be deposited with the Depository Trust Company ('DTC').

CHAPTER 22
Participation by US commercial banks in the international capital markets: the Glass-Steagall Act[1]

I THE GLASS-STEAGALL ACT

Four key provisions of the United States Banking Act 1933, which are referred to as the Glass-Steagall Act,[2] separate traditional commercial banking activity from investment banking activity or securities business. The Banking Act 1933 was part of the broad-ranging reform of the US domestic financial markets and institutions which also included the enactment of the Securities Act 1933 and the Securities Exchange Act 1934 in the aftermath of the Great Depression of the 1930s.[3]

i *Section 16*

Section 16[4] prohibits a US bank[5] from underwriting any issue of securities or stock and from dealing in securities for its own account. Section 16, however, does permit a bank to be involved in 'purchasing and selling such securities and stock without recourse solely upon the order and for the account of customers', as well as certain own account dealings permitted by the Comptroller of the Currency by regulations framed under s 16.

ii *Section 20*

Section 20[6] prohibits a US bank from being 'affiliated in any manner' described in 12 USC 221 a-(b) 'with any corporation, association, business

---

1 See also Mortimer and Slade 'Foreign Securities Activities of US Banks' IFLR, June 1987, 15.
2 48 Stat 162.
3 The latter statutes are discussed in detail in chapters 19 and 21.
4 12 USC 24.
5 Although s 16 by its terms is applicable only to 'national banks', para 20 of s 9 of the Federal Reserve Act (12 USC 35) makes s 16 applicable to member banks of the Federal Reserve System.
6 12 USC 377.

trust or other similar organisation *engaged principally* in the issue, floatation, underwriting or public sale or distribution at wholesale or retail or through syndicate participation of stocks, bonds, debentures, notes or other securities'. Affiliation is defined in 12 USC 221 a-(b) to include shareholder control, stock control or common board members.

The objective of this provision is to prevent a bank which is prohibited by s 16 from engaging in securities business from doing so through a specially incorporated investment banking subsidiary or affiliate.

iii *Section 21*

Section 21[7] prohibits any person or organisation from engaging both in securities business and from engaging in 'the business of receiving deposits'. This provision does not contain the requirement that the entity be principally engaged in securities business before the prohibition is triggered.

iv *Section 32*

Section 32[8] prohibits interlocking directorates or management between corporations[9] *'primarily engaged'* in the issue, flotation, underwriting, public sale or distribution, at wholesale or retail, or through syndicate participation of stocks, bonds or similar securities (ie securities firms) and member banks of the Federal Reserve System.

A parallel provision is found in s 4 of the Bank Holding Company Act 1956[10] which prohibits a bank holding company from owning controlling shares of a company that is not a bank[11] or a company in the business of banking. However, s 4(c)(8)[12] contains an important exception to this rule, permitting the Board of the US Federal Reserve Bank to permit the control of shares in a company 'the activities of which the Board ... has determined to be so closely related to banking or managing or controlling banks as to be a proper incident thereto ...'.[13]

---

7 12 USC 378.
8 12 USC 78.
9 As well as unincorporated association, and partnerships.
10 12 USC 1843.
11 S 2(c) defines a 'bank' as any institution 'which (1) accepts deposits that the depositor has a legal right to withdraw on demand and (2) engages in the business of making commercial loans'. See 12 USC s 1841(c).
12 12 USC 1843(c)(8).
13 As to the test to be applied to the question whether activities are 'so closely related to banking', see *National Courier Association v Board of Governors of the Federal Reserve System* 516 F2d 1229 (DC Cir 1975). See also Regulation Y 12 CFR 225 promulgated under s 4(c)(8) by the Federal Reserve Board as to what constitutes permissible non-banking activity.

II THE RATIONALE FOR THE GLASS-STEAGALL PROVISIONS

The reason for the legislative separation of investment banking from commercial banking was the view of Congress after the Great Depression of the 1930s 'that much of the financial difficulty experienced by banks could be traced to their involvement in investment banking activities both directly and through security affiliates'.[14] Justice Blackmun, in *Securities Industry Association v Board of Governors of the Federal Reserve System*[15] explained the policy and objectives of the provisions of the Glass-Steagall Act as follows:

> 'Congressional worries about commercial-bank involvement in investment-bank activities reflected two general concerns. The first was the inherent risks of the securities business. Speculation in securities by banks and their affiliates during the speculative fever of the 1920s produced tremendous bank losses when the securities markets went sour. In addition to the palpable effect that such losses had on the assets of affected banks, they also eroded the confidence of depositors in the safety of banks as depository institutions. This crisis of confidence contributed to the runs on the banks that proved so devastating to the solvency of many commercial banks.
>
> But the dangers that Congress sought to eliminate through the Act were considerably more than the obvious risk that a bank could lose money by imprudent investment of its funds in speculative securities. The legislative history of the Act shows that Congress also focused on "the more subtle hazards that arise when a commercial bank goes beyond the business of acting as fiduciary or managing agent and enters the investment banking business." *Camp*, 401 US, at 630, 28 L Ed 2d 367, 91 S Ct 1091. The Glass-Steagall Act reflects the 1933 Congress' conclusion that certain investment-banking activities conflicted in fundamental ways with the institutional role of commercial banks.
>
> The Act's legislative history is replete with references to the various conflicts of interest that Congress feared to be present when a single institution is involved in both investment and commercial banking. Congress observed that commercial bankers serve as an important source of financial advice for their clients. They routinely advise clients on a variety of financial matters such as whether and how best to issue equity or debt securities. Congress concluded that it was unrealistic to expect a banker to give impartial advice about such matters if he stands to realise a profit from the underwriting or distribution of securities. See, eg 75 Cong Rec 9912 (1932) (remarks of Sen Bulkley). Some legislators noted that this conflict is exacerbated by the considerable fixed cost that a securities dealer must incur to build and maintain a securities-distribution system. Explaining this concern, Senator Bulkley, a major sponsor of the Act, described the pressures that commercial banks had experienced through their involvement in the distribution of securities:
>
>> "In order to be efficient a securities department had to be developed; it had to have salesmen; and it had to have correspondent connections with smaller banks throughout the territory tributary to the great bank. Organisations were developed with enthusiasm and with efficiency ... But the sales departments were subject to fixed expenses which could not be reduced without the danger of so disrupting the organisation as to put the institution

---

14 Per Blackmun J in *Securities Industry Association v Board of Governors of the Federal Reserve System* 468 US 137 at 144.
15 468 US 137, 104 S Ct 2979.

at a disadvantage in competition with rival institutions. These expenses would turn the operation very quickly from a profit to a loss if there were not sufficient organisations and underwritings to keep the sales departments busy". Id, at 9911.

Congress also expressed concern that the involvement of a commercial bank in particular securities could compromise the objectivity of the bank's lending operations. Congress feared that the pressure to dispose of an issue of securities successfully might lead a bank to use its credit facilities to shore up a company whose securities the bank sought to distribute. See 1931 Hearings, pt 7, p 1064. Some in Congress feared that a bank might even make unsound loans to companies in whose securities the bank has a stake or to a purchaser of securities that the bank seeks to distribute. Ibid. Alternatively, a bank with loans outstanding to a company might encourage the company to issue securities through the bank's distribution system in order to obtain the funds needed to repay bank loans. 75 Cong Rec 9912 (1932) (remarks of Sen Bulkley). Congress also faced some evidence that banks had misused their trust departments to unload excessive holdings of undesirable securities. Camp, 401 US, at 633, 28 L Ed 2d 367, 91 S Ct 1091; 1931 Hearings, pt 1, p 237.'

This strict separation between commercial banking and investment banking has been eroded recently due to a series of decisions of the US Federal Reserve Board acting in its capacity as the agency responsible for the Bank Holding Company Act 1956. This erosion of the Glass-Steagall wall between investment and commercial banking in the US domestic capital markets is discussed elsewhere.[16]

III APPLICABILITY OF GLASS-STEAGALL TO EUROBONDS AND EURO COMMERCIAL PAPER

The importance of these provisions to the international bond markets, and the Euro Commercial Paper market[17] is that if these provisions were applied extraterritorially, US commercial banks would not be able (even through a foreign incorporated investment banking subsidiary) to underwrite or participate in an international bond issue or commercial paper, or act in an advisory capacity in respect of such issues.

While there was some doubt previously as to whether commercial paper[18] fell within the definition of 'security' in ss 16 and 20 of the Glass-Steagall Act, the matter has been put to rest by the US Supreme Court in *Securities Industry Association v Board of Governors of the Federal Reserve System* ('Bankers Trust I'),[19] where Blackmun J[20] held that while commercial paper

---

16 See two comprehensive reviews: Norton 'Up Against "the Wall": Glass-Steagall and the Dilemma of a De-regulated ("Re-regulated") Banking Environment' The Business Lawyer vol 42, no 2, February 1987, and Dale 'Glass-Steagall and US Banks' Securities Activities' [1990] 8 Jo of International Banking Law 321; see also Mortimer and Puleo 'The Bankers Trust Case: Pushing Open the Door' IFLR, October 1987.
17 The legal aspects of Euro Commercial Paper are discussed in Part VI.
18 The phrase refers to short-term unsecured negotiable promissory notes with maturities not exceeding nine months issued by prime quality corporations and placed with sophisticated investors, largely financial and other institutions.
19 (1989) 468 US 137, 82 Led 2d 607, 104 Sct 2979.
20 Expressing the views of Burger Ch J, White, Marshall Powell and Renquist JJ.

did not fall within the words 'bonds' or 'debentures', it clearly fell within the words 'notes' or 'other securities' in ss 16 and 21 of the Glass-Steagall Act. It had previously been held by the Federal Reserve Board in response to an application by Bankers Trust that commercial paper did not fall within the definition of a security within the Glass-Steagall Act. The Board's view was that 'if a particular kind of financial instrument evidences a transaction that is more functionally similar to a traditional commercial banking operation than to an investment transaction, then fidelity to the purpose of the Act would dictate that the instrument should not be viewed as a security'.[1] The Federal Reserve Board's view was rejected by the US District Court for the District of Columbia[2] but upheld by the US Court of Appeals for the District Court of Columbia.[3] The US Court of Appeals agreed with the Federal Reserve Board and went on to say that the word 'note' in the Glass-Steagall Act meant a long-term debt security such as a bond. The Supreme Court[4] reversed this decision and held that commercial paper fell within the Glass-Steagall prohibitions.

Subsequent rulings of the US Federal Reserve Board and the Federal Supreme Court have permitted US commercial banks to place commercial paper as agent in private placements of commercial paper. This is discussed below.

Subsequent to the ruling in Bankers Trust I the Federal Reserve Board granted permission to Bankers Trust to carry on activities merely as a placement agent for commercial paper relying on the exception in s 16 of the Glass-Steagall Act which permitted 'purchasing and selling such securities ... without recourse, solely upon the order and for the account of customers, and in no case for its own account'. Bankers Trust had stated to the Board that it would not underwrite such paper or purchase or repurchase paper placed by Bankers Trust or enter into a repurchase agreement with purchasers or make loans to purchasers of commercial paper secured by such paper as collateral. The US District Court for the District of Columbia, however, held that the Board's permission violated the Glass-Steagall prohibition in ss 16 and 21.[5] The court held that the permission in s 16 did not relate to placement of paper in the new issue or primary market but only to agency sales in the secondary markets. This ruling was, however, reversed by the US District Court of Appeals for the District of Columbia in 1986. The Appeal Court's ruling was affirmed by the Federal Supreme Court in *Security Industry Association v Board of Governors of the Federal Reserve System (Bankers Trust II)*.[6] In arriving at this conclusion the Court of Appeals had held first that the permissive language of s 16 was not subject to the prohibition in s 21 of the Glass-Steagall Act, and secondly, that s 16 was not confined to agency sales in secondary markets. The court went on to say that neither the solicitation of customers nor the giving of advice

---

1 See Blackmun J's citation of the Board's view at 468 US 137 at 141.
2 In *AG Becker Inc v Board of Governors of the Federal Reserve System* 519 F Supp 602 (1981).
3 By a divided vote in *AG Becker Inc v Board of Governors of Federal Reserve System* 224 US App DC 21, 693 F 2d 136 (1982).
4 See 468 US 137.
5 *Security Industry Association v Board of Governors* (1986) 627 F Supp 695.
6 807 F2d 1052 (DC Cir 1986) cert denied (1987) 483 US 1005, 97 Led 2d 734, 107 S Ct 3228.

to an issuer of paper took Bankers Trust outside the parameters of the exception in s 16 of the Glass-Steagall Act. Judge Bork, however, seemed to have held that only financial advice given after the issuer had decided to raise capital and concerning how he should raise it, was covered by the language of the exception in s 16, whereas advice given as to the necessity for raising capital might be outside the permission in s 16. The court also held that the prohibition on 'underwriting' imposed on banks by ss 16 and 21 of the Glass-Steagall Act related to public offerings of securities and did not apply to private placements of commercial paper with a small number of sophisticated investors who were large financial and other institutions (and not individuals) and where there were no public advertisements or solicitation of the general public.

While these liberalisations are important to the international markets, the active participation of US commercial banks in the international markets has been made possible otherwise. Participation by US commercial banks through foreign incorporated investment banking affiliates, in the underwriting and placing of international bonds and Euronotes, as well as acting as agents in Euro Commercial Paper issues, has been made possible by a key regulation of the Federal Reserve Board: Regulation K.[7]

Section 211.5(d) of Regulation K permits a foreign subsidiary of a US commercial bank to provide 'investment, financial, or economic advisory services'[8] and 'underwriting distributing in debt and equity securities'[9] (although the underwriting of equity securities is restricted to a maximum of $2 million or 20% of the capital and surplus of an issuer).[10] Further, Regulation K permits subsidiaries of bank holding companies (incorporated under the Bank Holding Company Act of 1956) to engage in other activities with the Federal Reserve Board's permission, which are considered by the Board to be 'usual in connection with the transaction of the business of banking... abroad...'.[11]

The result is that an overseas incorporated subsidiary of a US commercial bank is entitled to participate in underwriting and placing international bond issues as well as Euronotes[12] as well as acting as a placement agent in Euro Commercial Paper issues and, generally, provide investment banking and advisory services in respect of the issue of debt securities in the international markets.

It is also possible for a US commercial bank to participate in the international capital markets through so-called Edge Act corporations. Edge Act corporations are organisations chartered by the Federal Reserve Board under s 25A of the Federal Reserve Act 1916.[13] Though chartered as banks, Edge Act corporations were largely vehicles to enable US banks to engage in international banking under the supervision of the Federal Reserve. Under Regulation K, Edge Act corporations may engage in certain securities activities incidental to the conduct of their international business. The ability

---

7   12 CFR 211.
8   See 211.5(d)4.
9   S 211.5(d)13.
10 See 12 CFR 211.5(d).
11 See 12 CFR 211.5(d).
12 See ch 25 on Euronotes.
13 S 25A was an amendment to s 25 sponsored by Senator Walter Edge.

of such a corporation to participate in the international capital markets is more limited. Thus their ability to underwrite debt securities is confined to the debt obligations of the government or country in which they operate as well as debt obligations of agencies or instrumentalities of the national government or a municipality or other local or regional government entity. Even then there is a limit on the underwriting commitment which in aggregate amount may not exceed 10% of the banks' capital and surplus.[14]

Subsidiaries of Edge Act corporations have the wider powers conferred by s 211.5(d) of Regulation K.

---

14 See 12 CFR 211.3(b).

Part VI
Euro Commercial Paper and Euro Notes

CHAPTER 23
Definitions and structure

I WHAT ARE EURO COMMERCIAL PAPER[1] AND EURO NOTES?

'Euro Commercial Paper' ('ECP') and 'Euro Notes' are both phrases used in the international markets to refer to short-term debt securities in bearer form with maturities of at least seven days and up to a maximum of one year but, in practice, more typically with a maturity of 45 to 60 days. The term 'Euro Notes' is generally used when referring to short-dated instruments issued under structures called Revolving Underwriting Facilities (RUFs), Note Issuance Facilities (NIFs) or Short Term Note Issuance Facilities (SNIFs);[2] whereas the term 'Euro Commercial Paper' is generally used to refer to short-term debt instruments issued under a different issuing structure – a Euro Commercial Paper Programme.[3] The phrase 'commercial paper' is given a technical definition by the Banking Act 1987 (Exempt Transactions) (Amendment) Regulations 1990 as meaning 'a debt security which may not be redeemed in whole or in part until after seven days beginning with the date of issue but which must be redeemed within one year beginning with the date of issue'.

The structure which is termed a Euro Commercial Paper Programme is now the standard form in practice for issues of such short-term debt instru-

---

1 Three studies of the Euro Commercial Paper market, which concentrate on the commercial and financial aspects of such Paper, are: Heller (ed) *Euro Commercial Paper* (Euromoney Publications, 1988); Felix (ed) *Commercial Paper* (Euromoney Publications, 1987) which concentrates more on the US domestic market; and Bullock 'Euro Notes and Euro Commercial Paper' (Butterworths, 1987).
2 See the discussion at ch 25 below on these structures.
3 See, however, Penn Shea and Arora *The Law on Practice of International Banking*, writing in 1987, who state that the term Euro Note is to be used only when there is a commitment on the part of the arrangers to place the Notes. Beaumont has, however, pointed out that the presence or absence of a commitment to purchase the debt instrument distinguishes a committed RUF (see ch 25 below) from a NIF; in a NIF there is no underwritten commitment by the dealers to take the paper if it cannot be placed. (See the persuasive analysis of Beaumont in ch 7 of Bankson and Lee *Euro Notes*.) The presence or absence of a commitment, it is submitted with respect, does not assist in distinguishing Euro Commercial Paper from Euro Notes, and market practice favours the suggested distinction: see Piggott 'Developments in the London Eurocurrency Market' and Woolley 'The Euro Commercial Paper Boom' in Butterworth's JIBFL vol 1, no 1, June 1989.

ments. In 1990, a total of US $50.8 bn in value of short term paper was issued in the London markets compared with US $60.4 bn in value the year previous.[4]

Regardless of whether the debt instrument is called a Euro Note or Euro Commercial Paper, these instruments when issued in physical form would usually possess the following characteristics in practice:

(a) they are in bearer form and carry a promise by the issuer to pay the bearer of the instrument; and
(b) they are issued usually in denominations of US $500,000 (or sometimes US $1m) and, in the case of sterling denominated issues, a face value of £100,000; and
(c) they carry a legend on the face of the note that title is to pass on delivery to the instrument; and
(d) they possess a maturity period which is a minimum of seven days and a maximum of nine months, though it is more likely to be 45 to 60 days;[5] and
(e) they are issued without a coupon and at a discount.

Definitive or physical notes, *when issued*, may constitute a promissory note or negotiable instrument, and most commentators refer to Euro Notes or Euro Commercial Paper as such.[6] However, in practice, definitive physical paper in the form of notes is generally not issued in the modern ECP Programme.[7] A global note is issued instead which is stated to represent all the physical or definitive notes which would usually have been issued. Consequently, while ECP or Euro Notes in definitive physical form may be regarded as promissory notes or negotiable instruments, difficult legal issues arise in cases where there are no definitive notes issued. These issues are discussed below.[8]

The definitive notes or paper, it is submitted, will not qualify as a promissory note under s 83 of the Bills of Exchange Act 1882 and, consequently, will not be negotiable by virtue of that Act. Section 83 of that Act requires:

(a) an unconditional promise,
(b) in writing,
(c) made by one person to another,
(d) signed by the maker,
(e) engaging to pay,
(f) on demand or at a fixed or determinable future time,
(g) a sum certain in money,
(h) to bearer (or to the order of a specified person).

---

4   See the articles cited in the previous fn. The figures are from the Bank of England's Quarterly Bulletin, May 1991, p 241 and excludes Medium Term Notes (MTNs).
5   See Lucy Heller's *Euro Commercial Paper* ch 1 at p 11. She points out that there is little issuance of Paper with maturity under 30 days in the Euro markets whereas in the US domestic market the bulk of papers has a maturity under 30 days.
6   See Penn Shea and Arora *The Law and Practice of International Banking* ch 10 (10.16), p 206; McVicar 'Sterling Commercial Paper' Butterworth's JIBL, September 1986, 40; Woolley, fn 3 above; but cf Balfour 'Euro Notes and Commercial Paper: The English Regulatory Framework' [1986] 3 JIBL 137 and Beaumont, fn 3 above, who carefully refrain from referring to negotiable instruments.
7   See Balfour 'Euro Commercial Paper without Notes' IFLR, January 1986.
8   See pp 446 et seq.

Euro Notes and ECP in definitive physical form:

(a) do not contain an unconditional promise to pay bearer: the notes contain prohibitions as to the persons who may purchase such a note and further are subject to a number of conditions;[9] and
(b) do not contain a promise to pay a sum certain in money: the amounts payable depend on whether payments are subject to a withholding tax. Where a withholding tax is imposed on payments they need to be grossed up.

Consequently, ECP and Euro Notes do not fall within s 83 of the Act of 1882. However, it is extremely likely that definitive or physical notes issued under these structures would qualify as negotiable instruments under English law. As with the case of Eurobonds[10] the question under English law is whether market practice regards such notes as negotiable. It would seem that in market practice the definitive physical note or paper is regarded as negotiable.[11]

It is also necessary to decide whether the Euro Note or ECP in global and definitive form constitutes a 'debenture' under English law for a number of reasons:[12]

(a) If they are debentures, the prospectus provisions of Part III of the Companies Act 1985 will apply to issues of ECP or Euro Notes until those provisions are replaced by Part V of the Financial Services Act 1986.[13]
(b) If they are debentures, the prohibition in s 81 of the Companies Act 1985 will apply until it is repealed when Part V of FSA 1986 is brought into force.[14]
(c) The provisions in FSA 1986 apply to 'investments' as defined in Sch 1, Part I to the Act and 'debentures ... and other instruments creating or acknowledging indebtedness ... ' fall within para 2 of Sch 1, Part I to the Act.

The Companies Act itself contains an unhelpful definition of debenture in s 744 to the effect that a debenture 'includes debenture stock bonds and any other securities of a company whether constituting a charge on the assets of the company or not'. Consequently, for purposes of determining the meaning of the word 'debenture' in the Companies Act 1985, the formulae used by judges in the old common law cases need to be used. Chitty J, in a much cited passage in *Levy v Abercorris Slate Co*,[15] stated that a docu-

---

9 See ch 24 below.
10 See ch 9 above.
11 See McVicar *Sterling Commercial Paper*, fn 6 above; Penn Shea and Arora, fn 6 above; Woolley, fn 3 above, writing in June 1986 stated that there were US $16bn of ECP being traded at the time.
12 The meaning of the word 'debenture' in English law was considered previously and the reader is referred to ch 7. See the discussion at p 125 above.
13 See p 308 above.
14 S 81 is repealed by s 212 (3) and Sch 17, Part I of FSA 1986 when it is fully brought into effect. SI 1986/2246 brings these provisions into effect only in so far as a listing application has been made under Part IV of FSA 1986 but not otherwise.
15 (1987) 37 Ch D 260 at 264.

ment which creates or acknowledges a debt is a debenture.[16] On the basis of this broad formula it is submitted that the conclusion is quite clear, that ECP and Euro Notes in global or definitive form are debentures at common law and should be treated as such under the Companies Act 1985.

It is also submitted that since ECP and Euro Notes acknowledge and create indebtedness, they fall within para 2 (or 3) of Sch 1 to the FSA. Note (a) to para 2 of Sch 1 however does exclude from the definition of debenture 'any instrument acknowledging or creating indebtedness for, or for money borrowed to defray, the consideration payable under a contract for the supply of goods or services'. The exclusion would cover banker's acceptances where each instrument is directly related to a trading transaction. Since in practice neither ECP nor Euro Notes are directly trade related, in the sense that they are not issued to finance a trading transaction, this exclusion is generally inapplicable.

II THE MARKET FOR EURO COMMERCIAL PAPER AND EURO NOTES[17]

As far as issuers are concerned the issue of such notes or paper provides another avenue for obtaining short-term funds. For a company which has access to the Euro market it is generally a cheaper method of raising short-term finance than a short-term facility from a bank. Consequently, as Heller[18] has pointed out, ECP is an effective means of disintermediation which refined the concept already established by its predecessors, the RUF and NIF.[19] Early issuers in the market were US corporations who had already raised funds in the US commercial paper markets and came to London to obtain dollar financing in the international or Euro markets. Heller has also pointed out[20] that the yield differential between the domestic US commercial paper market and the US dollar denominated ECP market was a powerful factor in the growth of the US dollar segment of the Euro markets.[1] For investors it was a good alternative to placing short-term surplus cash on deposit with a bank, and it provided higher yields than bank deposits.[2] Woolley[3] has pointed out that generally investors are banks, insurance companies, pension funds, investment funds, large corporations and central banks.

The following discussion will focus on ECP Programmes since this structure has superseded the RUF and NIF structures in current practice as a framework for issuing short-term debt securities. Tables published by Euro-

---

16 See to the same effect Lindley J in *British India Steam Navigation Co v IRC* (1881) 7 QBD 165 at 173; Warrington LJ accepted and applied the formula of Chitty J cited above and adopted by Lindley J in *Lemon v Austin Friars Investment Trust Ltd* [1926] Ch 1 at 17.
17 See for a full discussion of the commercial and financial background Heller (ed) *Euro Commercial Paper* (Euromoney Publications, 1988).
18 Above, ch 1.
19 See ch 25 below.
20 Above, ch 1.
1 See Heller, above, ch 1; Woolley 'First Chicago's Euro Commercial Paper Facility' Butterworth's JIBFL vol 1 no 1 January 1986, p 19, vol 1, no 1, June 1986.
2 See articles cited in previous fn.
3 Above.

money Noteware[4] show that in 1985 there were 225 Euro Note facilities set up as compared with 51 ECP Programmes, while by year-end 1987, there were 152 Euro Note facilities set up as compared with 326 ECP Programmes.[5] RUF and NIF structures are nevertheless discussed in a later chapter.[6]

III STRUCTURE AND PROCEDURE IN RESPECT OF A EURO COMMERCIAL PAPER PROGRAMME

Under a modern Euro Commercial Paper Programme, a dealer (or a small group of dealers, usually around three to five) first agrees the terms under which the dealer(s) will purchase a prospective issuer's paper as principal, with a view to selling the paper to end investors. These terms are referred to as the 'ECP Programme Agreement', and constitute the standard terms and conditions which will apply if and when an issue of ECP (also referred to as 'notes' in this chapter) is made by a prospective issuer. There is no commitment at this stage on the part of the prospective issuer or the dealer to issue or purchase on the basis of the terms contained in the ECP Programme Agreement. Consequently, agreement needs to be reached on each occasion where an issue of paper is contemplated, as to the maturity date, the aggregate principal amount of the notes and the issue price.[7] If agreement is reached as to an issue of commercial paper between the issuer and the dealer(s), the terms and conditions of the programme agreement apply to each such issue.

Before the first issue of notes is effected under a programme, the issuer and the dealer may sometimes compile an information memorandum relating to the programme, which will describe the basic features of the notes, including currency and maturity range, the form of the note, and a very brief description of the issuer. The memorandum is very brief compared with a Eurobond offering circular.

The memorandum will be transmitted to prospective investors in advance of the issue by the dealers. When the terms of the notes of a specific issue have been agreed, the issuer will transfer a global note to Euroclear or Cedel (or more usually in practice, a bank in London which is a common depository for both) representing the notes which are 'issued'. The dealer or dealers will make payment through a paying agent against delivery of the global note. The dealers would themselves have sold or placed the paper with 'end' investors and in effect the issuer obtains its funds from such end investors. When the global note reaches maturity the issuer repays the face value of the global note. Since the maturity period is usually in the range of one to six months[8] there is little secondary trading, and definitive notes

---

4 Cited in Heller, fn 17 above, at p 10.
5 Even with this explosive growth the ECP market is dwarfed by the US market with US $360bn outstanding as against an estimated US $45bn in the ECP market: see Heller, fn 17 above, at p 11.
6 See ch 25.
7 The issue price will be a discounted value from the face value, the discount representing the interest payable on the Paper.
8 See Woolley cited in fn 1 above.

are hardly, if ever, issued. All trading is effected by electronic book entry on the records of Euroclear and Cedel.[9]

IV LEGAL DOCUMENTS

The entire structure of an ECP Programme is contained in four legal documents:

(a) the Euro Commercial Paper Programme Agreement;
(b) the Issuing and Paying Agency Agreement (IPA);
(c) the global note;
(d) the deed of covenant or deed poll.

The first of these will also contain the form of global note to be issued and the form of definitive note. The contents of these are discussed below.[10]

1 The Programme Agreement

As observed above, this agreement constitutes the standard terms and conditions on which the dealers will agree to purchase any commercial paper which may be issued by the issuer. It imposes no obligation on the dealers to purchase or on the issuer to issue any commercial paper. It simply sets up the framework for such issue and purchase. When an issuer wishes to raise funds through an issue of paper, several matters, including the amount of paper to be issued, the interest rate and discount, and maturity of notes, are negotiated and agreed as between issuer and dealer for each particular issue. The terms of the Programme Agreement would usually require that if agreement is reached as to price, amount and maturity of a note issue, the issuer will transfer a global note to Euroclear or Cedel and the securities account of the dealer at Euroclear or Cedel will be credited with the notes which that dealer has purchased.

It is usually made a condition precedent to the first issue of notes under the programme that certain documents must have been received by each dealer. These include the issuer's constitutional documents, all necessary internal corporate authorisations, any applicable external authorisations, legal opinions (which certify that the issuer may validly enter into the transactions) and any other necessary documents. These are necessary to ensure that the obligations of the issuer in respect of the commercial paper are valid and enforceable and are not void for lack of capacity or authority.[11]

Prior to each issue of notes under the programme (and not merely the first issue) the issuer is required to make certain representations and warran-

---

9 See Balfour 'Euro Commercial Paper Issues without Notes', IFLR, January 1986; and Woolley, above fn 3, p 437.
10 See pp 442–448 above.
11 See ch 2 above below for more detailed discussion of this aspect.

ties by virtue of the Programme Agreement to the dealers. The accuracy and veracity of these representations and warranties should be made a condition precedent to the obligations of the issuer to purchase the paper. These representations and warranties include at least the following:

(a) That the information memorandum, the annual report and accounts and any other documents supplied by the issuer are true and accurate in all respects and not misleading, that all opinions are honestly held and that no facts which would be material to a prudent investor have been omitted.

Such a clause is usually made a condition precedent to each issue so that, first, if a material non-disclosure or misrepresentation is discovered, the dealers can refuse to continue with any further issues.

Secondly, if there are material misrepresentations or non-disclosures, the dealers may be exposed to an allegation of a breach of the provisions of s 47(1) of the FSA which creates a criminal offence in respect of misstatements and omissions made in respect of transactions in 'investments', which includes bonds and commercial paper. The fact that the dealers obtained such representations and warranties would assist in negativing any allegation of recklessness on the part of the dealers, which is the minimum mens rea necessary to be established for the purposes of the offence under FSA 1986 s 47(1).

Thirdly, they assist in discharging any burden of proof placed on the dealers in establishing the absence of negligence under the Misrepresentation Act 1967 or of negativing negligence in tort law if they are sued in damages by end investors.

Fourthly, in the last resort they would enable the dealers to recover from the issuer any loss for which they might be held liable to end investors due to inaccuracies in the information memorandum.

(b) That since the date of the balance sheet (which is issued with the information memorandum) there has been no material adverse change in the financial or business condition or prospects of the issuer, which would affect the issuer's ability to repay the notes as they mature.

The legal purpose of this clause is the same as the previous clause discussed above.

(c) That the issuer's obligations under the Programme Agreement, the Agency Agreement[12] and the deed of covenant[13] are valid and binding obligations.

Under ordinary principles of contract law this clause is of use as a warranty or term of the contractual agreement, only if the contract arising on each issue of the notes is itself a valid and binding contract.[14] A clause in a void contract can have no independent contractual validity. In the event that the contracts relating to the issue of paper are void, the value of the

---

12 See p 445 below.
13 See p 446 below.
14 See the discussion above at ch 2.

clause lies in the fact that it would operate as a representation and consequently be actionable in tort in the event of negligence under the principle developed in the line of cases commencing with *Hedley Byrne & Co Ltd v Heller & Partners Ltd.*[15]

(d) That the issuer is not liable to a withholding tax on any payment due.[16]

This is a warranty which is commercially important since most investors would be reluctant to purchase if the payment on redemption was subject to withhold.

(e) That the obligations rank pari passu with the issuer's other unsecured obligations.

This warranty is necessary to prevent preferential payments to other unsecured creditors.[17]

The dealers' obligations to purchase notes are usually made conditional on the aggregate face value of the notes to be issued, plus the aggregate face value of notes then outstanding, not exceeding a specified maximum. The specification of such a maximum performs two functions. First, it indicates the maximum exposure which the dealers will accept in respect of the issuer. Secondly, in the event that the dealers agree to purchase notes on the assumption that other notes will be repaid on a day prior to issue, but the issuer fails to do so, the dealers have the ability to refuse to purchase the notes.

It is also necessary to have a condition precedent to each issue that the programme agent holds a global note duly executed by the issuer or on his behalf,[18] in order that the note may be issued virtually contemporaneously with the agreement as to aggregate maturity and terms. The obligations of the issuer should also include a covenant that the issuer (and guarantor if any) will provide financial and other information about itself or its subsidiaries as may be requested by the dealers from time to time.

Since ECP Programme Agreements do not actually impose obligations until and unless a note purchase agreement is entered into between the ECP dealers and the issuer there is no legal need to terminate the agreement. However, if new terms need to be negotiated for ECP to be issued in the future, it is extremely useful to have a termination provision. Consequently, a right to terminate the ECP Programme Agreement is conferred on the issuer and each dealer by giving a month's notice. Where one dealer out of a group of dealers is given a right to terminate it should be made clear that he may terminate only in relation to that dealer's participation in the programme, unless it is intended that he should have a right to terminate the entire programme on behalf of all the dealers.

---

15 [1964] AC 465.
16 On withholding tax see pp 79 and 198 above.
17 See the discussion at p 89 above.
18 See p 446 below.

2 The Issuing and Paying Agency Agreement ('IPA')

The agent in an ECP Programme is appointed as the agent of the issuer for a number of administrative purposes by the IPA, which is made between the agent and the issuer (or the guarantor). The agent is appointed, first, to authenticate and issue the global note representing the whole of the issue and to authenticate and issue definitive notes. Secondly, to pay sums due on the global note or the definitive notes as the case may be. For this purpose the agent is provided with a stock of global notes (and sometimes definitive notes if they are to be used) by the issuer and he is authorised by the issuer in the agency agreement to authenticate and issue such notes and deliver the same to the clearing house Euroclear or Cedel.

Once the issuer has agreed terms with one or more of the dealers for the issue of notes, the issuer is required to telephone the agent (to be confirmed by tested telex) to instruct him to authenticate and issue a global note, or definitive notes as the case may be, for each issue of ECP which the dealers have agreed to purchase. The issuer then confirms its instructions to the agent by tested telex, and sends a copy of such telex to the relevant dealer.

A dealer who has reached agreement with the issuer by telephone will confirm the terms of the agreement to the issuer by telex. It is important that the details set out in this telex are made conclusive as to the terms of the agreement in order to avoid disputes regarding the terms agreed.

The agent then prepares and authenticates the global note, or definitive notes as the case may be. All global notes are then delivered to a bank in London which acts as a common depository for Euroclear and Cedel; if definitive notes are being issued these are also delivered to a depository for Euroclear or Cedel. The agent instructs Euroclear or Cedel to credit the amount of notes to the account of each dealer with Euroclear, or Cedel, against payment of the aggregate issue prices of such notes. Each dealer which has agreed to purchase notes would have given corresponding instructions to Euroclear or Cedel.

All of the above would have occurred within two days preceding the actual date of issue of the notes. On the date of issue Euroclear or Cedel will credit the dealers' account with notes, and transfer funds to the agent's account.

An analysis of the procedure will reveal that the agent is exposed to legal risk at a number of points in the process and protective clauses become necessary.

(a) The agent may not have sufficient global notes when the request to issue is made; consequently, in practice his duty to authenticate and issue notes would be made conditional on the existence of such notes.

(b) The purchasers of all or some of the notes may fail to pay for the notes after the global note representing the whole issue is transferred to Euroclear. A clause is necessary to ensure that the agent is under no liability to pay the issuer for such notes, since the agent does not underwrite the issue of the notes. It is also necessary to make clear that Euroclear holds the global note for the issuer and not for the agent, in so far as payment has not been made for any part of the global note.

446 *Definitions and structure*

In addition, since the agent would already have transferred funds by way of same day transfer to the issuer, it is necessary to have a 'claw-back'[19] clause enabling the agent to demand immediate reimbursement for that part of the global note for which funds have not been received.

i *Repayment*

Repayment on the notes issued is also effected through the agent who receives repayment from the issuer and makes a same day transfer to investors through Euroclear or Cedel. Once again, the agent's position needs to be protected so as to ensure that he need not make a same day transfer on the maturity date, if he has reason to believe that funds will not be recovered from the issuer for purposes of transfer to investors. Secondly, if he does nevertheless make a transfer and does not receive from the issuer the whole or part of the sums which he has transferred to investors, the agent ought to be given an immediate right to recover such sums with interest from the issuer.

ii *Protective clauses*

Given the fiduciary position that an agent usually occupies in English law,[20] it is necessary to include a number of clauses for the protection of the agent. First, it must be made clear that since the agent acts for the issuer, the agent owes no fiduciary duties to purchasers of notes. Secondly, he is not liable for the validity of the Programme Agreement or the notes transferred under it to purchasers of notes. Thirdly, he must be given express power to delegate or obtain advice from accountants and lawyers.[1] Fourthly, he must be permitted to carry on any business with the issuer, dealers and investors and make profits from such business. This is necessary since in equity an agent owes fiduciary duties not to make secret profits or let his duty conflict with his interest in accordance with principles laid down in *Boardman v Phipps*[2] by the House of Lords.[3]

3 The global note and deed poll

As pointed out earlier, ECP Programme Agreements generally provide for the issue of a global note which represents the aggregate of the definitive or actual physical notes which ought to have been issued by the issuer on the date of issue. Actual or definitive notes are rarely, if ever, issued in practice. This practice is adopted because the security printing of definitives and their custody is costly, and both dealers and end investors do not generally demand physical possession of the notes or paper due to their short 'life span' to maturity. Where definitives are printed, as in the case of Euro-

---

19 See on such clauses the discussion at pp 59–61 above.
20 See the discussion in ch 4 in the context of an agent bank in a syndicated loan.
1 This is to exclude the common law rule against sub-delegation. See p 245 above.
2 [1967] 2 AC 46.
3 Discussed at pp 243–244 above.

bonds, they are warehoused with a common depositary for the Euroclear or Cedel system, and are hardly, if ever, physically traded. All trading occurs between dealers on the basis of an electronic book entry system at Euroclear or Cedel.[4]

The global note is thus issued as sole evidence of indebtedness of the issuer on the notional notes or paper, usually referred to as Underlying Notes. The global note is also stated to 'represent' the notional Underlying Notes. Trading occurs in the notional notes in multiples of $500,000, as between dealers, on a book entry system; and the notes are cleared through the clearing system by debiting and crediting the accounts of dealers who purchase and sell these notional notes. The physical global note evidencing the issue and representing the issuer's indebtedness is held by Euroclear or Cedel or a common depository for both.

Once the notes or paper matures the issuer transfers funds through the agent by way of repayment on the notes to Euroclear and/or Cedel and these clearing houses in turn credit the accounts of those persons or entities whose names appear on their books as 'holding' notes or paper.

So long as the issuer does not default, serious legal problems do not arise.

Suppose, however, that the issuer defaults on payment. Who may sue the issuer? In practice the only persons who would have an interest in suing would be those who have purchased the notional notes from the original dealers or from subsequent purchasers. They are not 'holders' of a negotiable instrument as that term is traditionally understood in English law,[5] and consequently may not be able to sue on the basis of a 'holding' of a negotiable instrument issued by the issuer of the notes. To overcome this problem the global note usually requires that the issuer must on the occurrence of any default issue actual or definitive notes to the holder of the global note. Euroclear and Cedel would then transfer the notes to those account holders who hold notional notes and they may then as holders of actual notes sue the issuer. However, it is not clear how this obligation to issue actual notes is enforceable, either as against the issuer or indeed Euroclear or Cedel, by those persons who are deemed to be the holders of notional notes.

The global note would itself usually provide that if no definitive or actual notes are issued within 30 days of default then the global note becomes void by its own terms. How then do the entities who purchased notional notes recover from the issuer?

The answer is that the issuer is required to and does execute at the very outset of the programme, a deed of covenant by way of deed poll.[6] The deed poll provides that in the event that the global note becomes void the issuer promises to pay on demand to each of the persons appearing on the books of Euroclear or Cedel as a person who has purchased the notional notes or paper, the aggregate value of notes which he 'holds' on the books of Euroclear and/or Cedel. These persons are referred to as 'account holders'. Who is an account holder for the purposes of the deed poll is determined by reference to the time at which the global note under its terms becomes

---

4 See pp 169 et seq above.
5 See pp 169–176 above.
6 See p 276 above on deed polls.

void. The issuer's obligations under the deed poll are declared to be independent obligations so that it is a fresh promise which does not relate in any way to the issue of the notes. The promise need not be supported by consideration since the deed is executed under seal.[7]

What happens where an account holder sells a notional note to another dealer after the crucial date, ie after the global note becomes void? Arguably no rights are acquired by the purchaser as against the issuer, unless a right under a deed poll is capable of being assigned. The deed, however, expressly covers this situation and provides that the contractual rights created under it may be assigned.

Suppose there is a dispute as to what amount of notional notes are held by an account holder in the Euroclear system? To handle this difficulty the records of Euroclear need to be made conclusive as between issuer and claimant as to the aggregate amount of notional notes held by the account holder.

It is submitted that this ingenious structure overcomes most of the practical and legal problems which arise in respect of ECP issues which are truly paperless.[8] There remains the difficult conceptual question as to the nature of the trading in this paperless market in negotiable instruments which have no physical existence. It is submitted that there is no neat or coherent analysis of the structure of this electronic market which can be advanced by reference to nineteenth century concepts of bearer negotiable instruments, which presuppose physical instruments. It is a situation in which English courts will need to be robust and recognise the commercial reality of the existence of an electronic negotiable instrument. Practice in the international capital markets favours and demands such recognition. Section 207 of the Companies Act 1989 does, however, make provision for regulation to be made enabling title to securities to be evidenced and transferred without a written instrument. Section 207 and regulations framed thereunder are to be in effect by 1 November 1991.[9] At the time of writing it appears, however, that 'dematerialisation' under s 207 will only cover UK corporate stock or bonds held within the TAURUS system of the London Stock Exchange.[10]

---

7 See p 276 above.
8 See Balfour 'Euro Commercial Paper Issues without Notes' IFLR, January 1986.
9 See art 4 of SI 1990/1392 made on 9 July 1990.
10 TAURUS is an acronym for Transferred and Automated Registration of Uncertificated Stock. See generally the DTI Consultative Paper of July 1990.

CHAPTER 24
The regulation of Euro Commercial Paper and Euro Note issues

I UK SECURITIES REGULATION

Under UK law Euro Commercial Paper and Euro Notes are regulated under the following statutes and regulations:

(a) the Banking Act 1987;
(b) the Companies Act 1985 (as amended by the Companies Act 1989);
(c) the Financial Services Act 1986 ('FSA');
(d) the Control of Borrowing Order 1958,[1] as amended, made by the Treasury under powers conferred by s 1 and 3(4) of the Borrowing (Control and Guarantees) Act 1946. The Order required the Bank of England's consent to the issue of certain debt securities. The Order is now only of academic interest since general consent has been conferred under the Order on 14 March 1989. Consequently, the provisions of the Order are not dealt with here.[2]
(e) the common law.

These are discussed below in the context of ECP and are equally appplicable to Euro Notes.

1 Banking Act 1987

i *The prohibition on the taking of 'deposits'*

Section 3 of the UK Banking Act 1987 contains a prohibition on the taking of 'deposits'.

> '(1) Subject to section 4 below, no person shall in the United Kingdom accept a deposit in the course of carrying on (whether there or elsewhere) a business which for the purposes of this Act is a deposit-taking business unless that person is an institution for the time being authorised by the Bank under the following provisions of this Part of this Act.'

---

1 SI 1958/1208.
2 The 1958 Order has been amended by the following statutory instruments: SI 1959/445 (revoked by SI 1967/69); SI 1967/69 (revoked by SI 1970/708); SI 1970/708 (revoked by SI 1985/1150); SI 1972/1218 (revoked by SI 1985/1150); SI 1975/12; SI 1977/1602 (revoked by SI 1985/1150); SI 1979/794 (revoked by SI 1985/1150); SI 1985/565 (revoked by SI 1985/1150); SI 1985/1150; SI 1986/770.

Under s 3(2) a breach of s 3(1) carries criminal sanctions. The problem under the Banking Act is that an issue of ECP by a commercial corporation may constitute the acceptance of a deposit and, consequently, since commercial companies who issue ECP are not usually entities which are 'authorised' under the Banking Act 1987, may constitute a breach of s 3 of the Act.

Due to s 3(3) a contravention of s 3 does not however make the contract in respect of the deposit void or unenforceable.[3]

The applicability of this provision to ECP issues by commercial companies may seem curious but a literal analysis of the provisions does lead to this conclusion.[4] Regulation of ECP issues under the Banking Act 1987 may nevertheless be justified as a matter of policy. An issue of short-term Certificates of Deposit (CDs) by a bank would fall within s 3, and the market for investors in CDs is co-extensive with the market for investors in ECP. As a matter of economic reality, a commercial corporation capable of raising funds from time to time is clearly obtaining funds from persons who would otherwise deposit those funds as deposits with banks. This is the process which is referred to as disintermediation, which eliminates the function of the banks as financial intermediaries.[5] Consequently, from the point of view of the banking community, it is justifiable to treat funds obtained by way of an ECP issue as 'deposits'.

Section 3 is applicable if three criteria are satisfied. First, there must be an 'acceptance of a deposit'. Secondly, it must be accepted 'in the course of carrying on... a deposit taking business' though it does not matter whether the business of deposit taking occurs in the UK or elsewhere. Thirdly, it is necessary that the deposit must have been accepted in the UK.[6]

(a) Meaning of 'deposit' A 'deposit' is defined in such a wide manner in s 5 of the Act that the act of receiving funds on the sale of ECP is potentially within the definition.

'(1) Subject to the provisions of this section, in this Act 'deposit' means a sum of money paid on terms—
  (a) under which it will be repaid, with or without interest or a premium, and either on demand or at a time or in circumstances agreed by or on behalf of the person making the payment and the person receiving it; and
  (b) which are not referable to the provision of property or services or the giving of security;
and references in this Act to money deposited and to the making of a deposit shall be construed accordingly.
(2) For the purposes of subsection (1)(b) above, money is paid on terms which are referable to the provision of property or services or to the giving of security if, and only if—
  (a) it is paid by way of advance or part payment under a contract for the sale, hire or other provision of property or services, and is repayable

---

3 Compare the sanction of unenforceability of contracts made in breach of s 3 of FSA 1986.
4 See the discussion below.
5 See Heller *Euro Commercial Paper* ch 2.
6 This latter requirement was not found in s 1(1) of the Banking Act 1979, though it is understood that the Bank of England interpreted it to mean that the deposit must be accepted in the UK before s 1(1) was triggered.

only in the event that the property or services is not or are not in fact sold, hired or otherwise provided;
(b) it is paid by way of security for the performance of a contract or by way of security in respect of loss which may result from the non-performance of a contract; or
(c) without prejudice to paragraph (b) above, it is paid by way of security for the delivery up or return of any property, whether in a particular state of repair or otherwise.'

The criteria laid down by s 5 are clearly applicable to acceptance of funds in the course of an ECP issue. There is, however, an exception in s 5(3) for any 'sum paid by ... an authorised person', that is, authorised under the Banking Act 1987. Consequently, it is arguable that if the issuer of ECP receives all funds from an entity authorised under the Banking Act 1987, who has as principal purchased all the paper issued, the funds so paid are not 'deposits' because they are 'sums paid' by an authorised person. The corresponding phrase used in the corresponding exception in the Banking Act of 1979 (which was superseded by the 1987 Act) was 'a loan made'.[7] The phrase 'sums paid' in the 1987 Act is wider than the phrase 'loans made' in the 1979 Act and consequently (whatever the position under the 1979 Act), it is submitted that if an ECP issue is structured so that a person or persons authorised under the Banking Act 1987 purchases all ECP issued, and pays over any sums due as consideration, such an issue would not be in breach of s 3. However, it is understood that the Bank of England does not consider that this provision exempts an ECP issue and has issued regulations (discussed below) providing a 'safe harbour' for ECP issues complying with certain criteria.[8]

Consequently, the markets have as a matter of caution acted on the basis of the Bank of England's interpretation, since the Bank of England is the authority charged with the function of enforcing s 3 of the Banking Act 1987.[9]

(b) 'Deposit-taking business' The second requirement of s 3 is that the deposit be accepted in the course of carrying on a deposit-taking business. Section 6 defines what constitutes this element:

'(1) Subject to the provisions of this section, a business is a deposit-taking business for the purposes of this Act if –
(a) in the course of the business money received by way of deposit is lent to others; or
(b) any other activity of the business is financed, wholly or to any material extent, out of the capital of or the interest on money received by way of deposit.

(2) Notwithstanding that paragraph (a) or (b) of subsection (1) above applies to a business, it is not a deposit-taking business for the purposes of this Act if –
(a) the person carrying it on does not *hold himself out* as accepting deposits on a day to day basis [*Italics added*]; and
(b) any deposits which are accepted are accepted *only on particular occasions*,

---

7 See the Banking Act 1979 s 1(5)(a).
8 See p 453 below.
9 See Banking Act 1987, s 1(1).

whether or not involving the issue of debentures or other securities. [*Italics added.*]

(3) For the purposes of subsection (1) above all the activities which a person carries on by way of business shall be regarded as a single business carried on by him.

(4) In determining for the purposes of subsection (2)(b) above whether deposits are accepted only on particular occasions regard shall be had to the frequency of those occasions and to any characteristics distinguishing them from each other.

(5) For the purposes of subsection (2) above there shall be disregard of any deposit in respect of the acceptance of which the person in question is exempt from the prohibition in section 3 above and any money received by way of deposit which is not used in the manner described in subsection (1) above.'

While s 6(1)(a) may be inapplicable to most issuers, s 6(1)(b) may be applicable, unless the two criteria set out in sub-s (2) above are satisfied. The criteria in sub-s (2) would not be satisfied in practice, in the context of an ECP programme.

It would be difficult to argue that there is no 'holding out' within s 6(2)(a) because the setting up of the programme itself constitutes a holding out to the dealers. Further, under the terms of a programme an issuer may frequently be offered funds by the dealers.

As regards s 6(2)(b), it would also be difficult to argue that the deposits are accepted only on 'particular occasions' given the frequency of issues in practice under any ECP programme. It is also not possible to rely on s 6(4) which requires consideration of 'any characteristics distinguishing' one deposit from another in order to determine whether deposits are accepted on a particular occasion. The phrase cannot apply to any variations in interest rates or in maturities in respect of deposits, for if it were so most deposits would be different from each other, and s 6 would have little applicability. On the other hand, it is difficult to envisage what other characteristics are to be taken into account. Given the ambiguity, little reliance can be placed on this provision in practice to exclude ECP issues from the prohibition in s 3.[10]

(c) Acceptance of a deposit 'in the United Kingdom' The third requirement of s 3 is that the deposit must be accepted in the UK regardless of where the deposit-taking business is carried on. There is no guidance on how the place of acceptance of a deposit is to be determined for these purposes. It is submitted that the answer depends on the location of the account of the issuer to which the funds from an ECP issue are transmitted. A deposit is 'accepted' at that location. This conclusion flows from the holding of Staughton J in *Libyan Arab Foreign Bank v Bankers Trust Co*[11] where his lordship held that a deposit is held at the location of the account. It is therefore submitted that the prohibition in s 3 should not apply where all sums received from the issue of ECP are credited to an offshore account of the issuer. This would usually be the case where the ECP is denominated in US dollars or other currency, but would not usually be in the case of sterling commercial paper issues.

---

10 See the narrow construction of what constituted 'a particular occasion' for these purposes under the corresponding provisions of the Banking Act of 1979 in the case of *SCF Finance Co Ltd v Masri (No 2)* [1987] 1 All ER 175.
11 [1988] 1 Lloyd's Rep 259.

ii Exempt Transactions Regulations

In order to permit the growth of a sterling commercial paper market the Bank of England first issued regulations on 29 April 1986 which permitted the issue of sterling commercial paper subject to certain conditions.[12] These Regulations have now been substantially revised by the Banking Act 1987 (Exempt Transactions)(Amendments) Regulations 1990.[13]

The regime introduced by the 1990 Regulations is intended to provide a 'safe harbour' not only to issuers of sterling commercial paper but also ECP denominated in other currencies.

(a) Who may issue? Under reg 13, the following entities are permitted to issue ECP:

(a) Companies whose shares or bonds are currently listed on the London Stock Exchange or on the Unlisted Securities Market ('USM') and which have a net asset value of £25m or more.
(b) Companies whose shares are not listed on the London Stock Exchange, but whose shares or debt securities are listed on a Recognised Overseas Exchange, may also issue commercial paper if they have a net asset value of £25m or more (as in the case of London listed companies).[14]
(c) A government of any country or territory or a public authority outside the UK whose debt securities are listed on the London Stock Exchange or on any Recognised Overseas Exchange.

A number of points need to be emphasised. First, the permission to issue is not confined to companies incorporated in the UK but is extended to any London listed company or a company whose shares are listed on a 'Recognised Overseas Exchange'. The definition of this phrase refers to overseas stock exchanges recognised by the London Stock Exchange for purposes of r 535 of the Stock Exchange Rules and not to exchanges recognised under s 40 of FSA 1986.

(d) Any entity whose commercial paper is to be guaranteed by a person authorised under the Banking Act 1987 or by a company whose shares are listed on the London Stock Exchange is also a qualifying issuer under reg 13(a)(iv). An entity whose ECP is guaranteed by a company whose shares are listed on a Recognised Overseas Exchange is not within this category. Finally, certain issuers specified under Sch 2, such as the Post Office and London Regional Transport, qualify.

(b) Conditions which need to be satisfied under the Regulations The commercial paper must possess certain characteristics.

(a) Each note must have a minimum redemption value of £100,000 or its currency equivalent, and it must not be capable of being transferred in whole or *in part* unless the debt security being transferred is not

---

12 See the Banking Act 1987 (Exempt Transactions) Regulations 1988 (SI 1988/646 as amended and substituted by SI 1989/465 of 14 March 1989) framed under powers conferred on the Treasury by s 4(4) of the Banking Act 1987.
13 SI 1990/20.
14 Reg 13(a)(ii) and 13(b).

less than £100,000 or its currency equivalent. It seems clear that this requirement applies both to the global note and the definitive note; a global note is capable of being transferred in part and for this reason the Regulations require that each part transferable is subject to the £100,000 test of minimum value.

(b) It must have a legend that it is 'commercial paper issued in accordance with regulations made under s 4 of the Banking Act 1987'.

(c) It must under reg 13(d)(iii) state the name of the issuer, and that it is not authorised, if this is the case, and whether it is guaranteed or not and if it is guaranteed the name of the guarantor and whether the guarantor is an authorised institution under the Banking Act 1987.

(d) The notes must contain a statement of compliance with the London Stock Exchange listing rules or the Rules of the USM if the issuer or guarantor is listed on the London Stock Exchange or the USM; if it is a company listed on a Recognised Overseas Exchange there must be a statement that it has complied with the requirements of Sch 3 of the Regulations; and in both cases that it reasonably believes that the issuer is unaware of circumstances which would 'significantly and adversely' affect its ability to redeem the paper when due.[15]

(e) In the case of an issuer which is listed on a Recognised Overseas Exchange Sch 3 requires that certain information relating to its financial and business position be delivered to the London Stock Exchange 14 days prior to the first issue of paper under a programme. The information required is broadly the same as that required to be delivered under the continuing obligations of disclosure and notification of information imposed on companies whose shares or bonds are listed on the London Stock Exchange.

(f) In the case of an issuer referred to in (e) above it must also provide certain information as to the debt securities to the Bank of England under arts 8 and 9 of Sch 3 of the Regulations. These are, first, that prior to the first issue of paper under the programme the Bank of England must be informed as to the total amount to be raised under the programme, the maturity periods of the paper (if known) and the purpose for which the proceeds are to be used. Secondly, a monthly report must be given to the Bank of England as to the amount of paper outstanding and how much has been issued and how much has been redeemed.

To summarise the position:

(a) It was submitted that Euro Commercial Paper issues, where the dealers are authorised persons under the Banking Act 1987, are outside the scope of the prohibition in s 3 of the Banking Act 1987. This is because the receipt of funds does not constitute a 'deposit' for purposes of the Act provided that the dealers are acting as principals and provided it may be said that the funds constitute a 'sum paid' by them to the issuer. However, the Bank of England it is understood takes a different view, and the market has acted in reliance of this view.[16]

---

15 See Reg 13(d)(iv).
16 See the Banking Act 1987 s 5(1) and (3).

(b) Where sums paid in respect of a Euro Commercial Paper issue are received at an off-shore account of the issuer, they do not constitute 'deposits' within the meaning of the Banking Act 1987 (s 3(1)) and are consequently outside the ambit of the prohibition in s 3 of the Banking Act 1987. In practice, only issues in sterling would not be capable of taking the benefit of this exception.

(c) In any event Euro Commercial Paper may be issued by an unauthorised entity who complies with the requirements of the Banking Act 1987 (Exempt Transactions) Regulations 1988 as amended by the Banking Act 1987 (Exempt Transactions)(Amendment) Regulations 1990.

iii *Prohibition on 'deposit advertisements'*

All 'deposit advertisements' must comply with any regulations made by the Treasury in respect of such advertisements: s 32(1). Regulations have in fact been issued under this section by the Banking Act 1987 (Advertisements) Regulations 1988.[17] Any person who issues or causes to be issued in the UK an advertisement, the issue of which is prohibited by the Regulations or which does not comply with the Regulations, is guilty of a criminal offence: s 32(3).

The question that arises under s 32 is whether information memoranda and screen displays, eg on Reuter, can constitute deposit advertisements and therefore be subject to the Regulations.

Section 32(5) and (6) defines a 'deposit advertisement'.

'(5) In this section "a deposit advertisement" means any advertisement containing –
   (a) an invitation to make a deposit; or
   (b) information which is intended or might reasonably be presumed to be intended to lead directly or indirectly to the making of a deposit;
and for the purposes of this section an advertisement includes any means of bringing such an invitation or such information to the notice of the person or persons to whom it is addressed and references to the issue of an advertisement shall be construed accordingly.
(6) For the purposes of this section—
   (a) an advertisement issued or caused to be issued by any person by way of display or exhibition in a public place shall be treated as issued or caused to be issued by him on every day on which he causes or permits it to be displayed or exhibited;
   (b) an advertisement inviting deposits with a person specified in the advertisement shall be presumed, unless the contrary is proved, to have been issued to the order of that person.'

It will be noticed, first, that the advertisement need not be in a document, and consequently, Reuter screen 'pages' could constitute an advertisement. Secondly, the advertisement need not contain an 'invitation' to make a deposit; it is sufficient that it 'might reasonably be presumed to be intended to lead directly or indirectly to the making of a deposit'.[18] Both an

---

17 SI 1988/645.
18 It may be noticed that this formula is narrower than the formula used in s 57(2) of the FSA. See the discussion on s 57 at ch 16, pp 296 et seq above.

information memorandum and a screen advertisement would clearly fall within this formula.

Thirdly, the prohibition in s 32 is restricted to advertisements issued in the UK, but even an advertisement issued outside the UK may fall within the prohibition under s 32(7):

> '(7) for the purposes of this section an advertisement issued outside the United Kingdom shall be treated as issued in the United Kingdom if it is directed to persons in the United Kingdom or is made available to them otherwise than in a newspaper, journal, magazine or other periodical publication published and circulating principally outside the United Kingdom or in a sound or television broadcast transmitted principally for reception outside the United Kingdom.'[19]

Fourthly, the advertisement must relate to the making of a 'deposit'. Consequently, in the situations where ECP issues do not constitute the taking of deposits the prohibition is inapplicable. Where ECP issues do constitute the taking of deposits, there are exemptions in the Advertisements Regulations[20] which are relevant to ECP issuers. Regulation 2(1) provides that the Regulations do not apply 'to a deposit advertisement unless it contains an invitation to make deposits only with offices of the deposit taker in the United Kingdom or another member State'. In the case of many ECP issues, in particular those denominated in a currency other than sterling, the deposit-taker, ie the issuer, does not accept a 'deposit' at its offices anywhere, since the 'deposit', ie the proceeds of the ECP issue, are credited to the account of the issuer at a bank. It is submitted, therefore, that, in practice, the Regulations have no application to ECP issues.

Additional exemptions are found in reg 2(2) to 2(5) of the Advertisements Regulations which are also relevant.[1]

Regulation 2(2) provides that in respect of advertisements issued by deposit-takers who carry on a deposit-taking business in any state of the European Community the advertisement is exempt if it 'does not indicate the offices with which the deposits are to be made'.

For this exemption to apply it must first be shown that the issuer is carrying on a deposit-taking business. Arguably if funds received from an ECP can constitute deposits, then the regular issue of such paper in London can constitute the carrying on of a deposit-taking business.

Secondly, it must be shown that the advertisement does not indicate the 'offices'. If the word 'offices' in reg 2(2) means offices of the deposit-taker, as in reg 2(1), then there is clearly no such indication in the information memorandum or on a Reuter screen or other screen display. However, even if it means 'any office', there is no indication in the information memorandum or the Reuter screen as to which office of which bank the account of the issuer should be credited with the proceeds of the issue (ie the deposit).

In conclusion, it is submitted that reg 2 exempts the information memorandum and any Reuter screen announcement or other screen display from

---

19 This provision mirrors s 207(3) of FSA 1986.
20 SI 1988/645.
1 Reg 2(1) is said to be 'subject to' these paragraphs and this means that even if the criteria in s 2(1) are not satisfied but one of the criteria in the later paragraphs is satisfied, the Regulations would not apply.

compliance with the Advertisement Regulations, and consequently, there should be no difficulty in practice with the prohibition in s 32(3) of the Banking Act 1987.

iv *Unsolicited calls*

Section 34(3) of the Banking Act 1987 contains a prohibition on making unsolicited calls on persons in the UK or elsewhere with a view to procuring the making of deposits in contravention of regulations made by the Treasury under s 34(1). An unsolicited call is defined in s 34(4) as a personal visit or oral communication without express invitation.[2] However, unlike under the provisions of the FSA, a breach of s 34(3) of the Banking Act does constitute a criminal offence under s 34.

2 Companies Act 1985

The provisions of the Companies Act 1985 which have an impact on a Euro Commercial Paper issue will soon be repealed and replaced by Part V of FSA 1986 and are discussed in detail in chapter 16; the other provisions of the FSA which are applicable to an ECP issue are discussed below.[3] However, at present there are two sets of provisions which need to be considered.

i *Prospectus provisions of the Companies Act 1985*

First, since ECP issues are not usually listed on the London Stock Exchange under Part IV of FSA 1986, the provisions of the Companies Act 1985 relating to prospectuses are at present applicable to ECP issues due to s 58 (if the issuer is a company incorporated in the UK) or s 72 (if the issuer is incorporated overseas). These sections provide that a UK or foreign company may not offer any shares or debentures by a prospectus unless it is a complying prospectus under the Companies Act 1985. Section 58(1) of the Act provides that 'if a company allots or agrees to allot its shares or debentures with a view to all or any of them being offered for sale to the public *any* document by which the offer for sale to the public is made is deemed for all purposes a prospectus issued by the company'. (Emphasis added.)

Given that the paper in global or definitive form constitutes a debenture,[4] it seems that an information memorandum issued by the company is potentially within the provisions of the Act. It does not matter that the document is not issued to the public by the company, nor that the paper is not directly offered for sale to the public by the company so long as (a) there is an allotment 'with a view to all or any of them being offered to the public' and (b) there is a document by which the offer for sale is made.

---

2 These provisions mirror s 56 of FSA 1986.
3 See p 459.
4 See p 440 above.

In practice an information memorandum never contains an offer for sale and indeed usually contains a legend to the effect that the document does not constitute an offer or invitation to purchase the notes described in it. The actual offer of paper is made orally by telephone. It is arguable that such a document is not caught by s 58(1) because a document which does not contain an offer to the public cannot constitute a prospectus.

However, it is equally arguable that where the offer is made orally by telephone and the information memorandum is so closely related to it in time and circumstances, the information memorandum is a document by which the offer is made to the public.

An alternative route is to use the exception contained in s 79(2) of the Companies Act 1985 which provides that an offer of debentures to professionals does not constitute an offer to the public.[5] This section previously applied only to offers by companies incorporated outside Great Britain,[6] but now, due to s 195 of FSA 1986, the exemption in s 79(2) is also available to companies incorporated in Great Britain in the case of 'short dated securities', which are defined as debentures repayable within five years from the date of issue.[7] Given that all Euro Commercial Paper and Euro Notes possess this characteristic it is possible for all issuers to take advantage of this exception.

Section 79(2), however, confines the exemption where the offer is made to persons 'whose ordinary business it is to buy or sell shares or debentures whether as principal or as agent'. It is submitted that this phrase is sufficiently wide to cover brokers, securities dealers, banks, insurance companies and probably fund managers; but it may not cover corporate treasurers.

The exclusion of corporate treasurers from the category of s 79(2) persons is of course a drawback, in practice, to the extensive use of this exception. Where placement of commercial paper is to be made to corporate treasury departments the oral offer route[8] may need to be adopted.

In order to take advantage of the exception in s 79(2), it is necessary to place contractual restrictions on the dealers, requiring them to sell the ECP issue only to persons falling within s 79(2). Suppose that the purchasers from the dealers, eg banks, resell the paper to non-professionals? Does the issuer lose the benefit of s 79? It is submitted that he does provided that he has taken all reasonable steps to ensure that the dealers will only sell to persons who are professionals within s 79(1), and he does not think it likely that resales will be made to non-professionals. The test is whether the allotment was made 'with a view to' notes or paper being offered for sale to the public. Selling restrictions imposed on the ECP dealers as to the persons to whom they may resell the paper should be sufficient to overcome any argument to the contrary, since the dealers are contractually bound to confine resale to persons coming within s 79(2) of the Companies Act 1985.

---

5 See the discussion ch 16, pp 308 et seq above.
6 Companies Act 1985 s 79(1).
7 Previously, s 195 was restricted to short dated debentures which must be repaid within a year but from 16 November 1989, s 202 of the Companies Act 1989 amended s 195 so that the exemption covers debentures repayable within five years from issue.
8 Above.

ii Section 81 of the Companies Act 1985

The second relevant prohibition is that under s 81 of the Companies Act 1985: no private company incorporated in Great Britain may offer debentures to the public. This means that for US multinationals, a subsidiary incorporated in Great Britain as a private limited company, cannot be used as a vehicle for a Euro Commercial Paper issue unless the issue can be said not to constitute an 'offer to the public' within the meaning of s 59 and s 60 of the Companies Act 1985.[9]

A subsidiary of a US multinational which is incorporated as a public limited company[10] is not subject to the prohibition. It is of course possible to convert a private company into a public limited company under the provisions of Part II of the Companies Act 1985[11] and it is also possible to issue commercial paper through an offshore financing vehicle which is not a public company.

The prohibition in s 81 will not apply if there is no offer to the public, and consequently the exception in s 79(2) of the Companies Act 1985 as extended by s 195 of FSA 1986 discussed above is equally applicable here.

3 Financial Services Act 1986 ('FSA')

The impact of the provisions of the FSA on ECP issues is similar to their impact on Eurobond issues and the relevant provisions in summary are as follows:

(a) the need for authorisation (s 3);
(b) the need to comply with s 57;
(c) the impact of Part V of the FSA;
(d) the need to comply with the unsolicited calls rules under s 56;
(e) the liability for criminal penalties for false or misleading statements under s 46(1) and for the liability to the offence of market manipulation under s 47(2).

The reader is referred to Part IV for detailed discussion of these provisions. A summary follows.

i The need for authorisation

It seems clear that commercial paper in global or definitive form constitutes a 'debenture or other instrument creating or acknowledging indebtedness' within the meaning of para 2 of Sch 1.[12] Consequently, selling or buying paper would constitute carrying on investment business falling within para 12 of Sch 1, while making arrangements for the issue of ECP would constitute

---

9 See also s 79(2) of the Act.
10 See Part I, Ch 1, s 1 of the Companies Act 1985.
11 See ss 43–48.
12 See *Levy v Abercorris Slate and Slab Co* (1887) 37 Ch D 260 at 264 per Chitty J who said that 'a document which creates a debt or acknowledges it' was a debenture. To the same effect see Lindley J in *British India Steam Navigation Co v IRC* (1881) 7 QBD 165 at 173; Warrington LJ in *Lemon v Austin Friars Investment Trust Ltd* [1926] Ch 1 at 17 following the two cases cited above.

an activity falling within para 13 of Sch 1 FSA. Any person engaging in such activity would need to be authorised unless that person falls within an exception to the prohibitions in FSA s 3 which prohibits an unauthorised person from carrying on investment business in the UK.

The issuer would not be caught by para 12 of Sch 1,[13] nor by para 13 (arranging deals in investments) because of the exemption in para 28 of FSA Sch 1 which excludes the activities of issuing and making arrangements for the issue of ECP from the ambit of paras 12 and 13 respectively of Sch 1 to the FSA.

The dealers would fall within para 12, and consequently would require to be authorised. In practice, they will usually be authorised persons and no breach of s 3 would occur.

Much trading activity in respect of commercial paper may also fall within the exempt transaction regime in Sch 5 to the FSA, and therefore outside the prohibition in FSA s 3. The buying and selling of commercial paper with maturities under one year is potentially within para 2(2)b of Sch 5 provided the transaction is effected as between institutions on the Bank of England's list maintained under FSA s 43 ('listed institutions').[14] Where the transaction of purchase and sale occurs between a listed institution and a commercial corporation the transaction will be exempt provided that the transaction is above the monetary limits specified in para 5(2)(b) of Sch 5, namely, £100,000 or its currency equivalent.[15] Commercial paper is usually issued in multiples of $500,000 and, consequently, the transactions in these instruments should in practice fall within Sch 5 as exempt transactions.

It is extremely important to note, however, that the exemption under FSA s 43 and Sch 5 covers only purchases and sales of commercial paper and arranging such deals (ie activity falling within paras 12 and 13 of FSA Sch 1).[16] It does not cover the giving of advice on an ECP issue (ie activity falling within para 15 of Sch 1). An arranger of an ECP issue would consequently need authorisation unless some other exception can be relied on in so far as advice is given which falls within para 15 of Sch 1 to the FSA.[17] In practice listed institutions active in the ECP market would also be authorised persons for purposes of the FSA.

ii *Advertising: s 57*

The information memorandum would constitute an investment advertisement and would require approval by an authorised person, if it is issued or caused to be issued in the UK by an unauthorised issuer, unless it is issued within an exemption to s 57. Since the issuer is generally not authorised under the FSA, the usual course of action is to ensure that the information memorandum is issued only to market professionals so that the prohibition in s 57 does not apply due to art 9 of the Financial Services Act 1986 (Invest-

---

13 See ch 15 above for a more detailed analysis.
14 See s 3 and s 43 read with Sch 5 to the FSA and paras 1 and 2(2)b of Sch 5.
15 At rates prevailing at the time of the transaction: para 8 of Sch 5.
16 See Schedule 5 to the FSA.
17 See discussion in ch 15 above.

ment Advertisements) (Exemptions) Order 1988.[18] This article permits the issue of advertisements by non-authorised persons to a number of specified persons including authorised persons, exempt persons and corporations who have a net asset value of £5m or more.[19] Consequently, all marketing materials need to be restricted to such persons and appropriate contractual clauses are necessary prohibiting the distribution of information to persons other than such persons.

Reuter screen and other electronic announcements would equally constitute investment advertisements, but in practice such announcements would be issued by authorised persons and, consequently, a breach of s 57 would not occur; otherwise its issue would need to be confined to persons specified in art 9 of the above Order.

iii Unsolicited calls: s 56

The 'cold calling' of investors with a view to placing ECP is caught by s 56, but this causes no difficulty in practice due to the exemptions available. These exemptions are the same as those applicable in the case of Eurobond issues, and were discussed in chapter 16.

4 Control of Borrowing Order (COBO)

This Order prohibits the issue of sterling securities where the aggregate amount is £3m or more unless the maximum amount to be raised by the issue and the time at which or the period during which the issue is to be made have been approved by the Bank of England on behalf of the Treasury: art 8A(2) read with art 8A(1) and Part I of the Order.[20] These provisions clearly apply to commercial paper. The detailed analysis by which this conclusion is reached is not dealt with here due to the fact that COBO is now a 'dead letter' after the General Consent of the Treasury was given under the Order for any transaction caught by COBO, effective on 14 March 1989.[1] COBO is to be revoked in the near future.[2] Prior to this General Consent it was necessary to obtain timing consent so as to enable the Bank of England to monitor the flow of new issues. As part of the process of timing consent the Bank operated a new issues queue whose basic purpose was to 'encourage maximum continuing flow of issues by seeking to maintain orderly conditions in the new issues markets', and in operating the queue the Bank's guiding principle was 'to try to avoid inadvertent clashes between large competing issues'.[3]

5 The information memorandum and liability for misstatements

As observed earlier the information memorandum is not as detailed as an offering circular in a Eurobond issue. In addition, other informational mater-

---

18 SI 1988/316. See the discussion on art 9 in ch 16.
19 See art 9(3).
20 The above proposition is the effect of the most convoluted drafting which an English lawyer can encounter.
1   See Bank of England Press Notice of 14 March 1989.
2   See the Press notice above.
3   See the Bank of England's Notice of 27 July 1987 'Capital Market Issues in Sterling'.

ial such as the issuer's (or guarantor's) annual report and account are also circulated to dealers and through them to end investors. The sources of liability in respect of all these documents are discussed below. It must be emphasised that liability under the following heads may potentially be imposed on the dealers as well as the issuer of notes.

i *Banking Act 1987 s 35*

Section 35 states as follows:

'(1) Any person who –
    (a) makes a statement, promise or forecast which he knows to be misleading, false or deceptive, or dishonestly conceals any material facts; or
    (b) recklessly makes (dishonestly or otherwise) a statement, promise or forecast which is misleading, false or deceptive,
is guilty of an offence if he makes the statement, promise or forecast or conceals the facts for the purpose of inducing, or is reckless as to whether it may induce, another person (whether or not the person to whom the statement, promise or forecast is made or from whom the facts are concealed) –
    (i) to make, or refrain from making, a deposit with him or any other person; or
    (ii) to enter, or refrain from entering into an agreement for the purpose of making such a deposit.
(2) This section does not apply unless –
    (a) the statement, promise or forecast is made in or from, or the facts are concealed in or from, the United Kingdom or arrangements are made in or from the United Kingdom for the statement, promise or forecast to be made or the facts to be concealed;
    (b) the person on whom the inducement is intended to or may have effect is in the United Kingdom; or
    (c) the deposit is or would be made, or the agreement is or would be entered into, in the United Kingdom.'

The extraterritorial nature of the offence also needs to be noted. If one of the facts specified in s 35(2) occurs in the UK, an offence may have been committed under s 35 of the Banking Act 1987, even though all other activity or conduct occurred overseas. Thus it is sufficient that the false statement, promise or forecast is made *in* or *from* the UK or, where this occurred overseas, that arrangements were made in the UK for the statement, promise or forecast to be made; it is also sufficient that the person who received the inducement was in the UK, or if that person was overseas the deposit was received in the UK.

It is also important to note that in determining whether the false statement or concealment etc was made 'for the purpose of inducing' or 'reckless as to whether it may induce' another person to make or agree to make a deposit, the dealers have the benefit of a number of exculpatory notices in the information memorandum. They are usually in a form such as:

'(a) The Dealers make no representation, express or implied, as to, and accept no responsibility for, the accuracy or completeness of any of the information in this Information Memorandum, which information has been obtained from

the Company and the Guarantor who have approved it and requested and authorised its delivery on their respective behalf.
(b) This Information Memorandum is not intended to provide the basis of any credit or other evaluation. Each potential purchaser should determine for itself the relevance of the information contained in this Information Memorandum as updated from time to time and its interest in the purchase of any Notes should be based upon such investigation as it deems necessary.
(c) The Dealers expressly do not undertake to review the financial condition or affairs of the Company or the Guarantor during the life of the programme, or to advise any recipient of this Memorandum of any information coming to their attention.'

While these may go a long way towards negativing any recklessness, the necessary exposure to criminal liability cannot be eliminated altogether by such clauses.

ii *Financial Services Act 1986 s 46(1)*

This is a provision analogous to s 35 of the Banking Act 1987 and was considered in ch 17. The question here is whether a false or inaccurate statement, promise or forecast knowingly made or a dishonest concealment of facts caused an investor to purchase ECP. Once again the dissemination of the information memorandum creates an exposure to a risk of a breach of s 47(1).[4] These risks are analogous to those arising under s 35 of the Banking Act 1987.

iii *Liability in contract law*

If there is any misrepresentation of fact (though not of opinion or law)[5] in the information memorandum, a recipient who relies on the information and purchases the security has an action to rescind the contract at common law[6] and further has an action for damages under the Misrepresentation Act 1967. In the latter case the action can subsist only if there is negligence on the part of the representor.[7] Arguably, the exculpatory protective clause included in the memorandum (referred to earlier) could either negative reliance on the part of the representee or negative any liability based on the existence of negligence. These issues were discussed in the context of information memoranda issued for syndicating loans and in the context of offering circulars distributed in Eurobond issues. The reader is referred to these discussions.[8]

It would seem that investors cannot take advantage of the provisions of the Misrepresentation Act 1967 as against the issuer if they purchase ECP from a dealer who acts as principal. The reason is that a representee can rely on the provisions of that Act only if he entered into a contract

---

4 See p 329 above.
5 See pp 48 et seq above.
6 *Redgrave v Hurd* (1881) 20 Ch D 1.
7 See the Misrepresentation Act 1967 s 2(1)(a). The burden of proving the absence of negligence is on the defendant representor.
8 See ch 3 above.

with the representor in consequence of the misrepresentation.[9] However, in such cases there may be liability in tort.

iv *Liability in tort*

End investors could sue either the issuer or the dealers in tort for any negligent misstatement, forecast or opinion, on the basis of the principles laid down by the House of Lords in *Hedley Byrne & Co Ltd v Heller & Partners Ltd*[10] and reformulated in *Caparo Industries plc v Dickman*.[11] Once again exculpatory clauses should enable the dealers to avoid liability on the basis that:

(a) it was not reasonable for investors to rely on the information memorandum vis-à-vis the dealers;
(b) given the disclaimers it was not within the reasonable foresight of the dealers that a party reading the memorandum would rely on the information vis-à-vis the dealers;
(c) the disclaimers are sufficiently wide to exempt the dealers from any tort liability which may arise;
(d) the court should not in the face of the clarity of the disclaimers impose liability on the dealers as a matter of policy.

v *Indemnities and other techniques*

The exposure of the dealers to actions by investors in contract and tort arising from any misstatement in the information memorandum or other information materials can and should also be the subject of an appropriate indemnity clause in the Programme Agreement.

In addition, each dealer is authorised by an express clause to provide copies of the information memorandum and other documents (such as the annual report and accounts) to potential purchasers of the notes, and secondly, each dealer is authorised to make statements on behalf of the issuers to such potential investors. Such a clause serves two purposes.

First, if there are inaccuracies and misrepresentations in the information materials distributed to investors, it will enable a dealer who is sued to join the issuer as principal to defend any action brought against that dealer. Secondly, it also strengthens the assertion which may be made by the dealers that the information documents, including the memorandum, were passed on by the dealers merely as a conduit pipe, and that therefore they have made no representation whatsoever. The agency clause ties in with the notice in the information memorandum addressed to investors which usually reads as follows:

> 'The Dealers make no representation, express or implied, as to and accept no responsibility for, the accuracy or completeness of any of the information in this Information Memorandum, which information has been obtained from the Company and the Guarantor who have approved it and requested and authorised its delivery on their respective behalf.'

---

9 See the Misrepresentation Act 1967 s 2(1).
10 [1964] AC 465.
11 [1990] 2 AC 605, HL. For a detailed discussion see ch 3 above.

II US SECURITIES REGULATION AND BANKING LEGISLATION

1 US Securities Act 1933 and the Securities Exchange Act 1934

The US Securities Act 1933 and the US Securities and Exchange Act 1934 and regulations framed thereunder are potentially applicable to the issue of ECP and Euro Notes in London's Euro markets since commercial paper constitutes a 'security' for purposes of these statutes.[12]

The legal considerations concerning the applicability of US securities laws to Euro Commercial Paper are similar to those applicable in the case of Eurobonds, subject to what is said below. The reader is consequently referred to the detailed discussion on this subject in Part V.

Issues of Euro Commercial Paper as well as of Euro Notes have been effected in the past within the 'safe harbour' provided under Release 4708 of the SEC discussed in chapter 20. ECP may now be issued within the 'safe harbour' provided by Regulation S (discussed in chapter 21) to the registration provisions of the Securities Act 1933.[13]

In addition to Regulation S,[14] there are two further exemptions available to an issuer of ECP.

i *Securities Act 1933 ('SA 1933') s 3(a)(3)*

First, s 3(a)(3) of SA 1933 exempts commercial paper meeting the criteria specified therein from the registration provisions of SA 1933.[15] The exemption is for:

'Any note, draft bill of exchange or banker's acceptance which *arises out of the current transaction* or the proceeds of which have been or are to be used for current transactions and which has a maturity at the time of issuance of not exceeding nine months, exclusive of days of grace, or any renewal thereof the maturity of which is likewise limited.' (Emphasis added.)

The interpretation of this provision has been significantly influenced by the SEC's interpretative Release 33-4142 of 20 September 1961, and is discussed below. It will be noticed that the two elements necessary under s 3(a)(3) are first that the instrument should not 'at the time of issuance' have a maturity of more than nine months, and secondly, that it arises 'out of a current transaction'.

The maturity requirement does not usually cause any difficulty. However, difficulties arise where the notes or paper have an automatic 'roll-over' (ie are automatically renewed). The SEC in Release 33-4412 has stated that paper with such a characteristic will not qualify for exemption under s 3(a)(3). However, where there is provision for the reissue of an equivalent amount of paper on the maturity of paper which has already been in issue, s 3(a)(3)

---

12 See the Securities Act 1933 s 2 and the Securities Exchange Act 1934 s 3(a)(10) and chapter 19.
13 Due to the short maturity of ECP strict 'lock-up' procedures developed under Release 4708 for Eurobonds have not been used in respect of ECP.
14 See ch 21.
15 See on registration provisions ch 19.

would be capable of being satisfied. If the paper is repayable on demand, the SEC has expressed the view in the above Release that the provision of s 3(a)(3) will not be regarded as being satisfied.

The 'current transactions' requirement is more difficult to interpret. The SEC in Release 33-4412 stated that where paper is issued for the following purposes, the current transactions exemption is not satisfied, ie where the paper is to be or is:

> 'used for the discharge of existing indebtedness unless such indebtedness is itself exempt under section 3(a)(3); the purchase or construction of plant; the purchase of durable machinery or equipment; the funding of commercial real estate development or financing; the purchase of real estate mortgages or other securities; the financing of mobile homes or home improvements; or the purchase or establishment of a business enterprise.'

The difficult question, however, is whether the issue of paper needs to be directly referable to a financing need created by a current transaction. 'No action' letters issued by the SEC have established[16] that the SEC has adopted a balance sheet approach to the question whether a note issue is related to current transactions. This means that the proceeds from the sale of paper need not identifiably be related to or be shown to be used for a particular transaction; it is sufficient if 'commercial paper outstanding at any one time does not exceed the dollar amount of current transactions to be financed'.[17] Thus, inventories and accounts receivable on a corporate balance sheet may be financed by commercial paper issues.[18]

The SEC has also extended the concept of 'current transactions' by 'no action' letters from the activities of ordinary commercial corporations to include the lending activities of foreign banks and US bank holding companies[19] and insurance companies.[20] The 'current transactions' concept has also been extended by the SEC to cover cash management and arbitrage programmes by commercial and industrial companies.[1] Acquisition finance is, however, regarded by the SEC as being outside even the most liberal interpretation of the 'current transactions' exception and Release 33-4412 expressly excludes acquisition financing.

Foreign governments have also been regarded as being capable of falling within the 'current transactions' requirement, provided the proceeds are to be used for commercial purposes. Thus, in relation to the Kingdom of Denmark[2] and the Kingdom of Spain[3] the SEC took the view that if

---

16 See an excellent article by Johnson 'Legal Considerations in the Establishment of a United States Commercial Paper Programme' in *Commercial Paper* Euromoney Publications, Richard Felix edn, 1987 ch 4.
17 Johnson, above, p 39.
18 See the 'no action' letters cited in Johnson, above, p 39, especially Atlantic Richfield (available 22 July 1985), Westinghouse Credit Corporation (available 4 May 1985) and Renault Acceptance BV (available 26 May 1977).
19 See 'no action' letters cited in Johnson, above, at p 40, and Sun Trust Banks Inc (available 15 November 1985).
20 See Nationale–Nederlander NV 'no action' letter (available 28 August 1981).
1 See 'no action' letter in Kellogg Company (available 7 October 1983) and the Gillette Company (available 15 May 1984) both of which are discussed by Johnson, above.
2 'No action' available 13 May 1985; see Johnson, above, at p 45.
3 'No action' available 1 August 1985; see Johnson, above, at p 45.

the proceeds were being used to finance state enterprises the exception in s 3(a)(3) would be available.

In addition to the requirements laid down in s 3(a)(3) of the Act, the SEC in their interpretative Release 33-4412 have also stated that the legislative history of the Securities Act 1933 makes it clear that the exception in s 3(a)(3) applies 'only to prime quality commercial paper of a type not ordinarily purchased by the general public'.

Release 33-4412 also required that commercial paper be 'of a type eligible for discounting by Federal Reserve banks' but this requirement is no longer insisted on.[4]

'Prime quality' standard is taken to mean investment grade paper as rated by Standard & Poor's or Moody's or any other recognised rating agency.[5]

The requirement that the paper is of a 'type not ordinarily purchased by the general public' is regarded as satisfied if the paper is issued in individual denominations of US $100,000 or multiples, although Johnson[6] has pointed out that smaller denominations have sometimes sufficed.[7]

Little reliance has been placed on this exception in practice in the ECP markets due to the complexity of the definition of 'current transactions', and the recurring need in consequence for 'no action' letters.

ii *SA 1933 s 4(2): private placement exception*

Section 4(2) of SA 1933 contains an exception from registration for 'transactions by an issuer not involving any public offering'. The parameters of this exception are enumerated in detail in r 506 of Regulation D issued by the SEC. Essentially, it requires a placement of paper with major institutional investors referred to as 'accredited investors'.[8]

Rule 506 requires the following:

(a) The paper should not be issued by means of any form of general solicitation or general advertising whether by means of brochures, advertisements in journals, newspapers, radio or television, or by means of presentations and seminars where those attending have been invited by public advertising or public solicitation.
(b) The paper should be offered only to 'accredited investors' as defined in r 501(a) of Regulation D, which include major US institutional investors, US banks (both national and state), regulated insurance companies in the US, investment companies registered under the US Investment Company Act 1940, certain qualifying employee benefit plans

---

4 See letter dated 20 February 1980 to the General Counsel of the Board of Governors of the Federal Reserve System from the General Counsel of the SEC, cited in Johnson, above, at p 38.
5 See for a discussion of rating agencies: Brian de Caires *Rating Agencies* in Lucy Heller (ed) *Euro Commercial Paper* (Euromoney Publications, 1988).
6 Above, at p 38.
7 It appears that in the Merryl Lynch, Pierce Fenner and Smith Incorporated 'no action' letter (available 5 September 1972) denominations of US $25,000 sufficed: see Johnson, above, at p 38.
8 See r 501(a) of Regulation D.

and corporate investors purchasing US $150,000 or more for their own account.
(c) Reasonable care should be exercised to ensure that purchasers are acquiring the paper as principal and not as an 'underwriter' as defined in s 2(11) of the Securities Act 1933. Regulation D specifies that for purposes of establishing that 'reasonable care' was taken, reasonable enquiry should have been made that the purchasers were acquiring for their own account; that there is a legend on each note stating that the note has not been registered under the Securities Act of 1933 and may not be sold or otherwise transferred without registration under the Act except by or through a dealer in a transaction exempt from the registration requirements of that Act; that written disclosure is made to each purchaser that the notes have not been registered under the 1933 Act and that the notes cannot be resold unless registered under that Act or under an applicable exemption.

The real difficulty of using this exception is that the doctrine of 'integration' applied by the SEC, r 502(a) of Regulation D, in effect states that during a period of six months prior to commencement of an offering under Regulation D or during a six-month period after completion of a Regulation D offering, there must not be a public offering of securities of the same type or class. A public offering of a same or similar class of securities as a Regulation D offering may result in the two offerings being integrated and being considered a public offering. If integration is applied by the SEC the exemption under Regulation D would be lost.

It would seem that an issue of paper under s 3(a)(3) of the Securities Act 1933 during the six months either side of a Regulation D offering could result in the doctrine of integration being applied. This exposure has in practice resulted in issuers preferring not to rely on the exception in an international offering of ECP.

iii Overall

Due to the complexities and uncertainty surrounding the exceptions under s 3(a)(3) and Regulation D, the practice in the international markets for the purpose of avoiding breaches of US law has been to confine issues to the foreign offerings exception under Release 4708[9] in the past, and now to offerings falling within the exception in Regulation S discussed in chapter 21.

iv Exposure of dealers

Where an issue is effected under SA 1933 s 3(a)(3), a commercial paper dealer is also exposed to civil action under s 12(2) for any untrue or misleading statement contained in the information memorandum.[10]

The extent of the exposure of a dealer under s 12(2) is highlighted in

---

9   July 1964.
10 While s 12(2) refers to a 'prospectus', there is no doubt that an information memorandum would fall within the definition of a prospectus in s 2(10) of the 1933 Act.

the case of *Franklin Savings Bank of New York v Levy*.[11] The court held in effect that where the issuer of paper becomes insolvent or bankrupt prior to maturity, the dealer may be liable to actions in damages under s 12(1) for an implied misrepresentation that the paper was of prime quality.

The analysis of the court was that paper sold under s 3(a)(3) was impliedly represented to be of 'prime quality' by reference to SEC Release 33-4412. A dealer is accordingly deemed to have made such a representation by the sale of paper in reliance of s 3(a)(3). If it transpired that the issuer became insolvent soon after the issue of paper prior its maturity, the implied representation is probably false, and the dealer is liable under s 12(1) unless the dealer could prove that it had exercised reasonable care.

This analysis also has another ramification. If the issuer's insolvency prior to maturity of the notes establishes that the notes were not of 'prime quality' at issue within the meaning of Release 33-4412, the issue falls outside s 3(a)(3) and the dealer may then be exposed to potential damages for loss suffered by investors under s 12(1). Section 12(1), it will be remembered,[12] provides an action for damages to any person who has suffered loss in consequence of buying a security sold in violation of s 5 of the Securities Act 1933.

A dealer may also be exposed to liability under s 10(b) and r 10(b)-5 of the Securities and Exchange Act of 1934. Despite the fact that s 3(a)(3) of the 1934 Act expressly excludes from the definition of security any note which has a maturity of not more than nine months at issue, the US courts have held that s 10(b) and therefore r 10(b)-5 applies to commercial paper. The Court of Appeal for the Second Circuit in *Zeller v Bogue Electric Manufacturing Corp*[13] based this conclusion on SEC Release 33-4412 arguing that only commercial paper satisfying the criteria in the Release qualified for exemption under s 3(a)(10). Essentially, the court held that to fall within the exemption the paper had to be 'prime quality' commercial paper of a type not ordinarily purchased by the general public.[14]

In a case where an issuer becomes insolvent soon after the issue of paper there would therefore be potential liability under the ruling in *Zeller* because the paper would probably not be regarded as being of prime quality due to the ruling in *Franklin Savings Bank of New York v Levy*.[15]

2 The Glass-Steagall Act

The US Banking Act of 1933, in four key provisions, separated traditional commercial loan and banking activity from investment banking.[16] These provisions are referred to as the Glass-Steagall Act, and as the 'Glass-Steagall Wall'. This Act needs to be considered by US commercial banks or their foreign subsidiaries which act as dealers in the ECP market. Generally speak-

---

11 551 F 2d 521 (2nd Circ 1977).
12 See ch 19 above.
13 476 F 2d 795 (2nd Cir) cert denied 414 US 908 (1973).
14 The Court followed *Sanders v John Nuveen & Co* 463 F 2d 1075 (7th Cir) cert denied 409 US 1009 (1972).
15 See above.
16 S 16 (12 USC s 24 (Seventh)(1982)), s 20 (12 USC s 377 (1945)) s 21 (12 USC s 378)(1982)) and s 32 (12 USC s 78)(1945)). See ch 22 for a full discussion.

ing, due to the provisions of Regulation K[17] of the Board of the Federal Reserve there is no difficulty in a US commercial bank's investment banking affiliate participating in the placement of an ECP issue as a placing agent. The reader is referred to the detailed discussion in chapter 22 on this subject.

---

17 12 CFR 211.

CHAPTER 25
Note issuance facilities (NIFs) and revolving underwriting facilities (RUFs)[1]

Prior to the development of the Euro Commercial Paper Programme structure, there were two basic structures which were used to issue short-dated debt instruments of under one year in maturity. These were referred to by various acronyms but the most common were NIFs and RUFs. These structures are now used only infrequently in current practice.

The fundamental difference between a NIF and a RUF was whether or not there was an underwriting obligation on the part of any bank or securities dealer to purchase notes which could not be placed in the market-place or to make advances in lieu of unsold securities. Where there was no such underwriting commitment, the structure was referred to as a Note Issuance Facility (NIF). In the alternative structure, a bank or group of banks agreed to purchase the paper themselves in the event of a failure to place the issuer's notes with investors. This form is appropriately termed the 'revolving underwriting facility' or RUF, due to the underwriting obligation undertaken by the dealers(s). In a number of facilities, however, the position was not as clear-cut, either intentionally or due to inadvertent drafting.[2]

I NOTE ISSUANCE FACILITIES (NIFs)

In the classic structure for an uncommitted NIF, the issuer seeks to place its paper through the mechanism of a specially appointed 'tender panel' of securities dealers. The issuer will appoint a 'tender agent' or 'facility agent' or 'manager' whose function will be to request competitive bids from the tender panel members for the issuer's paper, whenever the issuer requires short-term funds.

Neither the tender panel nor the issuer are under any obligation to ask for or make bids, and the issuer is not under any obligation to accept any or all of the bids if and when made by the tender panel. If and when bids are made by the panel the issuer has the option of choosing the best bids

---

1 See generally, Bankson and Lee (eds) *Euro Notes* (Euromoney Publications, 1985). The Bank of England's Quarterly Bulletin, May 1991, indicates that in 1988 there were US$10.6bn of RUFs/NIFs while in 1990 the value was US$3.0bn in value (see p 241).
2 This point is made clearly and persuasively by Beaumont 'The differences between NIFs and RUFs' in IFLR, June 1985, and reiterated by him in ch 7 of *Euro Notes*, above.

472 *Note issuance facilities (NIFs) and revolving underwriting facilities (RUFs)*

or none at all. The purpose of this structure is to give the issuer the best possible pricing for its paper which reduces the issuer's borrowing costs.

The mechanics which resulted from this structure were that:

(a) When the issuer required funds it would request the manager or tender agent to notify it of the prices at which the issuer's notes could be placed.

(b) The manager or tender agent would activate the tender panel by notifying the dealers that they should make tender offers; this is called a 'tender request notice'; and would usually be made four days prior to the completed issue of notes.

(c) The dealers would then notify their tender offers or bids to the 'manager' or 'tender agent' by telephone and/or confirmed telex latest on the third business day prior to the issue of the notes. The tender is made in specified form: the bid must be for an amount which is no larger than the amount agreed between the parties as the maximum amount of the issuer's notes which may be outstanding at any one time; it must be in multiples of 500,000 or one million of the currency of issue and must specify the interest rate or discount at which the dealer is prepared to purchase notes.

(d) The manager or tender agent will notify the issuer of these bids.

(e) The issuer accepts those bids which it considers attractive and rejects the others. The tender agent notifies each dealer of the acceptance or rejection of its tender offer.

(f) The issuer is then required to transfer definitive notes to Euroclear or Cedel and the subscribers to the notes will transfer same day funds to the issuer's account, outside the UK due to the requirements of the Banking Act 1987 discussed previously.

A number of points need to be made. First, under NIF structures, unlike in the case of the modern ECP Programme Agreement, actual or definitive notes were printed and issued on most issues of notes. Permanent global notes were generally not issued. The difficult questions with regard to the legal nature of the rights arising under a global note in a paperless ECP issue did not arise in this type of structure.[3] However, since all the definitives are delivered to the clearing houses, Euroclear and Cedel, and all trades are cleared and settled on the books of Euroclear or Cedel in the same way as for Eurobonds, legal issues similar to those discussed in respect of Eurobonds arise in respect of the negotiability of such Euro Notes and the reader is referred to chapter 9 on Eurobonds.

The fact that definitive notes are issued under a NIF structure means that there may be a negotiable instrument in existence if it is recognised as such by mercantile custom. Consequently, it is capable of conferring rights of action on the holder against the issuer under English law and there is no need therefore for a deed poll or deed of covenant to be executed in favour of subsequent purchasers of the notes.

Secondly, once the issuer has agreed to issue notes at the best prices offered, the tender agent or manager may purchase the aggregate of such notes as principal at the prices quoted by the successful bidders and then resell the

---

3 See the discussion in ch 23.

notes as principal to those dealers who tendered successful bids; alternatively, he could offer the notes as agent of the issuer.

Where the tender agent or manager is acting as principal in the transaction, the tender panel is required to make the bids on request to the manager or tender agent. The latter has an absolute discretion by virtue of the agreement between panel members and the manager or the tender agent whether to accept any of the bids or to reject any or all of the bids. However, in the agreement between the manager and the issuer, the manager is obliged to accept such bids as the issuer directs. The practical effect, therefore, is that there is no difference contractually whether the manager acts as agent or principal.

Thirdly, the manager or tender agent himself could make tenders for the notes, on the third business day prior to the date of issue of the notes. However, since the tender agent would have all the information concerning the bids from the tender panel at this stage, he is usually entitled to subscribe for only 10% of the total aggregate of notes to be issued. Tender panel members must be notified by the tender agent if the latter decides to exercise this right.

Fourthly, in addition to the tender agent, it is necessary to appoint:

(a) an issue agent to authenticate the issue, and transfer of the definitive notes on behalf of the issuer; and
(b) a paying agent who would make the payments on behalf of the issuer on maturity of the notes, and receive payments on behalf of the issuer; and
(c) a reference agent who would determine the LIBOR rate applicable (on a final and binding basis as between the parties) if the notes are to carry interest.

All these agents are agents of the issuer and have no obligations towards the panel members or sub-purchasers from such panel members. These agents are appointed by, and their functions specified in, a separate agreement between the issuer and such agents.

The manager or tender agent usually takes on the duties of reference agent, issue agent and paying agent (or at least one of the paying agents if there are more than one) and will be remunerated accordingly. All the points made previously with regard to an issuing and paying agent in an ECP Programme are equally applicable to the issuing and paying agent in a Euro Note issue.

Fifthly, the regulatory issues under the Banking Act 1987 and FSA 1986 are the same as those discussed in the context of an ECP Programme.[4] However, one comment needs to be made with regard to the need for a prospectus under Part III of the Companies Act 1985 so long as it remains in force. It is important to ensure that no document containing an offer of securities or by which such an offer is made comes into existence. To achieve this objective the offer telex in respect of the notes should emanate from the tender panel to the tender agent or manager and not the other way; it must be an offer to purchase.

The position of the tender panel and the procedure for tendering bids

---

4 See ch 24 above.

is usually provided for in a separate Tender Panel Agreement or Dealer agreement.

Since the tender panel members are under no legal obligation to make any bids if they do not wish to, there is relatively little exposure on their part to the financial prospects of the issuer on a medium or long-term basis. Consequently, protective clauses in the form of conditions precedent or representation and warranties are generally unnecessary. The tender panel members do, however, take the risk of the bankruptcy of the issuer once they have subscribed the notes, until the notes are resold by them or until maturity if the notes are held to maturity by the tender panel members. They are not protected during this period (potentially up to one year) by cross-default or other covenants usually found in Eurobonds[5] or syndicated loans.[6]

It is also necessary to prevent breaches of:

(a) the prospectus provisions in the Companies Act 1985 or Part V of FSA 1986 (when it repeals and replaces Part III of the Companies Act 1985);
(b) the advertising provisions in s 57 of FSA 1986

during the period of offer. Consequently, it is necessary that the dealer agreement (or tender panel agreements) contain appropriate selling restrictions governing the sub-sales of the notes by the tender panel members.

In order to prevent a breach of the prospectus provisions of Part III of the Companies Act 1985 or Part V of FSA 1986, it is necessary to restrict sub-sales to professionals as defined in s 79(2) or in the Regulations to be framed under Part V of the FSA respectively. The prohibition will thus take the form of a covenant and a representation that the dealers will not make any offer of notes which would violate these provisions.

As far as s 57 of FSA 1986 is concerned, it is necessary to distribute the information memorandum only to persons falling within art 9(3) of the Financial Services Act 1986 (Investment Advertisement)(Exemptions) Order 1988[7] to enable the dissemination of the information memorandum issued by a non-authorised person without breaching the prohibition in s 57. Once again the tender panel members must be subject to a legal obligation and be required to represent that they will not circulate any document except to such persons.

To satisfy both the provisions in the Companies Act 1985 and FSA 1986 discussed above, it may also be necessary to confine any Reuter screen quotation in respect of the notes if the Reuter screen pages are available to persons who may not be professionals for purposes of s 79 of the Companies Act or the Regulations to be framed under FSA Part V, as well as persons who do not fall within art 9(3) of the Order for purposes of FSA 1986.

Finally, it will be necessary to impose selling restrictions in respect of sales within the US and to US persons as discussed previously[8] to prevent violations of US securities laws.

---

5 See ch 5 above.
6 See chs 10 and ch 11 above.
7 SI 1988/316.
8 See ch 23.

1 The manager and tender panel members

The manager is exposed to legal liability to the tender panel in respect of:

(a) the accuracy of the information in the information memorandum which is circulated to tender panel members; and
(b) the validity and enforceability of the notes which it has sold.

The manager may protect itself in respect of (a) above by appropriate clauses in the information memorandum as discussed in respect of ECP issues and also by an express clause in the tender panel agreements which requires the dealers to make their own credit evaluation and not to rely on the information disseminated; a representation would also be obtained that they have not so relied by virtue of each purchase of notes.

With regard to (b) an express disclaimer may suffice.[9] The manager may also be exposed to further liability in respect of documents reaching the hands of sub-purchasers, and once again it may be possible to rely on the notices in the information memoranda discussed in respect of ECP issuers.[10] However, there is still some risk that a paternalistic court may impose fiduciary duties on the manager to ensure both the accuracy of informational materials as well as the legal validity of the notes for the benefit of the end investors.[11] It is submitted, however, that a court ought not to do so as a matter of policy, given the sophisticated nature of the investors in the Euro Note market; in this context it needs to be remembered that the notes are issued usually in multiples of half a million dollars or more.

2 The tender agent and the facility agreement

While there is little need to protect the position of the tender panel members, the position of the tender agent is different and requires protection by appropriate legal mechanisms. The relationship between the tender agent (or manager) and the issuer is regulated by the so-called Facility Agreement. Where the manager purchases the notes as principal his commitment is to purchase notes whenever the issuer accepts bids from the tender panel dealers. This obligation continues during the period of the 'facility' which is a fixed term as in the case of a medium-term loan agreement. Since the Facility Agreement enables the issuer to ask for and accept bids and issue paper on a continuous basis during the life of the facility, the manager needs to be protected in a manner similar to syndicate banks in a syndicated revolving facility.[12]

There is therefore a clear need to ensure that (a) the issuer is duly incorporated, and (b) has the necessary corporate power to issue the notes, and (c) that all necessary authorisations and consents external to the issuer have been obtained prior to the first issue and each fresh issue thereafter of the

---

9 See on similar disclaimers in syndicated loans ch 3.
10 See pp 462–464 above.
11 See the opinion of the court in *UBAF Ltd v European American Banking Corpn* [1984] QB 713 which deals with the position of an agent bank in a syndicated loan.
12 See ch 5 above.

notes. This is achieved by conditions precedent similar to those in bond issues[13] and syndicated loans.[14]

It is also necessary to ensure that the manager is under no obligation to make payment for notes it has purchased in accordance with the procedures set up, unless the manager has received funds from tender panel members who have tendered successful bids.

In addition to these conditions precedent, it is necessary that the legal ability of the issuer to enter into the Facility Agreement and issue the notes is made a representation and warranty of the issuer for the reasons discussed previously in respect of loans and bonds.[15] The validity of the legal obligations in the Facility Agreement and those contained in the notes should be a representation and warranty.

The accuracy of the information disseminated in the information memorandum and informational documents (including the latest report and accounts) must also be made a representation and warranty of the issuer prior to each issue of the notes and a condition precedent of each issue. This is fundamentally important to a manager despite any protective notices contained in the information memorandum similar to those discussed previously with regard to ECP issues. If there is any civil liability arising due to the inaccuracy of information, the manager can always claim from the issuer any loss for which the manager is held liable on the basis of such representations and warranties.

The right to terminate the Facility Agreement must also be carefully considered. This should include at least a right to terminate for:

(a) breach by the issuer of any representation, covenant or warranty in the Facility Agreement;
(b) failure by the issuer to pay any amount due on any note issued in pursuance of the facility;
(c) a cross-default clause[16] covering failure by the issuer to pay any other indebtedness when due, or breach of covenant under any other loan agreement.

It is also necessary to have an information covenant obliging the issuer to provide the manager with annual and semi-annual audited accounts and any other information which may reasonably be required by the manager for circulation to the tender panel members.

A negative pledge is generally regarded as unnecessary. It is essential, however, that where the issuer or any of its major subsidiaries creates a pledge charge or security interest over its assets, or any part of it, the manager should have the right to be informed of such an event and have the power to transmit such information to the tender panel, so that future issues of notes may be purchased (or not as the case may be) on the basis of such information.

---

13 See ch 10.
14 See ch 5.
15 See chs 5 and 10.
16 See ch 5 above.

II REVOLVING UNDERWRITING FACILITIES (RUFs)[17]

A RUF is essentially a NIF with one fundamental difference. In a NIF, the manager or arranger does not undertake an underwriting commitment, and the same is true of a dealer in an ECP Programme. If the notes or paper cannot be sold, the manager or ECP dealer may lose face in the markets but he is under no legal liability. On the other hand, in a RUF the banks and dealers who arrange the facility agree not only to place the notes of the issuer with investors but also agree that if they cannot do so they will purchase the notes themselves. In some cases, the underwriting obligation is either to purchase the notes or to make loans available to the issuer in lieu of purchasing unsold notes.

Due to this fundamental difference the underwriting banks and dealers will be paid an underwriting fee. The advantage to the issuer of the underwritten nature of the facility is that he has in effect a 'stand-by' committed credit facility which he may utilise when he requires funds. Due to this structure the issuer would also have the advantage of an assurance that during the life of the facility, he would have the ability to borrow funds (by issuing notes), and to repay and reborrow (by redeeming notes and issuing again), regardless of market conditions. The issuer in an uncommitted NIF or an ECP Programme would not have this assurance.

The underwriting banks are in a position similar to the managers of a Eurobond issue in the sense that they have a 'place or buy' obligation in relation to the notes. However, there is a vital difference between the legal position of managers of a Eurobond issue and the managers of a RUF. In a Eurobond issue, the underwriting obligation terminates on the closing date of the issue which is no longer than two weeks from launch.[18] The underwriting obligation of RUF managers continues for the full period of the facility and these periods were around ten years for the best issuers in practice. In this respect the legal position of the managers has much in common with that of syndicate managers in a revolving syndicated loan facility. To this extent the RUF is a truly hybrid financing structure. It provides for the issue of debt securities with the benefit of an underwriting obligation of a group of banks and dealers similar to those undertaken by managers in a Eurobond issue;[19] while at the same time the underwriting obligation also contains in effect a commitment to provide funds over the entire period of the facility if notes cannot be placed, and this period could even be ten years or more, so that it is similar to the commitment provided by a syndicate of banks in a syndicated revolving term loan.[20]

The similarity of the position of the underwriting banks in a RUF with that of syndicate banks in a revolving syndicated term loan has the conse-

---

17 See Bankson and Lee (eds) *Euro Notes* (Euromoney Publications, 1985) chs 2 and 3.
18 See ch 8.
19 See ch 10 above.
20 See also O'Kane in ch 7 of Bankson and Lee *Euro Notes*, where he points out that generally the best sovereign credits obtain commitments of ten years or more as in the case of Spain's RUF in 1984. He also points out that the commitment fees charged by banks reflect their long-term commitment. According to O'Kane, Sweden paid 1/8% per annum for its massive US $4bn RUF in September 1983. For other maturity examples see O'Kane at p 45.

quence that the legal relationship between the underwriting banks in a RUF and the issuer of notes has a legal structure which is similar to the legal relationship created between the borrower and the syndicate banks by a syndicated revolving term loan agreement.

Thus the conditions precedent to the first issue of notes are applicable to each subsequent issue. Similarly the representations and warranties are applicable to each issue of notes. The representations and warranties concerning the accuracy of the issuer's financial statements thus refer to the accuracy of the issuer's latest audited financial statements at the date of each issue of notes. The underwriting obligation in respect of each issue of notes is consequently made to depend on a number of factors:

(a) the accuracy of the latest financial information;
(b) the legality and continuing validity of all agreements;
(c) the continuing existence of corporate authority to issue notes;
(d) the continued availability of external consents and authorisations such as exchange control consent or central bank authorisation in the issuer's country;
(e) the absence of any changes in applicable regulations which would make performance of the issuer's obligations unlawful under the agreement;
(f) the absence of any breaches of covenants under the facility agreement;
(g) the continuing absence of any withholding tax in the home country of the issuer.

Many of these provisions are outside the control of the issuer, but all of these occurrences would affect the market for the issuer's paper adversely, and consequently would increase the probability that the issuer's paper may not be capable of being placed. In turn, these events increase the probability that the underwriting obligations of the banks and dealers will be triggered under the Facility Agreement. As Beaumont points out:

> 'It is the basic expectation on the part of the underwriters not to be left with unwanted Notes that result in a low underwriting fee and a low guaranteed yield on Paper actually taken up by them pursuant to their underwriting commitment. There is of course nothing to prevent the underwriters when negotiating the documentation from agreeing to provisions which involve a greater risk of being left with Paper but they would then no doubt wish to negotiate better remuneration.'[1]

In the event that the obligations of the underwriting banks are triggered at a time when interest rate quotations are not available on the London market, or deposits in the currency of issue are not available for any reason, it is necessary to have a Euro market disaster clause to release the underwriting banks from their obligation in respect of that particular issue of notes.[2]

The procedures for the placement of the notes which are to be issued under a RUF are the same as in the case of an uncommitted NIF. It may be effected by one of the managing underwriters or a group of dealers who undertake the duty to place notes in the market or, as is commonly the case, through a tender panel. The underwriting banks could and usually

---

1 In ch 7 of Bankson and Lee *Euro Notes*.
2 See ch 5 above on Euro market disaster clauses.

are also members of the tender panel where such a mechanism is being used. This, however, creates a commercial problem. The underwriting banks agree to underwrite a proportion of unsold notes up to a certain specified amount. Thus in a US $100m RUF an underwriting bank may agree to underwrite 10% of all unsold notes up to a maximum of US $10m. Now supposing this bank (A) is also a member of the tender panel, that it submits bids for US $10m of notes and this bid is accepted by the issuer; suppose further that US $20m of notes have not been sold; suppose also that other banks who are members of both the underwriting group and the tender panel have made unsuccessful bids. The question arises whether bank A should be required to take $2m of unsold notes in addition to the $10m for which it successfully bid. From a commercial point of view, banks in this position have insisted that their underwriting obligation should not be triggered, if they have bid successfully for notes as a member of the tender panel whereas other banks in the same position have not bid successfully (say, due to unrealistic pricing) and have triggered underwriting obligations. To deal with this problem, complicated formulae have to be inserted into the facility agreement which provide for the underwriting commitments to be varied in the case of underwriting banks who have bid successfully for notes as members of the tender panel.

If tender panel members are not to be subject to underwriting obligations, their position must be expressed in clear language. Beaumont[3] has given an example of the sort of problem which may arise if care is not taken to use clear language:

> 'Under the proposed agreement, each Tender Panel member undertook, on each occasion that a tranche of Notes was to be issued, to bid for at least a minimum proportion of such tranche, failing which it would be treated as having tendered for such minimum proportion at the lowest yield actually tendered by any Tender Panel member. This was a legally binding commitment, but how far did it go? Did it imply an obligation to tender a reasonable bid or merely a bona fide bid (however out of line with the bids tendered by others)? Would a tender at a very high yield, not then representative of market rates for the particular Issuer and designed to ensure that the Tender Panel member would not be successful in the tender (perhaps because of genuine change in its perception of the Issuer's creditworthiness), be in compliance with its obligation to bid? Might it, on the contrary, trigger the fall-back provision applying in the absence of a valid bid (that the Tender Panel member be treated as having bid at the lowest yield), particularly given the description of the standby as a 'committed' facility? If so, this deeming provision would apply at the very worst time for the Tender Panel member – when for some reason, which in reality would be a good commercial reason, the Paper was unattractive at any price. This result would be close to an underwriting commitment, though the conditions precedent did not deal with a material adverse change since the base date in the Issuer's financial position, nor was there any form of remuneration for such a commitment. Whatever the commercial terms were, as agreed between the Issuer and the arranger, the Tender Panel members' risks and obligations did not emerge in the documentation as clearly as they might and perhaps should have done.'

---

3   In *Euro Notes*, ch 7.

Index

Acquisitions,
   proper law of contract, and, 41–42
'Act of State' doctrine, 38–40
   appreciation, 40
   meaning in English law, 39–40
   proper law of contract, and, 38–40
Advertised securities,
   meaning, 346
Advertisements, 297–310
   approval, 304
   Companies Act 1985 Part II, 308–310
      repeal, 309
   exempt persons, 303–304
   Financial Services Act 1986, and, 297–310
   FSA 160 prohibition, 305–308
      'advertisement offering securities,' 306
      consequences of contravention, 307
      'primary offer', 306
      'secondary offer', 306–307
   'investment advertisements', 298–301
      exceptions, 301–304
   'issued in the UK', 298–301
      exceptions, 301–304
   listing particulars, consisting of, 301–302
   listing particulars, in connection with, 331–333
   meaning, 297
   misleading statements, 314–316.
      see also MISLEADING STATEMENTS
   prohibition in FSA s. 57, 298–304
   regulation of, 297–310
   unlisted Eurobond issues, and, 305
Agent bank, 58–67
   certification of compliance with conditions precedent by borrower, 58–59
   Chinese Wall, and, 64
   debtor and creditor relationship with syndicate, 60
   default, and, 61–64
      'actual knowledge', 62
      express clause, 62–63

Agent bank—*contd*
   default, and—*contd*
      effectiveness, 63–64
      other than payment of interest and principal, 63
   discretion to call default on own motion, 62
   duties as paying agent, 59–61
   duty to act on occurrence of default, 61–64
   exposure of borrower to insolvency of, 59–60
   failure to transfer funds to members of syndicate, 60
   fiduciary as, 64–67
      clauses seeking to negative existence of duty, 67
      conflict of duties, 66–67
      conflict of interest and duty, 65–66
      core of duty, 65
      disclosure of material facts, 66
      transfer of information, 67
   lead manager as, 58–67
   'monitoring' loan covenants, 61
   power to call default, 61–62
   times of transfer of funds, 59
   trustee, declaration as, 60–61
Asset sales,
   types of, 104–105
Assignments, 106–107
   'benefit of agreement' clause, and, 112–113
   confidentiality, and, 111
   equitable, 106–107
   Financial Services Act 1986, and, 134–137
   implied terms, and, 111
   legal, 106–107
   maturity stripping, and, 114
   notice of, 110–111
   obligations transferred, 109–110
      prohibition against, 112
   rescheduling, and, 113–114
   risk of default, and, 109

Assignments—*contd*
  set–off, and, 114
  sub–participation compared, 109–114
Associated securities
  meaning, 348

Basle Convergence Agreement, 115
Bond instruments
  negotiability,
    proper law of contract, and, 40
Bonds with equity warrants, 274–278
  deed poll, 276–277
  issue of shares, 277–278
    Agency Agreement, and, 278
  nature of warrant, 274–275
  subscription right, 275–276
    conditions precedent to, 277
    procedure for exercise, 277
Buying and selling,
  meaning, 136

Chinese Wall,
  consequence of, 64
Choice of law, 16–25
  certainty under legal documents, and, 20–23
    construction of contracts, 22–23
    subscription agreement in bond issue, 21
    syndicated loan, 21
  commercial factors, 16–25
  conceptual sophistication of system, 23
  familiarity, 24–25
  forum of potential litigation, 23–24
  freedom of choice under prospective proper law, 17–20. *See also* PARTY AUTONOMY
  English law, 17–19
  language, 23
  legal factors, 16–25
  'party autonomy', 17. *See also* PARTY AUTONOMY
  result predictability under legal documents, and, 20–23
Cold calling, 310–314
  business investors, 313–314
  market counterparties, 313
  meaning, 310
  non-private customers, and, 312
  non-private investors, and, 313
  overseas person, and, 311–312
  private customers, and, 312
  professional investors, 314
  regulation of, 310–314
Collective Investment Schemes, 130–134
  business other than investment business, and, 133
  complex security structures, and, 134
  conditions for, 130
  'contributions of the participants', 131–132
  day to day control, and, 131
  exceptions, 132–133

Collective Investment Schemes—*contd*
  'pooling', 132
  practical consequences, 133–134
  'property', 130–131
Company,
  power of directors to bind, 28–30
Construction of contracts,
  conflicting approaches, 22–23
Convertible Eurobonds, 251–278
  Equity convertibles. *See* EQUITY CONVERTIBLES
Corporate capacity,
  proper law of the contract, and, 27–34

Debenture
  meaning, 125–127
  whether syndicated loan constitutes, 125–127
Deposit
  meaning, 450–451
Deposit-taking business,
  meaning, 451–452
Directors,
  power to bind company, 28–30
Disposal,
  meaning, 136
Domestic bond issue, 147–149

Equity convertibles, 253–274
  attractions, 254–256
    investors, to, 255–256
    issues, to, 254–255
  'call option', and, 254
  conditions precedent to conversion, 272–273
  conversion period, 254
  conversion premium, 253
  conversion price, 253
  conversion privilege, 253, 256–262
    acceleration notices, 269
    additional notice provisions, and, 268
    adjustment of conversion price, and, 263–264
    allotment of 'equity securities', and, 272
    availability of unauthorised unissued capital, 270–271
    'call premium', and, 257
    capital maintenance, and, 272
    conflicting objectives of issuer and bond holder, 256–258
    contractual techniques, 262
    corporate action of issuer, and, 258–262
    corporate devices not caught by anti-dilution or notice provisions, 266–267
    distribution of corporate assets, and, 259
    distributions to shareholders prior to conversion in equal rights, 269
    issue of further shares by issuer, 258
    issue of shares at price below conversion price, 259

Equity convertibles—contd
  maintenance of listing, 269
  merger of corporate entities, and, 259–261
  notice provisions, 264–266
  prohibitions in relation to, 270
  protecting, 262–272
  subdivision of shares by company, 258
  takeover of issuer by hostile takeover bid, 261–262
  timing of conversion, 256–257
  transfer of assets of issuer, and, 267
  unusually large dividend distributions, 259
 conversion procedure, 272–273
 currency conversion, 253–254
 financial features, 253–254
 low coupon, 253
 right to dividends on conversion, 273–274
 right to interest on conversion, 273–274
Equity warrant. See BONDS WITH EQUITY WARRANTS
'Euro' bond markets, 3
 growth of, 8–10
Eurobonds, 143 et seq.
 advertising of issues,
  UK regulation, 297–316. See also ADVERTISEMENTS
 allotment, 157–158
 background, 145–149
 'call options', with, 216
 characteristics, 161–162
 closing of issue, 158–159
 commodity linked, 217
 conflict of laws, and, 165–169
  choice of law clause, and, 168
  issues, 166
  proprietary aspects of bonds instrument, 167
  'several laws' approach, 166
  single proper law expressed on face of instrument, 167
  warehousing with 'common depository', and, 167–168
 convertible. See CONVERTIBLE EUROBONDS
 covenants in instrument, 198–201
  level of protection, 200–201
 default acceleration, 204–213
  rationale for trustee control, 212–213
 default enforcement, 204–213
  rationale for trustee control, 212–213
 defaults, events of, 202–203
  cross-default provision, 202
 domestic bond issue, and, 147–149
 early redemption provisions, 195–196
 efficacy of 'no action' clause, 210–212
  early English case law, 210
  US case law, 210–211
  US policy, and, 211
 equity and other assets, linked to, 217
 equity convertibles, 217

Eurobonds—contd
 equity warrants, with, 217
 extendable, 197–198, 216
 'flip-flop', 215
 foreign bond issue, and, 147–149
 governing law, 161–176
 'grey market' trading, 155–156
 holder,
  legal relationship with issuer, 193–217
 holder control of trustee powers, 207–210
  exercise of discretion by trustee, and, 207–209
  judicial review of trustee's discretion, 209–210
 holder meetings, 222–223
 impact of trust deed on holder rights, 204–205
 impact of trustee on holder rights, 204–205
 incorporation by reference of terms of charterparty, and, 206
 interest, payment of, 193–195
  LIBOR, and, 194
  minimum level, 194
  taxation, and, 198
 interest rate, 213–215
  drop-lock FRNs, 214
  floating to fixed rate convertibles, 214
  FRNs, 213–214
  RRNs, 215
 zero coupon bonds, 214
 investment bank's perspective, 146–147
 investor's perspective, 146
 issue,
  fiscal agents, role of, 218–223. See also FISCAL AGENTS
  trustees, role of, 218–223
 issue procedures, 149–160
  'bought deal', 151
  development of, 149–150
  launch, 152–160
  mandate, 152
  pre-price deal, 150–151
  legal relationship with holder, 193–217
 issuer's perspective, 145–146
 launch, 152–160
  draft legal documents, 154
  'invitation telex', 152–153
  IPMA Recommendations, 153
  offering circular, 154–155
  prospectus, 154–155
 legal framework of marketing and distribution, 177–192. See also MARKETING AND DISTRIBUTION OF EUROBONDS
 legal relationship between issuer and holder, 193–217
 limitation period for actions in respect of principal, 203–204
 listing. See LISTING OF EUROBONDS
 'lock-up' period, 159–160
 mandatory early redemption, 196

Eurobonds—*contd*
  marketing of issues,
    UK regulation, 297–316. *See also* ADVERTISEMENTS
  matters which must appear on face of bond, 162
  maturity, 215–216
  negative pledge covenant, 199–201
    scope of, 200
  negotiability, 161–176
    characteristics, 162
    doors to, 163–165
    Euroclear/Cedel Systems, 169–174. *See also* EUROCLEAR/CEDEL CLEARANCE SYSTEMS
    negotiable instrument, as, 164–165
    promissory note, as, 164
  obligations arising on instrument, 193–204
  optional early redemption, 195–196
    'call' options, 195
    'put' options, 195–196
  pari passu covenant, 199
  perpetual, 215
  principal, payment of, 193–195
    taxation, and, 198
  purchase fund, subject to, 216
  purchase, fund, with, 197
  'put options', with, 216
  'ramping', 158
  redemption, 215–216
  retractable, 197–198, 216
  rights arising on instrument, 193–204
  serial notes, 216
  'short squeezes', 158
  signing, 156
    agreement between managers, 157
    selling group agreement, 157
    subscription agreement, 156
  sinking fund, subject to, 216
  sinking fund, with, 196–198
  stabilisation, 155–156
  temporary global bond (TGB). *See* TEMPORARY GLOBAL BOND
  trust deed provisions restricting individual holder rights,
    enforceability, 205–207
  trustees. *See* TRUSTEES UNDER EUROBOND TRUST DEEDS
  types of, 213–217
  warrants, with, 251–278
Euroclear/Cedel clearance systems, 169–174
  bailee, position of, 173
  English law, 172
  intentions of issuers and purchasers, 172–173
  legal issues, 171–174
  market practice, 169
  mechanics of transfer, 169–170
  rights and liabilities of parties, 171–172
Euro commercial paper, 435 *et seq.*
  Banking Act 1987, 449–457

Euro commercial paper—*contd*
  prohibition on taking of 'deposits', 449–452
    acceptance of deposit 'in the United Kingdom', 452
    deposit, meaning, 450–451
    'deposit-taking business', 451–452
  characteristics, 438
  Companies Act 1985, 457–459
    prospectus provisions, 457–459
  Control of Borrowing Order, 461
  debenture, whether, 439
  deed poll, 446–448
  exempt transactions Regulations, 453–455
    conditions to be satisfied under, 453–455
    who may issue, 453
  Financial Services Act 1986, 459–461
    advertising, 460–461
    authorisation, need for, 459–460
    unsolicited calls, 461
  global note, 446–448
  information memorandum, 461–464
    Banking Act 1987, s.35, 462–463
    contract law, liability in, 463–464
    Financial Services Act 1986, 463
    indemnities, 464
    misstatements, liability for, 461–464
    tort, liability in, 464
  Issuing and Paying Agency Agreement, 445–446
    protective clauses, 446
    repayment, 446
  legal documents, 442–448
  market for, 440–441
  meaning, 437–440
  procedure in respect of programme, 441–442
  programme agreement, 442–444
    termination provisions, 444
  prohibition on 'deposit advertisements', 455–457
  regulation of, 449–470
  requirements, 438
  structure in respect of programme, 441–442
  UK securities regulation, 449–463
  unsolicited calls, 457
  US legislation, 465–470
    Glass Steagall Act, 469–470
    Securities Act 1933, 465–469
      exposure of dealers, 468–469
      overall, 468
      private placement exception, 467–468
Eurocurrency, 2–3
  development of markets, 5–8
Eurodollars,
  meaning, 6
Euro notes, 435 *et seq. See also* EURO COMMERCIAL PAPER
Euro-securities, 148–149
Exchange contract,
  meaning, 36

Exchange control regulations, 34–37
International Monetary Fund Agreement, and, 35–37
'involving the currency of that member state', 36–37
proper law of contract, and, 34–37

Fiduciary,
agent bank as, 64–67
Financial Services Act 1986, 124–134, 283 *et seq.*
advertisements. *See* ADVERTISEMENTS
assignment, and, 134–137
investment business, and, 135–137
'authorisation', 283–296
'investment business, 284–289. *See also* INVESTMENT BUSINESS
collective investment schemes, 130–134. *See also* COLLECTIVE INVESTMENT SCHEMES
'debenture', 125–127
investment advertisements, 129–130
'investment business', and, 127–129. *See also* INVESTMENT BUSINESS
loan sales by traditional methods, and, 138
novation, and, 134–137
investment business, and, 135–137
offshore entities, 290–296
'overseas person', 290–296
'arranging deals in investments', 292
customers solicited in way not contravening provisions of Act, 293–296
draft EC Directives, 295–296
exception for transactions 'with or through' certain persons, 291–292
law governing, 290–291
marketing material, 294–295
unsolicited transactions, 293–296
para 2 or para 3 'investment', 124–127
sale of loan assets, and, 134–139
sub-participations, 137–138
syndicated loans, and, 124–134
TLCs, and, 138–139
TLIs, and, 138–139
TPCs, and, 138–139
unsolicited calls, 129–130
Fiscal agents, 218–223
bond holder meetings, 222–223
bond holders, position of, 221–222
delivery of bonds, 218–219
Eurobonds, and, 218–223
principal paying agent, 219–220
redemption of bonds, 220
replacement of bonds, 220–221
role of, 218–223
Foreign bond issue, 147–149
Forum,
choice of, 23–24

Glass Steagall Act, 141–142, 427–436
applicability to commercial paper, 430–433
rationale for provisions, 429–430
section 16, 427
section 20, 427–428
section 21, 428
section 32, 428
Governing law, 13 *et seq.*
nature of, 15–42
necessity for, 15–16
scope of, 15–42
Illegality,
subsequent to contract,
proper law of contract, and, 30–34

Information Memorandum, 48–55
contents, 48
liability of lead manager, and, 48–55
common law of tort, 49
contractual clauses, 51–54
contractual provisions, 54–55
disclaimers, 51–54
market practice, 51
negligence, and, 49
Unfair Contract Terms Act 1977, and, 52–53
Insider dealing,
stabilisation, and. *See* STABILISATION
Interest Equalisation Tax (I ET)
imposition in US, 9
International bond issues, regulations under UK laws, 279 *et seq.*
International bonds, 143 *et seq. See also* EUROBONDS
International Capital Markets,
participation by US commercial banks in, 427–436
regulation of, 279 *et seq.*
International finance
meaning, 2
traditional forms, 1–2
International financial market, 1–12
centre of, 10–11
description, 1–5
London, development in, 5–11
International Monetary Fund Agreement
exchange control regulations, and, 35–37
International Primary Markets Association (IPMA)
launch of Eurobonds, and, 153
International securities business,
meaning, 287–288
International securities self-regulating organisation,
meaning, 288
International syndicated loans, 43 *et seq. See also* SYNDICATED LOANS
Investment advertisement
meaning, 298–299, 300
Investment business, 127–129, 284–289

Investment business—*contd*
  advice, 128
  'arranging' loans, 127–128
  borrower, 128–129
  carried on in the UK, 289
  execution of documents, 127–128
  Financial Services Act 1986, under, 284–289
  'issue' of Eurobonds, and, 286–287
  listing on stock exchange, and, 287
  meaning, 284
  provision of facilities for trading in Eurobonds, 287
  specified activities, 285–286

Lead manager
  agent bank, as, 58–67
  due care and diligence, need for, 54
  information memorandum, and, 48–55. *See also* INFORMATION MEMORANDUM
  liability of, 48–57
  loan documentation, and, 55–57
    agency duty, 56
    express clauses, 57
    fiduciary duty, 56
    negligence, 56–57
  managing group, 47
  negligent misrepresentation, and, 50–51
  role of, 46–48
Legal documents,
  certainty, and, 20–23
  result predictability, and, 20–23
LIBOR
  syndicated loans, and, 77–78
Listing of Eurobonds, 317–339
  advertisements in connection with particulars, 331–333
    'specified', 332
  basic requirements, 321
  contents of particulars, 325–327
  continuing obligations, 336–339
    disclosure, 336–337
    functions for benefit of bond holders, 337–338
    local authorities, 338–339
    public international body, 338–339
  determining contents of particulars, 323
  documents, 322
  Extel cards, 327
  false or misleading particulars, 329–331
    civil liability, 329–331
    criminal liability, 329
  FSA section 146, 324
  legal basis of Rules, 320–321
  London, 318–320
    FSA 1986, s. 57, 319–320
    FSA 1986, s. 160, 319
    special provisions, 335–336
  'mutual recognition' provisions of Admissions Directive, under, 333–336
    additional information, 334

Listing of Eurobonds—*contd*
    material to be submitted to Stock Exchange, 335
  offer of participation to two market makers, 327
  preconditions to listing application, 321–322
  publication of particulars, 322–323
  reasons for, 317–318
  registration of particulars, 322–323
  requirements for, 321–327
  requirements of disclosure, 325–327
    issue guaranteed by state entity, where, 326
  security printing of definitive bonds, 327
  supplementary listing particulars, 328
  time, 322
  Yellow Book, section 7, 324–325
Loan facility
  sales of, 104–105
Loan sales, 103–104, 134–139
  Financial Services Act 1986, and, 134–139
  purposes of, 103–104
  UK regulation, and, 124–144
  US regulation, and, 124–144
London
  development of international financial market, 10–11

Marketing and distribution of Eurobonds, 177–192
  agreement between managers, 184–189
    authority of lead manager, 186–187
    bonds not fully subscribed, where, 185–186
    compliance with requirements of regulatory law, 189
    costs, 189
    netting-off provision, and, 185
    objectives, 184
    portion of amount of bonds issued unsold, 186
    power of managers to terminate issue, 188–189
    provisions strengthening lead manager control of issue, 186–189
    redistribution of primary underwriting obligation, 184–186
    'stabilising manager', 187–188
    variation of bonds, and, 188
  documents, 177–192
  selling group agreement, 189–192
    breach of selling restrictions, and, 191
    nature of, 189–190
    objectives, 190–191
    obligations of members, 190
    oral misrepresentation, and, 192
  US securities laws, and, 190
  subscription agreement, 178–184
    compliance with applicable regulatory laws, 182–184

Marketing and distribution of Eurobonds—*contd*
  subscription agreement—*contd*
    'conditions', 180–181
    Euromarket disaster clause, 182
    expert opinions, 181
    force majeure clauses, 181–182
    obligation of manager to transfer subscription monies on closing date, 179
    obligation of manager to underwrite, 179
    primary obligations, 178
    protection from major market disruptions, 181
  UK regulatory law, 182–183
  US regulatory law, 183–184
  underwriting agreement, 184–189
Mergers,
  proper law of contract, and, 41–42
Misleading statements, 314–316
  actus reus, 315
  'dishonest', 316
  extraterritorial ramifications, 315–316
  mens rea, 315

Negative pledge covenant, 89–97
  applicable law, 92–94
  'a security interest', 92–93
  'automatic security' clause, 96
  'borrowings', 92
  breach, effect of, 94–95
  core prohibition, 90
  enforcement, 94–97
  'equal security' clause, 95
  importance of, 97
  'indebtedness', 92
  inducing breach of contract, and, 96–97
  injunction to prevent breach, 95
  intangible movables, and, 94
  lex situs of fixed assets, and, 93–94
  liens arising by operation of law, and, 90
  proper law of agreement, and, 93
  registration, 97
  'same security' clause, 95
  width of, 90–91
Negligent misrepresentation,
  liability of lead manager, and, 50–51
New York, 'reasonable relation' rule, 19–20
Novation, 107
  Financial Services Act 1986, and, 134–137
Note issuance facilities, 471–476
  facility agreement, 475–476
  manager, 475
  mechanics, 472–474
  structure, 471
  tender agent, 475
  tender panel members, 475

Off market dealer,
  meaning, 347
Offshore transaction,
  meaning, 397–399

Party autonomy, 17–20
  English law, 17–19
  Contracts (Applicable Law) Act 1990, 18
  New York law, 19–20
  Rome Convention, and, 18–19
Pooling
  meaning, 132
PORTAL, 422–426
Proper law of contract, 25–27
  acquisitions, 41–42
  'Act of State' doctrine, and, 38–40
  corporate capacity, and, 27–34
    representation, need for, 29
  creation of security interests, 40–41
  exchange control regulations, and, 34–37. *See also* EXCHANGE CONTROL REGULATIONS
  illegality subsequent to contract, 30–34
  limitations of doctrine, 40–42
  limits to control of transaction by, 27–34
  matters governed by,
    English law, 25
  mergers, 41–42
  negotiability of bond instruments, and, 40
  power of directors to bind company, and, 28–30
  repayment of debt denominated in particular currency, 33–34
  Rome Convention, and, 26–27
Prospectus,
  meaning, 308–309

Regulation of international capital markets, 279 *et seq.*
Regulation S, 393 *et seq.*
  aims, 393–394
  creation of safe harbours, 394
  'directed selling efforts', prohibition on, 395–397
  effect of non-compliance with issuer safe harbour requirements, 407–408
  foreign issues with no substantial US market interest, 400–403
    meaning, 400
    'substantial US market interest', 400–403
  interaction with US tax laws, 409–416
  issuer conditions, 399–400
  issues of debt securities, 403–406
    offering restrictions, 404–406
    transitional restrictions, 403–404
  'offshore transaction', requirement of, 397–399
  reporting issues, 403–406
    offering restrictions, 404–406
    transactional restrictions, 403–404
  resale safe harbour, 408
  scope of, 394
  TEFRA D Regulations, 409–415. *See also* TEFRA D REGULATIONS
Trust Indenture Act 1939

Regulation S—*contd*
applicability of, 408–409
Revolving underwriting facilities, 477–479
conditions precedent, 478
nature of, 477
obligations of tender panel members, and, 479
procedures for placement of notes, and, 478–479
underwriting fee, 477
Risk asset ratios,
guidelines for calculation, 115
Risk participations, 105
Rome Convention,
party autonomy, and, 18–19
proper law of the contract, and, 26–27

Security,
meaning, 139
Security interests,
creation of,
proper law of the contract, and, 40–41
'Selling' bank assets
techniques of, 105–106
Stabilisation, 340–358
FSA 1986, section 47(2), 341–343
extraterritoral impact, 357–358
'false or misleading impression', 342–343
market manipulation, 341–343
insider dealing, and, 343–347
contrary arguments, 344–345
defences, 345–347
'unpublished price-sensitive information', 343–344
international, 357–358
nature of, 340
regulation of, 340–358
regulation under Securities Exchange Act 1934, 372–378
SIB Rules, 347–358
ancillary stabilising action, 353–354
associated securities, 348
legends, 351–352
permitted stabilising transactions, 353–355
preconditions to lawful stabilisation, 351–352
pre-stabilisation ramping, 352–353
price limits applicable to, 355
securities which may be stabilised, 348–349
stabilising manager, 350
stabilising period, 350–351
stabilisation register, 356
'squeezing the shorts', 354
warnings, 351–352
warrants to acquire, 348–349
SFA Rules, 356–357
Sub-participation, 108–109
assignment compared, 109–114
confidentiality, and, 111

Sub-participation—*contd*
Financial Services Act 1986, and, 137–138
maturity stripping, and, 114
notice of, 110–111
obligations transferred, 109–110
rescheduling, and, 113–114
risk of default, and, 109
set-off, and, 114
Supplementary listing particulars, 328
Syndicated loan
agent bank, 48, 58–67. *See also* AGENT BANK
alternative currencies, 79
asset disposal covenant, 86
certainty, need for, 21
collective investment schemes, 130–134. *See also* COLLECTIVE INVESTMENT SCHEMES
conditions precedent, 68–71
categories, 70–71
contingent, 69–70
documentation, 68
legal nature of, 70
nature of, 69
no events of default, 68–69
contents of agreement, 68–102
cost of funding, 81–82
covenants, 82–82
aim of, 82
'an event of default', 83–84
cross default' clause, 84
levels of performance, 82–83
maximum level of disclosure, 83
monitoring of compliance with, 83
'negative pledge', 83
preservation of borrower's asset base, 83
cross default, 98–100
purpose of clause, 99–100
currency of, 73–74
currency of repayment, 73–74
debenture, whether, 125–127
default clause, 98–100
documentation, 55–57
financial arrangements, 73–82
financial covenants, 84–85
current ratio, 85
debt service ratio, 85
debt to equity ratio, 84
minimum net worth, 85
minimum working capital, 85
financial information covenant, 86
Financial Services Act 1986, and, 124–134. *See also* FINANCIAL SERVICES ACT 1986
form of agreement, 47–48
frustration of contract, and, 78–79
funding mechanisms in international market,
special clauses, need for, 77–79
increased costs, 81–82
information memorandum. *See* INFORMATION MEMORANDUM
interest payments, 79–81

Index   489

Syndicated loan—contd
  investment advertisements, and, 129–130
  'investment business,' and, 127–129. See
      also INVESTMENT BUSINESS
  investment, whether, 124–127
  lead manager, 45–57. See also LEAD
      MANAGER
  legal structure, 45
  LIBOR rate, 77–78
  merger control covenants, 86–88
    objectives, 88
  monitoring covenants, 61
  negative pledge, 89–97. See also NEGATIVE
      PLEDGE COVENANT
  pari passu covenant, 89
  pre-payment, 75–77
  penalty, 75–76
  premium, 75–76
  relationship between syndicate bonds inter
      se, 100–102
  representations, 71–73
    effect, 71–72
    financial position of borrowing entity, 72
    revolving credit facility, and, 72–73
  sharing clauses, 101–102
  statement of purpose of, 74–75
  structure of agreement, 68–102
  UK regulation, and, 124–144
  unsolicited calls, and, 129–130
  US regulation, and, 124–144
  US securities regulation, and, 139–142
  use of proceeds of, 74–75
  warranties, 71–73
    effect, 71–72
    financial position of borrowing entity, 72
    revolving credit facility, and, 72–73
  withholding tax, 79–81

Takeover offer,
  meaning, 87
TEFRA C Regulations, 415–416
TEFRA D Regulations, 409–415
  certification, 412–413
  impact on Regulation S, 413–415
  restrictions on delivery, 412
  restrictions on offers and sales, 411–412
Temporary global bond (TGB), 174–176
  characteristics, 175–176
  exchangeability, 174–175
  nature of, 174
  negotiable instrument, whether, 175
  reasons for use, 175
  sui generis nature of, 175
  who is holder, 176
Transferable Loan Certificate, 116–119
  delivery, 117–118
  Financial Services Act 1986, and, 138–139
  issue mechanics, 117–119
  legal basis, 117
  persons who may accept offer, 118–119
  protective clauses, and, 118

Transferable Loan Certificate—contd
  signature, 117
  transfer for value, 118
  transfer mechanics, 117–119
Transferable Loan Instrument, 119
  debenture, as, 119
  Financial Services Act 1986, and, 138–139
  issue mechanics, 120–122
  nature of, 122–123
  negotiable instrument, whether, 122
  promissory note, whether, 122
  protection of transferee, 121–122
  registration, 121
  transfer mechanics, 120–122
Transferable Participation Certificates, 123
  Financial Services Act 1986, and, 138–139
Trustees under Eurobond trust deeds, 224–250
  accounts, 229, 230
  covenants, 229–231
  discretion, 228
  duties, 236–250
  duty not to allow duty as trustee to conflict
      with own interests, 243–245
  duty not to delegate, 245–246
  duty not to make incidental or secret profit,
      243
  duty not to traffic in or purchase trust
      property, 243
  duty to act with due skill and diligence,
      237–243
    advice and information from
        professionals and experts, 241
    attempted derogation, 237
    bona fide, 242
    breach of covenant, 239
    default, 239
    exclusion clauses, and, 243
    handling and investment of funds,
        241–242
    information, 240
    material prejudice, and, 241
    modification of terms of trust, and,
        240
    policing covenants of bonds and trust
        deed, 238–239
    provisions of trust deed, and, 238
    resolutions of bond holders, 240
  duty to provide information about matters
      affecting trust, 245
  functions, 228–236
  immunities, 236–250
  information, 229–230
  interpretation of trust deed, 235
  new, appointment of, 236
  liabilities, 236–250
  opinion as to material prejudice, 232
  power to modify terms of trust deed,
      231–232, 233–234
  powers, 228–236
  rationale for, 246–248
  regulation of contents of trust deeds,
      248–250

Trustees under Eurobond trust deeds—*contd*
  regulation of contents of trust
    deeds—*contd*
      necessity for, 249–250
    removal of, 235
    substitution of debtors, 234–235
    trust, nature of, 225–227
      beneficiaries, 227
      covenants as trust assets, 226
      English law sense, 227
    validly constituted trust, 227–228
    waiver of breaches of covenant, 231

UK laws,
  regulation of international bond issues, 279 *et seq.*
Unfair Contract Terms Act 1977,
  liability of lead manager, and, 52–53
Unsolicited call. *See* Cold calling
US commercial banks,
  participation in international capital markets, 427–436
US Securities Act 1933, 363–369
  anti-fraud provisions, 367–369
  consequences of breach, 365–367
    civil sanctions, 365–367
    criminal sanctions, 365
    SEC action, 365
  R 144A, 422–426
  section 5, 363–365
  section 12, 367–368
  section 17, 368–369
US Securities Exchange Act 1934, 369–372
  anti-fraud provision, 371–372
  broker/dealer registration, 369–370
  enforcement, 376–378
  R 15a-6, 416–420
    'comparably regulated' foreign broker/dealers, and, 420
    effecting transactions in securities with specified persons, 419–420
    furnishing of research reports, 417–418
    inducing transactions with US institutional investors, 419
    interaction with Regulation S, 420
    unsolicited transactions, 417
  regulation of stabilisation, 372–378
  'safe harbour' provisions, 374–375

US Securities Exchange Act 1934—*contd*
  remedies, 376–378
  section 15, 369–370
US securities laws, 359 *et seq.*
  extraterritoriality, 380–392
  choice of law, and, 381
    'conduct' based jurisdiction, 384–387
    'effects' doctrine, 382–384
    'intention of Congress', 380–381
    nationality, and, 385–387
    policy, 386–387
    SEC, and, 387–388
    SEC Release 4708 of July 1964, 388–392
  extraterritorial application, 362
  impact on international bond issues, 359 *et seq.*
  inter-action of Regulation S, TEFRA D and r 144A, 425
  'interstate commerce', and, 362
  legislative framework, 363–378
  PORTAL, 422–426
  r 144A, and, 425–426
  private placements, 422–426
  regulation of stabilisation,
    issue or distribution of securities, during, 372–378
  Regulation S, 393 *et seq. See also* REGULATION S
  Securities Act 1933, 363–369. *See also* US SECURITIES ACT 1933
  Securities Exchange Act 1934 369–372. *See also* US SECURITIES EXCHANGE ACT 1934
  Summary, 420–422
  Trust Indenture Act 1939, 378
US securities regulation, 139–142
  Glass Steagall Act, 141–142. *See also* GLASS STEAGALL ACT
US Trust Indenture Act 1939, 378

Warrants
  Eurobonds with, 251–278.
    See also BONDS WITH EQUITY WARRANTS

Yellow Book,
  listing, and, 324–325